The Pension Answer Book

Sixth Edition

Revised by: Stephen J. Krass
Krass & Lund, P.C.
New York City

(Original edition by Krass and Keschner)

THE PANEL ANSWER BOOK SERIES

This publication is designed to provide accurate and authoritative information in regard to the subject matter covered. It is sold with the understanding that the publisher is not engaged in rendering legal, accounting or other professional services. If legal advice or other professional assistance is required, the services of a competent professional person should be sought.

—From a *Declaration of Principles jointly adopted by a Committee of the American Bar Association and a Committee of Publishers and Associations.*

ISBN: 1-878375-33-4

Copyright © 1991

PANEL PUBLISHERS, INC.
A *Wolters Kluwer* Company

36 West 44th Street
Suite 1316
New York, NY 10036
(212) 790-2000

Printed in the United States of America

ABOUT PANEL PUBLISHERS, INC.

Panel Publishers derives its name from a panel of business professionals who organized in 1964 to publish authoritative, timely books, information services, and journals written by specialists to assist accountants, tax practitioners, attorneys, and other business professionals; human resources, compensation and benefits, and pension and profit-sharing professionals; and owners of small to medium-sized businesses. Our mission is to provide practical, solution-based "how-to" information to business professionals.

Also available in the Panel Answer Book Series:

Health Insurance Answer Book
Nonqualified Deferred Compensation Answer Book
Personnel Law Answer Book
The S Corporation Answer Book
Employee Benefits Answer Book

To order or for more information,
contact Panel Publishers, Inc.
36 W. 44th Street, New York, NY 10036
or call (212) 790-2090

The following editorial and production professionals have contributed to the publication of this book: Publisher, Richard H. Kravitz, CPA: Vice President, Editorial, Richard D. Walker, CPA; Director, New Product Development, Mark D. Persons, Esq.; Executive Editor, Isabelle Cohen; Senior Editor, JoAnne Haffeman; Editorial Assistants, Pat Dugal and Juanita Scarlett; Production Manager, Jan M. Lavin; and Assistant Production Manager, Carol Biedrzycki.

PANEL PUBLISHERS, INC.
Practical Solutions for Business Professionals

Dedication

To my wife, Sallie

for her faith and her love,
and without whom
this would not have been possible

About the Authors

STEPHEN J. KRASS, ESQ., is a member of the law firm of Krass & Lund, P.C. in New York City. Mr. Krass received his B.S. (Accounting) from The Ohio State University and LL.B. and LL.M. (Taxation) from New York University School of Law. Mr. Krass is one of the original co-authors of *The Pension Answer Book*. He is a member of the American Bar Association Sections on Taxation (Adjunct Member, Committee on Employee Benefits) and Real Property, Probate and Trust Law and the New York State Bar Association Sections on Taxation (Member, Employee Benefits Committee) and Trusts and Estates. He is on the Board of Directors of the Estate Planning Council of New York City and is a member of the Advisory Boards of the *CCH Financial and Estate Planning Reporter* and the *Journal of Pension Planning & Compliance*. Mr. Krass has been a panelist on AICPA programs and *The C.P.A. Report*. He has spoken at the N.Y.U. Institute on Federal Taxation; The American College-CCH National Conference on Financial Planning; Institute of Certified Financial Planners Annual Conference; International Association for Financial Planning; American Academy of Matrimonial Lawyers; Hofstra University-Center for Business Studies; New York Law School; C. W. Post Tax Institute; Iona College Tax Institute; New York State Society of Certified Public Accountants; and The Life Underwriters Association of the City of New York. Mr. Krass has been an instructor in the Long Island University Paralegal Program and is an Approved Sponsor of Continuing Professional Education by the New York State Board of Public Accountancy. He has contributed articles to *Taxes-The Tax Magazine, Journal of the Institute of Certified Financial Planners, Pension Actuary, The Practical Accountant, CLU Journal, CCH Financial and Estate Planning Reporter, The Journal of Financial Planning, Journal of Pension Planning & Compliance, Taxation for Accountants, Taxation for Lawyers,* and *Financial Planning To-*

day, and is a frequent lecturer on employee benefit plans, estate planning, and taxation.

STEVEN SCHMUTTER, ESQ., is a member of the law firm of Krass & Lund, P.C. Mr. Schmutter received his B.S. (*magna cum laude*) from the State University of New York at Binghampton, his J.D. from St. John's University School of Law, and his LL.M. (Taxation) from New York University School of Law. He has written on employee benefit plan topics.

STEVEN SULSKY, ESQ., is an associate of the law firm of Krass & Lund, P.C. Mr. Sulsky received his B.A. from the State University of New York at Binghampton, his J.D. from Boston University School of Law, and his LL.M. (Taxation) from New York University School of law. He has lectured on employee benefit plan topics.

RICHARD L. KESCHNER, ESQ., (1945–1989), was a sole practitioner in New York City. Mr. Keschner received his B.S. from Brooklyn College, his M.B.A. from Baruch College, and his J.D. from Brooklyn Law School.

Acknowledgments

I welcomed the opportunity to return to *The Pension Answer Book* after a three-year "break in service." Since the first edition, Congress has enacted TEFRA, TRA '84, REA, TRA '86, OBRA '86, OBRA '87, TAMRA and RRA '89. The goal of simplification in the qualified retirement plan area has not been achieved, and Treasury Department officials have admitted "there is little disagreement that pension law is one of the most complicated areas of tax law."

In view of the foregoing, *The Pension Answer Book* has grown from less than 400 questions to almost 1,000. I felt that this was the time to do a complete revision and major restructuring of *The Pension Answer Book*. With basic parity between corporate retirement plans and retirement plans of self-employed individuals, one effect of which is a reduction in the number of professionals incorporating their practices, separate chapters on "Self-Employed Persons," "Professional Practices," and "Closely Held Corporations" became redundant; hence, a single chapter entitled "Business Owners" has been created. With the increasing divorce rate and the allocation of retirement plan benefits to non-plan participant spouses, a new chapter, "Qualified Domestic Relations Orders," has been added to this edition. A new limitation on compensation used to calculate plan contributions and benefits now applies to employees of Fortune 500 corporations, not only to employee owners of small businesses. This has resulted in creating new questions and moving existing questions to another new chapter, "Contribution and Benefit Limitations." In fact, almost all chapters have been restructured to establish a better "flow" of the subject matter.

This sixth edition of *The Pension Answer Book* was beyond the reach of one person and there are many people to thank. I express my deepest appreciation to Steven Schmutter and Steven Sulsky, each of whom undertook the primary responsibility for the revision of eight chapters and who gave me invaluable assistance. This project required us to work late summer nights and long, hot weekends. To their wives, Sharon and Carol, to their children, Mindy, Jill, and Justin, and to my children, Stephanie, Caroline, and James, I thank them all so very much for their patience and understanding.

I am also very grateful to our secretary, Ildiko P. Balogh, who labored diligently on a portion of the manuscript. To my personal secretary, Susan Busani-Halevi, who coordinated this effort and labored so expertly and devotedly to ensure the completion of this sixth edition and who managed to bear with me in pressure-laden times, I express my heartfelt sympathy and extreme gratitude.

To my editor, JoAnne Haffeman, and to all the people at Panel Publishers, without whose assistance this edition would never have come to press, I say "thanks."

On behalf of all of us, I hope that you will find the sixth edition of *The Pension Answer Book* to be a better and more useful book and a welcome addition to your library.

SJK

How to Use the Book

The Sixth Edition of *The Pension Answer Book* is designed for professionals who need quick and authoritative answers to help them decide whether to institute or continue pension and other retirement plans, how to choose the plans most suited to their needs, and how to comply with the morass of federal requirements. This book uses simple, straightforward language and avoids technical jargon when possible. Citations of authority are provided as research aids for those who need to pursue particular items in greater detail. The question numbering system has been redesigned for greater ease of use.

This question-and-answer format, with its breadth of coverage and its plain-language explanations (plus numerous illustrative examples), offers a clear and useful guide to understanding the complex, but extremely important, area of qualified pension and profit sharing plans.

Numbering System: The questions are numbered consecutively within each chapter (e.g., 2:1, 2:2, etc.).

Detailed Listing of Questions: The detailed Listing of Questions that follows the Table of Contents in the front of this book helps the reader locate areas of immediate interest. This listing is like a detailed table of contents that provides both the question number and the page on which it appears.

Glossary: Because the pension area is replete with technical terms that have specific legal meanings, a special glossary of terms is provided following the question-and-answer portion of this book. Expressions not defined elsewhere, and abbreviations used throughout the book, are defined in the glossary, which is arranged in alphabetical order.

Index: At the back of this book is an index provided as a further aid to locating specific information. Key words included in the glossary are used in the index as well. *All references in the index are to question numbers rather than page numbers.*

Use of Abbreviations

Because of the breadth of subject area, a number of terms and statutory references are abbreviated throughout *The Pension Answer Book*. Among the most common of these shorthand references are:

- *Code*—The Internal Revenue Code of 1986.
- *ERISA*—The Employee Retirement Income Security Act of 1974, as amended.
- *IRS*—The Internal Revenue Service.
- *DOL*—The U.S. Department of Labor.
- *COBRA*—The Consolidated Omnibus Budget Reconciliation Act of 1985.
- *PBGC*—Pension Benefit Guaranty Corporation.
- *TRA '86*—The Tax Reform Act of 1986.
- *TAMRA*—The Technical and Miscellaneous Revenue Act of 1988.

For explanations of other abbreviations consult the Glossary.

Table of Contents

Listing of Questions XVII

Chapter 1: Overview 1-1

Chapter 2: Types and Choices of Plans 2-1

Chapter 3: Requirements for Qualification 3-1

Chapter 4: Eligibility and Participation 4-1

Chapter 5: Contribution and Benefit Limitations ... 5-1

Chapter 6: Integration with Social Security 6-1

Chapter 7: Funding Requirements 7-1

Chapter 8: Vesting 8-1

Chapter 9: Distribution Requirements 9-1

Chapter 10: Tax Deduction Rules 10-1

Chapter 11: Taxation of Distributions 11-1

Chapter 12: Life Insurance and Death Benefits 12-1

Chapter 13: Determination Letters 13-1

Chapter 14: Operating the Plan 14-1

Chapter 15: Reporting to Government Agencies ... 15-1

Chapter 16: Summary Plan Descriptions 16-1

Chapter 17: Fiduciary Responsibilities 17-1

Chapter 18: Prohibited Transactions 18-1

Chapter 19: Termination of the Plan 19-1

Chapter 20: Top-Heavy Plans 20-1

Chapter 21: 401(k) Plans 21-1

Chapter 22: Employee Stock Ownership Plans 22-1

Chapter 23: Multiemployer Plans 23-1

Chapter 24: Individual Retirement Plans 24-1

Chapter 25: Simplified Employee Pensions 25-1

Chapter 26: Rollovers 26-1

Chapter 27: Business Owners 27-1

Table of Contents

Chapter 28: Qualified Domestic Relations Orders .. 28-1

Glossary G-1

Index I-1

Listing of Questions

Chapter 1 Overview

Q. 1:1	Why should a company adopt a qualified retirement plan?	1-1
Q. 1:2	What is a qualified retirement plan?	1-2
Q. 1:3	What are the basic tax advantages of a qualified retirement plan?	1-2
Q. 1:4	Must a company incorporate to have a qualified retirement plan?	1-3
Q. 1:5	How does the deductibility of employer contributions differ between qualified and nonqualified plans?	1-3
Q. 1:6	How do qualified and nonqualified plans differ with regard to the taxation of employer contributions?	1-4
Q. 1:7	How do qualified and nonqualified plans differ with regard to coverage of employees and benefit or contribution limitations?	1-4
Q. 1:8	How is the employee affected by the employer's choice of a qualified or nonqualified plan?	1-4
Q. 1:9	What is the Employee Retirement Income Security Act?	1-5
Q. 1:10	What other acts have affected retirement plans?	1-5
Q. 1:11	Does the adoption of a qualified retirement plan by an employer constitute a contractual obligation to maintain the plan?	1-6
Q. 1:12	What cost will the company incur in adopting a qualified retirement plan?	1-6
Q. 1:13	Must the company contribute to the plan each year once it adopts a qualified retirement plan?	1-7
Q. 1:14	Must a qualified plan include all employees?	1-7
Q. 1:15	What are the most common eligibility requirements for participation in a qualified plan?	1-7
Q. 1:16	What statutory exclusions from participation in a qualified plan are permitted?	1-8
Q. 1:17	What other exclusions from participation in a qualified plan are permitted?	1-8

Q. 1:18   Can a company establish two qualified retirement plans?   1-9

Q. 1:19   What kinds of benefits may be provided under a qualified retirement plan?   1-9

Q. 1:20   May a qualified retirement plan provide life insurance benefits for participants?   1-10

Q. 1:21   May a qualified retirement plan provide health insurance?   1-10

Q. 1:22   Is a contribution to a qualified retirement plan adopted on the last day of the taxable year fully deductible?   1-11

Q. 1:23   May excess contributions made to a qualified retirement plan be returned to the company?   1-11

Chapter 2   Types and Choices of Plans

Q. 2:1   What are the basic choices among qualified retirement plans?   2-1

Q. 2:2   What is a defined contribution plan?   2-1

Q. 2:3   What is a defined benefit plan?   2-2

Q. 2:4   What is a money purchase pension plan?   2-3

Q. 2:5   What is a target benefit plan?   2-4

Q. 2:6   What is a profit sharing plan?   2-5

Q. 2:7   What is a thrift or savings plan?   2-6

Q. 2:8   What is a 401(k) plan?   2-7

Q. 2:9   What is a stock bonus plan?   2-7

Q. 2:10   What is an employee stock ownership plan?   2-8

Q. 2:11   What is a simplified employee pension?   2-8

Q. 2:12   What is a flat benefit plan?   2-8

Q. 2:13   What is a unit benefit plan?   2-8

Q. 2:14   How is the cost of providing benefits under a defined benefit plan determined?   2-9

Q. 2:15   Must the actuarial assumptions be set forth in the plan?   2-10

Q. 2:16   What is a Keogh plan?   2-10

Q. 2:17   What is a floor offset plan?   2-10

Q. 2:18   What is a cash balance plan?   2-11

Q. 2:19   What is an insured qualified retirement plan?   2-12

Q. 2:20   What is a custom-designed retirement plan?   **2-13**

Q. 2:21   What are master and prototype retirement plans?   **2-13**

Q. 2:22   How does a company's cash position affect its choice of a qualified retirement plan?   **2-13**

Q. 2:23   What type of retirement plan should a company adopt if profits fluctuate from year to year?   **2-13**

Q. 2:24   Are profit sharing plans best for small companies?   **2-14**

Q. 2:25   What type of qualified retirement plan is best for a company whose essential employees have reached an advanced age?   **2-14**

Q. 2:26   How can an ESOP or a stock bonus plan benefit a corporation and its stockholders?   **2-15**

Q. 2:27   Can the company take Social Security wage tax payments or benefits into consideration in its qualified retirement plan?   **2-16**

Q. 2:28   After the type of plan has been chosen, what options are available?   **2-16**

Chapter 3   Requirements for Qualification

Q. 3:1   What basic requirements must all retirement plans meet to qualify for favorable tax treatment?   **3-1**

Q. 3:2   Does a 401(k) plan qualify for favorable tax treatment?   **3-2**

Q. 3:3   Can an oral trust created in a state that recognizes its validity be used for a qualified retirement plan?   **3-3**

Q. 3:4   Can a trust that is not valid under local law be part of a qualified retirement plan?   **3-3**

Q. 3:5   Must all qualified retirement plans have trustees?   **3-3**

Q. 3:6   Does a retirement plan have to be submitted to IRS for approval?   **3-3**

Q. 3:7   Even if a retirement plan is not submitted to IRS for approval, must it nevertheless be amended periodically?   **3-4**

Q. 3:8   May an employee's benefits be reduced after retirement to reflect Social Security benefit increases?   **3-4**

Q. 3:9   May a participant assign his or her vested interest in a qualified retirement plan?   **3-5**

Q. 3:10   May a participant's qualified retirement plan benefits
           be attached or garnished?   3-5

Chapter 4   Eligibility and Participation

Q. 4:1   Must a company's qualified retirement plan cover all
           of its employees?   4-1
Q. 4:2   What minimum age and service requirements may
           be set by a qualified retirement plan?   4-1
Q. 4:3   May a qualified retirement plan set a maximum age
           limit for participation?   4-2
Q. 4:4   May a qualified retirement plan require two
           consecutive years of service for participation?   4-2
Q. 4:5   May conditions other than age and service be set
           for participation in a qualified retirement plan?   4-3
Q. 4:6   May the company require employee contributions as
           a condition of plan participation?   4-4
Q. 4:7   When must an employee who meets the plan's
           eligibility requirements begin to participate?   4-4
Q. 4:8   What is a year of service for a plan's service
           eligibility requirement?   4-5
Q. 4:9   What is an hour of service?   4-5
Q. 4:10   What is a one-year break in service?   4-5
Q. 4:11   What years of service must be taken into account
           for eligibility purposes?   4-6
Q. 4:12   May any years of service be disregarded for
           eligibility purposes?   4-6
Q. 4:13   May past service with a former employer be used
           for eligibility purposes in the qualified retirement
           plan of the present employer?   4-6
Q. 4:14   Is a maternity or paternity period of absence treated
           as a break in service?   4-7
Q. 4:15   What coverage requirements must a retirement plan
           satisfy to qualify for favorable tax treatment?   4-7
Q. 4:16   What is the ratio percentage test for the minimum
           coverage requirements?   4-8
Q. 4:17   What is the average benefit test for the minimum
           coverage requirements?   4-8
Q. 4:18   What is the classification test?   4-9
Q. 4:19   What is the average benefit percentage test?   4-9

Q. 4:20 When does an employee benefit under the qualified retirement plan? **4-10**

Q. 4:21 How are employees who terminated employment during the plan year treated for minimum coverage purposes? **4-11**

Q. 4:22 What is the family aggregation rule? **4-13**

Q. 4:23 What is the minimum participation requirement? **4-13**

Q. 4:24 What is a prior benefit structure? **4-14**

Q. 4:25 May a retirement plan that does not satisfy the minimum participation requirements be merged into another plan? **4-15**

Q. 4:26 Can an employee's waiver of participation in the employer's qualified retirement plan jeopardize the tax-favored status of the plan? **4-15**

Q. 4:27 What happens if a retirement plan fails to satisfy the minimum coverage or minimum participation requirements? **4-16**

Q. 4:28 Who is a highly compensated employee? **4-16**

Q. 4:29 How is compensation defined for purposes of determining who is a highly compensated employee? **4-17**

Q. 4:30 What are the determination year and look-back year for determining the group of highly compensated employees? **4-18**

Q. 4:31 Does the family aggregation rule affect the determination of who is a highly compensated employee? **4-18**

Q. 4:32 Do special coverage and participation rules apply to commonly controlled businesses? **4-18**

Q. 4:33 If an individual owns two corporations, each of which has employees, can a qualified retirement plan be adopted by only one of the corporations? **4-19**

Q. 4:34 When does common ownership result in a controlled group of corporations or businesses? **4-20**

Q. 4:35 Is there a separate line-of-business exception to the minimum coverage and minimum participation requirements? **4-20**

Q. 4:36 Who is a leased employee? **4-21**

Q. 4:37 Who is the employer of a leased employee? **4-21**

Q. 4:38 When is the leased employee first considered an employee of the recipient? **4-22**

Q. 4:39 What happens if the leased employee participates in the leasing organization's qualified retirement plan? 4-22

Q. 4:40 When will the leased employee not be treated as an employee of the recipient? 4-22

Q. 4:41 Can an employer utilizing the services of leased employees obtain IRS approval of its qualified retirement plan? 4-23

Chapter 5 Contribution and Benefit Limitations

Q. 5:1 How much may the company contribute to a defined contribution plan on behalf of a participant? 5-1

Q. 5:2 Will the $30,5-2 ceiling on the annual addition rise? 5-2

Q. 5:3 What does compensation mean for purposes of the annual addition limitation? 5-3

Q. 5:4 Does a withdrawn employee voluntary contribution that is replaced during the same year constitute part of the annual addition? 5-4

Q. 5:5 What is the maximum annual retirement benefit that a defined benefit plan may provide? 5-4

Q. 5:6 What does annual benefit mean? 5-5

Q. 5:7 What does average compensation mean for purposes of the annual retirement benefit limitations? 5-6

Q. 5:8 Is there a minimum number of years of participation or service required before a participant in a defined benefit plan qualifies for the maximum annual benefit? 5-6

Q. 5:9 What is the Social Security retirement age? 5-7

Q. 5:10 What happens if the employee's accrued benefit under a defined benefit plan exceeded the TRA '86 limitations? 5-7

Q. 5:11 What is the limitation year? 5-8

Q. 5:12 What happens if an employee participates in both a defined benefit plan and a defined contribution plan? 5-8

Q. 5:13 At what level of compensation will the 1.0 rule affect an employee? 5-10

Q. 5:14   What limits apply to employee contributions required
           under a qualified retirement plan?   5-10
Q. 5:15   Is any limit set on the amount that a participant can
           voluntarily contribute to a qualified retirement plan?   5-11
Q. 5:16   What tax advantages are gained when a qualified
           retirement plan permits participants to make
           voluntary contributions?   5-11
Q. 5:17   May a qualified retirement plan permit deductible
           employee contributions?   5-11
Q. 5:18   What is the family aggregation rule?   5-12

Chapter 6 Integration With Social Security

Q. 6:1   What does the integration of a qualified retirement
           plan with Social Security mean?   6-1
Q. 6:2   What types of qualified retirement plans can be
           integrated with Social Security?   6-2
Q. 6:3   What general rules apply to a defined contribution
           excess plan?   6-3
Q. 6:4   What is the excess contribution percentage?   6-3
Q. 6:5   What is the base contribution percentage?   6-3
Q. 6:6   What is the integration level?   6-4
Q. 6:7   How are the integration rules applied to contribution
           formulas under defined contribution excess plans?   6-4
Q. 6:8   Can the integration level in a defined contribution
           excess plan be other than the taxable wage base?   6-5
Q. 6:9   What general rules apply to a defined benefit
           excess plan?   6-6
Q. 6:10   What is the excess benefit percentage?   6-6
Q. 6:11   What is the base benefit percentage?   6-7
Q. 6:12   What is the maximum excess allowance?   6-7
Q. 6:13   How are the integration rules applied to benefit
           formulas under defined benefit excess plans?   6-7
Q. 6:14   Can benefits commence prior to Social Security
           retirement age in a defined benefit excess plan?   6-8
Q. 6:15   Can alternative integration levels be used in a
           defined benefit excess plan?   6-8
Q. 6:16   What general rules apply to a defined benefit offset
           plan?   6-9

Q. 6:17 What is the maximum offset allowance? 6-9
Q. 6:18 How are the integration rules applied to benefit formulas under defined benefit offset plans? 6-9
Q. 6:19 Can benefits commence prior to Social Security retirement age in a defined benefit offset plan? 6-10
Q. 6:20 Can alternative integration levels be used in a defined benefit offset plan? 6-11
Q. 6:21 What is average annual compensation? 6-11
Q. 6:22 What does covered compensation mean? 6-11
Q. 6:23 What is final average compensation? 6-13
Q. 6:24 What does compensation mean? 6-13
Q. 6:25 Can the termination of a defined benefit plan affect integration? 6-13
Q. 6:26 What special restrictions on integration apply to top-heavy plans? 6-14

Chapter 7 Funding Requirements

Q. 7:1 What are the minimum funding standards? 7-1
Q. 7:2 Are there funding requirements in addition to the minimum funding standards? 7-2
Q. 7:3 Which qualified retirement plans are not subject to the minimum funding standards? 7-2
Q. 7:4 What is an insurance contract plan? 7-3
Q. 7:5 Can a pension plan be converted to an insurance contract plan? 7-3
Q. 7:6 Can the employer contribute more than the amount needed to meet the minimum funding standards? 7-4
Q. 7:7 Must actuarial assumptions used in determining plan costs be reasonable? 7-4
Q. 7:8 Is there any penalty for overstatement of pension liabilities? 7-5
Q. 7:9 Can a pension plan's normal retirement age affect the minimum funding standards? 7-6
Q. 7:10 How are past service costs funded? 7-6
Q. 7:11 Do the pension plan's investment earnings affect the funding requirement? 7-7
Q. 7:12 How are assets valued in a defined benefit plan? 7-7
Q. 7:13 What is the funding standard account? 7-8
Q. 7:14 What is the full funding limitation? 7-9

Q. 7:15   Must separate funding standard accounts be maintained for each pension plan established by a controlled group of companies?   **7-10**

Q. 7:16   What happens if the company fails to make the required contribution to its pension plan?   **7-10**

Q. 7:17   Who is liable for failure to make contributions?   **7-10**

Q. 7:18   May IRS waive the minimum funding standards for a particular company?   **7-11**

Q. 7:19   What is the procedure for obtaining a waiver of the minimum funding standards?   **7-13**

Q. 7:20   Are there any notice requirements when a funding waiver request is filed?   **7-15**

Q. 7:21   Is any additional information required to be filed along with the funding waiver request?   **7-15**

Q. 7:22   May a pension plan be amended if a waiver of the funding standards is in effect for a particular year?   **7-15**

Q. 7:23   What alternative is available if IRS will not waive the minimum funding standards?   **7-16**

Q. 7:24   May an employer obtain an extension of an amortization period to help it meet the minimum funding standards?   **7-16**

Q. 7:25   May a contribution be timely for the minimum funding standards but not for tax deduction purposes?   **7-17**

Q. 7:26   Must quarterly contributions be made to a defined benefit plan?   **7-17**

Q. 7:27   Does the minimum funding requirement cease once a pension plan terminates?   **7-18**

Chapter 8   Vesting

Q. 8:1   What does vesting mean?   **8-1**

Q. 8:2   What is an accrued benefit?   **8-2**

Q. 8:3   Are minimum vesting standards set by law?   **8-2**

Q. 8:4   Do the minimum vesting standards apply to multiemployer plans?   **8-4**

Q. 8:5   Does the adoption of one of the minimum vesting schedules guarantee the retirement plan's qualification?   **8-5**

Q. 8:6   May a qualified retirement plan's vesting schedule be changed?   **8-5**

Q. 8:7 What is the period within which a participant may elect to stay under the old vesting schedule?   8-6

Q. 8:8 What vesting standards apply to an employee's own contributions?   8-6

Q. 8:9 What is a year of service for vesting purposes?   8-6

Q. 8:10 What years of service must be taken into account for vesting purposes?   8-6

Q. 8:11 May any years of service be disregarded for vesting purposes?   8-7

Q. 8:12 Is an employee's length of service ever irrelevant in determining his or her degree of vesting?   8-8

Q. 8:13 What vesting schedule is best for the employer?   8-8

Q. 8:14 How does a one-year break in service affect a previously nonvested participant's right to benefits?   8-10

Q. 8:15 How does a one-year break in service affect an employee if the qualified retirement plan requires the employee to have more than one year of service in order to be eligible to participate?   8-11

Q. 8:16 How does a one-year break in service affect a vested participant's right to benefits?   8-11

Q. 8:17 What is a forfeiture of benefits?   8-12

Q. 8:18 What happens to amounts forfeited by participants?   8-12

Q. 8:19 May a nonforfeitable benefit ever be forfeited?   8-13

Q. 8:20 Does a distribution (cash-out) of benefits affect how many years of service must be taken into account?   8-14

Q. 8:21 How can a reemployed participant restore (buy-back) forfeited benefits?   8-14

Q. 8:22 May a qualified retirement plan provide for the forfeiture of vested benefits on the death of an employee?   8-15

Q. 8:23 May any years of service be disregarded for accrual purposes?   8-15

Q. 8:24 Can a qualified retirement plan be amended to reduce accrued benefits?   8-16

Q. 8:25 Can accrued benefits be eliminated or reduced?   8-16

Q. 8:26 Can a qualified retirement plan be amended to reduce future accruals of benefits?   8-18

Q. 8:27 What benefits are not Section 411(d)(6) protected benefits?   8-18

Q. 8:28 What happens to a participant's benefits if the qualified retirement plan merges with another plan?   8-19

Chapter 9 Distribution Requirements

Q. 9:1 Must a qualified retirement plan provide benefits to a participant's surviving spouse? 9-1

Q. 9:2 Must a qualified retirement plan continue to pay benefits to a surviving spouse who remarries? 9-2

Q. 9:3 What is the annuity starting date? 9-2

Q. 9:4 What is the significance of the annuity starting date to survivor benefit requirements? 9-3

Q. 9:5 How do the automatic survivor benefit requirements apply to unmarried participants? 9-3

Q. 9:6 Are all qualified retirement plans required to provide automatic survivor benefits? 9-3

Q. 9:7 Are there any other conditions that must be satisfied, with respect to a participant, to be exempt from the automatic survivor rules? 9-4

Q. 9:8 What is a qualified joint and survivor annuity? 9-5

Q. 9:9 What is a qualified preretirement survivor annuity? 9-6

Q. 9:10 How is a survivor annuity treated for estate tax purposes? 9-7

Q. 9:11 What is the effect of a loan on the amount of a QPSA or QJSA? 9-7

Q. 9:12 Is spousal consent necessary for plan loans? 9-7

Q. 9:13 What is a transferee plan? 9-8

Q. 9:14 Do the automatic survivor annuity requirements apply to floor offset plans? 9-8

Q. 9:15 Must annuity contracts distributed to a participant or spouse by a plan satisfy the automatic survivor benefit requirements? 9-9

Q. 9:16 Must a frozen or terminated plan provide automatic survivor benefits? 9-9

Q. 9:17 Does it make any difference if PBGC is administering the plan? 9-9

Q. 9:18 To which benefits do the automatic survivor rules apply? 9-9

Q. 9:19 Can a qualified retirement plan treat married participants as not married under any circumstances? 9-10

Q. 9:20 May a participant waive the automatic survivor benefits? 9-11

Q. 9:21 Must the participant's spouse consent to the waiver of the QJSA or QPSA? 9-11

Q. 9:22 Must the waiver of the QPSA or QJSA specify an alternate beneficiary?   **9-12**

Q. 9:23 Must the waiver of a QJSA specify the optional form of benefit chosen?   **9-12**

Q. 9:24 Must the waiver of a QPSA specify the optional form of benefit chosen?   **9-13**

Q. 9:25 May a plan allow a spouse to give general consent to waive a QPSA or QJSA?   **9-13**

Q. 9:26 Does the nonparticipant spouse's consent to the waiver of a QJSA or a QPSA by the participant result in a taxable gift?   **9-14**

Q. 9:27 Should the plan document specifically set forth the spousal consent rules?   **9-14**

Q. 9:28 Must participants be notified of the QJSA?   **9-14**

Q. 9:29 Must participants be notified of the QPSA?   **9-15**

Q. 9:30 What happens if the plan fully subsidizes the cost of the QJSA or QPSA?   **9-15**

Q. 9:31 When did the survivor annuity benefit requirements become effective?   **9-16**

Q. 9:32 Can a qualified retirement plan provide optional ways in which to pay benefits?   **9-17**

Q. 9:33 Can a plan permit optional forms of benefit payment that favor highly compensated employees?   **9-17**

Q. 9:34 How is the determination made as to whether the current availability of an optional form of benefit is nondiscriminatory?   **9-18**

Q. 9:35 How is the determination made as to whether the effective availability of an optional form of benefit is nondiscriminatory?   **9-19**

Q. 9:36 May a qualified retirement plan deny a participant an optional form of benefit payment for which the participant is otherwise eligible?   **9-19**

Q. 9:37 Will a qualified retirement plan be considered discriminatory if it requires that an involuntary distribution be made?   **9-20**

Q. 9:38 What are the effective dates for the optional forms of benefit payment nondiscrimination rules?   **9-20**

Q. 9:39 Can a qualified retirement plan containing discriminatory optional forms of benefits be amended?   **9-21**

Q. 9:40 Should the plan administrator provide any notice that the qualified retirement plan's optional forms of benefit are being modified? **9-21**

Q. 9:41 What are Section 411(d)(6) protected benefits? **9-22**

Q. 9:42 Can a pattern of plan amendments result in an optional form of benefit? **9-23**

Q. 9:43 Can a plan provide that the employer may, through the exercise of discretion, deny a participant an optional form of benefit? **9-23**

Q. 9:44 When is the exercise of discretion by persons other than the employer treated as employer discretion? **9-24**

Q. 9:45 What is the scope of the administrative discretion exception? **9-24**

Q. 9:46 May a plan condition the availability of a Section 411(d)(6) protected benefit on objective criteria that are specifically set forth in the plan? **9-25**

Q. 9:47 May a plan be amended to add employer discretion or other conditions restricting the availability of a Section 411(d)(6) protected benefit? **9-26**

Q. 9:48 What are the effective dates of the Section 411(d)(6) protected benefit rules? **9-26**

Q. 9:49 Is there a transitional rule allowing amendment of plans containing prohibited discretion or consent provisions? **9-27**

Q. 9:50 May participants choose the way benefits will be paid to them? **9-27**

Q. 9:51 Is there a limitation on the amount of benefits that may be distributed to an individual in any one year? **9-27**

Q. 9:52 When must benefit payments to a participant begin? **9-28**

Q. 9:53 May a participant defer payment of benefits indefinitely? **9-28**

Q. 9:54 What is the required beginning date? **9-28**

Q. 9:55 When does a participant attain age 70-1/2? **9-29**

Q. 9:56 Can distributions be delayed until after the required beginning date? **9-29**

Q. 9:57 How much must be paid out each year? **9-30**

Q. 9:58 How is life expectancy determined? **9-31**

Q. 9:59 Can life expectancy be recalculated annually? 9-31

Q. 9:60 What distribution rules apply if the employee is a participant in more than one plan? 9-32

Q. 9:61 If distributions to an employee have begun prior to the employee's death, how must remaining distributions to the employee's beneficiaries be made? 9-32

Q. 9:62 If distributions to an employee have not begun prior to death, how must distributions be made to the employee's beneficiaries? 9-33

Q. 9:63 Is there a penalty for failure to make a required distribution? 9-34

Q. 9:64 How does the incidental death benefits rule affect benefit distributions? 9-34

Q. 9:65 What is the minimum distribution incidental benefit requirement? 9-35

Q. 9:66 What does the term normal retirement age mean? 9-35

Q. 9:67 May benefits commence earlier than the deadlines required under the law? 9-36

Q. 9:68 May participants be subject to penalty for early distribution of benefits? 9-36

Q. 9:69 What type of election by the participant is required to postpone the commencement of benefits? 9-37

Q. 9:70 May a participant receive benefit payments from a plan while still employed by the plan sponsor? 9-38

Q. 9:71 Can a qualified retirement plan provide early retirement benefits? 9-38

Q. 9:72 Can a qualified retirement plan make immediate distributions without the participant's consent? 9-39

Q. 9:73 What interest rate must be used to value benefits? 9-39

Q. 9:74 Does a participant have to formally apply for benefits? 9-40

Q. 9:75 What are the participant's rights if a claim for benefits is denied? 9-40

Chapter 10   Tax Deduction Rules

Q. 10:1 What are the basic requirements for deducting employer contributions to a qualified retirement plan? 10-1

Q. 10:2 When must contributions be made to be currently deductible? 10-2

Q. 10:3 May a contribution be timely for tax deduction purposes but not for the minimum funding standards? 10-2

Q. 10:4 May an employer deduct the fair market value of property other than money contributed to its qualified retirement plan? 10-3

Q. 10:5 May an employer make a timely contribution to the qualified retirement plan by check? 10-3

Q. 10:6 Is a contribution of the employer's promissory note a deductible payment? 10-4

Q. 10:7 What is the primary limitation on tax-deductible contributions to a profit sharing plan? 10-4

Q. 10:8 How are excess amounts contributed to a profit sharing plan treated for tax purposes? 10-4

Q. 10:9 How is the amount of nondeductible contributions computed? 10-5

Q. 10:10 When are nondeductible contributions for a given taxable year determined? 10-6

Q. 10:11 What happens if a deduction for plan contributions is subsequently disallowed? 10-6

Q. 10:12 Can the employer make up a missed profit sharing plan contribution? 10-6

Q. 10:13 What does compensation mean for purposes of the limits on deductible contributions to a profit sharing plan? 10-7

Q. 10:14 May a company make a deductible contribution to the profit sharing plan of an affiliated company? 10-7

Q. 10:15 What is the limit on tax-deductible contributions to defined contribution plans other than profit sharing plans? 10-8

Q. 10:16 What is the limit on tax-deductible contributions to a defined benefit plan? 10-9

Q. 10:17 How does a defined benefit plan's funding method affect its tax-deductible contributions? 10-9

Q. 10:18 Are excess amounts contributed to a defined benefit plan deductible in later years? 10-10

Q. 10:19 Are there any special limits on tax-deductible contributions if an employer maintains both a defined contribution plan and a defined benefit plan? 10-10

Q. 10:20 Are there any other limitations on the deductibility of employer contributions?   **10-11**

Q. 10:21 Will excess assets of an employer's overfunded defined benefit plan that are transferred to a defined contribution plan be considered taxable income to the employer?   **10-12**

Q. 10:22 Are excess amounts contributed to a combination of plans deductible?   **10-13**

Q. 10:23 May an employer deduct contributions to provide benefits to a participant in excess of Code Section 415 limits?   **10-13**

Q. 10:24 Are the employer's payment of plan expenses deductible?   **10-14**

Q. 10:25 How does the family aggregation rule affect the employer's tax deduction?   **10-14**

Chapter 11   Taxation of Distributions

Q. 11:1 In general, how are distributions from qualified retirement plans taxed?   **11-1**

Q. 11:2 Are any distributions from qualified retirement plans income tax-free?   **11-2**

Q. 11:3 How are annuity payments from a qualified retirement plan taxed?   **11-2**

Q. 11:4 What is a lump-sum distribution?   **11-3**

Q. 11:5 What does the term balance to the credit of an employee mean?   **11-4**

Q. 11:6 Can an employee who received installment payments later receive a lump-sum distribution from the same qualified retirement plan?   **11-5**

Q. 11:7 Are the tax benefits of a lump-sum distribution lost when an additional distribution is made in a subsequent taxable year?   **11-5**

Q. 11:8 What does separation from service mean?   **11-5**

Q. 11:9 Can a distribution from a qualified retirement plan to a disabled employee qualify as a lump-sum distribution?   **11-6**

Q. 11:10 How is a lump-sum distribution from a qualified retirement plan to the beneficiary of a deceased participant taxed?   **11-6**

Q. 11:11 Can the beneficiary of a deceased participant who received annuity payments from a qualified retirement plan receive a lump-sum distribution? **11-7**

Q. 11:12 How is a lump-sum distribution from a qualified retirement plan to an employee taxed? **11-7**

Q. 11:13 What special rules apply to a lump-sum distribution with regard to an individual who had attained age 50 before January 1, 1986? **11-8**

Q. 11:14 What tax options are available when a participant does not satisfy the five-year participation requirement? **11-9**

Q. 11:15 What portion of a lump-sum distribution is taxable? **11-9**

Q. 11:16 What is the tax treatment of a lump-sum distribution made in the form of employer securities? **11-10**

Q. 11:17 How is the tax on a lump-sum distribution computed using the five-year averaging method? **11-10**

Q. 11:18 How is the tax on a lump-sum distribution computed using the ten-year averaging method? **11-11**

Q. 11:19 What portion of a lump-sum distribution from a qualified retirement plan may be eligible for capital gains treatment? **11-12**

Q. 11:20 How is the number of months of plan participation computed? **11-14**

Q. 11:21 How is the distribution taxed if the retirement plan loses its qualified status? **11-14**

Q. 11:22 How does a recipient elect special forward averaging for a lump-sum distribution? **11-14**

Q. 11:23 Must all recipients of a single lump-sum distribution elect to use forward averaging? **11-15**

Q. 11:24 What is the income tax treatment of distributions of deductible employee contributions made by a participant? **11-15**

Q. 11:25 May any additional taxes be imposed on the recipient of a distribution from a qualified retirement plan? **11-16**

Q. 11:26 What are excess distributions? **11-16**

Q. 11:27 What distributions are taken into account to compute the individual's excess distributions? **11-16**

Q. 11:28 Is there a special rule regarding excess distributions when the individual receives a lump-sum distribution? **11-18**

Q. 11:29 What is the grandfather rule? 11-19

Q. 11:30 What portion of a distribution is treated as the recovery of an individual's initial grandfather amount? 11-19

Q. 11:31 What is the discretionary method? 11-20

Q. 11:32 What is the attained age method? 11-21

Q. 11:33 How is the amount of the excess distribution tax calculated when the special grandfather rule applies? 11-21

Q. 11:34 How is the special grandfather rule applied if an individual receives both a lump-sum distribution and a nonlump-sum distribution in the same year? 11-22

Q. 11:35 Is the excess distribution tax reduced by the early distribution tax? 11-22

Q. 11:36 Can a qualified retirement plan be amended to avoid the excess distribution tax? 11-23

Q. 11:37 May an additional estate tax be imposed at the participant's death? 11-23

Q. 11:38 Are there any limitations on loans from qualified retirement plans? 11-23

Q. 11:39 Is there a maximum repayment period for a loan from a qualified retirement plan? 11-25

Q. 11:40 Is interest paid on loans from qualified retirement plans deductible? 11-25

Q. 11:41 Is it necessary to obtain spousal consent for a loan from a qualified retirement plan? 11-26

Q. 11:42 Are there any other requirements applicable to loans from qualified retirement plans? 11-26

Chapter 12 Life Insurance and Death Benefits

Q. 12:1 Must a qualified retirement plan provide a death benefit to participants? 12-1

Q. 12:2 May a qualified retirement plan provide life insurance coverage for participants? 12-1

Q. 12:3 Is a company allowed a deduction for life insurance purchased under a qualified retirement plan? 12-2

Q. 12:4   What limits apply to the amount of life insurance that can be purchased for participants under a qualified retirement plan?   **12-2**

Q. 12:5   Does the purchase of life insurance affect retirement benefits?   **12-3**

Q. 12:6   What are the tax consequences to participants when their employer's qualified retirement plan provides life insurance protection?   **12-3**

Q. 12:7   What are P.S. 58 costs?   **12-4**

Q. 12:8   Must the P.S. 58 rates be used to determine the cost of pure life insurance included in a participant's gross income?   **12-5**

Q. 12:9   Are loans from insurance policies purchased under qualified retirement plans taxable?   **12-6**

Q. 12:10   Who receives the proceeds from life insurance purchased under a qualified retirement plan when a participant dies before retirement?   **12-6**

Q. 12:11   How are proceeds from life insurance purchased under a qualified retirement plan taxed for income tax purposes?   **12-6**

Q. 12:12   Are proceeds from life insurance purchased under a qualified retirement plan included in the participant's estate for tax purposes?   **12-7**

Q. 12:13   Can a participant recover the P.S. 58 costs tax-free when qualified retirement plan benefits are distributed?   **12-7**

Q. 12:14   Are P.S. 58 costs recovered tax-free by a deceased participant's beneficiary?   **12-8**

Q. 12:15   What advantage does a participant gain when the company's qualified retirement plan provides life insurance protection?   **12-8**

Q. 12:16   How are death benefit payments under a qualified retirement plan taxed?   **12-8**

Q. 12:17   Are any deceased participants entitled to an estate tax exclusion with respect to death benefit payments received from a qualified retirement plan?   **12-9**

Q. 12:18   Is a deceased participant's estate entitled to a marital deduction for death benefit payments received by the surviving spouse from a qualified retirement plan?   **12-10**

Q. 12:19   May any additional taxes be imposed on the estate of a decedent?   **12-10**

Q. 12:20 What is an excess retirement accumulation?   12-11
Q. 12:21 How are the deceased participant's aggregate
          interests calculated?   12-11
Q. 12:22 How is the present value of the single life annuity
          calculated for purposes of determining the amount
          of the participant's excess retirement
          accumulation?   12-12
Q. 12:23 Is the special grandfather rule applicable in
          determining the amount of a deceased
          participant's excess retirement accumulation?   12-13
Q. 12:24 Is there a special rule if the surviving spouse is
          the beneficiary of the deceased participant's
          aggregate interests?   12-13
Q. 12:25 Is the excess retirement accumulation tax
          deductible?   12-13
Q. 12:26 Who is liable for the excess retirement
          accumulation tax?   12-14
Q. 12:27 Whether or not the estate tax on an excess
          retirement accumulation is imposed, are postdeath
          distributions subject to the taxes on excess
          distributions or excess retirement accumulations?   12-14

Chapter 13   Determination Letters

Q. 13:1   What is an IRS determination letter?   13-1
Q. 13:2   Is a fee charged for a request for a determination
          letter?   13-1
Q. 13:3   Must an employer apply for a determination letter? 13-3
Q. 13:4   What does the term qualifies in operation mean?   13-3
Q. 13:5   What are the limitations of a favorable
          determination letter?   13-3
Q. 13:6   When should a retirement plan be submitted for
          IRS approval?   13-4
Q. 13:7   What are the filing requirements for obtaining a
          favorable determination letter?   13-5
Q. 13:8   What are the requirements regarding notice to
          employees?   13-6
Q. 13:9   Where is an application for a determination letter
          sent?   13-7

Q. 13:10 What happens to an application for a determination letter after it is sent to IRS?   13-9

Q. 13:11 How long does it take to obtain a determination letter?   13-10

Q. 13:12 What alternatives are available to an applicant if IRS proposes to issue an adverse determination letter?   13-10

Q. 13:13 Once a favorable determination letter is issued, may IRS subsequently revoke such qualification?   13-11

Chapter 14   Operating the Plan

Q. 14:1   Who is the plan administrator?   14-1

Q. 14:2   Can officers or owners of the company function as plan administrator?   14-2

Q. 14:3   What are the basic responsibilities of the plan administrator?   14-2

Q. 14:4   Which records should a plan administrator maintain?   14-2

Q. 14:5   May the plan administrator rely on information gathered by those performing ministerial functions?   14-4

Q. 14:6   What penalty is imposed for failure to comply with recordkeeping requirements?   14-4

Q. 14:7   Is withholding required on the distribution of benefits from a retirement plan?   14-4

Q. 14:8   Is there any liability for failure to withhold income taxes?   14-5

Q. 14:9   Which types of retirement plans are subject to the withholding rules on distributions?   14-5

Q. 14:10 How should a plan administrator handle oral inquiries from participants?   14-5

Q. 14:11 Must a recipient receive an explanation of the tax effects of a distribution from a qualified retirement plan?   14-6

Q. 14:12 May the plan administrator or trustee choose the form of distribution that will be made to a participant?   14-8

Q. 14:13 Can innocent errors in the operation of a qualified retirement plan result in disqualification of the plan? 14-8

Q. 14:14 What is the actuary's role in administering a qualified retirement plan? 14-8

Q. 14:15 What is the trustee's role in administering a qualified retirement plan? 14-9

Q. 14:16 What is the accountant's role in administering a qualified retirement plan? 14-9

Q. 14:17 Which plan officials must be bonded? 14-9

Q. 14:18 What are funds or other property for purposes of the bonding requirement? 14-10

Q. 14:19 What is handling of funds? 14-10

Q. 14:20 Are any fiduciaries exempt from the bonding requirements? 14-10

Q. 14:21 May a party in interest provide a bond in satisfaction of the bonding requirements? 14-11

Q. 14:22 Is bonding required for a plan with only one participant? 14-11

Chapter 15 Reporting to Government Agencies

Q. 15:1 What are IRS's reporting requirements? 15-1

Q. 15:2 Which Form 5500 series return is required for a particular qualified retirement plan? 15-1

Q. 15:3 Does the plan administrator have the option of filing Form 5500-C/R as Form 5500-C annually instead of as Form 5500-R? 15-3

Q. 15:4 Must any special schedules accompany the employer's annual return? 15-3

Q. 15:5 When is a Form 5500 series annual return due? 15-4

Q. 15:6 May the due date for filing a Form 5500 series annual return be extended? 15-4

Q. 15:7 Is the extension of time for filing the Form 5500 series annual return ever automatic? 15-5

Q. 15:8 What penalties may be imposed for late filing of the Form 5500 series annual return? 15-5

Q. 15:9 Are there any criminal penalties for violations of the reporting requirements? 15-6

Q. 15:10 Does a plan administrator's reliance on a third party to timely file the Form 5500 series annual return constitute reasonable cause for late filing?   **15-6**

Q. 15:11 Does the statute of limitations apply to the Form 5500 series annual return?   **15-7**

Q. 15:12 Does the filing of Form 5500 start the statute of limitations running with regard to a prohibited transaction?   **15-7**

Q. 15:13 Must a plan engage an independent accountant when it files its Form 5500 series annual return?   **15-7**

Q. 15:14 Where are the Form 5500 series annual returns filed?   **15-8**

Q. 15:15 Which special returns must be filed with IRS?   **15-9**

Q. 15:16 Which forms are used to report qualified retirement plan distributions?   **15-10**

Q. 15:17 What are the DOL reporting requirements?   **15-11**

Q. 15:18 Which types of plans are exempt from the reporting requirements of DOL?   **15-11**

Q. 15:19 Which forms must be filed with PBGC?   **15-12**

Q. 15:20 When are the PBGC premium forms due?   **15-12**

Q. 15:21 How does a change in the plan year affect the due dates for filing the PBGC premium forms?   **15-15**

Q. 15:22 Must PBGC Form 1 be filed after the plan is terminated?   **15-16**

Q. 15:23 What happens if the premium payment is late?   **15-16**

Q. 15:24 Can the late penalty charges be waived?   **15-16**

Q. 15:25 Are there any other notification requirements to PBGC?   **15-17**

Chapter 16   Summary Plan Descriptions

Q. 16:1 What is a summary plan description?   **16-1**

Q. 16:2 When must an SPD be furnished to a participant?   **16-2**

Q. 16:3 Where is the SPD filed?   **16-3**

Q. 16:4 What information must an SPD contain?   **16-3**

Q. 16:5 Is an SPD a legally binding document?   **16-4**

Q. 16:6 What is the purpose of a disclaimer clause?   **16-4**

Q. 16:7 Will a disclaimer in an SPD be recognized in a
lawsuit?   16-5
Q. 16:8 What happens if the plan is changed?   16-5
Q. 16:9 What constitutes a reportable material modification? 16-6
Q. 16:10 How often is an updated SPD due?   16-6
Q. 16:11 How is the five-year period for an updated SPD
measured?   16-6
Q. 16:12 What happens if the plan is terminated?   16-7
Q. 16:13 What documents other than an SPD can a
participant obtain?   16-7
Q. 16:14 Is there any special requirement if many plan
participants cannot read English?   16-8

Chapter 17 Fiduciary Responsibilities

Q. 17:1 Who is a fiduciary under ERISA?   17-1
Q. 17:2 What is rendering investment advice for the
purpose of determining fiduciary status?   17-3
Q. 17:3 What is a named fiduciary?   17-3
Q. 17:4 Are attorneys, accountants, actuaries, and
consultants who provide services to a plan
considered plan fiduciaries?   17-4
Q. 17:5 Do the fiduciary responsibility rules of ERISA apply
to a Keogh plan?   17-4
Q. 17:6 What is a self-directed account plan?   17-5
Q. 17:7 Is a participant or beneficiary who self-directs an
individual account considered a fiduciary?   17-5
Q. 17:8 Are any individuals prohibited from serving as
fiduciaries?   17-6
Q. 17:9 Can a trustee be appointed for life?   17-6
Q. 17:10 What is a fiduciary's basic duty?   17-6
Q. 17:11 What standard of care is a fiduciary held to?   17-7
Q. 17:12 How does the prudent man standard apply to
trustees or investment managers?   17-7
Q. 17:13 Would a transaction involving the plan that benefits
the employer result in a breach of fiduciary duty?   17-7
Q. 17:14 Must the assets of the plan be segregated?   17-8
Q. 17:15 What are plan assets when a plan invests in
another entity?   17-8

Q. 17:16   Are there any exceptions to the look-through rule?   **17-8**

Q. 17:17   What is an equity interest and a publicly offered
security?   **17-8**

Q. 17:18   What is an operating company?   **17-9**

Q. 17:19   What level of participation of benefit plan investors
is considered "significant"?   **17-10**

Q. 17:20   What is a benefit plan investor?   **17-10**

Q. 17:21   Are there any investments by a plan that may
never satisfy the exceptions to the look-through
rule?   **17-10**

Q. 17:22   When are participant contributions considered plan
assets?   **17-11**

Q. 17:23   What expenses relating to the plan may be paid
out of plan assets?   **17-12**

Q. 17:24   What are the consequences if plan assets are
used improperly?   **17-12**

Q. 17:25   Can a fiduciary be held liable for a breach of
duty?   **17-12**

Q. 17:26   Can a nonfiduciary be held liable for a breach of
duty?   **17-13**

Q. 17:27   May a fiduciary be held liable for breaches
committed by a co-fiduciary?   **17-14**

Q. 17:28   What should a fiduciary do if a co-fiduciary
commits a breach of duty?   **17-14**

Q. 17:29   Can a breaching fiduciary obtain contribution or
indemnity from other breaching co-fiduciaries?   **17-14**

Q. 17:30   Does ERISA authorize punitive damages for breach
of fiduciary duty?   **17-15**

Q. 17:31   Can the plan contain a provision relieving a
fiduciary of personal liability?   **17-16**

Q. 17:32   Is a release executed by a plan beneficiary freeing
plan fiduciaries from past liability under ERISA
valid?   **17-16**

Q. 17:33   Can fiduciary responsibility be delegated?   **17-16**

Q. 17:34   What is the liability of an investment manager for
its decisions regarding investment of plan assets?   **17-17**

Q. 17:35   Are there any limits on the investments a qualified
retirement plan can make?   **17-17**

Q. 17:36   May a qualified retirement plan borrow to make
investments?   **17-18**

Q. 17:37   What is the diversification requirement?   **17-18**

Q. 17:38   Must a plan make only blue chip investments?   **17-19**

Q. 17:39 How can a trustee or other plan fiduciary be protected from lawsuits for failure to meet the prudent man rule? **17-20**

Q. 17:40 May a qualified retirement plan invest in employer securities or employer real property? **17-20**

Q. 17:41 What is qualifying employer real property? **17-21**

Q. 17:42 What are qualifying employer securities? **17-22**

Q. 17:43 What does earmarking investments mean? **17-22**

Q. 17:44 What are pooled investment funds? **17-23**

Q. 17:45 Can plan assets be invested in a mutual fund? **17-23**

Chapter 18   Prohibited Transactions

Q. 18:1   What is a prohibited transaction? **18-1**

Q. 18:2   Who is a party in interest? **18-2**

Q. 18:3   How do the prohibited-transaction provisions under the Code differ from the prohibited-transaction provisions under ERISA? **18-3**

Q. 18:4   What penalties may be imposed on a party in interest or disqualified person for engaging in a prohibited transaction? **18-3**

Q. 18:5   How is a prohibited transaction corrected? **18-4**

Q. 18:6   May a plan purchase insurance to cover any losses to the plan resulting from a prohibited transaction? **18-4**

Q. 18:7   Are there any statutory exceptions to the prohibited-transaction provisions? **18-4**

Q. 18:8   Can an employer's contribution of property to a qualified retirement plan be a prohibited transaction? **18-5**

Q. 18:9   Can a party in interest obtain an exemption from the prohibited-transaction restrictions? **18-5**

Q. 18:10 Can a prohibited-transaction exemption be granted retroactively? **18-6**

Q. 18:11 Can a prohibited-transaction exemption be used to benefit the owner of a closely held corporation? **18-6**

Q. 18:12 What is a prohibited-transaction class exemption? **18-8**

Chapter 19 Termination of the Plan

Q. 19:1 Once a qualified retirement plan is established,
may the employer terminate it? 19-1

Q. 19:2 May a qualified retirement plan be terminated by a
formal declaration of the plan sponsor's board of
directors? 19-1

Q. 19:3 Which factors may cause a qualified retirement
plan to be terminated? 19-2

Q. 19:4 What is the effect of a plan termination on a
participant's accrued benefit? 19-2

Q. 19:5 What is a partial termination? 19-3

Q. 19:6 Does the adoption of a new qualified retirement
plan to replace another plan result in a
termination of the original plan? 19-5

Q. 19:7 Can termination of a qualified retirement plan
affect its tax-favored status for earlier years? 19-5

Q. 19:8 Is there a limit on the amount that a pension plan
may pay to participants in the first 10 years of
operation? 19-6

Q. 19:9 What is Title IV of ERISA? 19-7

Q. 19:10 What is the Pension Benefit Guaranty Corporation? 19-7

Q. 19:11 What are the Single Employer Pension Plan
Amendment Act and the Pension Protection Act? 19-7

Q. 19:12 What pension plans are insured by PBGC? 19-8

Q. 19:13 Are any qualified defined benefit plans exempt
from PBGC coverage? 19-8

Q. 19:14 What must plan sponsors pay as an insurance
premium to PBGC? 19-9

Q. 19:15 How is the number of participants determined for
insurance premium purposes? 19-9

Q. 19:16 Must a plan administrator notify PBGC when
certain significant events affecting a
single-employer defined benefit plan occur? 19-10

Q. 19:17 What is a standard termination? 19-11

Q. 19:18 What are benefit liabilities? 19-11

Q. 19:19 What is a distress termination? 19-12

Q. 19:20 What benefits under a single-employer defined
benefit plan are guaranteed by PBGC? 19-12

Q. 19:21 Does PBGC guarantee a benefit that becomes nonforfeitable solely as a result of the plan's termination?   19-13

Q. 19:22 Are there any limitations on the amount of the benefit PBGC will guarantee?   19-13

Q. 19:23 What is the maximum guaranteed monthly benefit for 1990?   19-14

Q. 19:24 What is the effect on PBGC's guarantees of a plan amendment prior to the plan's termination?   19-14

Q. 19:25 What is the effect of the plan's disqualification on the guaranteed benefit?   19-14

Q. 19:26 Can PBGC initiate the termination of a plan?   19-15

Q. 19:27 Can a plan covered by Title IV be terminated if the termination would violate an existing collective bargaining agreement?   19-16

Q. 19:28 Is there any restriction on the form of a benefit paid by a terminating defined benefit plan?   19-16

Q. 19:29 Who must be notified of the company's intention to terminate a defined benefit plan covered by Title IV--and when must this notice be given?   19-16

Q. 19:30 What is the relevance of the date of plan termination?   19-17

Q. 19:31 What factors are considered by PBGC in establishing a defined benefit plan's termination date?   19-17

Q. 19:32 Who is an affected party?   19-17

Q. 19:33 Are there any other notice requirements if the company intends to terminate a defined benefit plan?   19-18

Q. 19:34 What information is the plan administrator required to send to participants and beneficiaries in the Notice of Plan Benefits?   19-18

Q. 19:35 After the plan administrator's notice is sent to PBGC, does PBGC have to act within designated time limits?   19-19

Q. 19:36 May the 60-day period for PBGC to issue a notice of noncompliance be extended?   19-19

Q. 19:37 Assuming that PBGC does not issue a notice of noncompliance, when should final distribution of assets occur?   19-19

Q. 19:38 What is the method for the final distribution of assets?   19-20

Q. 19:39 How are plan assets allocated when a defined benefit plan is terminated? **19-20**

Q. 19:40 What does the phrase "all other benefits under the plan" cover? **19-21**

Q. 19:41 Can a distribution of plan assets be reallocated? **19-22**

Q. 19:42 Must PBGC be notified once final distribution of assets is completed? **19-22**

Q. 19:43 Does PBGC perform post-termination audits for compliance with the Title IV requirements? **19-23**

Q. 19:44 Does an employer incur any liability to PBGC for the payment of benefits to plan participants of an underfunded terminated plan? **19-23**

Q. 19:45 May excess assets remaining after the standard termination of a defined benefit plan be returned to the employer after payment of all plan benefit liabilities? **19-24**

Q. 19:46 May a defined benefit plan that did not originally provide for distribution of excess assets to the employer be amended to authorize such a distribution? **19-24**

Q. 19:47 May an employer terminate a defined benefit plan to recover any excess assets and adopt a new defined benefit plan covering the same employees? **19-25**

Q. 19:48 Is the employer liable for any taxes on the reversion? **19-26**

Q. 19:49 If an employer wants to withdraw from a plan maintained by two or more unrelated employers, would the withdrawal be considered a plan termination? **19-26**

Q. 19:50 What is a complete discontinuance of contributions under a profit sharing plan? **19-27**

Q. 19:51 Must a profit sharing plan provide for full vesting of benefits upon a complete discontinuance of contributions? **19-28**

Q. 19:52 Can a plan amendment result in the termination of the plan? **19-28**

Q. 19:53 Can a plan be amended to reduce or stop benefit accruals? **19-29**

Q. 19:54 Must terminating plans be amended to conform to TRA '86 qualification requirements? **19-29**

Q. 19:55 Must IRS be notified when a plan terminates? **19-29**

Chapter 20   Top-Heavy Plans

Q. 20:1	What is a top-heavy defined benefit plan?	20-1
Q. 20:2	How are accrued benefits calculated for purposes of determining whether a qualified retirement plan is top-heavy?	20-1
Q. 20:3	What is a top-heavy defined contribution plan?	20-2
Q. 20:4	Which qualified retirement plans are subject to the top-heavy rules?	20-2
Q. 20:5	Is a multiple employer plan subject to the top-heavy rules?	20-2
Q. 20:6	Are qualified nonelective contributions under a 401(k) plan taken into account for top-heavy purposes?	20-3
Q. 20:7	What is a top-heavy simplified employee pension?	20-3
Q. 20:8	Which factors must be considered in determining whether a qualified retirement plan is top-heavy?	20-3
Q. 20:9	What is a required aggregation group?	20-4
Q. 20:10	What is a permissive aggregation group?	20-4
Q. 20:11	Must collectively bargained retirement plans be aggregated with other retirement plans of the employer?	20-5
Q. 20:12	What is a top-heavy group?	20-5
Q. 20:13	How are separate retirement plans of related employers treated for purposes of the top-heavy rules?	20-6
Q. 20:14	How is a terminated retirement plan treated for purposes of the top-heavy rules?	20-7
Q. 20:15	How is a frozen retirement plan treated for purposes of the top-heavy rules?	20-7
Q. 20:16	What happens if an employee ceases to be a key employee?	20-7
Q. 20:17	How are plan distributions to employees treated for purposes of determining whether the qualified retirement plan is top-heavy?	20-8
Q. 20:18	Are death benefits treated as distributions for purposes of determining whether a qualified retirement plan is top-heavy?	20-8
Q. 20:19	How are rollovers and transfers treated for purposes of determining whether a retirement plan is top-heavy?	20-8

Q. 20:20 How are employee contributions treated for purposes of determining whether a qualified retirement plan is top-heavy?   **20-9**

Q. 20:21 When is the determination date?   **20-9**

Q. 20:22 If the employer has more than one qualified retirement plan, when is the top-heavy determination made?   **20-10**

Q. 20:23 Are there special qualification requirements that apply to top-heavy plans?   **20-11**

Q. 20:24 Who is a key employee?   **20-11**

Q. 20:25 Who is an officer of the employer for top-heavy plan purposes?   **20-11**

Q. 20:26 Do any organizations other than corporations have officers?   **20-12**

Q. 20:27 Who is one of the ten largest owners of the employer?   **20-12**

Q. 20:28 Who is a 5%-owner or a 1%-owner for top-heavy plan purposes?   **20-13**

Q. 20:29 Who is a non-key employee?   **20-13**

Q. 20:30 Who is a former key employee?   **20-13**

Q. 20:31 How is a beneficiary treated under the top-heavy plan rules?   **20-14**

Q. 20:32 What is the minimum vesting requirement for a top-heavy plan?   **20-14**

Q. 20:33 Which years of service must be taken into account for minimum vesting purposes?   **20-14**

Q. 20:34 Which benefits must be subject to the minimum top-heavy vesting requirement?   **20-15**

Q. 20:35 When a top-heavy plan ceases to be top-heavy, may the vesting schedule be changed?   **20-15**

Q. 20:36 Which top-heavy vesting schedule is more favorable to the employer?   **20-15**

Q. 20:37 What is the minimum benefit requirement for a top-heavy defined benefit plan?   **20-17**

Q. 20:38 What does annual retirement benefit mean for the minimum benefit requirement?   **20-18**

Q. 20:39 What is the minimum benefit required if the employee receives benefits other than at normal retirement age?   **20-18**

Q. 20:40 What does the term participant's average compensation mean for the minimum benefit requirement?   **20-18**

Q. 20:41 Which years of service are taken into account in determining the minimum annual benefit under a top-heavy defined benefit plan?   **20-18**

Q. 20:42 Which employees must receive a minimum benefit in a top-heavy defined benefit plan?   **20-20**

Q. 20:43 What is the minimum contribution requirement for a top-heavy defined contribution plan?   **20-20**

Q. 20:44 Do forfeitures affect the minimum contribution requirement?   **20-21**

Q. 20:45 What does participant's compensation mean for purposes of the minimum contribution requirement?   **20-21**

Q. 20:46 Which employees must receive the top-heavy defined contribution plan minimum contribution?   **20-21**

Q. 20:47 Can Social Security benefits or contributions be used to satisfy the minimum benefit and contribution requirements?   **20-22**

Q. 20:48 Can elective contributions under a 401(k) plan be used to satisfy the top-heavy minimum contribution rules?   **20-22**

Q. 20:49 Must an employer that has both a top-heavy defined benefit plan and a top-heavy defined contribution plan provide both a minimum benefit and a minimum contribution for non-key employees?   **20-23**

Q. 20:50 What is the limitation on compensation that may be taken into account under a top-heavy plan?   **20-24**

Q. 20:51 What happens if a key employee participates in both a defined benefit plan and a defined contribution plan?   **20-24**

Q. 20:52 At what level of compensation is a key employee excluded from participating in a second plan?   **20-25**

Q. 20:53 At what level of compensation will the top-heavy 1.0 rule have an effect on a key employee?   **20-26**

Q. 20:54 What is the special rule if two qualified retirement plans were adopted prior to 1984?   **20-26**

Q. 20:55 What happens if a key employee's combined fractions exceed 1.0?   **20-28**

Q. 20:56 If a key employee participates in both a defined benefit plan and a defined contribution plan, can his or her overall maximum limitation be computed under the regular 1.0 rule?   **20-28**

Q. 20:57 What is the concentration test for purposes of the
1.0 rule? **20-28**

Q. 20:58 What is an extra minimum benefit or extra
minimum contribution for purposes of the 1.0
rule? **20-29**

Q. 20:59 Must every qualified retirement plan be amended
to incorporate the top-heavy plan requirements? **20-30**

Chapter 21   401(k) Plans

Q. 21:1 What is a 401(k) plan? **21-1**

Q. 21:2 What is a cash-or-deferred election? **21-2**

Q. 21:3 When is an employee's election a cash-or-deferred
election? **21-3**

Q. 21:4 Does a 401(k) plan qualify for favorable tax
treatment? **21-3**

Q. 21:5 Are elective contributions to a 401(k) plan taxable
to the employee? **21-4**

Q. 21:6 Must a cash-or-deferred plan be a profit sharing
plan? **21-5**

Q. 21:7 May a self-employed individual participate in a
401(k) plan? **21-5**

Q. 21:8 What are the special nondiscrimination tests for a
401(k) plan? **21-5**

Q. 21:9 How is the ADP calculated for purposes of
applying the ADP test? **21-6**

Q. 21:10 How is the actual deferral ratio of an employee
calculated if an employer maintains more than
one 401(k) plan? **21-8**

Q. 21:11 What does compensation mean for purposes of the
ADP test? **21-8**

Q. 21:12 What contributions are counted for purposes of the
ADP test? **21-9**

Q. 21:13 What are elective contributions? **21-10**

Q. 21:14 What are qualified nonelective contributions and
qualified matching contributions? **21-10**

Q. 21:15 Is there a simple rule to follow in determining
whether the ADP test is satisfied? **21-12**

Q. 21:16 What are excess contributions? **21-12**

Q. 21:17 How are excess contributions corrected?   21-13

Q. 21:18 What happens if a 401(k) plan fails to correct excess contributions?   21-14

Q. 21:19 How are excess contributions recharacterized?   21-14

Q. 21:20 What are the tax consequences of the recharacterization of excess contributions?   21-15

Q. 21:21 When must the recharacterization of excess contributions occur?   21-15

Q. 21:22 Does the recharacterization of excess contributions result in a penalty tax to the employee?   21-16

Q. 21:23 Is there an excise tax on recharacterized excess contributions?   21-16

Q. 21:24 How is an excess contribution corrected by distribution?   21-16

Q. 21:25 How is a distribution of an excess contribution taxed?   21-17

Q. 21:26 Is there a dollar limitation on the amount of elective contributions?   21-17

Q. 21:27 To what time period does the dollar limitation on elective contributions apply?   21-18

Q. 21:28 How are excess deferrals corrected?   21-18

Q. 21:29 What are the tax consequences of making excess deferrals?   21-19

Q. 21:30 Are excess deferrals distributed after year-end to an employee nevertheless counted for purposes of the ADP test?   21-20

Q. 21:31 Must all contributions under a 401(k) plan be nonforfeitable?   21-20

Q. 21:32 What is a combined 401(k) plan?   21-21

Q. 21:33 When may distributions be made under a 401(k) plan?   21-22

Q. 21:34 What amounts may be distributed in the case of a participant's hardship?   21-23

Q. 21:35 What constitutes hardship?   21-23

Q. 21:36 How is a heavy and immediate financial need (Part 1) determined under the facts-and-circumstances test?   21-24

Q. 21:37 How is a heavy and immediate financial need (Part 1) determined under the safe-harbor test?   21-24

Q. 21:38 How is a hardship withdrawal determined to be necessary (Part 2) under the facts-and-circumstances test?   **21-25**

Q. 21:39 How is a hardship withdrawal determined to be necessary under (Part 2) the safe-harbor test?   **21-26**

Q. 21:40 Are matching contributions and nonelective contributions subject to the nonforfeitability and distribution requirements applicable to elective contributions?   **21-27**

Q. 21:41 What is a separate accounting under a 401(k) plan?   **21-27**

Q. 21:42 Can an employer maintain two or more 401(k) plans?   **21-27**

Q. 21:43 Can a CODA be part of a thrift or savings plan?   **21-28**

Q. 21:44 How does a CODA affect the employer's tax-deductible contributions?   **21-28**

Q. 21:45 How does a CODA affect the annual addition limitation?   **21-29**

Q. 21:46 Are elective contributions subject to payroll taxes?   **21-29**

Q. 21:47 Does a 401(k) plan require registration with the Securities and Exchange Commission?   **21-29**

Q. 21:48 What is the special nondiscrimination test for qualified plans with employer matching contributions and/or employee contributions?   **21-30**

Q. 21:49 How is the ACP calculated for purposes of applying the ACP test?   **21-30**

Q. 21:50 What contributions may be included for purposes of the ACP test?   **21-31**

Q. 21:51 When are contributions counted for purposes of applying the ACP test?   **21-32**

Q. 21:52 What other requirements must a plan subject to the ACP test meet?   **21-33**

Q. 21:53 What are excess aggregate contributions under the ACP test?   **21-34**

Q. 21:54 How are excess aggregate contributions corrected?   **21-34**

Q. 21:55 What is the tax treatment of excess aggregate contributions?   **21-35**

Q. 21:56 What is the multiple use limitation?   **21-36**

Q. 21:57 What are the family aggregation rules?   **21-38**

Chapter 22   Employee Stock Ownership Plans

Q. 22:1	What is an employee stock ownership plan?	22-1
Q. 22:2	When can participants exercise their put option?	22-2
Q. 22:3	How is an ESOP different from a stock bonus plan?	22-3
Q. 22:4	What is an exempt loan?	22-3
Q. 22:5	Do commercial lenders have a tax incentive to make loans to ESOPs?	22-3
Q. 22:6	What is a securities acquisition loan?	22-4
Q. 22:7	Which commercial lenders are eligible for the 50 percent interest exclusion?	22-5
Q. 22:8	May loans that qualify for the 50 percent interest exclusion be transferred to other lending institutions?	22-6
Q. 22:9	Is there a limit on the time period for which the 50 percent interest exclusion applies?	22-6
Q. 22:10	What are employer securities?	22-7
Q. 22:11	What is the limitation on tax-deductible contributions to an ESOP?	22-7
Q. 22:12	Are dividends paid on employer securities held by an ESOP ever deductible by the employer?	22-7
Q. 22:13	Are dividends paid to participants deductible even if participants can elect whether or not to receive them in a current cash payment?	22-8
Q. 22:14	How are dividends paid to ESOP participants taxed?	22-9
Q. 22:15	What is the limit on the amount that may be added to an ESOP participant's account each year?	22-9
Q. 22:16	Can a company obtain a tax deduction for stock contributions to its ESOP?	22-10
Q. 22:17	Can an ESOP be integrated with Social Security?	22-10
Q. 22:18	How can a company use an ESOP to help finance the acquisition of another company?	22-11
Q. 22:19	Are ESOPs used by publicly traded companies to defend against unwanted takeovers?	22-11
Q. 22:20	Can a profit sharing plan be converted to an ESOP?	22-12

Q. 22:21 How can an ESOP be used as an estate planning tool for the owner of a closely held corporation? **22-12**

Q. 22:22 Is there an estate tax deduction for sales of employer securities to an ESOP? **22-13**

Q. 22:23 What are qualified employer securities? **22-14**

Q. 22:24 What proceeds may be taken into account in determining the estate tax deduction? **22-15**

Q. 22:25 Is any statement required to be filed by the executor? **22-16**

Q. 22:26 Are there any penalties for the improper allocation or disposition of employer securities purchased by the ESOP in a qualified sale? **22-16**

Q. 22:27 What is the nonallocation period? **22-17**

Q. 22:28 Can an ESOP assume the estate tax liability of a deceased stockholder? **22-17**

Q. 22:29 How can an ESOP be used to provide a market for the stock of controlling shareholders in a closely held corporation? **22-18**

Q. 22:30 May gain on the sale of securities to an ESOP be deferred? **22-19**

Q. 22:31 Are all taxpayers eligible to elect deferral of gain upon the sale of securities to an ESOP? **22-19**

Q. 22:32 What are qualified securities? **22-19**

Q. 22:33 What is qualified replacement property? **22-19**

Q. 22:34 What is the replacement period? **22-20**

Q. 22:35 What other conditions apply before the deferral of gain is permitted? **22-20**

Q. 22:36 How does the selling shareholder elect not to recognize gain? **22-20**

Q. 22:37 What is the basis of qualified replacement property? **22-22**

Q. 22:38 What happens if the taxpayer who elects nonrecognition treatment later disposes of the qualified replacement property? **22-22**

Q. 22:39 Do all dispositions of qualified replacement property result in the recapture of gain? **22-22**

Q. 22:40 What is the statute of limitations when a selling shareholder elects nonrecognition of the gain on the sale of qualified securities? **22-23**

Q. 22:41 What happens if the ESOP disposes of qualified securities within three years of their acquisition? **22-23**

Q. 22:42 What is the amount of the excise tax on the disposition of qualified securities? 22-24

Q. 22:43 Are there any restrictions on the allocation of employer securities acquired by the ESOP in a transaction in which the seller elected nonrecognition of gain? 22-25

Q. 22:44 How can an ESOP be used to facilitate a buyout of shareholders in a closely held corporation? 22-26

Q. 22:45 How can an ESOP be used to finance a business? 22-27

Q. 22:46 May an ESOP enter into an agreement obligating itself to purchase stock when a shareholder dies? 22-27

Q. 22:47 Must plan participants be given voting rights with respect to their stock? 22-28

Q. 22:48 What is diversification of investments in an ESOP? 22-28

Q. 22:49 Who is a qualified participant? 22-28

Q. 22:50 What is the qualified election period? 22-29

Q. 22:51 What must an ESOP do to satisfy the diversification requirements? 22-29

Q. 22:52 What is the effect of the diversification or distribution of a participant's employer securities? 22-29

Q. 22:53 Are all employer securities held by an ESOP subject to diversification? 20-30

Q. 22:54 Are dividends paid to an ESOP subject to the diversification rules? 20-30

Q. 22:55 How is the determination made as to which employer securities are subject to diversification? 20-31

Q. 22:56 May any qualified participants in ESOPs that hold employer securities acquired after December 31, 1986 be excluded from making the diversification election? 22-32

Q. 22:57 May employer securities acquired before 1987 be diversified? 22-32

Q. 22:58 May an ESOP permit a qualified participant to elect diversification of amounts in excess of that required by statute? 22-32

Q. 22:59 Is a loan from a shareholder to an ESOP a prohibited transaction? 22-33

Q. 22:60 Must distributions under an ESOP commence by specified dates? 22-33

Q. 22:61 Must distributions under an ESOP be made at certain intervals? 22-33

Q. 22:62 Are distributions from an ESOP subject to the 10 percent additional tax on early distributions?   22-34

Q. 22:63 Which factors are used to value employer securities that are not readily tradable?   22-34

Q. 22:64 Is a participant's interest in an ESOP exempt from bankruptcy?   22-35

Chapter 23   Multiemployer Plans

Q. 23:1 What kind of retirement plan is used to provide retirement benefits for union workers?   23-1

Q. 23:2 What is a multiemployer plan?   23-2

Q. 23:3 What are the basic advantages of a multiemployer plan?   23-3

Q. 23:4 How are hours of service credited to an employee under a multiemployer plan?   23-3

Q. 23:5 Is a retirement plan maintained by two or more affiliated companies considered a multiemployer plan?   23-3

Q. 23:6 Are benefits under a multiemployer plan guaranteed?   23-4

Q. 23:7 When is a multiemployer plan insolvent?   23-4

Q. 23:8 What level of benefits is guaranteed?   23-4

Q. 23:9 What benefits are not guaranteed by PBGC?   23-5

Q. 23:10 What is the financial liability of an employer that withdraws from a multiemployer plan?   23-5

Q. 23:11 Can withdrawal liability be assessed against any employer that withdraws from a multiemployer plan?   23-6

Q. 23:12 What steps are involved in determining multiemployer plan withdrawal liability?   23-6

Q. 23:13 When is a participating employer considered to have withdrawn from a multiemployer plan?   23-6

Q. 23:14 Can an employer be held liable for withdrawal liability as a result of circumstances such as decertification of the union or a plant closing?   23-7

Q. 23:15 Does a participating employer have any liability if there is a partial withdrawal from the multiemployer plan?   23-8

Q. 23:16 What is a facility for purposes of a partial withdrawal?   **23-8**

Q. 23:17 Is withdrawal liability affected if employers are under common control?   **23-8**

Q. 23:18 Does a withdrawal occur if there is a change in business structure?   **23-9**

Q. 23:19 Does a withdrawal occur if there is a suspension of contributions during a labor dispute?   **23-10**

Q. 23:20 Who determines when a withdrawal from a multiemployer plan occurs?   **23-10**

Q. 23:21 Is a sale of employer assets considered a withdrawal from a multiemployer plan?   **23-10**

Q. 23:22 How is a withdrawing employer's share of the multiemployer plan's UVBs computed?   **23-11**

Q. 23:23 Can withdrawal liability be imposed if the multiemployer plan has no UVBs?   **23-12**

Q. 23:24 May multiemployer plan withdrawal liability be waived or reduced?   **23-12**

Q. 23:25 What happens if an employer reenters a plan after a prior withdrawal?   **23-13**

Q. 23:26 What withdrawal liability payments must the employer make while the abatement determination is made?   **23-13**

Q. 23:27 What is required for abatement of an employer's withdrawal liability upon reentry to the multiemployer plan?   **23-14**

Q. 23:28 What are the effects of an abatement?   **23-14**

Q. 23:29 What are the effects of a nonabatement?   **23-14**

Q. 23:30 How can a reentering employer elect nonabatement?   **23-15**

Q. 23:31 Does the value of the employer affect the amount of its withdrawal liability?   **23-15**

Q. 23:32 Does an insolvent employer have withdrawal liability?   **23-16**

Q. 23:33 What is the 20-year cap on a withdrawing employer's liability?   **23-17**

Q. 23:34 When is the employer notified of its liability for withdrawal from a multiemployer plan?   **23-17**

Q. 23:35 Is the initial determination of a withdrawing employer's liability presumptively correct?   **23-18**

Q. 23:36 May an employer contest the determination of its liability for withdrawing from a multiemployer plan?   **23-19**

Q. 23:37 Does the employer run any risk if it does not
demand arbitration of the plan sponsor's claim for
withdrawal liability?   23-20
Q. 23:38 When are withdrawal liability payments due?   23-20
Q. 23:39 What happens if a withdrawal liability payment is
missed?   23-21
Q. 23:40 Are owners of the employer personally liable for
withdrawal liability?   23-21
Q. 23:41 Are withdrawal liability claims entitled to priority in
bankruptcy proceedings?   23-22
Q. 23:42 What is a mass withdrawal from a multiemployer
plan?   23-22
Q. 23:43 What is the liability of an employer upon
termination of a multiemployer defined benefit
plan?   23-23
Q. 23:44 May a multiemployer plan exclude some newly
adopting employers from withdrawal liability?   23-23

Chapter 24   Individual Retirement Plans

Q. 24:1 What is an individual retirement plan?   24-1
Q. 24:2 What are the basic characteristics of an individual
retirement account?   24-2
Q. 24:3 What are the basic characteristics of an individual
retirement annuity?   24-2
Q. 24:4 Who is eligible to set up an IRA?   24-3
Q. 24:5 How much can be contributed to an IRA?   24-4
Q. 24:6 What penalty is imposed on an excess contribution
to an IRA?   24-4
Q. 24:7 Can active participants in qualified retirement plans
also make deductible IRA contributions?   24-5
Q. 24:8 What is active participation?   24-5
Q. 24:9 Who is an active participant?   24-5
Q. 24:10 What level of income affects an active participant's
deduction limitation?   24-7
Q. 24:11 If an individual is an active participant in a
qualified retirement plan, what are the applicable
IRA deduction limits?   24-7

Q. 24:12 May an individual who is ineligible to make a fully
          deductible IRA contribution make a nondeductible
          IRA contribution?   24-8
Q. 24:13 What are designated nondeductible IRA
          contributions?   24-9
Q. 24:14 May an individual who is eligible to make a
          deductible IRA contribution elect to treat such a
          contribution as nondeductible?   24-9
Q. 24:15 Is an individual required to report designated
          nondeductible contributions on his or her tax
          return?   24-9
Q. 24:16 What is the tax treatment of IRA withdrawals by
          an individual who has previously made both
          deductible and nondeductible contributions?   24-10
Q. 24:17 What is a spousal IRA?   24-11
Q. 24:18 When must IRA contributions be made?   24-12
Q. 24:19 Can an IRA deduction be claimed before the
          contribution is actually made?   24-12
Q. 24:20 Does the payment of a fee to the trustee of an
          IRA reduce the amount otherwise allowable as a
          contribution to the IRA?   24-13
Q. 24:21 Will the receipt of "free checking" by a customer
          who directs the IRA to invest in a bank's financial
          products constitute a prohibited transaction?   24-13
Q. 24:22 May an individual borrow money to fund an IRA?   24-14
Q. 24:23 May an individual make a contribution to an IRA
          with a credit card?   24-14
Q. 24:24 What is an employer-sponsored IRA?   24-14
Q. 24:25 Can employer-sponsored IRAs help an employer
          that has a qualified retirement plan satisfy
          coverage requirements?   24-15
Q. 24:26 What is a payroll-deduction IRA?   24-15
Q. 24:27 Does a payroll-deduction IRA expose the employer
          to ERISA liabilities and compliance requirements?   24-15
Q. 24:28 How does a simplified employee pension differ
          from an employer-sponsored IRA?   24-16
Q. 24:29 Are there restrictions on IRA distributions?   24-17
Q. 24:30 What is the minimum distribution requirement?   24-17
Q. 24:31 What is the penalty imposed for insufficient
          distributions from an IRA?   24-18
Q. 24:32 How are distributions from an IRA taxed?   24-18
Q. 24:33 Are amounts remaining in an IRA at death subject
          to federal estate taxes?   24-19

Q. 24:34 What is an inherited IRA?   24-20
Q. 24:35 Do special rules apply if the beneficiary is the IRA
          owner's surviving spouse?   24-20
Q. 24:36 What minimum distribution requirements apply after
          the IRA owner's death?   24-21
Q. 24:37 What is the penalty imposed on a premature
          distribution from an IRA?   24-21
Q. 24:38 May an IRA be transferred incident to divorce?   24-22
Q. 24:39 Can an IRA be reached by judgment creditors?   24-22

Chapter 25 Simplified Employee Pensions

Q. 25:1   What is a simplified employee pension?   25-1
Q. 25:2   Who is eligible to participate in a SEP?   25-1
Q. 25:3   Does the prohibition against discrimination in favor
          of highly compensated employees apply to a
          SEP?   25-2
Q. 25:4   May a SEP be integrated with Social Security?   25-3
Q. 25:5   Are contributions made to a SEP on an
          employee's behalf forfeitable?   25-4
Q. 25:6   How much may be contributed to an employee's
          IRA through a SEP?   25-4
Q. 25:7   How much can an employer deduct for
          contributions to a SEP?   25-4
Q. 25:8   When are contributions to a SEP deductible?   25-5
Q. 25:9   Which employers may adopt salary reduction
          SEPs?   25-5
Q. 25:10 What are the limits on elective deferrals to a SEP?   25-5
Q. 25:11 Is there a special nondiscrimination test for salary
          reduction SEPs?   25-6
Q. 25:12 How is an SEP established?   25-7
Q. 25:13 When may an employer use a model SEP?   25-7
Q. 25:14 Can a dissolved partnership's SEP be continued by
          its successor sole proprietors?   25-8
Q. 25:15 What are the annual reporting requirements of a
          SEP?   25-8
Q. 25:16 Are SEP contributions taxable to the employee?   25-9
Q. 25:17 How are SEP assets managed?   25-9

Q. 25:18 How are distributions from a SEP taxed?   25-9
Q. 25:19 How may assets be moved from a SEP without
          penalty?   25-30
Q. 25:20 May a distribution from a qualified retirement plan
          be rolled over into a SEP?   25-31
Q. 25:21 What advantages does a SEP offer to the
          business owner?   25-31
Q. 25:22 What are the drawbacks to the adoption of a
          SEP?   25-31

Chapter 26 Rollovers

Q. 26:1   What is a rollover?   26-1
Q. 26:2   What are IRA rollover accounts?   26-1
Q. 26:3   How does a rollover from one IRA to another
          work?   26-2
Q. 26:4   May an individual borrow from an IRA?   26-2
Q. 26:5   May more than one tax-free transfer between IRAs
          be made during a 12-month period?   26-3
Q. 26:6   May a beneficiary of an IRA roll over the proceeds
          at the death of the owner of the IRA?   26-3
Q. 26:7   What types of distributions from a qualified
          retirement plan may be rolled over?   26-4
Q. 26:8   What is a qualified total distribution?   26-4
Q. 26:9   Is a rollover available for a distribution from a
          terminated retirement plan?   26-4
Q. 26:10 What is a partial distribution?   26-5
Q. 26:11 How does the employee elect partial distribution
          treatment?   26-5
Q. 26:12 What are the tax consequences of electing partial
          distribution treatment?   26-5
Q. 26:13 May a retired employee who has received
          distributions from a qualified retirement plan roll
          over the remaining benefits to an IRA?   26-6
Q. 26:14 May a person who is over age 70½ roll over a
          qualified retirement plan distribution?   26-6
Q. 26:15 Is a rollover of qualified retirement plan benefits
          available to the spouse of a deceased employee?   26-7
Q. 26:16 How does a rollover from a qualified retirement
          plan to an IRA work?   26-7

Q. 26:17 When does the 60-day rollover period begin?   **26-8**

Q. 26:18 Can the 60-day rollover period be extended?   **26-8**

Q. 26:19 Can amounts in a rollover IRA be transferred to a qualified retirement plan?   **26-8**

Q. 26:20 Can a distribution from a disqualified retirement plan be rolled over?   **26-9**

Q. 26:21 What are the tax advantages and disadvantages of rolling over a qualified retirement plan distribution to an IRA?   **26-9**

Q. 26:22 Can an IRA rollover be revoked?   **26-10**

Chapter 27   Business Owners

Q. 27:1 How do the working owners of a closely held corporation benefit from a qualified retirement plan?   **27-1**

Q. 27:2 How can the adoption of a qualified retirement plan increase the wealth of the owner of a closely held corporation?   **27-2**

Q. 27:3 How does the adoption of a qualified retirement plan reduce a corporation's tax liability?   **27-3**

Q. 27:4 Can a self-employed individual set up a qualified retirement plan?   **27-3**

Q. 27:5 What tax advantage does a self-employed individual gain by adopting a qualified retirement plan?   **27-4**

Q. 27:6 Is it worthwhile for a self-employed individual to incorporate?   **27-4**

Q. 27:7 How should an existing qualified retirement plan be handled if a self-employed individual incorporates a business?   **27-5**

Q. 27:8 Who is a self-employed individual?   **27-6**

Q. 27:9 Who is an owner-employee?   **27-6**

Q. 27:10 What is earned income?   **27-6**

Q. 27:11 May an individual be both self-employed and an employee of another employer?   **27-7**

Q. 27:12 Can the bulk of qualified retirement plan contributions and benefits be set aside for the business owner and other essential employees under the terms of the plan?   **27-8**

Q. 27:13 May a qualified retirement plan lose its tax-favored status if only the business owner and other essential employees will receive benefits?   27-8

Q. 27:14 How much can a business owner contribute to the qualified retirement plan?   27-9

Q. 27:15 Is there any limit on tax-deductible contributions to a qualified retirement plan by a corporation?   27-10

Q. 27:16 How much may be contributed to a qualified retirement plan on behalf of a self-employed individual?   27-10

Q. 27:17 Do any special limitations apply to the deduction for contributions made to a defined benefit plan on behalf of a self-employed individual?   27-11

Q. 27:18 What type of qualified retirement plan should the business owner install?   27-11

Q. 27:19 What type of qualified retirement plan (or plans) should a business owner use to maximize retirement benefits?   27-13

Q. 27:20 How can the use of a normal retirement age earlier than 65 benefit the business owner?   27-14

Q. 27:21 How does integration with Social Security benefit the business owner?   27-15

Q. 27:22 Is a voluntary contribution feature attractive to the business owner?   27-15

Q. 27:23 Is it advantageous for the business owner to include life insurance protection in the qualified retirement plan?   27-16

Q. 27:24 May the company borrow from its qualified retirement plan to acquire assets needed in its business?   27-16

Q. 27:25 May a business owner borrow from the qualified retirement plan?   27-17

Q. 27:26 May a director of a corporation establish a qualified retirement plan based on the director's fees?   27-17

Q. 27:27 What happens if a business owner controls two corporations?   27-18

Q. 27:28 Does any special coverage requirement apply if an owner-employee controls another business?   27-18

Q. 27:29 What happens if the business owner sets up a management corporation?   27-19

Q. 27:30 Are there advantages gained by using a professional corporation together with a professional service partnership? 27-20

Q. 27:31 What is an affiliated service group? 27-20

Q. 27:32 Will IRS rule on the qualified status of the retirement plan of a member of an affiliated service group? 27-21

Q. 27:33 What is a personal service corporation? 27-23

Q. 27:34 Can the income of a personal service corporation be allocated to the employee-owner? 27-23

Q. 27:35 Who is an employee-owner? 27-24

Q. 27:36 What is one other organization for purposes of the personal service corporation rules? 27-24

Q. 27:37 Is there a safe harbor for a personal service corporation? 27-25

Q. 27:38 Is a retirement plan considered in determining whether the principal purpose of a personal service corporation is the avoidance of income taxes? 27-25

Q. 27:39 Is there any type of tax-favored qualified retirement plan for the business owner that is simple to adopt and inexpensive to operate? 27-25

Q. 27:40 Are corporate qualified retirement plan benefits exempt from the participants' creditors? 27-25

Q. 27:41 Can property in a qualified retirement plan covering self-employed individuals be reached by judgment creditors? 27-26

Q. 27:42 Is a professional's interest in the qualified retirement plan of a professional corporation exempt from creditors? 27-27

Chapter 28 Qualified Domestic Relations Orders

Q. 28:1 What is a qualified domestic relations order? 28-1

Q. 28:2 What is a domestic relations order? 28-2

Q. 28:3 Who is an alternate payee? 28-3

Q. 28:4 Does a QDRO violate the anti-assignment rule? 28-3

Q. 28:5 Do the QDRO rules apply to all qualified retirement plans? 28-4

Q. 28:6 Does a QDRO affect the qualification of a retirement plan? 28-5

Q. 28:7 Must a qualified retirement plan include provisions regarding QDROs? 28-5

Q. 28:8 What is the earliest retirement age exception? 28-5

Q. 28:9 What does earliest retirement age mean? 28-7

Q. 28:10 Must a qualified retirement plan establish a procedure to determine the qualified status of a DRO? 28-7

Q. 28:11 What happens when a qualified retirement plan receives a DRO? 28-7

Q. 28:12 Can the amounts segregated for an alternate payee under a QDRO be forfeited? 28-8

Q. 28:13 How does a QDRO affect the Qualified Pre-retirement Survivor Annuity and Qualified Joint Survivor Annuity requirements? 28-9

Q. 28:14 Must an alternate payee consent to a distribution from a qualified retirement plan? 28-10

Q. 28:15 Does a QDRO affect the maximum amount of the participant's benefits under a qualified retirement plan? 28-11

Q. 28:16 What are the income tax consequences of a QDRO to the participant? 28-11

Q. 28:17 What are the income tax consequences of a QDRO to an alternate payee spouse or former spouse? 28-12

Q. 28:18 Can an alternate payee roll over a distribution pursuant to a QDRO from a qualified retirement plan? 28-12

Q. 28:19 Does the 10 percent early distribution tax apply to a distribution made to an alternate payee pursuant to a QDRO? 28-13

Q. 28:20 How does a QDRO affect the excess distribution tax and the excess accumulation tax? 28-13

Q. 28:21 Are qualified retirement plan benefits subject to equitable distribution? 28-15

Q. 28:22 Can a QDRO be enforced by an attachment of the participant's monthly retirement benefits? 28-15

Q. 28:23 Can a QDRO be discharged in bankruptcy? 28-15

Chapter 1

Overview

For a company that wants to accumulate a substantial nest egg for its loyal employees—and the working owner—there is no better way to achieve this objective than through a tax-favored retirement plan. This chapter examines qualified retirement plans—what they are, their tax advantages, the types of costs the company can expect to incur, and the kinds of benefits that can be provided under the plan.

Q. 1:1 Why should a company adopt a qualified retirement plan?

A qualified retirement plan is one of the best tax shelters available. The company is allowed a current deduction for its contributions to the plan; the employee pays no tax on money contributed for his or her benefit until a distribution is made; earnings from investments made with funds in the plan accumulate tax-free; and distributions from the plan may be afforded favorable income tax treatment.

A qualified retirement plan is especially attractive to working owners of closely held corporations and to self-employed individuals. Their long-term service with their companies gives them the best opportunity to accumulate large sums of money through the tax-free build-up of capital. Although benefits must be provided for other employees as well, the owner usually receives a much larger benefit than the other employees.

The nontax reasons for adopting a qualified retirement plan include the following: (1) attracting employees; (2) reducing employee turnover; (3) increasing employee incentive; and (4) accumulating funds for retirement.

Q. 1:2 What is a qualified retirement plan?

There are two distinct elements embodied in the term qualified retirement plan. The first element is the term retirement plan. A retirement plan means any plan or program maintained by an employer or an employee organization (or both) that (1) provides retirement income to employees or (2) results in a deferral of income by employees for periods extending generally to the end of employment or beyond, regardless of how plan contributions or benefits are calculated or how benefits are distributed. [ERISA § 3(2)]

The second element is the term qualified, which means that the retirement plan is afforded special tax treatment for meeting a host of requirements of the Code. Qualified retirement plans fall into two basic categories: defined contribution plans and defined benefit plans. A defined contribution plan provides benefits based on the amount contributed to an employee's individual account plus any earnings and forfeitures of other employees that are allocated to the account. A defined benefit plan provides a definitely determinable annual benefit, that is, the benefits are determined on the basis of a formula contained in the plan.

When the term qualified retirement plan is used in this book, it refers to both defined contribution and defined benefit plans.

Q. 1:3 What are the basic tax advantages of a qualified retirement plan?

A qualified retirement plan is afforded special tax treatment. These tax advantages include the following:

- The sponsoring company is allowed an immediate tax deduction for the amount contributed to the plan for a particular year. [IRC § 404]
- Participants pay no current income tax on amounts contributed by the company on their behalf. [IRC §§ 402 and 403]

- Earnings of the plan are tax-exempt—permitting the tax-free accumulation of income and gains on investments. [IRC §§ 401 and 501]
- Reduced tax rates may apply to lump-sum distributions to certain participants. [IRC § 402(e)]
- Income taxes on a partial or qualified total distribution may be deferred by rolling over the distribution to an individual retirement account (IRA) or to another qualified retirement plan. [IRC §§ 402(a)(5), 402(e)(4), and 403(a)(4)]
- Income taxes on a partial or qualified total distribution to a deceased participant's spouse may be deferred by rolling over the distribution to an IRA. [IRC § 402(a)(7)]
- Installment or annuity payments are taxed only when they are received. [IRC §§ 72 and 403]

Q. 1:4 Must a company incorporate to have a qualified retirement plan?

No. The benefits of a qualified retirement plan are available to incorporated and unincorporated businesses alike. Sole proprietorships and partnerships can have retirement plans that are comparable to corporate retirement plans.

Q. 1:5 How does the deductibility of employer contributions differ between qualified and nonqualified plans?

Qualified retirement plans are given favorable tax treatment for meeting special requirements of the Code. There is no special tax treatment for nonqualified retirement plans. The basic difference between a qualified plan and a nonqualified plan is that contributions by the company to the nonqualified plan are not deductible until they are includible in the participant's income. This means the company does not get a current deduction for contributions made to a nonqualified plan. In contrast, contributions to a qualified plan are immediately deductible. [IRC §§ 83, 162, and 404]

Q. 1:6   How do qualified and nonqualified plans differ with regard to the taxation of employer contributions?

A participant in a qualified plan is not taxed until the benefits are distributed to the participant. This is also true in a nonqualified, unfunded plan. If the nonqualified plan is funded, however, the participant generally is taxed in the first year that the participant's rights are transferable or are not subject to a substantial risk of forfeiture. [IRC §§ 83 and 402(b)]

Q. 1:7   How do qualified and nonqualified plans differ with regard to coverage of employees and benefit or contribution limitations?

The nonqualified plan is designed primarily to provide retirement income for essential employees. Such a plan does not have to cover a broad spectrum of employees, as the qualified plan does. Furthermore, there are no limits on benefits or contributions, nor are there any reporting or bookkeeping requirements in connection with the nonqualified plan so long as it is not funded. [IRC § 401(a)]

Q. 1:8   How is the employee affected by the employer's choice of a qualified or nonqualified plan?

From the employee's standpoint, benefits paid under a nonqualified plan will usually be taxed at and after retirement when, presumably, the employee will be in a lower tax bracket. This same income tax advantage is available to those who participate in a qualified plan—but there are some additional tax benefits in that case. If the benefits are paid in a lump sum, for example, the distribution might qualify for forward averaging tax treatment (see Q. 11:12), which is a special method of tax computation that is unavailable for distributions from IRAs, simplified employee pensions (SEPs), and nonqualified plans. [IRC § 402(e)]

Q. 1:9   What is the Employee Retirement Income Security Act?

The Employee Retirement Income Security Act of 1974 (ERISA) became law on September 2, 1974. ERISA completely overhauled the federal pension law after Congress found that:

- Employees with long years of service were losing anticipated retirement benefits due to the lack of plan provisions relating to the vesting of benefits;
- Many plans lacked adequate funds to pay employees promised retirement benefits; and
- Plans were being terminated before enough funds had been accumulated to pay employees and their beneficiaries promised retirement benefits.

To protect the interests of retirement plan participants and their beneficiaries, ERISA established a new set of rules for participation in retirement plans, added mandatory schedules for the vesting of benefits, fixed minimum funding standards, set standards of conduct for administering the plan and handling plan assets, required disclosure of plan information, and established a system for insuring the payment of pension benefits.

Q. 1:10   What other acts have affected retirement plans?

- The Multiemployer Pension Plan Amendments Act of 1980 (MPPAA)
- The Economic Recovery Tax Act of 1981 (ERTA)
- The Tax Equity and Fiscal Responsibility Act of 1982 (TEFRA)
- The Tax Reform Act of 1984 (TRA '84)
- The Retirement Equity Act of 1984 (REA)
- The Single-Employer Pension Plan Amendments Act of 1986 (SEPPAA)
- The Tax Reform Act of 1986 (TRA '86)
- The Omnibus Budget Reconciliation Act of 1986 (OBRA '86)

- The Pension Protection Act (PPA), attached to The Omnibus Budget Reconciliation Act of 1987 (OBRA '87)
- The Technical and Miscellaneous Revenue Act of 1988 (TAMRA)
- The Revenue Reconciliation Act (RRA), Title VII of The Omnibus Budget Reconciliation Act of 1989 (OBRA '89)

Q. 1:11 Does the adoption of a qualified retirement plan by an employer constitute a contractual obligation to maintain the plan?

No. Although a qualified retirement plan must be a permanent plan (see Q. 1:13 and Q. 19:1), continuance of the plan is voluntary—it is not a contractual obligation of the company, except in the case of certain collectively bargained plans.

A carefully drafted plan and trust will specifically limit the company's obligation to maintain and fund the plan. In addition, the company should expressly retain the right to reduce, suspend, or discontinue contributions and the right to terminate the plan. (See Q. 19:2.)

Q. 1:12 What cost will the company incur in adopting a qualified retirement plan?

Professional fees vary, depending on the type of plan adopted by the company. However, the following types of services are generally required:

- Legal services for drafting the plan and trust and for submitting those and other required documents to IRS to obtain tax qualification;
- Accounting services; and
- Actuarial services to provide cost and benefit computations if a defined benefit plan is adopted.

It is also possible to adopt a master or prototype plan designed by an insurance company, a bank, or other investment-oriented company (a mutual fund, for example). (See Q. 2:21.) These institutions generally charge less for their services because they expect to profit from the products (e.g., life insurance policies) that may be required to be purchased.

Q. 1:13 Must the company contribute to the plan each year once it adopts a qualified retirement plan?

It depends on the type of plan adopted. IRS says that the adoption of a qualified retirement plan commits the company to maintaining the plan on a permanent basis. For this purpose, permanent means that, from the plan's inception, the company must intend to support the plan over a number of years. [Reg. § 1.401-1(b)(2)]

Annual contributions to a pension plan are required. Although there are exceptions to this rule, a company considering the adoption of a pension plan must recognize that it is undertaking a commitment to maintain and fund the plan. For details, see Chapter 7.

Annual contributions to a profit sharing plan are not usually required. Further, a company that has not done well in a particular year may decide to make either a minimal contribution or no contribution at all for that year (unless the plan itself mandates a contribution each year). Nevertheless, a profit sharing plan is not permanent unless contributions are "recurring and substantial." [Reg. § 1.401-1(b)(2)]

Q. 1:14 Must a qualified plan include all employees?

No. A company is permitted to exclude certain categories of employees from participation in its qualified plan. These exclusions are optional and apply only if they are specified in the plan. [IRC § 410]

Q. 1:15 What are the most common eligibility requirements for participation in a qualified plan?

The most common eligibility requirements are those relating to minimum age and length of service with the company.

A plan may exclude any employee who has not yet reached age 21. Plans of certain educational institutions may exclude employees who are under age 26. [IRC §§ 410(a)(1)(A)(i) and 410(a)(1)(B)(ii)]

In most instances, the plan requires an employee to complete a certain period of service before being eligible to participate. This service requirement usually does not exceed one year—otherwise the plan has to provide full and immediate vesting of benefits. Under no circumstances may the service requirement exceed two years. The service requirement for 401(k) plans cannot exceed one year. [IRC §§ 401(k)(2)(D), 410(a)(1)(A)(ii), and 410(a)(1)(B)(i)]

Q. 1:16   What statutory exclusions from participation in a qualified plan are permitted?

The two most common statutory exclusions from plan participation are minimum age and length of service requirements. (See Q. 1:15.)

Other than these exclusions, the most common statutory exclusion applies to union employees on whose behalf negotiations for retirement benefits have been conducted with the company. The company may exclude union employees from coverage, whether or not they are covered under a separate retirement plan, as long as retirement benefits were the subject of good-faith bargaining. Statutory exclusions for air pilots and nonresident aliens are also available. [IRC § 410(b)(3)]

Q. 1:17   What other exclusions from participation in a qualified plan are permitted?

Other exclusions—so-called plan exclusions—usually fall into the following categories: (1) classification by job description, (2) classification by geographic location of employment or by specific division of the company, and (3) classification by method of compensation (i.e., hourly as opposed to salaried). Bear in mind, however, that regardless of the plan's eligibility provisions, coverage of a sufficient number of employees not excluded by statute (see Q. 1:16) is needed to satisfy the minimum coverage requirements of the Code. Effective for plan years beginning after 1988, the minimum coverage requirements have become even stricter, and a new minimum participation requirement has been introduced. (See Q. 4:15 and Q. 4:23). [IRC §§ 401(a)(26) and 410(b)]

Q. 1:18   Can a company establish two qualified retirement plans?

Yes. The Code permits a company to maintain as many qualified plans as it chooses—provided all the plans meet the Code's requirements, including limitations on benefits and contributions.

Quite often, large companies establish separate plans for individual subsidiaries or divisions. These plans need not be comparable in all cases. Indeed, as explained at Q. 4:32 through Q. 4:35, not all divisions or subsidiaries of the same company or members of the controlled group must adopt a plan in order for another division, subsidiary, or member to maintain a plan for its employees.

Effective for plan years beginning after 1988, the minimum participation requirements severely curtail an employer's ability to maintain separate plans for individual subsidiaries or divisions and essentially eliminate the practice of establishing comparable plans. [IRC § 401(a)(26)]

Q. 1:19   What kinds of benefits may be provided under a qualified retirement plan?

Qualified plans are primarily intended to provide retirement benefits. Nevertheless, qualified plans also frequently provide benefits upon death, disability, early retirement, or some other termination of employment. These benefits are usually funded by a trust fund, insurance contracts, or a combination of the two.

A profit sharing plan need not be limited to retirement benefits; it may also provide for hardship distributions, for example. In addition, a profit sharing plan may permit distribution of all or some part of a participant's vested interest that has remained in the plan for at least two years prior to the distribution. [Rev. Rul. 71-224, 1971-1 CB 124; Rev. Rul. 71-295, 1971-2 CB 184; Rev. Rul. 73-553, 1973-2 CB 130]

A 10-percent excise tax applies to most premature distributions from qualified plans and IRAs. Consequently, a profit sharing plan can provide for in-service distributions of plan benefits after the passage of at least two years or because of hardship, but the distribution may be subject to the tax. [IRC § 72(t)]

Q. 1:20 May a qualified retirement plan provide life insurance benefits for participants?

Yes. However, different limits may apply to life insurance policies acquired under defined contribution plans and those acquired under defined benefit plans. (See Q. 12:4.) The following general rules also apply:

- The policies can be ordinary life, term life, universal life, retirement income, or endowment;
- The insurance must be incidental to the primary purpose of the plan (i.e., to provide benefits at retirement); and
- The participant pays tax on the cost of the current life insurance protection that is received each year.

Q. 1:21 May a qualified retirement plan provide health insurance?

Yes, although the rules governing how much health insurance can be acquired and for whom vary, depending on whether the plan is a pension plan or a profit sharing plan.

A pension plan may provide health insurance, but only for retired employees and their families. [IRC § 401(h); Reg. § 1.401-14]

A contribution allocated to an individual medical account under a pension plan is treated as part of an annual addition (see Q. 5:1) to a defined contribution plan. [IRC § 415(l)]

A profit sharing plan may provide health insurance benefits for all plan participants and their families. If this insurance is purchased with funds that have been in the plan for more than two years, there is no limit on how much the plan may pay for insurance coverage. If the plan uses other funds to buy the insurance, the amount of the premiums must be incidental, that is, the premiums may not exceed 25 percent of the funds allocated to the participant's account that have not been in the plan for at least two years. [*Reg.* § 1.401-1(b)(1)(ii); *Rev. Rul. 61-164,* 1961-2 CB 99]

Q. 1:22   Is a contribution to a qualified retirement plan adopted on the last day of the taxable year fully deductible?

Yes, if the plan and trust are executed by the end of the year and other procedural requirements established by IRS are met, then contributions made by the due date for filing the company's income tax return for that year (including extensions) are fully deductible. [IRC § 404(a)(6); *Rev. Rul. 81-114,* 1981-1 CB 207]

> **Example.** Sallie Corp., a calendar-year corporation, adopts a pension plan to become effective December 31, 1990. If the documents are executed by December 31, 1990, and the contribution is made by March 15, 1991 (or as late as September 16, 1991, if the company has received an extension until that time for filing its tax return), a full deduction will be allowed for 1990.

Q. 1:23   May excess contributions made to a qualified retirement plan be returned to the company?

If the company makes an excess contribution to its qualified retirement plan, that excess may be returned to the company only in the following circumstances:

- An actuarial error caused the excess funds to remain in the trust after the plan's termination and after the payment of all benefits to participants or their beneficiaries. [Reg. § 1.401-2]
- The contribution was conditioned on the initial qualification of the plan and the plan did not qualify. [ERISA § 403(c)(2)(B)]
- The contribution was conditioned on its deductibility and the deduction was denied. [ERISA § 403(c)(2)(C)]

- The excess contribution was made due to a mistake of fact. [ERISA § 403(c)(2)(A)]

In any event, the plan itself must permit the return of the excess contribution. And, in the last two situations, earnings attributable to the excess contribution may not be returned to the company. Losses attributable to the excess contribution will reduce the amount to be returned. Further, returns to the employer must be made within one year of the mistaken contribution, denial of qualification, or denial of the deduction. [Rev. Rul. 77-200, 1977-1 CB 98]

A 10-percent excise tax is now imposed on nondeductible contributions to a qualified plan (see Q. 10:9). [IRC § 4972]

Special rules apply to excess contributions made to a 401(k) plan. See Chapter 21.

Chapter 2

Types and Choices of Plans

The range of retirement plan alternatives is vast. There are defined contribution plans and defined benefit plans; there are pension plans and profit sharing plans. But before the relative merits of the various types of plans can be evaluated and the one most suited to the needs of a particular employer chosen, the employer must first know what each type of plan offers. This chapter provides descriptions of the different categories of retirement plans, examines the basic choices available to a company and offers guidelines for choosing the appropriate plan.

Q. 2:1 What are the basic choices among qualified retirement plans?

Qualified retirement plans generally fit into one of two categories: defined contribution plans (see Q. 2:2), and defined benefit plans (see Q. 2:3).

Q. 2:2 What is a defined contribution plan?

A defined contribution plan is a retirement plan that "provides for an individual account for each participant and for benefits based solely upon the amount contributed to the participant's account, and any income, expenses, gains and losses, and any forfeitures of accounts of other participants which may be allocated to such participant's account." [ERISA § 3(34); IRC § 414(i)]

Defined contribution plans include the following:

- Money purchase pension plans (see Q. 2:4)
- Target benefit plans (see Q. 2:5)
- Profit sharing plans (see Q. 2:6)
- Thrift or savings plans (see Q. 2:7)
- 401(k) plans (see Q. 2:8)
- Stock bonus plans (see Q. 2:9)
- Employee stock ownership plans (ESOPs) (see Q. 2:10)
- Simplified employee pensions (SEPs) (see Q. 2:11)

Three major consequences result when a retirement plan is classified as a defined contribution plan: (1) plan contributions are determined by formula and not by actuarial requirements (except for target benefit plans); (2) plan earnings and losses are allocated to each participant's account and do not affect the company's retirement plan costs; and (3) plan benefits are not insured by the Pension Benefit Guaranty Corporation (PBGC).

Q. 2:3 What is a defined benefit plan?

A defined benefit plan is a retirement plan "other than an individual account plan." In other words, a plan that is not a defined contribution plan is classified as a defined benefit plan. Under a defined benefit plan, retirement benefits must be definitely determinable. For example, a plan that entitles a participant to a monthly pension for life equal to 30 percent of monthly compensation is a defined benefit plan. [ERISA § 3(35); IRC § 414(j)] The most common types of defined benefit plans are flat benefit plans (see Q. 2:12) and unit benefit plans (see Q. 2:13).

If a plan is categorized as a defined benefit plan: (1) plan formulas are geared to retirement benefits and not to contributions (except for cash balance plans); (2) the annual contribution is usually actuarially determined; (3) certain benefits may be insured by PBGC; (4) early termination of the plan is subject to special rules; and (5) forfeitures reduce the company's cost of providing retirement benefits.

Q. 2:4 What is a money purchase pension plan?

A money purchase pension plan is a defined contribution plan in which the company's contributions are mandatory and are usually based solely on each participant's compensation.

The obligation to fund the plan makes a money purchase pension plan different from most profit sharing plans. In most profit sharing plans, there are generally no unfavorable consequences for the company if it fails to make a contribution; but, if the company maintains a money purchase pension plan, its failure to make a contribution can result in the imposition of a penalty tax. (See Q. 7:16.) Contributions must be made to a money purchase pension plan even if the company has no profits.

Forfeitures that occur because of employee turnover may reduce future contributions of the company or may be used to increase the benefits of remaining participants. [IRC § 401(a)(8)]

Retirement benefits are based on the amount in the participant's account at the time of retirement, that is, whatever pension the money can purchase.

The following is an example of a money purchase pension plan formula:

> The company shall contribute each plan year during which the plan is in effect on behalf of each participant an amount equal to 10 percent of compensation.

Under the formula, an equal percentage of compensation is allocated to each participant's account. The age and length of service of the participant are irrelevant for both contribution and allocation purposes, although length of service could be considered. [IRC § 411(b)(2); Reg. § 1.401-1(b)(1)(i)]

This concept is illustrated in the example at the top of page 2-4. The allocation in column (d) reflects a contribution formula that is not integrated with Social Security. When Social Security integration is considered, differences in compensation become more relevant. See Chapter 6 for more details.

Smith Corporation

Schedule of Contributions to
Money Purchase Pension Plan
for
Plan Year Ended December 31, 1990

(a)	(b)	(c)	(d)
			Allocation of
Participant	Age	Compensation	company contributions
Smith	45	$60,000	$6,000
Jones	30	10,000	1,000
Total		$70,000	$7,000

Q. 2:5   What is a target benefit plan?

A target benefit plan is a hybrid or cross between a defined benefit plan and a money purchase pension plan. It is like a defined benefit plan in that the annual contribution is determined by the amount needed each year to accumulate (at an assumed rate of interest) a fund sufficient to pay a projected retirement benefit (the target benefit) to each participant on reaching retirement age. Thus, if a target benefit plan contains a target formula, such as 40 percent of compensation, that is identical to the benefit formula in a defined benefit plan and is based on identical actuarial assumptions (e.g., interest rates, mortality, employee turnover), the employer's initial contribution for the same group of employees will be the same. [*Rev. Rul.* 76-464, 1976-2 CB 115]

However, this is where the similarity ends. In a defined benefit plan, if the actual experience of the plan differs from the actuarial assumptions used (for example, if the interest earned is higher or lower than the assumptions), then the employer either increases or decreases its future contributions to the extent necessary to provide the promised benefits. In a target benefit plan, however, the contribution, once made, is allocated to separate accounts maintained for each participant. Thus, if the earnings of the fund differ from those assumed, this does not result in any increase or decrease in employer contributions; instead, it increases or decreases the benefits payable to the participant.

In this regard, the target benefit plan operates like a money purchase pension plan. In fact, the only difference between a money purchase pension plan and a target benefit plan is that, in a money purchase pension plan, contributions are generally determined and allocated as a percentage of current compensation; in a target benefit plan, contributions are determined as if the plan were to provide a fixed benefit. In a money purchase pension plan, contributions for identically compensated employees are the same even though their ages differ; in a target benefit plan, age is one of the factors that determines the size of the contributions.

Because target benefit plans are defined contribution plans, they are subject to the limit on annual additions to a participant's account. (See Q. 5:1.)

Q. 2:6 What is a profit sharing plan?

A profit sharing plan is a defined contribution plan to which the company agrees to make "substantial and recurring," though generally discretionary, contributions. (See Q. 1:13.) Amounts contributed to the plan are invested and accumulate (tax-free) for eventual distribution to participants or their beneficiaries either at retirement, after a fixed number of years, or upon the occurrence of some specified event (e.g., disability, death, or termination of employment).

Unlike contributions to a pension plan, contributions to a profit sharing plan are usually keyed to the existence of profits. However, neither current nor accumulated profits are required for a company to contribute to a profit sharing plan. [IRC § 401(a)(27)]

Even if the company has profits, it can generally forgo or limit its contribution for a particular year if the plan contains a discretionary formula. The following is an example of such a formula:

> The company shall contribute each plan year during which the plan is in effect out of its earnings for its taxable year, or out of its accumulated earnings, an amount decided upon by the Board of Directors [or owner, partners, etc., as appropriate]. The contribution shall be allocated among the participants in the proportion that the compensation of each participant bears to the aggregate compensation of all the participants.

Under the allocation formula (the second sentence in the example), each participant receives the same percentage of the contribution as the participant's compensation bears to total compensation. The participant's length of service is irrelevant although this factor can be considered in the allocation formula if prohibited discrimination does not result. However, note that in a discretionary profit sharing plan, the actual amount to be allocated to each participant cannot be determined until the company decides upon its contribution for the year. [Reg. § 1.401-1(b)(1)(ii)]

Although many profit sharing plans adopt a discretionary contribution formula, others adopt a fixed formula. For example, a company may obligate itself to contribute to its profit sharing plan a specified percentage of each participant's compensation if profits exceed a specified level.

Similar to other defined contribution plans, retirement benefits are based on the amount in the participant's account at retirement. Unlike defined benefit plans, however, forfeitures arising from employee turnover may be reallocated among the remaining participants.

Q. 2:7   What is a thrift or savings plan?

A thrift or savings plan is a defined contribution plan in which employees are directly involved in contributing toward the ultimate benefits that will be provided. The plan can be in the form of a money purchase pension plan or a profit sharing plan.

These plans are contributory in the sense that employer contributions on behalf of a particular employee are geared to mandatory contributions by the employee. Employees can participate in the plan only if they contribute a part of their compensation to the plan.

Employer contributions are made on a matching basis, for example, 50 percent of the contribution made by the employee. The plan may permit the employer, in its discretion, to make additional contributions and may also include a voluntary contribution feature.

A contributory plan must satisfy a new nondiscrimination test that compares the relative contribution percentages of highly compensated employees with those of nonhighly compensated employees. (See Q. 5:14.)

Q. 2:8 What is a 401(k) plan?

A 401(k) plan is a qualified profit sharing or stock bonus plan that offers participants an election to receive company contributions in cash or to have these amounts contributed to the plan. A participant in a 401(k) plan does not have to include in income any company contributions to the plan merely because an election could have been made to receive cash instead. [IRC §§ 401(k)(2) and 402(a)(8)]

A 401(k) plan may also be in the form of a salary reduction agreement. Under this type of arrangement, each eligible employee may elect to reduce current compensation or elect to forgo a salary increase and have these amounts contributed to the plan. [Prop. Reg. § 1.401(k)-1(a)(3)(i)]

Benefits attributable to employer contributions to a 401(k) plan generally may not be distributed without penalty until the employee retires, becomes disabled, dies, or reaches age 59½. Contributions made by the employer to the plan at the employee's election are nonforfeitable (i.e., 100 percent vesting is required at all times). For a complete discussion on this subject, see Chapter 21.

Q. 2:9 What is a stock bonus plan?

A stock bonus plan is similar to a profit sharing plan except that benefit payments must be made in stock of the company. However, a stock bonus plan may distribute cash to a participant, subject to the participant's right to demand a distribution of employer securities. Further, if the plan permits cash distributions and the employer securities are not readily tradable on an established market, participants must be given the right to require the company to repurchase the stock it distributes to them under a fair valuation formula. [IRC § 401(a)(23); Reg. §§ 1.401-1(a)(2)(iii) and 1.401-1(b)(1)(iii)]

Q. 2:10   What is an employee stock ownership plan?

An ESOP is a special type of defined contribution plan (usually profit sharing or stock bonus) that can qualify for favorable tax treatment. For a discussion on ESOPs, see Chapter 22.

Q. 2:11   What is a simplified employee pension?

A SEP is a defined contribution plan that takes the form of an individual retirement account (IRA) but is subject to special rules. A SEP may be adopted by both incorporated and unincorporated businesses. For a discussion on SEPs, see Chapter 25.

Q. 2:12   What is a flat benefit plan?

Under this type of defined benefit plan, the benefit for each participant depends solely on compensation. The following is a typical formula used in a flat benefit plan:

> Each participant shall be entitled to a monthly pension, commencing at normal retirement date and thereafter payable for life, of an amount equal to 30 percent of monthly compensation.

Under this formula, a participant whose monthly compensation is $1,000 receives a monthly pension of $300; a participant whose monthly compensation is $2,000 receives a monthly pension of twice as much (i.e., $600).

Q. 2:13   What is a unit benefit plan?

This type of defined benefit plan recognizes service with the company by providing greater benefits for a long-service employee than for a short-term employee with the same average compensation. The following formula represents a type of unit benefit plan:

> Each participant shall be entitled to a monthly pension, commencing at normal retirement date and thereafter payable for

life, of an amount equal to one percent of monthly compensation multiplied by the number of years of service with the company.

Under this formula, a participant with a monthly compensation of $1,000 and 30 years of employment at retirement receives a monthly pension of $300, while a participant with the same monthly compensation but only 10 years of employment receives a monthly pension of $100.

The examples in Q. 2:12 and this Question reflect plan formulas that are not integrated with Social Security. When Social Security integration is considered, differences in compensation become more relevant. See Chapter 6 for more details on this issue.

Q. 2:14 How is the cost of providing benefits under a defined benefit plan determined?

The cost of funding the plan (other than a fully insured plan; see Q. 2:19) is determined actuarially. An actuary (generally one enrolled under the auspices of the Joint Board for the Enrollment of Actuaries) may take into consideration many factors in determining each year's plan contribution needed to fund the benefits the plan is to provide. [IRC § 412(c)] Among the most common actuarial assumptions are the following:

- Interest
- Mortality
- Employee turnover
- Salary scale

Each individual actuarial assumption is required to be reasonable or, if not, the assumptions, in the aggregate, must result in a total contribution equivalent to that which would be determined if each assumption were reasonable. Also, the actuarial assumptions must, in combination, offer the actuary's best estimate of anticipated experience under the plan. (See Q. 2:3.) [IRC § 412(c)(3); *Jerome Mirza & Assoc. Ltd. v. U.S.*, 882 F2d 229 (7th Cir. 1989)]

Q. 2:15 Must the actuarial assumptions be set forth in the plan?

The actuarial assumptions used to determine the cost of funding a defined benefit plan need not be set forth in the plan. However, the actuarial assumptions used to determine the value of a benefit (e.g., post-retirement interest and mortality) must be set forth in the plan in a manner that precludes employer discretion. In other words, the lump sum value of a participant's benefit and the present value of the monthly benefit must be the same (i.e., actuarially equivalent). If the post-retirement actuarial assumptions are not specified, the benefits under the defined benefit plan are not considered to be definitely determinable. (See Q. 2:3.) [IRC § 401(a)(25)]

Q. 2:16 What is a Keogh plan?

A Keogh, or H.R. 10, plan refers to a qualified retirement plan maintained by a self-employed individual, either a sole proprietor or a partner. The self-employed individual may take a tax deduction for annual contributions to the plan made on behalf of the individual and on behalf of any eligible employees. A Keogh plan may be either a defined contribution plan (see Q. 2:2) or a defined benefit plan (see Q. 2:3).

For more details, see Chapter 27.

Q. 2:17 What is a floor offset plan?

A floor offset plan is a hybrid arrangement in which the employer maintains a defined benefit plan and a defined contribution plan, and the benefits provided under the defined benefit plan will be reduced by the value of the participant's account in the defined contribution plan. In essence, the defined benefit plan provides a guaranteed floor benefit, but the amount is offset by the benefit provided under the defined contribution plan. [ERISA § 407(d)(9); Rev. Rul. 76-259, 1976-2 CB 111]

If the value of the participant's account in the defined contribution plan declines, the participant will be insulated from the risk of investment loss because the full amount of pension benefits will be received under the defined benefit plan. Alternatively, if the value of the participant's account exceeds the amount of the benefit under the defined benefit plan, the participant will receive benefits exclusively from the defined contribution plan. In other words, the participant has the best of both worlds: the participant is protected against any risk of adverse investment experience under the defined benefit plan and receives the favorable investment experience under the defined contribution plan.

The defined contribution plan component of this type of arrangement may be subject to certain restrictions that are not imposed on free-standing defined contribution plans. (See Q. 17:40.)

Q. 2:18 What is a cash balance plan?

A cash balance plan is a defined benefit plan (see Q. 2:3) but is a hybrid plan that exhibits features of both defined benefit and defined contribution plans (see Q. 2:2). The most recognizable feature of the cash balance plan is its use of a separate account for each participant. A cash balance account is established for each employee upon becoming a member of the plan.

If the plan is replacing an existing defined benefit plan, employees are credited with an opening balance, typically the actuarial present value of their accrued prior plan benefits. Thereafter, the employee's cash balance account receives additional credits. These are likely to be computed as a flat percentage of the employee's pay, such as 4 percent or 5 percent. In addition, employees' balances grow based on interest credits. The rate varies from year to year and is communicated to employees before the start of the year. As an example, it might be the yield on one-year Treasury bills. The interest rate is not tied to the actual investment performance of the plan's assets and is determined independently, based on specific provisions in the plan document. The plan may also set forth a minimum and/or maximum amount.

The amounts an employer contributes to the plan are determined actuarially to insure sufficient funds to provide for the benefits promised by the plan. The minimum funding standards apply to cash balance plans, as with other types of defined benefit plans. [IRC § 412]

One of the cash balance plan's advantages, from the employee's perspective, is that investment risks are borne by the employer as in any other defined benefit plan. This differs from a defined contribution plan (see Q. 2:2).

Cash balance plans provide higher benefits for younger employees and lower benefits for older employees, in contrast with traditional defined benefit plans. However, the costs of providing these benefits are also correspondingly higher for younger employees and lower for older employees, as compared with traditional defined benefit plans.

An employee's monthly pension is not determined solely by the amount in the employee's individual account at the time of retirement; if the balance in the account is less than the pension benefit promised, the employee will receive the higher promised benefit. However, if the cash balance account is greater than the promised benefit, the employee will receive a greater monthly benefit.

Q. 2:19 What is an insured qualified retirement plan?

An insured plan is a qualified retirement plan that is funded in whole or in part through the purchase of life insurance policies. The plan can be either split-funded or fully insured.

In a split-funded plan, there is partial funding of retirement benefits through insurance policies, with the balance of the retirement benefit coming from an investment fund. The portion of the plan's assets accumulated in the investment fund can be invested as the trustee determines.

In a fully insured plan, all company contributions are directed toward the purchase of insurance, normally in the form of retirement income policies or annuity contracts. One advantage of a fully insured plan is that the plan may qualify for an exemption from the minimum funding requirements. (See Q. 7:3.)

Qualified retirement plans can be attractive vehicles for acquiring life insurance. Premiums indirectly paid by the company in the form of plan contributions are deductible. Each insured participant reports taxable income, as determined under IRS tables, representing the cost of current life insurance protection. For further details, see Chapter 12.

Q. 2:20   What is a custom-designed retirement plan?

A custom-designed (or individually designed) retirement plan is a plan tailored to meet the needs of the client. The custom-designed plan reflects the company's desires and needs more fully than a master or prototype (see Q. 2:21) because the client has a greater variety of available options.

Q. 2:21   What are master and prototype retirement plans?

A master plan is a form of retirement plan in which the funding organization (trust, custodial account, or insurer) is specified in the sponsor's application. A prototype plan is a form of retirement plan in which the funding organization is specified in the adoption agreement.

Insurance companies, mutual funds, banks, brokerage firms, and other investment management firms have created IRS-approved master and prototype plans. The client adopts the plans by executing an adoption agreement and electing certain available options. Any change in the preapproved plan provisions causes the plan to lose its master or prototype status. [Rev. Proc. 89-9, 1989-1 CB 780]

Q. 2:22   How does a company's cash position affect its choice of a qualified retirement plan?

Because adoption of a pension plan entails a commitment to fund the plan, even if the company has no profits, a company experiencing a weak cash position would be ill-advised to establish that type of plan. Generally, it does not make good sense for a company to borrow funds to meet its pension obligations. In this situation, a profit sharing plan would be more appropriate.

Q. 2:23   What type of retirement plan should a company adopt if profits fluctuate from year to year?

A profit sharing plan is the only type of plan that can afford a company significant flexibility with respect to the contributions it makes from year to year. The typical profit sharing plan—probably more than 95 percent of all profit sharing plans maintained by small companies—specifies that the company's contribution is to be determined annually by its board of directors (or owners, partners, etc., as appropriate). The amount contributed in any year may vary from zero to 15 percent of the total compensation of all plan participants.

Q. 2:24 Are profit sharing plans best for small companies?

There is no general answer to this question. The decision about the type of retirement plan best suited for a small company must be made on the basis of all the facts and circumstances, including the owner's goals.

Profit sharing plans are usually recommended for recently formed companies because no profit pattern exists. Often, both a discretionary profit sharing plan and a 10 percent money purchase pension plan are recommended for the company. This combination permits a total contribution of 25 percent of compensation (as opposed to the 15 percent limitation for a profit sharing plan alone), but entails only a 10%-of-compensation commitment by the company, leaving the company some flexibility. [IRC §§ 404(a)(3)(A) and 404(a)(7)]

Remember, however, that a company's size is not always a factor in choosing the best plan. In many cases, a small company may decide to maximize its tax-deductible contributions. For example, a company with an older workforce that adopts a defined benefit plan increases the amount of the contribution that must be made each year to fund retirement benefits, which in turn increases the company's tax deduction. (See Q. 2:25.)

Q. 2:25 What type of qualified retirement plan is best for a company whose essential employees have reached an advanced age?

For a company whose essential employees have reached an advanced age, a defined benefit plan (see Q. 2:3) is a better choice than a defined contribution plan (see Q. 2:2) for the following reasons:

- A defined contribution plan limits the company's tax-deductible contributions on behalf of each employee regardless of age. Except for a target benefit plan (see Q. 2:5), age is not a factor in determining the company's contribution. Contributions on behalf of older employees are based on the same percentage of compensation as those made on behalf of younger employees. Since contributions are limited, there may not be sufficient time left before retirement to accumulate a desired amount for older employees.

- A defined benefit plan allows a company with older essential employees to make larger contributions to accumulate sufficient funds for retirement. The limit on contributions under a defined benefit plan is the amount necessary to fund the annual pension and this may far exceed the allowable contribution to a defined contribution plan. [IRC §§ 404(a)(1), 415(b), and 415(c)]

Q. 2:26 How can an ESOP or a stock bonus plan benefit a corporation and its stockholders?

An ESOP or a stock bonus plan (see Q. 2:9 and Q. 2:10), like all other qualified retirement plans, must be organized and operated for the exclusive benefit of the employees or their beneficiaries. This does not mean that the company and its stockholders cannot also derive a benefit from the plan. In fact, an ESOP or a stock bonus plan can benefit the company and its stockholders by

- Providing a market for the owner's closely held stock as a tax-favored alternative to a stock redemption;

- Giving the company tax deductions without affecting its cash flow; and

- Keeping company stock in what is generally considered friendly hands in the event of a hostile takeover of the company.

See Chapter 22 for more details.

Q. 2:27 Can the company take Social Security wage tax payments or benefits into consideration in its qualified retirement plan?

Yes. The company can combine (integrate) its qualified retirement plan with Social Security and thereby reduce the cost of maintaining its plan. For details on how this works, see Chapter 6.

Q. 2:28 After the type of plan has been chosen, what options are available?

After the employer has determined the most suitable plan, consideration must be given to the actual plan provisions. Among the employer's choices are the following:

- Eligibility requirements (see Chapter 4)
  —Length of service (Q. 4:2)
  —Minimum age (Q. 4:2)
  —Exclusion of union employees (Q. 1:16)
  —Other classification exclusions (Q. 4:18)
- Contributions or benefits
  —Defined contribution plan formula
  —Defined benefit plan formula
  —Integration with Social Security (Q. 6:1)
  —Voluntary contributions (Q. 5:15)
  —Mandatory contributions (Q. 5:14)
  —Minimum benefits or contributions (Q. 20:37 and Q. 20:43)
  —401(k) features (Q. 21:1)
- Vesting (see Chapter 8)
  —Cliff vesting
  —Graded vesting
  —Full and immediate vesting
  —Top-heavy vesting (Q. 20:32)
- Investment provisions (see Chapter 17)
  —Participant-directed accounts
  —Insurance benefits (Q. 12:2)
  —Loan provisions
- Methods of payment of benefits
  —Lump-sum distributions

—Annuities
—Installment distributions
• Miscellaneous provisions
—Designation of plan administrator (Q. 14:1)
—Definition of compensation
—Choice of plan year
—Normal retirement age (Q. 9:66)
—Rollover provision (Q. 26:86)
—Death benefits

Chapter 3

Requirements for Qualification

A company's retirement plan will receive favorable tax treatment only if the plan is qualified. The Code sets out a host of requirements that a retirement plan must meet in order to qualify. This chapter analyzes those requirements.

Q. 3:1 What basic requirements must all retirement plans meet to qualify for favorable tax treatment?

The four fundamental requirements for a qualified retirement plan are the following:

- The plan must be a definite written program.
- The plan must be communicated to the employees.
- The plan must be permanent.
- The plan must prohibit the use or diversion of funds for purposes other than the exclusive benefit of employees or their beneficiaries.

[IRC §§ 401(a)(1) and 401(a)(2); Reg. §§ 1.401-1 and 1.401-2]

The following requirements must also be met before a retirement plan qualifies for favorable tax treatment:

- The plan must satisfy minimum coverage and minimum participation requirements. For details, see Chapter 4. [IRC §§ 401(a)(3) and 401(a)(26)]
- Contributions or benefits under the plan may not discriminate in favor of highly compensated employees. [IRC § 401(a)(4)]

- The plan must meet requirements for the vesting of benefits. For details, see Chapter 8. [IRC § 401(a)(7)]

- The plan must provide for required minimum distribution of benefits. For details, see Chapter 9. [IRC § 401(a)(9)]

- Additional requirements apply to top-heavy plans. These additional requirements include minimum vesting rules, minimum benefits, and/or minimum contributions for employees who are not key employees. A retirement plan can qualify only if it contains provisions satisfying the top-heavy plan requirements that automatically take effect if the plan becomes top-heavy. For details, see Chapter 20. [IRC § 401(a)(10)(B)]

- With few exceptions, plans must provide for the payment of benefits in the form of a joint and survivor lifetime annuity and death benefits in the form of a preretirement survivor annuity. For details, see Chapter 9. [IRC § 401(a)(11)]

- The plan must provide that benefits may not be assigned or alienated. For details, see Q. 3:9. [IRC § 401(a)(13)]

- The plan must comply with rules regarding the commencement of benefit payments. For details, see Q. 9:52. [IRC § 401(a)(14)]

- The plan must limit the contributions that can be made to the plan on behalf of an employee (in the case of a defined contribution plan) or it must limit the benefits that can be paid to an employee (in the case of a defined benefit plan). For details, see Chapter 5. [IRC § 401(a)(16)]

- The plan must impose a $200,000 cap (subject to cost-of-living adjustments beginning in 1990) on the amount of compensation that can be taken into account. (See Q. 5:3) [IRC § 401(a)(17)]

- A defined benefit plan must specify the actuarial assumptions that are used. (See Q. 2:15.) [IRC § 401(a)(25)]

Q. 3:2   Does a 401(k) plan qualify for favorable tax treatment?

Yes, provided certain special requirements are met in addition to the regular retirement plan qualification requirements. For details, see Chapter 21.

Q. 3:3   Can an oral trust created in a state that recognizes its validity be used for a qualified retirement plan?

No. Since a qualified retirement plan must be a definite written program (see Q. 3:1), an oral trust, which may be valid under local law, will not meet the Code requirements for favorable tax treatment. [*Rev. Rul. 69-231*, 1969-1 CB 118]

Q. 3:4   Can a trust that is not valid under local law be part of a qualified retirement plan?

No. Contributions to a qualified retirement plan's trust must be made to a trust that is valid under local law. [*Rev. Rul. 69-231*, 1969-1 CB 118; *Rev. Rul. 81-114*, 1981-1 CB 207]

Q. 3:5   Must all qualified retirement plans have trustees?

No. The most common type of qualified retirement plan that has no trustee is an annuity plan funded solely through contracts issued by an insurance company. (See Q. 2:19.)

Q. 3:6   Does a retirement plan have to be submitted to IRS for approval?

A retirement plan may qualify for tax-favored status without first being submitted to IRS. Nevertheless, it is prudent to submit the retirement plan for IRS approval since this is the most important step that can be taken to preserve a retirement plan's qualified status. If, upon review of the application for a determination letter, IRS finds defects in the retirement plan, the timely filing of the application allows the plan to be retroactively corrected. The procedure for submitting a retirement plan to IRS is discussed in Chapter 13. [IRC § 401(b); Reg. § 1.401(b)-1]

There is another reason for applying for a determination letter from IRS with regard to the *initial* qualification of a retirement plan. If IRS does not approve the retirement plan, the employer may recover its contribution only if the employer made a timely request for the determination. In that case, the return of the employer's contribution must be made within one year after receipt of the adverse determination. [ERISA § 403(c)(2)(B); *Rev. Rul. 60-276*, 1960-2 CB 150]

Q. 3:7 Even if a retirement plan is not submitted to IRS for approval, must it nevertheless be amended periodically?

Yes. A retirement plan must be amended to comply with changes in laws, regulations, and rulings that affect retirement plans in general, or the specific type of retirement plan in particular, even if it is not submitted to IRS for approval. In one case, IRS revoked the retirement plan's qualification because the employer failed to make required plan amendments timely to comply with changes in law even though no such changes would have affected the operation of the plan. [*Basch Engineering, Inc.*, 59 TCM 482 (1990)] (See also Q. 11:21 and Q. 26:20.)

Formal amendments required as a result of TRA '86 (and other laws) need not be made until the last day of the plan year beginning in 1991. However, retirement plans must operate in conformity with the new rules as of each rule's effective date; and plan amendments, when made, must be retroactive to the applicable effective date. [*Rev. Proc. 89-65*, 1989-2 CB 786]

Q. 3:8 May an employee's benefits be reduced after retirement to reflect Social Security benefit increases?

No. A qualified retirement plan must provide that benefits cannot be reduced because of increases in Social Security benefits or wage base levels after (1) benefit payments commence to a participant or beneficiary or (2) a participant who has vested benefits under the plan separates from service. [IRC § 401(a)(15)]

Q. 3:9 May a participant assign his or her vested interest in a qualified retirement plan?

As a general rule, benefits provided under a qualified retirement plan may not be assigned or alienated. There are, however, exceptions to this rule.

A participant or beneficiary whose benefits are in pay status may assign or alienate the right to future benefit payments provided the following conditions are satisfied: (1) the assignment or alienation is voluntary and revocable; (2) the amount does not exceed 10 percent of any benefit payment; and (3) there is no direct or indirect defraying of plan administration costs. [IRC § 401(a)(13)(A); Reg. § 1.401(a)-13(d)(1)]

A loan made to a participant or beneficiary is generally not treated as an assignment or alienation if the loan is secured by the participant's vested interest and is not a prohibited transaction. (See Q. 27:25.) [IRC §§ 401(a)(13)(A) and 4975(d)(1); Reg. § 1.401(a)-13(d)(2)]

The prohibition against the assignment or alienation of retirement plan benefits does *not* preclude the enforcement of a federal tax levy or the collection by IRS on a judgment resulting from an unpaid tax assessment. [IRC § 6331; Reg. § 1.401(a)-13(b)(2); *U.S. v. Weintraub*, No. C-1-76-0032, USDC (SD Ohio, 1990)]

If a qualified domestic relations order (QDRO) (see Q. 28:1) requires the distribution of all or part of a participant's benefits to another individual, even though the participant is still employed, the distribution is not considered an assignment or alienation. [IRC §§ 401(a)(13)(B) and 414(p); Reg. § 1.401(a)-13(g)]

Q. 3:10 May a participant's qualified retirement plan benefits be attached or garnished?

According to IRS, an attachment, garnishment, levy, execution, or other legal or equitable process of or against a participant's qualified retirement plan benefits is not a voluntary assignment or alienation (see Q. 3:9) and, therefore, violates the anti-alienation rule. IRS has also held that a transfer of a participant's plan benefits, which violates the anti-alienation rule, results in the disqualification of the plan. [Reg. § 1.401(a)-13(d)(1); *Letter Ruling 8829009*]

Several courts have recognized an exception to the anti-alienation or assignment provision based on an employee's fraudulent or criminal conduct directed against his or her employer. [*Crawford v. La Boucherie Bernard Ltd.*, 815 F2d 117 (DC Cir. 1987); *St. Paul Fire & Marine Ins. Co. v. Cox*, 752 F2d 550 (11th Cir. 1985); *Brock v. Lindemann*, Civ. No. A3-84-1814-R (ND Tex. 1988); *Guidry v. National Sheet Metal Workers*, 641 F. Supp. 360 (D. Colo. 1986); but see *United Metal Products Corp. v. National Bank of Detroit*, 8 EBC 1244 (6th Cir. 1987); *Ellis National Bank of Jacksonville v. Irving Trust Co.*, 786 F2d 466 (2d Cir. 1986)]

Other courts have held that the bankruptcy laws create an implied exception to the anti-alienation rule. (See Q. 27:40 through Q. 27:42.)

Chapter 4

Eligibility and Participation

A company's retirement plan does not qualify for tax-favored status unless certain minimum standards for coverage of, and participation by, employees are met. This chapter examines those standards, describes the consequences of owning more than one company, and discusses important terms.

Q. 4:1   Must a company's qualified retirement plan cover all of its employees?

No. Certain minimum coverage and participation requirements, in terms of a percentage or a number of the company's workforce (see Q. 4:15 and Q. 4:23), must be satisfied. A retirement plan that meets the minimum coverage and participation requirements may qualify for favorable tax treatment even though some employees are excluded.

It is important to recognize that the coverage and participation requirements are minimum standards that must be satisfied by a qualified retirement plan. A company may use more liberal standards than those discussed in this chapter. [IRC §§ 401(a)(26) and 410(b)]

Q. 4:2   What minimum age and service requirements may be set by a qualified retirement plan?

A qualified retirement plan may require an employee to reach age 21 before becoming eligible to participate in the plan. A plan may also require an employee to complete one year of service (see Q. 4:8) with the company before becoming eligible to participate. [IRC § 410(a)(1)(a)]

For qualified retirement plans that provide full and immediate vesting (see Q. 8:12), an employer may condition participation on completion of more than one year of service. The maximum period for such plans is two years; however, for 401(k) plans, the maximum period is only one year. (See Q. 4:4 and Q. 21:4.) [IRC §§ 410(a)(1)(B) and 401(k)(2)(D)]

Q. 4:3 May a qualified retirement plan set a maximum age limit for participation?

No. A qualified retirement plan may not exclude from participation employees who are hired after reaching a specified maximum age. Previously, defined benefit and target benefit plans (see Q. 2:3 and Q. 2:5) could exclude employees who were hired within five years of the plan's normal retirement age (see Q. 9:66.). [Prop. Reg. §§ 1.410(a)-4A and 1.411(b)-2]

Q. 4:4 May a qualified retirement plan require two consecutive years of service for participation?

Qualified retirement plans that provide for immediate 100 percent vesting and require more than one year of service, but not more than two years of service, to be eligible to participate (see Q. 4:2 and Q. 8:12) may provide that years of service preceding a one-year break in service (see Q. 4:10) be disregarded if the employee has not yet met the service eligibility criterion. Thus, an employee who completes one year of service and then incurs a one-year break in service starts over again, either the next year or when the employee is rehired. However, the plan cannot require that the two years of service be consecutive. [IRC § 410(a)(5)(B); Reg. § 1.410(a)-8T]

> **Example.** CeeKay Corp. established a profit sharing plan in 1989 that operates on a calendar year basis. The plan provides that an employee must complete two years of service before becoming a participant and that the employee will be 100

percent vested upon completion of the two-year eligibility requirement. The following three employees all became employed by CeeKay on December 31, 1988:

Hours of Service Completed

Plan Year	Stephanie	Caroline	James
1989	1,000	1,000	1,000
1990	1,000	700	500
1991	1,000	1,000	1,000
1992	1,000	1,000	700
1993	1,000	1,000	1,000

Stephanie will have satisfied the plan's service requirement at the end of 1990; Caroline at the end of 1991 because 1989 may not be disregarded since she did not have a one-year break in service in 1990; and James at the end of 1993 because 1989 may be disregarded since he did have a one-year break in service in 1990.

Q. 4:5 May conditions other than age and service be set for participation in a qualified retirement plan?

Yes. A qualified retirement plan can impose other conditions for participation provided that the minimum coverage and minimum participation requirements are satisfied (see Q. 4:15 and Q. 4:23). For example, a plan could require that an employee not be employed within a specified job description (e.g., salesmen) to be eligible to participate (see Q. 1:17). [Reg. § 1.410(a)-3(d)]

The most common exclusion, other than exclusions based upon age and service, applies to union employees on whose behalf negotiations for retirement benefits have been conducted with the company. The company may exclude union employees from coverage, whether or not they are covered under a separate retirement plan, as long as retirement benefits were the subject of good-faith bargaining. Exclusions for air pilots and nonresident aliens are also permitted. [IRC § 410(b)(3)]

Q. 4:6   May the company require employee contributions as a condition of plan participation?

Yes. A company may adopt a plan—commonly called a thrift or savings plan (see Q. 2:7)—that gears employer contributions on behalf of an employee to contributions made by the employee. Other types of plans may also require contributions to be made by the employees (e.g., defined benefit plans). Since participation in these plans is usually limited to those employees who contribute, if required employee contributions are so burdensome that nonhighly compensated employees cannot afford to participate, the plan may fail to satisfy the minimum coverage and participation requirements (see Q. 4:15, Q. 4:23, and Q. 5:14).

Q. 4:7   When must an employee who meets the plan's eligibility requirements begin to participate?

An employee who meets the minimum age and service requirements of the Code (see Q. 4:2), and who is otherwise eligible to participate in the qualified retirement plan, must commence participation no later than the earlier of (1) the first day of the first plan year beginning after the date the employee met the eligibility requirements, or (2) the date six months after these requirements were met. [IRC § 410(a)(4)]

> **Example.** Ken began working for KD&M Corporation on October 1, 1989. He was 28 years old at that time. KD&M Corporation's qualified retirement plan operates on a calendar-year basis and requires that employees be at least age 21 and complete one year of service. Since Ken met the plan's eligibility requirements on October 1, 1990, he must start to participate in the plan no later than January 1, 1991. This is because January 1, 1991, the first day of the first plan year beginning after Ken has met the eligibility requirements, is earlier than April 1, 1991, the date six months after he has met these requirements.

Q. 4:8 What is a year of service for a plan's service eligibility requirement?

A year of service for eligibility purposes means a calendar year, a plan year, or any other consecutive 12-month period (the eligibility computation period) specified in the qualified retirement plan during which the employee completes at least 1,000 hours of service (see Q. 4:9). The period starts on the date employment commences. [IRC § 410(a)(3)(A)]

If the employee does not complete 1,000 hours of service during the initial eligibility computation period, the next period commences on the anniversary date of employment or, if provided in the plan, on the first day of the plan year during which the anniversary date falls. If the plan's service eligibility requirement is two years and the plan provides for the second year to start from the first day of the plan year, the employee will be credited with two years of service if 1,000 hours of service are completed during both the initial eligibility computation period and the plan year.

Q. 4:9 What is an hour of service?

An hour of service is any hour for which an employee is paid or is entitled to payment by the employer. An hour of service includes any hour for which payments are made due to an employee's vacation, sickness, holiday, disability, layoff, jury duty, military duty, or leave of absence, even if the employee no longer works for the company. An hour of service also includes any hour for which back pay is awarded. [DOL Reg. § 2530.200b-2]

Q. 4:10 What is a one-year break in service?

A one-year break in service means a calendar year, a plan year, or any other consecutive 12-month period designated in the plan during which an employee does not complete more than 500 hours of service (see Q. 4:9). [IRC §§ 410(a)(5)(C) and 411(a)(6)(A); DOL Reg. § 2530.200b-4]

An employee who works over 500 hours during the designated 12-month period does not incur a one-year break in service. An employee's one-year break in service has significance in terms of eligibility (see Q. 4:4 and Q. 4:12) and vesting of benefits (see Q. 8:11).

Q. 4:11 What years of service must be taken into account for eligibility purposes?

In general, all years of service with the employer must be counted. For the exceptions, see Q. 4:12. [IRC § 410(a)(5)]

Service with a predecessor of the employer must be counted if the successor-employer maintains the predecessor's qualified retirement plan. If the successor adopts a new retirement plan, recognition of service with the predecessor-employer is supposed to be decided under as-yet-unissued IRS regulations. [IRC § 414(a)]

Service with any member of a controlled group of corporations or with a commonly controlled entity (see Q. 4:32), whether or not incorporated, must be counted for eligibility purposes. Similarly, service with any member of an affiliated service group (see Q. 27:31) must be counted. [IRC §§ 414(b), 414(c), and 414(m)]

Q. 4:12 May any years of service be disregarded for eligibility purposes?

Yes. Qualified retirement plans may require up to two years of service as a prerequisite to participation. For plans that require two years of service as an eligibility requirement, a year of service (see Q. 4:8) preceding a one-year break in service (see Q. 4:10) need not be considered in determining whether an employee is eligible to participate (see Q. 4:4). [IRC §§ 410(a)(1)(B) and 410(a)(5)(B)]

Q. 4:13 May past service with a former employer be used for eligibility purposes in the qualified retirement plan of the present employer?

If the present employer maintains the qualified retirement plan of a predecessor employer, an employee's service with the predecessor counts as service for the present employer (see Q. 4:11).

A qualified retirement plan may provide that service as an employee with a predecessor business counts for purposes of meeting the service eligibility requirement, even if the predecessor business had no qualified retirement plan. Furthermore, service as a partner of a partnership may be counted in meeting the service requirement for participation in the plan of a successor corporation. [*Letter Ruling 7742003; Farley Funeral Homes, Inc.*, 62 TC 150 (1974)]

Q. 4:14   Is a maternity or paternity period of absence treated as a break in service?

For purposes of determining whether a one-year break in service (see Q. 4:10) has occurred for both participation and vesting purposes, an employee who is absent from work due to the birth or adoption of a child is treated as having completed, during the absence, the number of hours that normally would have been credited but for the absence, up to a maximum of 501 hours, so as to prevent a one-year break in service.

The hours of service are credited only in the year in which the absence begins (if necessary to prevent a break in service in that year) or in the following year. [IRC §§ 410(a)(5)(E) and 411(a)(6)(E)]

> **Example.** Before taking an approved maternity leave, Susan completed 750 hours of service during the 1990 plan year. Since the credit is not needed in 1990 to prevent a break in service, Susan is entitled to up to 501 hours of credited service in 1991.

Q. 4:15   What coverage requirements must a retirement plan satisfy to qualify for favorable tax treatment?

A retirement plan must satisfy one of two coverage tests in order to qualify for favorable tax treatment:

- The ratio percentage test (see Q. 4:16); or
- The average benefit test (see Q. 4:17).

A plan maintained by an employer that has no nonhighly compensated employees (see Q. 4:28) will automatically satisfy the coverage requirements. [IRC §§ 410(b)(1), 410(b)(2), and 410(b)(6)(F); Prop. Reg. § 1.410(b)-2]

Q. 4:16 What is the ratio percentage test for the minimum coverage requirements?

Under the ratio percentage test, the percentage of the nonhighly compensated active employees who benefit under the retirement plan must equal at least 70 percent of the percentage of the highly compensated active employees (see Q. 4:28) who benefit under the plan. [IRC § 410(b)(1); Prop. Reg. § 1.410(b)-2(b)(2)]

> **Example.** For a plan year, Debi Corporation's defined benefit plan covers 60 percent of its nonhighly compensated active employees and 80 percent of its highly compensated active employees. The plan's ratio percentage for the year is 75 percent (i.e., 60% divided by 80%) and thus satisfies the ratio percentage test.

For purposes of satisfying the minimum coverage requirements, employees who do not meet the plan's minimum age or service requirement (see Q. 4:2) are not counted. In addition, nonresident aliens who receive no earned income from sources within the United States and union members whose retirement benefits have been the subject of good-faith bargaining between the employer and the union do not count (see Q. 4:5). [IRC §§ 410(b)(3) and 410(b)(4); Prop. Reg. § 1.410(b)-6]

Q. 4:17 What is the average benefit test for the minimum coverage requirements?

Under the average benefit test, (1) the plan must benefit such employees as qualify under a classification set up by the employer and found by IRS not to be discriminatory in favor of highly compensated employees (see Q. 4:28), and (2) the average benefit percentage for nonhighly compensated employees of the employer must equal at least 70 percent of the average benefit percentage for highly compensated employees of the employer. [IRC § 410(b)(2); Prop. Reg. § 1.410(b)-2(b)(3)]

The classification test is described in Q. 4:18, and the average benefit percentage test in Q. 4:19.

Q. 4:18 What is the classification test?

The classification test is satisfied if, based on all the facts and circumstances, the classification set up by the employer is reasonable and is established under objective business criteria. In addition, the classification must be found to be nondiscriminatory based on either a safe harbor rule or a facts and circumstances test. The IRS safe harbor rule looks at the difference between the coverage percentage of the highly compensated employees (see Q. 4:28) and the coverage percentage of the nonhighly compensated employees. Generally, the safe harbor rule first looks at the percentage of all of the employer's employees who are nonhighly compensated employees (concentration percentage) and then creates both a safe harbor percentage and an unsafe harbor percentage. [Prop. Reg. § 1.410(b)-4]

> **Example.** Mikey Corp. has 200 employees; 120 are nonhighly compensated employees and 80 are highly compensated employees. The nonhighly compensated employees concentration percentage is 60 percent (120/200). Mikey Corp. maintains a retirement plan that excludes employees of a specified geographic location. The plan benefits 72 highly compensated employees so that the highly compensated employee benefiting percentage is 90 percent (72/80). Under the safe harbor rule, the IRS safe harbor percentage is 50 percent and the unsafe harbor percentage is 40 percent. If the plan benefits at least 45 percent (50% × 90%) of the nonhighly compensated employees, or 54 (45% × 120) employees, the classification is within the safe harbor and thus is considered nondiscriminatory. If the plan benefits less than 36 percent (40% times 90%) of the nonhighly compensated employees, or 44 (36% × 120) employees, the classification is within the unsafe harbor and thus is considered discriminatory. If the plan benefits from 44 to 53 nonhighly compensated employees, IRS may determine that the classification is nondiscriminatory based on all the facts and circumstances.

Q. 4:19 What is the average benefit percentage test?

In order for a qualified retirement plan to satisfy the average benefit percentage test, the benefits provided to nonhighly compensated employees under all plans of the employer must generally be at least 70 percent as great, on average, as the benefits provided to the employer's highly compensated employees (see Q. 4:28).

Satisfaction of the average benefit percentage test requires that the employer determine an employee benefit percentage for each employee taken into account for testing purposes and then separately average the percentages of all employees in the highly compensated and nonhighly compensated groups. Benefit percentages may be determined on either a contributions or a benefits basis. Generally, employee contributions and benefits attributable to employee contributions are not taken into account in calculating employee benefit percentages.

To simplify the calculations required to determine whether a plan satisfies the average benefit percentage test, a number of optional rules may be used. For example, the use of statistical sampling techniques and tables for converting benefits to contributions and contributions to benefits will help employers to determine more economically whether their qualified retirement plans satisfy the average benefit percentage test.

Because of the complexities attendant to the average benefit percentage test, IRS proposed regulations will not become effective until the plan year beginning on or after January 1, 1991. For plan years beginning before that date, the plan must be operated in accordance with a reasonable, good faith interpretation of the applicable Code provisions. Whether the plan is operated in accordance with a reasonable, good faith interpretation will generally be determined on the basis of all relevant facts and circumstances, including the extent to which an employer has resolved unclear issues in its favor. [Prop. Reg. §§ 1.410(b)-5 and 1.410(b)-10(d)]

Q. 4:20   When does an employee benefit under the qualified retirement plan?

For purposes of the minimum coverage rules, an employee must benefit under the qualified retirement plan to be taken into account for the percentage tests (see Q. 4:16 and Q. 4:17). An employee is treated as benefiting under the plan for a plan year:

- In the case of a defined contribution plan, only if the employee receives an allocation of contributions or forfeitures.

- In the case of a defined benefit plan, only if the employee receives a benefit accrual.

- In the case of a 401(k) plan, if the employee is eligible to make an elective contribution (see Q. 21:13), whether or not the employee actually does so.

- If the employee fails to accrue a benefit solely because of the Section 415 limits on benefits and annual additions (see Q. 5:1, Q. 5:5, and Q. 5:12).

- If the employee fails to accrue a benefit solely because of a uniformly applicable benefit limit under the plan.

- If the current benefit accrual is offset by the contributions or benefits under another plan.

In the case of a defined contribution plan, if no employee receives an allocation of contributions or forfeitures, the plan is treated as satisfying the minimum coverage requirements for the plan year. Thus, a defined contribution plan for which contributions cease and for which no forfeitures can be allocated satisfies the requirements. In the case of a defined benefit plan, if no employee accrues any additional benefits under the plan, the plan is treated as satisfying the requirements for the plan year. However, this special rule is not available with respect to a top-heavy plan that has required minimum contributions or benefit accruals (see Q. 20:37 and Q. 20:43) or to a plan where future compensation increases are taken into account in determining the accrued benefit under the plan. [Prop. Reg. § 1.410(b)-3(b)]

For the treatment of terminated employees, see Q. 4:21; and, for a discussion of the family aggregation rule, see Q. 4:22.

Q. 4:21   How are employees who terminated employment during the plan year treated for minimum coverage purposes?

An employee is not taken into account for purposes of the minimum coverage tests (see Q. 4:15) if:

1. The employee does not benefit (see Q. 4:20) under the plan for the plan year;

2. The employee is eligible to participate in the plan;

3. The plan has a minimum hours of service requirement or a requirement that an employee be employed on the last day of the plan year (last-day requirement) in order to accrue a benefit or receive an allocation for the plan year;

4. The employee fails to accrue a benefit or receive an allocation under the plan solely because of the failure to satisfy the minimum hours of service or last-day requirement; and

5. The employee terminates employment during the plan year with not more than 500 hours of service (see Q. 4:9) and the employee is not an active employee as of the last day of the plan year.

[Reg. § 1.410(b)-3(c)]

> **Example.** Norman of New Mexico, Inc. has 30 employees who are eligible under its profit sharing plan. The plan requires the employee to complete 1,000 hours of service during the plan year to receive an allocation of contributions or forfeitures. Ten employees do not receive an allocation because of their failure to complete 1,000 hours of service. Three of the ten employees completed less than 501 hours of service and terminated their employment. Two of the employees completed between 501 and 1,000 hours of service and terminated their employment. The remaining five employees did not terminate employment. The three terminated employees who completed less than 501 hours of service are not taken into account. The other seven employees who do not receive an allocation are taken into account but are treated as not benefiting under the plan.

The rule discussed above is effective for plan years beginning on or after January 1, 1990. For the 1989 plan year, any employee who was eligible to participate under the plan but who failed to accrue a benefit solely because of the failure to satisfy either a minimum hours of service requirement of 1,000 hours of service or less or a last-day requirement may be treated as benefiting under the plan. [Prop. Reg. § 1.410(b)-10(b)(2)]

Q. 4:22 What is the family aggregation rule?

A highly compensated employee (see Q. 4:28) who is a 5% owner or one of the ten most highly compensated employees and all family members of such highly compensated employee who are also employees of the employer are treated as a *single* highly compensated employee for purposes of the minimum coverage requirements.

If any member of such group is benefiting (see Q. 4:20) under the plan, the deemed single employee is treated as benefiting under the plan. If no member of such group is benefiting under the plan, the deemed single employee is treated as not benefiting under the plan.

Family includes the highly compensated employee's spouse, lineal descendants and ascendants, and spouses of lineal descendants or ascendants. [IRC §§ 410(b)(6)(A) and 414(q)(6); Prop. Reg. § 1.410(b)-8(c)]

Q. 4:23 What is the minimum participation requirement?

In addition to the minimum coverage requirements (see Q. 4:15), a minimum participation requirement must be met by each retirement plan of the employer in order to be qualified. To satisfy this latter requirement, a qualified retirement plan must benefit at least the lesser of (1) 50 employees, or (2) 40 percent of all employees. This requirement may not be satisfied by aggregating different plans of the employer. [IRC § 401(a)(26); Prop. Reg. §§ 1.401(a)(26)-1(a) and 1.401(a)(26)-2(a)]

> **Example 1.** S&C Professional Law Corporation employs two attorneys and no other employees. Each attorney may participate in a separate qualified retirement plan because each plan will cover 40 percent or more of the employees.
>
> **Example 2.** SC&J Professional Law Corporation employs three attorneys and no other employees. Each attorney may *not* participate in a separate qualified retirement plan because each plan will cover less than 40 percent of the employees.

Among the plans that are deemed to meet the minimum participation requirements automatically are:

- Defined contribution plans under which no employee receives an allocation of either contributions or forfeitures for the plan year. [Prop. Reg. § 1.401(a)(26)-2(b)(1)]

- Defined benefit plans under which no employee accrues any additional benefit for a plan year, *excepting* those minimum benefits provided for non-key employees under top-heavy plans (see Q. 20:37). [Prop. Reg. § 1.401(a)(26)-2(b)(2)]

Generally, an employee is deemed to benefit under the plan if the employee is deemed to benefit under the plan for the minimum coverage tests (see Q. 4:20); and employees not taken into account for the minimum coverage tests (see Q. 4:16) are, generally, not considered for the minimum participation test. [Prop. Reg. §§ 1.401(a)(26)-5 and 1.401(a)(26)-6]

The family aggregation rule (see Q. 4:22) does not apply for purposes of the minimum participation requirement.

Q. 4:24 What is a prior benefit structure?

Defined benefit plans (see Q. 2:3), but not defined contribution plans (see Q. 2:2), must also satisfy the minimum participation requirements (see Q. 4:23) with respect to a prior benefit structure. The prior benefit structure under a defined benefit plan for a plan year includes all benefits accrued to that time; therefore, the plan can have only one prior benefit structure.

Generally, the prior benefit structure satisfies the minimum participation requirement if at least 50 employees or 40 percent of the employees currently accrue meaningful benefits. Whether a plan is providing meaningful benefits is determined on the basis of all the facts and circumstances. This determination is intended to ensure that a plan functions as an ongoing defined benefit plan providing meaningful benefits to at least 50 employees of the employer or 40 percent of the employer's employees. A plan does not satisfy this requirement if it exists primarily to preserve accrued benefits for a small group of employees and thereby functions more as an individual plan for the small group of employees or for the employer. The relevant factors in making this determination include the following:

- The level of current benefit accruals;

- The comparative rate of accruals under the current benefit formula compared to prior rates of accrual under the plan;
- The projected accrued benefits under the current benefit formula compared to accrued benefits as of the close of the immediately preceding plan year;
- The length of time the current benefit formula has been in effect;
- The number of employees with accrued benefits under the plan; and
- The length of time the plan has been in effect.

[Prop. Reg. § 1.401(a)(26)-3]

Q. 4:25 May a retirement plan that does not satisfy the minimum participation requirements be merged into another plan?

Qualified retirement plans may be merged provided certain requirements are satisfied (see Q. 8:28).

Even though the minimum participation requirements (see Q. 4:23) became effective for plan years beginning after 1988, an IRS representative has advised that IRS will permit retroactive plan mergers up to the last day of the plan year beginning in 1990.

Q. 4:26 Can an employee's waiver of participation in the employer's qualified retirement plan jeopardize the tax-favored status of the plan?

Yes. For example, an employee who is otherwise eligible to participate in the employer's defined benefit plan that requires mandatory employee contributions as a condition of participation may be unable or unwilling to contribute and would therefore waive participation in the plan (see Q. 4:6). That employee is included in determining whether the company's retirement plan satisfies the minimum coverage and minimum participation tests (see Q. 4:15 and Q. 4:23). Therefore, the plan may lose its tax-favored status if too many employees waive participation.

An employee's decision not to make an elective contribution (see Q. 21:13) to a 401(k) plan is not a waiver of participation that would jeopardize the tax-favored status of the plan for purposes of the minimum coverage and minimum participation requirements (see Q. 4:20 and Q. 4:23). [Prop. Reg. §§ 1.410(b)-3(b)(2)(ii) and 1.401(a)(26)-3(b)(5)(b)]

Q. 4:27 What happens if a retirement plan fails to satisfy the minimum coverage or minimum participation requirements?

If a retirement plan fails to satisfy the qualification requirements of Section 401(a) (see Q. 3:1), the tax-exempt status of plan earnings is revoked, employer deductions for contributions may be deferred or eliminated, and all employees must include the value of vested plan contributions in income. [IRC § 402(b)(1)]

However, if the plan fails to satisfy the minimum coverage or minimum participation requirements (see Q. 4:15 and Q. 4:23), each highly compensated employee (see Q. 4:28) must include in income an amount equal to the employee's entire vested accrued benefit not previously included in income, not just current vested plan contributions. If, however, the plan is not qualified solely because it fails to satisfy either of the requirements, no adverse tax consequences are imposed on nonhighly compensated employees. [IRC § 402(b)(2)]

Q. 4:28 Who is a highly compensated employee?

Highly compensated employees are divided into two groups: highly compensated active employees and highly compensated former employees. [IRC § 414(q); Reg. § 1.414(q)-1T]

A highly compensated active employee is an employee who, during the determination year or the look-back year (see Q. 4:30),

- Was a more-than-5% owner of the employer (see Q. 20:28);
- Received compensation (see Q. 4:29) from the employer of more than $75,000 (adjusted for inflation);

- Received compensation from the employer of more than $50,000 (adjusted for inflation) and was a member of the top-paid group of employees; or

- Was an officer of the employer who received compensation of more than $45,000 (adjusted for inflation).

[IRC § 414(q)(1); Reg. § 1.414(q)-1T, Q&A 3]

For purposes of determining highly compensated active employees, the top-paid group of employees consists of the top 20 percent of the employer's employees ranked by compensation (see Q. 4:29). [IRC § 414(q)(4); Reg. § 1.414(q)-1T, Q&A 9]

The number of employees that can be considered officers is equal to 10 percent of all employees, or three, whichever is greater. In no case, however, can the total number of officers exceed 50. Thus, if the employer has fewer than 30 employees, no more than three can be considered officers. But, if no officer earned sufficient compensation to be a highly compensated employee, the highest paid officer will be included. [IRC § 414(q)(5); Reg. § 1.414(q)-1T, Q&A 10]

A former employee who was a highly compensated active employee at the time employment was terminated or in any determination year (see Q. 4:30) ending on or after the employee's 55th birthday is considered a highly compensated former employee. [Reg. § 1.414(q)-1T, Q&A 4]

A nonhighly compensated employee is any employee who is not a highly compensated employee.

Q. 4:29   How is compensation defined for purposes of determining who is a highly compensated employee?

The definition of compensation is the same as is used for purposes of the annual addition limitation applicable to defined contribution plans (see Q. 5:1). However, in addition, elective or salary reduction contributions to a 401(k) plan (see Q. 21:13), a cafeteria plan, or a tax-sheltered annuity are included. [IRC § 414(q)(7); Reg. § 1.414(q)-1T, Q&A 13]

Q. 4:30 What are the determination year and look-back year for determining the group of highly compensated employees?

The determination year is generally the plan year, and the look-back year is the 12-month period immediately preceding the determination year. [Reg. § 1.414(q)-1T, Q&A 14]

Q. 4:31 Does the family aggregation rule affect the determination of who is a highly compensated employee?

If any individual is a member of the family (see Q. 4:22) of a 5% owner or of a highly compensated employee (see Q. 4:28) in the group consisting of the ten most highly compensated employees, such individual is not considered a separate employee and any compensation paid to such individual is treated as if it were paid to the 5% owner or highly compensated employee [IRC § 414(q)(6); Reg. § 1.414(q)-1T, Q&A 11]

Q. 4:32 Do special coverage and participation rules apply to commonly controlled businesses?

For purposes of determining whether a retirement plan covers a sufficient number of employees to meet the minimum coverage requirements (see Q. 4:15) and the minimum participation requirements (see Q. 4:23), as well as other plan-related requirements, all employees of corporations which are members of a controlled group of corporations (see Q. 4:34) are treated as if they were employed by a single employer. A comparable requirement applies to affiliated service groups (see Q. 27:31), partnerships, sole proprietorships, and other businesses that are under common control. [IRC §§ 414(b), 414(c), and 414(m)]

However, the Tax Court has held that the employees of two failing corporations should not be aggregated with the employees of a sole proprietorship, all three of which were commonly controlled, when, under the circumstances, neither corporation was able, in good faith, to adopt a permanent retirement plan. IRS did not acquiesce in this decision. [*Sutherland*, 78 TC 395 (1982); *Non-acq.*, 1986-1 CB 1]

A separate line-of-business exception may apply, for purposes of the minimum coverage and participation requirements, to commonly controlled businesses but not to affiliated service groups (see Q. 4:35). [IRC §§ 401(a)(26)(G), 410(b)(5), and 414(r)]

Q. 4:33 If an individual owns two corporations, each of which has employees, can a qualified retirement plan be adopted by only one of the corporations?

Perhaps. For example, assume Herman owns all of the stock of Herman Corporation and Mabel Corporation. Herman Corporation maintains a retirement plan for its employees; Mabel Corporation does not.

The composition of Herman's employees is as follows:

Employee	Age	Service	Compensation
1	50	10 years	$150,000
2	35	6 years	20,000
3	30	4 years	10,000
4	28	Less than 1 year	10,000

The composition of Mabel's employees is as follows:

Employee	Age	Service	Compensation
5	45	2 years	$95,000
6	43	2 years	20,000
7	18	Less than 1 year	10,000

Employees 1, 2, 3, 5, and 6 satisfy the plan's eligibility requirements (age 21 and one year of service), and employees 1 and 5 are highly compensated employees (see Q. 4:28). Employees 4 and 7 need not be counted for purposes of the minimum participation and minimum coverage tests since they have not satisfied the plan's age and service requirements.

Since the retirement plan covers 60 percent of the employees who satisfy the eligibility requirements (i.e., 3 ÷ 5), the plan satisfies the minimum participation requirement (see Q. 4:23). In addition, the plan satisfies the ratio percentage test (see Q. 4:16) because the plan's ratio percentage is 70 percent or more (i.e., the coverage percentage of nonhighly compensated employees, 66⅔% (2 ÷ 3), divided by the coverage percentage of highly compensated employees, 50% (1 ÷ 2)).

Q. 4:34 When does common ownership result in a controlled group of corporations or businesses?

A controlled group of corporations exists if there is

1. A parent-subsidiary group of corporations connected through at least 80 percent stock ownership, or
2. A brother-sister group in which
   a. Five or fewer people own 80 percent or more of the stock value or voting power of each corporation, and
   b. The same five or fewer people together own more than 50 percent of the stock value or voting power of each corporation, taking into account the ownership of each person only to the extent such ownership is identical with respect to each organization.

[IRC § 1563(a); *U.S. v. Vogel Fertilizer Co.*, 102 S. Ct. 821 (1982)]

Q. 4:35 Is there a separate line-of-business exception to the minimum coverage and minimum participation requirements?

There is a separate line-of-business exception to the minimum coverage requirements (see Q. 4:15). If an employer operates two or more separate lines of business, the coverage tests may be applied separately to each separate line of business. However, this exception will apply only if the retirement plan satisfies the nondiscriminatory classification test (see Q. 4:17) on an employer-wide basis. If the retirement plan satisfied the ratio percentage test (see Q. 4:16), there would be no reason to apply the separate line-of-business exception. [IRC § 410(b)(5)]

To be treated as a separate line of business, a line of business must be separately maintained for *bona fide* business reasons and must satisfy each of the following:

- It must have at least 50 employees (excluding those who have not completed six months of service, normally work less than 17½ hours per week, normally work six months or less during the year, are under age 21, or are covered by a collective bargaining agreement);
- The employer must notify IRS that the line of business is being treated as separate; and
- The line of business must meet the guidelines to be prescribed in regulations or the employer must obtain a determination from IRS that the line of business may be treated as separate.

[IRC § 414(r)]

If the employer elects and IRS consents, the minimum participation requirements (see Q. 4:23) may be applied separately to each separate line of business of the employer. [IRC § 401(a)(26)(G)]

Q. 4:36 Who is a leased employee?

A leased employee is an individual who performs services for another person (the recipient) under an arrangement between the recipient and a third person (the leasing organization) who is otherwise treated as the individual's employer. The services performed by an individual for the recipient must be of a type that is historically performed by employees. [IRC §§ 414(n)(1) and 414(n)(2); Prop. Reg. § 1.414(n)-1(b)]

Q. 4:37 Who is the employer of a leased employee?

The leased employee (see Q. 4:36) is treated as the recipient's employee if the leased employee has performed services for the recipient pursuant to an agreement with the leasing organization on a substantially full-time basis for a period of at least one year and the services are of a type historically performed by employees in the recipient's business field. [IRC §§ 414(n)(1) and 414(n)(2); Prop. Reg. § 1.414(n)-1(b)]

Q. 4:38 When is the leased employee first considered an employee of the recipient?

The leased employee (see Q. 4:36) is treated as the recipient's employee after the leased employee has performed services for the recipient for a period of one year. Once this occurs, the leased employee's years of service for the recipient include the entire period for which he or she performed services for the recipient. [IRC § 414(n)(4); Prop. Reg. § 1.414(n)-2(d)]

Q. 4:39 What happens if the leased employee participates in the leasing organization's qualified retirement plan?

If the leasing organization maintains a qualified retirement plan, contributions or benefits for the leased employee (see Q. 4:36) are treated as if provided by the recipient to the extent those contributions or benefits are attributable to services performed by the leased employee for the recipient. [IRC § 414(n)(1)(B); Prop. Reg. § 1.414(n)-2(b)]

Q. 4:40 When will the leased employee not be treated as an employee of the recipient?

A leased employee (see Q. 4:36) will not be treated as the recipient's employee if leased employees do not constitute more than 20 percent of the recipient's nonhighly compensated workforce and each leased employee is covered by a qualified money purchase pension plan (see Q. 2:4) maintained by the leasing organization that provides the following:

- Immediate participation
- Full and immediate vesting
- A nonintegrated contribution rate of 10 percent of compensation

The immediate participation requirement does not apply to (1) employees who perform substantially all of their services for the leasing organization, and (2) employees whose compensation from the leasing organization for each of the four preceding plan years is less than $1,000. A money purchase pension plan meeting these requirements is referred to as a safe harbor plan. The term nonhighly compensated workforce means the aggregate number of individuals other than highly compensated employees (see Q. 4:28) who are employees of the recipient and have performed services for the recipient on a substantially full-time basis for one year or who are leased employees with respect to the recipient. [IRC § 414(n)(5); Prop. Reg. § 1.414(n)-2(f)]

Q. 4:41 Can an employer utilizing the services of leased employees obtain IRS approval of its qualified retirement plan?

Yes. An employer utilizing one or more leased employees (see Q. 4:36) may be able to obtain a favorable determination letter (see Q. 13:1) by following an application procedure developed by IRS. [Rev. Proc. 85-43, 1985-2 CB 501]

Chapter 5

Contribution and Benefit Limitations

ERISA set limits on the amount that could be allocated to an employee under a defined contribution plan and on the amount of the annual retirement benefit that could be provided to an employee under a defined benefit plan. These limits were subject to cost-of-living increases; and, because of the high rates of inflation in the late 1970s, these limits rose significantly. Congress reduced these limits in TEFRA and again in TRA '86. This chapter examines the defined contribution plan and defined benefit plan limitations now in effect.

Q. 5:1 How much may the company contribute to a defined contribution plan on behalf of a participant?

The Code sets limits on contributions and other additions made to a participant's account in a defined contribution plan (see Q. 2:2). Contributions and other additions are referred to as the annual addition to a participant's account. The annual addition is the sum of the following:

1. Employer contributions;

2. Employee contributions;

3. Forfeitures;

4. Amounts allocated to an individual medical account, which is part of a pension or annuity plan maintained by the employer; and

5. Amounts derived from contributions, which are attributable to

post-retirement medical benefits allocated to the separate account of a key employee (see Q. 20:24) under a welfare benefit fund maintained by the employer.

[IRC §§ 415(c)(2), 415(l), 419(e), and 419A(d)]

The annual addition with respect to a participant's account during any limitation year (see Q. 5:11) may not exceed the lesser of $30,000 (see Q. 5:2) or 25 percent of the participant's compensation (see Q. 5:3). [IRC § 415(c)(1)]

The annual addition limitation is best explained by an example:

Participant's compensation for 1990	$80,000
Employer contribution	11,000
Employee contribution	8,000
Forfeitures allocated to participant's account	5,000

Computation of Annual Addition

Employer contribution	$11,000
Employee contribution	8,000
Forfeitures	5,000
Annual addition	$24,000

The total amount to be allocated to the participant under the defined contribution plan will be $24,000 unless it exceeds the limitation amount, which is the lesser of $30,000 or 25 percent of the participant's compensation. Since the limitation for 1990 is $20,000 (25% of $80,000), the annual addition of $24,000 ($11,000 + $8,000 + $5,000) exceeds the limitation amount. The contributions and other additions to this participant's account therefore may not exceed $20,000.

See Q. 5:18 for a discussion of the family aggregation rule.

Q. 5:2   Will the $30,000 ceiling on the annual addition rise?

The dollar limitation on the annual addition is set at one-quarter of the dollar limitation applicable to defined benefit plans (see Q. 5:5). Therefore, the $30,000 ceiling cannot increase until the defined benefit plan ceiling increases to more than $120,000. [IRC § 415(c)(1)]

Q. 5:3   What does compensation mean for purposes of the annual addition limitation?

For annual addition limitation purposes (see Q. 5:1), compensation means the total compensation received from the employer for the limitation year (see Q. 5:11). For a self-employed individual (see Q. 27:8), compensation means earned income (see Q. 27:10). [IRC § 415(c)(3)]

Compensation includes:

- Wages, salaries, fees, and any other forms of earnings (commissions, tips, and bonuses), whether earned from sources inside or outside the United States;

- Employer-provided accident and health insurance benefits and medical reimbursement plan benefits, but only to the extent includible in the gross income of the employee;

- Moving expenses paid by an employer, but only to the extent not deductible by the employee under Section 217;

- The value of a nonqualified stock option granted to an employee by the employer, but only to the extent includible in the gross income of the employee for the taxable year in which it was granted; and

- The amount includible in gross income that results when an employee who receives restricted property makes an election to be taxed on it under Section 83(b).

[Reg. § 1.415-2(d)(1)]

Items not treated as compensation include:

- Elective or salary reduction contributions to a 401(k) plan to the extent not includible in the gross income of the employee for the year in which they are contributed;

- Employer contributions to a tax-sheltered annuity whether or not excludible from the gross income of the employee;

- Certain deferred compensation payments;

- SEP contributions that are excludible from the gross income of the employee;

- Amounts realized from the exercise of a nonqualified stock option or when restricted stock or property held by an employee becomes freely transferable or is no longer subject to a substantial risk of forfeiture; and

- Amounts realized from the sale, exchange, or other disposition of stock acquired under a qualified stock option.

[Reg. § 1.415-2(d)(2)]

The annual compensation of an employee taken into account under a qualified retirement plan may not exceed $200,000, with adjustments for inflation. For 1990, the compensation limit is $209,200. [IRC § 401(a)(17); IR 90-15 (Jan. 30, 1990)]

This definition of compensation applies only to the calculation of the annual addition limitation; a different definition of compensation may be used for the allocation or crediting of contributions under a defined contribution plan (see Q. 21.11).

See Q. 5:18 for a discussion of the family aggregation rule.

Q. 5:4 Does a withdrawn employee voluntary contribution that is replaced during the same year constitute part of the annual addition?

Yes. If employee voluntary contributions (see Q. 5:15) are withdrawn and then replaced during the same limitation year (see Q. 5:11), they are treated as part of the annual addition.

> **Example.** Sallie made employee voluntary contributions of $3,000 in January, 1990 and withdrew $2,000 in June. If she replaced the $2,000 within the same limitation year of the $3,000 contribution, she will be deemed to have made a total of $5,000 of employee voluntary contributions. [*Letter Ruling 8622044*]

Q. 5:5 What is the maximum annual retirement benefit that a defined benefit plan may provide?

The annual benefit (see Q. 5:6) that may be paid to a participant under a defined benefit plan (see Q. 2:3) is limited to the lesser of

(1) $90,000, with cost-of-living adjustments, or (2) 100 percent of the participant's average compensation (see Q. 5:7). [IRC § 415(b)(1)]

Cost-of-living adjustments to the $90,000 limit are tied to the annual cost-of-living increases in Social Security benefits. For 1990, the $90,000 limit has been increased to $102,582. [IRC § 415(d); IR 90-15 (Jan. 30, 1990)]

See Q. 5:18 for a discussion of the family aggregation rule.

Q. 5:6 What does annual benefit mean?

The term annual benefit means a retirement benefit payable annually in the form of a straight life annuity (with no ancillary or incidental benefits) under a defined benefit plan (see Q. 2:3) to which employees do not contribute and to which no rollover contributions are made. (Under a straight life annuity, payments terminate upon the death of the annuitant.) [IRC § 415(b)(2)(A)]

If benefits under a defined benefit plan are payable in a form other than a straight life annuity, the limits (see Q. 5:5) are adjusted to a benefit that is equivalent to a straight life annuity. But if benefits under the plan are payable in the form of a joint and survivor annuity (see Q. 9:8), no reduction in the annual benefit is required. [IRC § 415(b)(2)(B)]

If benefits under a defined benefit plan commence before the participant attains Social Security retirement age (see Q. 5:9), the $90,000 limit is reduced to the actuarial equivalent of a $90,000 annual benefit commencing at the Social Security retirement age. Similarly, if benefits commence after the Social Security retirement age, the $90,000 limit is increased to the actuarial equivalent of a $90,000 annual benefit commencing at the Social Security retirement age. [IRC §§ 415(b)(2)(C) and 415(b)(2)(D)]

In adjusting the benefit limits for payment in a form other than a straight life annuity or for payments commencing before the Social Security retirement age, the interest rate assumption cannot be less than the greater of 5 percent or the interest rate specified in the plan. The interest rate for an adjustment if the payments commence after the Social Security retirement age cannot exceed the lesser of 5 percent or the rate specified in the plan. [IRC § 415(b)(2)(E)]

Q. 5:7 What does average compensation mean for purposes of the annual retirement benefit limitations?

For purposes of the limitation on a participant's annual retirement benefit under a defined benefit plan (see Q. 2:3), average compensation means the average compensation for the high three years. A participant's high three years is the period of consecutive years (not more than three) during which the participant both was an active participant in the plan and had the greatest aggregate compensation from the employer. It should be noted that IRS regulations use the high three years of service, not years of participation. [IRC § 415(b)(3); Reg. § 1.415-3(b)(3)]

For purposes of calculating average compensation, the definition of compensation parallels the definition used to calculate the annual addition limitation. The $200,000 compensation limitation also applies. (See Q. 5:3.)

See Q. 5:18 for a discussion of the family aggregation rule.

Q. 5:8 Is there a minimum number of years of participation or service required before a participant in a defined benefit plan qualifies for the maximum annual benefit?

If a participant has less than ten years of participation with the employer at retirement, the dollar limitation ($90,000) is reduced by 10 percent for each year of *participation* less than ten. The maximum percentage limitation (100 percent of the participant's average compensation) is reduced by 10 percent for each year of *service* less than ten. In both cases, the reduction in the limitation is never more than 90 percent. [IRC § 415(b)(5)]

> **Example 1.** Stephanie has seven years of service but only five years of plan participation at retirement in 1990, and her average compensation is $102,582. Stephanie's maximum annual benefit is $51,291 [the lesser of $51,291 (5/10 × $102,582) or $71,807 (7/10 × 100% × $102,582)].
>
> **Example 2.** If Stephanie's average compensation is $70,000, the maximum annual benefit is $49,000 [the lesser of $51,291 (5/10 × $102,582) or $49,000 (7/10 × 100% × $70,000)].

In any event, the annual benefit payable to a participant under a defined benefit plan does not exceed the limitation (see Q. 5:5) if the following conditions are met:

1. The annual benefit payable to a participant under the plan (and under all other defined benefit plans of the employer) does not exceed $10,000 for the plan year or for any prior plan year; and

2. The employer has not at any time maintained a defined contribution plan in which the participant participated.

Therefore, if a participant's average compensation is less than $10,000, the annual benefit under the plan could be $10,000—more than the participant's average compensation. If the participant has less than ten years of service with the employer, however, the $10,000 amount is reduced by 10 percent for each year less than ten (the reduction is never more than 90 percent). [IRC § 415(b)(4)]

Q. 5:9 What is the Social Security retirement age?

For purposes of calculating adjustments to the dollar limitation ($90,000) on benefits payable under a defined benefit plan (see Q. 2:3), Social Security retirement age means the age used as the retirement age under the Social Security Act (rounded to the next lower whole number) and depends on the calendar year of birth.

Year of birth	Social Security retirement age
Before 1938	65
After 1937 but before 1955	66
After 1954	67

[IRC § 415(b); Social Security Act § 216(l)]

Q. 5:10 What happens if the employee's accrued benefit under a defined benefit plan exceeded the TRA '86 limitations?

If the defined benefit plan was in existence on May 6, 1986, the employee was a participant as of the first day of the first plan year beginning after 1986, and the employee's accrued benefit (see Q. 8:2), as of the end of the plan year beginning before 1987, exceeded the TRA '86 maximum allowable benefit (see Q. 5:5 and Q. 5:6), the higher accrued benefit is preserved. [TRA '86 § 1106(i)]

Q. 5:11 What is the limitation year?

The limitation year, with respect to any qualified retirement plan maintained by the employer, is the calendar year. However, instead of using the calendar year, an employer may elect to use any other consecutive 12-month period as the limitation year. The election is made by the adoption of a written resolution by the employer. This requirement is satisfied if the election is made in connection with the adoption of the plan or any amendments to the plan. [Reg. § 1.415-2(b)]

Q. 5:12 What happens if an employee participates in both a defined benefit plan and a defined contribution plan?

If an employee participates in both a defined benefit plan (see Q. 2:3) and a defined contribution plan (see Q. 2:2) that are maintained by the same employer, a special formula is used to determine the combined maximum limit on benefits and contributions. [IRC § 415(e)]

For an employee who participates in both plans, the sum of the defined benefit plan fraction and the defined contribution plan fraction cannot exceed 1.0.

To arrive at the overall maximum limitation, take the following steps:

1. Compute a defined benefit plan fraction. The numerator of this fraction is the projected annual retirement benefit determined at year end. The denominator is the lesser of 1.25 times the dollar limitation for the current year or 1.4 times the percentage limitation for the current year. [IRC § 415(e)(2)]

2. Compute a defined contribution plan fraction. The numerator

of this fraction is the total of the annual additions to the participant's account for all years determined at year end. The denominator is the lesser of 1.25 times the dollar limitation or 1.4 times the percentage limitation for the current year and all years of prior service. [IRC § 415(e)(1)]

Each plan may contain a fail-safe provision that freezes the annual addition or benefit accrual at a level that prevents the limitation from being exceeded. For purposes of the 1.0 rule, the reduction, if any, in the defined benefit plan dollar limitation is based upon years of service, not years of participation (see Q. 5:8). [IRC § 415(b)(5)(B)]

> **Example.** Mr. James, age 45, incorporates his business in January, 1990. The corporation adopts a 100 percent defined benefit plan and a 10%-of-compensation money purchase pension plan. Mr. James earns $102,582 in 1990. Here is how the 1.0 rule works:
>
> 1. The defined benefit plan fraction is .8 [$102,582/$128,228 (the lesser of 1.25 × $102,582 or 1.4 × $102,582)].
> 2. The defined contribution plan fraction is .286 [$10,258/ $35,904 (the lesser of 1.25 × $30,000 or 1.4 × $25,646)].
> 3. The two fractions total 1.086.

At this point, the 1.0 rule comes into play—one of the fractions must be reduced. If the 10%-of-compensation contribution formula under the defined contribution plan is reduced to 7 percent, the defined contribution plan fraction will be .2 [$7,181 (7% × $102,582)/$35,904]. Then, the total of the fractions will be 1.0.

The cost to fund the 100%-of-compensation defined benefit plan varies from participant to participant. Note that contributions under a defined benefit plan depend upon the participant's age and the actuarial assumptions, such as interest and retirement age, used by the actuary to calculate that cost. Thus, the combination of a defined benefit plan and a defined contribution plan may provide the employee with a greater tax deduction.

For details on tax deduction rules, see Chapter 10; and, for details on top-heavy combined plans, see Q. 20:51 through Q. 20:58.

Q. 5:13 At what level of compensation will the 1.0 rule affect an employee?

If the employee's annual compensation exceeds $91,195, the 1.0 rule requires a reduction in one of the plans (see Q. 5:12). Under the rule, at $91,195 of compensation, the total of the fractions of a 100 percent defined benefit plan ($91,195/$127,673 = .714) plus a 10 percent defined contribution plan ($9,120/$31,918 = .286) equals 1.0.

If the maximum dollar limits increase (see Q. 5:1 and Q. 5:5), the threshold level of compensation for equivalency will also increase, but not necessarily in proportion to the percentage increase in the dollar limits.

Q. 5:14 What limits apply to employee contributions required under a qualified retirement plan?

A special nondiscrimination test, the actual contribution percentage (ACP) test, applies to required (i.e., mandatory) employee contributions under all qualified defined contribution plans (see Q. 2:2 and Q. 21:48 through Q. 21:55). If the plan satisfies the special requirements regarding such employee contributions, the plan will not be discriminatory. [Prop. Reg. §§ 1.401(a)(4)-2(d) and 1.401(a)(4)-6(d)]

Since a defined benefit plan does not separately account for required employee contributions (such contributions are not allocated or credited to separate accounts), the special nondiscrimination test does not apply; but, the plan will generally be deemed nondiscriminatory only if such employee contributions are made at the same rate, expressed as a percentage of compensation, by all employees under the plan. [Prop. Reg. § 1.401(a)(4)-6(c)]

If required employee contributions are so burdensome that non-highly compensated employees cannot afford to participate, the plan may fail to satisfy the coverage requirements (see Chapter 4) and not be a qualified retirement plan.

Required employee contributions made to a defined contribution plan are considered employee contributions that must satisfy the annual addition limitation (see Q. 5:1).

Q. 5:15 Is any limit set on the amount that a participant can voluntarily contribute to a qualified retirement plan?

The same special nondiscrimination test (see Q. 5:14) applies to employee voluntary contributions. Since employee voluntary contributions under a defined benefit plan (see Q. 2:3) will be separately accounted for, there is no limit on the amount of employee voluntary contributions made to either a defined contribution plan or a defined benefit plan as long as the ACP test and other special requirements are satisfied. (See Q. 21:48 through Q. 21:55.)

However, under all circumstances, whether the employee voluntary contributions are made to a defined contribution plan or a defined benefit plan, these contributions are considered employee contributions that must satisfy the annual addition limitation (see Q. 5:1).

Q. 5:16 What tax advantaes are gained when a qualified retirement plan permits participants to make voluntary contributions?

Although participants cannot deduct their voluntary contributions to the plan, they do get the advantage of having their contributions build up free of tax under the protection of the qualified retirement plan's tax shelter.

Q. 5:17 May a qualified retirement plan permit deductible employee contributions?

The law permitting deductible employee contributions was repealed. [TRA '86 § 1101(b)]

Although deductible employee contributions are no longer permitted, separate accounting by the employer or plan administrator is required with respect to any such contributions that were ever made to the plan to ensure that an employee who later receives a distribution from the plan is able to compute the tax due correctly. However, assets purchased by the plan with deductible employee contributions need not be segregated from other plan assets. [*Notice 82-13, 1982-1 CB 360*]

Distributions of deductible employee contributions (including earnings) are taxed as ordinary income in the year received, unless they are rolled over (that is, transferred tax-free) to an IRA or to another qualified retirement plan. Distributions of deductible employee contributions may also be subject to the early distribution tax (see Q. 9:68).

Q. 5:18 What is the family aggregation rule?

If an individual is a member of the family of a 5% owner or of one of the ten most highly compensated employees, the compensation of that individual is treated as if paid to (or on behalf of) a single 5% owner or highly compensated employee. Family members include the employee's spouse and any lineal descendant who has not attained age 19 before the close of the year. [IRC §§ 401(a)(17) and 414(q)(6)]

> **Example.** S&M Corporation adopts a 25%-of-compensation money purchase pension plan for calendar year 1990. There are two participants, Stanley, who earns $209,200, and his wife, Marjorie, who also earns $209,200. Because of the family aggregation rule, their combined compensation cannot exceed $209,200 (see Q. 5:3). The contribution for each is calculated as follows:
>
> 1. Each is deemed to earn $104,600 ($209,200 ÷ 2).
> 2. The contribution for each is $26,150 (25% × $104,600).
> 3. The total contribution is $52,300 ($26,150 + $21,150).
>
> If the family aggregation rule did not apply, the total contribution would be $60,000 [(lesser of $30,000 or 25% × $209,200) × 2].

The family aggregation rule does not apply to the annual addition limitation (see Q. 5:1), nor does it apply to the limitation on the annual retirement benefit that a defined benefit plan may provide (see Q. 5:5).

Chapter 6

Integration With Social Security

A company can make its qualified retirement plan part of an overall retirement scheme that includes Social Security; this combination is called integration. This chapter examines how integration works in light of the extensive changes brought about by TRA '86 and the opportunity it affords the company to provide benefits favorable to shareholder-employees and key personnel without running afoul of the prohibition against discrimination.

Q. 6:1 What does the integration of a qualified retirement plan with Social Security mean?

Every employer is already paying for a retirement plan for its employees—Social Security. By integrating (combining) its private retirement plan with Social Security, the employer gets the benefit of its Social Security tax payments. The employer in effect makes its qualified retirement plan part of one overall scheme that combines both Social Security and the employer's private plan.

Technically, an integrated plan means a qualified retirement plan that is not considered discriminatory merely because the benefits provided under the plan favor highly compensated employees (see Q. 4:28), as long as the difference in benefits is attributable to what IRS refers to as permitted disparity, i.e., Social Security integration.

Permitted disparity, or integration, can mean a substantial saving for the employer because the cost of the employer's qualified retirement plan can be reduced. [IRC §§ 401(a)(5) and 401(l); Prop. Reg. §§ 1.401(l)-2 and 1.401(l)-3]

Q. 6:2 What types of qualified retirement plans can be integrated with Social Security?

Both defined contribution plans (see Q. 2:2) and defined benefit plans (see Q. 2:3) can be integrated with Social Security.

A defined contribution excess plan is a defined contribution plan under which the rate at which employer contributions (and forfeitures) are allocated to the accounts of participants with respect to compensation above a level specified in the plan (expressed as a percentage of such compensation) is greater than the rate at which employer contributions (and forfeitures) are allocated with respect to compensation at or below such specified level (expressed as a percentage of such compensation). [Prop. Reg. § 1.401(l)-1(b)(3)(i)]

A defined benefit excess plan is a defined benefit plan under which the rate of employer-derived benefits provided by the plan with respect to compensation above a level specified in the plan (expressed as a percentage of such compensation) is greater than the rate with respect to compensation at or below such specified level (expressed as a percentage of such compensation). [Prop. Reg. § 1.401(l)-1(b)(3)(ii)]

A defined benefit offset plan is a defined benefit plan that is not a defined benefit excess plan and that provides that each participant's employer-derived benefit is reduced by an amount specified (either directly or by formula) in the plan or by a specified percentage of the participant's final average compensation (see Q. 6:23). A plan is not a defined benefit offset plan for permitted disparity purposes merely because the participant's employer-derived benefit is reduced by benefits provided under another qualified retirement plan maintained by the employer or because the participant's employer-derived benefit under a plan that considers service with a prior employer for purposes of eligibility, vesting, and benefit accrual is reduced by benefits attributable to such service provided under a qualified retirement plan maintained by the prior employer. [Prop. Reg. § 1.401(l)-1(b)(4)]

For purposes of the integration rules, target benefit plans (see Q. 2:5) are generally treated like defined benefit plans. [Prop. Reg. § 1.401(l)-3(i)]

Q. 6:3   What general rules apply to a defined contribution excess plan?

A defined contribution excess plan (see Q. 6:2) will be considered to integrate properly with Social Security only if the excess contribution percentage (ECP; see Q. 6:4) does not exceed the base contribution percentage (BCP; see Q. 6:5) by more than the lesser of (1) the BCP or (2) the greater of 5.7 percentage points, or the percentage equal to the rate of tax attributable to the old age insurance portion of the Old-Age, Survivors, and Disability Insurance (OASDI) as of the beginning of the plan year. [IRC § 401(l)(2); *Notice 89-70*, 1989-1 CB 730]

For purposes of the integration rules, target benefit plans (see Q. 2:5) are generally treated like defined benefit plans. [Prop. Reg. § 1.401(l)-3(i)]

Q. 6:4   What is the excess contribution percentage?

The ECP is the percentage of compensation at which employer contributions (and forfeitures) are allocated to the accounts of participants with respect to compensation of participants *above* the integration level (see Q. 6:6) specified in the defined contribution plan (see Q. 2:2) for the plan year. [IRC § 401(l)(2)(B)(i)]

Q. 6:5   What is the base contribution percentage?

The BCP is the percentage of compensation at which employer contributions (and forfeitures) are allocated to the accounts of participants with respect to compensation of participants *at* or *below* the integration level (see Q. 6:6) specified in the defined contribution plan (see Q. 2:2) for the plan year. [IRC § 401(l)(2)(B)(ii)]

Q. 6:6 What is the integration level?

The integration level is the amount of compensation specified in the defined contribution plan (see Q. 2:2) or the defined benefit plan (see Q. 2:3) at or below which the rate of contributions or benefits provided under the plan is less than the rate with respect to compensation above such level. Any method or formula for determining the integration level in effect for a plan year must apply to all participants on a consistent basis for purposes of determining a participant's accrued benefit attributable to service during such year. The plan must specify the integration level in effect for the plan year for each participant, which in no event can exceed the taxable wage base (TWB) in effect as of the beginning of the plan year. The TWB is the maximum amount of earnings in any calendar year that may be considered wages for Social Security purposes. For 1990, this amount is $51,300.

For defined contribution excess plans (see Q. 6:2), the integration level of the plan cannot exceed the TWB in effect as of the beginning of the year (see Q. 6:8).

For defined benefit excess plans (see Q. 6:2), generally the integration level of the plan is covered compensation (see Q. 6:15 and Q. 6:22). [IRC § 401(l)(5)(A); Prop. Reg. § 1.401(l)-1(b)(5); Notice 89-70, 1989-1 CB 730]

Q. 6:7 How are the integration rules applied to contribution formulas under defined contribution excess plans?

The following examples illustrate whether or not a defined contribution excess plan properly integrates (see Q. 6:2 and Q. 6:3):

> **Example 1.** J.T. Corporation has a money purchase pension plan with a calendar year plan year. For the 1990 plan year, the plan provides that each participant will receive a contribution of 5 percent of compensation up to the TWB (see Q. 6:6) and 10 percent of compensation in excess of the TWB. The plan integrates properly because the ECP (see Q. 6:4), 10 percent, does not exceed the BCP (see Q. 6:5), 5 percent, by more than the lesser of 5 percentage points or 5.7 percentage points.

Example 2. Assume the same facts as above except that the plan provides that, with respect to compensation in excess of the TWB, each participant will receive a contribution for the plan year of 10.7 percent of such excess compensation. The plan does not integrate properly because the ECP, 10.7 percent, exceeds the BCP, 5 percent, by more than the lesser of 5 percentage points or 5.7 percentage points.

Q. 6:8 Can the integration level in a defined contribution excess plan be other than the taxable wage base?

The integration level (see Q. 6:6) of a defined contribution excess plan (see Q. 6:2) cannot exceed the TWB (see Q. 6:6) in effect at the beginning of the plan year. [Prop. Reg. § 1.401(l)-1(b)(5)]

However, there are two alternative approaches that may be used for determining integration levels below the TWB in a defined contribution excess plan:

1. An acceptable integration level is a uniform dollar amount for all participants no greater than the greater of $10,000 or 20 percent of the TWB in effect as of the beginning of the plan year.

2. Another acceptable integration level is any uniform dollar amount greater than the amount in (1) above that is less than the TWB in effect as of the beginning of the plan year provided the limitation of 5.7 percentage points is reduced and a proportionate reduction is made relating to the old age portion of the OASDI tax. If the integration level is more than the greater of $10,000 or 20 percent of the TWB but not more than 80 percent of the TWB, the 5.7 percentage points factor is reduced to 4.3 percentage points. If the integration level is more than 80 percent but less than 100 percent of the TWB, the 5.7 percentage points factor is reduced to 5.4 percentage points.

Example. For the 1990 plan year, a profit sharing plan uses an integration level of $30,000, which is less than 80 percent of the taxable wage base of $51,300 but more than $10,260 (the greater of $10,000 or 20% × $51,300). Consequently, the 5.7

percentage points factor must be replaced by 4.3 percentage points.

[*Notice 89-70*, 1989-1 CB 730]

Q. 6:9 What general rules apply to a defined benefit excess plan?

A defined benefit excess plan (see Q. 6:2) will be considered to integrate properly if the excess benefit percentage (EBP; see Q. 6:10) does not exceed the base benefit percentage (BBP; see Q. 6:11) by more than the maximum excess allowance (MEA; see Q. 6:12). Also, benefits must be based on average annual compensation (see Q. 6:21).

Furthermore, any optional form of benefit, preretirement benefit, actuarial factor, or other benefit or feature provided with respect to compensation above the integration level (see Q. 6:6) must also be provided with respect to compensation below the integration level. Thus, for example, if a lump-sum distribution option, calculated using particular actuarial assumptions, is available for benefits relating to compensation above the integration level, the same lump-sum option must be available on an equivalent basis for benefits based on compensation up to the integration level. [IRC § 401(l)(3); Prop. Reg. § 1.401(l)-3(b)]

For purposes of the integration rules, target benefit plans (see Q. 2:5) are generally treated like defined benefit plans. [Prop. Reg. § 1.401(l)-3(i)]

Q. 6:10 What is the excess benefit percentage?

The EBP is the percentage of compensation at which employer-derived benefits are accrued with respect to compensation of participants *above* the integration level (see Q. 6:6) specified in the defined benefit plan for the plan year. [IRC § 401(l)(3)(A)]

Q. 6:11   What is the base benefit percentage?

The BBP is the percentage of compensation at which the employer-derived benefits are accrued with respect to compensation of participants *at or below* the integration level (see Q. 6:6) specified in the defined benefit plan for the plan year. [IRC § 401(l)(3)(A)]

Q. 6:12   What is the maximum excess allowance?

The MEA with respect to benefits attributable to any year of service taken into account under the defined benefit plan equals the lesser of (1) the BBP (see Q. 6:11), or (2) .75 percentage point. With respect to total benefits under the plan, the MEA is the lesser of (1) the BBP, or (2) .75 percentage point multiplied by the participant's years of service (not in excess of 35) taken into account under the plan. In no event may the MEA exceed the BBP. [IRC § 401(l)(4)(A)]

Q. 6:13   How are the integration rules applied to benefit formulas under defined benefit excess plans?

The following examples illustrate whether or not a defined benefit excess plan properly integrates (see Q. 6:2 and Q. 6:9):

Example 1. M.P. Corporation maintains a defined benefit excess plan. The formula is .5 percent of the participant's average annual compensation (see Q. 6:21) up to covered compensation (see Q. 6:22) for the plan year plus 1.25 percent of the participant's average annual compensation for the plan year in excess of the participant's covered compensation for the plan year, multiplied by the participant's years of credited service with the company up to a maximum of 35 years. The plan formula provides a benefit that exceeds the MEA (see Q. 6:12) because the EBP (see Q. 6:10), 1.25 percent, for the plan year exceeds the BBP (see Q. 6:11), .5 percent, for the plan year by more than the BBP, .5 percentage point.

Example 2. If the BBP in Example 1 was .75 percent, the plan would integrate properly because the EBP (1.25%) would not exceed the BBP (.75%) by more than the MEA (.75 percentage point). [Prop. Reg. § 1.401(l)-3(b)(7)]

Q. 6:14 Can benefits commence prior to Social Security retirement age in a defined benefit excess plan?

Yes; but, if benefits commence prior to the Social Security retirement age (see Q. 5:9), the .75 percentage point factor (see Q. 6:12) is reduced depending on the age at which benefits commence and the participant's Social Security retirement age. [Prop. Reg. § 1.401(l)-3(e)]

Q. 6:15 Can alternative integration levels be used in a defined benefit excess plan?

Yes; however, the use of an integration level (see Q. 6:6) for any participant other than such participant's covered compensation (see Q. 6:22) may result in an adjustment to the .75 percentage point factor (see Q. 6:12). There is a safe harbor integration level for a plan year of a uniform dollar amount not exceeding the greater of $10,000 or one-half of the covered compensation of an individual attaining Social Security retirement age (see Q. 5:9) in the plan year that does not require an adjustment.

Another alternative that does not require an adjustment is use of a transitional definition of covered compensation for plan years 1989 through 1994, which was published by IRS and which is the average of the Social Security taxable wage bases during the 35-year period ending with the last day of the year preceding the year in which the participant attains (or will attain) Social Security retirement age.

Furthermore, a defined benefit plan may determine covered compensation without the required reduction by using a simplified table of covered compensation each year published by IRS. [IRC § 401(l)(5)(E); Prop. Reg. §§ 1.401(l)-1(b)(9), 1.401(l)-3(b)(4), and 1.401(l)-3(d)(1); Notice 89-70, 1989-1 CB 730]

Q. 6:16 What general rules apply to a defined benefit offset plan?

A defined benefit offset plan (see Q. 6:2) will be considered to integrate properly if the participant's accrued benefit is not reduced by reason of the offset by more than the maximum offset allowance (MOA; see Q. 6:17) and benefits are based on average annual compensation (see Q. 6:21). [IRC §§ 401(l)(3)(B) and 401(l)(4)(B)]

For purposes of the integration rules, target benefit plans (see Q. 2:5) are generally treated like defined benefit plans. [Prop. Reg. § 1.401(l)-3(i)]

Q. 6:17 What is the maximum offset allowance?

The MOA with respect to a participant for any year of service is the lesser of (1) 50 percent of the benefit that would have accrued without regard to the offset, or (2) .75 percent of the participant's final average compensation (see Q. 6:23). With respect to total benefits under the defined benefit offset plan, the MOA is the lesser of (1) 50 percent of the benefit which would have accrued without regard to the offset, or (2) .75 percent of the participant's final average compensation multiplied by the participant's years of service (not in excess of 35) taken into account under the plan. In no event may the MOA exceed 50 percent of the benefit that would have accrued without regard to the offset. [IRC § 401(l)(4)(B)]

Q. 6:18 How are the integration rules applied to benefit formulas under defined benefit offset plans?

The following examples illustrate whether or not a defined benefit offset plan properly integrates (see Q. 6:2 and Q. 6:16):

Example 1. Jill Corporation maintains a defined benefit offset plan. The formula provides that, for each year of credited service with the company up to a maximum of 35 years, a participant receives a normal retirement benefit equal to 2 percent of the participant's average annual compensation (see Q. 6:21), reduced by .75 percent of the participant's final average compensation up to covered compensation (see Q. 6:22 and Q. 6:23). Mindy retires at her Social Security retirement age (see Q. 5:9) with 40 years of service. At the time of her retirement, Mindy has average annual compensation of $16,000 and final average compensation (up to covered compensation) of $14,000. Under the plan benefit formula, Mindy is entitled to receive a normal retirement benefit of $7,525 [$11,200 (2% × 35 years × $16,000) minus $3,675 (.75% × 35 years × $14,000)]. The MOA (see Q. 6:17), as applied to Mindy, is not exceeded because the offset under the plan (1) does not exceed .75 percent of her final average compensation (up to covered compensation) for any year of credited service with the company, (2) does not exceed the cumulative MOA of 26.25 percent (.75% × 35 years) of her final average compensation (up to covered compensation), and (3) does not exceed 50 percent of the normal retirement benefit she would have been entitled to receive under the plan with respect to her average annual compensation not in excess of her final average compensation (up to covered compensation) if no offset had been applied.

Example 2. Assume the same facts as in Example 1, except that the plan provides no limit on the years of credited service with Jill Corporation taken into account in determining benefits under the plan. Mindy retires at her Social Security retirement age. Under the plan's benefit formula, she is entitled to receive a normal retirement benefit of $8,600 [$12,800 (2% × 40 years × $16,000) minus $4,200 (.75% × 40 years × $14,000)]. The plan benefit formula provides an offset that exceeds the MOA because the offset exceeds the cumulative MOA of 26.25 percent (.75% × 35 years) of Mindy's final average compensation (up to covered compensation). [Prop. Reg. § 1.401(l)-3(c)(6)]

Q. 6:19 Can benefits commence prior to Social Security retirement age in a defined benefit offset plan?

Yes; but, if benefits commence prior to Social Security retirement age (see Q. 5:9), the .75 percent factor (see Q. 6:17) is reduced depending on the age at which benefits commence and the participant's Social Security retirement age. [Prop. Reg. § 1.401(l)-3(e)]

Q. 6:20   Can alternative integration levels be used in a defined benefit offset plan?

The .75 percent factor (see Q. 6:17) is applicable if the offset for each participant is based on such participant's final average compensation up to covered compensation (see Q. 6:22 and Q. 6:23). The use of an integration level for any participant other than such participant's covered compensation *may* result in an adjustment to the .75 percent factor. Similar to defined benefit excess plans, certain safe harbors and alternatives to the use of a participant's covered compensation in determining the offset applicable to a participant are available (see Q. 6:15). [Prop. Reg. §§ 1.401(l)-3(c)(4) and 1.401(l)-3(d)(2); *Notice 89-70*, 1989-1 CB 730]

Q. 6:21   What is average annual compensation?

Average annual compensation means the participant's highest average annual compensation for (1) any period of at least three consecutive years, or (2) if shorter, the participant's full period of service. [IRC § 401(l)(5)(C); Prop. Reg. § 1.401(l)-1(b)(8)]

Q. 6:22   What does covered compensation mean?

Covered compensation means the average (without indexing) of the Social Security wage bases for the 35 calendar years ending with the year an individual attains Social Security retirement age (see Q. 5:9). A defined benefit plan can be integrated with Social Security on the basis of each individual employee's covered compensation. Covered compensation does not refer to the amount of compensation that the employee actually earned, but reflects the ceiling for Social Security wages over the years.

1990 COVERED COMPENSATION TABLE

Calendar Year of Birth	Year of Social Security Retirement Age	Exact Covered Compensation	Rounded Covered Compensation
1925	1990	$18,312	$18,600
1926	1991	19,668	19,800
1927	1992	21,012	21,000
1928	1993	22,356	22,200
1929	1994	23,688	23,400
1930	1995	25,008	25,200
1931	1996	26,340	26,400
1932	1997	27,672	27,600
1933	1998	28,992	28,800
1934	1999	30,324	30,600
1935	2000	31,656	31,800
1936	2001	32,928	33,000
1937	2002	34,212	35,400
1938	2004	36,696	36,600
1939	2005	37,932	37,800
1940	2006	39,180	39,000
1941	2007	40,392	40,200
1942	2008	41,544	41,400
1943	2009	42,636	42,600
1944	2010	43,692	43,800
1945	2011	44,724	45,000
1946	2012	45,720	45,600
1947	2013	46,680	46,800
1948	2014	47,496	47,400
1949	2015	48,216	48,000
1950	2016	48,840	48,600
1951	2017	49,380	49,200
1952	2018	49,824	49,800
1953	2019	50,208	50,400
1954	2020	50,544	50,400
1955	2022	51,024	51,000
1956	2023	51,204	51,000
1957 or later	2024 or later	51,300	51,600

IRS has provided alternative definitions of covered compensation. In lieu of using the definition of covered compensation specified above, defined benefit plans may use alternative definitions of covered compensation (see Q. 6:15 and Q. 6:20). [IRC § 401(l)(5)(E); Prop. Reg. § 1.401(l)-1(b)(9)]

Q. 6:23 What is final average compensation?

Final average compensation means the participant's average annual compensation (see Q. 6:21) for (1) the three consecutive year period ending with the current year, or (2) if shorter, the participant's full period of service, but does not include compensation for any year in excess of the taxable wage base (see Q. 6:6) in effect at the beginning of such year. [IRC § 401(l)(5)(D); Prop. Reg. § 1.401(l)-1(b)(7)]

Q. 6:24 What does compensation mean?

Compensation means compensation as defined under the plan, provided that such definition is reasonable and nondiscriminatory. A definition of compensation that is significantly less inclusive than the maximum amount of compensation that may be taken into account under the Code is not reasonable if such less inclusive definition results in the avoidance of the MEA (see Q. 6:12) or the MOA (see Q. 6:17). In addition, a definition of compensation is not reasonable if it provides that compensation is a uniform percentage of a basic definition of compensation. [IRC §§ 401(l)(5)(B) and 414(s); Prop. Reg. § 1.401(l)-1(b)(6)]

Q. 6:25 Can the termination of a defined benefit plan affect integration?

Yes. If an integrated defined benefit plan is terminated and the plan assets exceed the present value of the accrued benefits, the use of the excess funds to increase benefits under the plan must not violate the integration rules. [*Rev. Rul. 80-229*, 1980-2 CB 133]

Q. 6:26 What special restrictions on integration apply to top-heavy plans?

A top-heavy defined benefit plan (see Q. 20:1) must provide each participant who is a non-key employee with a minimum annual retirement benefit, and a top-heavy defined contribution plan (see Q. 20:3) must provide each participant who is a non-key employee with a minimum annual contribution. A top-heavy plan cannot take into account Social Security benefits or contributions to satisfy these minimum requirements (see Q. 20:37, Q. 20:43, and Q. 20:47). [IRC § 416(e); Reg. § 1.416-1, Question M-11]

Chapter 7

Funding Requirements

To ensure that sufficient money will be available to pay promised retirement benefits to employees when they retire, certain qualified retirement plans are subject to minimum funding requirements. This chapter examines the funding requirements—which qualified retirement plans must meet them, how they work, and how they are enforced.

Q. 7:1 What are the minimum funding standards?

To ensure that sufficient money will be available to pay promised retirement benefits to employees when they retire, minimum funding standards have been established for defined benefit plans (see Q. 2:3), money purchase pension plans (see Q. 2:4), and target benefit plans (see Q. 2:5). [ERISA §§ 301 and 302; IRC § 412; Prop. Reg. § 1.412(a)-1]

For defined benefit plans, employers are required each year to fund the retirement benefits earned that year by the employees (the normal cost). In addition, formulas are established for amortizing over stated periods the cost of retirement benefits for employees' services in the past for which funds have not yet been set aside (past service liabilities), the cost of retroactively raising the level of benefits by plan amendments, and for making up experience losses and increases in liabilities attributable to changes in actuarial assumptions.

For a money purchase pension plan, the amount required to be contributed each year is based on the plan's contribution formula. For example, if the employer has a money purchase pension plan with a 10%-of-compensation formula and the participants' aggregate compensation for the year totals $80,000, the employer's required contribution is $8,000.

In a target benefit plan, the required contribution is based on the participant's compensation, age, and an assumed interest rate that is specified in the plan document.

Certain qualified retirement plans are not subject to minimum funding standards (see Q. 7:3).

Q. 7:2 Are there funding requirements in addition to the minimum funding standards?

Yes. There is an additional funding requirement that generally applies to defined benefit plans (other than multiemployer plans or defined benefit plans having 100 or fewer participants) with assets less than their current liability for the plan year. For this purpose, current liability means all liabilities to participants and their beneficiaries under the plan. [ERISA § 302(d); IRC § 412(l)]

Q. 7:3 Which qualified retirement plans are not subject to the minimum funding standards?

The minimum funding standards do not apply to profit sharing, stock bonus, 401(k), or employee stock ownership plans (see Chapter 2). Pension plans funded exclusively by the purchase of certain insurance contracts (insurance contract plans; see Q. 7:4) are also exempt from the funding standards. [IRC §§ 412(h) and 412(i)]

Other retirement plans that are not subject to the minimum funding standards include:

1. Plans that do not provide for employer contributions after September 2, 1974 (such as plans to which only employees contribute);

2. Unfunded, nonqualified plans that are maintained by the employer primarily to provide deferred compensation for selected management or highly compensated employees; and

3. Supplemental plans that provide benefits in excess of the lim-

its on contributions and benefits under the Code. [ERISA § 301(a)]

Q. 7:4   What is an insurance contract plan?

An insurance contract plan is a pension plan that is funded exclusively by individual insurance contracts and meets the following requirements:

• The insurance contracts provide for level annual premiums from the time the employee commences plan participation until retirement age.

• Benefits under the plan are equal to the benefits provided under the contracts.

• Benefits are guaranteed by an insurance company licensed to do business in the state in which the plan is located.

• Premiums must be paid timely or the contracts must have been reinstated.

• No rights under the contracts were subject to a security interest during the plan year.

• No policy loans were outstanding during the plan year.

A pension plan that is funded exclusively by group insurance contracts having the same characteristics as those listed above is also considered to be an insurance contract plan. [ERISA § 301(b); IRC § 412(i); Reg. § 1.412(i)-(1)]

Q. 7:5   Can a pension plan be converted to an insurance contract plan?

Yes. Although the conversion of an existing pension plan to a plan that is funded exclusively by insurance contracts might cause the premium payments to begin after an employee commences participation in the plan (see Q. 7:4), the converted plan may be considered to be an insurance contract plan for future years. [*Rev. Rul. 81-196*, 1981-2 CB 107]

Q. 7:6 Can the employer contribute more than the amount needed to meet the minimum funding standards?

Yes. However, the additional amount contributed might not increase the employer's current tax deduction. (See Q. 10:15 and 10:16.)

If the additional amount is not deductible, the additional contribution will, however, increase the tax-free accumulation of earnings in the pension plan, which will eventually reduce the cost of funding the plan. However, a tax is imposed on the employer equal to 10 percent of the nondeductible contributions to the plan (see Q. 10:9). [IRC §§ 412(c)(6), 412(c)(7), and 4972]

Q. 7:7 Must actuarial assumptions used in determining plan costs be reasonable?

Yes. In the case of a defined benefit plan, all plan costs, liabilities, interest rates, and other factors must be determined on the basis of actuarial assumptions and methods (1) each of which is reasonable (taking into account the experience of the plan and reasonable expectations), or that, when taken together, produce a total contribution that is the same as if each assumption and method were reasonable; and (2) which, in combination, offer the actuary's best estimate of anticipated experience under the plan. [ERISA § 302(c)(3); IRC § 412(c)(3)]

The actuarial assumptions used to determine the cost of funding a defined benefit plan need not be set forth in the plan (see Q. 2:15). However, even if the actuarial assumptions and methods are set forth in the plan, that does not mean they will always be reasonable or acceptable. [Rev. Rul. 78-48, 1978-1 CB 115]

In one case, the court agreed with IRS that use of a 5 percent interest rate was not reasonable and that an 8 percent interest rate was appropriate at a time when safe investments were yielding approximately 12 percent or more. The court agreed with IRS that "the reasonableness of an actuary's assumption must be evaluated in light of the plan's experience and reasonable expectations." [Jerome Mirza & Assoc., Ltd. v. U.S., 882 F2d 229 (7th Cir. 1989); see also Letter Ruling 9031001]

In another case, IRS recalculated a corporation's tax deduction by rejecting the actuarial assumptions contained in the corporation's defined benefit plan. IRS concluded that the actuarial assumptions contained in the plan did not reflect current plan experience. IRS determined that a more appropriate interest rate was 8 percent (instead of the plan's assumed 5½% rate), and that the normal retirement age for this one-participant plan should have been age 65, rather than age 55 as provided for in the plan. As a result of these modifications by IRS, no deduction for the taxable year involved was allowable. [*Letter Ruling 8552001*]

According to a letter issued by an IRS Assistant Commissioner (Employee Plans and Exempt Organizations) on May 25, 1990, IRS has expanded its defined benefit plan actuarial examination program. IRS is questioning the funding of defined benefit plans where the annual contribution per participant indicates that the actuaries may have exceeded the contribution limits for any of the following reasons:

1. Using an inappropriate funding method;
2. Exceeding the maximum benefit limitation under Section 415;
3. Using an unreasonably low interest rate not supported by the facts and circumstances of the plan; or
4. Employing an unreasonably low retirement age not supported by the facts and circumstances of the plan.

Q. 7:8 Is there any penalty for overstatement of pension liabilities?

Yes. Effective for returns due after December 31, 1989 (determined without regard to extensions), a 20 percent penalty tax is imposed on the underpayment of tax created by a substantial overstatement of pension liabilities. The penalty tax is imposed if the actuarial determination of pension liabilities is between 200 percent and 399 percent of the amount determined to be correct; but, if the actuarial determination is 400 percent or more of the correct amount, the penalty tax is increased to 40 percent. No penalty will be imposed if the underpayment attributable to the substantial overstatement is $1,000 or less. [IRC §§ 6662(a), 6662(f), and 6662(h)]

For pension liabilities that are overstated after October 22, 1986, but before the above penalty tax became effective, and that result in an underpayment of tax, a percentage of the underpayment is added to the tax as follows:

If the claimed pension liability is the following % of the correct valuation	The applicable percentage is:
150% or more, but not more than 200% 10	
More than 200%, but not more than 250% 20	
More than 250% 30	

[IRC § 6659A prior to repeal]

Q. 7:9 Can a pension plan's normal retirement age affect the minimum funding standards?

Yes. Each actuarial assumption used to determine pension plan costs should be reasonable and must offer the actuary's best estimate of anticipated experience under the plan. [ERISA § 302(c)(3); IRC § 412(c)(3)] Therefore, an assumption that employees will retire at the normal retirement age specified in the plan, ignoring the fact that employees normally retire at earlier or later ages, would not be reasonable (see Q. 7:7).

Q. 7:10 How are past service costs funded?

If a defined benefit plan was adopted after January 1, 1974, costs relating to an employee's service before the adoption of the plan must be amortized over not more than 30 years from the date the plan was adopted. Increases or decreases in past service costs resulting from an amendment to the plan must be amortized over not more than 30 years from the time the amendment takes effect.

For plans in existence on January 1, 1974, past service liabilities on the first day of the plan year beginning after December 31, 1975, may be amortized over not more than 40 years. Increases or decreases in past service liabilities arising thereafter must be amortized over not more than 30 years. [IRC § 412(b)(2)]

There is an additional funding requirement for many plans (see Q. 7:2) that generally requires the amortization of unfunded old liability over 18 plan years. Unfunded old liability is generally the unfunded current liability of the plan as of the beginning of the first plan year beginning after December 31, 1987. [IRC § 412(l)(3)]

Q. 7:11 Do the pension plan's investment earnings affect the funding requirement?

Yes. Experience gains and losses—that is, when the defined benefit plan's actual investment growth and earnings are either higher or lower than was actuarially estimated—must be amortized over a period of not more than five years from the time the gain or loss is determined. For experience gains and losses occurring in plan years beginning before 1988, the period for amortizing experience gains and losses was 15 years. The 15-year amortization period is retained for multiemployer plans (see Q. 23:2). [IRC §§ 412(b)(2)(B)(iv) and 412(b)(3)(B)(ii)]

An experience gain reduces the amount of funding required, and an experience loss increases the amount of funding required. Increases or decreases in costs resulting from a change in the Social Security law or from changes in the amount of wages taken into account under an integrated pension plan (see Q. 6:1) are treated as experience gains or losses. [IRC § 412(c)(4)]

Q. 7:12 How are assets valued in a defined benefit plan?

For funding purposes, assets in a defined benefit plan are valued on the basis of any reasonable actuarial method of valuation that takes into account fair market value. To be considered a reasonable actuarial method of valuation, the method must result in an actuarial value between 80 percent and 120 percent of the current fair market value. Special rules apply to the valuation of bonds or other evidences of indebtedness. [IRC § 412(c)(2); Reg. § 1.412(c)(2)-1]

For purposes of the minimum funding standards, a defined benefit plan's assets must be valued every year (every three years prior to 1989). To ease difficulties brought about by this change, IRS has granted automatic approval to change the valuation date for defined benefit plans to the last day of the plan year beginning in 1989. For the immediately following plan year, the valuation date should be changed back to the first day of the plan year. [IRC §§ 412(c)(5) and 412(c)(9); *Announcement 90-90*, 1990-31 IRB]

Q. 7:13 What is the funding standard account?

Each pension plan subject to the minimum funding standards (see Q. 7:1) must maintain a funding standard account—a device used to ease the administration of the funding rules. Each year, the funding standard account is charged with amounts that must be paid to satisfy the minimum funding standards and is credited with the plan contributions made, any decrease in plan liabilities, and experience gains. If the pension plan meets the minimum funding standards (the charges equal the credits) at the end of any plan year, the funding standard account will show a zero balance. If the employer has contributed more than the minimum amount required for any year (the credits exceed the charges), the account will show a positive balance and the employer is credited with interest on the excess. If the employer contributed less than the minimum amount required for any year (the charges exceed the credits), the account will show an accumulated funding deficiency. An excise tax is imposed on that deficiency (see Q. 7:16). [IRC § 412(b)]

The following examples illustrate how the funding standard account works.

> **Example 1.** In 1989, MuMu Corporation established a defined benefit plan that is subject to the minimum funding requirements. For the plan's first year, the normal cost (the cost of benefits earned during the year) is $80,000. Past service costs (the cost of benefits for employees' services before the plan was adopted) are $1,000,000. The actuarially assumed rate of interest is 6 percent. MuMu contributed $148,537 to the plan. The funding standard account is charged with $80,000 of normal cost and $68,537, which represents amortization of the past service costs of $1,000,000 at 6 percent over 30 years.

Since the total charges ($148,537) equal the contribution, the funding standard account has a zero balance.

Example 2. In 1990, MuMu amends its defined benefit plan to increase benefits, so that past service costs rise by $100,000. The plan's normal cost is now $85,000. In addition, the plan had an experience gain (the plan's actual investment growth was higher than that actuarially estimated) of $5,000. MuMu contributed $170,000 to the plan in 1990. The funding standard account for 1990 is credited with the $170,000 contribution plus $1,120 (representing amortization of the $5,000 experience gain at 6% over five years), for a total credit of $171,120. The funding standard account is charged with $85,000 normal cost and $68,537 for amortizing past service costs over 30 years plus $6,854 for amortizing past service costs resulting from the plan amendment over 30 years, for a total charge of $160,391. Since the account's credits exceed the charges by $10,729 ($171,120 − $160,391), the funding standard account has a positive balance of $10,729. Add to this $644, representing interest on the $10,729 at 6 percent, and the account has a balance of $11,373 to be credited to future years.

Q. 7:14 What is the full funding limitation?

The term full funding limitation means the excess, if any, of the lesser of (1) 150 percent of current liability, or (2) the accrued liability (including normal cost) under the defined benefit plan, over the value of plan assets. If plan assets equal or exceed plan liabilities, the plan is fully funded and no contribution is required. Furthermore, because of the full funding limitation, there may be no contribution or a decreased contribution even if the accrued liability under the plan exceeds plan assets. In any case, no deduction is allowed for a contribution made when the plan is fully funded. In future years, if plan liabilities (for full funding limitation purposes) increase and exceed the value of plan assets, the employer will have to make contributions to satisfy the minimum funding requirements. [IRC §§ 404(a)(1)(A), 412(c)(6), and 412(c)(7)]

Q. 7:15   Must separate funding standard accounts be maintained for each pension plan established by a controlled group of companies?

Yes. Even though identical, but separate, pension plans are established by members of a controlled group of companies (see Q. 4:34), separate funding standard accounts (see Q. 7:13) must be maintained for each plan. [ERISA § 302(b)(1); IRC § 412(b)(1); Rev. Rul. 81-137, 1981-1 CB 232]

Q. 7:16   What happens if the company fails to make the required contribution to its pension plan?

There is an excise tax for failure to comply with the minimum funding standard (see Q. 7:1) equal to 10 percent (5% for multiemployer plans; see Q. 23:2) of the amount of the accumulated funding deficiency. If the accumulated funding deficiency is not corrected, an excise tax equal to 100 percent of such uncorrected amount is imposed. Accumulated funding deficiency means the excess of the total charges to the funding standard account for all plan years over the total credits to such account for such years. [IRC §§ 412(a), 4971(a), 4971(b), and 4971(c)]

The failure to meet minimum funding standards triggers a reportable event notice requirement to PBGC if the present value of unfunded vested benefits under the pension plan equals or exceeds $250,000 (see Q. 19:16). [ERISA § 4043; PBGC Reg. § 2615.16]

In addition, if a quarterly payment (see Q. 7:26) or any other payment required by the minimum funding standards is not made, PBGC must be notified within ten days of the due date of the payment if the unpaid balance exceeds $1 million. Furthermore, a lien is created in favor of the plan upon all property of the employer if the delinquency exceeds $1 million. [ERISA § 302(f); IRC § 412(n)]

Q. 7:17   Who is liable for failure to make contributions?

Liability for contributions to a pension plan (other than a multiemployer plan; see Q. 23:2) is joint and several among the employer-sponsor and the members of the controlled group of which the employer is a member. Also, all members of the controlled group are subject to the lien (see Q. 7:16) in favor of a pension plan maintained by any member if the contributions are late. [IRC §§ 412(c)(11) and 412(n)]

Furthermore, if an employer fails to make a required payment to meet minimum funding requirements or a required quarterly payment (see Q. 7:25 and Q. 7:26) within 60 days after it is due, the employer must notify each participant and beneficiary of such failure. This notice requirement does not apply to multiemployer plans; nor does it apply if the employer has a funding waiver request pending with IRS. This notice requirement is in addition to the requirement that participants be notified of the filing of an application for a funding waiver (see Q. 7:20). [ERISA § 101(d)]

Q. 7:18 May IRS waive the minimum funding standards for a particular company?

Yes. IRS may grant a waiver of the minimum funding standards for any year in which the employer is unable to make the necessary contributions without "temporary substantial business hardship" ("substantial business hardship" for multiemployer plans; see Q. 23:2) and if meeting the funding requirement would harm the interests of the plan's participants. [IRC § 412(d)(1)]

IRS examines several factors in deciding whether to waive the funding standards:

1. Is the employer operating at a loss?
2. Is there substantial unemployment or underemployment in the industry?
3. Are sales and profits of the industry depressed or declining?
4. Will the pension plan be continued only if the waiver is granted?

These factors are not all-inclusive. Furthermore, IRS has to be convinced that the employer's business hardship is temporary. IRS has granted a conditional waiver of the minimum funding standards to a company that has experienced net losses, but whose financial situation was improving. [*Letter Ruling 9031040*] However, IRS has denied requests for waivers of the minimum funding standards to companies whose prospects of recovery were tenuous. [*Letter Rulings 9033039* and *9033040*]

Legislative history indicates that a waiver should not be granted to an employer if it appears that the employer will not recover sufficiently to make its waived contributions. Chances for a waiver are improved if the plan's assets are greater than the benefits to which the participants are entitled. [IRC § 412(d)(2)]

As a practical matter IRS, in its efforts to avert plan terminations, generally approves a hardship waiver request if it can find reasonable grounds for doing so. In one case, IRS required the owner, as a condition for granting the waiver, to reduce his accrued benefit until plan assets became sufficient to meet plan liabilities. [*Letter Ruling 7945047*] In another case, IRS granted a conditional waiver of the minimum funding standards subject to the adoption of an amendment ceasing the accrual of benefits for participants who were also shareholders. [*Letter Ruling 8847079*]

There are other rules with respect to funding waivers:

- The number of waivers allowed within a 15-year period is three (five for multiemployer plans).
- If the employer applying for a funding waiver is a member of a controlled group, not only must the employer-applicant meet the standards, but the standards must be met as if all members of the controlled group are treated as a single employer.
- The amortization period of a waived funding deficiency is five years (15 years for multiemployer plans).
- The interest rate used for computing the amortization charge is the greater of (1) 150 percent of the federal mid-term rate or (2) the plan interest rate.
- IRS is authorized to require security when outstanding waived amounts are $1 million or more.

[ERISA § 303(a); IRC §§ 412(b), 412(d), and 412(f)]

Q. 7:19   What is the procedure for obtaining a waiver of the minimum funding standards?

The request for a waiver of the minimum funding standards is made to the IRS National Office and not to the local IRS Key District Office.

The employer must furnish evidence that (1) the minimum funding standards cannot be satisfied without temporary substantial business hardship, and (2) meeting the funding standards would adversely affect the interests of the plan's participants in the aggregate. The request should include the following items:

- A statement concerning the employer's business, its history and ownership, any recent or contemplated changes that might affect its financial condition, and whether the employer is to be aggregated with any other entity (see Q. 4:34).

- The current and preceding two years' financial statements (the balance sheets and profit and loss statements). Uncertified statements are acceptable if certified statements have not been prepared. If the employer files financial reports with the Securities and Exchange Commission, the most recent ones should be submitted. If neither the statements nor reports are available, copies of federal income tax returns may be submitted.

- A comprehensive discussion of the nature and extent of the business hardship, and statements that (1) discuss the prospects of recovery and why recovery is likely, (2) describe actions taken or planned to effect recovery, and (3) explain when and to what extent it is anticipated that required contributions can reasonably be expected to resume.

- Facts concerning the plan and its coverage of employees (e.g., the name of the plan, the date it was adopted).

- Copies of the current plan document and summary plan description.

- A description of any plan amendments that affected plan costs.

- Actuarial reports for the preceding two plan years.

- A statement of how the plan is funded (e.g., trust funds, insurance policies).
- The contribution history for the current plan year and prior two plan years.
- The plan year for which the waiver is requested and the approximate contribution required to meet the minimum funding standards.
- Copy of the most recent annual report, with appropriate schedules attached.
- A statement as to whether the plan is subject to PBGC jurisdiction (see Q. 19:12).
- A statement as to whether any other matters are currently or about to be pending before any court, IRS, DOL, or PBGC.
- Information concerning the granting of any prior waivers.
- Information concerning any other plans maintained by the employer.

[Rev. Proc. 83-41, 1983-1 CB 775; Rev. Proc. 88-29, 1988-1 CB 828]

In addition to the above, a defined contribution plan subject to the minimum funding standards must adopt an amendment to the plan specifying how the waived contribution will be made up and allocated to the plan participants. [Rev. Rul. 78-223, 1978-1 CB 125]

If, in addition to the waiver request, the employer wants to receive a determination letter with respect to the amendment, it should submit the waiver request as part of the determination letter request to the IRS Key District Office and include all of the above information. For more details, see Chapter 13.

The application for a waiver generally should be submitted no earlier than 180 days prior to the beginning of the plan year for which the waiver is being requested, because the evidence required to support the request may not be available. Furthermore, requests must be submitted no later than the fifteenth day of the third month following the close of the plan year for which the waiver is required. This deadline may be extended upon a showing of good cause for the late filing. [IRC § 412(d)(4); Rev. Proc. 83-41, 1983-1 CB 775; Rev. Proc. 88-29, 1988-1 CB 828]

Requests for a waiver only should be addressed to:
Commissioner of Internal Revenue
Attention: OP:E:A
1111 Constitution Avenue, N.W.
Washington, D.C. 20224

Q. 7:20 Are there any notice requirements when a funding waiver request is filed?

Yes. The applicant must give advance notice of the waiver application to (1) each participant in the plan, (2) each beneficiary under the plan, (3) each alternate payee (see Q. 28:3), and (4) each employee organization representing participants in the plan. The notice must include a description of the extent to which the plan is funded for benefits that are guaranteed by PBGC and the extent to which the plan is funded for benefit liabilities. [ERISA § 303(e)(1); IRC § 412(f)(4)(A); Rev. Proc. 88-29, 1988-1 CB 828]

Q. 7:21 Is any additional information required to be filed along with the funding waiver request?

Yes. The employer must provide a list of all prior plan years for which IRS has granted it a waiver. This list must include the amount waived for each plan year, the outstanding balance of the amortization base established by the waiver, and any conditions regarding the waiver.

The employer must also provide a copy of the letter that was sent to each union representing plan participants and indicate whether it mailed or hand delivered the letter to the union, to enable IRS to verify this notice requirement. [Rev. Proc. 88-29, 1988-1 CB 828; Rev. Proc. 88-5, 1988-1 CB 587]

Q. 7:22 May a pension plan be amended if a waiver of the funding standards is in effect for a particular year?

Yes, but the funding waiver automatically ends if one of the following types of plan amendments is adopted:

- An amendment increasing plan benefits;
- An amendment changing the accrual of benefits if the change would increase the plan's liabilities; or
- An amendment changing the rate at which benefits become nonforfeitable if the change would increase the plan's liabilities.

These amendments will not cause a funding waiver to cease if (1) DOL decides that the amendment is reasonable and has only a small impact on plan liabilities, (2) the amendment merely repeals a retroactive plan amendment reducing benefits, or (3) the amendment must be made for the plan to remain qualified for tax-favored status. [IRC §§ 412(f)(1) and 412(f)(2)]

Q. 7:23   What alternative is available if IRS will not waive the minimum funding standards?

To keep the pension plan in compliance with the minimum funding standards, owners of the company may have to waive their benefits irrevocably. In small pension plans, the costs attributable to the owners' benefits are usually a large portion of the required contribution. Thus, if the owners are permitted to waive their contributions or benefits, the amount that has to be contributed to the pension plan to meet the minimum funding standards may be reduced substantially.

Q. 7:24   May an employer obtain an extension of an amortization period to help it meet the minimum funding standards?

Yes. An extension may be granted by IRS if the employer shows the extension would provide adequate protection for participants and their beneficiaries and denial of the extension would (1) risk the continuation of the pension plan or might cause a curtailment of retirement benefits or employee compensation, and (2) be adverse to the interests of the participants. (Extending an amortization period reduces each year's pension outlay by spreading out the cost of funding benefits over a greater number of years.) [IRC § 412(e)(1); Rev. Rul. 79-408, 1979-2 CB 191; Rev. Proc. 79-61, 1979-2 CB 575]

In addition to the information required when a waiver is sought (see Q. 7:19), an application for an extension must include the following information:

- The unfunded liability (past service costs, for example) for which the extension is sought;
- The reasons an extension is being sought;
- The length of the desired extension (up to a maximum of 10 years); and
- A numerical illustration showing how annual plan costs will be affected.

Q. 7:25   May a contribution be timely for the minimum funding standards but not for tax deduction purposes?

Yes. Contributions made after the close of a plan year may relate back to that year if they are made within 8½ months (2½ months for multiemployer plans; see Q. 23:2) after the close of the plan year. This special deadline does not extend the time limit for making a contribution for tax deduction purposes, that is, payment by the due date, including extensions, for filing the employer's federal income tax return (see Q. 10:3). [ERISA § 302(c)(10)(A); IRC § 412(c)(10); Reg. § 1.412(c)-12]

This special deadline applies only for purposes of minimum funding and the excise tax (see Q. 7:16) imposed for failure to meet the funding requirements. Employer contributions to its plan after the due date for filing its federal income tax return (including extensions) but within 8½ months after the close of the plan year are not deductible as contributions for the closed year. Although the minimum funding standards may be met, the tax deduction requirements are not. [*Letter Ruling 7949018*]

Q. 7:26   Must quarterly contributions be made to a defined benefit plan?

Yes. Quarterly contribution payments are required to be made to a defined benefit plan (other than a multiemployer plan; see

Q. 23:2). The quarterly payments are due 15 days after the end of each quarter of the plan year. The percentage of each required quarterly payment is being phased-in until 1992, when the required quarterly payment will be equal to 25 percent of the required annual payment. In 1990, the applicable percentage of each quarterly payment is 12.5 percent; and, in 1991, it will be 18.75 percent. The required annual payment is the lesser of (1) 90 percent of the amount required to be contributed to the plan for the plan year in order to meet minimum funding, or (2) 100 percent of the amount so required for the preceding plan year. Quarterly contributions are not required for the first plan year. [ERISA § 302(e); IRC § 412(m); Notice 89-52, 1989-1 CB 692]

An underpayment of a required quarterly payment requires that the funding standard account (see Q. 7:13) be charged with interest at a rate equal to the greater of (1) 175 percent of the federal mid-term rate, or (2) the rate of interest used to determine costs by the plan. However, the interest is offset by the assumed interest rate under the plan. [IRC § 412(m); Notice 89-52, 1989-1 CB 692]

Q. 7:27 Does the minimum funding requirement cease once a pension plan terminates?

Generally, the minimum funding standards apply to a pension plan until the end of the plan year in which the plan terminates and do not apply to the plan in later years. Therefore, the funding standard account (see Q. 7:13) must be maintained through the end of the plan year in which the pension plan terminates, even if the termination occurs before the last day of the plan year.

For details on plan terminations, see Chapter 19.

Chapter 8

Vesting

One of the major features of a qualified retirement plan is the requirement that it provide for the vesting of benefits according to one of several schedules set by law. Thus, at a certain point, a nonforfeitable interest in benefits under the plan is acquired by an employee. This chapter examines what vesting means, the minimum requirements set by law, and how vesting works.

Q. 8:1 What does vesting mean?

Vesting represents the nonforfeitable interest of participants in their (1) account balances under a defined contribution plan (see Q. 2:2) or (2) accrued benefits under a defined benefit plan (see Q. 2:3).

> **Example.** Assume a participant is 40 percent vested (that is, he or she has a nonforfeitable right to 40% of the benefit accrued in the plan). In a defined contribution plan, the participant's vested accrued benefit is equal to 40 percent of the balance in the account. In a defined benefit plan, the participant has a nonforfeitable right to 40 percent of the normal retirement benefit that has been accrued. Thus, if the accrued normal retirement benefit is $150 a month, the participant has a nonforfeitable right to $60 a month.

Vesting is directly related to an employee's length of service with the employer (or group of employers). (See Q. 8:3.)

Special vesting rules apply to top-heavy plans (see Q. 20:32).

Q. 8:2 What is an accrued benefit?

A participant's accrued benefit is the benefit that has accumulated up to a particular point in employment. Earning accrued benefits does not mean that a participant has a nonforfeitable (that is, vested) right to those benefits. The nonforfeitability of an accrued benefit is determined by the retirement plan's vesting schedule.

Defined contribution plans (see Q. 2:2) must provide separate accounts with respect to each participant's accrued benefit. This means that a participant's accrued benefit is the balance of the participant's individual account. [IRC § 411(a)(7)(A)(ii)]

Defined benefit plans (other than those funded solely through insurance contracts) are required to include a procedure for determining a participant's accrued benefit that satisfies one of three alternative benefit accrual formulas. Generally, accrued benefits are determined with reference to the benefits that are payable at normal retirement age (see Q. 9:66) and that accrue over the period of the employee's participation in the plan. The alternative formulas limit the amount of back loading (providing a higher rate for accrual of benefits for later years of service than for earlier years); however, they do not require the same rate of benefit accrual each year. Front loading (providing a higher rate for accrual of benefits for earlier years of service than for later years) is permitted, although such front loading also may be limited. [IRC § 411(b)(1); Prop. Reg. § 1.411(b)-2(b)(3); *Rev. Rul. 85-131*, 1985-2 CB 138; *Notice 87-21*, 1987-1 CB 458 (Q&A 16); *Notice 89-45*, 1989-1 CB 684; *Jerome Mirza & Assocs., Ltd. v. U.S.*, 882 F2d 229 (7th Cir. 1989)]

Q. 8:3 Are minimum vesting standards set by law?

Yes. Two minimum vesting schedules apply to a participant's accrued benefit (see Q. 8:2) derived from employer contributions. [IRC § 411(a)(2); Reg. §§ 1.411(a)-3T(b), 1.411(a)-3T(c), and 1.411(a)-3T(e)] These schedules, either one of which may be used, are as follows:

Five-Year Vesting

Years of service	Nonforfeitable percentage
Less than 5	0
5 or more	100

Seven-Year Graded Vesting

Years of service	Nonforfeitable percentage
Less than 3	0
3	20
4	40
5	60
6	80
7 or more	100

Example 1. Stanley Corporation's retirement plan provides for plan participation after the completion of one year of service and provides for 100 percent vesting after five years of plan participation rather than service. The plan does not satisfy the minimum vesting standards because, under the plan, an employee becomes 100 percent vested only after completion of *more than* five years of service. Vesting based upon years of participation is permitted as long as the minimum vesting standards are satisfied. [*Ferrara v. Allentown Physician Anesthesia Assocs., Inc.,* 711 F. Supp. 206 (DC ED Pa. 1989)]

Example 2. Marjorie Corporation's retirement plan contains the following vesting schedule:

Years of service	Nonforfeitable percentage
1 or less	0
2	10
3	25
4	45
5	65
6	75
7 or more	100

The plan does not satisfy the minimum vesting standards because the nonforfeitable percentage after six years of service (75%) is less than the percentage required at that time (80%). The fact that the nonforfeitable percentage for years prior to the sixth year of service is greater than the percentage required is immaterial.

These new minimum vesting standards apply to plan participants who perform an hour of service in any plan year beginning after 1988.

Q. 8:4 Do the minimum vesting standards apply to multiemployer plans?

A multiemployer plan (see Chapter 23) may use a 10-year cliff vesting schedule (that is, an employee with at least ten years of service is 100% vested), but only for participants covered under the plan pursuant to a collective bargaining agreement.

Employees are not covered under a collective bargaining agreement unless they are represented by a bona fide employee representative who is a party to the agreement. Consequently, an employee of the multiemployer plan or an employee of the union is not covered pursuant to the collective bargaining agreement even though the employee is covered under the plan pursuant to an agreement with the plan or with the union on behalf of the employee.

Plan participants not covered pursuant to a collective bargaining agreement must have a nonforfeitable right to accrued benefits derived from employer contributions under either the five-year cliff or the seven-year graded vesting schedule (see Q. 8:3).

For employees covered by a multiemployer plan pursuant to a collective bargaining agreement ratified before March 1, 1986, the effective date of the new minimum vesting standards is the plan year beginning after the earlier of: (1) January 1, 1991, or (2) the later of (a) January 1, 1989, or (b) the date the last such collective bargaining agreement terminates.

Example. A calendar-year multiemployer plan is maintained pursuant to a three-year collective bargaining agreement, which expired on February 28, 1989. The plan must be in compliance with the new vesting rules for its plan year commencing on January 1, 1990, the first plan year beginning after February 28, 1989. However, the new vesting rules apply to plan participants who are employees of the plan or of the union as of the plan year beginning after December 31, 1988, if they have an hour of service after that date.

[IRC §§ 411(a)(2)(C) and 414(f)(1)(B); Reg. § 1.411(a)-3T(d) and 1.411(a)-3T(e)]

Q. 8:5 Does the adoption of one of the minimum vesting schedules guarantee the retirement plan's qualification?

Unless there has been a pattern of abuse or actual misuse in the operation of a retirement plan, the use of one of the two minimum vesting schedules (see Q. 8:3) will satisfy the plan's qualification requirements. The intentional dismissal of employees to prevent vesting may indicate a pattern of abuse. See Chapter 20 for details relating to vesting under a top-heavy plan. [IRC § 411(d)(1); Prop. Reg. § 1.411(d)-1(b); Rev. Proc. 89-29, 1989-1 CB 893]

Q. 8:6 May a qualified retirement plan's vesting schedule be changed?

Yes. Like other provisions in a qualified retirement plan, the vesting schedule may be amended by the employer, even after IRS has approved the plan as adopted initially.

If the vesting schedule is amended, however, each participant in the qualified retirement plan on the date the amendment is adopted or becomes effective (whichever is later) who has completed at least three years of service may elect, during the election period (see Q. 8:7), to stay under the old vesting schedule. A participant's failure to make that election means that the participant is subject to the new schedule—provided that the participant was notified of the right to elect. An amendment of the vesting schedule may not cause any participant to forfeit (directly or indirectly) vested benefits regardless of length of service. [IRC § 411(a)(10); Reg. § 1.411(a)-8T(b)(1)]

A new determination letter should be obtained, particularly if the plan's vesting schedule has been made less liberal. See Chapter 13 for details.

Q. 8:7 What is the period within which a participant may elect to stay under the old vesting schedule?

A participant must have at least 60 days to elect the old vesting schedule. In addition, the election period must begin no later than the date on which the amendment is adopted and end no earlier than the latest of the following:

- 60 days after the amendment is adopted;
- 60 days after the amendment becomes effective; or
- 60 days after the participant "is issued written notice of the plan amendment by the employer or plan administrator."

[IRC § 411(a)(10)(B); Reg. § 1.411(a)-8T(b)(2)]

Q. 8:8 What vesting standards apply to an employee's own contributions?

Whether contributions are mandatory or voluntary, the employee at all times must have a nonforfeitable right to 100 percent of the benefits derived from the employee's own contributions. [IRC § 411(a)(1); Reg. §§ 1.411(a)-1(a)(2) and 1.411(c)-1]

Q. 8:9 What is a year of service for vesting purposes?

For purposes of determining a participant's vested benefits, a year of service means a 12-month period specified in the qualified retirement plan during which the participant completes at least 1,000 hours of service (see Q. 4:9). [IRC § 411(a)(5)]

Q. 8:10 What years of service must be taken into account for vesting purposes?

In general, all years of service with the employer must be counted. For the exceptions, see Q. 8:11. [IRC § 411(a)(4)]

Service with a predecessor of the employer must be counted if the successor-employer maintains the predecessor's qualified retirement plan. If the successor adopts a new retirement plan, recognition of service with the predecessor-employer is supposed to be decided under as-yet-unissued IRS regulations. IRS has said that, in the case of a predecessor-partnership, service with the partnership could be counted for vesting purposes under the successor-corporation's retirement plan, even though the corporation did not continue the partnership's retirement plan. [IRC § 414(a); *Letter Ruling 7742003*]

Service with any member of a controlled group of corporations or with a commonly controlled entity (see Q. 4:34), whether or not incorporated, must be counted for vesting purposes. Similarly, service with any member of an affiliated service group (see Q. 27:31) must be counted. [IRC §§ 414(b), 414(c), and 414(m)]

A multiple-employer defined benefit plan that does not credit vesting service attributable to periods for which an *employer* does not make required contributions to the plan does not satisfy the minimum vesting requirements. [*Rev. Rul. 85-130*, 1985-2 CB 137]

Q. 8:11 May any years of service be disregarded for vesting purposes?

Yes. There are limited exceptions to the general rule that all years of service with an employer must be counted for vesting purposes (see Q. 8:10). [IRC § 411(a)(4)]

The following years of service may be disregarded:

- Years of service before the employee reached age 18;
- Years of service before the qualified retirement plan went into effect;
- Years of service during which the *employee* declined to make required (mandatory) contributions; and
- Years of service before a one-year break in service (see Q. 4:10) if the number of consecutive one-year breaks in service equals or exceeds the greater of five or the number of prebreak years of service, and the participant did not have any nonforfeitable right to the accrued benefit (see Q. 8:14).

Q. 8:12 Is an employee's length of service ever irrelevant in determining the degree of vesting?

Yes. In any of the following circumstances an employee is fully vested (that is, has a nonforfeitable right to 100% of the employer-provided account balance or accrued benefit) regardless of how many years of service the employee has completed:

- The employee reaches normal retirement age (see Q. 9:66). [IRC §§ 411(a) and 411(a)(8)]
- The qualified retirement plan is terminated, a partial termination of the plan has occurred (see Q. 19:5), or plan contributions are completely discontinued. [IRC § 411(d)(3)]
- The minimum service requirement for participation is more than one year of service (see Q. 4:21 and Q. 4:4). [IRC § 410(a)(1)(B)(i)]
- The plan is a qualified 401(k) plan and the accrued benefit is derived from employer contributions made pursuant to the employee's election. See Chapter 21 for details. [IRC § 401(k)(2)(C)]

A plan may also provide for full vesting under any of these circumstances:

- The employee reaches the early retirement age set by the qualified retirement plan.
- The employee becomes disabled.
- The employee dies.

Q. 8:13 What vesting schedule is best for the employer?

It depends on how long the employees usually stay with the employer.

> **Example.** Keren Corporation adopted a 5%-of-compensation money purchase pension plan on January 1, 1989. Sharon completes a year of service on January 1, 1990 and joins the plan. Sharon earns $20,000 a year. Below is a calculation of

Sharon's benefits under the seven-year graded and five-year cliff vesting schedules (see Q. 8:3):

	7-Year		5-Year	
Plan Year	Contribution/ Account Balance	Vesting Percentage/ Vested Benefits	Contribution/ Account Balance	Vesting Percentage/ Vested Benefits
1	0 / 0		0 / 0	
2	$1,000 / $1,000	0% / $0	$1,000 / $1,000	0% / $0
3	$1,000 / $2,000	20% / $400	$1,000 / $2,000	0% / $0
4	$1,000 / $3,000	40% / $1,200	$1,000 / $3,000	0% / $0
5	$1,000 / $4,000	60% / $2,400	$1,000 / $4,000	100% / $4,000
6	$1,000 / $5,000	80% / $4,000	$1,000 / $5,000	100% / $5,000
7	$1,000 / $6,000	100% / $6,000	$1,000 / $6,000	100% / $6,000

In plan years 3 and 4, less vested benefits are provided under the five-year cliff vesting schedule; and, in plan years 5 and 6, less vested benefits are provided under the seven-year graded vesting schedule. Thus, if employees customarily leave before completing five years of service, five-year cliff vesting is more favorable to the employer; but, if they leave after completing five or six years of service, the seven-year graded schedule is more favorable to the employer. After seven years of service, both schedules provide equal benefits.

As an alternative, Keren Corporation could require employees to complete two years of service to become eligible, but then employees must be 100 percent vested immediately (see Q. 8:12). With a two-year service requirement and 100 percent immediate vesting, Sharon's benefits would be as follows:

Plan Year	Contribution/ Account Balance	Vesting Percentage/ Vested Benefits
1	$\dfrac{0}{0}$	
2	$\dfrac{0}{0}$	
3	$\dfrac{\$1,000}{\$1,000}$	$\dfrac{100\%}{\$1,000}$
4	$\dfrac{\$1,000}{\$2,000}$	$\dfrac{100\%}{\$2,000}$
5	$\dfrac{\$1,000}{\$3,000}$	$\dfrac{100\%}{\$3,000}$
6	$\dfrac{\$1,000}{\$4,000}$	$\dfrac{100\%}{\$4,000}$
7	$\dfrac{\$1,000}{\$5,000}$	$\dfrac{100\%}{\$5,000}$

In plan years 3 and 4, the least vested benefits still occur under five-year cliff; in plan year 5, the least vested benefits still occur under seven-year graded; in plan year 6, the most vested benefits are still created under five-year cliff; and, in plan year 7 and in all subsequent plan years, the least vested benefits occur under the two-year schedule. Therefore, if employees customarily leave after completing seven or more years of service, the two-year schedule will be most favorable to the employer.

Q. 8:14 How does a one-year break in service affect a previously nonvested participant's right to benefits?

A nonvested participant's years of service before any period of consecutive one-year breaks in service (see Q. 4:10) may be disregarded for vesting purposes if the number of consecutive one-year breaks in service equals or exceeds the greater of five or the participant's years of service before the break. [IRC § 411(a)(6)(D)]

Example. Ceekay Corporation's profit sharing plan, which operates on a calendar-year basis, requires an employee to complete one year of service to become a participant. Under the plan's vesting provision, a participant becomes 100 percent vested after five years of service. Caroline began working for Ceekay on January 1, 1986, separated from service on December 15, 1987, and is rehired on January 12, 1991. Caroline's two years of service before her break in service must be counted because her consecutive one-year breaks in service are less than five.

A participant's prebreak years of service do not have to be taken into account until a year of service is completed after reemployment. [IRC § 411(a)(6)(B)]

Q. 8:15 How does a one-year break in service affect an employee if the qualified retirement plan requires the employee to have more than one year of service in order to be eligible to participate?

Qualified retirement plans that provide for immediate 100 percent vesting but require more than one year of service to be eligible to participate (see Q. 4:12 and Q. 8:12) may provide that years of service preceding a one-year break in service (see Q. 4:10) be disregarded if the employee has not yet met the service eligibility criterion. Thus, an employee who completes one year of service and then incurs a one-year break in service starts over again when rehired. [IRC § 410(a)(5)(B)]

Q. 8:16 How does a one-year break in service affect a vested participant's right to benefits?

The years of service of a vested participant in a defined contribution plan (see Q. 2:2) or a fully insured defined benefit plan (see Q. 2:19) completed after a one-year break in service (see Q. 4:10) need not be counted for purposes of computing the participant's right to benefits derived from employer contributions accruing before the one-year break in service if the participant has at least five consecutive one-year breaks in service. [IRC § 411(a)(6)(C)]

Example. Jay-Kay Corporation has a profit sharing plan in which James participated. At the time James separated from service, he had a nonforfeitable right to 20 percent of his accrued benefit but no distribution was made. In 1990, after incurring a one-year break in service, James is rehired and becomes an active participant in the plan once again. The plan is not permitted to disregard James' postbreak service for purposes of computing the vested percentage of his prebreak accrued benefit.

If a participant's prebreak years of service are required to be taken into account, such years of service need not be counted until the participant completes a year of service after resuming employment. [IRC § 411(a)(6)(B)]

Q. 8:17   What is a forfeiture of benefits?

If an employee terminates employment before becoming 100 percent vested, the employee may be entitled to some benefits. This will usually depend on the number of years the employee worked for the company. Thus, if, at the time of termination, the employee's account balance in a profit sharing plan is $10,000 and the employee is 60 percent vested, the vested benefit is $6,000 (60% of $10,000). The balance in the account that is not vested at the time of termination generally will be forfeited when the employee receives a distribution or, if earlier, after the employee incurs five consecutive one-year breaks in service (see Q. 4:10). [IRC § 411(a)(6)(C)]

Q. 8:18   What happens to amounts forfeited by participants?

Only defined benefit plans (see Q. 2:3) are restricted in the application of forfeitures. Forfeitures under a defined benefit plan must be used to reduce future employer contributions and may not be used to provide additional benefits for remaining participants. Defined contribution plans (see Q. 2:2) may provide that forfeitures be used either to reduce contributions or to increase benefits provided under the plan. [IRC § 401(a)(8)]

IRS has ruled that a profit sharing plan may provide for the allocation of forfeitures to participants on the basis of their account balances provided such allocation does not discriminate in favor of highly compensated employees. [*Rev. Rul. 81-10*, 1981-1 CB 172; Reg. § 1.401-4(a)(1)(iii)]

Q. 8:19 May a nonforfeitable benefit ever be forfeited?

The courts have differed on whether forfeitures can be imposed because of employee dishonesty (so-called bad boy clauses) or violation of a promise not to compete. Some courts say such forfeitures are not permitted. Other courts have ruled that if the forfeiture provisions do not cause a forfeiture of an amount greater than what would result under the minimum vesting standards (see Q. 8:3), the forfeiture is allowed. [*Noell v. American Design, Inc. Profit Sharing Plan*, 764 F2d 827 (8th Cir. 1985); *Montgomery v. Lowe*, (DC ED Texas 1981); *Hepple v. Roberts & Dybdahl, Inc.* (8th Cir. 1980); *Marshall v. Edison Bros.*, 593 F2d 30 (8th Cir. 1979); *Nedrow v. MacFarlane and Hays Co.* (DC Mich. 1979)]

According to IRS, vested benefits in excess of the benefits required to be nonforfeitable under the statutory alternatives (see Q. 8:3) may be forfeited because of an employee's misconduct or dishonesty. The qualified retirement plan must provide the specific criteria for application of this bad boy clause, and its use cannot be discriminatory in operation.

> **Example 1**. Mikey Corporation's retirement plan provides that an employee is fully vested after the completion of three years of service. The plan also provides that, if the employee works for a competitor, he forfeits his rights in the plan. Such a provision could result in a prohibited forfeiture; but, if the plan limited the forfeiture to employees who completed less than five years of service, the plan would not fail to satisfy the minimum vesting requirements.

> **Example 2**. Sallie Corporation's retirement plan has a seven-year graded vesting provision and provides for forfeiture of benefits if an employee with less than five years of service terminates employment and works for a competitor. This is permissible because the plan could have had five-year vesting.

[Reg. §§ 1.411(a)-4T(c) and 1.411(d)-4, Q&A 6; *Rev. Rul. 85-31*, 1985-1 CB 153]

Q. 8:20 Does a distribution (cash-out) of benefits affect how many years of service must be taken into account?

Yes. Upon termination of the employee's participation in a qualified retirement plan, the plan may disregard service for which the employee has received (1) an involuntary distribution of the present value of the employee's nonforfeitable benefit up to a maximum of $3,500, or (2) a voluntary distribution of the present value of the nonforfeitable benefit. [IRC §§ 411(a)(7)(B) and 411(a)(11); Reg. § 1.411(a)-7(d)(4)]

In order to disregard the prior service of a participant who resumes employment and participation under the qualified retirement plan and who previously received a distribution of less than the present value of the accrued benefit, the plan must provide the participant with the opportunity to repay the entire amount of the distribution (see Q. 8:21). [IRC § 411(a)(7)(C); Reg. § 1.411(a)-7(d)(4)]

Q. 8:21 How can a reemployed participant restore (buy-back) forfeited benefits?

In most situations, upon reemployment, a participant is entitled to repay a prior distribution from the qualified retirement plan and to have any forfeited benefits restored. This buy-back provision must permit the employee to pay back the full amount distributed. The plan can require repayment by the reemployed participant before the earlier of (1) five years after reemployment, or (2) when the participant incurs a period of five consecutive one-year breaks in service commencing after the distribution. Thus, the employer is not required to offer this buy-back right to a participant who has five consecutive one-year breaks in service after the distribution. [IRC § 411(a)(7)(C)]

A defined benefit plan may require that any repayment include interest on the full amount of the distribution. The maximum interest rate that may be charged upon repayment is 120 percent of the federal mid-term rate in effect on the first day of the plan year during which repayment occurs. [IRC §§ 411(a)(7)(C), 411(c)(2)(C), and 1274; Reg. § 1.411(a)-7(d)(2)(ii)(B)]

Q. 8:22 May a qualified retirement plan provide for the forfeiture of vested benefits on the death of an employee?

Yes, with the following exception: the surviving spouse of a participant in a qualified retirement plan subject to the survivor annuity requirements must be paid an annuity based on the participant's vested accrued benefit unless the participant waived the coverage with the spouse's consent. (See Q. 9:20.) [IRC § 401(a)(11)]

A qualified retirement plan may not provide for the forfeiture of vested benefits derived from employee contributions, whether mandatory or voluntary (see Q. 8:8). However, a forfeiture does not occur merely because benefits derived from contributions of both the employer and the employee are paid out in the form of an annuity that stops on the employee's death. [Reg. § 1.411(a)-4(b)(1)(ii)]

Q. 8:23 May any years of service be disregarded for accrual purposes?

Yes. A qualified retirement plan may impose a limitation on the amount of benefits an employee may accrue or the number of years of service that will be taken into account in determining an employee's accrued benefit (see Q. 8:2). Therefore, a qualified retirement plan may disregard an employee's service that occurs after the specified benefit level or the specified number of years of service has been reached. However, a retirement plan may not cease an employee's accrual of benefits (or reduce the rate of accrual) solely because the employee attains a certain age. [IRC § 411(b)(1)(H); Prop. Reg. § 1.411(b)-2]

> **Example**. James Corporation maintains a defined benefit plan under which the participant's normal retirement benefit will be based on the highest annual salary earned by the participant during the time of employment. The plan further provides that each participant will accrue an interest in the benefit at the rate of 4 percent per year of service. The plan does, however, limit the number of years of service that will be taken into account in determining each participant's retirement benefit to

20. Therefore, a participant's normal retirement benefit will be limited to 80 percent of the participant's highest annual salary. This type of accrual scheme is permissible despite the fact that an older participant is more likely to be affected by the plan provision.

Q. 8:24   Can a qualified retirement plan be amended to reduce accrued benefits?

Generally, no. A qualified retirement plan may not be amended to eliminate or reduce a Section 411(d)(6) protected benefit (see Q. 9:41) that has already accrued unless IRS approves a request to amend the plan or the elimination or reduction satisfies certain requirements (see Q. 8:25). This is the rule even if such elimination or reduction is contingent upon the employee's consent. However, a plan may (subject to certain notice requirements) be amended to eliminate or reduce Section 411(d)(6) protected benefits with respect to benefits not yet accrued as of the later of the amendment's adoption date or effective date (see Q. 8:26). [IRC §§ 411(d)(6) and 412(c)(8); ERISA §§ 204(g), 302(c)(8), and 4281; Reg. § 1.411(d)-4, Q&A 2]

Q. 8:25   Can accrued benefits be eliminated or reduced?

It is permissible to eliminate or reduce accrued benefits (see Q. 8:2) if any of the following circumstances are present:

- The amendment constitutes timely compliance with a change in law affecting plan qualification; IRS gives Section 7805(b) relief; and the elimination or reduction is made only to the extent necessary to comply with the plan qualification rules. An amendment will not treated as necessary if it is possible to satisfy the applicable qualification requirement through other modifications to the plan (e.g., by expanding the availability of an optional form of benefit to additional employees).

- A qualified retirement plan that provides a range of three or more actuarially equivalent joint and survivor annuity options may be amended to eliminate any of such options, other than the options with the largest and smallest optional survivor payment percentages. The amendment is permissible even if the effect of such amendment is to change the option that is the qualified joint and survivor annuity (QJSA) (see Q. 9:8).

> **Example**. A retirement plan provides three joint and survivor annuity options with survivor payments of 50 percent, 75 percent, and 100 percent, respectively. The options are uniform with respect to age and are actuarially equivalent. The employer may eliminate the option with the 75 percent survivor payment, even if this option had been the QJSA under the plan.

- If a qualified retirement plan includes an optional form of benefit under which benefits are distributed in specified property (other than cash), such optional form may be modified for distributions after plan termination by substituting cash for the property, but only to the extent that, on plan termination, an employee has the opportunity to receive the optional form of benefit in the specified property. However, if the employer that maintains the terminating plan also maintains another plan that provides an optional form of benefit in the specified property, this exception is not available.

> **Example.** Ess-Kay Corporation maintains a stock bonus plan under which a participant, upon termination from employment, may elect to receive benefits in a lump-sum distribution in the company's stock. This is the only plan maintained by Ess-Kay under which distributions in employer stock are available. Ess-Kay decides to terminate the stock bonus plan. If such plan is amended to make available a lump-sum distribution in employer stock on plan termination, the plan will not fail the anti-cutback rule solely because the optional form of benefit providing a lump-sum distribution in employer stock on termination of employment is modified to provide that such distribution is available only in cash.

[Reg. § 1.411(d)-4, Q&A 2(b)]

Other circumstances permitting elimination or reduction of accrued benefits include amendments to provide for certain involuntary distributions, to eliminate provisions authorizing loans and certain plan-to-plan transfers, and to make a *de minimis* change in the timing of an optional form of benefit (see Q. 9:32). In addition, special rules have been provided for amendments to Employee Stock Ownership Plans (ESOPs) (see Q. 22:1). [Reg. § 1.411(d)-4, Q&A 2(d)]

Q. 8:26 Can a qualified retirement plan be amended to reduce future accruals of benefits?

Yes. However, an amendment to a qualified retirement plan subject to the minimum funding requirements (see Q. 7:1) that provides for a "significant reduction in the rate of future benefit accrual" will not be effective unless the plan administrator (see Q. 14:1) provides written notice to all participants, any alternate payee under a qualified domestic relations order (QDRO) (see Q. 28:1), and each employee organization representing participants. That notice, which must set forth the amendment and its effective date, is required to be sent to such parties after adoption of the amendment and at least 15 days prior to its effective date. The reduction may result in either a termination or partial termination of the plan. See Chapter 19 for details. [ERISA § 204(h)]

Q. 8:27 What benefits are not Section 411(d)(6) protected benefits?

Examples of benefits that are not Section 411(d)(6) benefits and, therefore, may be reduced or eliminated by an amendment to a qualified retirement plan are:

- Ancillary life insurance protection;
- Accident or health insurance benefits;
- Social Security supplements described in Section 411(a)(9);
- The availability of loans (other than the distribution of an employee's accrued benefit upon default under a loan);
- The right to make certain after-tax employee contributions or elective deferrals;
- The right to direct investments;
- The right to a particular form of investment (for example, investment in employer stock or securities or investment in cer-

tain types of securities, commercial paper, or other investment media);

- The allocation dates for contributions, forfeitures, and earnings, the time for making contributions (but not the conditions for receiving an allocation of contributions or forfeitures for a plan year after such conditions have been satisfied), and the valuation dates for account balances;
- Administrative procedures for distributing benefits, such as provisions relating to the particular dates on which notices are given and by which elections must be made; and
- Rights that derive from administrative and operational provisions, such as mechanical procedures for allocating investment experience among accounts in defined contribution plans.

[Reg. § 1.411(d)-4, Q&A 1(d)]

Q. 8:28 What happens to a participant's benefits if the qualified retirement plan merges with another plan?

In case of a merger or consolidation of qualified retirement plans or a transfer of assets or liabilities from one qualified retirement plan to another, each participant must be entitled to receive a benefit after the merger that is at least equal to the value of the benefit the participant would have been entitled to receive before the merger. (The before-and-after merger benefits are determined as if the plan had been terminated.) [IRC § 401(a)(12); Reg. § 1.401(a)-12]

The plan administrator (see Q. 14:1) of a merged plan must apprise the appropriate IRS District Director of the merger by completing Parts I and II of Form 5310 and filing the form at least 30 days before the event. No request for a determination letter is required; however, additional actuarial data are required for a defined benefit plan and, of course, IRS may request additional documentation with regard to any filing.

Chapter 9

Distribution Requirements

Numerous rules govern the timing and form of benefit distributions. This chapter examines qualified joint and survivor annuity (QJSA) requirements, qualified preretirement survivor annuity (QPSA) requirements, limits on optional forms of benefit, when distributions must commence, and related matters.

Q. 9:1 Must a qualified retirement plan provide benefits to a participant's surviving spouse?

If a married participant with vested benefits dies before the annuity starting date (see Q. 9:3), a QPSA (see Q. 9:9) must, with certain exceptions, be provided to the participant's surviving spouse. A QPSA must be provided whether or not the participant separated from service before death. If a married participant survives until the annuity starting date, all vested benefits must, with certain exceptions, be paid in the form of a QJSA (see Q. 9:8). The QPSA and the QJSA must be provided by all qualified retirement plans except certain profit sharing plans (see Q. 9:6), but may be waived if the applicable notice, election, and spousal consent requirements are satisfied (see Q. 9:20 through Q. 9:25). Also, the automatic survivor benefit requirements do not apply to a payment of the benefit before the annuity starting date if the present value of the married participant's benefit is $3,500 or less. [IRC §§ 401(a)(11) and 417]

It is possible that one portion of a married participant's benefit may be subject to a QJSA and another portion to a QPSA at the same time. For example, a participant in a money purchase pension plan may have separate accounts for employer contributions and employee contributions. An in-service withdrawal of all or part of the employee contribution account would be subject to the QJSA. The QPSA would apply to the employer contribution account if the participant died prior to the annuity starting date. [Reg. § 1.401(a)-20, Q&A 9]

Q. 9:2 Must a qualified retirement plan continue to pay benefits to a surviving spouse who remarries?

Yes. The remarriage of a surviving spouse does not affect a qualified retirement plan's obligation to continue to pay benefits to the surviving spouse under the QPSA or QJSA. The plan must continue to pay benefits to the surviving spouse as long as the participant and surviving spouse are married on the date of the participant's death with respect to a QPSA, and on the annuity starting date with respect to a QJSA. [Reg. § 1.401(a)-20, Q&A 25(b)]

Q. 9:3 What is the annuity starting date?

The annuity starting date is the first day of the first period for which a benefit is payable as an annuity. For benefits payable in any other form, it is the first day on which all events have occurred that entitle the participant to the benefit. For example, if an annuity is scheduled to begin on January 1, 1990, the annuity starting date is January 1, 1990, even though the first payment is not made until July 1, 1990. If the benefit is a deferred annuity, the annuity starting date is the date on which the annuity payments are scheduled to commence, not the date that the deferred annuity is elected or the date the deferred annuity contract is distributed. [IRC § 417(f)(2)(A); Reg. § 1.401(a)-20, Q&A 10(b)]

There is a special rule that applies to disability benefits. The annuity starting date of a disability benefit is the first day of the first period for which the disability benefit becomes payable, unless it is an auxiliary benefit. An auxiliary disability benefit is disregarded in determining the annuity starting date. A disability benefit is considered auxiliary if it is not taken into account in determining the disabled participant's retirement benefit under the plan. [IRC § 417(f)(2)(B); Reg. § 1.401(a)-20, Q&A 10(c)]

Q. 9:4 What is the significance of the annuity starting date to survivor benefit requirements?

The annuity starting date (see Q. 9:3) determines whether benefits are payable as a QJSA, QPSA, or any other selected optional form of benefit. If a participant is living on the annuity starting date, the benefits must be payable as a QJSA. If the participant dies before the annuity starting date, the surviving spouse must receive a QPSA.

The annuity starting date is also relevant in determining when a participant may waive a QJSA and when a spouse may consent to the waiver. Such waivers and consents are effective only if made within 90 days before the annuity starting date. Since, under a deferred annuity, the annuity starting date is the date on which the payments are to commence (see Q. 9:3), the QJSA cannot be waived until 90 days before such time. [Reg. § 1.401(a)-20, Q&A 10(a)]

Q. 9:5 How do the automatic survivor benefit requirements apply to unmarried participants?

A QJSA (see Q. 9:8) for an unmarried participant is a life annuity (i.e., payments cease on the participant's death). Thus, an unmarried participant must be provided with a life annuity unless the participant elects another form of benefit.

There is no requirement to provide a QPSA (see Q. 9:9) with respect to an unmarried participant who dies before the annuity starting date. [Reg. § 1.401(a)-20, Q&A 25(a)]

Q. 9:6 Are all qualified retirement plans required to provide automatic survivor benefits?

The automatic survivor benefit requirements (see Q. 9:1) apply to defined benefit plans (see Q. 2:3) and also to defined contribution plans subject to minimum funding requirements (i.e., money purchase pension and target benefit plans; see Q. 7:1).

The automatic survivor benefit requirements also apply to participants in a profit sharing plan, stock bonus plan, or a 401(k) plan unless:

1. The plan provides that, upon the participant's death, the participant's vested benefit (reduced by any security interest held by the plan by reason of a loan outstanding to such participant) is payable in full to the participant's surviving spouse (unless the participant has elected with spousal consent that such benefit be paid instead to a designated beneficiary) (see Q. 9:18);

2. The participant does not elect the payment of benefits in the form of a life annuity; and

3. With respect to the participant, the plan is not a direct or indirect transferee plan (see Q. 9:13) or a floor offset arrangement (see Q. 9:14).

[IRC § 401(a)(11); Reg. § 1.401(a)-20, Q&A 3(a)]

If a participant elects a life annuity option provided by a plan otherwise exempt from the automatic survivor benefit requirements, the participant's benefits under the plan will be subject to automatic survivor requirements thereafter. Generally, plans eligible to avoid the automatic survivor benefit requirements will offer benefits only in the form of a single sum distribution or over a fixed period that is less than the participant's life expectancy. [Reg. § 1.401(a)-20, Q&A 4]

Q. 9:7 Are there any other conditions that must be satisfied, with respect to a participant, to be exempt from the automatic survivor rules?

Yes. In order for a participant in a profit sharing plan (or other defined contribution plan not subject to the minimum funding standards) (see Q. 9:6) to be exempt from the automatic survivor rules:

1. The benefit payable to the participant's surviving spouse must be available within a reasonable period after the participant's death (whether the period is reasonable will be determined on the basis of facts and circumstances; however, 90 days will be deemed to be reasonable); and

2. The benefit must be adjusted for gains or losses occurring after

the participant's death in accordance with plan provisions specifying the adjustment of account balances for other plan distributions.

[Reg. § 1.401(a)-20, Q&A 3(b)]

Q. 9:8 What is a qualified joint and survivor annuity?

A QJSA is an immediate annuity for the life of the participant, with a survivor annuity for the life of the participant's spouse. The amount of the survivor annuity may not be less than 50 percent, nor more than 100 percent, of the amount of the annuity payable during the time that the participant and spouse are both alive. The QJSA must be at least the actuarial equivalent of an annuity for the life of the participant only. [IRC § 417(b)]

A qualified retirement plan may have more than one form of joint and survivor annuity satisfying the QJSA requirements. In that event, the joint and survivor annuity with the greatest actuarial value is the QJSA. If one or more are actuarially equivalent, the plan must designate which one is the automatic form of payment. In any event, the QJSA for a married participant must be at least equal to the most valuable optional form of benefit payable to the participant at the time of the election. [IRC § 417(b); Reg. § 1.401(a)-20, Q&A 16]

A participant must be allowed to receive a QJSA at the participant's earliest retirement age, which is generally the earliest date on which the participant could receive a distribution from the plan. The participant (but not the participant's spouse) must consent to the distribution in the form of a QJSA before the participant's benefits are immediately distributable. A participant's benefits are immediately distributable at the later of normal retirement age (see Q. 9:66) or age 62. Once benefits are immediately distributable, a QJSA may be distributed without the participant's consent (but see Q. 9:32 through Q. 9:49 on optional forms of benefit). Distributions may not be made at any time in a form other than a QJSA unless the participant so elects and the participant's spouse consents. [Reg. § 1.401(a)-20, Q&A 17; Reg. § 1.417(e)-1(b)]

Q. 9:9 What is a qualified preretirement survivor annuity?

A QPSA is an immediate annuity for the life of the surviving spouse of a participant who dies before the annuity starting date (see Q. 9:3). Under a QPSA, each payment to the surviving spouse will be the same as (or the actuarial equivalent of) the payment that would have been made to the surviving spouse under the plan's QJSA (see Q. 9:8) if:

1. In the case of a participant who dies after attaining the earliest retirement age (see Q. 9:8) under the plan, the participant had retired with an immediate QJSA on the day before the participant's death; or

2. In the case of a participant who dies upon or before attaining the earliest retirement age under the plan, the participant had: (a) separated from service on the date of death, (b) survived to the earliest retirement age, (c) retired with an immediate QJSA at the earliest retirement age, and (d) died on the day after the day on which the earliest retirement age would have been attained. (If the participant had separated from service prior to death, the amount of the QPSA is calculated by reference to the actual date of separation from service rather than the date of death to prevent the participant from accruing benefits after separation from service.)

Example. Dan, who is married, participates in a pension plan, and early retirement age under the plan is age 50. The plan must provide automatic survivor coverage in the form of a QJSA and a QPSA. In 1990, Dan reached age 50 but did not elect early retirement. Although Dan continues to work after age 50, a QPSA must be provided for his wife in the event he dies before he retires.

The QPSA may be payable from a defined benefit plan (see Q. 2:3) to the surviving spouse at any time, but must be available to the surviving spouse no later than the month in which the participant would have reached the earliest retirement age under the plan. A defined benefit plan may provide that the QPSA is forfeited if the surviving spouse does not survive until the QPSA is payable under the plan. Similarly, the plan may provide that the QPSA is forfeited if the surviving spouse elects to defer payment of the QPSA, but does not survive until the deferred commencement date. [IRC § 417(c); Reg. § 1.401(a)-11, Q&A 18, 19, and 22(a)]

The QPSA provided under a defined contribution plan (see Q. 2:2) must be available to the surviving spouse within a reasonable time after the participant's death. The QPSA may not be less valuable than 50 percent of the vested account balance of the participant as of the date of the participant's death. [IRC § 417(c)(2); Reg. § 1.401(a)-20, Q&A 20 and 22(b)]

Q. 9:10 How is a survivor annuity treated for estate tax purposes?

The value of a surviving spouse's interest in a QPSA or QJSA is included in the participant's gross estate for estate tax purposes. The marital deduction is allowable unless the deceased participant's executor elects not to take the deduction (see Q. 12:16 and Q. 12:18). [IRC §§ 2039 and 2056(b)(7)(C)]

Q. 9:11 What is the effect of a loan on the amount of a QPSA or QJSA?

In determining the amount of the QPSA or QJSA, the accrued benefit (see Q. 8:2) is reduced by any security interest held by the plan by reason of a loan outstanding to the participant if, at the date of death or benefit payment, the security interest is treated as payment of the loan under the plan. The plan may offset any loan outstanding at the participant's death that is secured by the participant's account balance against the spousal benefit. [IRC § 417(c); Reg. § 1.401(a)-20, Q&A 24(d)]

Q. 9:12 Is spousal consent necessary for plan loans?

Yes, if the participant's accrued benefit (see Q. 8:2) is used as security for the loan. Consent is required even if the accrued benefit is not the primary security for the loan. Spousal consent is not required, however, if the total accrued benefit subject to the security is $3,500 or less. Spousal consent must be obtained within 90 days of the date that the loan is so secured in the same manner as the consent to the waiver of the QJSA or QPSA is obtained (see Q. 9:21). For purposes of spousal consent, any renegotiation, extension, renewal, or other revision of a loan is treated as a new loan. [Reg. § 1.401(a)-20, Q&A 24]

Q. 9:13 What is a transferee plan?

Although profit sharing plans, stock bonus plans, and 401(k) plans are generally not subject to the automatic survivor benefit requirements (see Q. 9:1 and Q. 9:6), these plans become subject to such requirements to the extent the plan is a transferee plan with respect to any participant. A plan is a transferee plan with respect to a participant if it is a direct or indirect transferee of that participant's benefits held on or after January 1, 1985, by:

- A defined benefit plan;
- A defined contribution plan subject to the minimum funding standards (see Q. 7:1); or
- A defined contribution plan that is subject to the automatic survivor benefit requirements with respect to that participant.

Neither a transfer made before 1985, nor a rollover contribution (see Q. 26:1) made by a participant at any time, is treated as a transfer that subjects a plan to the survivor benefit rules with respect to the participant. Even if a plan is a transferee plan with respect to a participant, the automatic survivor benefit requirements apply only to benefits attributable to the transferred assets, as long as there is an acceptable separate accounting between the transferred assets and other plan benefits. If a separate accounting is not maintained for the transferred assets, the survivor benefit requirements apply to all benefits payable with respect to the participant under the plan. [IRC § 401(a)(11)(B)(iii)(III); Reg. § 1.401(a)-20, Q&A 5]

Q. 9:14 Do the automatic survivor annuity requirements apply to floor offset plans?

Yes. If benefits of a plan not otherwise subject to the survivor annuity requirements (see Q. 9:1 and Q. 9:6) are used to offset benefits that would otherwise accrue under a plan subject to the survivor annuity requirements (e.g., a defined benefit plan), the floor offset plan (see Q. 2:17) will be subject to survivor annuity requirements. [Reg. § 1.401(a)-20, Q&A 5; ERISA § 407(d)(9)]

Q. 9:15 Must annuity contracts distributed to a participant or spouse by a plan satisfy the automatic survivor benefit requirements?

Yes. If a plan is required to provide automatic survivor benefits (see Q. 9:1), such benefits may not be eliminated or reduced because the plan uses annuity contracts to provide benefits or because such a contract is held by a participant or spouse instead of a plan trustee. [Reg. § 1.401(a)-20, Q&A 2]

Q. 9:16 Must a frozen or terminated plan provide automatic survivor benefits?

Benefits under a plan that is subject to the survivor benefit requirements must be provided in the form of a QJSA (see Q. 9:8) or QPSA (see Q. 9:9) even if the plan is frozen or terminated. [Reg. § 1.401(a)-20, Q&A 6]

Q. 9:17 Does it make any difference if PBGC is administering the plan?

No. If PBGC (see Q. 19:10) is administering a plan, it will pay benefits in the form of a QPSA or QJSA. [Reg. § 1.401 (a)-20, Q&A 7]

Q. 9:18 To which benefits do the automatic survivor rules apply?

Benefits derived from both employer and employee contributions are subject to the automatic survivor benefit requirements (see Q. 9:1).

For defined benefit plans (see Q. 2:3), the automatic survivor benefit requirements apply only to benefits in which the participant was vested immediately before death. They do not apply to benefits to which the participant's beneficiary becomes entitled by reason of death or to the proceeds of a life insurance contract maintained by the plan for the participant to the extent such proceeds exceed the present value of the participant's vested benefits existing immediately before death.

For defined contribution plans (see Q. 2:2), the survivor annuity requirements apply to all vested benefits, whether vested before or upon death, including the proceeds of insurance contracts. This rule also applies in determining the vested benefits that must be paid to the surviving spouse under a defined contribution plan exempt from the survivor annuity requirements since such a plan is required to pay all death benefits to the surviving spouse (see Q. 9:6). [IRC §§ 401(a)(11) and 417(f)(1); Reg. § 1.401(a)-20, Q&A 11, 12, and 13]

Q. 9:19 Can a qualified retirement plan treat married participants as not married under any circumstances?

Yes. A qualified retirement plan is not required to treat a participant as married unless the participant was married throughout the one-year period ending on the earlier of the participant's annuity starting date (see Q. 9:3) or date of death. However, if the participant marries within one year of the annuity starting date and dies after that date, the participant's spouse is still entitled to the QJSA, provided the marriage lasted for at least one year. This is true even if the spouse and the participant are not married on the date of the participant's death, except as may be provided in a Qualified Domestic Relations Order (QDRO) (see Q. 28:1). [IRC § 417(d); Reg. § 1.401(a)-20, Q&A 25(b)(2) and (3)]

Also, a qualified retirement plan can refuse payment of a survivor annuity to a participant's surviving spouse who pleaded guilty to the murder of the participant. [*Letter Ruling 9008079*]

Q. 9:20 May a participant waive the automatic survivor benefits?

A plan required to provide automatic survivor benefits must also provide the participant with an opportunity to waive the QJSA (see Q. 9:8) or the QPSA (see Q. 9:9) during the applicable election period. In addition, the participant is permitted to revoke any election during this period. There is no limit on the number of times the participant may waive the QJSA or QPSA or revoke a waiver. [IRC § 417(a)(1)]

The applicable election period is:

1. In the case of a QJSA, the 90-day period ending on the annuity starting date (see Q. 9:3), or

2. In the case of a QPSA, the period beginning on the first day of the plan year in which the participant attains age 35 and ending on the date of the participant's death.

[IRC § 417(a)(6); Reg. § 1.401(a)-20, Q&A 10 and 33]

Q. 9:21 Must the participant's spouse consent to the waiver of the QJSA or QPSA?

Yes. A spouse's consent to the participant's waiver of the QJSA or the QPSA is effective only if

1. The spouse consents to the waiver in writing;

2. The election designates a beneficiary (or a form of benefit) that may not be changed without spousal consent (unless the consent expressly allows such amended designations);

3. The spouse's consent acknowledges the effect of the election; and

4. The consent is witnessed by a plan representative or notary public.

The consent must be given within the applicable election period (see Q. 9:20). Spousal consent is not required if the participant establishes to the satisfaction of the plan representative that there is no spouse or the spouse cannot be located. Also, spousal consent is not required if there is a court order stating that the participant is legally separated or has been abandoned unless a QDRO (see Q. 28:1) provides otherwise. [IRC § 417(a)(2); Reg. § 1.401(a)-20, Q&A 27]

A spouse's consent to the waiver of the QJSA or QPSA is binding only on that spouse; it is not binding on a subsequent spouse of the participant. A plan may preclude a spouse from revoking the consent to the waiver once it has been given, but a plan may also permit a spouse to revoke the consent and render ineffective the participant's prior election to waive the QJSA or QPSA. [Reg. § 1.401(a)-20, Q&A 29 and 30]

Q. 9:22 Must the waiver of the QPSA or QJSA specify an alternate beneficiary?

Yes. The participant's waiver of a QPSA and QJSA, and the spouse's consent, must specify the nonspouse beneficiary (or class of beneficiaries) who will receive the benefit. For example, if the spouse consents to the participant's election to have benefits payable upon the participant's death before the annuity starting date (see Q. 9:3) paid to the participant's children, the participant may not subsequently change beneficiaries (to someone other than a child) without the consent of the spouse unless the change is back to a QPSA or the spouse gave a general consent (see Q. 9:25). If the spouse consents only to the designation of a trust as beneficiary, no further spousal consent to the designation of trust beneficiaries is required. [Reg. § 1.401(a)-20, Q&A 31(a)]

Q. 9:23 Must the waiver of a QJSA specify the optional form of benefit chosen?

Yes. Both the participant's waiver of a QJSA and the spousal consent must specify the particular optional form of benefit (see Q. 9:41). A participant who has waived a QJSA with spousal consent in favor of another form of benefit may not subsequently change the optional form of benefit without the spouse's consent unless the change is back to a QJSA or the spouse gave a general consent (see Q. 9:25). If the plan so provides, the participant may change the optional form of benefit after the spouse's death or a divorce (other than as provided in a QDRO; see Q. 28:1). [Reg. § 1.401(a)-20, Q&A 31(b)(1)]

Q. 9:24 Must the waiver of a QPSA specify the optional form of benefit chosen?

No. A participant's waiver of a QPSA and the spouse's consent need not specify the optional form of any preretirement benefit. A participant may subsequently change the form of the preretirement benefit without obtaining further spousal consent. However, the participant may not change the nonspouse beneficiary without spousal consent (see Q. 9:22). [Reg. § 1.401(a)-20, Q&A 31(b)(2)]

Q. 9:25 May a plan allow a spouse to give general consent to waive a QPSA or QJSA?

Yes, a plan may permit a spouse to execute a general consent. A general consent will enable the participant to waive a QPSA or QJSA and change a designated beneficiary or the optional form of benefit without further spousal consent. Alternatively, the spouse may give a limited general consent, that is, the spouse consents only to changes with respect to certain beneficiaries or forms of benefits.

A general consent executed after October 21, 1986, will not be valid unless the general consent acknowledges that the spouse (1) has the right to limit consent to a specific beneficiary and a specific optional form of benefit, and (2) voluntarily elects to relinquish both such rights. A general consent, including a limited general consent, is effective only if it is made during the applicable election period (see Q. 9:20). [Reg. § 1.401(a)-20, Q&A 31(c)]

Q. 9:26   Does the nonparticipant spouse's consent to the waiver of a QJSA or a QPSA by the participant result in a taxable gift?

No. Such consent by the nonparticipant spouse before the participant's death does not result in a taxable transfer for purposes of the gift tax. After the participant's death, the surviving spouse may be able to disclaim the survivor benefit and avoid the gift tax. [IRC §§ 2503(f) and 2518]

Q. 9:27   Should the plan document specifically set forth the spousal consent rules?

It is highly recommended to ensure that plan representatives obtain valid spousal consents. One court ordered a plan to pay the QPSA to the surviving spouse because the plan "by its own terms" did not require that spousal consent meet the requirements of the Code and ERISA. [*Profit-Sharing Plan for Employees of Republic Financial Servs., Inc. v. MBank Dallas, N.A.*, 683 F. Supp. 592 (ND Tex. 1988)]

Q. 9:28   Must participants be notified of the QJSA?

A plan that is required to provide a QJSA (see Q. 9:6 and Q. 9:8) must give each participant a written explanation of

1. The terms and conditions of the QJSA;
2. The participant's right to make, and the effect of, an election to waive the QJSA;
3. The rights of the participant's spouse; and
4. The right to make, and the effect of, a revocation of an election.

Participants must also be furnished with a general description of the eligibility conditions and other material features of the optional forms of benefit, as well as sufficient information to explain the relative values of the optional forms of benefit. This explanation must be given to the participant within a reasonable period before the annuity starting date (see Q. 9:3). The plan must provide this

explanation to both vested and nonvested participants. [IRC §
417(a)(3)(A); Reg. § 1.401(a)-11(c) and 1.401(a)-20, Q&A 34 and 36]

Q. 9:29 Must participants be notified of the QPSA?

A plan that is required to provide a QPSA (see Q. 9:6 and Q. 9:9)
must give each participant a written explanation of the QPSA similar to the explanation required for the QJSA (see Q. 9:28). This
explanation must be given to both vested and nonvested participants
within whichever of the following applicable periods ends last with
respect to a participant:

1. The period beginning with the first day of the plan year in
   which the participant attains age 32 and ending at the end of
   the plan year preceding the plan year in which the participant
   attains age 35;

2. The period beginning one year before and ending one year
   after the individual becomes a participant;

3. The period beginning one year before and ending one year
   after the survivor benefit applicable to the participant is no
   longer subsidized (see Q. 9:30);

4. The period beginning one year before and ending one year
   after the survivor benefit requirements become applicable to
   the participant; or

5. In the case of a participant who separates from service before
   age 35, the period beginning one year before and ending one
   year after the separation.

[IRC § 417(a)(3)(B); Reg. § 1.401(a)-20, Q&A 35 and 36]

Q. 9:30 What happens if the plan fully subsidizes the cost of the QJSA or QPSA?

If a plan fully subsidizes a QJSA (see Q. 9:8) or QPSA (see Q. 9:9)
and does not permit a participant to waive the benefit or to designate another beneficiary, it need not provide the required written
explanation (see Q. 9:28 and Q. 9:29). If a plan that subsidizes the
cost of the QJSA or QPSA offers such election, the plan must satisfy

the election, consent, and notice requirements. [IRC § 417(a)(5); Reg. § 1.401(a)-20, Q&A 37]

A fully subsidized QJSA is one under which no increase in cost or decrease in benefits to the participant could possibly result from the participant's failure to elect another benefit. For example, if a plan provides a joint and survivor annuity and a lump-sum option, the plan does not fully subsidize the joint and survivor annuity (even if the actuarial value of the joint and survivor annuity is greater than the amount of the lump-sum payment) because, in the event of the participant's early death, the participant would receive less under the annuity than under the lump-sum option. Similarly, if a plan provides for a life annuity of $100 per month and a joint and 100 percent survivor benefit of $99 per month, the plan is not fully subsidizing the joint and survivor benefit.

A QPSA is fully subsidized if the participant's benefit is not reduced because of the QPSA coverage and the participant is not charged for the QPSA coverage. Therefore, a QPSA is fully subsidized in a defined contribution plan because the participant's account balance is not reduced by the QPSA coverage and no charge is made against the account for such coverage. [Reg. § 1.401(a)-20, Q&A 38]

Q. 9:31 When did the survivor annuity benefit requirements become effective?

The survivor annuity benefit provisions generally became effective for plan years beginning after 1984, but the spousal-consent rules (see Q. 9:21) became effective on January 1, 1985. Thus, a waiver by a participant made in 1985, but before the first day of the first plan year to which the survivor annuity benefit provisions apply, is not effective unless the participant's spouse subsequently consents to the election. A participant's election to waive the QPSA (see Q. 9:9), and spousal consent to the waiver made before August 23, 1984 (the effective date of REA), are not valid; a new election and consent must be executed by the participant and the participant's spouse. [REA §§ 302(a) and 303(c)(3); Reg. § 1.401(a)-20, Q&A 39, 43, and 44; *Letter Ruling 9008003; Lucaskevge v. Mollenberg*, 11 EBC 1355 (WD NY 1989); *The Manitowac Eng'g and Salaried Em-*

ployees' Deferred Profit Sharing Plan v. Powalisz, 8 EBC 1094 (D. Wis. 1987)]

Q. 9:32 Can a qualified retirement plan provide optional ways in which to pay benefits?

Yes. However, the optional forms of benefit provided by a qualified retirement plan must comply with IRS guidelines. Generally, each optional form of benefit must (1) be provided in a way that does not discriminate in favor of highly compensated employees (see Q. 4:28 and Q. 9:33 through Q. 9:40), and (2) be available to eligible employees without employer discretion (see Q. 9:41 through Q. 9:49). [IRC §§ 401(a)(4) and 411(d)(6); Reg. §§ 1.401(a)-4 and 1.411(d)-4; Prop. Reg. § 1.401(a)(4)-4]

If a plan offers optional forms of benefit, the different forms must be actuarially equivalent and the plan must specify the actuarial assumptions to be used in calculating the equivalent benefits. [IRC § 401(a)(25); *Rev. Rul. 79-90,* 1979-1 CB 155]

Q. 9:33 Can a plan permit optional forms of benefit payment that favor highly compensated employees?

No. A qualified retirement plan must provide benefits that do not discriminate in favor of highly compensated employees (see Q. 4:28). If a plan provides for optional forms of benefit payment, for example, different forms of distribution commencing at the same time or the same form of distribution commencing at different times, the availability of each of these optional forms of benefit payment is subject to this nondiscrimination requirement. This is true whether or not the particular benefit option is the actuarial equivalent (see Q. 2:14 and Q. 2:15) of any other form of benefit under the plan. To meet the nondiscrimination requirement, the optional form of benefit must be both currently available (see Q. 9:34) and effectively available (see Q. 9:35) in a nondiscriminatory manner. It is not necessary, however, to apply a nondiscriminatory test to the actual receipt of each optional form of benefit. [IRC § 401(a)(4); Reg. § 1.401(a)-4, Q&A 1 and 2; Prop. Reg. § 1.401(a)(4)-4]

Q. 9:34 How is the determination made as to whether the current availability of an optional form of benefit is nondiscriminatory?

An optional form of benefit must be currently available to a group of employees that satisfies one of the minimum coverage tests (see Q. 4:15). Generally, current availability is determined on the basis of current facts and circumstances. However, certain specified conditions on the availability of an optional form of benefit (e.g., minimum age or service, disability, or hardship) are disregarded in determining whether a benefit is currently available to an employee.

If an employer eliminates an optional form of benefit with respect to *future* benefit accruals, the current availability test is treated as satisfied for all years after the elimination if the optional form satisfied the nondiscrimination requirement immediately prior to its elimination.

> **Example**. A profit sharing plan that provides for a lump-sum distribution available to all employees on termination of employment is amended in 1990 to eliminate the lump-sum option with respect to benefits accrued after January 1, 1991. As of January 1, 1991, the lump-sum optional form of benefit is available to a group of employees that satisfies the ratio percentage test (see Q. 4:16). As of January 1, 1995, all nonhighly compensated employees who were entitled to the lump-sum optional form of benefit have terminated employment and taken a distribution of their benefits. The only remaining employees who are eligible to take a portion of their benefits in a lump sum on termination of employment are highly compensated employees. Because the availability of the lump-sum optional form of benefit satisfied the current availability test as of January 1, 1991, the availability of such optional form of benefit will be deemed to continue to satisfy the current availability test.

[Reg. § 1.401(a)-4, Q&A 2(a)(2) and (b); Prop. Reg. § 1.401(a)(4)-4]

Q. 9:35 How is the determination made as to whether the effective availability of an optional form of benefit is nondiscriminatory?

This determination must be based on all the surrounding facts and circumstances of the employer maintaining the plan. A condition with respect to the availability of a particular optional form of benefit payment violates the effective availability test if it substantially favors highly compensated employees (see Q. 4:28).

> **Example.** Amy Corporation maintains a qualified retirement plan in which all of its eligible employees participate. Under the plan, a participant is entitled to receive a retirement benefit at age 65. Also, an employee who terminates employment after age 55 with at least 30 years of service may also receive early retirement benefits. Both of Amy Corporation's highly compensated employees, but only two of Amy Corporation's eight non-highly compensated employees, may become eligible to receive early retirement benefits because they were hired before age 35. Even though the early retirement benefit is currently available to all participants, because age and service requirements are disregarded, it does not meet the effective availability test because the availability conditions substantially favor highly compensated employees. [Reg. § 1.401(a)-4, Q&A 2(a)(3); Prop. Reg. § 1.401(a)(4)-4]

Q. 9:36 May a qualified retirement plan deny a participant an optional form of benefit payment for which the participant is otherwise eligible?

No. Even though this type of provision may satisfy the nondiscrimination requirements in certain circumstances, such a provision impermissibly results in the employer or some person other than the participant having discretion as to the optional form of benefit payment (see Q. 9:43). [IRC § 411(d)(6)]

Q. 9:37   Will a qualified retirement plan be considered discriminatory if it requires that an involuntary distribution be made?

No. A qualified retirement plan will not be treated as discriminatory merely because it provides for an involuntary distribution if the present value of an employee's benefit is $3,500 or less (see Q. 9:72). Thus, a plan may require a lump-sum distribution to terminating employees whose benefits have a present value of $3,500 or any lower amount. However, this rule does not permit employer discretion in deciding whether or not to cash out involuntarily a terminating employee. [IRC §§ 411(a)(11) and 417(e); Reg. §§ 1.401(a)-4, Q&A 4 and 1.411(d)-4, Q&A 2(b)(2)(V); Prop. Reg. § 1.401(a)(4)-4]

Q. 9:38   What are the effective dates for the optional forms of benefit payment nondiscrimination rules?

The regulations on discrimination in optional forms of benefit payment became effective January 30, 1986, with respect to new plans, i.e., plans either adopted or made effective on or after such date.

With respect to existing plans, i.e., plans both adopted and in effect prior to January 30, 1986, the regulations are effective for the first day of the first plan year commencing on or after January 1, 1989. The delayed effective date for existing plans is applicable only if the optional form of benefit and any condition causing the availability of such optional form of benefit to be discriminatory were both adopted and in effect before January 30, 1986. Otherwise, the rules are effective with respect to such optional form of benefit payment as if the plan were a new plan. [Reg. § 1.401(a)-4, Q&A 6]

Before the issuance and finalization of the cited regulations, IRS had ruled that restrictions on the availability of a distribution option could result in prohibited discrimination. [Rev. Rul. 85-59, 1985-1 CB 135]

Q. 9:39 Can a qualified retirement plan containing discriminatory optional forms of benefits be amended?

Yes. If the availability of an optional form of benefit in an existing qualified retirement plan is discriminatory, the plan must be amended either to eliminate the optional form or to make the availability of the optional form nondiscriminatory. The availability of an optional form of benefit may be made nondiscriminatory by making the benefit available to a sufficient number of additional nonhighly compensated employees (see Q. 4:28) or by imposing nondiscriminatory objective criteria on its availability so that the group of employees to whom the benefit is available is nondiscriminatory. The plan sponsor may also amend the plan in that manner if the availability of an optional form of benefit may reasonably be expected to discriminate.

The plan sponsor must select one of the alternatives with respect to each affected optional form on or before the applicable effective date (see Q. 9:38) for the plan. This is an operational requirement and does not require a plan amendment prior to the date the plan must be amended to meet the requirements of TRA '86. [Reg. § 1.401(a)-4, Q&A 5]

Q. 9:40 Should the plan administrator provide any notice that the qualified retirement plan's optional forms of benefit are being modified?

Yes. Although there is no special reporting requirement regarding modification of a qualified retirement plan's optional forms of benefit, a plan administrator is required to file with DOL and to furnish to participants a summary of material modifications within 210 days after the close of the plan year in which the modification is adopted (see Q. 16:8 and Q. 16:9).

However, even before a modification is formally adopted, it is prudent for the plan administrator to give prompt notice of any such modification to participants. Giving prompt notice to participants would reconcile the conflict between ERISA's mandate that the plan be administered in accordance with the terms of its plan documents and IRS's operational requirement that the plan be administered consistent with a conforming plan amendment that has not yet been adopted. [ERISA §§ 104 and 404(a)(1)(D); DOL Reg. § 2520.104b-3]

Q. 9:41   What are Section 411(d)(6) protected benefits?

Accrued benefits, early retirement benefits, retirement-type subsidies, and optional forms of benefit are Section 411(d)(6) protected benefits that may not be eliminated, reduced, or made subject to employer discretion except to the extent permitted by regulations. (See Q. 8:27 for examples of benefits that are not Section 411(d)(6) protected benefits.)

An optional form of benefit is a form of distribution of benefits from a qualified retirement plan that is identical with respect to all features relating to the specified distribution form. The plan provides separate optional forms of benefit to the extent there are any differences in any features relating to the form of distribution, including payment schedule, timing, commencement, medium of distribution, portion of the benefit to which such distribution features apply, and election rights with respect to such features.

> **Example 1.** A plan permits each participant to receive a benefit under the plan as a lump-sum distribution, a level monthly distribution over 10 years, a single life annuity, a joint and 50 percent survivor annuity, a joint and 75 percent survivor annuity, a joint and 50 percent survivor annuity with a benefit increase for the participant if the beneficiary dies before a specified date, or a joint and 50 percent survivor annuity with a 10-year certain feature. Each of these forms of benefit payment is an optional form of benefit, whether or not their values are actuarially equivalent.

> **Example 2.** A plan provides a single life annuity that begins in the month of termination of employment and a single life annuity that begins after five consecutive one-year breaks in service (see Q. 4:10). They are optional benefit forms because they begin at different times.

Example 3. A profit sharing plan permits loans that are secured by an employee's account balance. In the event of default on such a loan, there is an execution on the account balance. Such execution is a distribution of the employee's accrued benefit under the plan. A distribution of an accrued benefit contingent on default under a plan loan secured by such accrued benefits is an optional form of benefit under the plan. [IRC § 411(d)(6); Reg. § 1.411(d)-4, Q&A 1]

Q. 9:42 Can a pattern of plan amendments result in an optional form of benefit?

Yes. Generally, benefits are considered to be provided as an optional form of benefit only if such optional form is provided under the terms of the qualified retirement plan. If, however, an employer establishes a pattern of repeated plan amendments providing for similar benefits in similar situations for limited periods of time, those benefits may be treated as provided under the terms of the plan without regard to the limited periods of time. For example, a pattern of repeated plan amendments making single sum distributions available only to certain participants for a limited period may result in single sum distributions being treated as provided under the terms of the plan to all participants, without regard to any restrictions provided by the terms of the plan. [Reg. § 1.411(d)-4, Q&A 1(c)]

Q. 9:43 Can a plan provide that the employer may, through the exercise of discretion, deny a participant an optional form of benefit?

Generally, no. A qualified retirement plan that permits an employer, through the exercise of discretion, to deny a participant a Section 411(d)(6) protected benefit (see Q. 9:41) violates the anticutback rule (see Q. 8:24). In other words, to the extent benefits have accrued, the discretionary denial of the optional form of the benefit is not permitted. In addition, a pension plan that permits employer discretion to deny the availability of a Section 411(d)(6) protected benefit will fail to satisfy the requirement that all benefits be definitely determinable. This is so even if the plan specifically limits the employer's discretion to choose among optional forms of benefit that are actuarially equivalent. However, a plan may permit limited administrative discretion (see Q. 9:45). [Reg. § 1.411(d)-4, Q&A 1 and 4(a)]

Q. 9:44 When is the exercise of discretion by persons other than the employer treated as employer discretion?

For the purposes of determining impermissible employer discretion, the employer is considered to include a plan administrator, fiduciary, trustee, actuary, independent third party, and other persons. Thus, if a qualified retirement plan permits any person—other than the participant and the participant's spouse—to exercise discretion to limit or deny the availability of an optional form of benefit, the plan violates these rules. [IRC §§ 401(a) and 411(d)(6); Reg. § 1.411(d)-4, Q&A 5]

Q. 9:45 What is the scope of the administrative discretion exception?

A qualified retirement plan may permit limited discretion with respect to the ministerial or mechanical administration of the plan, including the application of objective plan criteria specifically set forth in the plan. The following are examples of permissible provisions of limited administrative discretion:

1. Commencement of benefit payments as soon as administratively feasible after a stated date or event;

2. Employer authority to determine whether objective criteria specified in the plan (see Q. 9:46) have been satisfied; and

3. Employer authority to determine, pursuant to specific guidelines set forth in the plan, whether the participant or spouse is dead or cannot be located.

[Reg. § 1.411(d)-4, Q&A 4(b)]

Q. 9:46 May a plan condition the availability of a Section 411(d)(6) protected benefit on objective criteria that are specifically set forth in the plan?

The availability of a Section 411(d)(6) protected benefit (see Q. 9:41) may be limited to employees who satisfy certain objective conditions. The conditions must be ascertainable, clearly set forth in the qualified retirement plan, and not subject to the employer's discretion, except to the extent reasonably necessary to determine whether the objective conditions are met. In addition, the availability of the Section 411(d)(6) protected benefit must meet the nondiscrimination requirements.

For example, a plan may provide that the lump-sum benefit distribution option is not available to participants for whom life insurance is not available at standard rates. A plan may also provide that an otherwise permissible lump-sum distribution option may be available only in the event of extreme financial need, determined under standards specifically set forth in the plan. Another example is a provision making a lump-sum distribution available only upon the execution of a covenant not to compete, provided that the plan sets forth objective conditions with respect to employees required to execute a covenant, its terms, and the circumstances requiring execution of the covenant.

On the other hand, a plan may not condition the availability of Section 411(d)(6) protected benefits on factors that are within the employer's control. For example, the availability of an optional form of benefit payment from a defined benefit plan may not be conditioned on the level of the funding of the plan because the amount of plan funding is within the employer's discretion.

A plan may limit the availability of a Section 411(d)(6) protected benefit (e.g., a lump-sum distribution) in an objective manner. For example, a plan may provide that lump-sum distributions of $25,000 and less are available without limit, and lump-sum distributions in excess of $25,000 are available for a given year only to the extent that the total amount of such distributions for that year does not exceed $5 million. However, the plan must then also provide an objective and nondiscriminatory method for determining which particular lump-sum distributions will and will not be distributed because of the $5 million limitation. [Reg. § 1.411(d)-4, Q&A 6]

In a case decided before the IRS regulations were issued, a "good health standard" in terms of expected mortality for determining eligibility for lump-sum payments was satisfactory. [*Medei v. Bethlehem Steel Corp. and General Pension Board,* 617 F. Supp. 372 (ED Pa. 1985)]

Q. 9:47 May a plan be amended to add employer discretion, or other conditions restricting, the availability of a Section 411(d)(6) protected benefit?

No. The addition of employer discretion or restrictive conditions with respect to a Section 411(d)(6) protected benefit that has already accrued violates the anti-cutback rule. The addition of conditions, even if they are objective conditions, is impermissible if it results in any further restrictions. However, conditions and restrictions may be imposed prospectively to benefits accrued after the later of the adoption or effective date of the amendment. [Reg. § 1.411(d)-4, Q&A 7]

Q. 9:48 What are the effective dates of the Section 411(d)(6) protected benefit rules?

The final rules relating to Section 411(d)(6) protected benefits are effective January 30, 1986, but there are significant exceptions.

For existing plans, these rules became effective for the first day of the first plan year commencing on or after January 1, 1989. Plans that were adopted and in effect prior to August 1, 1986, are existing plans for this purpose.

For new plans, these rules are effective August 1, 1986. Plans that were adopted or made effective on or after August 1, 1986, are considered new plans for purposes of these rules. However, a new plan that received a favorable determination letter (see Q. 13:1) with respect to an application submitted prior to July 11, 1988, is treated as an existing plan with respect to Section 411(d)(6) protected benefits. [Reg. § 1.411(d)-4, Q&A 9]

Q. 9:49 Is there a transitional rule allowing amendment of plans containing prohibited discretion or consent provisions?

Yes. If an existing plan (see Q. 9:48) provides for employer discretion with respect to the availability of an optional form of benefit payment, the plan must be amended to eliminate such discretion or to eliminate the optional form of benefit payment subject to a consent or discretion provision.

Any amendment to eliminate employer discretion or an optional form of benefit payment must be applied in operation beginning on the applicable effective date (see Q. 9:48). If the plan satisfies the operational requirement, the plan amendment conforming to the operational procedure selected need not be adopted until the time plan amendments for TRA '86 must be adopted. [Reg. § 1.411(d)-4, Q&A 8]

Q. 9:50 May participants choose the way benefits will be paid to them?

Yes, if the qualified retirement plan itself provides alternatives, although the participant's spouse may have to consent (see Q. 9:21). Retirement benefits are taxed when paid, not if merely made available to the participant. Thus, a deferral of the receipt of benefits also defers the taxation of the benefits. [IRC § 402(a)(1)]

Q. 9:51 Is there a limitation on the amount of benefits that may be distributed to an individual in any one year?

No. However, there is a 15 percent tax on the amount of any excess distributions (see Q. 11:25 through Q. 11:36) made to any individual during any calendar year. [IRC § 4980A(a)]

Q. 9:52 When must benefit payments to a participant begin?

The plan must provide that, unless the participant elects to defer payment, payment of benefits to the participant will begin not later than the sixtieth day after the close of the plan year in which the latest of the following events occurs:

1. The participant reaches the plan's normal retirement age (see Q. 9:66) or age 65, whichever is earlier;

2. The tenth anniversary of the employee's participation in the plan is reached; or

3. The participant terminates service with the employer.

[IRC § 401(a)(14); Reg. § 1.401(a)-14(a)]

Q. 9:53 May a participant defer payment of benefits indefinitely?

No. The qualified retirement plan must provide that (1) the entire interest of the participant be distributed to the participant not later than the required beginning date (see Q. 9:54), or (2) the participant's interest be paid out in installments that start on or before the required beginning date. The installments must be paid over (1) the life of the participant, (2) the lives of the participant and the participant's designated beneficiary, or (3) a period not extending beyond the life expectancy of the participant or the joint life expectancies of the participant and the participant's designated beneficiary. [IRC § 401(a)(9)(A)]

Q. 9:54 What is the required beginning date?

For participants who reach age 70½ in 1989 or later, the required beginning date is April 1 of the calendar year following the calendar year in which the participant reaches age 70½. [IRC § 401(a)(9)(C)]

For participants who reached age 70½ before 1989, the determination of the required beginning date depended on whether the participant was a 5% owner (see Q. 20:28). For 5% owners, the required beginning date was the April 1 following the calendar year in which age 70½ was reached; for all other participants who attained age 70½ before 1988, the required beginning date is deferred until the April 1 following the calendar year in which the participant retires or becomes a 5% owner. A transitional rule applies to employees who are not 5% owners and who attained age 70½ in 1988. Those participants are treated as having retired in 1989, and their required beginning date was April 1, 1990. [IRC § 401(a)(9)(C); Prop. Reg. § 1.401(a)(9)-1, Q&A B-2; *Notice 89-42,* 1989-1 CB 683]

Q. 9:55 When does a participant attain age 70½?

A participant attains age 70½ as of the date six months after the participant's seventieth birthday. For example, a participant whose birthday is June 30, 1920 attains age 70½ on December 30, 1990, and a participant whose birthday is August 31, 1920 attains age 70½ on February 28, 1991. [Prop. Reg. § 1.401(a)(9)-1, Q&A B-3]

Q. 9:56 Can distributions be delayed until after the required beginning date?

Yes, but only if the participant made a valid election under Section 242(b)(2) of TEFRA before 1984. In that case, the participant can defer distributions until the participant actually retires. However, if the Section 242(b)(2) election is revoked after the participant's required beginning date, the total amount of distributions that would have been required by the revocation date (see Q. 9:57) must be distributed by the end of the calendar year after the year of revocation. [Prop. Reg. § 1.401(a)(9)-1, Q&A J-1 and J-4; *Notice 83-23,* 1983-2 CB 418]

A revocation of a Section 242(b)(2) election does not result from (1) the change in the employer's form of business from corporation to partnership, or (2) the revocation of the election with respect to another plan within a commingled trust. [*Letter Rulings 9013011* and *8938073*]

Q. 9:57 How much must be paid out each year?

If the employee's benefit is in the form of an individual account (e.g., defined contribution plans), the annual distribution must equal at least the quotient obtained by dividing the participant's applicable account balance by the applicable life expectancy. The applicable account balance is the account balance as of the plan's last valuation date in the calendar year immediately preceding the calendar year for which the distribution is being made. The applicable life expectancy is the life expectancy of the employee, or the joint life expectancies of the employee and the employee's designated beneficiary, if any (see Q. 9:58 and Q. 9:59).

A year for which a distribution must be made is called a distribution calendar year. Generally, the first distribution calendar year is the year in which the participant reaches age 70½ (see Q. 9:54 and Q. 9:56). The distribution for the first distribution calendar year must be made by April 1 of the following year. Distributions for subsequent distribution calendar years must be made by December 31 of such year. Thus, if the participant attains age 70½ in 1990 and defers the initial distribution until 1991, two minimum distributions must occur in 1991. The minimum distribution for 1990 must occur by April 1, 1991, and the minimum distribution for 1991 must occur by December 31, 1991. However, for purposes of calculating the December 31, 1991 minimum distribution, the applicable account balance is reduced by the amount of the required distribution for the first distribution calendar year actually made in 1991 by April 1, 1991. [Prop. Reg. § 1.401(a)(9)-1, Q&A F-1 and F-5]

Annuity distributions under a defined benefit plan must be paid in periodic payments at intervals not longer than one year, over (1) the life of the participant, (2) the lives of the participant and the participant's designated beneficiary, or (3) a period certain not extending beyond the life expectancy of the participant or the joint life expectancies of the participant and the participant's designated beneficiary. Once payment begins over a period certain, the period certain cannot be extended. Payments under the annuity must either be nonincreasing, or increase only under certain circumstances (e.g., in accordance with a specified cost-of-living index). The annuity may vary with the investment performance of the underlying assets. [Prop. Reg. § 1.401(a)(9)-1, Q&A F-3]

The amount distributed in satisfaction of the minimum distribution requirement is determined annually. No credit is given for amounts distributed in previous years that exceeded the required amount. [Prop. Reg. § 1.401(a)(9)-1, Q&A F-2]

Q. 9:58 How is life expectancy determined?

Life expectancy is calculated using the ages of the employee and the employee's designated beneficiary in the calendar year in which the employee attains age 70½ (or retires, if the required beginning date is deferred; see Q. 9:54). Unless life expectancy is being recalculated (see Q. 9:59), the life expectancy so calculated is reduced by one for each succeeding calendar year. Life expectancies must be determined by using the expected return multiples in Tables V (single life) and VI (joint lives) of Regulation § 1.72-9. If more than one individual is a designated beneficiary (e.g., the employee's children), the designated beneficiary with the shortest life expectancy is used to determine the applicable life expectancy. [Prop. Reg. § 1.401(a)(9)-1, Q&A E-1, 3, 4, and 5]

Q. 9:59 Can life expectancy be recalculated annually?

Yes. The life expectancy of the employee and/or the employee's spouse can be recalculated annually. The life expectancy of a beneficiary other than a spouse cannot be recalculated. The plan can either specify whether life expectancies will be recalculated or allow the employee to elect whether to recalculate life expectancy. The election becomes irrevocable as of the date of the first required distribution.

The employee's life expectancy (or the joint life expectancies of the employee and the employee's spouse) is recalculated annually by using the appropriate table (see Q. 9:58) to redetermine the employee's life expectancy (or the joint life expectancies of the employee and the employee's spouse), using the employee's (and spouse's) attained age on the employee's (and spouse's) birthdays in that year. Upon the death of the employee (or the employee's spouse), the recalculated life expectancy of the deceased employee or spouse will be reduced to zero in the year following the year the employee (or spouse) died, and the employee's entire remaining interest must be distributed in the year the last life expectancy is reduced to zero. [Prop. Reg. § 1.401(a)(9)-1, Q&A E-6, 7, and 8]

Q. 9:60 What distribution rules apply if the employee is a participant in more than one plan?

If the employee is a participant in more than one plan, the employee must receive a minimum distribution from each plan. [Prop. Reg. § 1.401(a)(9)-1, Q&A H-1]

Separate accounts under a plan are generally aggregated for purposes of the minimum distribution requirements. Aggregation is not required if different beneficiaries are designated for each separate account; in that event, each separate account may separately satisfy the requirements. [Prop. Reg. § 1.401(a)(9)-1, Q&A H-2]

Q. 9:61 If distributions to an employee have begun prior to the employee's death, how must remaining distributions to the employee's beneficiaries be made?

If the employee dies after distributions have begun, the remaining portion of the employee's benefits must be distributed to the beneficiary at least as rapidly as under the method of distribution in effect on the date of the employee's death. For this purpose, distributions are treated as having begun only if the employee dies after the required beginning date.

> **Example.** John retires in 1990 at age 65½ and begins receiving installment distributions from a plan over the joint life expectancies of John and his wife. Benefits are not treated as having begun until April 1, 1996 (the April 1 following the calendar year in which John will attain age 70½). Thus, if John dies before April 1, 1996 (his required beginning date), distributions to his wife must be made in accordance with the rules regarding distributions that begin after an employee has died (see Q. 9:62). However, if John made an irrevocable election at retire-

ment to receive distribution in the form of an annuity, distribution will be considered to have begun on the actual date payments started, even if John dies before his required beginning date. [IRC § 401(a)(9)(B)(i); Prop. Reg. § 401(a)(9)-1, Q&A B-4 and 5]

Q. 9:62 If distributions to an employee have not begun prior to death, how must distributions be made to the employee's beneficiaries?

If the employee dies before distributions begin, death benefits can be distributed in one of two methods.

The first method (the five-year rule) requires that the entire interest of the employee be distributed on or before December 31 of the year in which the fifth anniversary of the employee's death occurs. [IRC § 401(a)(9)(B)(ii); Prop. Reg. § 1.401(a)(9)-1, Q&A C-1 and 2]

The second method (the exception to the five-year rule) requires that the employee's benefit payable to a designated beneficiary be distributed over the beneficiary's life or over a period not extending beyond the beneficiary's life expectancy. If the beneficiary is not the employee's spouse, distributions must commence on or before December 31 of the year after the year in which the employee died. If the beneficiary is the employee's spouse, the first distribution can be deferred to December 31 of the year in which the employee would have reached age 70½. [IRC §§ 401(a)(9)(B)(ii) and 401(a)(9)(B)(iii); Prop. Reg. § 1.401(a)(9)-1, Q&A C-1 and 3]

The plan may adopt a provision specifying which method will apply to distributions after the employee's death. Alternatively, the plan may permit employees or beneficiaries to elect the method of distribution. If, however, the plan is silent as to which method applies if no election is made, distributions must be made in accordance with the exception to the five-year rule if the employee's beneficiary is the employee's spouse and, in all other cases, in accordance with the five-year rule. [Prop. Reg. § 1.401(a)(9)-1, Q&A C-4]

Q. 9:63   Is there a penalty for failure to make a required distribution?

Yes. A nondeductible excise tax is imposed on the payee (i.e., participant or beneficiary) of 50 percent of the difference between the amount required to be distributed (see Q. 9:57) and the amount actually distributed in any year. IRS may waive the excise tax if the payee establishes that the shortfall was due to reasonable error and that reasonable steps are being taken to correct the deficiency. The tax will not apply to distributions made in accordance with a properly executed Section 242(b)(2) election (see Q. 9:56). [IRC § 4974; Prop. Reg. § 54.4974-2, Q&A 2]

Q. 9:64   How does the incidental death benefits rule affect benefit distributions?

Any benefits payable to a beneficiary because of the participant's death must be incidental to the qualified retirement plan's primary purpose of providing retirement benefits to the participant (see Q. 12:4).

If a participant elects installment payments to himself or herself and a designated beneficiary, more than 50 percent of the entire projected distribution of benefits must be payable to the participant during the participant's lifetime. Further, if the designated beneficiary is the participant's spouse, and the spouse is substantially younger than the participant, this requirement may be applicable even if the form of distribution is a QJSA (see Q. 9:8). [Rev. Ruls. 72-240 and 72-241, 1972-1 CB 108; IRC §§ 401(a)(11) and 417]

A qualified retirement plan is generally required to provide an QPSA (see Q. 9:9) to the surviving spouse of a vested participant who dies before the annuity starting date. Since a QPSA is considered a part of the preretirement death benefit, both the QPSA and any other death benefit must be considered together to determine whether the total death benefits provided are incidental. If a plan provides a preretirement death benefit equal to 100 times the employee's projected monthly benefit and a QPSA, the incidental death benefits rule will be violated. This problem may be remedied by:

* Eliminating the preretirement death benefit; or
* Offsetting the preretirement death benefit by the value of the QPSA.

[*Rev. Rul. 85-15*, 1985-1 CB 132]

Q. 9:65 What is the minimum distribution incidental benefit requirement?

Distributions made during or after a participant's first distribution calendar year must satisfy the minimum distribution incidental benefit (MDIB) requirement and the incidental death benefits rule (see Q. 9:64) as well as the minimum distribution requirements (see Q. 9:57). Thus, distributions must satisfy both incidental requirements even if the amount required to be distributed under such requirements exceeds the amount required under the general minimum distribution rules. Prior to 1989, distributions were required to satisfy the minimum distribution requirements and either the incidental death benefits rule or the MDIB requirements.

For individual account and annuity distributions, the amount that must be distributed to meet the MDIB requirement is determined by dividing the employee's benefit by the applicable divisor specified in the proposed regulations. The applicable divisor is based on the joint life expectancies of the employee and a hypothetical individual ten years younger than the employee. However, if the employee's beneficiary on the required beginning date is the employee's spouse, satisfaction of the minimum distribution requirement (see Q. 9:57) will automatically satisfy the MDIB requirement. [IRC § 401(a)(9)(G); Prop. Reg. § 1.401(a)(9)-2, Q&A 1A-7]

Q. 9:66 What does the term normal retirement age mean?

Normal retirement age means the earlier of (1) the time specified in the plan as the normal retirement age, or (2) the later of the time a participant attains age 65 or the fifth anniversary of the participant's date of initial plan participation. A qualified retirement plan must provide that an employee's right to his or her benefits is nonforfeitable once the employee reaches the plan's normal retirement age (see Q. 8:12). [IRC §§ 411(a) and 411(a)(8)]

Ordinarily, a defined benefit plan uses a normal retirement age of 65. However, a plan will not fail to qualify merely because it provides for a normal retirement age earlier than 65. (Planning aspects relating to the use of a normal retirement age earlier than 65 are discussed in Q. 27:20.) [Rev. Rul. 78-120, 1978-1 CB 117]

Unlike defined benefit plans, the normal retirement age used by a defined contribution plan (Q. 2:2) other than a target benefit plan does not affect the company's plan contribution. Thus, for example, a profit sharing plan may permit a participant to retire at age 55 and receive full benefits under the plan at that time even if employees in the particular industry involved customarily retire at a later age. [Rev. Rul. 80-276, 1980-2 CB 131]

Q. 9:67 May benefits commence earlier than the deadlines required under the law?

Yes. The law and regulations only establish the time by which the plan must begin paying benefits (see Q. 9:52 and Q. 9:53). As long as participants are not treated in a discriminatory manner (see Q. 9:33 through Q. 9:40), benefits may begin earlier.

Plan benefits are taxed only when they are paid to the employee or a beneficiary. They are not taxed if they are merely made available (see Q. 9:50). It is not necessary, therefore, to draft a plan so that a participant does not have an absolute, unrestricted right to demand payment of benefits upon satisfying certain plan provisions. [IRC § 402(a)(1)]

Q. 9:68 May participants be subject to penalty for early distribution of benefits?

Yes. The individual's tax is increased by 10 percent of the amount distributed from a qualified retirement plan and includible in income, unless the distribution is:

1. Made on or after the date the employee attained age 59½;

2. Made to a beneficiary (or to the estate of the employee) after the death of the employee;

3. Attributable to the employee's disability;

4. Part of a series of substantially equal periodic payments (not less frequently than annually), made for the life (or life expectancy) of the employee or the joint lives (or joint life expectancies) of such employee and the employee's beneficiary, that begin after the employee separates from service and are not thereafter modified (other than by reason of death or disability) before the later of (a) the end of the five-year period that begins with the date of the first payment, or (b) the employee's attainment of age 59½ (see Q. 24:37);

5. Made to an employee after separation from service after attainment of age 55;

6. A dividend paid with respect to certain stock held by an Employee Stock Ownership Plan (ESOP) (see Q. 22:14);

7. A payment to an alternate payee pursuant to a QDRO (see Q. 28:1); or

8. An amount not in excess of the total expenses deductible for the year under Section 213 by the participant (determined without regard to whether the taxpayer itemizes deductions for the relevant taxable year).

[IRC § 72(t)]

Exceptions 5, 7, and 8 above are not applicable to a distribution from an individual retirement plan; and, for exception 4 to apply, separation from service is not required. (For rules governing early distributions from individual retirement plans, see Q. 24:37.)

The 10 percent penalty tax can be avoided if the early distribution qualifies for rollover treatment and it is rolled over into another qualified plan or an IRA. See Chapter 26 for more information on rollovers.

Q. 9:69 What type of election by the participant is required to postpone the commencement of benefits?

A qualified retirement plan that permits an election by a participant to postpone the receipt of benefits beyond the latest of the three dates referred to in Q. 9:52 must require that the election be made by submitting to the plan administrator a written statement (signed by the participant) describing the benefit and the date payments will begin. [Reg. § 1.401(a)-14(b)(2)]

However, an election to postpone the payment of benefits cannot be made if it would cause benefits payable under the plan, with respect to the participant, to begin after the required beginning date (see Q. 9:54) or to violate the incidental death benefits rule (see Q. 9:64). [IRC § 401(a)(9); Reg. § 1.401(a)-14(b)(3)]

Q. 9:70 May a participant receive benefit payments from a plan while still employed by the plan sponsor?

Yes, provided the participant has reached the plan's normal or early retirement age. [*Rev. Rul. 80-276*, 1980-2 CB 131; *Letter Rulings 8311071* and *8137048*]

Q. 9:71 Can a qualified retirement plan provide early retirement benefits?

Yes. However, if a defined benefit plan permits a participant to receive an early retirement benefit if the participant meets certain age and service requirements (e.g., age 55 and 30 years of service), the plan must also permit a former participant who fulfilled the service requirement, but separated from service before meeting the age requirement, to receive benefit payments when he or she meets the age requirement. [IRC § 401(a)(14); Reg. § 1.401(a)-14(C)]

> **Example.** A defined benefit plan provides a benefit of $100 a month at age 65, or an actuarially reduced benefit at age 55 for employees with 30 years of service who are still employed when they reach age 55. An employee who separates from service at age 50 with 30 years of service would have the right to actuarially reduced benefits at age 55.

A plan was permitted to pay a more valuable early retirement benefit to participants electing periodic payments than to participants electing single-sum distributions. Those electing single-sum distributions received the benefits they were entitled to, but they did not receive the supplemental payments made to the early retirees who elected to receive periodic payments. [*DeNobel v. Vitro Corp.*, 885 F2d 1180 (4th Cir. 1989)]

Q. 9:72 Can a qualified retirement plan make immediate distributions without the participant's consent?

A qualified retirement plan may provide for an involuntary, immediate distribution of the present value of the benefits under either a QJSA (see Q. 9:8) or a QPSA (see Q. 9:9) if the present value does not exceed $3,500. The plan may pay benefits in the form of a QJSA or a QPSA at any time after the benefits are no longer immediately distributable (see Q. 9:8), whether or not the present value exceeds $3,500. A plan may provide that a participant may elect a QJSA at any time without spousal consent. [Reg. § 1.417(e)-1(b)(1)]

No single-sum distribution may be made after the annuity starting date (see Q. 9:3) unless the participant (and spouse or surviving spouse, if applicable) consents in writing to the distribution, whether or not the present value exceeds $3,500. [IRC §§ 411(a)(11) and 417(e); Reg. §§ 1.411(a)-11(c)(3) and 1.417(e)-1(b)(2)]

Q. 9:73 What interest rate must be used to value benefits?

Generally, the interest rate used to value benefits is the applicable interest rate, which is the interest rate that would be used by PBGC for purposes of determining the present value of a lump-sum distribution on plan termination. [IRC § 417(e)(3)(B)] If a defined benefit plan uses interest rates in addition to the applicable interest rate to value benefits, the interest rate producing the greatest benefit must be used. [Reg. § 1.417(e)-1(d)(4)]

The applicable interest rate is used to value the participant's vested benefit if the present value of the benefit does not exceed $25,000, and 120 percent of that rate is used if the present value exceeds $25,000. (If 120% of the applicable interest rate is used, the present value cannot be less than $25,000.) Note that the applicable interest rate may be a series of interest rates. For example, the applicable interest rate could be 8 percent for the first 5 years over which the benefits are valued, 8.25 percent for the next ten years, and 8.5 percent for the following years. [Reg. § 1.417(e)-1(d)(2)]

Q. 9:74 Does a participant have to formally apply for benefits?

No. However, failure to apply for benefits would result in the participant receiving the benefit in the form of a QJSA, if applicable, or in the normal form of benefit under the terms of the plan, rather than an optional form of benefit that the participant might have preferred. If the participant has received notice of the QJSA and optional forms of benefit no less than 30 days and no more than 90 days after the annuity starting date (see Q. 9:3), a QJSA can be distributed without the participant's consent after the participant reaches normal retirement age (see Q. 9:66), or age 62, if later. [Reg. § 1.411(a)-11(c)(2)]

ERISA requires that every plan establish and maintain reasonable claims procedures, which must be described in the summary plan description (SPD) (see Q. 16:1). DOL regulations further provide that a claim is filed when the requirements of a "reasonable claim filing procedure" of a plan have been met. [DOL Reg. § 2560.503-1]

Q. 9:75 What are the participant's rights if a claim for benefits is denied?

If the claim for benefits is denied, either in part or in full, the plan administrator must furnish written notice to the participant or beneficiary explaining why the claim was denied. Moreover, the plan must afford a reasonable opportunity to the participant or beneficiary to have a full and fair review of that decision. [ERISA § 503]

Chapter 10

Tax Deduction Rules

One of the primary tax advantages of a qualified retirement plan is that a current deduction is allowed for the company's contributions to a plan that provides future benefits. This chapter examines when a contribution must be made in order to be deductible on a current basis and the limits set on the amount of a tax-deductible contribution.

Q. 10:1 What are the basic requirements for deducting employer contributions to a qualified retirement plan?

For such a contribution to be tax-deductible, it must be an "ordinary and necessary" business expense and must be compensation for services actually rendered. Thus, for example, a contribution on behalf of a stockholder may be made only if the stockholder is also an employee actually rendering services to the corporation. Also, the contribution, when considered together with the employee's regular compensation, must be "reasonable in amount" for the services rendered. Reasonable current compensation and the plan contribution may include additional amounts for previously uncompensated prior services. [IRC §§ 162 and 404; Reg. § 1.404(a)-1(b); *Bianchi*, 66 TC 324 (1976), *aff'd*, 533 F2d 93 (2d Cir. 1977)]

A contribution on behalf of a self-employed individual (see Q. 27:8) satisfies the ordinary-and-necessary business expense requirement if it does not exceed the individual's earned income for the year determined without regard to the deduction for the contribution (see Q. 27:10). [IRC § 404(a)(8); Reg. § 1.404(a)(8)-1T]

Q. 10:2 When must contributions be made to be currently deductible?

Tax-deductible contributions to a qualified retirement plan may be made at any time during the taxable year and *even after the end of the taxable year* up to the due date (including extensions) for the filing of the employer's federal income tax return for the particular year. Timely contributions made after the end of the taxable year are deductible for that taxable year if either (1) the employer designates in writing to the plan administrator or trustee that the contribution is for the preceding year, or (2) the employer claims the contribution as a deduction on its tax return for the preceding year. Such a designation, once made, is irrevocable. [IRC § 404(a)(6); *Rev. Rul. 76-28, 1976-1 CB 106*]

The employer's timely mailing of the contribution is adequate. Thus, a contribution mailed and bearing a postage cancellation date no later than the due date of the employer's tax return, including extensions, is timely even if the trust received it after such due date. [*Letter Ruling 8536085*]

A bookkeeping entry showing that a portion of the employer's certificate of deposit (CD) belonged to a qualified retirement plan as of the deadline for tax-deductible contributions is not timely payment of the contribution. [*Rollar Homes, Inc.*, 53 TCM 471 (1987)]

An employer mistakenly made out and mailed its plan contribution check for the taxable year to PBGC. The check was returned by PBGC, and the contribution was paid late. IRS ruled that the contribution was not timely made and, therefore, was not deductible for that taxable year. [*Letter Ruling 9031033*]

Q. 10:3 May a contribution be timely for tax deduction purposes but not for the minimum funding standards?

Yes. The rules regarding timeliness for tax deduction purposes are based on the employer's *taxable* year and are independent of the rules regarding timeliness for purposes of the minimum funding standards (see Q. 7:1), which are based on the *plan* year. Tax-deductible plan contributions may be made after the end of the taxable year if payment is made by the due date (including extensions) for filing the employer's federal income tax return for that taxable year (see Q. 10:2). For purposes of the minimum funding standards, contributions made after the end of the plan year may relate back to that year if they are made within 8½ months after the end of the plan year. [IRC § 412(c)(10)(A); Rev. Rul. 77-82, 1977-1 CB 121]

Q. 10:4 May an employer deduct the fair market value of property other than money contributed to its qualified retirement plan?

Yes. If property is contributed, the employer may deduct the fair market value of the property at the time of the contribution. However, if the fair market value exceeds the employer's basis in the property, the employer has a taxable gain equal to the excess. But if the basis exceeds the fair market value, there is no recognizable loss to the employer. [IRC §§ 267 and 1001; Rev. Rul. 75-498, 1975-2 CB 29; Rev. Rul. 73-583, 1973-2 CB 146; Rev. Rul. 73-345, 1973-2 CB 11]

If an employer purchases real estate from its qualified retirement plan for an amount in excess of the real estate's fair market value, such excess is considered a contribution to the plan. [Letter Ruling 8949076] However, that purchase by the employer or the contribution of property by an employer may be considered a prohibited transaction (i.e., a transfer, sale, or exchange of assets between a party in interest and the plan) in some circumstances (see Q. 18:8).

Q. 10:5 May an employer make a timely contribution to the qualified retirement plan by check?

Yes. The contribution will be considered timely even if the plan trustee receives payment after the deadline for a deductible contribution (see Q. 10:2) if the employer mails the check to the plan trustee before such deadline, the check is promptly presented for payment, and it is paid in the regular course of business. However, the contribution is not timely if the trustee delays presentation of the check because of the employer's financial problems. Also, the contribution was not considered timely in one case because the employer could not explain why the check was not negotiated until two weeks after the contribution deadline. [*Flomac, Inc.*, 53 TCM 305 (1987); *Walt Wilger Tire Co., Inc.*, 38 TCM 287 (1979); *Cain-White & Co., Inc.*, 37 TCM 1829 (1978)]

If the check bounces, no contribution is deemed to have been made. [*Springfield Productions, Inc.*, 38 TCM 74 (1979)]

Q. 10:6 Is a contribution of the employer's promissory note a deductible payment?

No. The employer must make a timely contribution in cash or its equivalent to obtain a tax deduction for its contribution for the current or preceding taxable year (see Q. 10:2). Since the contribution by the employer of its own promissory note is merely a promise to pay, it is not considered a payment of cash or its equivalent. [*Don E. Williams Co. v. U.S.*, 429 US 569 (1977); Rev. Rul. 80-140, 1980-1 CB 89]

A contribution of the employer's own promissory note is also a prohibited transaction (see Q. 18:1).

Q. 10:7 What is the primary limitation on tax-deductible contributions to a profit sharing plan? 401(k)

The primary limitation on tax-deductible contributions to a profit sharing plan is 15 percent of the total compensation (see Q. 10:13) paid to all participants during the taxable year. [IRC § 404(a)(3)(A); Reg. § 1.404(a)-9(c)] See Q: 10:13

Q. 10:8 How are excess amounts contributed to a profit sharing plan treated for tax purposes?

There is an excise tax imposed on the employer equal to 10 percent of the portion of any contribution to any qualified retirement plan that is not deductible (see Q. 10:9 through Q. 10:11). [IRC § 4972]

Amounts contributed in excess of the primary limitation (see Q.

10:7) are generally carried forward and may be deducted in later years. However, the total amount deductible in a later taxable year, including the contribution to the profit sharing plan for that year, is limited to 15 percent of the compensation of the participants in the later year. [IRC § 404(a)(3)(A); Reg. § 1.404(a)-9(e); Rev. Rul. 83-48, 1983-1 CB 93; Rev. Rul. 73-608, 1973-2 CB 147]

> **Example.** Elliot Corporation contributes $30,000 to its profit sharing plan in 1988, $32,000 in 1989, and $36,000 in 1990. If $27,000 is 15 percent of the total compensation paid to all participants in 1988, Elliot's deduction for 1988 would be limited to $27,000, and $3,000 ($30,000 − $27,000) would be carried over to later years. Elliot would be subject to an excise tax of $300 (10% × $3,000). If $33,000 is 15 percent of compensation in 1989, Elliot's deduction for 1989 is $33,000 ($32,000 + $1,000 carried over from 1988), and the excise tax would be $200 [10% × ($3,000 − $1,000)]. If $38,000 is 15 percent of compensation in 1990, Elliot's deduction for 1990 is $38,000 ($36,000 plus the remaining $2,000 carried over from 1988).

Q. 10:9 How is the amount of nondeductible contributions computed?

Nondeductible contributions are defined as the sum of (1) amounts contributed by an employer to a qualified retirement plan for a taxable year in excess of the amount allowable as a deduction for that taxable year, plus (2) the unapplied amounts from the preceding taxable year.

The unapplied amounts from the preceding taxable year are the amounts subject to the excise tax in the preceding taxable year reduced by the sum of (1) the portion that is returned to the employer during the taxable year, plus (2) the portion that is deductible during the current taxable year.

> **Example.** Rachel Corporation makes a nondeductible contribution of $100,000 for its 1989 taxable year. Rachel contributes $75,000 in 1990 when its deductible limit is $150,000. In 1991, it contributes $75,000 when its deductible limit is $100,000. Rachel must pay an excise tax of $10,000 for 1989 (10% ×

$100,000) and $2,500 for 1990 [10% × ($100,000 + $75,000 − $150,000)]. It owes no excise tax for 1991 [10% × ($25,000 + $75,000 − $100,000)]. [IRC § 4972(c)]

Q. 10:10 When are nondeductible contributions for a given taxable year determined?

Nondeductible contributions for purposes of the excise tax are determined as of the close of the employer's taxable year. If, however, a nondeductible contribution is returned by the due date of plan contributions for the year (see Q. 1:23 and Q. 10:2), the returned amount is not treated as a nondeductible contribution and is not subject to the tax (see Q. 10:9). [IRC § 4972(c)(3)]

For defined benefit plans, IRS may approve a request for the return of nondeductible contributions made to satisfy quarterly contribution requirements (see Q. 7:16) for plan years that began in 1989. The request must be made no later than 2½ months after the close of the plan year for which the deduction is disallowed (or July 31, 1990, if later). [*Rev. Proc. 89-35, 1989-1* CB 917; *Announcement 90-77, 1990-23* IRB]

Q. 10:11 What happens if a deduction for plan contributions is subsequently disallowed?

The excise tax applies to contributions for which the deduction is disallowed. [*General Explanation of TRA '86,* Title XI, D2, p. 748]

Q. 10:12 Can the employer make up a missed profit sharing plan contribution?

If an employer made less than the full 15 percent contribution (see Q. 10:7) in a taxable year beginning before January 1, 1987, it may carry over the unused difference, known as the unused pre-87 limitation carryforward, and make a larger tax-deductible contribution in a subsequent year, provided the plan is still qualified.

However, the combined regular deduction and unused pre-87 limitation carryforward may not exceed the lesser of (1) 25 percent of that year's total compensation, or (2) 15 percent of that year's compensation plus the total amount of the unused pre-87 limitation carryforward. Also, to avoid disqualifying the plan, the employer's contribution must be limited so that the amount allocated to any participant's account does not exceed the annual addition limitation (see Q. 5:1). [IRC §§ 401(a)(16) and 404(a)(3)(A)]

Q. 10:13 What does compensation mean for purposes of the limits on deductible contributions to a profit sharing plan?

Compensation generally includes the total compensation of all plan participants paid or accrued during the taxable year. Even if, for purposes of allocating employer contributions, the plan defines compensation as base salary only, other forms of compensation (e.g., overtime, bonuses, and commissions) are included for purposes of the profit sharing plan deduction limitations. [Reg. § 1.404(a)-9(b); Rev. Rul. 80-145, 1980-1 CB 89]

If a terminated employee does not receive a share of the employer's contribution for the year of termination, such employee's compensation is not included for deduction limitation purposes. [Dallas Dental Labs, 72 TC 117 (1979); Rev. Rul. 65-295, 1965-2 CB 148]

There is a $200,000 per participant compensation cap that applies to the computation of deductions. The $200,000 limit is adjusted for inflation and is $209,200 for 1990. [IRC § 404(l); IR 90-15 (Jan. 30, 1990)]

See Q. 10:25 for a discussion of the family aggregation rule.

Q. 10:14 May a company make a deductible contribution to the profit sharing plan of an affiliated company?

Yes. Although contributions to a profit sharing plan are not required to be based on profits (see Q. 2:6), a profit sharing plan may require profits in order to make a contribution. If a member of an affiliated group of corporations cannot make a contribution to its profit sharing plan because it has no current or accumulated earnings or profits, another member of the affiliated group may make a contribution for the employees of the unprofitable member. But the contribution is deductible only if both members participate in the same profit sharing plan; the contribution is not deductible if they maintain separate plans. [IRC §§ 404(a)(3)(B) and 1504; Reg. § 1.404(a)-10(a)(1)]

Q. 10:15 What is the limit on tax-deductible contributions to defined contribution plans other than profit sharing plans?

Generally, the deduction for defined contribution plans that are pension plans (e.g., money purchase and target benefit plans; see Q. 2:4 and Q. 2:5) is the amount necessary to meet minimum funding standards (see Q. 7:1). Thus, the deductible amount of the employer's contribution to a money purchase or target benefit pension plan is ordinarily the sum of amounts required to be contributed on behalf of each plan participant. [IRC § 404(a)(1)(A); Prop. Reg. § 1.412(b)-1(a)]

However, in computing the amount deductible for contributions to any type of defined contribution plan (see Q. 2:2), if the annual addition (see Q. 5:1) of any participant under the plan is more than the amount allowed by law, the excess amount of the company contribution will not be deductible (see Q. 10:23). [IRC § 404(j)(1)(B)]

> **Example.** Jeannie Corp. establishes a money purchase pension plan in 1990 for its only employee, Jeannie Jones. The plan provides a 25%-of-compensation contribution formula. Jones's compensation is $150,000 and the contribution under the formula is $37,500. The excess portion of the company's contribution for 1990 of $7,500 ($37,500 − $30,000) will not be deductible. In addition, the nondeductible contribution will be subject to a nondeductible 10 percent excise tax penalty (see Q. 10:8 and Q. 10:9).

Q. 10:16   What is the limit on tax-deductible contributions to a defined benefit plan?

Under the level cost method, the employer may deduct the amount needed to fund each employee's past and current service credits distributed as a level amount over the employee's remaining years of future service. If the amount attributable to three or fewer employees is more than 50 percent of the remaining costs, the unfunded costs for these employees must be spread over a period of at least five years. [IRC § 404(a)(1)(A)(ii)]

Under the normal cost method, the employer may deduct the normal cost of the plan plus the amount needed to amortize the unfunded portion of past service costs equally over ten years. [IRC § 404(a)(1)(A)(iii)]

If the contribution needed to satisfy the minimum funding requirement exceeds the amount calculated under either of these two methods (whichever the plan adopts), the deductible limit is the minimum funding amount. [IRC § 404(a)(1)(A)(i)]

No deduction is allowed for any contribution to fund a retirement benefit in excess of any participant's annual benefit limit (see Q. 10:23). [IRC § 404(j)(1)(A)]

In any event, the deductible limit cannot exceed the full funding limitation. [IRC § 404(a)(1)(A)]

For details, see Chapter 7.

Q. 10:17   How does a defined benefit plan's funding method affect its tax-deductible contributions?

The amount of deductible contributions cannot exceed the cost based on reasonable funding methods and actuarial assumptions. [IRC § 412(c)(3); Reg. § 1.404(a)-3(b)]

For example, a contribution calculated on the basis of an assumption that plan assets would earn interest at a rate of 5 percent was unreasonable in view of the availability of investments with a significantly higher interest rate. Further, the calculation under the normal cost method in a plan's first year of existence unreasonably failed to allocate costs between the normal cost of benefits accrued for service during the year of the contribution and the cost of benefits accrued during the year for past service, which must be amortized over ten years. [*Jerome Mirza & Assocs., Ltd. v. U.S.*, 882 F2d 229 (7th Cir. 1989); *Custom Builders, Inc.*, 58 TCM 696 (1989); *Letter Ruling 9030001*]

An assumption that employees will retire at the normal retirement age specified in the plan, ignoring the fact that employees normally retire later, may be unreasonable and result in a nondeductible contribution (see Q. 2:14). [*Rev. Rul. 78-331*, 1978-2 CB 158]

Q. 10:18 Are excess amounts contributed to a defined benefit plan deductible in later years?

The excess contributions may be carried over and deducted in later years. For example, suppose that for 1989 the maximum deduction is $20,000 and the employer contributes $25,000 to the plan. There is a $5,000 carryover that is tax-deductible only in a later year in which a full contribution is not made. So, if in 1990 the maximum deduction is $22,000 and the employer contributes $20,000 to the plan, $2,000 of the $5,000 carryover can be deducted for that year. [IRC § 404(a)(1)(E)]

Excess amounts contributed to a defined benefit plan (or any other qualified retirement plan) are subject to an excise tax equal to 10 percent of the nondeductible contributions (see Q. 10:9 and Q. 10:10). [IRC § 4972]

Q. 10:19 Are there any special limits on tax-deductible contributions if an employer maintains both a defined contribution plan and a defined benefit plan?

If no employee is covered by both plans, the regular deduction limitations apply with respect to each plan. But, if at least one employee is covered by any combination of defined contribution and defined benefit plans maintained by the same employer, a special deduction limitation applies: the greater of (1) 25 percent of the aggregate compensation of all participants, or (2) the amount necessary to meet the minimum funding standard for the defined benefit plan (see Q. 7:1). This limitation is applied after the regular limitations have been determined for each plan. [IRC § 404(a)(7)]

> **Example.** Elliot Corporation maintains a defined benefit plan and a money purchase pension plan. Elliot's employees participate in both plans. In 1990, Elliot must make a contribution equal to 30 percent of the participant's aggregate compensation to fund both plans. The contribution to the defined benefit plan is an amount equal to 20 percent of the participant's aggregate compensation. Elliot will not be able to deduct the full amount of both contributions, and the portion that is not deductible (5% of aggregate compensation) is subject to an excise tax (see Q. 10:9 and Q. 10:10).

To alleviate the impact of the paired plan deduction limitation and the excise tax on nondeductible contributions, the defined contribution plan may provide that required contributions will be limited to amounts that are deductible.

Aggregate compensation includes the total compensation paid or accrued during the taxable year of all employees who are participants in either the defined benefit plan or the defined contribution plan, or both (see Q. 10:13). [Reg. § 1.404(a)-13(a)]

If an employee is covered by both a defined contribution plan and a defined benefit plan, a special rule governs the overall benefits of the employee (see Q. 5:12).

See Q. 10:25 for a discussion of the family aggregation rule.

Q. 10:20 Are there any other limitations on the deductibility of employer contributions?

Yes. For certain employers engaged in the production of property or the acquisition of property for resale, the uniform capitalization rules require the capitalization of a portion of contributions to various employee benefits plans, including qualified retirement plans. [IRC § 263A]

Essentially, an employer covered by the uniform capitalization rules that maintains a qualified retirement plan must first calculate its otherwise allowable deductible contribution under the generally applicable limits under Section 404 and then allocate that amount between production or inventory costs, which must be capitalized, and other costs, which are deductible. OBRA '87 repealed an exception that had exempted past service costs from the capitalization requirements. The effective date of this change generally requires that past service costs incurred after December 31, 1987, be capitalized. [IRC § 263A(a); *General Explanation of TRA '86*, Title VIII, D, p. 513; *Notice 88-86*, 1988-2 CB 401]

Q. 10:21   Will excess assets of an employer's overfunded defined benefit plan that are transferred to a defined contribution plan be considered taxable income to the employer?

Yes. However, the employer may deduct the amount transferred as a contribution to the defined contribution plan, subject to applicable deduction limits (see Q. 10:7 and Q. 10:15). [GCM 39744 (1988)]

> **Example.** JCS Corporation maintains two qualified retirement plans: a defined benefit plan that is overfunded, and a profit sharing plan. JCS terminates its defined benefit plan; and, after all benefits are paid to plan participants, it transfers the defined benefit plan's excess assets to the profit sharing plan. JCS deducted all of its contributions to the defined benefit plan when made. JCS must recognize income upon the transfer from the defined benefit plan to the profit sharing plan. JCS will be entitled to a deduction for the transferred funds if its contribution to the profit sharing plan during the year of the transfer and the amount of transferred funds are less than or equal to 15 percent of the compensation of plan participants.

Also, although GCM 39744 does not specifically address the question, it appears that the amount transferred from the defined benefit plan would also be subject to the 15 percent excise tax on reversions (see Q. 19:48) unless the defined contribution plan is an ESOP. [IRC § 4980]

Q. 10:22   Are excess amounts contributed to a combination of plans deductible?

If an amount is contributed by the employer to both a defined benefit plan and a defined contribution plan in excess of the deduction limitation (see Q. 10:19), the excess contribution may be deducted in the succeeding taxable years. However, the total deduction in any succeeding year, including the contributions for that year, is limited to 25 percent of the compensation of the participants during that year. [IRC § 404(a)(7)(B); Reg. § 1.404(a)-13(c)]

Excess amounts contributed to any qualified retirement plan (or combination of plans) are subject to an excise tax equal to 10 percent of the nondeductible contributions (see Q. 10:9). [IRC § 4972]

Q. 10:23   May an employer deduct contributions to provide benefits to a participant in excess of Section 415 limits?

No. The deductible limit for a contribution to a defined contribution plan is reduced to the extent the contribution produces an annual addition in excess of the Section 415 limit for the year. Similarly, no deduction is allowed for the portion of a contribution to a defined benefit plan to fund a benefit for any participant in excess of the annual benefit limitation for the year. For details on contribution and benefit limits, see Chapter 5. [IRC § 404(j)(1)]

In calculating the contribution to a defined benefit plan, anticipated cost-of-living increases in the allowable annual retirement benefit (see Q. 5:5) cannot be taken into account before the year in which the increase first becomes effective. [IRC § 404(j)(2); *Feichtinger*, 80 TC 239 (1983)]

> **Example**. SS Corporation sponsors a defined benefit plan for its only employee, Steve Smith, who is currently age 55 and has average annual compensation for plan purposes of $120,000. The plan provides an annual retirement benefit of 100 percent of compensation in the form of a straight life annuity at the normal retirement age of 65. Any portion of the company's contribution for the 1990 year that funds the excess

benefit of \$17,418 (\$120,000 − \$102,582) will not be deductible and will be subject to a 10 percent excise tax. That result is not changed by the fact that it is reasonable to project that Steve will be entitled to receive an annual benefit of \$120,000 at retirement due to cost-of-living increases in the allowable annual retirement benefit.

Q. 10:24 Are the employer's payment of plan expenses deductible?

Many qualified retirement plans provide that general administrative expenses may be paid from plan assets unless paid by the employer. If the employer pays the administrative fees (e.g., the fees of trustees and actuaries) directly, or indirectly by reimbursing the trust, the amounts paid are deductible under Section 162 or Section 212 to the extent they satisfy the requirements of those sections. [Rev. Rul. 84-146, 1984-2 CB 61; Letter Rulings 9001002, 8941010, 8941009, 8940014, 8940013]

However, brokers' commissions incurred in connection with non-recurring transactions such as the purchase and sale of plan assets are not separately deductible under Section 162 or Section 212. Instead, amounts paid by the employer directly to the broker, or indirectly to the trust as reimbursement for the brokers' commissions, are treated as having been contributed to the trust and used to provide benefits. Consequently, such contributions are deductible, subject to the limits of Section 404. [Rev. Rul. 86-142, 1986-2 CB 60]

Q. 10:25 How does the family aggregation rule affect the employer's tax deduction?

Generally, no more than \$200,000 of compensation for each participant may be taken into account in determining the limit on deductible contributions (see Q. 10:13). In addition, the compensation of an employee who is either a 5% owner or one of the ten most highly compensated employees of the employer is aggregated with the compensation of the family members of such employee, and the \$200,000 limit is applied to the total compensation of all family members. For this purpose, the employee's family includes the employee's spouse and lineal descendants who have not attained age 19 before the end of the year. [IRC §§ 404(l) and 414(q)(6)]

Example. Delta Corporation adopts a profit sharing plan for calendar year 1990. There are four participants—husband Dean ($200,000), wife Debbie ($200,000), 18 year old daughter Denise ($30,000), and 17 year old son Don ($10,000). The maximum tax deductible contribution is limited to $31,380 ($209,200 × 15%) (see Q. 10:7), which will be allocated among the family members as follows:

Dean	$14,264
Debbie	14,264
Denise	2,139
Don	713
Total	$31,380

The family aggregation rule does not apply to the annual addition limitation (see Q. 5:1 and Q. 5:18), so the total family contribution can exceed $30,000.

Chapter 11

Taxation of Distributions

The form and time of payment of distributions from a qualified retirement plan depend primarily on the type of plan. Defined benefit plans generally pay benefits in the form of an annuity on the participant's early or normal retirement date. Defined contribution plans generally pay benefits in a single lump-sum payment upon the participant's termination of employment. Some retirement plans also permit participants to receive distributions prior to their retirement or termination of employment as in-service withdrawals or loans. This chapter discusses the tax treatment of the various forms of distribution.

Q. 11:1   In general, how are distributions from qualified retirement plans taxed?

Generally, all distributions from qualified retirement plans are includible in the recipient's gross income when received. The taxation of a distribution that qualifies as a qualified total distribution (see Q. 26:8) or a partial distribution (see Q. 26:10) may be postponed through a tax-free rollover to an individual retirement account (IRA) or another qualified retirement plan. (See Chapter 26 for more details.) In some cases, favorable tax treatment may be available for a lump-sum distribution (see Q. 11:4). A distribution received from a qualified retirement plan in the form of a loan will not be taxable if certain requirements are met (see Q. 11:38 through Q. 11:42). [IRC §§ 72 and 402]

In certain instances, penalty taxes are imposed on distributions that exceed certain amounts (see Q. 11:25) and distributions that commence too early (see Q. 9:68) or too late (see Q. 9:63).

Distributions to beneficiaries generally are also included in the deceased participant's estate for federal estate tax purposes. Such distributions may also be subject to penalty taxes if they exceed certain amounts (see Q. 11:37).

Q. 11:2 Are any distributions from qualified retirement plans income tax-free?

Yes, if the participant has an investment in the contract (also known as basis). [IRC §§ 72(b) and 72(c)]

A participant's investment in the contract or basis includes:

- The participant's after-tax contributions to the qualified retirement plan (i.e., voluntary or mandatory contributions).
- PS-58 costs (see Q. 12:7 and Q. 12:13).
- Loans from the qualified retirement plan to the participant that were treated as taxable distributions (see Q. 11:38 through Q. 11:42).

Q. 11:3 How are annuity payments from a qualified retirement plan taxed?

Annuity payments from a qualified retirement plan under which the participant has no investment in the contract or basis (see Q. 11:2) are taxed as ordinary income in the year received by the participant or beneficiary. [IRC § 72(m)]

If a participant has basis, a portion of each distribution is considered a return of the participant's investment in the contract and is therefore not taxable. The following formula applies to determine the part of each payment that is excluded from taxable income.

$$\frac{\text{Investment in the contract}}{\text{Expected return under the annuity}} \times \text{Annual annuity payment}$$

The expected return is determined at the time the payments commence on the basis of unisex life expectancy tables. The ratio of the participant's investment in the contract to the expected return under the contract is then applied to each annuity payment to derive the nontaxable portion. [IRC §§ 72(b)(1) and 72(e)(8); Reg. § 1.72-9; Notice 88-118, 1988-2 CB 450]

The participant may not exclude from income an amount greater than the participant's investment in the contract. Thus, once the participant recovers the entire basis, all remaining payments are fully taxable. [IRC § 72(b)(2)]

If the participant dies before recovering the entire investment in the contract, the unrecovered basis can be deducted on the participant's last income tax return. [IRC § 72(b)(3)]

Q. 11:4 What is a lump-sum distribution?

A lump-sum distribution is a distribution from a qualified retirement plan of the balance to the credit of an employee (see Q. 11:5) made within one taxable year of the recipient. The distribution must be made on account of the employee's death, attainment of age 59½, separation from service (except for self-employed individuals; see Q. 27:8), or disability (self-employed individuals only). [IRC § 402(e)(4)(A)]

A distribution will not qualify as a lump-sum distribution unless the employee was a plan participant for at least five of the employee's taxable years prior to the year of distribution. This requirement does not apply to a beneficiary receiving a distribution after the participant's death. [IRC § 402(e)(4)(H); Prop. Reg. § 1.402(e)-2(e)(3); Deisenroth, 58 TCM 838 (1989); Letter Ruling 8805025]

Lump-sum distributions may qualify for favorable income tax treatment (see Q. 11:12). Further, the participant (or surviving spouse) may elect to defer payment of taxes by rolling over the distribution into an IRA or another qualified retirement plan. See Chapter 26 for details.

Q. 11:5 What does the term balance to the credit of an employee mean?

Balance to the credit of an employee means either the vested (nonforfeitable) account balance that will be distributed from a defined contribution plan (see Q. 2:2) or the vested (nonforfeitable) accrued benefit that will be distributed from a defined benefit plan (see Q. 2:3).

In determining whether a distribution is the balance to the credit of the employee, all qualified profit sharing plans must be aggregated, all qualified stock bonus plans must be aggregated, and all qualified pension plans (defined benefit, money purchase, and target benefit plans) must be aggregated. Because only similar plans of the employer are required to be aggregated, a distribution to the employee from a profit sharing plan may qualify as a lump-sum distribution even though the employee still has an interest in a pension plan maintained by the employer. [IRC § 402(e)(4)(C)]

Only the vested portion of an employee's account balance or accrued benefit is taken into account in determining the balance to the credit. For this purpose, amounts attributable to deductible employee contributions (see Q. 11:24) are ignored. Accordingly, a partially vested employee who receives a distribution of the entire vested balance may qualify for lump-sum distribution tax treatment. However, if the employee is reemployed and is credited with additional vesting with respect to the employee's preseparation benefits, the tax benefits the employee received earlier will be recaptured. [IRC §§ 402(e)(4)(A) and 402(e)(6)(B)]

The balance to the credit does not include amounts payable to an alternate payee under a qualified domestic relations order (QDRO). See Chapter 28. [IRC § 402(e)(4)(M)]

To qualify as a lump-sum distribution, the balance to the credit of the employee must be paid within one taxable year of the recipient. Thus, if more than one payment is planned, all the payments must be made within the same calendar year (most individuals are calendar-year taxpayers). However, if an individual receives lump-sum distributions from both a pension plan and a profit sharing plan of the same employer in the same taxable year, the individual must elect forward averaging treatment for both distributions or neither will qualify for forward averaging. The same rule applies if an individual receives lump-sum distributions from qualified retirement plans of different employers in the same taxable year. [IRC §§ 402(e)(4)(A) and 402(e)(4)(B); *Blyler*, 67 TC 878 (1977); *Letter Ruling 9003061*]

Q. 11:6 Can an employee who received installment payments later receive a lump-sum distribution from the same qualified retirement plan?

No. If an employee separates from service, receives benefits in installment payments, and then takes the balance to the employee's credit under the qualified retirement plan in a subsequent taxable year in lieu of the remaining installment payments, the payout will not qualify as a lump-sum distribution. [Prop. Reg. § 1.402(e)-2(d)(1)(ii)(C); *Letter Ruling 8917020*]

Q. 11:7 Are the tax benefits of a lump-sum distribution lost when an additional distribution is made in a subsequent taxable year?

Not necessarily. If a distribution constituted the balance to the credit of the employee at the time it was made and all other requirements are satisfied (see Q. 11:4 and Q. 11:5), it is treated as a lump-sum distribution even if additional amounts are credited and distributed to the employee in a later taxable year. The additional distribution, however, is not a lump-sum distribution. [Prop. Reg. § 1.402(e)-2(d)(1)(ii)(B); *Rev. Rul. 69-190*, 1969-1 CB 131; *Rev. Rul. 56-558*, 1956-2 CB 290; *Letter Rulings 9009055* and *8952010*]

Q. 11:8 What does separation from service mean?

Separation from service and termination of employment are synonymous. Separation from service does not occur when the employee continues on the same job for a different employer as a result of a corporate transaction (i.e., merger or sale) or continues on the same job for the same employer after the sale of a shareholder's shares. [*Dickson*, TCM 1990-177; *Edwards v. Commissioner*, No. 89-2833 (4th Cir. 1990); *Rev. Rul. 80-129*, 1980-1 CB 86; *Rev. Rul. 79-336*, 1979-2 CB 187; *Rev. Rul. 81-141*, 1981-1 CB 204; *Rev. Rul. 81-26*, 1981-1 CB 200; *Letter Ruling 8441071*]

Distribution need not be made in the year of the employee's termination of employment to be considered made "on account of" the employee's separation from service. Thus, distributions from qualified retirement plans that permit distributions to be deferred until a specified age or time may qualify as lump-sum distributions. [*Letter Rulings 8949102, 8541094, and 8541116*]

A distribution to a self-employed individual (see Q. 27:8) cannot qualify as a lump-sum distribution solely by reason of separation from service. [IRC § 402(e)(4)(A); *Letter Ruling 8945053*]

Q. 11:9 Can a distribution from a qualified retirement plan to a disabled employee qualify as a lump-sum distribution?

No, unless the employee terminates employment at that time (see Q. 11:8). On the other hand, a distribution from a qualified retirement plan to a disabled self-employed individual (see Q. 27:8) can be a lump-sum distribution. [IRC § 402(e)(4)(A)]

Although two courts [*Wood*, 590 F2d 321 (9th Cir. 1979); *Masterson v. U.S.*, 478 F. Supp. 454 (DC Ill. 1979)] have ruled that amounts paid to a disabled employee under the disability retirement provisions of a qualified retirement plan are tax-free disability payments, IRS and other courts have ruled that such amounts are taxable. [IRC § 105(c); *Rev. Rul. 85-105*, 1985-2 CB 53; *Berman*, 58 TCM 916 (1989); *Beisler v. Commissioner*, 787 F2d 1325 (9th Cir. 1986); *Mabry*, 50 TCM 336 (1985); *Caplin v. U.S.*, 718 F2d 544 (2d Cir. 1983); *Christensen v. U.S.*, 7 EBC 1110 (D. Minn. 1986); *Gibson*, No. 83-2682 GA (WD Tenn. 1986)]

Q. 11:10 How is a lump-sum distribution from a qualified retirement plan to the beneficiary of a deceased participant taxed?

If the beneficiary is the surviving spouse of the deceased participant, the same options that would have been available to the participant (see Q. 11:12) are available to the spouse. Other beneficiaries have the same options, *except* they cannot take advantage of a tax-free rollover to an IRA (see Q. 26:6). [IRC §§ 402(a)(7) and 402(e)(4)]

The five-year participation requirement (see Q. 11:4 and Q. 11:12) for electing forward averaging does not apply to distributions due to death. [IRC § 402(e)(4)(H)]

Q. 11:11 Can the beneficiary of a deceased participant who received annuity payments from a qualified retirement plan receive a lump-sum distribution?

Yes. A distribution to an employee before the employee's death, in the form of annuity payments after retirement, will not prevent the employee's beneficiary from receiving a lump-sum distribution. [Prop. Reg. § 1.402(e)-2(d)(1)(ii)(B); *Rev. Rul. 69-495*, 1969-2 CB 100]

Q. 11:12 How is a lump-sum distribution from a qualified retirement plan to an employee taxed?

An employee who has attained age 59½ and who has completed at least five years of plan participation prior to the year of distribution has four income tax options:

1. The ordinary income portion of the distribution (amount attributable to post-1973 plan participation) might qualify for five-year forward averaging, and the rest of the distribution (amount attributable to pre-1974 plan participation) might qualify as long-term capital gain. (See Q. 11:17 and Q. 11:19.)

2. The entire distribution may be reported as ordinary income and might qualify for five-year forward averaging (see Q. 11:17).

3. The entire distribution may be reported as ordinary income without electing five-year forward averaging. [IRC § 402(a)(1)]

4. All or part of the distribution may be rolled over to an IRA or to another qualified retirement plan; no tax is paid on the amount rolled over; and the rest is taxed as ordinary income without the availability of electing five-year forward averaging. [IRC § 402(a)(5)]

For options available when the participant has not satisfied the five-year participation requirement, see Q. 11:14.

An individual who receives a lump-sum distribution and who had attained age 50 before January 1, 1986, is eligible to elect special tax treatment (see Q. 11:13).

If more than one lump-sum distribution is received in a single taxable year, all such distributions received that year must be aggregated, and the election to use forward averaging will apply to the aggregate amount. Only one election to use forward averaging treatment is permitted after the employee has attained age 59½. If the employer maintains more than one qualified retirement plan, special rules apply. (See Q. 11:5.) [IRC §§ 402(e)(4)(A), 402(e)(4)(B), and 402(e)(4)(C)]

Q. 11:13 What special rules apply to a lump-sum distribution with regard to an individual who had attained age 50 before January 1, 1986?

If an individual who had attained age 50 before January 1, 1986, receives a lump-sum distribution, neither the requirement that an individual be at least age 59½ (see Q. 11:12) to use forward averaging tax treatment nor the phase-out of the capital gains tax treatment of the pre-1974 portion of the distribution (see Q. 11:19) will apply.

Forward averaging can be either five-year averaging at the rates in effect at the time of distribution or ten-year averaging at the rates in effect during 1986. Under either alternative, capital gains will be taxed at a flat 20 percent rate.

Only one election to use forward averaging (and capital gains treatment) is permitted. Thus, an individual who makes an election under the special rule for individuals who attained age 50 before January 1, 1986, will be unable to make another election under the general rule after attaining age 59½. [TRA '86 §§ 1122(h)(5), 1122(h)(3)(A)(ii), and 1122(h)(3)(B)(ii)]

Q. 11:14 What tax options are available when a participant does not satisfy the five-year participation requirement?

Forward averaging is not an option, so only two tax choices are available:

1. A tax-free rollover into an IRA or another qualified retirement plan, or

2. Inclusion of the distribution in gross income for the year of receipt.

Q. 11:15 What portion of a lump-sum distribution is taxable?

Several adjustments that reduce the taxable amount of a lump-sum distribution are made before any tax is computed. The amount of the employee's investment in the contract (see Q. 11:2) is subtracted from the distribution in computing the taxable amount. If any part of the distribution is made in employer securities, special rules apply (see Q. 11:16).

If the recipient elects to use forward averaging, a minimum distribution allowance reduces the tax on relatively small distributions. The allowance, which is subtracted in computing the taxable amount of the payout, is the lesser of $10,000 or one-half of the total taxable amount of the payout, reduced by 20 percent of the excess of the total amount over $20,000. In effect, there is no minimum distribution allowance if the total taxable amount is $70,000 or more. [IRC § 402(e)(1)(D)]

> **Example.** Assume Sallie receives a lump-sum distribution of $50,000 in cash from a qualified retirement plan, has no basis, and the entire payment is ordinary income (i.e., attributable to post-1973 plan participation). The minimum distribution allowance is the lesser of $10,000 or one-half the total taxable amount. Because it is less than $25,000 (i.e., one-half of $50,000), the $10,000 figure applies. The $10,000 figure is then reduced by 20 percent of the excess of the taxable amount of

the payment over $20,000, or $6,000 (20% of $30,000). This makes the minimum distribution allowance $4,000 and the taxable amount of the distribution $46,000.

Q. 11:16 What is the tax treatment of a lump-sum distribution made in the form of employer securities?

Special rules apply to appreciated stock or other securities of the employer that are included in a lump-sum distribution. The gain on the securities while they were held by the qualified retirement plan (the net unrealized appreciation) is not subject to tax until the securities are sold by the recipient, at which time the gain is eligible for capital gains treatment. The basis of the securities (the value when contributed to the plan) is includible in income upon distribution. If the value of the securities at the time of distribution is less than basis, the total value of the securities is taxable in accordance with the general rules applicable to lump-sum distributions. [IRC § 402(e)(4)(D); Prop. Reg. § 1.402(a)-1(b)(1); Reg. § 1.402(a)-1(b)(2)]

The recipient of a distribution that includes employer securities may elect to have the net unrealized appreciation included in income at the time the distribution is received rather than taxed as a capital gain at the time the securities are sold. This election is made on the recipient's tax return for the year in which the distribution is received. [IRC § 402(e)(4)(J); Notice 89-25 (Q&A 1), 1989-1 CB 662]

Q. 11:17 How is the tax on a lump-sum distribution computed using the five-year averaging method?

The tax computed using the five-year averaging method is separate from and in addition to the regular income tax. To avoid double taxation, the ordinary income portion is deducted from the recipient's gross income. The tax on lump-sum distributions for which five-year averaging is elected is computed using IRS Form 4972.

There are three basic steps in computing the tax on ordinary income using five-year averaging.

Step one: Subtract the minimum distribution allowance (see Q. 11:15) from the ordinary income portion of the distribution.

Step two: Divide the net amount determined in Step one by 5 and compute the initial separate tax on this figure using the rate table for single individuals (regardless of the recipient's marital status).

Step three: Multiply the initial separate tax determined in Step two by 5.

Multiple lump-sum distributions received during the current year and the five preceding taxable years (for which forward averaging was elected) are added together in computing the tax using the five-year averaging method. The resulting tax is reduced by taxes paid with respect to the ordinary income tax portions of the earlier distributions. The effect of this six-year look-back rule is to increase the tax rate applied to the current year's distribution. Because of this look-back rule, tax savings can result from delaying the receipt of a lump-sum distribution so that an earlier distribution falls outside the six-year period. Note, however, that *only one* election to use forward averaging may be made after 1986.

[IRC §§ 402(e)(1)(B), 402(e)(2), and 402(e)(3)]

Q. 11:18   How is the tax on a lump-sum distribution computed using the ten-year averaging method?

Ten-year forward averaging is available only if the participant had attained age 50 before January 1, 1986 (see Q. 11:13). Since ten-year forward averaging remains keyed to the 1986 income tax rates, the following schedule may be used to calculate the tax on a lump-sum distribution for which this averaging method is elected:

If the adjusted total taxable amount is:		*The ten-year averaging tax is:*		
At least	*But not over*	*This amount*	*Plus this %*	*Of the excess over*
. . . .	$ 20,000	Zero	5.5	Zero
$ 20,000	21,583	$ 1,100	13.2	$ 20,000
21,583	30,583	1,309	14.4	21,583

If the adjusted total taxable amount is:		The ten-year averaging tax is:		
				Of the
At least	But not over	This amount	Plus this %	excess over
30,583	49,417	2,605	16.8	30,583
49,417	67,417	5,769	18.0	49,417
67,417	70,000	9,009	19.2	67,417
70,000	91,700	9,505	16.0	70,000
91,700	114,400	12,977	18.0	91,700
114,400	137,100	17,063	20.0	114,400
137,100	171,600	21,603	23.0	137,100
171,600	228,800	29,538	26.0	171,600
228,800	286,000	44,410	30.0	228,800
286,000	343,200	61,570	34.0	286,000
343,200	423,000	81,018	38.0	343,200
423,000	571,900	111,342	42.0	423,000
571,900	857,900	173,880	48.0	571,900
857,900	....	311,160	50.0	857,900

See Q. 11:17 regarding the six-year look-back rule.

Q. 11:19 What portion of a lump-sum distribution from a qualified retirement plan may be eligible for capital gains treatment?

Generally, no portion of a lump-sum distribution from a qualified retirement plan is eligible to be taxed under separate tax rates applicable to capital gains. [IRC § 402(a)(2) before repeal by TRA '86 § 1122(b)(1)(A)]

However, an individual who had attained age 50 before January 1, 1986, may elect to treat the capital gain portion of a lump-sum distribution under the 1986 tax provisions. This means that the capital gain portion will be taxed at a flat 20 percent tax rate. (See Q. 11:13.)

For all other individuals, the capital gain portion of the lump-sum distribution is subject to a five-year phase-out under which a certain percentage (see below) of the amount that would have been treated as long-term capital gain under the prior rules will continue to be treated as long-term capital gain subject to the rate of tax in effect at the time of the distribution. [TRA '86 § 1122(h)(4)(A)]

For purposes of determining the percentage of the capital gain portion of a lump-sum distribution that will be treated as long-term capital gain, the following percentages apply:

In the case of a distribution during calendar year	The phase–out percentage is:
1987	100
1988	95
1989	75
1990	50
1991	25
1992 or later	0

[TRA '86 § 1122(h)(4)(B)]

An employee (or the employee's beneficiaries) who is able to treat the portion attributable to pre-1974 participation as long-term capital gain may also irrevocably elect to use forward averaging on the entire distribution. This election is significant because, as a capital gain, part of a lump-sum distribution might otherwise be subject to the alternative minimum tax. [IRC § 402(e)(4)(L) before repeal by TAMRA § 1011(A)(b)(8)(G); *Brown*, 93 TC No. 59 (1989)]

The allocation between the capital gain portion and the ordinary income portion is made on the basis of the number of months of active participation before 1974 as compared with the total number of months of plan participation. The portion of the taxable amount of a distribution that is taxed as long-term capital gain is determined as follows:

$$\text{Taxable amount} \times \frac{\text{Number of months of plan participation before 1974}}{\text{Number of months of plan participation}}$$

[IRC § 402(a)(2) before repeal by TRA '86 § 1122(b)(1)(A)]

If the qualified retirement plan from which the distribution is made had assets transferred to it from another qualified retirement plan or if the distributee plan was merged into the plan making the distribution, the period of active participation includes both participation in the distributing plan and participation in the distributee plan. [*Letter Rulings 8934051* and *8535116*]

Q. 11:20 How is the number of months of plan participation computed?

To compute an employee's number of months of participation, any part of a calendar year prior to 1974 in which the employee participated in the plan is counted as 12 months and any part of a calendar month after 1973 in which the employee participated in the plan is counted as one month. [Prop. Reg. § 1.402(e)-2(d)(3)(ii)]

> **Example.** If an employee commenced participation in a plan on December 22, 1969, and terminated employment on May 2, 1990, the employee would have 60 (12 × 5) months of pre-1974 participation and 197 [(12 × 16) + 5] months of post-1973 participation, for a total of 257 months of participation. If the total taxable amount of the distribution received by the employee is $257,000, the capital gain portion is $60,000 (60/257 × $257,000) and the ordinary income portion is $197,000 (197/257 × $257,000).

Q. 11:21 How is the distribution taxed if the retirement plan loses its qualified status?

If IRS revokes the favorable determination letter previously issued to the retirement plan, the plan is no longer qualified and a distribution from the retirement plan will not be treated as a lump-sum distribution. [Reg. §§ 1.402(a)-1(a)(1)(ii), 1.402(a)-1(a)(1)(v), and 1.402(b)-1(b); *Cass v. Commissioner*, 774 F2d 740 (7th Cir. 1985); *Baetens v. Commissioner*, 777 F2d 1160 (6th Cir. 1985); *Woodson v. Commissioner*, 651 F2d 1094 (5th Cir. 1981); but see *Greenwald v. Commissioner*, 366 F2d 538 (2d Cir. 1966)]

Q. 11:22 How does a recipient elect special forward averaging for a lump-sum distribution?

Form 4972, Tax on Lump-Sum Distributions, is used for electing five-year and ten-year averaging and computing the tax. The form must be attached to the individual's tax return for the year in which the distribution is received. [Prop. Reg. § 1.402(e)-3(c)(2)]

Plan administrators must issue Form 1099-R (Total Distributions From Profit-Sharing, Retirement Plans, Individual Retirement Arrangements, Insurance Contracts, Etc.) to let the recipient know the amount of the distribution and the breakdown between ordinary income and capital gain. This statement must be issued to the recipient by January 31 of the year following the distribution, and a copy must be sent to IRS by the end of February.

Q. 11:23 Must all recipients of a single lump-sum distribution elect to use forward averaging?

No. When more than one person receives a payment qualifying as a lump-sum distribution (for example, if the payments are made to several beneficiaries on the participant's death), any eligible recipient may elect to use forward averaging even if the others do not. Similarly, any recipient may decide to treat amounts attributable to pre-1974 participation as ordinary income instead of capital gain (see Q. 11:19). [TIR-1426, 12/15/75; Ann. 76-51, 1976-15 IRB 30]

Form 4972 (see Q. 11:22) is used to make the election and compute the tax.

Q. 11:24 What is the income tax treatment of distributions of deductible employee contributions made by a participant?

Distributions of deductible employee contributions (see Q. 5:17), including earnings, are taxed as ordinary income in the year received. They do not qualify for forward averaging tax treatment as a lump-sum distribution (see Q. 11:4) or the $5,000 income tax exemption for death benefits (see Q. 12:16). If a distribution is premature (i.e., made before the participant reaches age 59½, dies, or is disabled), a penalty tax equal to 10 percent of the amount distributed may be imposed (see Q. 9:68). [IRC §§ 72(o) and 72(t)]

Distributions of deductible employee contributions may be rolled over to an IRA or another qualified retirement plan on a tax-free basis. See Chapter 26.

Q. 11:25 May any additional taxes be imposed on the recipient of a distribution from a qualified retirement plan?

In addition to penalty taxes imposed on distributions that commence too early (see Q. 9:68 and Q. 11:35) or too late (see Q. 9:63), a 15 percent excise tax is imposed on excess distributions (see Q. 11:26). The individual, with respect to whom the excess distributions are made, is liable for this additional tax. [IRC §§ 4980A(a) and 4980A(b); Reg. § 54.4981A-1T, Q&A a-1]

Q. 11:26 What are excess distributions?

The term excess distributions means the aggregate amount of retirement plan distributions (see Q. 11:27) made with respect to any individual during any calendar year to the extent that such amount exceeds the greater of (1) $112,500 (as adjusted for inflation), or (2) $150,000. For 1990, the $112,500 amount has increased to $128,228. This is known as the threshold amount (see Q. 11:29). [IRC § 4980A(c)(1); Reg. § 54.4981A-1T, Q&A a-2 and a-9]

> **Example.** Stella commences receiving annual distributions from three retirement plans in 1990: $90,000 from a defined benefit plan; $55,000 from a profit sharing plan; and $30,000 from an IRA. Stella did not make a grandfather election (see Q. 11:29). Since Stella's total retirement distributions ($175,000) in 1990 exceed the $150,000 threshold amount by $25,000, the excise tax will be $3,750 (15% × $25,000).

See Q. 11:28 regarding special treatment of lump-sum distributions.

Q. 11:27 What distributions are taken into account to compute the individual's excess distributions?

All distributions from qualified retirement plans, tax-sheltered annuities, and IRAs must be taken into account in determining the amount of excess distributions for the calendar year. [Reg. § 54.4981A-1T, Q&A a-3 and a-6]

The following amounts, whether or not they are actually distributed during the year or currently includible in income, are also included:

1. Amounts payable to an alternate payee under a QDRO (see Q. 28:1) if not taxable to the alternate payee (e.g., a child);

2. Payments received under an annuity contract previously distributed from a plan;

3. P.S. 58 costs (see Q. 12:7 and Q. 12:13);

4. Loans that are treated as taxable distributions (see Q. 11:38 through Q. 11:42);

5. Amounts includible in income because of plan disqualification; and

6. Net unrealized appreciation in employer securities (see Q. 11:16) when distributed.

[IRC § 4980A(e); Reg. § 54.4981A-1T, Q&A a-5 and a-8]

The following amounts, however, are not included:

1. Amounts received by any person as a result of the participant's death;

2. Amounts payable to an alternate payee under a QDRO (see Q. 28:1) if taxable to the alternate payee (e.g., spouse or former spouse);

3. Amounts attributable to the individual's investment in the contract (e.g., a distribution that is excluded from gross income because it is treated as a recovery of nondeductible contributions from an IRA) (see Q. 11:2);

4. Any amount rolled over into an IRA or another qualified retirement plan (see Chapter 26);

5. The distribution of an annuity contract from a plan;

6. Certain inherited benefits;

7. Any health coverage or any distribution of medical benefits provided to retirees under a pension or certain other plans to the extent that the coverage or distribution is excludable from an individual's gross income; and

8. Distributions of excess deferrals, excess contributions, excess aggregate contributions, and excess IRA contributions, including any income attributable to such amounts.

[IRC §§ 401(k)(8), 401(m)(6), 402(g)(2), 408(d)(4), 408(d)(5), and 4980A(c)(2); Reg. § 54.4981A-1T, Q&A a-4, a-5, a-7, a-8, and d-10; *Letter Rulings 9013008, 9013020, and 9013076*]

Q. 11:28   Is there a special rule regarding excess distributions when the individual receives a lump-sum distribution?

Yes. If the retirement distributions with respect to any individual include a lump-sum distribution (see Q. 11:4) for which the individual elects forward averaging or capital gains tax treatment (see Q. 11:12 and Q. 11:13), the lump-sum distribution is treated separately from the other distributions and is subject to a threshold amount that is five times the threshold amount ($112,500 indexed or $150,000 unindexed) that applies to nonlump-sum distributions (see Q. 11:26). [IRC § 4980A(c)(4); Reg. § 54.4981A-1T, Q&A c-1]

> **Example 1.** In 1990, Stephanie, age 60, receives a lump-sum distribution of $750,000 from a qualified retirement plan and elects five-year income averaging. Stephanie did not make a grandfather election (see Q. 11:29) so her threshold amount is $150,000. Stephanie's distribution consists solely of an amount in the lump-sum category. Stephanie's threshold amount equals $750,000 (5 × $150,000). Because Stephanie's threshold amount ($750,000) equals the amount of her distribution from the plan ($750,000), no part of her lump-sum distribution is treated as an excess distribution subject to the 15 percent excise tax.

> **Example 2.** Assume the same facts, except that Stephanie receives an additional distribution from an IRA of $150,000. Stephanie's distributions consist of two categories, the lump-sum category (qualified retirement plan: $750,000) and the nonlump-sum category (IRA: $150,000). A separate threshold amount is subtracted from Stephanie's IRA distribution. This threshold amount equals $150,000, the same initial threshold amount that is applied against the lump-sum distribution prior to the multiplication by 5. Because Stephanie's threshold amount ($150,000) equals the amount of her distribution from the IRA ($150,000), no part of her distribution from the IRA is treated as an excess distribution subject to the 15 percent excise tax.

Q. 11:29   What is the grandfather rule?

An individual whose total benefits in all retirement plans (see Q. 11:27) on August 1, 1986 (initial grandfather amount) had a value in excess of $562,500 was eligible to elect the special grandfather rule. The special grandfather rule permits an individual to offset distributions by the portion of the initial grandfather amount recovered during the year of distribution. The election had to be made no later than the due date of the individual's timely filed 1988 income tax return.

The $112,500 indexed threshold amount is used by individuals who elected the special grandfather rule. The $150,000 unindexed threshold amount is used by individuals who did not elect or were ineligible to elect the special grandfather rule. When the indexed $112,500 amount exceeds the unindexed $150,000, the higher indexed amount will be available to all individuals, whether or not the grandfather election was made.

If an individual elected the special grandfather rule, the individual also had to elect one of two alternative grandfather recovery methods (see Q. 11:31 and Q. 11:32) to determine the rate at which the initial grandfather amount would be recovered.

The excess distribution tax does not apply to the portion of the distribution that represents the recovery of the initial grandfather amount. The initial grandfather amount is then reduced by the amount that is treated as a recovery thereof. When an individual's initial grandfather amount has been reduced to zero, the special rule no longer applies and the entire amount of any subsequent excess distributions will be subject to the 15 percent excise tax. [IRC § 4980A(f); Reg. § 54.4981A-1T, Q&A b-1 through b-14 and c-1]

Q. 11:30   What portion of a distribution is treated as the recovery of an individual's initial grandfather amount?

The total amount of all retirement distributions received between August 1 and December 31, 1986, is treated as a recovery of the initial grandfather amount. The portion of retirement distributions received after December 31, 1986, that is treated as a recovery of the initial grandfather amount is calculated under the method of recovery elected (see Q. 11:29).

The amount that is treated as a recovery of the initial grandfather amount is then applied, on a dollar-for-dollar basis, as a reduction from the remaining unrecovered grandfather amount. After the entire initial grandfather amount has been recovered, the excise tax rules apply to excess distributions without regard to any grandfather amount.

[IRC § 4980A(f); Reg. § 54.4981A-1T, Q&A b-1]

Q. 11:31   What is the discretionary method?

Under the discretionary method, 10 percent of the total retirement distributions received by an individual during a calendar year will be treated as a recovery of the initial grandfather amount. This method also allows an individual to elect to accelerate the rate of recovery to 100 percent of the distributions received.

> **Example.** Susan had, as of December 31, 1986, a grandfather amount of $800,000. She made the required election to use the special grandfather rule and chose the discretionary method of recovery. In 1989, Susan received total retirement distributions of $100,000. With regard to her 1989 distributions, 10 percent, or $10,000, was treated as a recovery of her initial grandfather amount. In 1990, Susan receives $200,000 of distributions. With her 1990 tax return, Susan files Form 4972 electing to accelerate her recovery rate to 100 percent. This election will cause the entire $200,000 of 1990 retirement distributions to be treated as a recovery of Susan's initial grandfather amount. By making this election, Susan avoids the excise tax on the excess portion of her 1990 distributions because the entire $200,000 represents a recovery of a portion of her initial grandfather amount.

The acceleration election will also be effective for all years subsequent to the election. The election may be made (or revoked retroactively) on an individual's (amended) tax return. However, with respect to deceased individuals, the acceleration election may not be made on an amended return filed after the individual's death for a year in which a return was filed before the individual's death. [IRC § 4980A(f); Reg. § 54.4981A-1T, Q&A b-12]

Q. 11:32 What is the attained age method?

Under the attained age method, the rate of recovery is calculated based on a formula that takes into account the individual's age both on August 1, 1986, and at the end of the year in which the retirement distributions are received. The recovery rate is derived from a fraction whose numerator is the difference between the individual's attained age, in months, on August 1, 1986, and the individual's age in months at age 35 (420 months). The denominator of this fraction is the difference between the individual's attained age, in months, on December 31 of the calendar year in which the retirement distributions are received and the individual's age in months at age 35 (420 months). As a result, the rate of recovery diminishes as the individual ages. [IRC § 4980A(f); Reg. § 54.4981A-1T, Q&A b-13]

> **Example.** Christopher had an unrecovered amount of $1 million as of December 31, 1989. Christopher elected the special grandfather rule and the attained age method of recovery. If Christopher was born on December 1, 1944, his attained age on August 1, 1986, was 500 months. In 1990, Christopher received total distributions of $300,000. His attained age on December 31, 1990, was 553 months. Therefore, of the $300,000 distributed in 1990, $180,451 [$300,000 × ((500 − 420)/(553 − 420))] represents a recovery of Christopher's initial grandfather amount.

Q. 11:33 How is the amount of the excess distribution tax calculated when the special grandfather rule applies?

The 15 percent excise tax is applied to the amount by which the total retirement distribution exceeds the greater of (1) the threshold amount (see Q. 11:26) applicable for the year in which the distribution is made, or (2) the initial grandfather amount recovered in that year. This means there is no tax benefit for the recovered grandfather amount up to the threshold amount. [IRC § 4980A(f); Reg. § 54.4981A-1T, Q&A b-4]

> **Example.** Peter's unrecovered initial grandfather amount on December 31, 1989, is $600,000. Peter elected the discretionary

method (see Q. 11:31) of recovery. In 1990, Peter receives IRA distributions totaling $728,228 and makes an acceleration election. Even though the grandfather amount recovered ($600,000) is exempt from the excise tax, the remaining $128,228 is subject to the tax. The amount exempt from the excise tax is the greater of (1) the grandfather amount recovered or (2) the threshold amount, not the total of both amounts.

Q. 11:34 How is the special grandfather rule applied if an individual receives both a lump-sum distribution and a nonlump-sum distribution in the same year?

If, in any calendar year, an individual receives both a lump-sum distribution and a nonlump-sum distribution, the grandfather amount will be recovered ratably from each of the two categories of distributions. The ratable recovery is required even if the distribution in one category is less than that category's threshold amount while the distribution in the other category exceeds the applicable threshold amount. [Reg. § 54.4981A-1T, Q&A c-1(b)]

Q. 11:35 Is the excess distribution tax reduced by the early distribution tax?

Yes, the 15 percent excess distribution tax is offset by the 10 percent early distribution tax (see Q. 9:68) but only to the extent that the early distribution tax is applied to the excess distribution. The early distribution tax is still applicable to the amount of the distribution that is not an excess distribution. [IRC § 4980A(b); Reg. § 54.4981A-1T, Q&A c-4]

> **Example.** In 1990, Sharon, age 35, receives total distributions of $200,000. She did not elect the special grandfather rule (see Q. 11:29), and her threshold amount is therefore $150,000. The excess distribution tax is $7,500 (15% × $50,000). The entire distribution is subject to an early distribution tax of $20,000 (10% × $200,000). Of that amount, $5,000 (10% × $50,000) may be offset against the excess distribution tax because $5,000 represents the early distribution tax applicable to the excess portion of the distribution. Therefore, Sharon will owe a total

of $22,500 [$20,000 + ($7,500 − $5,000)] in additional taxes on her 1990 distribution.

Q. 11:36 Can a qualified retirement plan be amended to avoid the excess distribution tax?

If a plan sponsor chooses, it can amend a qualified retirement plan to limit future benefit accruals provided certain notice requirements are satisfied (see Q. 8:26). [Reg. § 54.4981A-1T, Q&A c-2; ERISA § 204(h)]

However, a qualified retirement plan may not be amended to reduce accrued benefits in order to avoid the excess distribution tax. An amendment reducing accrued benefits generally is a violation of plan qualification requirements (see Q. 8:24). [Reg. § 54.4981A-1T, Q&A c-3]

Q. 11:37 May an additional estate tax be imposed at the participant's death?

Amounts accumulated in a decedent's retirement plans as of the date of death may be subject to an additional 15 percent estate tax on excess retirement accumulations (see Q. 12:19 through Q. 12:27 for details).

Q. 11:38 Are there any limitations on loans from qualified retirement plans?

Yes. Loans from qualified retirement plans are subject to a number of limitations and requirements (see Q. 11:39).

Even if all of the requirements are satisfied, any loan in excess of a maximum specified amount is treated as a taxable distribution. In addition, a taxable plan loan may also be subject to the early distribution tax (see Q. 9:68) and the excess distribution tax (see Q. 11:25).

A loan from a qualified retirement plan to a participant or beneficiary is not treated as a taxable distribution to the extent the loan (when added to the outstanding balance of all other loans from the plan) does *not* exceed the lesser of:

1. $50,000 reduced by the excess (if any) of:
   - The highest outstanding balance of loans from the plan during the one-year period ending on the day before the date on which such loan was made, over
   - The outstanding balance of loans from the plan on the date such loan was made; or
2. The greater of:
   - 50 percent of the present value of the participant's vested benefit under the plan (determined without regard to any deductible employee contributions (see Q. 5:17)), or
   - $10,000.

[IRC § 72(p)(2)(A)]

For the purpose of applying the loan limits, all qualified retirement plans maintained by the same employer and all qualified retirement plans maintained by a member of a controlled group (see Q. 4:34) or an affiliated service group (see Q. 27:31) are treated as one plan. [IRC § 72(p)(2)(D)]

Any amount received as a loan made under an insurance contract purchased under a qualified retirement plan is treated as a loan made from the plan. [IRC § 72(p)(5)]

> **Example.** On April 3, 1990, Dan borrowed $40,000 from his employer's qualified retirement plan, and he repaid $30,000 on December 3, 1990. On March 6, 1991, Dan's vested interest under the plan is $150,000, and he wishes to make another loan. Until December 4, 1991, Dan can borrow only $10,000 more. Here's why:

Highest outstanding loan balance	$40,000
Balance on March 6, 1991	10,000
Reduction in maximum loan amount	$30,000

Maximum loan amount	$50,000
Reduction	30,000
Reduced loan limit	$20,000
Balance on March 6, 1991	10,000
Maximum loan not a distribution	$10,000

Q. 11:39 Is there a maximum repayment period for a loan from a qualified retirement plan?

A loan to a participant from a qualified retirement plan must be required to be repaid within five years or it is treated as a taxable distribution at the time the loan is made. However, the five-year repayment period does not apply to a loan used to acquire any dwelling unit that within a reasonable time is to be used (determined at the time the loan is made) as the principal residence of the participant. [IRC § 72(p)(2)(B)]

The loan repayment schedule must provide for level amortization. That is, repayment must be made in substantially equal installments consisting of principal and interest and must be made not less frequently than quarterly over the term of the loan. Accordingly, the participant cannot repay the loan in one balloon payment at the end of the loan term. [IRC § 72(p)(2)(C)]

Q. 11:40 Is interest paid on loans from qualified retirement plans deductible?

The deductibility of interest on a loan from a qualified retirement plan is first determined under the general rules governing the deductibility of interest. Notwithstanding the general rules, interest on plan loans is *never* deductible if the loan is made to a key employee (see Q. 20:24), whether or not the plan is top-heavy, or the loan is secured by elective contributions made under a 401(k) plan (see Q. 21:1). [IRC §§ 72(p)(3) and 163; *Letter Ruling 8933019*]

Q. 11:41 Is it necessary to obtain spousal consent for a loan from a qualified retirement plan?

A qualified retirement plan that is subject to the automatic survivor benefit requirements (see Q. 9:1) must provide that no portion of a participant's accrued benefit may be used as security for a plan loan unless the participant's spouse consents to the loan within the 90-day period ending on the date the security agreement becomes effective. The consent must satisfy the requirements applicable to the QPSA and QJSA election procedures (see Q. 9:21). [IRC § 417(a)(4)]

Q. 11:42 Are there any other requirements applicable to loans from qualified retirement plans?

Yes. Another set of requirements must be met to avoid a plan loan from being subject to an excise tax. An excise tax is imposed on certain prohibited transactions (e.g., loans) between a plan and a disqualified person (see Chapter 18 for details). However, an exemption is provided for any loan by a qualified retirement plan to a participant or beneficiary who is a disqualified person if the following requirements are met:

1. The loan must be available to all participants and beneficiaries on a reasonably equivalent basis;

2. The loan must be made in accordance with specific provisions in the plan;

3. Loans must not be made available to highly compensated employees (see Q. 4:28) in amounts greater than the amounts made available to other employees;

4. The loan must bear a reasonable rate of interest; and

5. The loan must be adequately secured.

[IRC § 4975(d); Rev. Rul. 89-14, 1989-1 CB 111]

A shareholder-employee (i.e., a more-than-5% shareholder) of an S corporation may not borrow from the corporation's qualified retirement plan, and the law prohibits a qualified retirement plan from lending to an owner-employee (see Q. 27:9) or to the owner-employee's spouse and certain other relatives. [IRC §§ 401(a)(13) and 4975(d)]

According to IRS, the loan may be secured by the participant's vested accrued benefit; but, according to DOL, no more than one-half of the vested accrued benefit may be used to secure the loan. [IRC § 401(a)(13)(A); Reg. § 1.401(a)-13(d)(2); DOL Reg. § 2550.408b-1; DOL Advisory Opinion 89-30A]

Chapter 12

Life Insurance and Death Benefits

Although the primary purpose of a qualified retirement plan is to pay retirement benefits, the plan may also provide life insurance coverage for participants. Limits on life insurance coverage and the tax consequences of including insurance in a qualified retirement plan are examined in this chapter. A discussion of how death benefit payments by qualified retirement plans are taxed is also included.

Q. 12:1 Must a qualified retirement plan provide a death benefit to participants?

Generally, a qualified retirement plan is not required to provide a death benefit with respect to employer contributions if the employee dies while a participant in the plan. However, in the case of married participants, a qualified retirement plan is required to provide a death benefit to the participant's surviving spouse unless an election and consent to waive such benefits have been made. [IRC §§ 401(a)(11), 411(a)(3), and 417(a)]

For details on preretirement survivor annuities and joint and survivor annuities, see Chapter 9.

Q. 12:2 May a qualified retirement plan provide life insurance coverage for participants?

Yes, but the primary purpose of a company's qualified retirement plan must be to pay retirement benefits to participants. Any life insurance coverage provided under the qualified retirement plan must be incidental to the provision of retirement benefits. (See Q. 12:4).

Q. 12:3 Is a company allowed a deduction for life insurance purchased under a qualified retirement plan?

The portion of employer contributions to its qualified retirement plan that is used to purchase life insurance on behalf of plan participants is deductible.

However, if life insurance is provided under a qualified retirement plan for a self-employed individual (see Q. 27:8), the cost of current life insurance protection (see Q. 12:6 through Q. 12:8) is not deductible. [IRC § 404(e); Reg. § 1.404(e)-1A(g)]

Q. 12:4 What limits apply to the amount of life insurance that can be purchased for participants under a qualified retirement plan?

The basic restriction is that the amount of life insurance coverage must be incidental to the plan's retirement benefits. [Reg. § 1.401-1(b)(1)]

For a defined contribution plan (see Q. 2:2), life insurance coverage is considered incidental if less than 50 percent of the company's contributions to the plan on behalf of the participant is used to purchase whole life insurance or no more than 25 percent is used to purchase term life insurance. [Rev. Rul. 54-51, 1954-1 CB 147; Rev. Rul. 57-213, 1957-1 CB 157; Rev. Rul. 66-143, 1966-1 CB 79; Rev. Rul. 69-408, 1969-2 CB 58; Rev. Rul. 76-353, 1976-2 CB 112]

For a defined benefit plan, life insurance coverage is generally considered incidental if the amount of the insurance does not exceed 100 times the participant's projected monthly benefit. For example, if a participant can expect a $1,000 monthly benefit, life insurance coverage of up to $100,000 can be provided for the participant under the defined benefit plan. However, life insurance coverage may exceed the 100 times limit and still be considered incidental. [*Rev. Rul. 60-83*, 1960-1 CB 157; *Rev. Rul. 61-121*, 1961-2 CB 65; *Rev. Rul. 68-31*, 1968-1 CB 151; *Rev. Rul. 68-453*, 1968-2 CB 163; *Rev. Rul. 74-307*, 1974-2 CB 126]

Q. 12:5 Does the purchase of life insurance affect retirement benefits?

If part of the company's contributions to its defined contribution plan goes toward the purchase of life insurance coverage, there may be less available for participants at retirement. This will be so if the return on the investment in life insurance is less than the return on the trust fund investments. Although retirement benefits may be reduced, death benefits will be substantially increased.

Using company contributions to pay for life insurance under a defined benefit plan does not affect the amount of a participant's retirement benefit. However, because participants are promised a fixed level of benefits at retirement, the company may have to increase its contributions to cover any shortfall in funding for those benefits resulting from the use of company contributions to pay insurance premiums.

Q. 12:6 What are the tax consequences to participants when their employer's qualified retirement plan provides life insurance protection?

The tax law allows participants to postpone payment of income taxes on retirement benefits payable to them from a qualified retirement plan. Participants pay no tax until they receive those benefits. They do, however, incur some tax cost when their employer's qualified retirement plan provides life insurance. Because participants receive a present benefit—current life insurance protection—they must include the value of that benefit in their gross incomes for the year in which employer contributions or trust earnings are used to pay life insurance premiums.

A participant must pay tax on the term cost of insurance protection paid for with employer contributions or trust earnings if, upon death, the proceeds of the life insurance policy on the participant's life are payable to either (1) the participant's estate or beneficiary, or (2) the trustee of the plan, if the trustee is required by the plan's provisions to pay such proceeds to the participant's estate or beneficiary. [IRC § 72(m)(3)(B); Reg. § 1.72-16(b)]

The amount included in a participant's gross income, which is determined under special IRS tables that contain the P.S. 58 costs (see Q. 12:7), is often well below the premium paid by the plan for the insurance. [Rev. Rul. 55-747, 1955-2 CB 228; Rev. Rul. 66-110, 1966-1 CB 12]

If a self-employed individual is covered by a life insurance policy under a qualified retirement plan, the individual will not be taxed with P.S. 58 costs because the cost of the current life insurance protection is not deductible to the employer. (See Q. 12:3.) [IRC §§ 72(m)(3)(B) and 404(e); Reg. § 1.404(e)-1A(g)]

Q. 12:7 What are P.S. 58 costs?

IRS rulings set forth the method of calculating the amount of a participant's current taxable income as a result of receiving life insurance protection under a company's qualified retirement plan (see Q. 12:6). [Rev. Rul. 55-747, 1955-2 CB 228; Rev. Rul. 66-110, 1966-1 CB 12]

The participant's current taxable amount is determined by applying the one-year premium term rate (the P.S. 58 rates) at the participant's age to the difference between the face amount of the policy and its cash surrender value at the end of the year.

The P.S. 58 rates are shown in the chart on page 12-5.

> **Example.** Keren, age 35, is a participant in her company's qualified retirement plan. The plan provides Keren with a life insurance policy on her life in the face amount of $40,000. At year end, the policy had a cash surrender value of $2,000. Keren must include $121.98 in her current taxable income [$38,000 ($40,000 − $2,000) multiplied by $3.21, divided by 1,000].

One-Year Term Premiums for $1,000 of Life Insurance Protection

Age	Premium	Age	Premium	Age	Premium
15	$1.27	37	$ 3.63	59	$ 19.08
16	1.38	38	3.87	60	20.73
17	1.48	39	4.14	61	22.53
18	1.52	40	4.42	62	24.50
19	1.56	41	4.73	63	26.63
20	1.61	42	5.07	64	28.98
21	1.67	43	5.44	65	31.51
22	1.73	44	5.85	66	34.28
23	1.79	45	6.30	67	37.31
24	1.86	46	6.78	68	40.59
25	1.93	47	7.32	69	44.17
26	2.02	48	7.89	70	48.06
27	2.11	49	8.53	71	52.29
28	2.20	50	9.22	72	56.89
29	2.31	51	9.97	73	61.89
30	2.43	52	10.79	74	67.33
31	2.57	53	11.69	75	73.23
32	2.70	54	12.67	76	79.63
33	2.86	55	13.74	77	86.57
34	3.02	56	14.91	78	94.09
35	3.21	57	16.18	79	102.23
36	3.41	58	17.56	80	111.04
				81	120.57

Q. 12:8   Must the P.S. 58 rates be used to determine the cost of pure life insurance included in a participant's gross income?

No. If the insurance company's rates for individual one-year term policies available to all standard risks on an initial issue insurance basis are lower, the lower rates may be utilized. [Rev. Rul. 66-110, 1966-1 CB 12; Rev. Rul. 67-154, 1967-1 CB 11; Letter Ruling 9023044]

Q. 12:9   Are loans from insurance policies purchased under qualified retirement plans taxable?

If a participant receives a loan from an insurance policy purchased under a qualified retirement plan (as well as any assignment or pledge of the policy), it is treated as a loan made from the plan. Generally, such loans are not taxable. However, if the policy loan exceeds the Code limitations on loans from qualified retirement plans, the loan is treated as a taxable distribution to the participant. (See Q. 11:2 for details.) [IRC § 72(p)(5)]

Q. 12:10   Who receives the proceeds from life insurance purchased under a qualified retirement plan when a participant dies before retirement?

Generally, if a participant dies while working for the company, the proceeds from life insurance purchased under a qualified retirement plan will be paid to designated beneficiaries. If the participant fails to designate a beneficiary or if the sole designated beneficiary predeceases the participant, the life insurance proceeds generally will be paid to the participant's estate in accordance with the provisions of the policy. See Q. 9:1 through Q. 9:31 for a discussion of the automatic survivor annuity requirements and their effect on the participant's right to designate a beneficiary.

If there is a death benefit under the plan (other than life insurance) and there is no designated beneficiary, the provisions of the plan will determine who will receive the death benefit. [Jensen v. Estate of McGowan, 101 Nev. 182, 697 P2d 1380 (1985)]

Q. 12:11   How are proceeds from life insurance purchased under a qualified retirement plan taxed for income tax purposes?

The amount of the proceeds that is equal to the cash surrender value of the policy is included in the beneficiary's gross income. Any proceeds in excess of the cash surrender value of the insurance policy are not subject to federal income tax. However, the beneficiary's taxable amount is subject to a $5,000 death benefit exclusion and is reduced further by the P.S. 58 costs that were included in the deceased participant's gross income during such participant's lifetime (see Q. 12:6; they are treated as a tax-free return of the participant's investment.) [IRC § 101; Reg. § 1.72-16(b)]

If the participant's surviving spouse receives the proceeds, payment of income tax may be postponed by rolling over the taxable amount of the proceeds to an individual retirement account (IRA). In that case, the surviving spouse will not incur income tax liability until withdrawals are made from the IRA. For details on rollovers, see Chapter 26.

If all of the benefits payable under the qualified retirement plan—including the life insurance proceeds—are distributed within one taxable year, the recipient may be able to elect forward averaging income tax treatment for the entire distribution. See Chapter 11 for more details.

Q. 12:12 Are proceeds from life insurance purchased under a qualified retirement plan included in the participant's estate for tax purposes?

Yes. Life insurance proceeds (and other death benefits) paid under a qualified retirement plan are included in the participant's gross estate. [IRC § 2039]

See Q. 12:19 through Q. 12:26 regarding additional estate tax liability that may apply to a deceased participant.

Q. 12:13 Can a participant recover P.S. 58 costs tax-free when qualified retirement plan benefits are distributed?

Yes. When an insurance policy purchased under a qualified retirement plan is distributed to a participant who had reported P.S. 58 costs as income (see Q. 12:6), the total P.S. 58 costs that were included in gross income can be recovered tax-free from the benefits received under the plan. However, these costs can be recovered only if the original insurance policy is distributed to the employee. If the life insurance is surrendered and the cash value and investment fund are used to purchase an annuity, the P.S. 58 costs are not part of the participant's cost for the annuity because the benefits will not be provided under the same contract. However, if the participant elects an annuity settlement option under the original policy, the P.S. 58 costs are recoverable. [IRC § 72; Reg. § 1.72-16(b); Rev. Rul. 67-336, 1967-2 CB 66]

In addition, if the policy is surrendered by the plan's trustee and the cash surrender value is distributed to the participant, the participant's P.S. 58 costs are not recoverable.

Q. 12:14 Are P.S. 58 costs recovered tax-free by a deceased participant's beneficiary?

Yes. P.S. 58 costs can be recovered tax-free by the beneficiary of the life insurance proceeds in the event of the participant's death. [Reg. § 1.72-16(c); Rev. Rul. 63-76, 1963-1 CB 23]

Q. 12:15 What advantage does a participant gain when the company's qualified retirement plan provides life insurance protection?

By purchasing life insurance protection through the company's qualified retirement plan, the participant is able to shift a personal expense (not tax-deductible) to the plan without adverse tax consequences (see Q. 12:3).

The income tax advantage of buying life insurance through the company's qualified retirement plan is even greater for a participant who could otherwise buy insurance only by paying a very high premium because of ill health. Instead of making large out-of-pocket premium payments, the participant merely includes the P.S. 58 costs (see Q. 12:6) in gross income.

Q. 12:16 How are death benefit payments under a qualified retirement plan taxed?

Death benefits payable under a qualified retirement plan are generally included in the deceased participant's gross estate. For the exceptions, see Q. 12:17. [IRC § 2039]

The participant's beneficiary is subject to income tax on death benefit payments. The income tax treatment depends on how the beneficiary receives the death benefit payments. Forward averaging treatment may be available for a lump-sum distribution (see Q. 11:10). If an annuity is purchased, ordinary income tax rates apply to amounts received under the annuity contract.

Death benefit payments up to $5,000 are exempt from income tax. The $5,000 exemption is not available if the participant had a nonforfeitable right to receive the payment while the participant was alive. However, the exemption is available in any event for a lump-sum distribution. If there are two or more beneficiaries, the exemption is still $5,000 and must be apportioned between or among them. [IRC § 101(b)(2); Reg. §§ 1.101-2(a) and 1.101-2(c); Rev. Rul. 71-146, 1971-1 CB 34]

For rules on the taxation of life insurance proceeds, see Q. 12:11 and Q. 12:14.

Q. 12:17 Are any deceased participants entitled to an estate tax exclusion with respect to death benefit payments received from a qualified retirement plan?

Yes. The repeal of the $100,000 estate tax exclusion by TRA '84 does not apply to a participant who was receiving benefit payments under the plan prior to 1985 and who, prior to July 18, 1984, irrevocably elected the form of the benefit that the beneficiary would receive.

Furthermore, the total estate tax exclusion previously available if the participant had died before 1983 continues to apply if the participant was receiving benefit payments (i.e., was in pay status) under the plan prior to 1983, and had already irrevocably elected the form of benefit that the beneficiary would receive.

The estate tax exclusion remains available if the participant terminated employment before 1985 (in the case of the $100,000 exclusion) or 1983 (in the case of the total exclusion), irrevocably elected the form of benefit to be paid in the future, and was not in pay status as of the applicable date. [IRC § 2039; TEFRA § 245(c) as amended by TRA '84 § 525; Reg. § 20.2039-1T, Q&A-1; Letter Ruling 8630028]

A participant was in pay status on the applicable date with respect to an interest in the plan if the participant irrevocably elected the form of benefit and received at least one payment under such form of benefit. [Reg. § 20.2039-1T, Q&A-2]

As of the applicable date, an election of the form of benefit is irrevocable if, as of such date, a written election had been made specifying the form of distribution (e.g., lump-sum, annuity) and the period over which the distribution would be made (e.g., life annuity, term certain). An election is considered revocable if the form or period of the distribution could be determined or altered after the applicable date. But, it will not be considered revocable just because the beneficiaries were not designated as of such date or could be changed thereafter. [Reg. § 20.2039-1T, Q&A-3]

Q. 12:18 Is a deceased participant's estate entitled to a marital deduction for death benefit payments received by the surviving spouse from a qualified retirement plan?

A marital deduction is allowed for any property included in the deceased participant's estate that passes from the decedent to the surviving spouse. [IRC § 2056]

Death benefit payments from a qualified retirement plan to a deceased participant's surviving spouse will qualify for the marital deduction and will be deducted from the deceased participant's gross estate for estate tax purposes. This deduction will also be available if the surviving spouse receives the death benefit payments in the form of a qualified preretirement survivor annuity (see Q. 9:9) and the deceased participant's executor does *not* elect to forgo the deduction. [IRC §§ 2039 and 2056(b)(7)(C); *Letter Ruling 9008003;* see also *Rev. Rul. 89-89,* 1989-2 CB 231]

Q. 12:19 May any additional taxes be imposed on the estate of a decedent?

The estate of a participant may be subject to an additional estate tax equal to 15 percent of the deceased participant's excess retirement accumulation (see Q. 12:20). Neither the unified credit nor the credit for state death taxes allowable in the computation of the estate tax may be used to offset this additional estate tax. Further, neither the marital deduction (see Q. 12:18) nor the charitable deduction for estate tax purposes is available. [IRC §§ 4980A(d)(1) and 4980A (d)(2); Reg. § 54.4981A-1T, Q&A d-1 and d-8]

Q. 12:20 What is an excess retirement accumulation?

For purposes of determining the additional estate tax (see Q. 12:19), an excess retirement accumulation generally means the excess (if any) of:

1. The value of the deceased participant's aggregate interests (see Q. 12:21) in qualified retirement plans, tax-sheltered annuities, and IRAs as of the date of death (or, in the case of any alternate valuation election, the applicable valuation date), over

2. The present value of a single life annuity (see Q. 12:22) with annual payments equal to the excess distribution threshold amount (see Q. 11:26). [IRC §§ 4980A(c)(1) and 4980A(d)(3); Reg. § 54.4981A-1T, Q&A d-2]

Q. 12:21 How are the deceased participant's aggregate interests calculated?

Generally, the aggregate interests include all amounts payable to beneficiaries under any qualified retirement plan (including payments under a joint and survivor annuity or preretirement survivor annuity), tax-sheltered annuity, or IRA. [IRC § 4980A(d)(3)(A); Reg. § 54.4981A-1T, Q&A d-5]

However, the deceased participant's aggregate interests do not include (1) benefits that represent the participant's investment in the contract (e.g., P.S. 58 costs, nondeductible voluntary employee contributions, nondeductible IRA contributions); (2) amounts payable to an alternate payee spouse or former spouse pursuant to a qualified domestic relations order (QDRO) (see Q. 28:1 and Q. 28:3); (3) life insurance proceeds reduced by the cash surrender value of the policy immediately before the deceased participant's death; and (4) amounts inherited from other deceased individuals (see Q. 12:27).

[IRC §§ 4980A(d)(3)(A) and 4980(A)(d)(4); Reg. § 54.4981A-1T, Q&A d-6]

Q. 12:22 How is the present value of the single life annuity calculated for purposes of determining the amount of the participant's excess retirement accumulation?

The present value of the single life annuity is calculated using the applicable interest rate and mortality assumptions in effect on the date of the participant's death. [IRC §§ 4980A(d)(3)(B) and 7520; Reg. §§ 54.4981A-1T, Q&A d-7 and 20.2031-7; Notice 89-60, 19891 CB 700]

For purposes of this calculation, the amount of each annual payment under the single life annuity is equal to the greater of $150,000 (unindexed) or $112,500 (indexed). If the special grandfather rule (see Q. 11:29) is applicable, each annual payment is $112,500 (indexed) even if no grandfather amount remains. For 1990, the indexed amount is $128,228. [IR 90-15, January 30, 1990]

The interest rate used to calculate present value may change each month; the mortality assumption will change at least once every ten years. [IRC § 7520]

Below is the present value of a single life annuity for ages 40 to 85 based upon a 10 percent assumed interest rate and using the most current mortality table:

Age at Death	Present Value Multiplier	PV/SLA at $150,000	PV/SLA at $128,228
40	9.2945	1,394,175.00	1,191,815.15
41	9.2465	1,386,975.00	1,185,660.20
42	9.1959	1,379,385.00	1,179,171.87
43	9.1424	1,371,360.00	1,172,311.67
44	9.0859	1,362,885.00	1,165,066.79
45	9.0264	1,353,960.00	1,157,437.22
46	8.9637	1,344,555.00	1,149,397.32
47	8.8978	1,334,670.00	1,140,947.10

Age at Death	Present Value Multiplier	PV/SLA at $150,000	PV/SLA at $128,228
48	8.8287	1,324,305.00	1,132,086.54
49	8.7567	1,313,505.00	1,122,854.13
50	8.6818	1,302,270.00	1,113,249.85
51	8.6037	1,290,555.00	1,103,235.24
52	8.5220	1,278,300.00	1,092,759.02
53	8.4365	1,265,475.00	1,081,795.52
54	8.3476	1,252,140.00	1,070,396.05
55	8.2550	1,238,250.00	1,058,522.14
56	8.1586	1,223,790.00	1,046,160.96
57	8.0581	1,208,715.00	1,033,274.05
58	7.9536	1,193,040.00	1,019,874.22
59	7.8449	1,176,735.00	1,005,935.84
60	7.7326	1,159,890.00	991,535.83
61	7.6169	1,142,535.00	976,699.85
62	7.4980	1,124,700.00	961,453.54
63	7.3760	1,106,400.00	945,809.73
64	7.2507	1,087,605.00	929,742.76
65	7.1213	1,068,195.00	913,150.06
66	6.9876	1,048,140.00	896,005.97
67	6.8492	1,027,380.00	878,259.22
68	6.7063	1,005,945.00	859,935.44
69	6.5595	983,925.00	841,111.57
70	6.4093	961,395.00	821,851.72
71	6.2564	938,460.00	802,245.66
72	6.1009	915,135.00	782,306.21
73	5.9425	891,375.00	761,994.89
74	5.7805	867,075.00	741,221.95
75	5.6144	842,160.00	719,923.28
76	5.4437	816,555.00	698,034.76
77	5.2689	790,335.00	675,620.51
78	5.0906	763,590.00	652,757.46
79	4.9103	736,545.00	629,637.95
80	4.7295	709,425.00	606,454.33
81	4.5501	682,515.00	583,450.22
82	4.3730	655,950.00	560,741.04
83	4.1993	629,895.00	538,467.84
84	4.0287	604,305.00	516,592.14
85	3.8608	579,120.00	495,062.66

Q. 12:23   Is the special grandfather rule applicable in determining the amount of a deceased participant's excess retirement accumulation?

Yes. If the grandfather election (see Q. 11:29) was made, the excess retirement accumulation is equal to the deceased participant's aggregate interests (see Q. 12:21) minus the greater of (1) the unrecovered grandfather amount on the date of death or (2) the present value of a single life annuity (see Q. 12:22). [IRC § 4980A(f)(2)(B); Reg. §§ 54.4981A-1T, Q&A d-3 and d-4]

The unrecovered grandfather amount is the portion of the grandfather amount not previously recovered by the participant as of the date of death (see Q. 11:30). [Reg. § 54.4981A-1T, Q&A b-11 through b-14]

Q. 12:24   Is there a special rule if the surviving spouse is the beneficiary of the deceased participant's aggregate interests?

Yes. If the surviving spouse is the beneficiary of at least 99 percent of the deceased participant's aggregate interests (see Q. 12:21), the surviving spouse may elect to have such interests and any retirement distribution attributable to such interests treated as belonging to the surviving spouse. [IRC § 4980A(d)(5)]

If the surviving spouse makes the election, no additional estate tax will be imposed on the deceased participant's estate. However, the surviving spouse may, upon receipt of such interests, be subject to the excess distribution tax (see Q. 11:25) unless the distribution is rolled over to an IRA (see Q. 26:6). [Reg. § 54.4981A-1T, Q&A d-10]

Q. 12:25   Is the excess retirement accumulation tax deductible?

The additional estate tax is an administrative expense deductible either for estate tax purposes or for income tax purposes on a fiduciary income tax return if the estate or a trust is the beneficiary of the excess retirement accumulation. If the beneficiary is other than the deceased participant's estate or a trust, the tax is deductible only for estate tax purposes. [IRC §§ 642(g) and 2053(c)(1)(B)]

Q. 12:26   Who is liable for the excess retirement accumulation tax?

The deceased participant's estate is liable for the excise tax. [IRC § 4980(A)(d)(1)]

Additionally, the rules generally applicable for purposes of determining the apportionment of the estate tax apply to the apportionment of the excess retirement accumulation tax. The deceased participant's will or the applicable state apportionment law may provide that the estate is entitled to recover the tax. However, absent such a provision either in the will or under applicable state law, the estate is *not* entitled to recover the tax from the beneficiary. [Reg. § 54.4981A-1T, Q&A d-8A]

Q. 12:27   Whether or not the estate tax on an excess retirement accumulation is imposed, are postdeath distributions subject to the taxes on excess distributions or excess retirement accumulations?

Whether or not the additional estate tax is imposed (see Q. 12:19), postdeath distributions may be disregarded for purposes of the taxes on both excess distributions and excess retirement accumulations. Thus, a beneficiary who is receiving distributions with respect to a participant after the participant's death is not required to aggregate those amounts with any other retirement distributions or accumulations except for a surviving spouse who made a spousal election (see Q. 12:24). If the surviving spouse did not make a spousal election and rolled over the distribution, then postdeath distributions will be disregarded only if the surviving spouse did not commingle the rollover with any other IRA funds. [IRC § 4980A(d)(3)(A); Reg. § 54.4981A-1T, Q&A d-10; *Letter Rulings 9013076, 9013020,* and *9013008*]

Chapter 13

Determination Letters

Before a company commits itself to making substantial contributions to a retirement plan, it must be certain that the plan qualifies for favorable tax treatment. This chapter discusses the procedure for submitting the retirement plan to IRS for an advance ruling on the plan's tax status.

Q. 13:1   What is an IRS determination letter?

Although not required, an employer has the option of seeking an advance determination as to the qualified status of its retirement plan by IRS, rather than waiting for IRS to review the plan in connection with an audit. This written advance determination is called a determination letter. A favorable determination letter indicates that, in the opinion of IRS, the terms of the plan conform to the requirements of the Code. For more details, see Chapter 3. [Rev. Proc. 80-30, 1980-1 CB 685; Rev. Proc. 90-20, 1990-15 IRB 23]

A determination letter may also be requested when the retirement plan is amended or terminated.

Q. 13:2   Is a fee charged for a request for a determination letter?

Prior to September 30, 1990, IRS charged a user fee for each request for a determination letter (as well as for letter rulings, opinion letters, and other similar rulings or determinations). The user fee program ended September 30, 1990, since legislation has not been enacted to extend it. IRS has announced that a request submitted after September 29, 1990, should not be accompanied by a user fee; however, if an extension is subsequently enacted by Congress and is made retroactive to that date, an announcement detailing the method for paying applicable fees will be issued by IRS.

Prior to September 30, 1990, each request had to be accompanied by payment of the user fee (check or money order) attached to IRS Form 8717. Any determination letter request not accompanied by full payment was returned to the applicant for resubmission. The fee was refundable only in certain situations (e.g., if IRS refused to rule on an issue properly requested, it issued an erroneous ruling, or the ruling issued was not responsive).

The amount of the user fee depended on the type of request and the number of plan participants; some examples are listed below:

Determination of Qualification

Individually designed plans (Form 5300):

100 or more participants	$825
Fewer than 100 participants	$700
Adopters of master and prototype plans, volume submitter plans (Form 5307)	$125
Short amendments (Form 6406)	$125

Determination on Termination (Form 5310)

100 or more participants	$375
Fewer than 100 participants	$225

[OBRA '87 § 10511; Rev. Proc. 90-17, 1990-12 IRB 13; Announcement 90-113, 1990-41 IRB]

Q. 13:3 Must an employer apply for a determination letter?

No. However, the advantage of obtaining a favorable determination letter is that the employer is afforded some assurance that its retirement plan is qualified and will remain so if it qualifies in operation (see Q. 13:4), if it is not amended (other than as may be required by IRS), and if there is no change in law. Receipt of a favorable determination letter allows the employer to make contributions to the retirement plan with the knowledge that its deductions for those contributions will most likely be allowed should IRS audit its tax returns.

See Q. 3:6 for a discussion of timely filed determination letter requests and an employer's ability to recover its contributions to a disqualified retirement plan.

Q. 13:4 What does the term qualifies in operation mean?

Generally, a retirement plan qualifies in operation if it is maintained according to the terms on which the favorable determination letter was issued. However, conditions may develop in operation that may jeopardize the qualification of the retirement plan. Examples of common operational features that arise after issuance of a favorable determination letter and that may adversely affect the favorable determination include the following:

- Failure to meet nondiscrimination requirements (see Q. 27:12);
- Rapid turnover of lower paid employees (see Q. 8:5);
- Contributions or benefits in excess of the limitations under Section 415 (see Chapter 5); or
- Not providing top-heavy minimums (see Chapter 20).

Q. 13:5 What are the limitations of a favorable determination letter?

A determination letter applies only to qualification requirements regarding the form of the retirement plan. For example, a determination letter does not consider whether actuarial assumptions are reasonable for funding purposes or whether a specific contribution is deductible. The determination as to whether a retirement plan qualifies is made from the information in the written plan document and the supporting information submitted by the employer. Therefore, the determination letter may not be relied upon if

- There has been a misstatement or omission of material facts;
- The facts subsequently developed are materially different from the facts on which the determination was made; or
- There is a change in applicable law.

Also, the determination letter applies only to the employer and its participants on whose behalf the determination letter was issued. A determination letter may include one or more caveats that affect the scope of reliance represented by the letter.

Q. 13:6   When should a retirement plan be submitted for IRS approval?

A retirement plan should be submitted for IRS approval as early as possible. Amendments needed to qualify a retirement plan can be made retroactively until the company's federal income tax return for the year is due (including extensions) or at a later time if allowed by IRS. If the retirement plan is submitted to IRS before the tax return is due, IRS will extend the time limit for amending the plan. If the retirement plan is submitted after the company's tax return is due, IRS may not allow the company to amend its plan retroactively, particularly if the changes that need to be made are significant. [IRC § 401(b); Reg. § 1.401(b)-1]

Qualified retirement plans must be amended to comply with the requirements of TRA '86 (and other laws) by the last day of the plan year beginning in 1991. However, the plan must comply in operation with the new rules as of each rule's effective date; and plan amendments, when made, must be retroactive to the applicable effective date (see Q. 3:6 and Q. 3:7). [*Rev. Proc. 89-65,* 1989-2 CB 786; *Letter Ruling 9018062*]

Q. 13:7 What are the filing requirements for obtaining a favorable determination letter?

Before the actual application may be filed, notice of the filing must first be given to all interested parties. (See Q. 13:8.) The application should then be sent to the District Director of the district that covers the employer's principal place of business. Documents that should accompany the request include the following:

• Copies of the plan and trust

• Executed power of attorney (if the application is made on behalf of the employer)

• Employee census (Form 5302)

• IRS application—Form 5300 or 5307 (for both defined benefit and defined contribution plans)

• Form 8717 and applicable user fee (see Q. 13:2)

• Copy of latest favorable determination letter

In the case of certain amendments to a retirement plan, Form 6406 may be filed as an alternative to Form 5300. The instructions to Form 6406 require that only the actual amendments, along with various explanatory information, and not the entire plan document, be included with Form 6406.

Form 5309 should be filed together with Form 5300 if the application relates to an employee stock ownership plan (ESOP). See Chapter 22.

Form 5310 should be used when the employer intends to terminate a retirement plan. Form 6088, Distributable Benefits From Employee Pension Benefit Plans, should be included with the filing of Form 5310. Generally, IRS will not issue a determination letter with respect to the termination unless the retirement plan has been amended to meet the requirements of TRA '86 that are in effect at the time of termination. [Rev. Proc. 88-9, 1988-1 CB 634; Notice 87-57, 1987-2 CB 368] However, IRS has provided some relief with respect to terminating retirement plans (see Q. 19:54).

For details with regard to requesting a determination letter for an affiliated service group, see Q. 27:32.

Q. 13:8 What are the requirements regarding notice to employees?

All interested parties must be given notice that an application for a determination letter will be made. Generally, this means all current employees eligible to participate in the retirement plan must be notified. If that notice is given by posting or in person, it must be given not less than seven days, and not more than 21 days, before the application is filed. If notice is given by mail, it must be given not less than ten days, and not more than 24 days, before the application is filed. (The postmark date is what counts.) [IRC § 7476(b); Reg. §§ 1.7476-1 and 1.7476-2; Reg. § 601.201(o)(3)(xv); *Rev. Proc. 80-30* (§ 7.02), 1980-1 CB 685]

The notice must contain the following information:

- Brief description of the class of interested parties to whom the notice is addressed;
- Name of plan, plan identification number, and name of plan administrator;
- Name and identification number of the applicant;
- Description of class of employees eligible to participate;
- Description of the procedures for employees to submit comments to IRS or to request DOL to do so;
- That an application for a determination letter will be sent to IRS, the address of the IRS office, and the purpose of the application (e.g., initial qualification);
- Whether IRS has ever issued a determination letter as to the qualified status of the plan; and
- The procedure whereby certain additional information may be obtained by the interested parties. This additional information consists of

  — An updated copy of the plan and related trust agreement

  — A copy of the application

  — Other documents, whether sent to or from IRS in connection with this application

  — Any other information that affects the rights of the interested parties

An employer that fails to give proper notice to interested parties is barred from appealing IRS's refusal to issue a determination letter to the Tax Court. [IRC § 7476(b); Reg. §§ 601.201(o)(3)(xviii) through 601.201(o)(3)(xx); *Rev. Proc. 80-30*, 1980-1 CB 685]

Q. 13:9 Where is an application for a determination letter sent?

Nine IRS districts are designated as key districts. Each key district has a division known as the Employee Plans/Exempt Organization (EP/EO) Division. The other districts are associate districts. Each key district has as few as two, or as many as nine, associate districts.

The application for a determination letter with all supporting documents and forms should be sent to the IRS key district that has jurisdiction over the employer. For example, an Albany-based employer files its application with the Brooklyn (New York) district because the Brooklyn district is the key district for Albany.

If employer is in IRS district covering:	*Send application to this key district address:*
Albany, Augusta, Boston, Brooklyn, Buffalo, Burlington, Hartford, Manhattan, Portsmouth, Providence	Internal Revenue Service EP/EO Division P.O. Box 1680, GPO Brooklyn, New York 11202
Baltimore, District of Columbia, Pittsburgh, Richmond, Newark, Philadelphia, Wilmington, any U.S. possession or foreign country	Internal Revenue Service EP/EO Division P.O. Box 17010 Baltimore, Maryland 21203
Atlanta, Birmingham, Columbia, Fort Lauderdale, Greensboro, Jackson, Jacksonville, Little Rock, Nashville, New Orleans	Internal Revenue Service EP/EO Division P.O. Box 941 Atlanta, Georgia 30370

Cincinnati, Cleveland, Detroit, Indianapolis, Louisville, Parkersburg	Internal Revenue Service EP/EO Division P.O. Box 3159 Cincinnati, Ohio 45201
Dallas, Albuquerque, Austin, Cheyenne, Denver, Houston, Oklahoma City, Phoenix, Salt Late City, Wichita	Internal Revenue Service EP/EO Division Mail Code 4950 DAL 1100 Commerce Street Dallas, Texas 75242
Chicago, Aberdeen, Des Moines, Fargo, Helena, Milwaukee, Omaha, St. Louis, St. Paul, Springfield	Internal Revenue Service EP/EO Division 230 South Dearborn DPN 20-6 Chicago, Illinois 60604
Honolulu, Laguna Niguel, Las Vegas, Los Angeles, San Jose	Internal Revenue Service EP Application Receiving Room 5127 P.O. Box 536 Los Angeles, California 90053-0536
Sacramento, San Francisco	Internal Revenue Service EP Application Receiving Stop SF 4446 P.O. Box 36001 San Francisco, California 94102
Anchorage, Boise, Portland, Seattle	Internal Revenue Service EP Application Receiving P.O. Box 21224 Seattle, Washington 98111

[Rev. Proc. 90-17, 1990-12 IRB 13]

Q. 13:10 What happens to an application for a determination letter after it is sent to IRS?

After the application is stamped "received," it is reviewed by an individual known as a perfecter. The perfecter reviews the application and related documents for completeness and to ensure that it has been sent to the proper district. If the application is incomplete, it may be returned to the employer.

Once the perfecter is satisfied that the application is complete, case and file folder numbers are assigned to the application. The file folder number has nine digits; the case number has nine digits followed by the letters EP. In each instance, the first two digits reflect the district code; thus, for example, an application of a Brooklyn employer bears case and file folder numbers beginning with 11, the Brooklyn district code.

Data are then fed from the application through a computer terminal to one of the IRS Service Centers. The Service Center, in turn, performs two functions with those data. First, the Service Center issues Form 4646B, Deferred Compensation Plan, which is an acknowledgment to the applicant of IRS's receipt of the application. In addition to identifying data regarding the applicant, this acknowledgment contains the case and file folder numbers and the IRS control date, which starts the 270-day review period (see Q. 13:11). Second, the Service Center generates preaddressed labels that are affixed to the annual reporting forms that are sent to the applicant.

The application is then either screened out for the early issuance of a favorable determination letter or winds its way through clerical functions and is assigned to a group. The group manager assigns the application to an employee plans specialist, depending on the degree of difficulty, the size of the applicant, and the workload of the specialists in the group. The application is assigned about 60 to 90 days after the control date.

The specialist reviews the application and contacts the applicant or authorized representative if additional information is needed. If everything is in order, the specialist recommends the issuance of a favorable determination letter and, if the group manager agrees with the recommendation, the file is sent to the Review Staff. Not all applications receive this second level of review. Although some applications are subject to mandatory review, most are subjected to a random sampling review.

Assuming again that everything is in order and the reviewer agrees with the specialist, the district apprises the Service Center of its recommendation and a computer-generated favorable determination letter is issued to the applicant. The applicant's authorized representative receives a copy of the determination letter.

Q. 13:11   How long does it take to obtain a determination letter?

Generally, a determination letter is issued within 180 days after the application is filed. Form 4646B (see Q. 13:10) generally provides an estimate of the time period to process the application; it typically reflects 145 days.

IRS has a maximum of 270 days to rule after it receives an application for a determination. If IRS fails to act within this period, the employer can ask the Tax Court for a favorable ruling (technically, a declaratory judgment) notwithstanding IRS's inaction.

On the other hand, IRS must wait at least 60 days after it receives the application before it can issue a determination letter. This gives IRS a chance to review any comments made by interested parties. (See Q. 13:8.) [IRC § 7476; Rev. Proc. 80-30, 1980-1 CB 685]

Q. 13:12   What alternatives are available to an applicant if IRS proposes to issue an adverse determination letter?

Generally, IRS is inclined to issue a favorable determination letter to an applicant even if this means accepting amendments in proposed form as a basis for closing a case. There are circumstances, however, in which the applicant cannot satisfy the employee plans specialist (by amendment or otherwise) that a favorable determination letter should be issued. Three courses of action are then available to the applicant. The applicant can:

1. Request the employee plans specialist to seek technical advice from IRS's National Office;

2. Withdraw the application; or

3. Appeal the proposed adverse determination letter.

Requests for technical advice are made only when the issue involved satisfies certain criteria established by IRS. Chances of going this route are remote.

Withdrawal of an application at best restores the status quo. On occasion, withdrawal might even lead the employee plans specialist to issue an information report to the Examination Division (formerly, the Audit Division) to consider selecting the employer's tax return for examination to see whether a tax deduction was claimed for the employer's contribution to the plan.

Appeal is the usual course of action. An appeal may be taken to an IRS Regional Office within time limits established by IRS. If the Appeals Officer sustains the district's position, the next appeal is to the IRS National Office. Finally, if that office sustains the district's position, the applicant must petition the Tax Court for a declaratory judgment that its retirement plan is qualified on or before the ninety-first day after the date of issuance of the final adverse determination. Failure to exhaust all IRS administrative remedies bars an applicant from proceeding in the Tax Court. However, an employer whose plan qualification request is unduly delayed by IRS is deemed to have exhausted administrative remedies. [IRC § 7476; *Tipton and Kalmbach, Inc.*, 43 TCM 1345 (1982)]

Q. 13:13 Once a favorable determination letter is issued, may IRS subsequently revoke such qualification?

Courts have generally held that in order for IRS to revoke a prior favorable determination letter, a material change of fact must have occurred since the time of the initial IRS review of the employer's retirement plan. However, the failure to amend a retirement plan on a timely basis after initial IRS approval may cause the plan to lose its qualified status. [*Lansons, Inc.*, 622 F2d 774 (5th Cir. 1980); *Boggs v. Commissioner*, 784 F2d 1166 (4th Cir. 1986), *vac'g and rem'g* 83 TC 132 (1984); *Halligan et al.*, 51 TCM 1203 (1986); *Basch Eng'g, Inc.*, 59 TCM 482 (1990)]

Chapter 14

Operating the Plan

The role of the plan administrator was given consider-able significance by ERISA. Responsibility for adminis-tering a qualified retirement plan was clearly placed with the plan administrator. This chapter explains who the plan administrator is, what the plan administrator's responsibilities are, and which records must be main-tained.

Q. 14:1 Who is the plan administrator?

Generally, the plan administrator is a person specifically desig-nated by the qualified retirement plan as the administrator (1) by name, (2) by reference to the person or group holding a named position, (3) by reference to a procedure for designating an adminis-trator, or (4) by reference to the person or group charged with the specific responsibilities of plan administrator. If no person or group is designated, the employer is the administrator (in the case of a qualified retirement plan maintained by a single employer). The employer's board of directors (in the case of a corporation) may authorize a person or group to fulfill the responsibilities of adminis-trator. In any case, if a plan administrator cannot be determined, the plan administrator is the person or persons actually responsible for control, disposition, or management of the property received by the qualified retirement plan. [ERISA § 3(16)(A); IRC § 414(g); Reg. § 1.414(g)]

Q. 14:2   Can officers or owners of the company function as plan administrator?

Yes. In small companies, a company officer or owner usually is designated as plan administrator. In large companies, three or more people (a committee) may be designated collectively as plan administrator.

Q. 14:3   What are the basic responsibilities of the plan administrator?

The plan administrator is responsible for managing the day-to-day affairs of the qualified retirement plan. Specifically, these responsibilities include the following:

- Hiring attorneys, accountants, consultants, and, for certain qualified retirement plans, actuaries;
- Determining eligibility for plan participation, vesting, and accrual of benefits;
- Advising participants or beneficiaries of their rights and settlement options;
- Ruling on claims for benefits;
- Directing distribution of benefits;
- Preparing reports for participants, IRS, DOL, and PBGC (see Chapter 15); and
- Keeping service records, benefit records, vesting records, and participant information.

Q. 14:4   Which records should a plan administrator maintain?

The plan administrator is required to maintain records relating to the operation of the qualified retirement plan that will provide in sufficient detail the necessary information from which required reports (to IRS, DOL, and PBGC) may be verified, explained, or clarified. These records must be kept available for at least six years after the filing date of the reports. [ERISA § 107]

The plan administrator must also maintain records to determine the benefits due or that may become due in order to be able to report that information to any plan participant who:

- Requests the information (but not more than once in any 12-month period);
- Terminates service with the company; or
- Has a break in service.

[ERISA § 209]

Thus, a plan administrator should maintain the following records:

Service: Precise records must be kept of time worked by all employees so that determinations of eligibility, vesting, or benefit accrual may be substantiated. These records have to be maintained for many years, even though a participant may have terminated employment and distributions may have been made.

Benefits: Detailed records should be maintained to project benefits for highly paid participants to ensure that their benefits do not exceed the limitations provided by law. These records should also be maintained if a qualified retirement plan provides for deferred payment of benefits. For example, a participant who terminates employment at a young age might not receive benefits until a later age.

Vesting: The vesting alternatives under ERISA and the Code require calculations under specific formulas. In some cases, participants may be under different vesting schedules, requiring meticulous administrative records. For example, if a vesting schedule is changed by amendment, certain participants may elect to remain under the old vesting schedule (see Q. 8:6). See also Q. 20:32 through Q. 20:36 regarding vesting under top-heavy plans, which may require dual recordkeeping for vesting purposes.

Deductible employee contributions: Although no longer permitted, separate accounting for past contributions, if any, is still required (see Q. 5:17).

Plan administrators are also required to retain all plan records necessary to support or validate PBGC premium payments. The records, which include actuarial calculations, must be kept for six years after the filing due date. For the consequences of a plan administrator's failure to maintain those records, see Q. 14:6. [PBGC Reg. § 2610.11]

Q. 14:5   May the plan administrator rely on information gathered by those performing ministerial functions?

Yes, provided the plan administrator has exercised prudence in selecting and retaining these people. The plan administrator should consider whether those gathering information are competent, honest, and responsible. [DOL Reg. § 2509.75-8, FR-11]

Q. 14:6   What penalty is imposed for failure to comply with recordkeeping requirements?

PBGC may audit the records of a defined benefit plan covered by PBGC (see Q. 19:12 and Q. 19:13) regarding the calculation of the premium owed each year to the agency. If it is determined that the plan's records do not support the amount of unfunded vested benefits reported in the PBGC forms, PBGC will "deem" the variable-rate portion of the premium to be the maximum $34 amount per participant (see Q. 19:14). [PBGC Reg. § 2610.11]

Q. 14:7   Is withholding required on the distribution of benefits from a retirement plan?

Taxable distributions from a retirement plan (see Q. 14:9) are subject to income tax withholding unless the recipient of the distribution elects out of the withholding. The withholding rules apply to both periodic payments (e.g., annuities) and nonperiodic payments (e.g., lump-sum distributions). In addition to withholding, plan administrators are also subject to recordkeeping and reporting responsibilities. (See Q. 15:16.) [IRC §§ 3405(a) and 3405(b)]

The option to elect out of withholding is not available if the payment is delivered outside of the United States or its possessions unless the payee certifies to the payor that the payee is not (1) a U.S. citizen or resident alien or (2) a tax-avoiding expatriate under Section 877. [IRC § 3405(d)(13); Notice 87-7, 1987-1 CB 420]

Q. 14:8   Is there any liability for failure to withhold income taxes?

Yes. Generally, the plan administrator (or payor) will be liable for the tax that should have been withheld as well as any penalties if a taxable distribution is made from a retirement plan (see Q. 14:9) and the recipient of the distribution does not elect out of the withholding or if automatic withholding applies (see Q. 14:7). [IRC § 6672(a); Temp. Reg. § 35.3405-1, G-2 and G-20]

Q. 14:9   Which types of retirement plans are subject to the withholding rules on distributions?

All qualified and nonqualified retirement plans—including individual retirement accounts (IRAs) of any type—are subject to the withholding rules. [IRC § 3405(d)]

Q. 14:10   How should a plan administrator handle oral inquiries from participants?

Numerous questions by participants can be expected. The plan administrator can insist that inquiries be in writing unless the effect of that request is to make it difficult for participants to inquire about the plan (e.g., if the participants are not fluent in English).

The danger, of course, in responding orally to complex questions about the plan is that since there is no record of what was said, a participant may claim at a later date that the information provided by the plan administrator was misleading. Thus, the plan administrator should limit the number of individuals authorized to answer questions concerning the plan or its benefits. Such a policy should be conveyed to participants and strictly adhered to. Those authorized to answer questions should maintain a log for recording inquiries. They should also respond in writing to inquiries that they believe may affect an individual's benefits in order to have a record of what was said.

Q. 14:11   Must a recipient receive an explanation of the tax effects of a distribution from a qualified retirement plan?

Yes. Plan administrators are required to give recipients of certain distributions a written explanation of the rules relating to the taxation of amounts as capital gains (see Q. 11:19), the income forward averaging method for the ordinary income portion of lump-sum distributions (see Q. 11:17 and Q. 11:18), and the exclusion from gross income for amounts rolled over into eligible retirement plans (see Q. 26:1). This notice must be provided to the recipient of any qualified total distribution or any partial distribution (see Q. 26:7), not later than two weeks after the distribution is made. [IRC § 402(f); Reg. § 1.402(f)-1]

This requirement may be satisfied by providing each recipient of a qualified total distribution or a partial distribution a copy of the notice set forth below. Additional information may be provided to recipients, except that such information may not be inconsistent with the following IRS notice:

Q: Under what circumstances may an individual continue to use the special 10-year averaging rules for lump-sum distributions from qualified pension, profit sharing, stock bonus or annuity plans?

A: In general, the special 10-year forward averaging rules on lump-sum distributions are available for 1986, but have been replaced with special 5-year averaging rules for 1987 and later years. The special 5-year averaging is calculated in the same manner as the 10-year averaging except the amount is treated as if it were spread out over 5 years instead of 10 years. The special 5-year averaging rule generally may not be used unless the individual is age 59½ at the time of the distribution and may be used only once.

Q: What is a lump-sum distribution?

A: A lump-sum distribution refers to a specific type of distribution from a qualified pension, profit sharing, stock bonus or annuity plan that satisfies very specific requirements. Generally, lump-sum distribution means a distribution (after 5 or more years of participation in the plan) of the entire amount in the plan (the balance to the credit) within 1 taxable year that is made because of the employee's death or separation from service or after the employee is disabled or reaches age 59½.

Q: What special rules apply for capital gains treatment of lump-sum distributions?

A: In general, the special capital gains rules for the pre-1974 portion of a lump-sum distribution are eliminated. However, a special transition rule allows limited use of capital gains treatment between 1987 and 1991.

Q: Is there a special rule for individuals who reached age 50 before January 1, 1986?

A: There is an exception to the general rule that special treatment for lump-sum distributions is only available to those who have reached age 59½. Individuals who reached age 50 by January 1, 1986, may, in general:

1. Elect to use the special 5-year averaging provisions (using the tax rates in effect in the year of distribution), or the 10-year averaging provisions (using the 1986 tax rates), and

2. Elect to apply the pre-TRA '86 capital gains rules (using a 20% rate).

Only one election is available with respect to an individual and, if made, it eliminates the ability to elect 5-year averaging and capital gains treatment after age 59½.

Q: Certain distributions from a qualified pension, profit sharing or stock bonus plan, qualified annuity plan or Section 403(b) tax-sheltered annuity contract may be rolled over to an IRA, as may distributions from other IRAs. Did TRA '86 change any of the rules as to when rollovers can be made?

A: In general, distributions from a qualified pension, profit sharing or stock bonus plan, qualified annuity plan or Section 403(b) tax-sheltered annuity contract or custodial account may be rolled over to an IRA only if the distribution satisfies certain conditions. There are two types of distributions (other than distributions from other IRAs) that are eligible for rollover to an IRA. First, when the amount distributed from a qualified plan or annuity contract is a lump-sum distribution [as described earlier] or is distributed as a result of a plan termination. Second, when the amount distributed from a qualified plan or annuity contract is a partial distribution. Under TRA '86, a distribution is a partial distribution that can be rolled over to an IRA only if the distribution is an amount equal to at least 50 percent of the account balance and the distribution was made due to the death or disability of the employee or on account of the employee's separation from service.

[IRC § 402(f); *Announcement 87-2*, 1987-12 IRB 38]

Q. 14:12 May the plan administrator or trustee choose the form of distribution that will be made to a participant?

No. See Q. 9:41 through Q. 9:50 regarding discretion with respect to distributions from a qualified retirement plan.

Q. 14:13 Can innocent errors in the operation of a qualified retirement plan result in disqualification of the plan?

Yes. One qualified retirement plan, for example, was disqualified (i.e., lost its tax-favored status) after IRS determined that the plan was discriminatory because contributions had been allocated solely for the benefit of a shareholder-employee when, in fact, five additional employees were eligible for coverage. It did not matter that this situation resulted from an honest mistake. Furthermore, the company's offer to cure the discrimination retroactively was rejected. Although the Code authorizes retroactive corrections for defects in the retirement plan itself, there is no statutory authority for a retroactive correction of a mistake in the operation of the retirement plan. [IRC § 401(b); *Myron v. U.S.*, 550 F2d 1145 (9th Cir. 1977); see also *Buzzetta Construction Corp. v. Commissioner*, 92 TC 641 (1989)]

Q. 14:14 What is the actuary's role in administering a qualified retirement plan?

The actuary's primary function is to determine the amount needed by an employer's defined benefit plan to pay promised retirement benefits to participants. Assumptions and methods used by the actuary are basic to the application of the minimum funding standards (see Q. 7:1). The actuary is called upon to certify the amount of tax-deductible dollars the employer must contribute to its defined benefit plan.

If a defined benefit plan is not funded solely through insurance, the services of an enrolled actuary are required, that is, an actuary who is licensed to practice before the government agencies responsible for administering ERISA. Some enrolled actuaries may work for insurance companies and others may be employed by accounting firms or firms specializing in actuarial services. [ERISA §§ 3041, 3042, and 3043; IRC § 7701(a)(35)]

Q. 14:15 What is the trustee's role in administering a qualified retirement plan?

The trustee holds title to plan assets and is responsible for managing the assets unless this responsibility has been delegated to an investment manager. For details on the trustee's investment responsibilities, see Chapter 17.

Q. 14:16 What is the accountant's role in administering a qualified retirement plan?

The accountant's role may entail preparing statements of plan assets, auditing the plan's books and records, and preparing reports to government agencies. A plan with 100 or more participants requires special reports by an independent qualified public accountant. (See Q. 15:13.)

Q. 14:17 Which plan officials must be bonded?

Generally, every fiduciary (anyone who has some discretionary authority or control over the plan or its assets; see Chapter 17), and anyone who handles funds or other property of the plan, must be bonded. The bond must cover at least 10 percent of the amount handled by the bonded individual; it may not be for less than $1,000 and need not be for more than $500,000. [ERISA §§ 3(21) and 412]

Q. 14:18   What are funds or other property for purposes of the bonding requirement?

The term funds or other property is intended to encompass all property that is or may be used as a source for the payment of benefits to plan participants. It includes property in the "nature of quick assets" (e.g., cash, checks, negotiable instruments) and property that is readily convertible into cash for distribution as benefits.

Although the term does not include permanent assets used in plan operation (land and buildings, furniture and fixtures), land and buildings that are investments of a qualified retirement plan will be covered by the term other property. [DOL Reg. § 2580.412-4]

Q. 14:19   What is handling of funds?

A person handles funds or other property of a qualified retirement plan whenever that person's duties or activities are such that there is risk that the funds or other property could be lost if that person, acting alone or with others, engaged in dishonest or fraudulent conduct. Under this definition, handling is generally considered to include situations in which there is:

- Physical contact with cash, checks, or property;
- The power to secure physical possession of the cash, checks, or similar property;
- The authority to cause a transfer of property such as mortgages or securities to oneself or another; or
- Disbursement of funds or other property including the power to sign or endorse checks.

[DOL Reg. § 2580.412-6]

Q. 14:20   Are any fiduciaries exempt from the bonding requirements?

Yes. A bond generally is not required from:

- A bank that is subject to federal regulation and federally insured;

- A savings and loan association subject to federal regulation if it is the plan administrator; and
- An insurance company that provides or underwrites, in accordance with state law, plan benefits for any plan other than one established or maintained for the insurance company's employees.

[ERISA § 412(a); DOL Reg. §§ 2580.412-23 through 2580.412-32]

Q. 14:21 May a party in interest provide a bond in satisfaction of the bonding requirements?

No. A bond may not be procured from any entity in which the qualified retirement plan or a party in interest (see Q. 18:2), directly or indirectly, has any significant control or financial interest. [ERISA § 412(c); DOL Reg. §§ 2580.412-33 through 2580.412-36]

Q. 14:22 Is bonding required for a plan with only one participant?

In the case of a qualified retirement plan covering only the owner (i.e., the shareholder or sole proprietor), or the owner and the owner's spouse, the qualified retirement plan is not subject to the bonding requirements. However, if the plan's only participant is not the owner, this exception does not apply. Furthermore, if a partnership's qualified retirement plan covers only partners (or partners and their spouses), the qualified retirement plan is not subject to the bonding requirements (see Q. 17:5). [DOL Reg. § 2510.3-3]

Chapter 15

Reporting to Government Agencies

Once a qualified retirement plan has been put into operation, the plan administrator has the responsibility of filing certain information returns, reports, and statements with the agencies that administer the federal pension laws—IRS, DOL, and PBGC. This chapter sets forth guidelines for the plan administrator to follow in meeting these reporting requirements.

Q. 15:1 What are IRS's reporting requirements?

Each employer that maintains a qualified retirement plan is required to file an annual report. The annual report is commonly referred to as the Form 5500 series return/report.

The appropriate Form 5500 series return/report (Form 5500, 5500-C/R, or 5500EZ) must be filed for each qualified retirement plan (see Q. 15:2) for each plan year in which the plan has assets. Therefore, the year of complete distribution of all plan assets is the last year for which a return/report must be filed. [IRC §§ 6058 and 6059]

Q. 15:2 Which Form 5500 series return is required for a particular qualified retirement plan?

Qualified retirement plans with 100 or more participants must file Form 5500 each year. Qualified retirement plans with two or more but fewer than 100 participants must file Form 5500-C/R, which takes the place of separate Forms 5500-C and 5500-R for plan years beginning in 1989. The Form 5500-C/R must be filed as Form 5500-C for the first plan year, at least once every three plan years thereafter, and for the final plan year. For the plan years that Form 5500-C is not required, Form 5500-C/R may be filed as Form 5500-R, a brief registration statement.

If the plan has between 80 and 120 participants (inclusive) at the beginning of the plan year, the plan may file the same series of forms (Form 5500 or 5500-C/R) that it filed for the previous year.

Form 5500-C is enforcement-oriented and, according to IRS, PBGC, and DOL, "will provide the information necessary for each Agency to monitor compliance with ERISA. The 5500-R is designed to ensure that the Agencies receive annually certain minimal information to permit the continuous review of small plans." [Notice of Adoption of Revised Forms, filed with the Federal Register of July 31, 1980]

Form 5500EZ, Annual Return of One-Participant (Owners and Their Spouses) Pension Benefit Plan, may be used for certain qualified retirement plans. A one-participant plan is defined as a qualified retirement plan that covers only:

1. The owner of a business or both the owner and spouse, and the business, whether or not incorporated, is wholly owned by the owner, or both the owner and spouse, or

2. Partners (or the partners and their spouses) in a business partnership.

Form 5500EZ cannot be used if the plan sponsor is a member of an affiliated service group (see Q. 27:31), controlled group of corporations (see Q. 4:34), or group of businesses under common control (see Q. 4:32), or leases employees (see Q. 4:37). In addition, if the plan satisfies the coverage requirements (see Q. 4:15) only when combined with another plan, Form 5500EZ cannot be used. A qualified retirement plan that cannot use Form 5500EZ must use Form 5500-C/R.

Employers with one-participant plan or plans that have total assets of $100,000 or less at the end of the plan year are not required to file any Form 5500 series return/report for the plan year. [Instructions to 1989 IRS Form 5500EZ]

Q. 15:3 Does the plan administrator have the option of filing Form 5500-C/R as Form 5500-C annually instead of as Form 5500-R?

Yes. Plan administrators and sponsors may file a Form 5500-C for any year in which a Form 5500-R registration statement could have been filed. If the Form 5500-C is filed, the three-year filing cycle starts again (see Q. 15:2). [Instructions to 1989 IRS Form 5500-C/R]

Q. 15:4 Must any special schedules accompany the employer's annual return?

Yes. Schedule A (Form 5500), Insurance Information, must be attached to Forms 5500 and 5500-C/R if any benefits under the qualified retirement plan are provided by an insurance company. However, Schedule A is not needed if Form 5500EZ is filed or if a Form 5500-C/R is filed but the plan covers only a sole owner of a trade or business (or owner and owner's spouse) or partners (or partners and their spouses). [ERISA § 103(e)]

Schedule B (Form 5500), Actuarial Information, must be attached to the annual return of most defined benefit plans. [IRC § 6059]

Schedule C (Form 5500), Service Provider and Trustee Information, must be attached to Form 5500 to report:

1. Service providers receiving, directly or indirectly, $5,000 or more in compensation for services rendered to the plan during a plan year (see Instructions to IRS Form 5500 Schedule C for exceptions);

2. Trustee information; and

3. Information relating to the termination of all persons who acted as accountants, enrolled actuaries, insurance carriers, custodians, administrators, investment managers, and trustees of the plan during the plan year.

[Instructions to 1989 Schedule C to IRS Form 5500]

Schedule P (Form 5500), Annual Return of Fiduciary of Employee Benefit Trust, may be completed by a fiduciary (trustee or custodian) and filed as an attachment to Form 5500, 5500-C/R, or 5500EZ. It is strongly recommended that Schedule P be filed because it starts the running of the statute of limitations under Section 6501(a) for the trust. (See Q. 15:11.) [Instructions to 1989 Schedule P to IRS Form 5500]

Schedule SSA (Form 5500), Annual Registration Statement Identifying Separated Participants With Deferred Vested Benefits, is used to inform IRS of plan participants who separated from service but were not paid retirement benefits. The Instructions to IRS Form 5500 Schedule SSA describe when a separated participant must be reported on Schedule SSA. [IRC § 6057]

Also, if the current value of a qualified retirement plan's assets is less than 70 percent of the current liability under the plan, the percentage must be disclosed on the annual report. [ERISA § 103(d)(11)]

Q. 15:5   When is a Form 5500 series annual return due?

Unless an extension is granted (see Q. 15:6 and Q. 15:7), the appropriate Form 5500 series annual return is due by the last day of the seventh month following the close of the plan year (July 31 for calendar-year plans). Note that the due date relates to the plan year and not to the employer's taxable year. [ERISA § 104]

> **Example.** Just-In Corporation files its federal income tax return on a calendar-year basis. Just-In maintains a qualified retirement plan with a plan year end of January 31. For the plan year ending January 31, 1991, the Form 5500 series annual report is due August 31, 1991.

Q. 15:6   May the due date for filing a Form 5500 series annual return be extended?

Yes. An extension of up to 2½ months may be granted for filing the Form 5500 series return. Form 5558, Application for Extension of Time to File Certain Employee Plan Returns, must be filed in sufficient time before the regular due date to permit IRS to consider and act on the application. A detailed statement of the reason for an extension must be attached to the application. (See Q. 15:7.)

Q. 15:7   Is the extension of time for filing the Form 5500 series annual return ever automatic?

Yes. An automatic extension of the due date for filing is available to an employer if all of the following conditions are met:

• The plan year coincides with the employer's taxable year;

• The employer has been granted an extension of time to file its federal income tax return to a date later than the due date for its Form 5500 series annual return; and

• A copy of the income tax extension is attached to the Form 5500 series annual return.

Example. Just-In Corporation files its federal income tax return on a calendar-year basis. Just-In maintains a qualified retirement plan with a plan year end of January 31. Just-In receives extensions to file its federal income tax return through September 15, 1991. Is the August 31, 1991 due date for filing the Form 5500 series annual return automatically extended? No, because the plan year does not coincide with the tax year. However, if the plan year was a calendar year, the due date would have been extended from July 31, 1991 to September 15, 1991.

Q. 15:8   What penalties may be imposed for late filing of the Form 5500 series annual return?

One or more of the following five penalties may be imposed or assessed for late or incomplete filings after the date they are due unless there was reasonable cause for the improper filing:

1. DOL may assess a civil penalty against a plan administrator of up to $1,000 a day for the late filing of Form 5500. In addition, a Form 5500 series return rejected by DOL because it lacks material information will be treated as if it had not been filed. In other words, the plan administrator can be assessed a penalty for an incomplete as well as an untimely but complete filing.

2. A penalty of $25 a day (up to a maximum of $15,000) is imposed for each day a 5500 series return is overdue.

3. A plan administrator who fails to include all required sepa-

15-5

rated participants in a timely filed annual registration statement (Schedule SSA) (see Q. 15:4) is subject to a penalty of $1 a day for each separate participant (the maximum penalty is $5,000).

4. A penalty of $1,000 is imposed if an actuarial report (Schedule B) (see Q. 15:4) is not filed for a defined benefit plan.

5. A penalty of $1 a day (up to a maximum of $1,000) is imposed if a notification of change of status of a plan is not filed on time.

[ERISA §§ 104(a)(4) and 502(c)(2); IRC §§ 6652(e), 6652(d)(1), 6692, and 6652(d)(2)]

Q. 15:9 Are there any criminal penalties for violations of the reporting requirements?

Yes. Willful violations of the reporting and disclosure requirements of ERISA can result in penalties up to a maximum of $5,000 in the case of an individual ($100,000 for any other entity), one year imprisonment, or both. [ERISA § 501]

In addition, it is a criminal offense to knowingly make a false statement or conceal or fail to disclose any fact needed to prepare reports required by Title I of ERISA. The maximum penalties are a $10,000 fine, five years imprisonment, or both. [18 U.S.C. § 1027] This provision has been applied to:

- A service provider that provided the plan with false information regarding his profits, which the plan needed to complete its Form 5500. [*U.S. v. Martorano*, 767 F2d 63 (3d Cir. 1985)]

- A participant who submitted false information to his plan. [*U.S. v. Bartkus*, 816 F2d 255 (6th Cir. 1987)]

Q. 15:10 Does a plan administrator's reliance on a third party to timely file the Form 5500 series annual return constitute reasonable cause for late filing?

No. A circuit court has upheld the imposition by IRS of a $5,000 penalty against an employer for the late filing of Form 5500-C, even though the employer relied on a bank to file the return on time, because the responsibility for timely filing remains with the employer or plan administrator. [IRC § 6058(a); *Alton Ob-Gyn, Ltd. v. U.S.*, 789 F2d 515 (7th Cir. 1986)]

Q. 15:11   Does the statute of limitations apply to the Form 5500 series annual return?

The filing of Schedule P (Form 5500), Annual Return of Fiduciary of Employee Benefit Trust, (see Q. 15:4) with the Form 5500 series annual return starts the running of the statute of limitations for any tax-exempt trust that is part of a qualified retirement plan. [IRC § 6033(a)]

The Tax Court has held that the filing of Form 5500-C for 1980 without Schedule P attached started the running of the statute of limitations because the Form disclosed the plan's trustees and was signed by a trustee under penalty of perjury. However, the 1979 Form 5500-C did not start the running of the statute of limitations because it did not disclose the plan's trustees. [*Martin Fireproofing Profit Sharing Plan and Trust*, 92 TC 1173 (1989)]

Q. 15:12   Does the filing of Form 5500 start the statute of limitations running with regard to a prohibited transaction?

Yes, if it discloses the transaction. Although Form 5330 is the appropriate form to report a prohibited transaction for the purpose of computing any excise taxes that may be owed (see Q. 18:4), in a Tax Court case, IRS conceded that the filing of a Form 5500 series annual return that adequately discloses the facts of the transaction is sufficient to start the statute of limitations running for prohibited transactions. [*Rutland*, 89 TC 1137 (1987)]

Q. 15:13   Must a plan engage an independent accountant when it files its Form 5500 series annual return?

In the case of a plan with 100 or more participants, a certified public accountant or licensed public accountant (or an individual certified by DOL) must conduct an audit of the plan's books and records. The accountant must issue an opinion, which is to be included in the annual report, covering:

1. The financial statements and schedules covered by the annual report;

2. The accounting principles and practices reflected in the report;

3. The consistency of the application of those principles and practices; and

4. Any changes in accounting principles having a material effect on the financial statements. [ERISA §§ 103(a)(3) and 109(b); DOL Reg. § 2520.103-1(b)(5)]

If the plan has fewer than 100 participants at the beginning of the plan year, an accountant's opinion is not required. [DOL Reg. § 2520.104-46]

Q. 15:14 Where are the Form 5500 series annual returns filed?

Returns should be filed at the IRS Service Center indicated below:

Location of the principal office of the plan sponsor or plan administrator	Internal Revenue Service Center address
Connecticut, Delaware, District of Columbia, Foreign Address, Maine, Maryland, Massachusetts, New Hampshire, New Jersey, New York, Pennsylvania, Puerto Rico, Rhode Island, Vermont, Virginia	Holtsville, NY 00501
Alabama, Alaska, Arkansas, California, Florida, Georgia, Hawaii, Idaho, Louisiana, Mississippi, Nevada, North Carolina, Oregon, South Carolina, Tennessee, Washington	Atlanta, GA 39901

Arizona, Colorado, Illinois, Indiana, Iowa, Kansas, Kentucky, Michigan, Minnesota, Missouri, Montana, Nebraska, New Mexico, North Dakota, Ohio, Oklahoma, South Dakota, Texas, Utah, West Virginia, Wisconsin, Wyoming	Memphis, TN 37501
All Form 5500EZ filers	Andover, MA 05501

Q. 15:15 Which special returns must be filed with IRS?

Form 5310 is filed as part of an application for a determination letter from IRS concerning the termination of a qualified retirement plan, or to notify IRS of a consolidation or merger or the transfer of plan assets and liabilities. Form 5310 must be filed for a plan merger or consolidation or a transfer of plan assets or liabilities at least 30 days before the event. Although there is no legal requirement to file for a determination letter regarding a plan's termination, it is strongly suggested that Form 5310 be filed with IRS (see Q. 19:55).

Another special return is Form 5330, Return of Excise Taxes Related to Employee Benefit Plans. This form is used to report a prohibited transaction and any penalty tax due, by the person who engaged in the prohibited transaction (see Chapter 18). [IRC § 4975]

Form 5330 is also used for paying penalty taxes if the employer failed to meet the minimum funding standards. (See Q. 7:1.) [IRC § 4971]

Form 5330 is also used to report and pay the tax on:

• Certain ESOP dispositions;

• Nondeductible contributions to qualified retirement plans;

• Excess contributions to 401(k) plans;

• Certain prohibited allocations of qualified securities by an ESOP; and

• Reversions of qualified retirement plan assets to employers.

[IRC §§ 4978, 4978A, 4972, 4979, 4979A, and 4980; 1989 Instructions to IRS Form 5330]

Form 5330 is generally due on or before the last day of the seventh month after the end of the taxable year of the employer or other person required to file Form 5330. An extension of up to six months may be requested by filing Form 5558 (see Q. 15:6). However, to report reversions, Form 5330 must be filed by the last day of the month following the reversion. To report excess contributions to 401(k) plans, Form 5330 must be filed by the due date of the employer's income tax return for the year during which occurs the end of the plan year to which the excise tax applies.

Q. 15:16 Which forms are used to report qualified retirement plan distributions?

The reporting requirements are met by filing Form W-2P for all periodic payments and nonperiodic payments that are not total distributions. Total distributions are reported on Form 1099-R.

Those receiving qualified retirement plan payments must receive the appropriate form by January 31 of the year after the payment. Copy A of Form W-2P must also be sent with Form W-3 to the Social Security Administration by the last day in February. Form 1099-R information is summarized on Form 1096, which must be filed with IRS by the last day in February. *Note:* If magnetic media are used to transmit Forms 1099-R to IRS, Form 4804 (not Form 1096) must accompany such submission. [Instructions to 1990 IRS Form 1096]

The failure to timely file a required report can result in a $25 per day penalty up to a maximum of $15,000. [IRC § 6652(e)]

Forms W-2P and 1099-R are also used to report corrective distributions of excess deferrals and excess contributions to 401(k) plans (see Q. 21:28 and Q. 21:17). [*Notice 89-32*, 1989-1 CB 671, corrected by *Announcement 89-69*, 1989-24 IRB 78]

IRS has announced that Forms W-2P and 1099-R will be combined into a single revised Form 1099-R for use beginning with distributions in 1991. [*Announcement 90-79*, 1990-25 IRB 28]

Generally, the filing of Form W-2P or Form 1099 with respect to each payee satisfies information reporting requirements with respect to income tax withholding. For failing to report withholding taxes or keep necessary records, IRS may impose a penalty of $50 for each affected individual, up to a maximum of $50,000 in a calendar year. [IRC §§ 6047(d) and 6704; Reg. § 35.3405-1, Q&A E-9]

Q. 15:17 What are DOL reporting requirements?

Unless a qualified retirement plan is exempt from the reporting and disclosure requirements of ERISA (see Q. 15:18), the following reports are required:

1. Annual reports (Form 5500 series annual return/report);
2. Summary plan descriptions (SPDs);
3. Summary description of material modifications to the plan or SPD (sometimes referred to as SMMs); and
4. Supplementary or terminal reports. [ERISA §§ 101 and 104]

To avoid duplicate reporting, annual reports are filed only with IRS. Copies of the reports are supplied to DOL by IRS.

Some of these reports must also be distributed to participants. See Chapter 16 for more details.

Q. 15:18 Which types of plans are exempt from the reporting requirements of DOL?

There is a general exemption for individual retirement accounts (IRAs), governmental plans, church plans, and excess benefit plans (unfunded plans providing benefits above the limits on contributions and benefits for tax purposes). [ERISA § 4(b)]

There is also an exemption for "plans without employees," that is, plans in which the only participants are an individual and the individual's spouse if that individual is the only owner of the business (whether incorporated or not). In the case of any other family relationship, the exemption does not apply. For example, if the only plan participants are brothers, or father and son, the reporting requirements apply. This exemption does not apply to the requirement to file the annual Form 5500 series return/report with IRS (see Q. 15:2). [DOL Reg. § 2510.3-3]

Q. 15:19 Which forms must be filed with PBGC?

PBGC Form 1 (including Schedule A) and PBGC Form 1-ES are used to report premiums due to the PBGC. Qualified retirement plans with fewer than 500 participants file only PBGC Form 1, along with their total premium payment, by the final filing due date (see Q. 15:20).

The plan administrator of any qualified retirement plan (single-employer or multiemployer) that reported 500 or more participants on its PBGC Form 1 for the prior year must file a PBGC Form 1-ES to make its premium payment initially (the flat-rate portion of the premium for single-employer plans) on the basis of an estimated participant count. This filing and payment must be made by the first filing due date (see Q. 15:20). Using the actual participant count, such single-employer and multiemployer plans must thereafter file PBGC Form 1 to make a reconciliation filing and pay the final fixed per participant premium. In addition, all single-employer plans must file a Schedule A with PBGC Form 1 and pay the variable-rate portion of the premium. (It should be noted that if all the information needed to file PBGC Form 1 is known before the first filing due date, PBGC Form 1 should be filed instead of Form 1-ES. If Form 1-ES is filed, it will be necessary to file PBGC Form 1 by the final filing due date.) [Instructions to 1989 Annual Premium Payment Package]

A plan that was at the full funding limitation (see Q. 7:14) for the preceding plan year is not liable for the variable-rate portion of the premium. This exemption is retroactive to plan years beginning in 1988. Plans that qualified for the exemption in 1988 and 1989 may either request a refund (see Q. 15:21) or credit earlier premium payments against premiums owed in 1990. [PBGC Reg. § 2610.24(a)(5)]

Q. 15:20 When are the PBGC premium forms due?

If the plan has 500 or more participants for the plan year, the plan sponsor must file a PBGC Form 1-ES by the last day of the second full calendar month following the close of the preceding plan year (first filing due date). For single-employer plans, only the flat-rate portion of the premium is due by the first filing due date; the variable-rate portion is due and PBGC Form 1 must be filed by the final filing due date (see below). For multiemployer plans, the entire premium is due by the first filing due date.

If the plan has fewer than 500 participants for the plan year, the plan sponsor must file the Form 1 (single-employer plans must also file Schedule A to Form 1) and pay the entire premium by the fifteenth day of the eighth full calendar month following the month in which the plan year began (final filing due date). If the full amount due is not paid by the applicable date(s), the plan will be subject to late payment interest and penalty charges. (See Q. 15:23.) [PBGC Reg. §§ 2610.25 and 2610.34]

> **Example 1.** A single-employer plan has a plan year beginning July 1 and ending June 30. It had 950 participants as of the first day of its first plan year, July 1, 1989. For its second plan year beginning July 1, 1990, the plan must file a PBGC Form 1-ES on the first filing due date, August 31, 1990, using an estimated participant count to determine the flat-rate portion of the premium. The plan must file its PBGC Form 1 and pay any outstanding balance of the flat-rate portion of the premium plus the variable-rate portion by the final filing due date, March 15, 1991.

> **Example 2.** A multiemployer plan has a July 15 to July 14 plan year. It had 1,500 participants as of the first day of the plan's first year, July 15, 1989. The first filing due date for the plan's second plan year beginning July 15, 1990 is September 30, 1990, and the plan must generally file a PBGC Form 1-ES on that date, using an estimated participant count to determine the amount of the premium. The plan must make a final reconciliation filing on PBGC Form 1 by the final filing due date, March 15, 1991.

New and newly covered single-employer and multiemployer plans, regardless of the number of plan participants, are not required to pay estimated premiums. Such plans are required to file and pay the applicable premium for the first time by the latest of the following dates:

- The fifteenth day of the eighth full calendar month following the later of the month in which the plan year began or the month in which the plan first became effective for benefit accruals for future service;

- The ninetieth day after the date of the plan's adoption; or
- The ninetieth day after the date on which the plan became covered under ERISA Title IV.

[PBGC Reg. §§ 2610.25 and 2610.34]

> **Example 1.** A new plan has a plan year beginning January 1, 1991, and ending December 31, 1991. The plan was adopted on October 1, 1990, but became effective for benefit accruals on January 1, 1991. The filing due date is September 15, 1991.

> **Example 2.** A professional service employer maintains a plan with a plan year beginning on January 1, 1990, and ending December 31, 1990. If this plan has always had fewer than 25 participants, it is not a covered plan under Section 4021 of ERISA. On October 15, 1990, the plan has 26 participants for the first time. It is now a covered plan and will continue to be a covered plan regardless of the plan's future participant count. The filing due date is January 13, 1991, i.e., 90 days after the plan became covered under Title IV.

An extension of the due date granted by IRS for filing Form 5500 (Annual Report/Report of Employee Benefit Plan) does not extend the due date for filing PBGC Form 1.

PBGC Form 1-ES and Form 1 should be mailed with premium payments to:

> Pension Benefit Guaranty Corporation
>
> P.O. Box 105655
>
> Atlanta, Georgia 30348-5655

PBGC Form 1-ES and Form 1, along with premium payments, may be hand delivered to:

> Retail Lockbox Processing Center
>
> PBGC Lockbox 105655
>
> 1740 Phoenix Highway
>
> College Park, Georgia 30349

[PBGC Reg. § 2610.4]

Q. 15:21 How does a change in the plan year affect the due dates for filing the PBGC premium forms?

If the plan year is changed, two sets of PBGC forms must be filed: one for the old plan year and another for the new plan year. Each filing and premium payment must reflect a full 12-month plan year.

Plans that change their plan years as a result of a plan amendment must follow the due date rules for the short year as though it were a regular plan year (Q. 15:20).

For the plan year following the short year, the first filing due date is the later of (1) the last day of the second full calendar month following the close of the short plan year; or (2) 30 days after the date the amendment changing the plan year was adopted. The final filing due date is the later of (1) the fifteenth day of the eighth full calendar month following the month in which the plan year begins; or (2) 30 days after the date the amendment changing the plan year was adopted. [PBGC Reg. § 2610.25(b)(3)]

> **Example 1.** A plan amendment adopted on October 1, 1990, and made effective retroactively to February 1, 1990, changes a calendar-year plan to one with a plan year beginning February 1. The plan's 1989 Form 1 reported 350 plan participants. The final filing due date for the plan year that began on January 1, 1990, was September 15, 1990. The final filing due date for the new plan year, which began on February 1, 1990, was October 15, 1990.

> **Example 2.** A plan changes its plan year from one that begins January 1 to one that begins June 1. The change is adopted on December 1, 1989. This results in a short plan year beginning January 1, 1990, and ending May 31, 1990. The plan's 1989 Form 1 reported 100 plan participants. The final filing due date is September 15, 1990, for the plan year that began January 1, 1990, and would have otherwise ended December 31, 1990. The final filing due date is February 15, 1991, for the new plan year beginning June 1, 1990, and ending May 31, 1991.

Refunds for duplicate premium payments for overlapping periods must be requested by writing to:

Pension Benefit Guaranty Corporation

FOD/Premium Operations Division (33700)

2020 K Street, N.W.

Washington, DC 20006-1860

The employer must include copies of the relevant PBGC Forms 1, and the PBGC will calculate the amount of the refund and send it to the employer. [PBGC Reg. § 2610.22(d)]

Q. 15:22 Must PBGC Form 1 be filed after the plan is terminated?

The obligation to file PBGC Form 1 and make the required premium payment continues until the end of the plan year in which either the plan's assets are distributed or a trustee is appointed under ERISA. Any required premium payments will be for a full plan year and may not be prorated. However, a refund for premium payments applicable to the months after final distribution may be obtained by using the procedure for overlapping payments resulting from a change of plan year (see Q. 15:21). [PBGC Reg. §§ 2610.25(e) and 2610.34(c)]

Q. 15:23 What happens if the premium payment is late?

Late payment charges are assessed if PBGC receives a premium payment after the due date. The interest charge is based on the number of days the payment is late. The late filing penalty is the greater of 5 percent of the late payment for each late month (or part thereof), or $25, but not more than 100 percent of the unpaid premiums. [PBGC Reg. § 2610.8]

Q. 15:24 Can the late penalty charges be waived?

Generally, if the plan administrator can show substantial hardship or otherwise demonstrate good cause, PBGC may waive the penalty (but not interest) charge. [PBGC Reg. § 2610.8(b)]

Q. 15:25   Are there any other notification requirements to PBGC?

Yes. PBGC must be notified within ten days of the due date for a required plan contribution (Q. 7:16) if the aggregate unpaid balance, including interest, exceeds $1,000,000. [ERISA § 302(f)(4)]

Chapter 16

Summary Plan Descriptions

One of the major obligations of a plan administrator is the preparation of a summary of the plan for distribution to participants and beneficiaries. This chapter examines summary plan descriptions (SPDs)—what they are, the information they must contain, and the legal pitfalls to avoid.

Q. 16:1 What is a summary plan description?

An SPD is a booklet that describes the plan's provisions and the participants' benefits, rights, and obligations in simple language. Plan administrators must supply an SPD to each plan participant and each beneficiary receiving benefits under the plan. [ERISA §§ 102(a)(1) and 104(b)]

Q. 16:2 When must an SPD be furnished to a participant?

An SPD must be furnished to each participant and beneficiary no later than (1) 90 days after becoming a participant or first receiving benefits, as the case may be, or (2) within 120 days after the plan first becomes subject to the reporting and disclosure requirements of ERISA. [ERISA § 104(b)]

In the case of a new plan that provides that it is effective only upon IRS approval, the 120-day period does not begin until the day after such condition is satisfied (i.e., the day after the IRS issues a favorable determination letter). (See Q. 13:1.) [DOL Reg. § 2520.104b-

2(a)(3)] Conversely, if the plan is adopted retroactively, the 120-day period begins to run at the time of adoption.

Q. 16:3 Where is the SPD filed?

The SPD must be filed with DOL no later than the time it is furnished to plan participants and beneficiaries. The SPD is filed at the following address:

> SPD, Pension and Welfare Benefits Administration
>
> Room N-5644
>
> U.S. Department of Labor
>
> 200 Constitution Avenue, N.W.
>
> Washington, DC 20210

[DOL Reg. § 2520.104a-3]

Q. 16:4 What information must an SPD contain?

An SPD must contain the following information:

1. Name of the plan;
2. Name and address of the employer whose employees are covered by the plan;
3. Employer identification number (EIN) assigned by IRS to the employer;
4. Plan number;
5. Type of plan (e.g., defined benefit pension plan, money purchase pension plan, profit sharing plan);
6. Type of administration of the plan (e.g., employer self-administration, contract administration, insurer administration);
7. Name, business address, and business telephone number of the plan administrator;

8. Name of the person designated as agent for the service of legal process, and the address at which the agent may be served (and a statement that a plan trustee or administrator may also be served);

9. Name, title, and business address of each trustee;

10. Plan's requirements regarding eligibility for participation and benefits, including the plan's normal retirement age;

11. Statement describing any joint and survivor benefits;

12. Description of the vesting provisions under the plan, including contingent top-heavy provisions, and circumstances that may result in disqualification, ineligibility, or denial, loss, forfeiture, or suspension of benefits;

13. Statement as to whether the plan is maintained pursuant to one or more collective bargaining agreements and, if so, a statement that copies of such agreement are available to participants and beneficiaries;

14. Statement as to whether the plan is covered by termination insurance from PBGC and, if so, a description of the guaranty provisions;

15. Plan's fiscal year end;

16. Source of contributions to the plan (employer and/or employee contributions) and the method used to calculate the amount of the contributions;

17. Plan's provisions governing termination of the plan, including the rights and benefits of participants and the disposition of assets;

18. Plan's procedures regarding claims for benefits and the remedies available for disputing denied claims; and

19. Statement of ERISA rights available to plan participants.

Bear in mind that technical jargon is out—the idea is simplicity and the goal is being understood by the average plan participant. Clarifying examples and illustrations are recommended. [ERISA § 102(b); DOL Reg. § 2520.102-3; DOL ERISA Tech. Rel. 84-1; DOL Opinion No. 85-05A]

Q. 16:5 Is an SPD a legally binding document?

The status of an SPD is not entirely clear. Plan administrators must make sure that they do not make any false or misleading representations in an SPD that will haunt them later. The plan may be bound by a statement in the SPD that is inconsistent with the plan, even if the inconsistency is inadvertent. [*Heidgerd v. Olin Corp.*, No. 89-7869 (2d Cir. 1990); *Edwards v. State Farm Mutual Automobile Ins. Co.*, 851 F2d 134 (6th Cir. 1988); *McKnight v. Southern Life and Health Ins. Co.*, 758 F2d 1566 (11th Cir. 1985)]

Q. 16:6 What is the purpose of a disclaimer clause?

Disclaimer language (see below) is a possible means of insulating plan assets and the plan administrator from liability should the SPD prove to be misleading, incomplete, or contradictory to the actual provisions of the plan. Participants and their beneficiaries are placed on notice that the plan itself is the controlling document, and that they should not rely solely upon the representations in the SPD. [*Kolentus v. Avco Corp.*, 798 F2d 949 (7th Cir. 1986)]

The following is a sample disclaimer clause:

> Please read this summary carefully. This summary is written in simple, nontechnical language, and it is intended to help you to understand how this plan will benefit you and your loved ones. The plan and trust documents are also available for you to read. Although these documents are written in technical language, they may be helpful to you.
>
> If it appears to you that any of the provisions of the plan or trust documents are not in agreement with the statements made in this summary, please bring this to the attention of the plan administrator. Keep in mind that, if there is any conflict between this summary and the provisions of the plan or trust documents, the terms of the plan or trust will govern. You should rely solely on the provisions of the plan and trust documents.

Q. 16:7   Will a disclaimer in an SPD be recognized in a lawsuit?

At present, there are no governmental prohibitions against the use of a disclaimer in an SPD. Nothing is risked, therefore, by including the disclaimer.

The courts have held that a participant or beneficiary cannot use an SPD to sue for relief under ERISA unless the lawsuit also asserts a claim arising under the plan itself. However, the courts have left the door open for a participant to sue on other than ERISA grounds on the basis of inaccurate or misleading statements in the SPD. In any event, it is reasonable to expect that a claim based on willful or negligent misrepresentations in an SPD would be upheld even when a disclaimer is included in the SPD. [*O'Brien v. Sperry Univac*, 458 F. Supp. 1179 (D. DC 1978); *McKnight v. Southern Life and Health Ins. Co.*, 758 F2d 1566 (11th Cir. 1985)]

Q. 16:8   What happens if the plan is changed?

Any change in the provisions of the plan or in the administration of the plan that constitutes a material modification (see Q. 16:9) must be disclosed to participants and beneficiaries in the form of a summary description of material modifications (SMM) to the plan, which must be distributed within 210 days after the close of the plan year in which the material modification is adopted. [DOL Reg. § 2520.104b-3]

The SMM must also be filed with DOL within the same 210-day period, at the following address:

SMM, Pension and Welfare Benefits Administration

Room N-5644

U.S. Department of Labor

200 Constitution Avenue, N.W.

Washington, DC 20210

[DOL Reg. § 2520.104a-4]

Q. 16:9 What constitutes a reportable material modification?

Basically, a material modification exists when there is a change or modification to any of the information required to be included in the SPD (see Q. 16:4). [DOL Reg. § 2520.104b-3]

For example, the elimination of a special retirement benefit that allowed participants not eligible for normal retirement benefits to qualify for reduced retirement benefits was held to be a material modification of a plan. [*Baker v. Lukens Steel Co.*, 793 F2d 509 (3d Cir. 1986)]

Q. 16:10 How often is an updated SPD due?

Generally, the plan administrator is required to furnish to each participant and each beneficiary receiving benefits under the plan an updated SPD every five years that incorporates all plan amendments made within that five-year period. The updated SPD must be furnished no later than 210 days after the end of the fifth plan year after the previous SPD. This requirement for an updated SPD must be met even if SMMs have been issued (see Q. 16:8). However, even if there have been no amendments to the plan, another copy of the original SPD must be distributed every ten years. [ERISA § 104(b); DOL Reg. § 2520.104b-2]

Q. 16:11 How is the five-year period for an updated SPD measured?

Each time an SPD is distributed and filed with DOL, the five-year period begins anew. If the plan distributes an updated SPD less than five years after the previous one was distributed, a new five-year period begins at that time. [DOL Reg. § 2520.104b-2(b)]

Example. The plan administrator of the Justin Corporation profit sharing plan distributed the first SPD on March 1, 1988. On January 4, 1989, the vesting provisions of the calendar-year plan were amended and an SMM (see Q. 16:8) was timely filed on July 29, 1990 (210 days after the end of the plan year of the amendment). An updated SPD will be due on July 29, 1994 (210 days after December 31, 1993, the end of the plan year of the fifth anniversary of the original SPD). If a new SPD (instead of the SMM) had been distributed on July 29, 1990, the next SPD would be due July 29, 1996.

Q. 16:12   What happens if the plan is terminated?

If the plan terminates before the date by which an original or an updated SPD is required, the SPD requirement is waived if, and only if, all distributions to participants and beneficiaries have been completed. [DOL Reg. § 2520.104a-3(c)]

Q. 16:13   What documents other than an SPD can a participant obtain?

Other than an SPD, a participant is entitled to obtain, without charge and without request, a summary of material modifications to the plan and a summary annual report.

Upon request, other documents must be furnished to a participant by the plan administrator. These include:

1. A statement of the participant's total accrued benefits;

2. The plan instrument;

3. The latest annual report (Form 5500 series return);

4. The trust agreement; and

5. The collective bargaining agreement or any other document under which the plan is established.

A reasonable charge (not to exceed $.25 a page) may be imposed for copies of these items (other than the annual benefit statement). [ERISA § 105(a); DOL Reg. § 2520.104b-30] The plan administrator's failure to provide these documents within 30 days after the participant's request may subject the administrator to fines. In addition, the failure may result in a participant's complaint to the local DOL field office, with the possibility of an ensuing investigation of the plan.

Q. 16:14   Is there any special requirement if many plan participants cannot read English?

Yes. If a sufficient number of plan participants (generally, 25% for plans with less than 100 participants, 10% for plans with 100 or more participants) are literate only in the same non-English language, then the plan administrator must give these participants an SPD with a notice written in their own language. This notice must inform such participants of the availability of assistance sufficient to enable them to become informed as to their rights under the plan. [DOL Reg. § 2520.102-2(c)]

Chapter 17

Fiduciary Responsibilities

Plan administrators, trustees, and fiduciaries must take special care to carry out their responsibilities properly. Carelessness in the investment of plan assets, for example, can mean financial ruin for these individuals. This chapter examines the meaning of fiduciary responsibility under ERISA, when a fiduciary can be held personally liable for losses sustained by the plan, how liability can be avoided, and guidelines for investing plan assets.

Q. 17:1 Who is a fiduciary under ERISA?

A fiduciary under ERISA is any person who

- Exercises any discretionary authority or control over the plan's management;
- Exercises any authority or control over the management or disposition of the plan's assets;
- Renders investment advice for a fee or other compensation with respect to plan funds or property; or
- Has any discretionary authority or responsibility in the plan's administration.

[ERISA § 3(21)(A)]

The test for determining fiduciary status is a functional one. In other words, if a person or entity has or exercises any of the functions described in Section 3(21)(A) of ERISA, the person or entity will be deemed to be a fiduciary. [*Eaves v. Penn*, 587 F2d 453 (10th Cir. 1978); *Blatt v. Marshall and Lassman*, 812 F2d 810 (2d Cir. 1987)]

17-1

Those performing purely ministerial functions within guidelines established by others are not plan fiduciaries. DOL regulations list the following job categories as ministerial:

- Application of rules to determine eligibility for participation or benefits;
- Calculation of service and compensation for benefit purposes;
- Preparing communications to employees;
- Maintaining participants' service and employment records;
- Preparing reports required by government agencies;
- Calculating benefits;
- Explaining the plan to new participants and advising participants of their rights and options under the plan;
- Collecting contributions and applying them as specified in the plan;
- Preparing reports covering participants' benefits;
- Processing claims; and
- Making recommendations to others for decisions with respect to plan administration.

[DOL Reg. § 2509.75-8, D-2]

A broker or dealer registered under the Securities Exchange Act of 1934 is not deemed to be a fiduciary solely because the broker-dealer executes securities transactions on behalf of the plan in the ordinary course of its business, provided

1. The broker-dealer is not affiliated with a plan fiduciary, and
2. The plan fiduciary specifies
   - The security to be purchased or sold;
   - The price range within which the security is to be purchased or sold;
   - The time span, but not exceeding five days, during which the security may be purchased or sold; and
   - The minimum or maximum quantity of the security that may be purchased or sold within such price range.

[DOL Reg. § 2510.3-21(d)(1)]

Q. 17:2 What is rendering investment advice for the purpose of determining fiduciary status?

A person is rendering investment advice to a plan only if such person (1) makes recommendations as to valuing, buying, holding, or selling securities or other property, and (2) has, directly or indirectly, (a) discretionary authority or control over buying or selling securities or other property for the plan, whether or not pursuant to an agreement, arrangement, or understanding, or (b) regularly renders advice to the plan pursuant to a mutual agreement, arrangement, or understanding that such advice will serve as a primary basis for plan investment decisions and that such advice will be based on the particular needs of the plan regarding such matters as investment policies or strategy, overall portfolio composition, or diversification of plan investments. [DOL Reg. § 2510.3-21(c)(1)]

A broker's practice of recommending investments will not make that broker a fiduciary in the absence of any agreement, arrangement, or understanding referred to in item (2)(b) above. [*Farm King Supply, Inc. Integrated Profit Sharing Plan and Trust v. Edward D. Jones & Co.*, 884 F2d 288 (7th Cir. 1989)]

Q. 17:3 What is a named fiduciary?

Every plan is required to have at least one named fiduciary. A named fiduciary is one or more persons designated in the plan by name or title as responsible for operating the plan. The purpose of the requirement is to enable employees and other interested parties to ascertain the person responsible for plan operations. A plan covering employees of a corporation can designate the corporation as the named fiduciary. However, DOL regulations suggest that "a plan instrument which designates a corporation as 'named fiduciary' should provide for designation by the corporation of specified individuals or other persons to carry out specified fiduciary responsibilities under the plan. . . ." [ERISA § 402(a)(1); DOL Reg. § 2509.75-5, FR-1 and FR-3]

Q. 17:4 Are attorneys, accountants, actuaries, and consultants who provide services to a plan considered plan fiduciaries?

No. They are not considered plan fiduciaries solely because they render such services. However, they will be regarded as fiduciaries if they exercise discretionary authority or control over the management or administration of the plan or some authority or control over plan assets. [DOL Reg. § 2509.75-5, D-1; *Procacci v. Drexel Burnham Lambert*, No. 89-0555 (ED Pa. 1989); *Brock v. Self*, 632 F. Supp. 1509 (WD La. 1986)]

Recent cases have held that attorneys and accountants do not possess or exert the necessary discretionary authority or control respecting management of the plan to cause them to be fiduciaries under ERISA. [*Anoka Orthopaedic Assocs., P.A. v. Lechner*, No. 89-5200 (8th Cir. 1990); *Brown v. Roth*, 729 F. Supp. 391 (D. NJ 1990); *Useden v. Acker*, 721 F. Supp. 1233 (SD Fla. 1989); *Nieto v. Ecker*, 845 F2d 868 (9th Cir. 1988) (attorneys); *Painters of Philadelphia District Council No. 21 Welfare Fund v. Price Waterhouse*, 879 F2d 1146 (3rd Cir. 1989) (accountants)]

Q. 17:5 Do the fiduciary responsibility rules of ERISA apply to a Keogh plan?

Generally, if the plan covers self-employed individuals as well as common-law employees, the fiduciary responsibility provisions of ERISA are applicable. However, the fiduciary responsibility provisions of ERISA do not apply to plans that cover only self-employed individuals. A plan covering only the owner-employee (see Q. 27:9) and the owner-employee's spouse is not a plan providing retirement income to employees. Plans in which only sole proprietors or partners participate are not considered employee benefit plans, and sole proprietors, partners, and their spouses are not considered employees for ERISA's fiduciary responsibility rules. [ERISA § 3(3); DOL Reg. §§ 2510.3-3(b) and 2510.3-3(c); *Robertson v. Alexander Grant & Co.*, 798 F2d 868 (5th Cir. 1986); *Schwartz v. Gordon*, 761 F2d 864 (2d Cir. 1985)]

Q. 17:6 What is a self-directed account plan?

A self-directed account plan is an individual account plan described in Section 3(34) of ERISA that permits a participant to make an independent choice, from a broad range of investment alternatives, regarding the manner in which any portion of the assets in the participant's individual account is invested. [ERISA § 404(c); Prop. DOL Reg. § 2550.404c-1(b)(1)]

According to DOL, the broad range of investment alternatives must

1. Permit the participant to materially affect the potential return and riskiness of the assets in the participant's account;

2. Include investments that offer

   • Capital preservation and generation of income

   • Capital appreciation

   • Income, with a high degree of liquidity

3. Enable diversification of investments; and

4. Include a relatively "safe" investment option, that is, a fully insured interest-bearing deposit in a bank or similar financial institution or a pooled investment fund whose assets consist only of cash and securities issued or guaranteed by the United States or one of its agencies.

[Prop. DOL Reg. § 2550.404c-1(b)]

Q. 17:7 Is a participant or beneficiary who self-directs an individual account considered a fiduciary?

No. If the plan permits self-directed accounts, participants will not be considered fiduciaries solely because they exercise control over assets in their individual accounts. The consequences are twofold. First, other plan fiduciaries generally would have no cofiduciary liability on account of participants' investment decisions. Second, because the participants are not fiduciaries, no prohibited transaction under ERISA would result if their exercise of control over the assets in their accounts caused the trust to engage in transactions with parties in interest (see Q. 18:2). [ERISA § 404(c); Prop. DOL Reg. §§ 2550.4-04c-1(a) and 2550.404c-1(e)]

Q. 17:8 Are any individuals prohibited from serving as fiduciaries?

Yes. A person who has been convicted of any of a wide range of crimes, including robbery, bribery, extortion, and fraud, cannot serve as a plan fiduciary for a period of 13 years after the conviction or after the end of imprisonment, whichever is later. A person who knowingly violates the rule is subject to a maximum fine of $10,000 or five years' imprisonment or both. [ERISA § 411]

Q. 17:9 Can a trustee be appointed for life?

No. DOL has ruled that the appointment of a trustee for life, or the ability to remove a trustee only upon misfeasance or incapacity to perform the duties of the position, is inconsistent with ERISA's fiduciary responsibility provisions. [DOL Advisory Opinion No. 85-41A]

Trustees did not breach their fiduciary duty by approving a trust amendment that transferred the power to appoint and remove trustees from a single joint council of local unions to three joint councils. The amendment only affected the distribution of power among the various unions and did not entrench current trustees. [*International Brotherhood of Teamsters v. The New York State Teamsters Council Health and Hospital Fund*, 1990 U.S. App. Lexis 8409 (2nd Cir. 1990)]

Q. 17:10 What is a fiduciary's basic duty?

The basic duty of a fiduciary is to act solely in the interest of the plan's participants and beneficiaries and for the exclusive purpose of providing benefits for participants and their beneficiaries (and defraying reasonable administrative costs of the plan).

A fiduciary must also act prudently, diversify the investment of the plan's assets and act in a manner consistent with the plan's documents. [ERISA § 404(a)]

Q. 17:11   What standard of care is a fiduciary held to?

A fiduciary is subject to the prudent man standard of care; that is, the fiduciary must act "with the care, skill, prudence, and diligence under the circumstances then prevailing that a prudent man acting in a like capacity and familiar with such matters would use in the conduct of an enterprise of a like character and with like aims." [ERISA § 404(a)(1)(B)]

Q. 17:12   How does the prudent man standard apply to trustees or investment managers?

A trustee or other fiduciary responsible for investing the plan's assets must, in order to satisfy the prudent man standard, consider the following factors:

1. The composition of the portfolio with regard to diversification;
2. The liquidity and current return of the portfolio relative to the anticipated cash flow requirements of the plan; and
3. The projected return of the portfolio relative to the funding objectives of the plan.

In addition, the trustee or other fiduciary must determine that the particular investment or investment strategy is reasonably designed to further the purposes of the plan, taking into consideration the risk of loss and the opportunity for gain (or other return) associated with the investment or the investment strategy. [DOL Reg. § 2550.404a-1]

Q. 17:13   Would a transaction involving the plan that benefits the employer result in a breach of fiduciary duty?

Not necessarily. A transaction that incidentally benefits the employer will not violate the rule that a fiduciary act solely in the interest of the plan's participants and beneficiaries as long as the fiduciary correctly concludes, on the basis of a careful, thorough, and impartial inquiry, that the transaction is in the interests of participants and beneficiaries. [*Donovan v. Bierwirth*, 680 F2d 263 (2d Cir. 1982), *cert. denied*, 459 US 1069 (1982); see also *Phillips v. Amoco Oil Co.*, 799 F2d 1464 (11th Cir. 1986), *cert. denied*, 481 US 1016 (1987)]

Q. 17:14 Must the assets of the plan be segregated?

Yes. The plan's assets must be segregated from the employer's property and held in trust. [ERISA § 403(a)]

Q. 17:15 What are plan assets when a plan invests in another entity?

Generally, the plan's assets will include its investment in an entity but not any of the underlying assets of such entity. However, if the plan's equity interest in an entity is neither a publicly offered security nor a security issued by an investment company registered under the Investment Company Act of 1940, the plan's assets will include both the equity interest and an undivided interest in each of the underlying assets (the look-through rule). In that event, any person who has any authority or control over the management of the underlying assets or provides investment advice for a fee with respect to such assets is a fiduciary of the investing plan. [DOL Reg. § 2510.3-101(a)]

Q. 17:16 Are there any exceptions to the look-through rule?

The look-through rule will not apply if:

- The equity interest (see Q. 17:17) is in an operating company (see Q. 17:18); or
- The amount of equity participation in the entity by benefit plan investors is not significant (see Q. 17:19 and Q. 17:20).

[DOL Reg. § 2510.3-101(a)(2)]

Q. 17:17 What is an equity interest and a publicly offered security?

An equity interest is any interest in an entity other than an instrument that is treated as indebtedness under applicable local law and that does not have substantial equity features. Examples include a profits interest in a partnership, an undivided interest in property, and a beneficial interest in a trust.

A publicly offered security is a security that is freely transferable, is part of a widely held class of securities, and covered under certain federal securities registration rules.

> **Example 1.** A plan acquires debentures issued by the Jaykay Corporation pursuant to a private offering. All of Jaykay's shareholders are benefit plan investors. Jaykay is engaged primarily in investing and reinvesting in precious metals on behalf of its shareholders, so it is not an operating company. By their terms, the plan's debentures are convertible to common stock of Jaykay at the plan's option. At the time of the plan's acquisition of the debentures, the conversion feature is incidental to Jaykay's obligation to pay interest and principal. The plan's assets do not include an interest in the underlying assets of Jaykay because the plan has not acquired an equity interest in Jaykay.

> **Example 2.** Assume the same facts in Example 1, except the plan exercises its option to convert the debentures to common stock, thereby acquiring an equity interest in Jaykay. Assuming that the common stock is not a publicly offered security and that there has been no change in the composition of the other equity investors in Jaykay, the plan's assets would then include an undivided interest in the underlying assets of Jaykay. As a result, employees of Jaykay with authority or control over the assets of Jaykay would be fiduciaries of the plan.

[DOL Reg. §§ 2510.3-101(b) and 2510.3-101(j)(1)]

Q. 17:18   What is an operating company?

An operating company is generally an entity that is primarily engaged, directly or through subsidiaries, in the production or sale of a product or services other than the investment of capital. Also, a venture capital operating company or a real estate operating company will be treated as an operating company. [DOL Reg. § 2510.3-101(c)]

An entity is a venture capital operating company if at least 50 percent of its assets (other than short-term investments made pending long-term commitments) are invested in an operating company (other than a venture capital operating company) as to which the investing entity has and exercises the right to substantially participate in or influence the management of the operating company. [DOL Reg. § 2510.3-101(d)]

An entity is a real estate operating company if at least 50 percent of its assets are invested in managed or developed real estate and the investing entity has the right to substantially participate directly in the management or development activities. In addition, the investing entity, in the ordinary course of its business, must actually engage in real estate management or development activities. [DOL Reg. § 2510.3-101(e)]

Q. 17:19 What level of participation of benefit plan investors is considered "significant"?

Equity participation in an entity is significant on any date if, immediately after the most recent acquisition or redemption of any equity interest (see Q. 17:17) in the entity, 25 percent or more of the value of any class of equity interest in the entity is held by benefit plan investors (see Q. 17:20). [DOL Reg. § 2510.3-101(f)(1); DOL Advisory Opinion No. 89-05A]

Q. 17:20 What is a benefit plan investor?

The term benefit plan investor includes

1. An employee benefit plan as defined by ERISA;
2. A qualified retirement plan, individual retirement account, or individual retirement annuity; or
3. Any entity whose underlying assets include plan assets as a result of a plan's investment in that entity.

[DOL Reg. § 2510.3-101(f)(2)]

Q. 17:21 Are there any investments by a plan that may never satisfy the exceptions to the look-through rule?

Yes. If a plan acquires or holds an interest in any entity (other than a licensed insurance company) established or maintained to provide any pension or welfare benefit to participants or beneficiaries of the investing plan, none of the exceptions may apply. As a result, the assets of the plan will include its investment and an undivided interest in the underlying assets of that entity.

> **Example.** A qualified retirement plan acquires a beneficial interest in a trust that is not an insurance company licensed to do business in a state. Under this arrangement, the trust will provide the plan benefits that are promised to the participants and beneficiaries under the terms of the plan. The plan's assets include its beneficial interest in the trust and an undivided interest in each of the trust's underlying assets. Thus, persons with authority or control over trust assets would be fiduciaries of the qualified retirement plan. [DOL Reg. §§ 2510.3-101(h)(2) and 2510.3-101(j)(12)]

Q. 17:22 When are participant contributions considered plan assets?

Amounts paid by participants, or withheld by the employer from participants' wages, as contributions to a plan will be considered to be plan assets as of the earliest of the date on which the contributions can reasonably be segregated from the general assets of the employer. That date can be no later than 90 days after the date on which the contributions are received by the employer or would have been paid to the employee in cash if not withheld from wages. [DOL Reg. § 2510.3-102(a)]

> **Example.** Cee & Ess Company employs a small number of people at a single payroll location. Cee & Ess maintains a contributory profit sharing plan in which there is 100 percent participation. Because the small number of participants are all in a single location, the company could reasonably be expected to transmit participant contributions to the trust within ten days of the close of each pay period. Therefore, the assets of the plan would include the participants' contributions as of that date. [DOL Reg. § 2510.3-102(b)(2)]

Q. 17:23   What expenses relating to the plan may be paid out of plan assets?

Generally, plan assets are held exclusively to provide benefits to participants or beneficiaries and to defray reasonable expenses of administering the plan. Plan assets may therefore be used to pay plan expenses that are reasonably related to plan administration and authorized by the plan.

Services provided in conjunction with establishing the plan, terminating the plan, and other plan design functions would not properly be paid out of the plan. Payment of PBGC premiums is proper if the plan is silent or explicitly states that the plan may pay the premiums. However, the payment would be improper if the document indicates that the plan sponsor will pay them. [ERISA §§ 403(c)(1) and 404(a)(1); DOL Information Letter, March 2, 1987]

Q. 17:24   What are the consequences if plan assets are used improperly?

An improper payment of plan assets for expenses other than reasonable plan administration expenses would be a breach of fiduciary duty and would subject the fiduciary to personal liability for the breach (see Q. 17:25). In addition, the payment may be a prohibited transaction if the payment is made to, on behalf of, or for the benefit of, a party in interest (see Q. 18:2 and Q. 18:4) and does not qualify for a statutory or administrative exemption under ERISA or the Code (see Q. 18:7 through Q. 18:9). Finally, the payment may be considered a violation of the exclusive benefit provision in the Code and result in plan disqualification (see Q. 11:21).

Q. 17:25   Can a fiduciary be held liable for a breach of duty?

Yes. ERISA permits a civil action to be brought by a participant, beneficiary, or other fiduciary against a fiduciary for a breach of duty. The fiduciary is personally liable for any losses to the plan resulting from the breach of duty, and any profits obtained by the fiduciary through the use of plan assets must be turned over to the plan. The court may require other appropriate relief, including re-moval of the fiduciary. [ERISA §§ 409 and 502(a)(2)]

A fiduciary, however, cannot be held liable for a breach of fiduci-ary duty that was committed prior to the fiduciary becoming a fiduciary. Although the fiduciary may not be liable for the original breach, if the fiduciary knows about the breach, the fiduciary should take steps to remedy the situation. Failure to do so might constitute a subsequent independent breach of fiduciary duty by the successor fiduciary.

> **Example.** John Smith has no existing relationship with the plan. He negotiates an agreement to provide investment advice to the plan, which will render him a fiduciary. He will not be liable for any investment decisions made prior to his becoming a fiduciary that are held to have been imprudent and, conse-quently, a fiduciary breach. [ERISA § 409(b); *Baeten v. Van Ess*, 446 F. Supp. 868 (ED Wis. 1977); DOL Opinion Letter 76-95]

For breaches of fiduciary duties (or knowing participation therein) on or after December 19, 1989, DOL imposes a penalty of 20 percent of the amount payable pursuant to a court order or settlement agree-ment with DOL. DOL may waive or reduce the penalty if the fiduci-ary or other person (1) acted responsibly and in good faith, or (2) will not otherwise be able to restore all plan losses without severe financial hardship. [ERISA § 502(l)]

Q. 17:26 Can a nonfiduciary be held liable for a breach of duty?

Some courts have imposed liability on nonfiduciaries who:

• Have actual knowledge that a breach is occurring; and

• Take action that furthers or completes the breach.

[*Freund v. Marshall & Isley Bank*, 485 F. Supp. 629 (WD Wis. 1979); see also *Brock v. Hendershott*, 840 F2d 339 (6th Cir. 1988); *Thornton v. Evans*, 692 F2d 1064 (7th Cir. 1982); *Mid-Jersey Trucking Industry–Local 701 v. Omni Funding Group*, 731 F. Supp. 161 (D. NJ 1990); *Brock v. Gerace*, 635 F. Supp. 563 (D. NJ 1986); but see *Nieto v. Ecker*, 845 F2d 868 (9th Cir. 1988)]

Q. 17:27   May a fiduciary be held liable for breaches committed by a co-fiduciary?

Yes, if the fiduciary:

* Knowingly participates in or tries to conceal a co-fiduciary's breach;

* Enables a co-fiduciary to commit a breach by failing to meet the fiduciary's specific responsibilities; or

* Knowing of a co-fiduciary's breach, fails to make a reasonable effort to remedy it. [ERISA § 405(a)]

    Example. Tom and Tracey are co-trustees. The trust specifies that they cannot invest in commodity futures. If Tom suggests to Tracey that she invest part of the plan assets in commodity futures and Tracey does so, both Tom and Tracey may be held personally liable for any losses sustained by the plan. Similarly, if Tracey invests in commodity futures and tells Tom about it, Tom could be held personally liable for any losses if he conceals the investment or fails to make a reasonable effort to correct it.

Q. 17:28   What should a fiduciary do if a co-fiduciary commits a breach of duty?

The fiduciary must try to remedy the breach. For example, if an improper investment was made, the fiduciary might consider disposing of the asset. Alternatively, the fiduciary might notify the company of the breach, institute a lawsuit against the co-fiduciary, or bring the matter before DOL. The fiduciary's resignation as a protest against the breach, without making reasonable efforts to prevent it, will not relieve the fiduciary of liability. [ERISA § 405(a)(3); DOL Reg. § 2509.75-5, FR-10]

Q. 17:29   Can a breaching fiduciary obtain contribution or indemnity from other breaching co-fiduciaries?

The courts have generally held that no right of contribution or indemnity exists under ERISA. [*Call v. Sumitomo Bank of Califor-*

nia, 881 F2d 626 (9th Cir. 1989); Kim v. Fujikawa, 871 F2d 1427 (9th Cir. 1989); Mutual Life Ins. Co. of N.Y. v. Yampol, 706 F. Supp. 596 (ND Ill. 1989); cf. Free v. Briody, 732 F2d 1331 (7th Cir. 1984)]

Q. 17:30 Does ERISA authorize punitive damages for breach of fiduciary duty?

The Supreme Court has held that punitive damages are not available to a beneficiary in an action against the plan fiduciary for an alleged breach of fiduciary duty when the alleged breach was the untimely processing of the beneficiary's claim for benefits. Remedies available to the beneficiary in such instances would include only recovery of the benefits owed, clarification of the beneficiary's right to present or future benefits, or removal of the breaching fiduciary. [Metropolitan Life Ins. Co. v. Russell, 473 US 134 (1985)]

However, the Supreme Court expressly left open certain issues— for instance, whether a plan, as opposed to a participant or beneficiary, could recover punitive damages and whether a participant or beneficiary could recover such damages when the injurious conduct was not a breach of fiduciary duty but a violation of other sections of ERISA or of the terms of the plan. Most courts since the Russell decision have concluded that punitive damages under such circumstances are likewise unavailable under ERISA. [Drinkwater v. Metropolitan Life Ins. Co., 846 F2d 821 (1st Cir. 1988), cert. denied, 109 S. Ct. 261 (1988); Varhola v. Doe, 820 F2d 809 (6th Cir. 1987); Kleinhans v. Lisle Savings Profit Sharing Trust, 810 F2d 618 (7th Cir. 1987); Sommers Drug Stores Co. Employee Profit Sharing Trust v. Corrigan Enters., Inc., 793 F2d 1456 (5th Cir. 1986), cert. denied, 479 US 1034 (1987); Powell v. Chesapeake and Potomac Tel. Co. of Va., 780 F2d 419 (4th Cir. 1985), cert. denied, 476 US 1170 (1986); Guintoli v. Garvin Buybutler Corp., 726 F. Supp. 494 (SD NY, 1990); Bone v. Association Management Servs., Inc., 632 F. Supp. 493 (SD Miss. 1986); but see California Digital Defined Benefit Pension Plan v. Union Bank, 705 F. Supp. 489 (CD Cal. 1989); Schoenholtz v. Doniger, 657 F. Supp. 899 (SD NY 1987)]

Q. 17:31 Can the plan contain a provision relieving a fiduciary of personal liability?

No, but the plan may buy insurance to cover liability or losses due to acts or omissions of fiduciaries if the insurance company is given a right to sue the breaching fiduciary. A fiduciary may buy insurance to cover the fiduciary's own liability. [ERISA § 410]

Q. 17:32 Is a release executed by a plan beneficiary freeing plan fiduciaries from past liability under ERISA valid?

Yes. A release that is part of a settlement of a bona fide dispute over past fiduciary breaches is valid, but not one relating to the performance of future fiduciary duties. [*Blessing v. Struthers-Dunn, Inc.*, No. 85-1362 (ED Pa., July 31, 1985)]

Q. 17:33 Can fiduciary responsibility be delegated?

Yes. For example, the trust instrument can provide that one trustee has responsibility for one-half of the plan assets and a second trustee has responsibility for the other half of the plan assets. Neither trustee would be liable for the acts of the other except under the co-fiduciary liability rules of Section 405(a) of ERISA. (See Q. 17:27.) [ERISA § 405(b)]

If the plan expressly so provides, the named fiduciaries can allocate among themselves or delegate to others their fiduciary duties, other than the management or control of the plan's assets. The management or control of the plan's assets can be delegated only to an investment manager. [ERISA §§ 405(c)(1) and 402(c)(3)]

An effective allocation or delegation will generally relieve the named fiduciary from liability for the acts of the person to whom such duties are allocated or delegated. The named fiduciary, however, is not relieved of liability under the co-fiduciary rules of Section 405(a) of ERISA. [ERISA § 405(c)(2)]

Q. 17:34 What is the liability of an investment manager for its decisions regarding investment of plan assets?

An investment manager is a bank, insurance company, or registered investment advisor that acknowledges in writing that it is a fiduciary with respect to the plan (see Q. 17:1). Therefore, any failure to comply with fiduciary standards may result in a breach of fiduciary duty, and the investment manager will be liable for any losses to the plan resulting from the breach. In addition, the investment manager may be required to disgorge any profits derived from the breach.

> **Example.** An investment manager who bought and sold on behalf of a plan was found to have engaged in churning the plan's portfolio. Over 17 months, there were approximately 94 transactions. The churning transactions resulted in a loss of $47,000, while the broker received commissions of $9,700 in one three-month period. The investment manager was held liable for the losses to the plan and was ordered to return the commissions to the plan. [*Dasler v. E. F. Hutton and Co.*, 694 F. Supp. 624 (D. Minn. 1988)]

Q. 17:35 Are there any limits on the investments a qualified retirement plan can make?

There are no specific dollar or percentage limits placed on the amount a qualified retirement plan can invest in any particular type of asset (other than qualifying employer securities or qualifying employer real property; see Q. 17:40). Nor are there any limits on the types of investments that can be made. Investments in such tangible assets as real estate, gold, art, or diamonds are permitted, even though these investments may not generate current income for the plan and generally lack liquidity. However, see the discussion regarding a fiduciary's standard of care at Q. 17:11 and Q. 17:12.

Limits on investments in qualifying employer securities or qualifying employer real property are discussed at Q. 17:40. The consequences of investments by self-directed accounts in collectibles are discussed at Q. 17:43.

Q. 17:36 May a qualified retirement plan borrow to make investments?

Yes. There is no prohibition against any particular method by which a qualified retirement plan invests its assets. However, securities purchased on margin are considered acquisition indebtedness, subject to the unrelated business income tax on the income—both dividends and gains—resulting from its acquisition indebtedness. [IRC §§ 511 and 514; *Ocean Cove Corp. Retirement Plan and Trust v. U.S.*, 657 F. Supp. 776 (SD Fla. 1987); *Elliot Knitwear Profit Sharing Plan v. Commissioner*, 614 F2d 347 (3d Cir. 1980), *aff'g* 71 TC 765 (1979)]

However, when a plan borrows money to acquire or improve real estate, the debt generally is not considered acquisition indebtedness, so the income or gain from the real estate is not treated as unrelated business taxable income. [IRC § 514(c)(9)]

Q. 17:37 What is the diversification requirement?

A trustee (or any other fiduciary responsible for investing plan assets) is required to discharge the trustee's duties "by diversifying the investments of the plan so as to minimize the risk of large losses, unless under the circumstances it is clearly not prudent to do so." [ERISA § 404(a)(1)(C)]

The degree of investment concentration that would violate the diversification rule cannot be stated as a fixed percentage but depends on the facts and circumstances of each case. However, factors that should be considered include

- The purposes of the plan
- The amount of plan assets
- Financial and industrial conditions
- The type of investment made
- Diversification along geographic lines
- Diversification along industry lines
- The date the investment matures

So, for example, if the trustee is investing in real estate mortgages, the trustee should not invest a disproportionate amount in mortgages within a particular area or on a particular type of property even if that investment would result in social gains to a particular community. [H. Conf. Rep. No. 1280, 93d Cong., 2d Sess., reprinted in 1974 U.S. Code Cong. & Admin. News 5038, 5084–5085]

One court held that trustees violated the diversification rule when over 65 percent of the plan's assets were invested in commercial first mortgages secured by property located in one area. The lack of diversification caused too much risk that the value of the assets would decline in the event of a severe economic downturn in the area where the property securing the mortgages was located. As a result, the investments in the aggregate were held to be imprudent. [*Brock v. Citizens Bank of Clovis*, 841 F2d 344 (10th Cir.), *cert. denied*, 109 S.Ct. 82 (1988)]

Another court held that an investment company that invested over 70 percent of a plan's assets in long-term government bonds failed to properly diversify plan assets. The investment company failed to determine the plan's particular cash flow needs, and was forced to sell some bonds at a loss to meet the plan's need for cash. [*GIW Industries, Inc. v. Trevor, Stewart, Burton & Jacobsen, Inc.*, 845 F2d 729 (11th Cir. 1990)]

It is possible to meet the diversification requirement by investing plan assets in a bank's pooled investment fund (see Q. 17:44), a mutual fund (see Q. 17:45), or insurance or annuity contracts if the bank, mutual fund, or insurance company diversifies its investments. Although the diversification requirement does not apply to employee stock ownership plans (ESOPs), an ESOP must offer certain participants the right to elect to diversify the stock acquired after 1986 and allocated to their accounts (see Q. 22:48 through Q. 22:58).

Q. 17:38 Must a plan make only blue chip investments?

No. DOL says "although securities issued by a small or new company may be a riskier investment than securities issued by a blue chip company, the investment in the former company may be entirely proper under . . . [the] prudence rule." [Preamble to DOL Reg. § 2550.404a-1]

The degree of risk that the trustee takes in making investments depends in part on the type of plan the employer maintains. In a defined contribution plan (e.g., a profit sharing plan), benefits received by a plan participant are based on the employer's contributions, increased or decreased by the return on plan investments. Thus, it may be appropriate to consider some speculative investments in a defined contribution plan.

In a defined benefit plan, a rate of return on investments above that assumed by the actuary reduces required contributions, and a rate of return below the assumed rate increases required contributions. Thus, investments will normally be of a nature that will return at least as much as the actuary has assumed. It is likely, therefore, that speculative investments will have less appeal than in a defined contribution plan.

Q. 17:39   How can a trustee or other plan fiduciary be protected from lawsuits for failure to meet the prudent man rule?

In acting prudently, trustees or other fiduciaries should also act defensively, building a record to defend their actions. Fiduciaries should, for example:

- Keep detailed records of the actions taken and the factors that went into the decisions;
- Make sure these records describe in detail the relevant circumstances prevailing at the time—that is, outline the conditions under which the action was taken; and
- Make sure all reasonable steps have been taken to acquire the information needed to make informed decisions.

Q. 17:40   May a qualified retirement plan invest in employer securities or employer real property?

A plan subject to ERISA generally may not acquire or hold qualifying employer securities (see Q. 17:42) or qualifying employer real property (see Q. 17:41) if the total fair market value of such assets exceeds 10 percent of the fair market value of the plan's assets at the time of acquisition. The 10 percent limitation does not apply to an eligible individual account plan that specifically authorizes such investments. An eligible individual account plan is defined as

- A profit sharing, stock bonus, thrift, or savings plan;
- An ESOP; or
- A money purchase pension plan in existence on the date of ERISA's enactment that invested primarily in qualifying employer securities at that time. [ERISA § 407]

Individual account plans that are part of a floor offset arrangement—an arrangement under which the plan's benefits are taken into account in determining a participant's benefits under a defined benefit plan—established after December 17, 1987, do not fall within this exception. [ERISA § 407(d)(3)(C)]

In addition, the two plans that constitute the floor offset arrangement will be treated as a single plan for purposes of the 10 percent limit.

> **Example.** Corporation A and Corporation B each have floor offset arrangements with assets of $200,000 divided equally between their defined benefit and profit sharing plans. Corporation A established its floor offset arrangement in 1985; Corporation B's was established in 1988. Up to $10,000 of the assets of Corporation A's defined benefit plan and up to $100,000 (which is 100% of the assets) of Corporation A's profit sharing plan can be invested in qualifying employer securities—for a total of $110,000. In contrast, the amount of Corporation B's qualifying employer securities held by the floor offset arrangement may not exceed $20,000 (10% of its assets in the aggregate). [ERISA § 407(d)(9)]

Q. 17:41 What is qualifying employer real property?

Employer real property is real property leased to an employer of employees covered by the plan or an affiliate of the employer. Such real property is qualifying only if it is dispersed geographically, suitable for more than one use, and held without violation of the other ERISA fiduciary rules (other than diversification and prohibited transaction rules). [ERISA §§ 406(d)(2) and 406(d)(4)]

Q. 17:42   What are qualifying employer securities?

Employer securities are stock or marketable obligations issued by an employer of employees covered by the plan or an affiliate of the employer. Stock acquired after December 17, 1987, will be qualifying employer securities only if (1) not more than 25 percent of the aggregate amount of stock of the same class issued and outstanding at the time of acquisition is held by the plan, and (2) at least 50 percent of such aggregate amount is held by persons independent of the issuer. For stock acquired on or before December 17, 1989, plans have until December 31, 1992 to comply with the new rules. [ERISA §§ 407(d)(5) and 407(f)]

Q. 17:43   What does earmarking investments mean?

Earmarking in a defined contribution plan allows each participant, on a nondiscriminatory basis, an opportunity to invest funds contributed to the plan on the participant's behalf as the participant sees fit in any investment vehicle that the trustees are willing to administer. Traditional retirement plan investments—blue chip stocks, bonds, and real estate—can be passed over in favor of more speculative investments such as new stock issues, diamonds, gold, art, and antiques. However, amounts invested in collectibles under an earmarked plan will be treated as distributions for tax purposes. Collectibles are defined as works of art, rugs, antiques, precious metals, stamps, coins, and any other tangible property specified as a collectible by IRS. [IRC § 408(m)]

There is no place for earmarking of employer contributions in a defined benefit plan since there are no individual accounts and investment gains or losses affect the amount the employer must contribute to the plan rather than the level of benefits payable to participants. However, earmarking of voluntary or rollover contributions by participants may be appropriate. Earmarking has the added advantage of relieving the plan's trustees of liability for poor investment decisions made by the participant (see Q. 17:6).

Q. 17:44 What are pooled investment funds?

Pooled investment funds are commingled funds maintained by a bank on behalf of many qualified retirement plans. When a bank is appointed as trustee and the qualified retirement plan's assets are invested by the bank, the company retains only a limited choice in directing the investment of the plan's assets.

Generally, the bank has a dual fund arrangement—a fixed-income fund and a common stock fund—that permits the company to direct the proportion of its contributions invested in each fund.

The pooling of funds makes it possible to offer small plans the economies and security of a large plan. This investment vehicle may be a particular attraction to small and medium-sized plans, that is, any plan in which the annual contribution is below, for example, $100,000.

To participate in a pooled investment fund, the company maintaining the plan must adopt the bank's collective trust as part of its own trust and authorize investments in the bank's trust.

A trustee must, of course, be prudent in selecting and retaining the bank that directs the plan's investments.

Q. 17:45 Can plan assets be invested in a mutual fund?

Yes. Mutual funds are a common investment vehicle, especially for small plans desiring professional investment management but not wishing to go the route of bank trusteeship, or for plans that are too small to participate in a bank's pooled investment fund. A trustee must, of course, be prudent in selecting and retaining the mutual fund in which plan assets are invested, taking into account the wide variety of funds available with different investment goals.

Chapter 18

Prohibited Transactions

Both ERISA and the Code prohibit certain classes of transactions between a plan and parties in interest to the plan, regardless of the fairness of the particular transaction involved or the benefit to the plan. In addition, fiduciaries are prohibited from engaging in certain conduct that would affect their duty of loyalty to the plan. This chapter examines the nature of prohibited transactions, the penalties that apply when a prohibited transaction occurs, and the statutory, administrative, and class exemptions to the prohibited-transaction rules.

Q. 18:1 What is a prohibited transaction?

A prohibited transaction occurs under ERISA if a plan fiduciary causes the plan to engage in a transaction that the fiduciary knows or should know constitutes a direct or indirect:

1. Sale, exchange, or lease of any property between the plan and a party in interest;

2. Loan or other extension of credit between the plan and a party in interest;

3. Furnishing of goods, services, or facilities between the plan and a party in interest;

4. Transfer of plan assets to a party in interest or the use of plan assets by or for the benefit of a party in interest; or

5. Acquisition of employer securities or employer real property in

excess of the limits set by law (see Q. 17:40). [ERISA § 406(a)(1)]

In addition, ERISA prohibits a fiduciary from:

1. Dealing with plan assets (see Q. 17:15) in the fiduciary's own interest or for the fiduciary's own account;
2. Acting in any transaction involving the plan on behalf of a party whose interests are adverse to the interests of the plan or its participants or beneficiaries; or
3. Receiving any consideration for the fiduciary's own personal account from any person dealing with the plan in connection with any transaction involving plan assets. [ERISA § 406(b)]

For example, receipt of commissions by a fiduciary's wholly owned subsidiary on loans from a plan to unrelated borrowers is a prohibited transaction. [*Murphy v. Dawson*, No. 88-2992 (4th Cir. 1989)]

Q. 18:2 Who is a party in interest?

Under ERISA, the following are parties in interest with respect to a plan:

1. Any fiduciary, counsel, or employee of the plan;
2. A person providing services to the plan;
3. An employer any of whose employees are covered by the plan, and any direct or indirect owner of 50 percent or more of such employer;
4. A relative, that is, spouse, ancestor, lineal descendant, or spouse of a lineal descendant, of any of the persons described in (1), (2), or (3) above;
5. An employee organization, any of whose members are covered by the plan;
6. A corporation, partnership, estate, or trust of which at least 50 percent is owned by any person or organization described in (1), (2), (3), (4), or (5) above;
7. Officers, directors, 10%-or-more shareholders, and employees of any person or organization described in (2), (3), (5), or (6) above; and

8. A 10%-or-more partner of or joint venturer with any person or organization described in (2), (3), (5), or (6) above. [ERISA § 3(14)]

Q. 18:3 How do the prohibited-transaction provisions under the Code differ from the prohibited-transaction provisions under ERISA?

The prohibited-transaction provisions under the Code are in many respects the same as those under ERISA. However, the Code uses the term disqualified person rather than party in interest and does not require knowledge on the part of a fiduciary that the transaction or conduct is prohibited. The definition of the terms party in interest under ERISA and disqualified person under the Code are nearly identical, but the term party in interest is slightly more inclusive (i.e., the ERISA, but not the Code, definition includes counsel to and employees of the plan, and all employees—not only highly compensated employees—of the employer).

In addition, the prohibited-transaction provisions under the Code apply to individual retirement accounts (IRAs) while ERISA's prohibited-transaction provisions do not. [IRC § 4975(c)]

Q. 18:4 What penalties may be imposed on a party in interest or disqualified person for engaging in a prohibited transaction?

Under the Code, a penalty tax equal to 5 percent of the amount involved in the transaction is imposed on the disqualified person (other than a fiduciary acting solely in that capacity) for each year or part thereof that the transaction remains uncorrected. An additional tax equal to 100 percent of the amount involved is imposed if the prohibited transaction is not timely corrected. (See Q. 18:5.) [IRC §§ 4975(a) and 4975(b)]

Under ERISA, any fiduciary (see Q. 17:1) who engages in a prohibited transaction is personally liable for any losses to the plan and must restore to the plan any profit made by the fiduciary through the use of the plan's assets. Also, the civil penalty imposed by DOL for certain breaches of fiduciary duty applies to prohibited transactions (see Q. 17:25), but the penalty is reduced by any penalty tax imposed under Section 4975. [ERISA §§ 409(a) and 502(l)]

Q. 18:5   How is a prohibited transaction corrected?

A prohibited transaction is corrected by undoing the transaction to the extent possible, but in any event placing the plan in a financial position no worse than the position it would have been in had the party in interest acted under the highest fiduciary standards. [IRC § 4975(f)(5)]

Q. 18:6   May a plan purchase insurance to cover any losses to the plan resulting from a prohibited transaction?

Yes, a plan may carry insurance to protect itself from loss due to the conduct of a fiduciary. However, a plan cannot contain a provision relieving a fiduciary from liability for actions taken with respect to a prohibited transaction. [ERISA § 410]

Q. 18:7   Are there any statutory exceptions to the prohibited-transaction provisions?

There are numerous statutory exceptions to the prohibited-transaction provisions. Some of the most common are as follows:

- Loans made by a plan to a party in interest who is a plan participant or beneficiary if such loans (1) are available to all participants and beneficiaries on a reasonably equivalent basis, (2) are not made available to highly compensated employees in an amount greater than the amount made available to other employees, (3) are made in accordance with specific provisions regarding such loans set forth in the plan, (4) bear a reasonable rate of interest, and (5) are adequately secured.
- Services rendered by a party in interest to a plan that are necessary for the establishment or operation of the plan if no more than reasonable compensation is paid.
- A loan to an employee stock ownership plan (ESOP), provided the interest rate is not in excess of a reasonable interest rate (see Q. 22:4).

- Ancillary services provided by a federal or state supervised bank or similar financial institution that is a fiduciary (see Q. 17:1) to the plan, provided (1) the bank or similar financial institution has adopted adequate internal safeguards to ensure that provision of the ancillary service is consistent with sound banking and financial practice, and (2) no more than reasonable compensation is paid for such services.

- The acquisition or sale by a plan of qualifying employer securities (see Q. 17:42) or the acquisition, sale, or lease by a plan of qualifying employer real property (see Q. 17:41) if (1) the acquisition, sale, or lease is for adequate consideration, (2) no commission is charged, and (3) the restrictions and limitations of Section 407 of ERISA are satisfied. [ERISA §§ 408(b) and 408(e); IRC § 4975(d); DOL Opinion 90-04A]

Q. 18:8 Can an employer's contribution of property to a qualified retirement plan be a prohibited transaction?

Yes. According to DOL, the contribution of property to a pension plan (e.g., defined benefit or money purchase pension plan) is a prohibited transaction because the contribution discharges the employer's legal obligation to contribute cash to the plan. On the other hand, if the plan is not a pension plan (e.g., profit sharing plan), the contribution of property is not a prohibited transaction because it is purely voluntary and does not relieve the employer of an obligation to make cash contributions to the plan. [DOL Opinions 81-69A and 90-05A]

Q. 18:9 Can a party in interest obtain an exemption from the prohibited-transaction restrictions?

DOL may grant an exemption from the prohibited-transaction rules if the exemption is (1) administratively feasible, (2) in the interests of the plan and of its participants and beneficiaries, and (3) protective of the rights of the plan's participants and beneficiaries. [ERISA § 408(a); IRC § 4975(c)(2)]

IRS has granted DOL primary authority to issue rulings and regulations on, and grant exemptions from, the prohibited-transaction restrictions.

Q. 18:10   Can a prohibited-transaction exemption be granted retroactively?

Yes, but only under very limited circumstances. DOL generally will grant a retroactive exemption only if the applicant acted in good faith and the safeguards necessary for the grant of a prospective exemption were in place when the prohibited transaction occurred. DOL generally will not grant a retroactive exemption if the transaction resulted in a loss to the plan or was inconsistent with the general fiduciary responsibility provisions of Sections 403 and 404 of ERISA. [DOL Tech. Rel. 85-1]

Q. 18:11   Can a prohibited-transaction exemption be used to benefit the owner of a closely held corporation?

Yes. Although the continued well-being of the plan is the prime consideration in qualifying for an exemption from the prohibited-transaction restrictions, the fact that the corporation or a shareholder also benefits from the transaction will not preclude the granting of an exemption. For example, it may be possible for the corporation to borrow from its cash-rich qualified retirement plan or to sell assets to the plan to improve the business's cash flow without incurring a penalty. As the following case histories illustrate, DOL is willing to approve an exemption even if the corporation or shareholder will reap a substantial benefit from the transaction with the qualified retirement plan.

Business financing: Leep Homes, a corporation engaged in building homes in California, received approval from DOL to enter into a sale-leaseback arrangement for its model homes with its profit sharing and defined benefit plans. Investments in the corporation's model homes were estimated to yield the plans a net return of 10 percent and would be limited to 25 percent of each plan's assets. Leep would buy the land and incur all development expenses. The purchase price was set at Leep's costs for building the homes.

An independent real estate investment advisor was to check out the model homes and have the power to reject any home offered to the plans. Leep was to pay all maintenance expenses and taxes. The plan's trustee was to have an option to sell the homes back to Leep at cost or fair market value, whichever was greater. Any offers to buy from third parties would be reviewed by the real estate advisor; Leep, however, would have a right of first refusal. Elwood J. Leep, sole stockholder of Leep Homes, was to personally guarantee the corporation's lease payments. [PT Exemption 80-61]

Loan to corporation: DOL granted a New York law firm an exemption that permitted the corporation's defined benefit plan to make loans to the law firm on a recurring basis over a five-year period. The proceeds of the loans were to be used by the corporation to buy automobiles. [PT Exemption 82-125]

Selling an unwanted asset: A doctor's professional corporation had a profit sharing plan that permitted him (as well as all other participants) to direct the investment of funds for his own account. Several years ago, he had the plan invest in residential farmland. The land cost the plan $55,000 plus $30,000 spent on improvements. Since the land supported only subsistence agricultural activities and yielded little or no income, the land was not helping to build much of a nest egg for the doctor's retirement.

The plan received approval from DOL to sell the land to the doctor for $88,000, its then current value. After selling the land, which represented a substantial part of the assets in the doctor's account, the plan was able to invest in other assets yielding a much higher return. [PT Exemption 80-38]

Sale by parties in interest to plan: DOL granted an exemption to participants in a medical corporation's profit sharing plan that enabled the participants to sell promissory notes to their respective individual plan accounts. The promissory notes, which were issued by an unrelated third party, were held by the participants and sold for cash to their respective fully vested individual plan accounts at fair market value. [PT Exemption 82-143]

Lease of facilities: A professional corporation's profit sharing and money purchase pension plans acquired medical facilities and then sought to lease them to the plans' sponsor. Based on evidence that the terms of the lease were at least as favorable to the plans as those they could obtain from an unrelated party, the transaction was exempted. [PT Exemption 83-124]

Loan to plan: DOL granted an exemption, on both a retroactive and a prospective basis, to loans by an insurance company to a qualified retirement plan, of the maximum loan values of life insurance policies held by the plan on the lives of the plan participants. [PT Exemption 86-13]

Q. 18:12 What is a prohibited-transaction class exemption?

In addition to the statutory and administrative exemptions from the prohibited-transaction rules, DOL can grant a class exemption under which a party in interest or disqualified person (see Q. 18:2 and Q. 18:3) who meets the requirements of the class exemption will automatically be entitled to relief from the prohibited-transaction rules.

The following is a brief summary of some of the transactions for which prohibited-transaction class exemptions (PTCEs) have been issued. Many of these exemptions have detailed requirements that are not summarized here.

PTCE 86-128: PTCE 86-128 allows broker-dealers who are plan fiduciaries to effect or execute securities transactions for a fee. The exemption also allows sponsors of pooled separate accounts and other pooled investment funds to use their affiliates to effect or execute securities transactions for such accounts if certain conditions are met. [51 FR 41686]

PTCE 75-1: PTCE 75-1 permits certain transactions among employee benefit plans, broker-dealers, reporting dealers, and banks. Under this exemption, the prohibited-transaction provisions of ERISA will not apply to the purchase or sale of securities between a broker-dealer registered under the Securities and Exchange Act of 1934 and an employee benefit plan during the existence of an underwriting or selling syndicate with respect to such securities or a reporting dealer who is a market maker. The exemption also allows the extension of credit between a broker-dealer and a plan. [40 FR 50845]

PTCE 84-14: PTCE 84-14 permits parties in interest to engage in various transactions involving plan assets that would otherwise be prohibited transactions if, among other conditions, the plan assets are managed by persons defined in the exemption as qualified professional asset managers (QPAMs). QPAMs can be banks, savings and loans, insurance companies, and investment managers that are regulated by applicable state or federal law and meet certain financial standards. A major condition of the exemption is the requirement that the QPAM maintain independence from the entities in which the plan invests by retaining full authority over the terms of transactions and investment decisions. [49 FR 9494, as amended by 50 FR 41430]

PTCE 81-6: Securities lending arrangements between a security owner and a broker-dealer may enable the owner to increase its return on its assets. PTCE 81-6 permits such arrangements provided neither the borrower nor any affiliate of the borrower has any discretionary authority with respect to the investment of plan assets involved in the transaction. [46 FR 7527, as amended by 52 FR 18754]

PTCE 77-3: PTCE 77-3 permits the acquisition and sale of shares of an open-end mutual fund registered under the Investment Company Act of 1940 by an employee benefit plan covering only employees of the mutual fund, the investment advisor, or principal underwriter of the mutual fund, or any affiliate thereof (whether or not such mutual fund, investment advisor, principal underwriter, or affiliate is a fiduciary of the plan). [42 FR 18734]

PTCE 79-13: PTCE 79-13 permits the acquisition and sale of shares of a closed-end mutual fund that is registered under the Investment Company Act of 1940 by an employee benefit plan covering only employees of the mutual fund, the investment advisor of the fund, or any affiliate thereof (whether or not the mutual fund, investment advisor, or affiliate is a fiduciary of the plan). [44 FR 25533]

Chapter 19

Termination of the Plan

To qualify for tax-favored status, an employer's qualified retirement plan must be permanent. Nevertheless, an employer may amend the plan, terminate the plan, or stop contributing to the plan. This chapter examines how these actions may affect plan participants and the plan status, and discusses the rules regarding the termination of qualified retirement plans.

Q. 19:1 Once a qualified retirement plan is established, may the employer terminate it?

Yes. Although the employer must have intended the plan to be permanent, it may be terminated if the plan permits it. In addition, in the case of a defined benefit plan (see Q. 2:3) covered by Title IV of ERISA (see Q. 19:9, Q. 19:12, and Q. 19:13), the applicable termination rules must be satisfied.

Defined contribution plans (see Q. 2:2) and defined benefit plans not covered by Title IV of ERISA are not subject to these rules. However, not less than 15 days before the effective date of termination, the plan administrator must provide a written notice to each participant and beneficiary in a terminating pension plan (see Q. 19:53). [ERISA § 204(h)]

Q. 19:2 May a qualified retirement plan be terminated by a formal declaration of the plan sponsor's board of directors?

Although the plan sponsor's board of directors should adopt a resolution authorizing the termination of a qualified retirement plan, certain substantive and/or notice requirements must also be met to implement a plan termination (see Q. 19:17 and Q. 19:19).

The date that a plan subject to PBGC jurisdiction is deemed to terminate can be no earlier than the date determined under applicable PBGC provisions. In the case of any other qualified retirement plan, the date of termination is generally established by the terms of the plan and by the actions of the company officials (e.g., a meeting of the board of directors). [Reg. § 1.411(d)-2; Rev. Rul. 79-237, 1979-2 CB 190 and Rev. Rul. 89-87, 1989-2 CB 81]

However, IRS has clarified that a termination will not occur if plan assets are not distributed as soon as administratively feasible, even if the plan has been terminated in accordance with Title IV of ERISA. (See Q. 19:55.)

Q. 19:3 Which factors may cause a qualified retirement plan to be terminated?

A defined benefit plan covered by the Title IV program will be considered to be terminated only if the conditions and procedures prescribed by PBGC are satisfied (see Q. 19:17 and Q. 19:19).

Whether a defined contribution plan is terminated is generally a question to be determined with regard to all the facts and circumstances in a particular case. For example, a plan may be terminated when, in connection with the winding up of the company's trade or business, the company begins to discharge its employees (see Q. 19:5). However, a plan is not terminated merely because a company consolidates or replaces that plan with a comparable plan (see Q. 19:6). [Reg. § 1.401-6(b)] Similarly, a plan is not terminated merely because the company sells or otherwise disposes of its trade or business if the acquiring company continues the plan as a separate and distinct plan of its own or consolidates or replaces that plan with a comparable plan.

Q. 19:4 What is the effect of a plan termination on a participant's accrued benefit?

A qualified retirement plan must provide that (1) upon its full or partial termination, or (2) in the case of a profit sharing plan, upon complete discontinuance of contributions under the plan, "the rights of all affected employees to benefits accrued to the date of such termination, partial termination, or discontinuance, to the extent funded as of such date, or the amounts credited to the employees' accounts, are nonforfeitable." [IRC § 411(d)(3)]

The practical effect of a plan termination, therefore, is that each affected participant becomes 100 percent vested in the participant's accrued benefit as of the date of termination if the plan has sufficient assets to cover the benefit.

Generally, a participant who is partially vested need not become 100 percent vested upon termination of the plan if the participant separates from service and is paid the vested accrued benefit prior to the date of termination. However, a partially vested participant who terminates service, is not paid the vested accrued benefit, and does not incur a one-year break in service (see Q. 4:10) prior to the date of termination, must become 100 percent vested upon termination of the plan. [GCM 39310 (Nov. 29, 1984)]

Some IRS district offices have interpreted the above rule to require that all nonvested former participants with breaks in service of less than five years be fully vested. (See Q. 8:16.) [IRC §§ 411(a)(6)(B) and 411(a)(6)(C)]

Q. 19:5 What is a partial termination?

Generally, whether or not a partial termination of a qualified retirement plan has occurred will be determined on the basis of all the facts and circumstances. Under applicable regulations, a partial termination may be found to have occurred when a significant group of employees covered by the plan is excluded from coverage, as a result of either an amendment to the plan or their discharge by the employer. Similarly, a partial termination may be held to have occurred when benefits or employer contributions are reduced or the eligibility or vesting requirements under the plan are made less liberal. However, if a partial termination of a qualified retirement plan occurs, the provisions of the Code and regulations apply only to the part of the plan that is terminated. [Reg. §§ 1.401-6(b)(2) and 1.411(d)-2(b)(3)]

If a determination letter on the continued qualification of the plan after the partial termination is desired, Form 5300 (see Q. 13:7) should be filed with IRS.

> **Example 1.** A partial termination of a qualified retirement plan occurred when the employer's business was closed and 12 of the 15 participating employees were discharged upon refusing the opportunity to transfer to the employer's new business location. [*Rev. Rul.* 73-284, 1973-1 CB 139]

> **Example 2.** An employer established a qualified retirement plan that covered the employees in the two divisions of its business. At a time when the plan covered 165 employees, the employer closed down one division. In connection with the closing, the services of 95 participants under the plan were terminated. Because a significant number of employees who had been covered under the employer's qualified retirement plan were discharged in connection with the winding up of part of the business, IRS said there was a partial termination of the plan. [*Rev. Rul.* 81-27, 1981-1 CB 228]

> **Example 3.** In two successive years, an employer experienced reductions in its workforce of 34 percent and 51 percent, respectively, as a result of adverse economic conditions. The Tax Court ruled that, based on all the facts and circumstances, a partial termination occurred in each year. [*Tipton & Kalmbach, Inc.*, 83 TC 154 (1984)]

> **Example 4.** A corporation maintaining pension and profit sharing plans operated two divisions: One manufactured paint, and the other produced other types of wallcoverings. As a result of a split-off of one of the divisions to a new corporation, 16 employees (representing 14.7% of the participating employees) were transferred and were no longer eligible to participate in the original corporation's plans. In reviewing these facts, a court held that there was not a "significant percentage" of participants affected by the corporation's actions and that a partial termination of the plans did not occur. [*Babb v. Olney Paint Co.*, 764 F2d 240 (4th Cir. 1985); see also *Kreis v. Charles O. Townley, M.D. & Assocs., P.C.*, 833 F2d 74 (6th Cir. 1987)]

Q. 19:6 Does the adoption of a new qualified retirement plan to replace another plan result in a termination of the original plan?

Not necessarily. A qualified retirement plan is not considered to be terminated if it is either replaced by or converted into a comparable plan. For this purpose, a comparable plan is defined as a qualified retirement plan covered by the same limitations on deductions as the original plan. Since stock bonus plans, employee stock ownership plans (ESOPs), and profit sharing plans are generally covered by the same limitations on deductions, these plans are considered to be comparable. [Reg. §§ 1.381(c)(11)-1(d)(4) and 1.401-6(b)(1)]

On the other hand, a defined benefit plan covered by Title IV is considered to be terminated if an amendment is adopted to convert the plan to a defined contribution plan, such as a profit sharing plan, an ESOP, or a stock bonus plan. However, the amendment will not take effect unless and until the requirements for a standard or distress termination under Title IV are satisfied (see Q. 19:17 and Q. 19:19). [ERISA § 4041(e)]

Q. 19:7 Can termination of a qualified retirement plan affect its tax-favored status for earlier years?

Yes. The termination of a plan, or the complete discontinuance of contributions to a profit sharing plan, can result in the retroactive disqualification of the plan, causing the disallowance of tax deductions for the employer. This will depend on whether the plan was intended as a permanent program for the exclusive benefit of employees or a temporary device to set aside funds for the benefit of highly compensated employees, and whether the plan was discriminatory in operation.

Generally, IRS will not treat the termination as a device to benefit highly compensated employees if the termination is caused by a change in circumstances that would make it financially impractical to continue the plan. When termination of the plan occurs within a few years of its adoption, the reasons for termination will be examined closely. IRS will not assume the plan was temporary if the termination is for a "valid business reason" or on account of "business necessity."

Form 5310, Application for Determination Upon Termination, provides some insight into IRS's views as to what reasons for plan termination it considers valid, notwithstanding the presumed permanence of the plan. The listed reasons include:

- A change in ownership by merger
- The liquidation or dissolution of the employer
- A change in ownership by sale or transfer
- The existence of adverse business conditions
- The adoption of a new plan

If the plan termination is due to adverse business conditions, IRS requires an explanation of why such adverse conditions require the plan's termination.

When the termination occurs after ten years of active operation, IRS will usually not challenge the plan on these grounds even though a valid business reason for the termination is lacking. [Rev. Rul. 72-239, 1972-1 CB 107]

Q. 19:8 Is there a limit on the amount that a pension plan may pay to participants in the first ten years of operation?

Yes. A plan that substantially funds benefits for older, higher-paid employees at a more rapid pace than for younger, lower-paid employees (e.g., a defined benefit plan) is limited in the amount that it may pay out. The restriction applies if

1. The plan is terminated within ten years of its establishment;
2. Benefits become payable within ten years of the plan's establishment or before the full current costs for the first ten years have been funded; or
3. The plan is amended before the end of the ten-year period and the amendment substantially increased benefits. In this situation, a new ten-year limitation period would begin.

[Reg. § 1.401-4(c)]

Q. 19:9 What is Title IV of ERISA?

Title IV of ERISA established the rules regarding the termination of many defined benefit plans. In addition, it established an insurance program to guarantee that participants and beneficiaries will receive certain pension benefits promised under an employer's defined benefit plan if the plan does not have sufficient assets to cover certain benefits in the event of the plan's termination. The program was designed to be self-financed, funded with premiums paid by sponsors of covered plans.

Q. 19:10 What is the Pension Benefit Guaranty Corporation?

ERISA established PBGC as a wholly owned government corporation to administer the termination rules and to establish the mechanism for insuring benefits under Title IV. [ERISA § 4002]

Q. 19:11 What are the Single Employer Pension Plan Amendments Act and the Pension Protection Act?

SEPPAA was enacted as a sweeping reform of the single-employer defined benefit plan termination rules of Title IV. SEPPAA was designed to bolster an increasingly overburdened plan termination insurance program and correct a system that, in some instances, encouraged employers to terminate a plan, avoid their obligations to pay benefits, and shift unfunded pension liabilities to PBGC. PPA was designed to protect the fiscal integrity of the Title IV program, for example, by increasing premium rates and limiting the circumstances in which an employer may terminate its defined benefit plan.

As a result of SEPPAA and PPA, a defined benefit plan may be voluntarily terminated (i.e., terminated by the plan administrator) only if the conditions for either a standard or a distress termination are satisfied (see Q. 19:17 and Q. 19:19). In addition, these laws expanded the employer's liability upon termination if the plan is underfunded (see Q. 19:44).

Q. 19:12 What pension plans are insured by PBGC?

To be entitled to coverage, the plan must be a defined benefit plan (see Q. 2:3). In addition, the plan must:

1. Have been in effect for at least one year;

2. Be maintained by an employer engaged in commerce or in an industry or activity that affects commerce, or by a labor organization that represents employees who are engaged in commerce or in activities affecting commerce; and

3. Be a qualified pension plan, or have been operated in practice as a qualified pension plan for the five plan years prior to the termination.

[ERISA § 4021(a)]

Q. 19:13 Are any qualified defined benefit plans exempt from PBGC coverage?

Excluded from plan termination insurance coverage are defined benefit plans that are established and maintained:

- For government employees (or to which the Railroad Retirement Acts apply);

- For church employees, unless the plan elects under Section 410(d) to be covered and has notified PBGC that it wishes to have this section of the law apply to it;

- Outside the United States for nonresident aliens;

- Exclusively for one or more substantial owners (i.e., the sole owner of the trade or business, a more-than-10% partner, or a more-than-10% stockholder); or

- By professional service employers that at no time have had more than 25 active participants.

In addition to the aforementioned plans, all defined contribution plans (e.g., profit sharing, money purchase pension, ESOPs, stock bonus) as well as certain nonqualified plans are excluded from Title IV coverage. [ERISA § 4021(b)]

Q. 19:14 What must plan sponsors pay as an insurance premium to PBGC?

The basic annual premium rate is $16 for each participant in a single-employer pension plan during the plan year. [ERISA § 4006(a)(3)(A)(i)] In addition, each plan year a variable-rate component must be paid for underfunded plans equal to $6 for every $1,000 of unfunded vested benefits, divided by the number of participants for whom premiums are being paid as of the close of the preceding plan year. However, if an employer contributed to a plan during any of the five years preceding 1988, then, for the first five years after 1987, the variable amount is reduced by $3 for each plan year in which the employer made contributions. Because this variable premium may not exceed $34 per participant, the total premium amount for each participant cannot exceed $50. [ERISA § 4006(a)(3)(E)]

For multiemployer plans, that is, plans maintained under a collective bargaining agreement to which two or more employers contribute, the annual PBGC premium is $2.60 per participant. [ERISA § 4006(a)(3)(A)(iii)]

The total amount of premiums is determined on the basis of the number of plan participants. (See Q. 19:15.)

Q. 19:15 How is the number of participants determined for insurance premium purposes?

The participant count is made as of the last day of the prior plan year, except that, for a new plan, the count is made as of the date on which the plan becomes subject to PBGC jurisdiction. [PBGC Reg. § 2610.22]

The following categories of individuals are considered participants:

- All individuals accruing benefits or retaining or earning credited service under the plan;
- Former employees with vested rights to either immediate or deferred benefits;
- Retirees receiving or eligible to receive benefits;

- Deceased participants whose beneficiaries are receiving benefits; and
- Any other "participants" as defined under the plan.

Certain individuals to whom an insurance company has made an irrevocable commitment to pay benefits are not considered participants. The number of participants in the above categories should equal the total number reported on the Form 5500 series annual report for the plan for the prior plan year. [PBGC Reg. § 2610.2]

Q. 19:16 Must a plan administrator notify PBGC when certain significant events affecting a single-employer defined benefit plan occur?

Yes. The plan administrator may be required to notify PBGC within 30 days after the plan administrator knows or has reason to know of a reportable event.

The 30-day notice is always required for the following:

- Inability to pay benefits when due;
- Failure to meet minimum funding standards (see Q. 7:1) if the present value of unfunded vested benefits equals or exceeds $250,000;
- Bankruptcy, liquidation, or dissolution of a plan sponsor; and
- Certain transactions involving a change of employer.

PBGC has waived the notice requirement for those reportable events that would have minimal impact on the plan, the employer, or PBGC, and for those reportable events about which IRS or DOL is required by ERISA to notify PBGC. Examples of these events include:

- Plan disqualification
- Decrease in benefits
- DOL finding of an ERISA violation
- Plan merger, consolidation, or transfer
- Certain corporate reorganizations

- A determination by IRS that there has been a complete or partial termination

[ERISA §§ 4043(a) and 4043(b); PBGC Reg. § 2615]

Q. 19:17   What is a standard termination?

A single-employer defined benefit plan may be voluntarily terminated under Title IV's standard termination procedures only if it is determined that when the final distributions are made, the assets of the plan will be sufficient to cover all benefit liabilities (see Q. 19:18) as of the termination date. In addition:

- The plan administrator must provide a 60-day advance notice of termination to affected parties (see Q. 19:32);
- A notice containing specified information (completed by the plan administrator), together with an enrolled actuary's certification, must be sent to PBGC;
- A notice containing required information must be sent to participants and beneficiaries regarding benefits to be paid; and
- PBGC must not have issued a notice of noncompliance stating that it has reason to believe that the standard termination requirements have not been met or that the plan does not have sufficient assets for benefit liabilities.

[ERISA § 4041(b)]

Q. 19:18   What are benefit liabilities?

Benefit liabilities under a single-employer defined benefit plan are defined as "the benefits of employees and their beneficiaries under the plan (within the meaning of § 401(a)(2) of the Internal Revenue Code of 1986)." [ERISA § 4001(a)(16)]

If a plan does not have sufficient assets for benefit liabilities, the plan sponsor may consider making a contribution to the plan. However, because of the rules relating to deductibility of contributions and funding requirements, the contribution may not be allowed. In this circumstance, some limited relief is offered whereby contributions made to a plan under a standard termination are deductible, but only to the extent they are guaranteed by PBGC. [IRC § 404(g), clarified by OBRA '89, § 11841]

Q. 19:19 What is a distress termination?

If a defined benefit plan cannot satisfy the conditions for a standard termination, it can be voluntarily terminated only if the conditions for a distress termination of a single-employer plan are satisfied. This type of termination may occur if the employer contributing to the plan and each member of its controlled group meet at least one of the following conditions:

- Liquidation in bankruptcy or insolvency proceeding.
- Reorganization in bankruptcy or insolvency proceeding. In addition, the bankruptcy petition must be filed prior to the proposed date of plan termination, and the bankruptcy or other appropriate court must determine that, unless the plan is terminated, the employer and all the members of the controlled group will be unable to pay their debts under a reorganization plan and unable to continue without a reorganization.
- Termination of the plan is required to enable payment of debts while staying in business or to avoid unreasonably burdensome pension costs caused by a decline of the employer's covered workforce.

If PBGC determines that the requirements of a distress termination have been met, additional information may be required of the plan administrator and the enrolled actuary in order to determine the sufficiency of plan assets. PBGC must then notify the plan administrator as soon as possible after reaching its determination. [ERISA § 4041(c)]

Q. 19:20 What benefits under a single-employer defined benefit plan are guaranteed by PBGC?

When a single-employer defined benefit plan terminates under the distress termination procedures, PBGC will guarantee the payment of "certain benefits." The characteristics of this type of benefit are that:

1. It is a pension benefit;

2. It is nonforfeitable (see Q. 19:21) on the date of plan termination; and

3. A participant must be entitled to the benefit. The benefit will be guaranteed to the extent it does not exceed the limitations set forth in ERISA and its regulations (see Q. 19:22 through Q. 19:25). [ERISA §§ 4022(a) and 4022(b); PBGC Reg. § 2613.3]

Under a special rule, a qualified preretirement survivor annuity is not treated as forfeitable solely because the participant has not died as of the termination date. [ERISA § 4022(e)]

Q. 19:21 Does PBGC guarantee a benefit that becomes nonforfeitable solely as a result of the plan's termination?

No. Although the plan must provide for 100 percent vesting upon termination (see Q. 19:4), a benefit that vests because of this rule is not a guaranteed benefit. [ERISA § 4022(a)]

Q. 19:22 Are there any limitations on the amount of the benefit PBGC will guarantee?

Yes. PBGC's guarantee may be subject to one or more statutorily prescribed benefit limitations (see Q. 19:23 through Q. 19:25). For example, the guarantee may not exceed the maximum monthly benefit limitation amount, which is expressed in terms of an annuity that is payable for the life of the participant commencing at age 65. The maximum guaranteed benefit is adjusted annually to reflect inflation and cost-of-living increases.

Furthermore, the guaranteed benefit may not exceed the actuarial equivalent of a monthly benefit in the form of a life annuity commencing at age 65. Accordingly, if a benefit is payable at an earlier age, the maximum guaranteed benefit is actuarially reduced to reflect the earlier commencement of the receipt of the benefit. [ERISA § 4022(b); PBGC Reg. § 2621.4]

Q. 19:23 What is the maximum guaranteed monthly benefit for 1990?

The maximum monthly guaranteed benefit for plans terminating in 1990 is $2,164.77. This amount applies even though a participant may not retire and receive the benefit until years after the termination of the plan. [ERISA § 4022(b)(3); Appendix A to 29 C.F.R. Part 2621]

Q. 19:24 What is the effect on PBGC's guarantees of a plan amendment prior to the plan's termination?

If an amendment is adopted within five years of the termination and adds a new benefit or increases the value of benefit for any participant who is not a substantial owner (see Q. 19:13), PBGC's guarantee will be subject to a phase-in rule. Such increases include any changes that advance a participant's entitlement (such as liberalization of the participation or vesting requirement), a reduction in the normal or early retirement ages, or a change in the form of benefit. Increases due to salary increases or additional years of service are not subject to this rule. Under this five-year phase-in rule, a benefit increase will be subject to the following formula: multiply the number of years a benefit increase has been in effect by the greater of 20 percent of the monthly increase or $20 per month (but not in excess of the actual increase). [ERISA § 4022(b)(7); PBGC Reg. §§ 2621.2 and 2621.6]

Any benefits provided under a plan to a participant who is a substantial owner, and thereafter any amendment benefiting a substantial owner, will be subject to a 30-year phase-in rule. [ERISA § 4022(b)(5); PBGC Reg. § 2621.7]

Q. 19:25 What is the effect of the plan's disqualification on the guaranteed benefit?

PBGC will not guarantee any benefits that accrue *after* IRS has disqualified a plan or an amendment. [ERISA § 4022(b)(6); PBGC Reg. § 2621.8]

Q. 19:26 Can PBGC initiate the termination of a plan?

Yes. PBGC may institute termination proceedings in federal court if it finds that:

- Minimum funding standards (see Q. 7:1) have not been satisfied;
- The plan will be unable to pay benefits when due;
- A distribution of more than $10,000 was made to a substantial owner in any 24-month period for reasons other than death and, after the distribution, there are unfunded vested liabilities; or
- The possible long-run liability of the employer to PBGC is expected to increase unreasonably if the plan is not terminated. [ERISA § 4042(a)]

However, PBGC must institute termination proceedings whenever it determines that a single-employer defined benefit plan does not have enough assets to pay benefits that are currently due. [ERISA § 4042(a)]

Furthermore, PBGC may cease the termination of a plan and restore the plan to its status prior to termination if circumstances change. In a much publicized case, the Supreme Court allowed PBGC to restore terminated defined benefit plans. LTV Corporation (LTV) filed for bankruptcy. At that time, LTV maintained three underfunded defined benefit plans all covered by PBGC. PBGC instituted proceedings to involuntarily terminate the plans. Subsequently, LTV established new plans that provided benefits lost by the termination. In effect, the new "follow-on" plans provided benefits equal to the difference between the promised benefits under the terminated plans and PBGC guaranteed benefits. PBGC objected and determined to restore the plans. The Supreme Court upheld PBGC's authority to return responsibility for funding the terminated plans to the plan sponsor. Employers may now be discouraged from using "follow-on" plans to shift the burden of paying benefits from the plan sponsor to PBGC. [ERISA § 4047; *PBGC v. LTV Corp.*, No. 89-390 (S. Ct. June 18, 1990)]

Q. 19:27 Can a plan covered by Title IV be terminated if the termination would violate an existing collective bargaining agreement?

The authority of PBGC to terminate a plan under these circumstances will depend on whether the termination is initiated by the plan administrator or PBGC. If the plan administrator attempts to terminate the plan under the standard or distress termination provisions, PBGC may not proceed with the termination. However, PBGC's authority to institute involuntary termination proceedings for such a plan is not limited by the fact that the termination would violate the collective bargaining agreement. [ERISA § 4041(a)(3); PBGC Opinion Letter No. 87-4]

Q. 19:28 Is there any restriction on the form of a benefit paid by a terminating defined benefit plan?

Yes. The general rule is that a benefit be paid in annuity form, unless the participant elects an optional form of benefit under the terms of the plan. [ERISA § 4041(b)(3)(A)(i); PBGC Reg. § 2617.4] However, an exception exists for small amounts of benefits. PBGC and any other plan administrator of a terminating plan may choose to pay a benefit in a single payment without the consent of the participant if the present value of the benefit is $3,500 or less. [PBGC Reg. §§ 2613.8 and 2617.4]

Q. 19:29 Who must be notified of the company's intention to terminate a defined benefit plan covered by Title IV—and when must this notice be given?

The plan administrator must provide to all affected parties written notice of the company's intention to terminate a defined benefit plan covered by Title IV at least 60 days before the proposed date of termination. [ERISA § 4041(a)(2)] Although PBGC Prop. Reg. § 2617.12 (September 1987) states that the notice may not be issued earlier than 180 days prior to the plan termination date, later guidelines issued by the PBGC (December 22, 1989) state that a proposed termination date may not be later than the ninetieth day after issuance of the Notice of Intent to Terminate (NOIT).

Q. 19:30 What is the relevance of the date of plan termination?

The termination date is critical for determining the rights of the participants and beneficiaries to the benefits under the plan that are guaranteed by PBGC, the employer's liability to PBGC for any underfunding, and PBGC's exposure for guaranteed benefits. [ERISA § 4048; *Audio Fidelity Corp. v. PBGC*, 624 F2d 513 (4th Cir. 1980)]

Q. 19:31 What factors are considered by PBGC in establishing a defined benefit plan's termination date?

The date of termination will depend on whether the termination is filed by the plan administrator under the standard or distress termination procedures or whether PBGC has initiated the termination (see Q. 19:26). However, in a termination other than one initiated by PBGC, the date must be prospective and at least 60 days after the NOIT is given to affected parties (see Q. 19:29 and Q. 19:32). [ERISA § 4041(a)(2)]

Q. 19:32 Who is an affected party?

An affected party, for purposes of a termination subject to PBGC's jurisdiction, is:

- A participant;
- A beneficiary of a deceased participant;
- A beneficiary who is an alternate payee under a Qualified Domestic Relations Order (see Chapter 28);
- Any employee organization representing plan participants;
- PBGC (in the case of a distress termination; see Q. 19:19); or
- Any person designated in writing to receive notice on behalf of an affected party.

[ERISA §§ 4001(a)(21), 4041(a)(2), and 4041(c)(1)(A)]

Q. 19:33 Are there any other notice requirements if the company intends to terminate a defined benefit plan?

Yes. Effective for standard terminations with respect to which the NOIT was issued on or after February 1, 1990, notice must be provided to PBGC by filing PBGC Form 500, Standard Termination Notice Single-Employer Plan Termination. Schedule EA-S, Standard Termination Certification of Sufficiency, attached to Form 500, must be used by the enrolled actuary to certify that the plan is projected to have sufficient assets to provide all benefit liabilities. [ERISA § 4041(b)(2)(A)]

In addition, no later than on the date that the notice is given PBGC, the plan administrator must provide each participant and beneficiary with a Notice of Plan Benefits (see Q. 19:34). [ERISA § 4041(b)(2)(B)]

Q. 19:34 What information is the plan administrator required to send to participants and beneficiaries in the Notice of Plan Benefits?

The plan administrator must send a notice to each participant and beneficiary that (1) specifies the amount of the individual's benefits as of the proposed termination date, and the form of benefit on the basis of which the amount was determined; and (2) includes the following information used in determining the individual's benefits:

- Length of service
- Age of the participant or beneficiary
- Wages
- Assumptions (including the interest rate)
- Such other information as PBGC may require

[ERISA § 4041(b)(2)(B)]

Q. 19:35 After the plan administrator's notice is sent to PBGC, does PBGC have to act within designated time limits?

Yes. Within 60 days after the plan administrator notifies PBGC (see Q. 19:33), PBGC must issue to the plan administrator a notice of noncompliance if it (1) has reason to believe that any of the notice requirements have not been met, or (2) otherwise determines, on the basis of information provided by affected parties (see Q. 19:32) or otherwise obtained by PBGC, that there is reason to believe that the plan assets are not sufficient for benefit liabilities (see Q. 19:18). [ERISA § 4041(b)(2)(C)]

Q. 19:36 May the 60-day period for PBGC to issue a notice of noncompliance be extended?

Yes. PBGC and the plan administrator may extend the 60-day period (see Q. 19:35) for the noncompliance notice by jointly signing a written agreement before expiration of the initial 60-day period. Additional extensions are also permitted. [ERISA § 4041(b)(2)(C)]

Q. 19:37 Assuming that PBGC does not issue a notice of noncompliance, when should final distribution of assets occur?

The plan administrator must commence the final distribution of assets, pursuant to a standard termination, "as soon as practicable" after expiration of the 60-day (or extended) period (see Q. 19:35 and Q. 19:36), assuming that plan assets are sufficient to meet benefit liabilities (see Q. 19:18), determined as of the termination date, when the final distribution occurs. [ERISA § 4041(b)(2)(D)]

Although PBGC Prop. Reg. § 2617.18(a) (September 1987) states that the final distribution of plan assets must be made within 30 days after the expiration of the 60-day period, later guidelines issued by the PBGC (December 22, 1989) interpret "as soon as practicable" to mean that final distribution of plan assets must be completed within 180 days after the expiration of the 60-day period.

Q. 19:38   What is the method for the final distribution of assets?

The plan administrator must distribute the plan's assets in accordance with the required allocation of assets (see Q. 19:39). In distributing the assets, the plan administrator must:

1. Purchase irrevocable commitments from an insurer to provide for all benefit liabilities (and any other benefits to which assets are required to be allocated); or

2. Otherwise fully provide the benefit liabilities (and any other benefits to which assets are required to be allocated) in accordance with the plan's provisions and any applicable PBGC regulations.

[ERISA § 4041(b)(3)]

In order to have a valid termination, the benefits of all participants must be distributed. Before a reversion of excess assets occurs (see Q. 19:45), all plan liabilities must first be satisfied. [IRC § 401(a)(2); ERISA § 4044(d)]

If a participant cannot be located, a request can be sent to the Social Security Administration or IRS. If the participant still cannot be located, PBGC has advised that unclaimed *de minimis* benefits in a terminating plan should be placed in a separate bank account opened in the missing participant's name. PBGC guidelines (December 22, 1989) included in the instructions to PBGC Form 501 offer similar advice. According to the instructions, if the benefit of a participant who cannot be located is $3,500 or less, the amount may be deposited into a bank account. If the amount is greater than $3,500, the administrator should purchase an irrevocable commitment (e.g., annuity contract) to provide benefits for the participant. [PBGC Opinion Letter No. 89-4 (July 26, 1989)]

Q. 19:39   How are plan assets allocated when a defined benefit plan is terminated?

There are six categories into which plan assets must be divided upon termination of a single-employer defined benefit plan. The assets are assigned to these categories, starting with the first category, until the value of the assets has been exhausted. On termination of a defined benefit plan, the assets are allocated in the following order:

1. Employee voluntary contributions;

2. Employee mandatory contributions;

3. Annuity payments in pay status at least three years before the termination of the plan (including annuity payments that would have been in pay status for at least three years if the employee had retired then) based on the provisions of the plan in effect during the five years before termination of the plan under which the benefit would be the least;

4. All other guaranteed insured benefits, determined without regard to the aggregate limit on benefits guaranteed with respect to a participant under all multiemployer and single-employer plans;

5. All other vested benefits; and

6. All other benefits under the plan (see Q. 19:40).

[ERISA § 4044(a)]

Q. 19:40   What does the phrase "all other benefits under the plan" cover?

According to PBGC and IRS, the statutory language in Section 4044(a)(6) of ERISA encompasses only those benefits that participants have accrued as of the date of termination (or in the case of benefit subsidies protected by the Retirement Equity Act (REA), benefits to which participants may become entitled in the future). [PBGC Opinion Letter No. 87-11; GCM 39665]

The Supreme Court has agreed with the PBGC and IRS positions and held that the "all other accrued benefits" category under Section 4044(a)(6) of ERISA covers participants' accrued forfeitable benefits, but not unaccrued benefits. [*Mead Corp. v. Tilley*, 109 S. Ct. 2156 (1989); see also *May v. The Houston Post Pension Plan*, No. 89-2249 (5th Cir. 1990) and *Blessitt v. Retirement Plan for Employees of Dixie Engine Co.*, 848 F2d 1164 (11th Cir. 1988)]

Q. 19:41   Can a distribution of plan assets be reallocated?

Yes. The traditional rules provide that if the asset allocation discriminates in favor of officers, shareholders, or highly paid employees, the allocation (see Q. 19:39) may be changed to the extent necessary to avoid the prohibited discrimination. Furthermore, if the plan is terminated early (generally, before it has been in existence for ten years), a reallocation of assets may be made to avoid discrimination, and benefits payable to the 25 highest paid employees may be restricted. (See Q. 19:8.) [ERISA § 4044(b)(4); Reg. §§ 1.401-4(c), 1.411(d)-2(a)(2)(ii), and 1.411(d)-2(e)]

However, although these traditional rules remain, the law also provides that a defined benefit plan cannot terminate in a standard termination unless it has sufficient assets to cover all benefit liabilities of the plan, which would obviate any such reallocation. [ERISA § 4041(b)(1)(D)]

Q. 19:42   Must PBGC be notified once final distribution of assets is completed?

Yes. Within 30 days after the final distribution of assets is completed, the plan administrator must send PBGC a notice certifying that the assets have been distributed in accordance with the required order of allocation of assets and that all benefits have been distributed in accordance with either method of distribution described in Q. 19:38. PBGC Form 501, Post-Distribution Certification for Standard Terminations, has been designed for this purpose. [ERISA § 4041(b)(3)(B)]

Q. 19:43   Does PBGC perform post-termination audits for compliance with the Title IV requirements?

Yes. PBGC is believed to be selectively conducting post-termination compliance audits. The data request may include copies of the following:

- The plan and trust documents
- Applicable labor contracts
- Applicable insurance contracts to fund the plan
- Actuarial reports and enrolled actuary's worksheets
- The plan's financial statement as of the termination date
- Benefit data for each participant
- Election and spousal consent forms

Q. 19:44 Does an employer incur any liability to PBGC for the payment of benefits to plan participants of an underfunded terminated plan?

Yes. When PBGC incurs liabilities for benefits in the case of a distress termination or a termination instituted by the PBGC, it can obtain reimbursement from the contributing employer or a member of its controlled group. If more than one employer jointly sponsors a plan, the liability to PBGC is separately applicable to each such entity.

Any trade or business, whether or not incorporated, can be a member of the contributing employer's controlled group if a prescribed control or ownership test is satisfied. In that case, it will be jointly and severally liable to reimburse PBGC. [ERISA §§ 4062(b) and 4001(b)]

The liability of a contributing employer or member of its controlled group generally is the total amount of the unfunded benefit liabilities to all participants and beneficiaries as of the termination date, plus interest at a reasonable rate calculated from the termination date. [ERISA § 4062(b)]

If the liability to PBGC is not paid, a lien in favor of PBGC arises in an amount equal to the lesser of (1) the unfunded benefit liabilities or (2) 30 percent of the collective net worth of the contributing employers of a plan and members of the controlled group (but treating as zero any negative net worth). [ERISA §§ 4062(d)(1) and 4068(a)]

Q. 19:45 May excess assets remaining after the standard termination of a defined benefit plan be returned to the employer after payment of all plan benefit liabilities?

Yes, provided that the distribution does not contravene any other provision of law, the excess was the result of an "erroneous actuarial computation," and the plan specifically permits the distribution of excess assets in this situation. (See Q. 19:38 and Q. 19:46 through Q. 19:48.) [ERISA § 4044(d); Reg. § 1.401-2]

In one case, an employer recovered $275 million to use in expanding and improving its ongoing business. [*Walsh v. The Great Atlantic & Pacific Tea Co.*, 4 EBC 2577 (3d Cir. 1983), *aff'g* 96 FRD 632 (D. NJ 1983)]

In another case, the court held that a 1959 plan provision that "in no event and under no circumstances" could plan assets be returned to the employer precluded any subsequent amendment to the plan to allow such a reversion upon termination of the plan. [*Bryant v. International Fruit Products, Inc.*, 7 EBC 2562 (6th Cir. 1986), *den'g and reh'g* 793 F2d 118 (6th Cir. 1986)]

Further, if an overfunded plan with mandatory employee contributions is terminated, certain assets attributable to such contributions must be distributed to participants and beneficiaries. [ERISA § 4044(d)(3)(B)]

Q. 19:46 May a defined benefit plan that did not originally provide for distribution of excess assets to the employer be amended to authorize such a distribution?

Yes. However, for defined benefit plans covered by PBGC (see Q. 19:12 and Q. 19:13), any amendment providing for a reversion, or increasing the amount that may revert to the employer, is not effective before the fifth calendar year following the date of the adoption of such an amendment. A special rule provides that a distribution to the employer will not be treated as failing to satisfy this rule if the plan has been in effect for fewer than five years.

For plans that, as of December 17, 1987, have no provision relating to the distribution of plan assets to the employer, the new rule applies to such amendments that were adopted more than one year after the effective date of the new law. For plans that, as of December 17, 1987, provide for the distribution of plan assets to the employer, the new law applies to any amendment made after December 17, 1987. [ERISA § 4044(d)(2)]

Q. 19:47 May an employer terminate a defined benefit plan to recover any excess assets and adopt a new defined benefit plan covering the same employees?

Yes, if the plan specifically permits the recovery of excess assets and:

- All employees covered by the original plan are given notice of the termination and adoption;
- All accrued benefits are vested as of the termination date and annuities are purchased to cover those benefits;
- The plan's funding method is changed to take into consideration the termination and adoption, and IRS approves the change in funding method;
- No other termination and adoption will be made in the next 15 years; and
- The new plan is intended to be permanent. [PBGC News Release 84-23, on the Joint Implementation Guidelines for Termination of Defined Benefit Plans]

Recent legislation has sought to prohibit employers from terminating plans in order to recover excess assets, but thus far the measures have been only temporary. For example, in 1988, Treasury directed IRS to suspend defined benefit plan termination approvals for several months in cases in which the employer would recover all or a portion of the assets. [Treasury Department News Release, October 24, 1988]

Q. 19:48 Is the employer liable for any taxes on the reversion?

Yes. The amount of the reversion is taxable to the employer as ordinary income. Furthermore, a nondeductible excise tax equal to 15 percent of the amount of the reversion is imposed upon the employer. [IRC § 4980]

A special provision in OBRA '89 offers some relief to overfunded defined benefit plans. Present law provides a tax-favored arrangement to accumulate assets to provide post retirement medical benefits through a separate account in a pension plan. [IRC § 401(h)]

Under the special provision, a one-time transfer of certain excess assets is permitted from the pension portion of a defined benefit plan to the Section 401(h) account that is part of such plan. The assets transferred are not includible in the gross income of the employer and are not subject to the 15 percent excise tax on reversions. The transfer of assets to a Section 401(h) account is required to occur before 1992, and in a plan year beginning after 1989. The retirement benefits of plan participants are subject to the same rules that apply if the plan had terminated on the date of the transfer. Thus, each participant's retirement benefits are to be nonforfeitable and an annuity is to be purchased to fund such benefits.

Only one transfer of excess assets may qualify under the provision. The amount of excess pension assets that may be transferred and used for retiree health benefits is limited to the amount reasonably estimated to be the amount the employer will pay or incur for qualified current retiree health liabilities. [OBRA '89, §§ 11321 and 11322]

Q. 19:49 If an employer wants to withdraw from a plan maintained by two or more unrelated employers, would the withdrawal be considered a plan termination?

No. The general rule is that such a withdrawal would not constitute a plan termination. However, the withdrawal of one or more employers may result in a partial termination of the plan (see Q. 19:5). [Reg. § 1.411(d)-2(b)]

Q. 19:50   What is a complete discontinuance of contributions under a profit sharing plan?

Instead of directly defining a complete discontinuance, IRS describes what it is and what it is not.

First, IRS regulations distinguish a complete discontinuance from a suspension of contributions under a plan that is "merely a temporary cessation of contributions by the employer." The regulations provide that "a complete discontinuance of contributions may occur although some amounts are contributed by the employer under the plan if such amounts are not substantial enough to reflect the intent on the part of the employer to continue to maintain the plan. The determination of whether a complete discontinuance of contributions under the plan has occurred will be made with regard to all the facts and circumstances in the particular case, and without regard to the amount of any contributions made under the plan by employees." [Reg. § 1.411(d)-2(d)]

Second, the regulations state that, in any case in which a suspension of a profit sharing plan is considered a discontinuance, the discontinuance becomes effective no later than the last day of the taxable year that follows the last taxable year for which a substantial contribution was made under the profit sharing plan. [Reg. § 1.411(d)-2(d)(2)]

> **Example.** SOS Corporation maintains a calendar-year profit sharing plan. The last "substantial" contribution made by the corporation was on November 14, 1989. If a discontinuance of contributions was deemed to have occurred, it would become effective no later than December 31, 1990.

Employees who become eligible to enter a plan subsequent to its discontinuance receive no benefits, nor do any additional benefits accrue to any of the participants unless employer contributions are resumed. IRS, therefore, takes the position that discontinuance of contributions is equivalent to a plan termination.

What if an employer has no profits? IRS says that the failure of an employer to make contributions to its profit sharing plan for five consecutive years due solely to the absence of current or accumulated earnings and profits is not a discontinuance of contributions if the plan requires the employer to resume contributions as soon as it has profits. [*Rev. Rul. 80-146,* 1980-1 CB 90] Since current or accumulated profits are no longer required for the employer to make tax deductible contributions to a profit sharing plan, such failure to make contributions may ripen into a discontinuance. [IRC § 401(a)(27)]

Q. 19:51 Must a profit sharing plan provide for full vesting of benefits upon a complete discontinuance of contributions?

Yes. A Tax Court decision upheld IRS's position that a profit sharing plan did not qualify merely because it did not provide for full vesting of participants' accrued benefits on complete discontinuance of contributions. Even though IRS conceded that there never was a discontinuance of contributions, and no employee's rights to benefits were ever adversely affected, the absence of such a provision from a plan was, according to the court, a sufficient defect in the instrument to disqualify the plan, resulting in the disallowance of the employer deduction. [*Tionesta Sand and Gravel, Inc.,* 73 TC 758 (1980), *aff'd,* 3d Cir. in unpublished opinion (2/27/81)]

Q. 19:52 Can a plan amendment result in the termination of the plan?

Yes. If benefits or employer contributions to the plan are reduced, or vesting or eligibility requirements are made less liberal, the plan is considered to be curtailed. Full vesting of a portion of the benefits may be required if IRS decides that the curtailment is a partial termination of the plan. (See Q. 19:5.)

If an employer seeks to amend a defined benefit plan covered by Title IV to convert it to a defined contribution plan, the termination rules of Title IV must be satisfied first before the former plan is treated as terminated. [ERISA § 4041(e)]

Q. 19:53   Can a plan be amended to reduce or stop benefit accruals?

Yes, but if the amendment provides for a significant reduction in the rate of future benefit accrual, certain notice requirements must be satisfied. After adoption of the amendment and no less than 15 days before the effective date of a plan amendment that significantly reduces future accruals, each participant, beneficiary who is an alternate payee under a QDRO (see Chapter 28), and labor organization representing plan participants must be provided with written notice of the amendment and its effective date. This rule applies to amendments to defined benefit plans and to defined contribution plans subject to the funding standards of Section 302 of ERISA, namely, money purchase pension plans and target benefit plans. [ERISA § 204(h)]

Q. 19:54   Must terminating plans be amended to conform to TRA '86 qualification requirements?

Yes. Generally, all plans must be amended to comply with the qualification requirements (and other rules) effective at the time of termination. [Rev. Proc. 88-9, 1988-1 CB 634; Notice 87-57, 1987-2 CB 368]

IRS has provided some temporary relief for employers faced with making their plans comply with TRA '86 requirements. Employers that adopted Model Amendment 4 by December 31, 1989 were not required to amend their plans to comply with the TRA '86 post-1988 requirements (although they were still required to comply with the TRA '86 pre-1989 requirements, as well as those of OBRA '86 and OBRA '87). [Notice 88-131, 1988-2 CB 546; Notice 89-92, 1989-2 CB 410]

Q. 19:55   Must IRS be notified when a plan terminates?

Just as there is no legal requirement to file a request for a favorable determination letter with IRS with regard to a new or amended plan, there is no requirement regarding a plan's termination. How-ever, a plan administrator must notify IRS on the annual return/report for the year in which the plan terminates. In addition, an annual return/report must be filed every year (even after a plan terminates) until all assets are distributed from the trust.

It is strongly suggested that plan administrators file Form 5310 (see Q. 13:7) with IRS requesting a favorable determination letter with regard to a plan's termination. IRS is conducting a pilot exami-nation program of 400 retirement plans that have terminated without seeking a determination letter. If results show that problems exist, IRS will institute a special examination program in 1991. [*An-nouncement 90-96, 1990-34 IRB*]

IRS has issued a revenue ruling explaining that a termination of a qualified retirement plan is not complete until the final distribution of plan assets. However, if the "terminated" retirement plan fails to distribute its assets as soon as administratively feasible following the established plan termination date, IRS will not treat the plan as being terminated.

The ruling provides that whether a distribution is made as soon as administratively feasible is to be determined under all the facts and circumstances of the given case but, generally, a distribution that is not completed within one year following the date of plan termina-tion specified by the employer will be presumed not to have been completed as soon as administratively feasible. If a plan's assets are not distributed as soon as administratively feasible, the plan is con-sidered to be an ongoing plan and must meet the requirements of Section 401(a) in order to maintain its qualified status. For example, such a plan remains subject to the minimum funding requirements under Section 412 (see Q. 7:1) and the information reporting require-ments of Sections 6057 and 6058 (and, in the case of a defined benefit plan, the actuarial reporting requirements of Section 6059). It is not clear under the ruling whether a pending determination letter request on the plan's termination or a delay caused by the termina-tion procedures of Title IV of ERISA (applicable to certain defined benefit plans) will excuse a distribution delay of more than one year. [*Rev. Rul. 89-87, 1989-2 CB 81*]

Chapter 20

Top-Heavy Plans

A qualified retirement plan that primarily benefits key employees—a top-heavy plan—can qualify for tax-favored status only if, in addition to the regular qualification requirements, it meets several special requirements. This chapter examines what top-heavy plans are and the special requirements these plans must satisfy.

Q. 20:1   What is a top-heavy defined benefit plan?

A defined benefit plan (see Q. 2:3) is top-heavy if, as of the determination date (see Q. 20:21), the present value of the accrued benefits of all key employees (see Q. 20:24) exceeds 60 percent of the present value of the accrued benefits of all employees. [IRC § 416(g)(1)(A)(i); Reg. § 1.416-1, Question T-1(c)]

Q. 20:2   How are accrued benefits calculated for purposes of determining whether a qualified retirement plan is top-heavy?

Solely for determining whether the present value of cumulative accrued benefits for key employees exceeds 60 percent of the present value of cumulative accrued benefits for all employees (90% for purposes of the super-top-heavy plan rules, see Q. 20:57), the accrued benefit of an employee (other than a key employee) is determined by the method that is used for benefit accrual purposes under all qualified retirement plans maintained by the employer or, if there is no such single method used under all the plans, as if the benefit accrues no more rapidly than the slowest permitted rate under the fractional accrual rule. [IRC § 416(g)(4)(F)]

Q. 20:3   What is a top-heavy defined contribution plan?

A defined contribution plan (see Q. 2:2) is top-heavy if, as of the determination date (see Q. 20:21), the total of the accounts of all key employees (see Q. 20:24) exceeds 60 percent of the total of the accounts of all employees. [IRC § 416(g)(1)(A)(ii); Reg. § 1.416-1, Questions T-1(c) and M-16]

Q. 20:4   Which qualified retirement plans are subject to the top-heavy rules?

Generally, all defined benefit plans (see Q. 2:3) and defined contribution plans (see Q. 2:2) are subject to the top-heavy rules. A simplified employee pension (SEP) is also subject to the top-heavy rules (see Q. 20:7 and Q. 25:1). [Reg. § 1.416-1, Question G-1]

Q. 20:5   Is a multiple employer plan subject to the top-heavy rules?

Yes. A multiple employer plan is subject to the top-heavy rules. A multiple employer plan is a qualified retirement plan to which more than one employer contributes and that is not the subject of a collective bargaining agreement.

If five employers contribute to a multiple employer plan and the accrued benefits of the key employees (see Q. 20:24) of one employer exceed 60 percent of the accrued benefits of all employees of that employer, the plan is top-heavy with respect to that employer. If the retirement plan fails to satisfy the top-heavy rules for the employees of *that employer, all five employers* will be maintaining a retirement plan that is not qualified. [IRC § 413(c); Reg. § 1.416-1, Questions G-2 and T-2]

Q. 20:6 Are qualified nonelective contributions under a 401(k) plan taken into account for top-heavy purposes?

Yes. Qualified nonelective contributions to a 401(k) plan (see Q. 21:14) may be taken into account for the purpose of satisfying the minimum top-heavy contribution requirement. Also, matching contributions to a 401(k) plan may not be treated as elective contributions in order to satisfy the actual deferral percentage (ADP) test (see Q. 21:12) if they are allocated to non-key employees in order to satisfy the minimum top-heavy contribution requirement (see Q. 20:43, Q. 20:46, and Q. 20:48). [Prop. Reg. §§ 1.401(k)-1(e)(7)(ii) and 1.416-1, Questions M-18 and M-19]

Q. 20:7 What is a top-heavy simplified employee pension?

A SEP (see Q. 25:1) is top-heavy if, as of the determination date (see Q. 20:21), the total of the accounts of all key employees (see Q. 20:24) exceeds 60 percent of the total of the accounts of all employees. However, at the employer's election, top-heavy status may be determined by taking into account only the total employer contributions (rather than account balances) to the SEP. [IRC §§ 408(k)(1) and 416(i)(6)]

Q. 20:8 Which factors must be considered in determining whether a qualified retirement plan is top-heavy?

To determine whether a qualified retirement plan is top-heavy, it is necessary to consider:

1. Which employers must be treated as a single employer (see Q. 20:13);

2. What the determination date is for the plan year (see Q. 20:21);

3. Which employees are or formerly were key employees (see Q. 20:24);

4. Which former employees have not performed any services for the employer during the five-year period ending on the determination date;

5. Which plans of such employers are required or permitted to be aggregated in determining top-heavy status (see Q. 20:9 and Q. 20:10); and

6. The present value of the accrued benefits of key employees, former key employees, and non-key employees.

[Reg. § 1.416-1, Question T-1(a)]

Q. 20:9   What is a required aggregation group?

A required aggregation group consists of each retirement plan of the employer in which a key employee (see Q. 20:24) is a participant in the plan year containing the determination date (see Q. 20:21) or any of the four preceding plan years and any other retirement plan of the employer that enables a retirement plan covering a key employee to satisfy the coverage and nondiscriminatory benefit requirements (see Q. 4:1 and Q. 5:14). [IRC § 416(g)(2)(A); Reg. § 1.416-1, Question T-6]

> **Example 1.** Elaine Corporation maintains a defined benefit plan covering key employees and other salaried employees and also maintains a second defined benefit plan covering hourly employees. The first defined benefit plan by itself does not satisfy the coverage or nondiscriminatory benefit requirements but does so when the two plans are considered together. The two defined benefit plans constitute a required aggregation group. If the first plan by itself satisfies the coverage and non-discriminatory benefit requirements, the second plan would not be part of the required aggregation group.

> **Example 2.** A sole proprietor terminated his qualified retirement plan in 1989. In 1990, the sole proprietor incorporated and established a corporate qualified retirement plan. In determining whether the corporate plan is top-heavy, the sole proprietor's terminated retirement plan and the corporate retirement plan are part of a required aggregation group.

Q. 20:10   What is a permissive aggregation group?

A permissive aggregation group consists of each retirement plan of the employer that is required to be aggregated (see Q. 20:9) and any other retirement plan of the employer that is not part of the required aggregation group but satisfies the coverage and nondiscriminatory benefit requirements (see Q. 4:1 and Q. 5:5) when considered together with the required aggregation group. [IRC § 416(g)(2)(A)(ii); Reg. § 1.416-1, Question T-7]

In Example 1 in Q. 20:9, suppose that the second defined benefit plan was not part of the required aggregation group. If so, the second plan could be permissively aggregated with the first retirement plan only if the benefits or contributions under the second retirement plan were comparable to those under the first plan.

Q. 20:11 Must collectively bargained retirement plans be aggregated with other retirement plans of the employer?

Collectively bargained retirement plans that include a key employee (see Q. 20:24) must be included in the required aggregation group for the employer (see Q. 20:9). Collectively bargained retirement plans that do not include a key employee may be included in a permissive aggregation group (see Q. 20:10). However, the special qualification requirements applicable to top-heavy plans (see Q. 20:23) generally do not apply to collectively bargained retirement plans, whether or not they include a key employee. [IRC §§ 416(i)(4) and 7701(a)(46); Reg. § 1.416-1, Questions T-3, T-7, and T-8]

Q. 20:12 What is a top-heavy group?

If a required aggregation group (see Q. 20:9) is a top-heavy group, each retirement plan that is required to be included in the aggregation group is treated as a top-heavy plan. If, however, the group is not top-heavy, no retirement plan in the required aggregation group is treated as a top-heavy plan.

If a permissive aggregation group (see Q. 20:10) is top-heavy, only those retirement plans that are part of the required aggregation group are subject to the special qualification requirements (see Q. 20:23) placed on top-heavy plans. Retirement plans that are not part of the required aggregation group are not subject to these added requirements. If a permissive aggregation group is not top-heavy, on the other hand, the top-heavy requirements do not apply to any retirement plan in the group.

An aggregation group is a top-heavy group if, as of the determination date (see Q. 20:21), the sum of

1. The present value of the accumulated accrued benefits for key employees (see Q. 20:24) under all defined benefit plans included in the group, and

2. The account balances of key employees under all defined contribution plans included in the group

exceeds 60 percent of the same amount determined for all employees under all retirement plans included in the group. [IRC § 416(g)(2)(B); Reg. § 1.416-1, Questions T-9, T-10, and T-11]

> **Example.** Nat Corporation maintains a defined benefit plan covering key employees and other salaried employees and also maintains a second defined benefit plan covering hourly employees that enables the first plan to satisfy the coverage and nondiscriminatory benefit requirements. If the present value of the total accrued benefits for all key employees exceeds 60 percent of the present value of the total accrued benefits for all employees under both plans, both plans are considered top-heavy plans. If, however, the first plan satisfied the coverage and nondiscriminatory benefit requirements by itself, the two plans would not constitute an aggregation group and only the first plan would be a top-heavy plan.

Q. 20:13 How are separate retirement plans of related employers treated for purposes of the top-heavy rules?

The aggregation group rules (see Q. 20:9 and Q. 20:10) and the top-heavy group rules (see Q. 20:12) apply to all retirement plans of related employers if the related employers are treated as a single employer for retirement plan purposes. [IRC §§ 414(b), 414(c), and 414(m); Reg. § 1.416-1, Question T-1(b)]

Q. 20:14 How is a terminated retirement plan treated for purposes of the top-heavy rules?

A terminated retirement plan must be aggregated with the employer's other retirement plans if it was maintained within the five-year period ending on the determination date (see Q. 20:21) for the plan year in question and would be part of a required aggregation group (see Q. 20:9) for that plan year had it not been terminated. (A terminated retirement plan is a retirement plan that has formally terminated, has ceased crediting service for benefit accruals and vesting, and has been or is distributing plan assets to the participants.)

No additional vesting, benefit accruals, or contributions must be provided for participants in a terminated retirement plan. [IRC § 416(g)(3); Reg. § 1.416-1, Question T-4]

Q. 20:15 How is a frozen retirement plan treated for purposes of the top-heavy rules?

A frozen retirement plan must provide minimum benefits or contributions (see Q. 20:37 and Q. 20:43) and provide top-heavy vesting (see Q. 20:32). (A frozen retirement plan is a retirement plan that has ceased crediting service for benefit accruals, but has not distributed all assets to the participants.) [Reg. § 1.416-1, Question T-5]

Q. 20:16 What happens if an employee ceases to be a key employee?

If an employee ceases to be a key employee (see Q. 20:24) and continues to work for the employer, that employee is treated as a non-key employee and the employee's accrued benefit under the defined benefit plan and account balance under the defined contribution plan are disregarded for purposes of determining whether the retirement plan is top-heavy for each plan year following the last plan year for which the employee was a key employee. [IRC § 416 (g)(4)(B); Reg. § 1.416-1, Questions T-1(d) and T-12]

Q. 20:17   How are plan distributions to employees treated for purposes of determining whether the qualified retirement plan is top-heavy?

The present value of the accrued benefit of an employee in a defined benefit plan, or the account balance of an employee in a defined contribution plan, includes any amount distributed with respect to the employee under the plan within the five-year period ending on the determination date (see Q. 20:21). This rule applies whether or not the employee is a key employee (see Q. 20:24) and applies to distributions made to a beneficiary of an employee (see Q. 20:31). [IRC § 416(g)(3); Reg. § 1.416-1, Question T-30]

If the employee does not render any services to the employer at any time during the five-year period ending on the determination date (see Q. 20:21), the present value of the employee's accrued benefit or account balance is not taken into account for purposes of top-heavy plan testing. [IRC § 416(g)(4)(E); Reg. § 1.416-1, Question T-1(d)]

Q. 20:18   Are death benefits treated as distributions for purposes of determining whether a qualified retirement plan is top-heavy?

Death benefits up to the present value of the deceased participant's accrued benefit immediately prior to death are treated as distributions for top-heavy testing purposes, but any death benefits in excess of this amount are not taken into account. For example, the distribution from a defined contribution plan, including the cash value of life insurance policies, of a participant's account balance on account of the participant's death is treated as a distribution for top-heavy testing purposes. [Reg. § 1.416-1, Question T-31]

Q. 20:19   How are rollovers and transfers treated for purposes of determining whether a retirement plan is top-heavy?

The rules for handling rollovers and plan-to-plan transfers depend on whether the rollovers and transfers are unrelated (both initiated by the employee and made from a qualified retirement plan maintained by one employer to a qualified retirement plan maintained by another employer) or related (either not initiated by the employee or made to a qualified retirement plan maintained by the same or a related employer).

In the case of unrelated rollovers or transfers, (1) the qualified retirement plan making the distribution always counts the distribution (see Q. 20:17), and (2) the qualified retirement plan accepting the rollover or transfer does not consider it if it was accepted after 1983, but considers it if it was accepted prior to 1984.

In the case of related rollovers or transfers, the qualified retirement plan making the rollover or transfer does not count it as a distribution, but the qualified retirement plan accepting the rollover or transfer counts it. The rules for related rollovers do not depend on whether the rollover or transfer was accepted prior to 1984. [IRC § 416(g)(4)(A); Reg. § 1.416-1, Question T-32]

Q. 20:20 How are employee contributions treated for purposes of determining whether a qualified retirement plan is top-heavy?

For purposes of determining the present value of accumulated accrued benefits under a defined benefit plan and the sum of the account balances under a defined contribution plan, benefits derived from both employer contributions and employee contributions (whether mandatory or voluntary) are taken into account. However, accumulated deductible employee contributions (see Q. 5:17) under a qualified retirement plan are disregarded. [Reg. § 1.416-1, Question T-28]

Q. 20:21 When is the determination date?

The date on which a qualified retirement plan is determined to be top-heavy is called the determination date. The determination date for a new retirement plan is the last day of the first plan year; for an existing plan, it is the last day of the preceding plan year. [IRC § 416(g)(4)(c); Reg. § 1.416-1, Question T-22]

> **Example.** Charles Corporation established a calendar-year defined contribution plan on January 1, 1990. On December 31, 1990 (the last day of the first plan year), the accounts of the key employees exceed 60 percent of all employees' accounts

under the plan. For 1990, the plan is top-heavy. The plan will also be top-heavy for the 1991 plan year because the determination date for the 1991 plan year is the last day of the 1990 plan year.

Q. 20:22 If the employer has more than one qualified retirement plan, when is the top-heavy determination made?

When two or more retirement plans are aggregated (see Q. 20:9 and Q. 20:10), the present value of the accrued benefits or account balances is determined separately for each plan as of each plan's determination date (see Q. 20:21). The retirement plans are then aggregated by adding the results of each plan as of the determination dates that fall within the same calendar year. The combined results indicate whether or not the retirement plans are top-heavy. [Reg. § 1.416-1, Question T-23]

> **Example.** David Corporation maintains two qualified retirement plans, Plan A and Plan B, each covering a key employee. Plan A's plan year commences July 1 and ends June 30. Plan B's plan year is the calendar year. For Plan A's plan year commencing July 1, 1990, the determination date is June 30, 1990. For Plan B's 1991 plan year, the determination date is December 31, 1990. These plans must be aggregated.

On the respective determination dates of each plan, separate calculations of the present value of the accrued benefits of all employees are made. The determination dates, June 30, 1990, and December 31, 1990, fall within the same calendar year. Accordingly, the present values of accrued benefits or account balances with respect to each of these determination dates are combined for purposes of determining whether the plans are top-heavy. If, after combining the two, the total results show that the plans are top-heavy, Plan A will be top-heavy for the plan year commencing July 1, 1990, and Plan B will be top-heavy for the 1991 calendar plan year.

Q. 20:23 Are there special qualification requirements that apply to top-heavy plans?

Yes. In addition to the qualification requirements that apply to all retirement plans, a top-heavy plan must satisfy the following requirements:

1. Minimum vesting (see Q. 20:32); and

2. Minimum benefits or contributions (see Q. 20:37 and Q. 20:43).

[IRC § 416(a); Reg. § 1.416-1, Questions T-35, T-36, and T-37]

Q. 20:24 Who is a key employee?

A key employee is an employee who, at any time during the plan year containing the determination date (see Q. 20:21) or any of the four preceding plan years, is (or was):

- An officer having annual compensation in excess of 50 percent of the annual dollar limitation for defined benefit plans in effect for such plan year (see Q. 20:25 and Q. 5:1);
- One of the ten largest owners of the employer having annual compensation in excess of the annual addition limitation in effect for such plan year (see Q. 20:27 and Q. 5:1);
- A 5%-owner (see Q. 20:28); or
- A 1%-owner whose annual compensation exceeds $150,000 (see Q. 20:28).

[IRC § 416(i)(1)(A); Reg. § 1.416-1, Question T-12]

Q. 20:25 Who is an officer of the employer for top-heavy plan purposes?

The determination as to whether an employee is an officer is made on the basis of all the facts and circumstances, including, for example, the source of the employee's authority, the term for which the employee was elected or appointed, and the nature and extent of the employee's duties. As generally accepted in connection with corporations, the term "officer" means an administrative executive who is in regular and continued service. It implies continuity of service and excludes those employed for a special and single transaction, or those with only nominal administrative duties. So, for example, all the employees of a bank who have the title of vice-president or assistant vice-president are not automatically considered officers. An employee who does not have the title of an officer but has the authority of an officer is an officer for purposes of the key employee test. [Rev. Rul. 80-314, 1980-2 CB 152; Reg. § 1.416-1, Question T-13]

The number of employees that can be considered officers is equal to 10 percent of all employees, or three, whichever is greater. In no case, however, can the total number of officers exceed 50. Thus, if the employer has fewer than 30 employees, no more than three can be considered officers. [IRC § 416(i)(1)(A); Reg. § 1.416-1, Question T-14]

Q. 20:26 Do any organizations other than corporations have officers?

Sole proprietorships, partnerships, unincorporated associations, trusts, and labor organizations may have officers. [Reg. § 1.416-1, Question T-15]

Q. 20:27 Who is one of the ten largest owners of the employer?

The ten largest owners are the ten employees owning the largest interest in the employer. An employee who has some ownership interest is considered to be one of the top ten owners unless at least ten other employees own a greater interest than the employee owns.

In determining the ten employees owning the largest interests in the employer, only employees with annual compensation in excess of the annual addition limitation for such plan year (see Q. 5:1) and having more than a 1/2 percent ownership interest are taken into account as key employees. If two employees have the same interest in the employer, the employee with the greater annual compensation is treated as having a larger interest. [IRC § 416(i)(1); Reg. § 1.416-1, Question T-19]

Example. Twenty-five employees at Allyson Corporation have a 4 percent interest in the employer. Compensation for 15 of these employees ranges from $25,000 to $45,000. Compensation for the other ten employees ranges from $60,000 to $75,000. Only the latter ten employees are considered key employees for top-heavy plan testing purposes.

Q. 20:28   Who is a 5%-owner or a 1%-owner for top-heavy plan purposes?

A 5%-owner is a person who owns, directly or indirectly, more than 5 percent of the stock of the corporation. A 1%-owner is a person who owns, directly or indirectly, more than 1 percent of the stock of the corporation. A 1%-owner is a key employee (see Q. 20:24) only if his or her annual compensation from the employer is more than $150,000.

If the employer is not a corporation, the ownership test is applied to the person's capital or profits interest in the employer. In determining ownership percentages, each employer, whether related or unrelated (see Q. 4:34), is treated as a separate entity. But for purposes of determining whether an employee has compensation of more than $150,000, compensation from each related entity is aggregated. [IRC §§ 416(i)(1)(B) and 416(i)(1)(C); Reg. § 1.416-1, Questions T-16, T-17, T-18, T-20, and T-21]

Q. 20:29   Who is a non-key employee?

Any employee who is not a key employee (see Q. 20:24) is a non-key employee. [IRC § 416(i)(2)]

Q. 20:30   Who is a former key employee?

A former key employee is an individual who, when employed by the employer, was once a key employee (see Q. 20:24). For example, an individual, who was a 5%-owner in 1990, sold all of his or her interest in the employer before the end of the year and retired. Even though the individual is no longer an employee or owner, he or she will be treated as a key employee for each plan year through the 1995 plan year. For the 1996 plan year and subsequent plan years, the individual will be treated as a former key employee.

Former key employees are non-key employees and are excluded entirely from the calculation in determining top-heaviness. [Reg. § 1.416-1, Questions T-1(d) and T-12]

Q. 20:31 How is a beneficiary treated under the top-heavy plan rules?

For purposes of the top-heavy plan rules, the terms key employee, former key employee, and non-key employee include their beneficiaries. [IRC § 416(i)(5); Reg. § 1.416-1, Question T-12]

Q. 20:32 What is the minimum vesting requirement for a top-heavy plan?

A top-heavy plan must contain either a three-year vesting provision or a six-year graded vesting provision. [IRC § 416(b)(1); Reg. § 1.416-1, Questions V-1 and V-5]

Under three-year vesting, an employee who completes at least three years of service (see Q. 20:33) must be 100 percent vested. Under six-year graded vesting, an employee must become vested as determined under the following table:

Completed years of service	Vested percentage
2	20
3	40
4	60
5	80
6 or more	100

Q. 20:33 Which years of service must be taken into account for minimum vesting purposes?

The rules for determining an employee's years of service for vesting under non-top-heavy plans (see Chapter 8) also apply for the minimum vesting requirements under top-heavy plans. Thus, years of service completed before 1984 (the year top-heavy rules went into effect) and years of service completed after 1983 (including years when the plan is not top-heavy) are counted for minimum vesting purposes. [IRC § 416(b)(2); Reg. § 1.416-1, Question V-2]

Q. 20:34 Which benefits must be subject to the minimum top-heavy vesting requirement?

All benefits must be subject to the minimum top-heavy vesting requirement. These benefits include benefits accrued before a retirement plan becomes top-heavy. However, when a retirement plan becomes top-heavy, the accrued benefit of an employee who does not have an hour of service after the plan becomes top-heavy is not required to be subject to the minimum vesting requirement. [Reg. § 1.416-1, Question V-3]

Q. 20:35 When a top-heavy plan ceases to be top-heavy, may the vesting schedule be changed?

Yes. When a top-heavy plan ceases to be top-heavy, the vesting schedule may be changed to one that would otherwise be permitted. However, in changing the vesting schedule, any portion of the benefit that was nonforfeitable before the plan ceases to be top-heavy must remain nonforfeitable, and any employee with three or more years of service must be given the option of remaining under the prior (i.e., top-heavy) vesting schedule (see Q. 8:6). [IRC § 411(a)(10); Reg. § 1.416-1, Question V-7]

Q. 20:36 Which top-heavy vesting schedule is more favorable to the employer?

It depends on how long the employees usually stay with the employer.

> **Example.** Rena Corporation adopted a 10%-of-compensation money purchase pension plan on January 1, 1989. Bob completes a year of service on January 1, 1990 and enters the plan. Bob earns $10,000 a year. Set forth below is a calculation of

Bob's benefits under the six-year graded and three-year cliff vesting schedules (see Q. 20:32):

Plan Year	6-Year Contribution/ Account Balance	6-Year Vesting Percentage/ Vested Benefits	3-Year Contribution/ Account Balance	3-Year Vesting Percentage/ Vested Benefits
1	0 0		0 0	
2	$1,000 $1,000	20% $200	$1,000 $1,000	0% $0
3	$1,000 $2,000	40% $800	$1,000 $2,000	100% $2,000
4	$1,000 $3,000	60% $1,800	$1,000 $3,000	100% $3,000
5	$1,000 $4,000	80% $3,200	$1,000 $4,000	100% $4,000
6	$1,000 $5,000	100% $5,000	$1,000 $5,000	100% $5,000

In plan year 2, less vested benefits are provided under the three-year cliff vesting schedule; in plan years 3, 4, and 5, less vested benefits are provided under the six-year graded vesting schedule. Thus, if employees customarily leave before completing three years of service, three-year cliff vesting is more favorable to the employer; if they leave after completing three years of service, the six-year graded schedule is more favorable to the employer. After six years of service, both schedules provide equal benefits.

As an alternative, Rena Corporation could require employees to complete two years of service to become eligible but then employees must be 100 percent vested immediately (see Q. 8:12). With a two-year service requirement and 100 percent immediate vesting, Bob's benefits would be as follows:

Plan Year	Contribution/ Account Balance	Vesting Percentage/ Vested Benefits
1	0 / 0	
2	0 / 0	
3	$1,000 / $1,000	100% / $1,000
4	$1,000 / $2,000	100% / $2,000
5	$1,000 / $3,000	100% / $3,000
6	$1,000 / $4,000	100% / $4,000

In plan year 2, the least vested benefits occur under three-year cliff and the two-year schedule; in plan years 3 and 4, the least vested benefits occur under six-year graded; in plan years 5 and 6, and in all subsequent plan years, the least vested benefits occur under the two-year schedule.

Therefore, if employees customarily leave after completing five or more years of service, the two-year schedule will be most favorable to the employer maintaining a top-heavy plan.

Q. 20:37 What is the minimum benefit requirement for a top-heavy defined benefit plan?

Under a top-heavy defined benefit plan, the annual retirement benefit (see Q. 20:38) of a non-key employee (see Q. 20:29) must not be less than the employee's average compensation (see Q. 20:40) multiplied by the lesser of:

1. 2 percent times the number of years of service (see Q. 20:41); or

2. 20 percent.

Benefits attributable to employer contributions are considered, but benefits attributable to employee contributions must be ignored.

[IRC §§ 416(c)(1)(A) and 416(c)(1)(B); Reg. § 1.416-1, Questions M-1, M-2, M-5, and M-6]

Q. 20:38 What does annual retirement benefit mean for the minimum benefit requirement?

Annual retirement benefit means a benefit attributable to employer contributions payable annually in the form of a single life annuity (with no ancillary benefits) beginning at the retirement plan's normal retirement age. [IRC § 416(c)(1)(E); Reg. § 1.416-1, Question M-2(d)]

If benefits under the defined benefit plan are payable in a form other than a straight life annuity (under a straight life annuity payments terminate upon the death of the annuitant), the minimum benefit is adjusted downward to a benefit that is equivalent to a straight life annuity. For example, if the annuity payments under the defined benefit plan are guaranteed for a period of ten years (i.e., if the participant dies within the ten-year period, payments will be made to his or her beneficiary for the rest of the period), the minimum annual retirement benefit (see Q. 20:37) is reduced by 10 percent. [Reg. § 1.416-1, Question M-3]

Q. 20:39 What is the minimum benefit required if the employee receives benefits other than at normal retirement age?

If the benefit commences at a date other than at normal retirement age (see Q. 9:66), the employee must receive an amount that is at least the actuarial equivalent of the minimum single life annuity benefit (see Q. 20:37 and Q. 20:38) commencing at normal retirement age. The employee may receive a lower benefit if the benefit commences before normal retirement age and must receive a higher benefit if the benefit commences after normal retirement age. [Reg. § 1.416-1, Question M-3]

Q. 20:40   What does the term participant's average compensation mean for the minimum benefit requirement?

A participant's average compensation means the participant's compensation averaged over a period of no more than five consecutive years (the testing period) during which the participant had the greatest aggregate compensation from the employer. [IRC § 416(c)(1) (D)(i); Reg. § 1.416-1, Questions M-2(c) and T-21]

A year need not be taken into account during the testing period if it ends in a plan year beginning before 1984 or begins after the close of the last plan year in which the plan was a top-heavy plan. [IRC § 416(c)(1)(D)(iii); Reg. § 1.416-1, Question M-2(c)]

Q. 20:41   Which years of service are taken into account in determining the minimum annual benefit under a top-heavy defined benefit plan?

A year of service generally means a year during which the employee completes 1,000 hours of service. The rules for determining years of service parallel those for calculating vesting (see Q. 8:3, Q. 8:9 through Q. 8:11). However, the following years of service are not taken into account for determining the minimum annual retirement benefit:

1. A year of service within which ends a plan year for which the defined benefit plan is not top-heavy; and

2. A year of service completed in a plan year beginning before 1984.

[IRC § 416(c)(1)(C); Reg. § 1.416-1, Question M-2(b)]

The minimum annual benefit under a top-heavy defined benefit plan (see Q. 20:37) is the lesser of (1) 2 percent of the employee's compensation multiplied by his or her years of service, or (2) 20 percent of his or her compensation. This determination of the employee's total years of service is important only if the total is less than ten, because if years of service equal or exceed ten, the 20 percent minimum can be used.

In one circumstance, IRS allowed the top-heavy minimum accrued benefit to start to accrue when the employee became a participant. According to the facts, a non-key employee was hired January 1, 1985 and became eligible to participate in the company's defined benefit plan on January 1, 1988. For purposes of the top-heavy rules, IRS stated that the minimum accrued benefit starts to accrue when an employee becomes a participant, so that in the circumstances of the above case, the accrued benefit as of January 1, 1988 was zero. *The foregoing was offered as general information and was not to be construed as a ruling relating to any actual case.*

Q. 20:42 Which employees must receive a minimum benefit in a top-heavy defined benefit plan?

Each non-key employee (see Q. 20:29) who is a participant and who has at least 1,000 hours of service during the year must receive a minimum benefit in a top-heavy defined benefit plan for that period. A non-key employee may not fail to receive a minimum benefit merely because the employee was not employed on a specified date (e.g., the last day of the plan year). Similarly, a non-key employee who is excluded from participation (or who accrues no benefit) because either (1) the employee's compensation is below a stated amount or (2) the employee fails to make mandatory employee contributions, must nevertheless accrue a minimum benefit. [Reg. § 1.416-1, Questions M-1 and M-4]

Q. 20:43 What is the minimum contribution requirement for a top-heavy defined contribution plan?

Under a top-heavy defined contribution plan, the employer's contribution for each non-key employee (see Q. 20:29) must not be less than 3 percent of compensation (see Q. 20:45). However, if the highest contribution percentage rate for a key employee (see Q. 20:24) is less than 3 percent of compensation, the 3 percent minimum contribution rate is reduced to the rate that applies to the key employee. [IRC §§ 416(c)(2)(A) and 416(c)(2)(B); Reg. § 1.416-1, Questions M-1, M-7, M-8, and M-9]

Example. Aviva Corporation established a calendar-year defined contribution plan (see Q. 2:2) on January 1, 1990. The plan is top-heavy and contains a contribution formula of 2 percent of compensation below the taxable wage base and 4 percent of compensation in excess of the taxable wage base. Andrea, the highest paid key employee, earns $60,000 and the contribution on her behalf is $1,374 [(2% × $51,300) + 4% × ($60,000 − $51,300)]. Because her contribution rate is 2.29 percent ($1,374/$60,000), Aviva Corporation has to contribute only 2.29 percent of compensation for each non-key employee.

Q. 20:44 Do forfeitures affect the minimum contribution requirement?

Under the minimum contribution rules (see Q. 20:43), reallocated forfeitures are considered as employer contributions. For example, if no amount is contributed by the employer under a profit sharing plan for any key employee but forfeitures are allocated to key employees, contributions may be required under the minimum contribution rules for non-key employees. [Reg. § 1.416-1, Question M-7]

Q. 20:45 What does participant's compensation mean for purposes of the minimum contribution requirement?

The term participant's compensation means the participant's total compensation from the employer during the year—even though compensation, as defined in the plan, may exclude certain forms of compensation (bonuses, for example). [IRC §§ 415(c)(3) and 416(c)(2)(A); Reg. § 1.416-1, Questions M-7 and T-21]

Q. 20:46 Which employees must receive the top-heavy defined contribution plan minimum contribution?

Those non-key employees (see Q. 20:29) who are participants and have not separated from service at the end of the plan year, whether or not they have completed 1,000 hours of service, must receive the top-heavy defined contribution plan minimum contribution. A non-key employee who is excluded from participation (or who accrues no benefit) because (1) the employee declines to make mandatory contributions to the plan, or (2) the employee declines to make elective contributions under a 401(k) plan (see Q. 20:48 and Q. 21:13) is considered an employee covered by the plan for purposes of the minimum contribution requirement. [Reg. § 1.416-1, Question M-10]

Q. 20:47 Can Social Security benefits or contributions be used to satisfy the minimum benefit and contribution requirements?

No. A top-heavy plan cannot take benefits or contributions under Social Security into account to satisfy the minimum benefit requirement (see Q. 20:37) or the minimum contribution requirement (see Q. 20:43). Thus, the required minimum benefit or contribution for a non-key employee may not be eliminated or reduced by integrating the plan with Social Security. [IRC § 416(e); Reg. § 1.416-1, Question M-11]

Q. 20:48 Can elective contributions under a 401(k) plan be used to satisfy the top-heavy minimum contribution rules?

No. Elective contributions to a 401(k) plan (see Q. 21:13) on behalf of non-key employees may not be treated as employer contributions for the purpose of satisfying the top-heavy minimum contribution requirement. However, in determining the percentage at which contributions are made for the key employee with the highest percentage, elective contributions on behalf of key employees are taken into account (see Q. 20:6, Q. 20:43, and Q. 20:46). [Prop. Reg. §§ 1.401(k)-1(e)(7)(ii) and 1.416-1, Question M-20]

Q. 20:49   Must an employer that has both a top-heavy defined benefit plan and a top-heavy defined contribution plan provide both a minimum benefit and a minimum contribution for non-key employees?

No. If a non-key employee (see Q. 20:29) participates in both a top-heavy defined benefit plan and a top-heavy defined contribution plan maintained by an employer, the employer is not required to provide the non-key employee with both the minimum benefit and the minimum contribution.

There are four safe-harbor rules a top-heavy plan may use in determining which minimum an employee must receive. Because the defined benefit minimums are generally more valuable, if each employee covered under both a top-heavy defined benefit plan and a top-heavy defined contribution plan receives the defined benefit minimum, receipt of that minimum will satisfy the standards. A safe-harbor defined contribution minimum is provided by IRS. If the contributions and forfeitures under the defined contribution plan equal 5 percent of compensation each year the plan is top-heavy, that minimum will also satisfy the standards.

The other two safe-harbor rules are:

1. Using a floor offset under which the defined benefit minimum is provided in the defined benefit plan and is offset by the benefits provided under the defined contribution plan; and

2. Proving by use of a comparability analysis that the plans provide aggregate benefits at least equal to the defined benefit minimum.

[IRC § 416(f); Reg. § 1.416-1, Questions M-12, M-13, and M-15; *Rev. Rul. 76-259*, 1976-2 CB 111; *Rev. Rul. 81-202*, 1981-2 CB 93]

Example. Alicia, a non-key employee, participates in a top-heavy money purchase pension plan that provides an annual contribution rate of 5 percent of compensation and a top-heavy defined benefit plan that provides a retirement benefit equal to 8 percent of compensation. The employer is not required to provide an additional retirement benefit for Alicia under the defined benefit plan.

Q. 20:50 What is the limitation on compensation that may be taken into account under a top-heavy plan?

Only the first $200,000 (adjusted for inflation) of an employee's compensation may be taken into account, regardless of whether the plan is top-heavy (see Q. 5:3). For 1990, this amount has increased to $209,200. [IRC § 401(a)(17)]

Q. 20:51 What happens if a key employee participates in both a defined benefit plan and a defined contribution plan?

If a key employee (see Q. 20:24) participates in both a defined benefit plan and a defined contribution plan that are included in a top-heavy group (see Q. 20:12), the overall maximum limitation for the key employee is computed under a more restrictive formula unless certain requirements are met (see Q. 20:56).

For combined plans in a top-heavy group, the sum of the defined benefit plan fraction and the defined contribution plan fraction cannot exceed 1.0 (the same rule that applies in a non-top-heavy situation; see Q. 5:12). However, the denominator of each fraction is calculated differently.

To arrive at the overall maximum limitation, take the following steps:

1. *Compute a defined benefit plan fraction.* The numerator of this fraction is the projected annual retirement benefit determined at year end. The denominator is the lesser of 1.0 (instead of 1.25) times the dollar limitation for the current year or 1.4 times the percentage limitation for the current year. [IRC §§ 415(e)(2) and 416(h)(1)]

2. *Compute a defined contribution plan fraction.* The numerator of this fraction is the total of the annual additions to the participant's account for all years determined at year end. The denominator is the lesser of 1.0 (instead of 1.25) times the dollar limitation or 1.4 times the percentage limitation for the current year and all years of prior service. [IRC §§ 415(e)(3) and 416(h)(1); Reg. § 1.416-1, Question T-33]

3. Add the two fractions. The total may not exceed 1.0.

[IRC § 415(e)(1)]

Each plan may contain a fail-safe provision (see Q. 5:12).

Example. Mr. James incorporates his business in January 1990. The corporation adopts a 100 percent defined benefit plan and a 10%-of-compensation money purchase pension plan that are included in a top-heavy group. Mr. James earns $91,195 in 1990. Here is how the top-heavy 1.0 rule works:

1. The defined benefit plan fraction is .889 [$91,195/$102,582 (i.e., the lesser of 1.0 × $102,582 or 1.4 × $91,195)].

2. The defined contribution plan fraction is .304 [$9,120/ $30,000 (i.e., the lesser of 1.0 × $30,000 or 1.4 × $22,799)].

3. The two fractions total 1.193.

At this point, the top-heavy 1.0 rule comes into play so that one of the fractions must be reduced. If the 10%-of-compensation contribution formula under the defined contribution plan is reduced to 3.65 percent, the defined contribution plan fraction will be .111 [$3,329 (i.e., 3.65 percent × $91,195)/$30,000]. Then, the total of the fractions will be 1.0.

Q. 20:52 At what level of compensation is a key employee excluded from participating in a second plan?

If either the defined benefit plan fraction or the defined contribution plan fraction is 1.0, the key employee is excluded from participating in a second plan.

If the key employee's annual compensation is $102,582 or more and the key employee's annual retirement benefit under the defined benefit plan is $102,582 (the current maximum; see Q. 5:5), the defined benefit plan fraction is 1.0 [$102,582/$102,582 (i.e., the lesser of 1.0 × $102,582 or 1.4 × $102,582)].

If the key employee's annual compensation is $120,000 or more and his or her annual addition (see Q. 5:1) under the defined contribution plan is $30,000 (the current maximum; see Q. 5:1), the defined contribution plan fraction is 1.0 [$30,000/$30,000 (i.e., the lesser of 1.0 × $30,000 or 1.4 × $30,000)].

If the maximum dollar limits increase (see Q. 5:2 and Q. 5:5), the level of compensation at which a key employee is excluded from a second plan will also increase.

Q. 20:53 At what level of compensation will the top-heavy 1.0 rule have an effect on a key employee?

If the employee's annual compensation exceeds $73,273, the top-heavy 1.0 rule requires a reduction in one of the plans. (See Q. 20:51.) At $73,273 or less, the 1.0 rule as applied to combined plans in a non-top-heavy group will be equivalent to the top-heavy 1.0 rule.

Under the non-top-heavy rule, at $73,273 of compensation, the total of the fractions of a 100% defined benefit plan ($73,273/$102,582 = .714) plus a 10% defined contribution plan ($7,327/$25,645 = .286) equals 1.0. Under the top-heavy rule, at $73,273 of compensation, the total of the fractions of the same 100% defined benefit plan ($73,273/$102,582 = .714) plus the same 10% defined contribution plan ($7,327/$25,645 = .286) also equals 1.0.

If the maximum dollar limits increase (see Q. 5:2 and Q. 5:5), the threshold level of compensation for equivalency will also increase, but not necessarily in proportion to the percentage increase in the dollar limits.

Q. 20:54 What is the special rule if two qualified retirement plans were adopted prior to 1984?

If the employer adopted both a defined benefit plan and a defined contribution plan prior to 1984 (the defined contribution plan must have been in existence on or before July 1, 1982), the plan administrator may make a special election to calculate the denominator of the defined contribution plan fraction for each participant for all limitation years (see Q. 5:11) ending before 1983.

This calculation is made in two steps. First, the denominator of the fraction for the 1982 limitation year is determined. Then, the denominator is multiplied by a transition fraction.

The numerator of the transition fraction is the lesser of:

1. $41,500 (instead of $51,875—the amount used in a non-top-heavy situation); or
2. 1.4 times 25 percent of the participant's compensation for the 1981 limitation year.

The denominator of the fraction is the lesser of:

1. $41,500; or
2. 25 percent of the participant's compensation for the 1981 limitation year.

[IRC §§ 415(e)(6) and 416(h)(4)]

> **Example.** Dr. Jones incorporated his medical practice in January 1975. His compensation for each of the years 1975 through 1982 was $185,000. The corporation adopted a 25%-of-compensation money purchase pension plan (a defined contribution plan) in 1977 and a defined benefit plan in 1982.
>
> The denominator of the defined contribution plan fraction for 1982 was $266,600, and Dr. Jones earned $185,000 in 1981. The numerator of the transition fraction is $41,500 [the lesser of $41,500 or $64,750 (i.e., 1.4 × 25% × $185,000)]; the denominator is also $41,500 [the lesser of $41,500 or $46,250 (i.e., 25% × $185,000)]. The transition fraction is 1.0 (i.e., $41,500/$41,500), and the adjusted denominator of the defined contribution plan fraction remains $266,600 (i.e., 1.0 × $266,600). In this example, electing the transition rule is of no value.
>
> If Dr. Jones earned less than $166,000 in 1981, the transition fraction would exceed 1.0 and Dr. Jones would therefore benefit by electing to use the transition fraction.

Q. 20:55 What happens if a key employee's combined fractions exceed 1.0?

In some cases, the total of a key employee's defined benefit plan fraction and defined contribution plan fraction may exceed 1.0 at the time he or she becomes subject to this rule. In that event, the key employee is permitted no further benefit accruals under the defined benefit plan and no additional employer contributions (including forfeitures and voluntary nondeductible contributions) under the defined contribution plan until the total of these fractions becomes less than 1.0. [IRC § 416(h)(3)]

Q. 20:56 If a key employee participates in both a defined benefit plan and a defined contribution plan, can his or her overall maximum limitation be computed under the regular 1.0 rule?

Yes. The 1.0 rule (see Q. 5:12), which applies to an employee covered by two qualified retirement plans that are not top-heavy, also applies to a key employee covered by two qualified retirement plans in a top-heavy group (rather than the more restrictive rule that is usually applied; see Q. 20:51) if these additional requirements are met:

1. A concentration test is satisfied (see Q. 20:57); and
2. An extra minimum benefit or extra minimum contribution is given to non-key employees (see Q. 20:58).

[IRC § 416(h)(2); Reg. § 1.416-1, Questions T-33 and M-14]

Q. 20:57 What is the concentration test for purposes of the 1.0 rule?

One of the two requirements (see Q. 20:56) that must be satisfied before a key employee is subject to the less restrictive 1.0 rule (see Q. 5:12) is the concentration test. This test is generally satisfied with respect to a key employee for a year if, as of the last determination date (see Q. 20:21):

1. The present value of the accumulated accrued benefits for key employees under the defined benefit plan; *plus*

2. The sum of the account balances of key employees under the defined contribution plan is not greater than 90 percent of the same amount determined for all participants under the retirement plans.

[IRC § 416(h)(2)(B); Reg. § 1.416-1, Question T-33]

Qualified retirement plans may be permissively aggregated to avoid exceeding the 90 percent amount. (See Q. 20:10.) [Reg. § 1.416-1, Question T-34]

Q. 20:58 What is an extra minimum benefit or extra minimum contribution for purposes of the 1.0 rule?

The second requirement (see Q. 20:56) that must be satisfied before a key employee is subject to the less restrictive 1.0 rule (see Q. 5:12) is that non-key employees must be given an extra minimum benefit or an extra minimum contribution.

To satisfy this requirement, any one of the four safe-harbor rules (see Q. 20:49) may be used with the following modifications. Each non-key employee in the defined benefit plan accrues an extra benefit, which is not less than:

1. 1 percent of his or her average annual compensation multiplied by years of service with the employer; or

2. 10 percent of his or her average annual compensation, whichever is less.

This extra minimum benefit generally is determined in the same manner as the minimum benefit required for a top-heavy defined benefit plan. (See Q. 20:37.)

The defined contribution minimum is increased to 7½ percent of compensation. If the floor offset or comparability analysis approach is used, each non-key employee in the defined benefit plan will accrue the extra 1 percent benefit discussed above. [IRC § 416(h)(2)(A)(ii); Reg. § 1.416-1, Questions T-33, M-14, and M-15]

Q. 20:59 Must every qualified retirement plan be amended to incorporate the top-heavy plan requirements?

The additional rules for top-heavy plans are tax-qualification requirements. A top-heavy plan will be a qualified retirement plan, and a trust forming part of a top-heavy plan will be a qualified trust, only if the additional requirements are met. Other than governmental plans and collectively bargained plans that are not top-heavy, any retirement plan qualifies for tax-favored status only if the plan includes provisions that will automatically take effect if the plan becomes a top-heavy plan and that meet the additional qualification requirements for top-heavy plans. [IRC § 401(a)(10)(B); Reg. § 1.416-1, Questions G-1 and T-38]

Chapter 21

401(k) Plans

Qualified plans containing cash-or-deferred arrangements, commonly known as 401(k) plans, are one of the most popular and widely offered employee benefit plans. This chapter describes how a 401(k) plan operates and the special qualification requirements that must be satisfied. This chapter also describes the special qualification requirements applicable to qualified retirement plans that provide for employer matching contributions and/or employee voluntary contributions.

Q. 21:1 What is a 401(k) plan?

A 401(k) plan is a qualified profit sharing or stock bonus plan that contains a cash-or-deferred arrangement (CODA). Under a CODA, an eligible employee may make a cash-or-deferred election (see Q. 21:2) to have the employer make a contribution to the plan on the employee's behalf or pay an equivalent amount to the employee in cash. The amount contributed to the plan under the CODA on behalf of the employee is called an elective contribution (see Q. 21:13). Subject to certain limitations (see Q. 21:8 and Q. 21:26), elective contributions are excluded from the employee's gross income for the year in which they are made and are not subject to taxation until distributed. For purposes of many of the rules applicable to 401(k) plans, elective contributions are considered employer contributions.

A 401(k) plan may be a stand-alone plan (permit elective contributions only) or may also permit other types of employer contributions and/or employee voluntary contributions. However, a 401(k) plan is the only method available under which employees may defer compensation on an elective, pretax basis to a qualified retirement plan. [IRC § 401(k); Reg. §§ 1.401(k)-1(a), 1.401(k)-1(e), and 1.401(k)-1(g)(4); Preamble to the Proposed Regulations, TD 8217]

Q. 21:2 What is a cash-or-deferred election?

Under a 401(k) plan, an employee can elect to have the employer make an elective contribution to the plan on the employee's behalf or to receive an equivalent amount in cash. This is known as a cash-or-deferred election. The election may take the form of a compensation reduction agreement between the employee and the employer under which the employee elects to reduce cash compensation or to forgo an increase in cash compensation and to have the employer contribute such amount to the plan on the employee's behalf. A cash-or-deferred election may be made at any time permitted under the plan, but may be made only with respect to amounts that are not currently available (see Q. 21:3) to the electing employee as of the date of the election. [IRC § 401(k)(2)(A); Reg. §§ 1.401(k)-1(a)(2), 1.401(k)-1(a)(3)(i), and 1.401(k)-1(a)(3)(ii)]

> **Example 1.** Adam Corporation gives each employee an annual bonus of 10 percent of compensation payable on January 30 each year with respect to the previous calendar year. Under Adam Corporation's profit sharing plan, each eligible employee may elect prior to January 30 to receive all or part of the bonus in cash or to have Adam Corporation contribute such amount to the plan on the employee's behalf. This constitutes a cash-or-deferred election under a CODA.

> **Example 2.** Dana Corporation maintains a profit sharing plan under which each eligible employee may elect to have Dana Corporation contribute up to 10 percent of the employee's compensation for each payroll period during the plan year or to receive an equivalent amount in cash. The election must be made prior to the date on which such compensation is to be paid to the employee. This constitutes a cash-or-deferred election under a CODA.

Q. 21:3 When is an employee's election a cash-or-deferred election?

A qualified cash-or-deferred election does not occur if amounts contributed to a plan at the employee's election are either currently available to the employee or designated as after-tax employee voluntary contributions. Compensation is currently available if it has been paid to the employee or if the employee is able currently to receive the cash at the employee's discretion. An amount is not currently available if there is a significant restriction on the employee's right to receive the amount currently or if the employee may under no circumstances receive the amount before a particular time in the future. Contributions of amounts that were currently available to the employee at the time of the election are treated as employee voluntary contributions and are included in the employee's gross income at the time they are contributed to the plan. [Reg. §§ 1.401(k)-1(a)(3)(i), 1.401(k)-1(a)(3)(ii), 1.401(k)-1(a)(5)(ii), and 1.402(a)-1(d)(2)]

In addition, an employee's elective contributions are treated as not having been made pursuant to a cash-or-deferred election if they are made pursuant to a one-time irrevocable election by the employee to have a specified amount or percentage of the employee's compensation contributed by the employer to the plan for the duration of the employee's employment. The election must be available either at the employee's inception of employment or when the employee first becomes eligible under any plan of the employer, and must relate to all plans of the employer, including those not in existence at the time the election is made. [Reg. § 1.401(k)-1(a)(3)(iii)]

Q. 21:4 Does a 401(k) plan qualify for favorable tax treatment?

Yes, provided certain special qualification requirements are met in addition to the regular plan qualification requirements (see Chapter 3 for details). The special qualification requirements are as follows:

- The plan must permit the employee to elect either to have the employer make a contribution to the plan on the employee's behalf or to receive an equivalent amount in cash (see Q. 21:1).

- The plan must not allow distributions to employees with respect to amounts attributable to elective contributions merely because of the completion of a stated period of plan participation or the passage of a fixed number of years (see Q. 21:33).

- Employees' rights to their benefits derived from elective contributions must be nonforfeitable (i.e., 100% vested) (see Q. 21:31).

- The employer must not condition the availability of any other benefit (except for employer matching contributions) on the employee's electing, or not electing, to make elective contributions under a CODA in lieu of receiving cash. [IRC § 401(k)(4)(A); Prop. Reg. § 1.401(k)-1(e)(6)]

- The plan meets the special nondiscrimination test with respect to the amount of elective contributions made to the plan each plan year (see Q. 21:8). [IRC § 401(k)(3); Reg. § 1.401(k)-1(b)(2)(i)]

- The plan does not condition participation on completion of more than one year of service with the employer. [IRC § 401(k)(2)(D); Prop. Reg. § 1.401(k)-1(e)(5)]

- The amount of elective contributions made to the plan on behalf of each employee does not exceed the applicable limit (see Q. 21:26). [IRC § 402(g)(1); Prop. Reg. § 1.402(g)-1]

Q. 21:5 Are elective contributions to a 401(k) plan taxable to the employee?

Elective contributions made to a plan under a qualified CODA are not includible in the employee's gross income. Income taxes are postponed until the employee receives a distribution from the plan. In addition, earnings on elective contributions are accumulated tax-free until distributed. [Reg. §§ 1.401(k)-1(a)(4) and 1.402(a)-1(d)(2)]

A plan that includes a CODA that is not qualified (the arrangement does not satisfy the special requirements; see Q. 21:4) may, nevertheless, be a qualified plan under the regular plan qualification requirements (see Chapter 3). However, if the plan satisfies only the regular requirements, contributions to the plan made at the election of the employee for the plan year are considered employee voluntary contributions and are includible in the employee's gross income. [Reg. §§ 1.401(k)-1(a)(5) and 1.402(a)-1(d)(1)]

Q. 21:6   Must a cash-or-deferred plan be a profit sharing plan?

Generally, a CODA must be part of a profit sharing or stock bonus plan and cannot be part of a pension plan. There is a limited exception for pre-ERISA money purchase pension plans and rural electric cooperative plans. [IRC §§ 401(k)(1), 401(k)(2), 401(k)(6), and 401(k)(7); Reg. §§ 1.401(k)-1(a)(1), 1.401(k)-1(g)(11), 1.401(k)-1(g)(12), and 1.401(k)-1(h)(3)]

Elective contributions to profit sharing plans may be made without regard to whether or not the employer has current or accumulated profits. [IRC § 401(a)(27)]

Q. 21:7   May a self-employed individual participate in a 401(k) plan?

Yes. The term employee for purposes of 401(k) plans includes a self-employed individual (see Q. 27:8). If the self-employed individual is a sole proprietor, the individual is treated as his or her own employee. If the self-employed individual is a partner, the individual is treated as an employee of the partnership. The compensation of a self-employed individual is his or her earned income (see Q. 27:10). [IRC § 401(c)(1); Reg. § 1.401(k)-1(g)(1); Notice 88-127, 1988-2 CB 538]

Q. 21:8   What are the special nondiscrimination tests for a 401(k) plan?

A qualified 401(k) plan must meet a special actual deferral percentage (ADP) test, which is designed to limit the extent to which elective contributions made on behalf of highly compensated employees (see Q. 4:28) may exceed the elective contributions made on behalf of nonhighly compensated employees. If the ADP test is satisfied, the plan is treated as satisfying Section 401(a)(4) (prohibiting discrimination as to contributions and benefits) with respect to elective contributions. [IRC § 401(k)(3)(C); Prop. Reg. § 1.401(k)-1(b)(2)(i)]

The ADP test for the plan year will be satisfied if:

1. The ADP for the plan year for highly compensated employees does not exceed the ADP for such plan year for nonhighly compensated employees multiplied by 1.25; or

2. The ADP for the plan year for highly compensated employees does not exceed the ADP for such plan year for nonhighly compensated employees multiplied by 2.0, provided that the ADP for the highly compensated employees does not exceed the ADP for the nonhighly compensated employees by more than two percentage points. [IRC § 401(k)(3); Prop. Reg. § 1.401(k)-1(b)(4)(ii)]

Example. A 401(k) plan has a 12 percent ADP for highly compensated employees and an 8 percent ADP for nonhighly compensated employees for the 1990 plan year. The plan does not meet the ADP test because (1) 12 percent exceeds 8 percent multiplied by 1.25, and (2) the ADP of highly compensated employees exceeds the ADP of nonhighly compensated employees by more than two percentage points.

Q. 21:9   How is the ADP calculated for purposes of applying the ADP test?

The ADP is calculated by first determining the actual deferral ratio (ADR) (expressed as a percentage) of each eligible employee's elective contributions (including qualified nonelective contributions and qualified matching contributions that are treated as elective contributions; see Q. 21:14) for the plan year to the employee's compensation (see Q. 21:11) for the plan year. For example, if Ellen's compensation is $50,000 and she made elective contributions of $3,000, her ADR is 6 percent ($3,000 ÷ $50,000).

The ADP for the highly compensated employees is then determined by taking the average of the ADRs (expressed as a percentage) for all eligible highly compensated employees. For example, if there are three highly compensated employees with ADRs of 5 percent, 7 percent, and 3 percent, the ADP is 5 percent (5% + 7% + 3% =

15% ÷ 3). This procedure is then performed for the group of eligible nonhighly compensated employees. The ADP test (see Q. 21:8), comparing the ADP of the highly compensated employees to the ADP of the nonhighly compensated employees, is then applied. The ADRs and ADP for each group are calculated to the nearest one-hundredth of 1 percent. [IRC § 401(k)(3)(B); Reg. § 1.401(k)-1(g)(8)(i)]

Example. Lucille Corp., with six eligible employees, maintains a 401(k) plan. Each employee may elect to receive up to 15 percent of compensation (or $7,000, adjusted for inflation, if less) in cash or to have part or all of this amount contributed to the plan as an elective contribution. The employees make the following elections:

Highly compensated	Compensation	Elective contribution	Percentage of compensation
A	$70,000	$7,000	10
B	60,000	4,500	7.5
			17.5

Nonhighly compensated	Compensation	Elective contribution	Percentage of compensation
C	$20,000	$1,000	5
D	15,000	0	0
E	10,000	350	3.5
F	10,000	350	3.5
			12.0

The ADP for the highly compensated employees is 8.75 percent (17.5% ÷ 2); the ADP for the nonhighly compensated employees is 3 percent (12% ÷ 4). The plan fails the ADP test (see Q. 21:8) because the ADP of highly compensated employees is more than the ADP of the nonhighly compensated employees multiplied by 1.25, and the ADP of the highly compensated employees exceeds the ADP of the nonhighly compensated employees by more than two percentage points.

See Q. 21:56 and Q. 21:57 for discussions of the multiple use limitation and the family aggregation rules.

Q. 21:10 How is the actual deferral ratio of an employee calculated if an employer maintains more than one 401(k) plan?

For purposes of the ADP test, if a highly compensated employee is eligible to participate in more than one 401(k) plan of the employer, the ADR is calculated by treating all such plans in which the highly compensated employee may participate as one plan. If the plans have different plan years, all plans having plan years ending with or within the same calendar year are combined. [IRC § 401(k)(3)(A); Prop. Reg. § 1.401(k)-1(g)(8)(ii)]

> **Example.** Steve, who earns $100,000, may make elective contributions under two of Dolly Corporation's 401(k) plans. If Steve makes elective contributions of $5,000 to one and $1,000 to the other, Steve's ADR is 6 percent ($5,000 + $1,000 ÷ $100,000).

Q. 21:11 What does compensation mean for purposes of the ADP test?

For purposes of determining the availability of making elective contributions (see Q. 21:13) by an employee, the term compensation must satisfy a general nondiscriminatory definition, that is, the definition cannot discriminate in favor of highly compensated employees. For certain purposes, such as allocating nonelective contributions, an employer may elect to include elective contributions in the definition of compensation; but, for the ADP test, compensation, *before* reduction for elective contributions, is always used. [IRC §§ 401(k)(9) and 414(s); Reg. §§ 1.401(k)-1(g)(9)(ii) and 1.414(s)-1T(d)(1)(ii)]

If an employee begins, resumes, or ceases to be eligible to make elective contributions during a plan year, the employee's compensation for the entire plan year is taken into account. For the first plan year, the employee's compensation during the entire 12-month period ending on the last day of the plan year is taken into account. [Prop. Reg. § 1.401(k)-1(g)(9)(ii)]

The amount of compensation used for purposes of the ADP test may not exceed $200,000. This amount is adjusted annually to reflect increases in the cost of living. For 1990, the applicable amount is $209,200. [IRC § 401(a)(17)]

Q. 21:12 What contributions are counted for purposes of the ADP test?

In applying the ADP test, a participant's elective contributions (see Q. 21:13) are taken into account, but only if the following two requirements are satisfied:

1. The elective contribution is allocated to the employee as of a date within the plan year; and
2. The elective contribution relates to compensation that either
   - Would have been received by the employee in the plan year but for the employee's cash-or-deferred election (see Q. 21:2), or
   - Is attributable to services performed by the employee in the plan year and, but for the employee's cash-or-deferred election, would have been received by the employee within 2½ months after the close of the plan year.

For purposes of the first requirement, an elective contribution is considered to be allocated to the employee as of a date within the plan year if the allocation is not contingent upon the employee's participation in the plan or performance of services on any later date, and the elective contribution is actually paid to the plan no later than the end of the 12-month period immediately following the plan year to which it relates.

Elective contributions that do not meet these requirements may not be taken into account in applying the ADP test for the plan year for which they are made or for any other plan year. Instead, they must satisfy the nondiscrimination requirements of Section 401(a)(4) (without the application of the ADP test) for the plan year for which they are allocated as if they were the only employer contributions for that plan year. [Reg. § 1.401(k)-1(b)(6)]

In addition, for purposes of applying the ADP test, all or any part of qualified nonelective contributions and qualified matching contributions (see Q. 21:14) made to any plan of the employer with respect to those employees who are eligible under the 401(k) plan being tested may, if the plan so provides, be treated as elective contributions. [IRC § 401(k)(3)(D); Prop. Reg. § 1.401(k)-1(b)(3)]

Qualified nonelective contributions may be used to satisfy the ADP test even though they are also used to satisfy the actual contribution percentage (ACP) test (see Q. 21:48). However, if qualified matching contributions are used to satisfy the ADP test, they may not also be used to satisfy the ACP test, nor are they subject to that test. [Prop. Reg. § 1.401(m)-1(b)(1)]

Q. 21:13 What are elective contributions?

Elective contributions are those contributions made to a plan by the employer on an employee's behalf pursuant to the employee's cash-or-deferred election (see Q. 21:2). Any amount that is contributed to the plan pursuant to a special one-time irrevocable election, that is designated as an employee voluntary contribution or that is currently available to the employee at the time of the election, is not treated as an elective contribution (see Q. 21:3). [Reg. §§ 1.401(k)-1(a)(2), 1.401(k)-1(a)(3), and 1.401(k)-1(g)(4)]

Elective contributions cannot be used to satisfy the top-heavy minimum contribution requirement. (See Q. 20:48.)

Q. 21:14 What are qualified nonelective contributions and qualified matching contributions?

A nonelective contribution is an employer contribution made to the plan (other than a matching contribution) that the employee could not have elected to receive in cash. [Reg. § 1.401(k)-1(g)(5)]

A matching contribution is an employer contribution made to the plan on behalf of an employee because of an after-tax voluntary contribution or an elective contribution made by or on behalf of such employee. [Reg. § 1.401(k)-1(g)(6)]

To be qualified, nonelective contributions and matching contributions must satisfy the distribution (see Q. 21:33) and vesting (see Q. 21:31) requirements as though they were elective contributions and, for plan years beginning after 1988, amounts attributable to such contributions are not distributable merely because of the employee's hardship. [Reg. §§ 1.401(k)-1(g)(7)(i) and 1.401(k)-1(g)(7)(ii); Prop. Reg. §§ 1.401(k)-1(b)(3) and 1.401(k)-1(g)(7)(iii)]

To be qualified, the following requirements must also be satisfied to the extent applicable:

1. The nonelective contributions, *including* those qualified non-elective contributions treated as elective contributions for purposes of the ADP test, must satisfy the nondiscrimination requirements of Code Section 401(a)(4).

2. The nonelective contributions, *excluding* those qualified non-elective contributions treated as elective contributions for purposes of the ADP test and those qualified nonelective contributions treated as matching contributions for purposes of the ACP test, must satisfy the nondiscrimination requirements of Section 401(a)(4).

3. The matching contributions must satisfy the requirements of Section 401(m). Those qualified nonelective contributions and qualified matching contributions treated as elective contributions for purposes of the ADP test are disregarded.

4. Except as provided in (1) and (3) above, the qualified nonelective contributions and qualified matching contributions treated as elective contributions for purposes of the ADP test must not be taken into account in determining whether any other contributions or benefits satisfy Section 401(a)(4) and must not be taken into account in determining whether employee contributions or other matching contributions meet the requirements of Section 401(m).

5. Qualified nonelective contributions must not be treated as elective contributions if the effect is to increase the difference between the ADP for the eligible highly compensated employees and the actual ADP for all other eligible employees.

6. The qualified nonelective contributions and qualified matching contributions must satisfy the allocation rules (see Q. 21:12).

7. The plan year of the plan that includes the CODA and takes qualified nonelective contributions and qualified matching contributions into account in determining whether elective contri-

butions satisfy the ADP test must be the same as the plan year of the plan or plans to which the qualified nonelective contributions and qualified matching contributions are made. [Prop. Reg. § 1.401(k)-1(b)(3)]

Q. 21:15 Is there a simple rule to follow in determining whether the ADP test is satisfied?

Yes. If the ADP for the nonhighly compensated employees is less than 2 percent, the ADP for the highly compensated employees can be up to two times higher. If the ADP for the nonhighly compensated employees is between 2 and 8 percent, the ADP for the highly compensated employees can be two percentage points higher. If the ADP for the nonhighly compensated employees is more than 8 percent, the ADP for the highly compensated employees can be up to 1.25 times higher.

For example, a 4 percent ADP for the nonhighly compensated employees means that an ADP of 6 percent (4% + two percentage points) for the highly compensated employees is not discriminatory. Likewise, an ADP of 10 percent for the nonhighly compensated employees permits an ADP of 12.5 percent (10% × 1.25) for the highly compensated group. [IRC § 401(k)(3); Prop. Reg. § 1.401(k)-1(b)(4)(ii)]

Q. 21:16 What are excess contributions?

An excess contribution for a plan year is the excess of the elective contributions (including qualified nonelective and matching contributions that are treated as elective contributions) made on behalf of highly compensated employees for the plan year over the maximum amount of such contributions permitted under the ADP test (see Q. 21:8) for such plan year. [IRC § 401(k)(8)(B); Reg. § 1.401(k)-1(g)(13)]

The ADP test compares the elective contribution percentage for highly compensated employees with the elective contribution percentage for nonhighly compensated employees. If the ADP test is failed, there is an excess contribution made to the plan. However, correction of the excess contribution (see Q. 21:17) is done on an individual employee basis.

The amount of the excess contribution allocated to a highly compensated employee for a plan year is determined by the following leveling method, under which the ADR of the highly compensated employee with the highest ADR is reduced to the extent required to:

1. Enable the plan to satisfy the ADP test; or
2. Cause such highly compensated employee's ADR to equal the ratio of the highly compensated employee with the next highest ADR.

This process is repeated until the plan satisfies the ADP test. For each highly compensated employee, the amount of excess contributions is equal to (1) the total elective contributions made on behalf of the employee (determined without regard to the above described reduction) minus (2) the amount determined by multiplying the employee's ADR (as reduced under the above described procedure) by the employee's compensation used in determining the ADR.

The total elective contributions in (1) above ordinarily include qualified nonelective contributions and qualified matching contributions that are treated as elective contributions. However, if a highly compensated employee's share of excess contributions is recharacterized for a plan year in order to correct the excess contribution (see Q. 21:17), that share may not exceed the actual amount of elective contributions made on the employee's behalf for that plan year. [Reg. § 1.401(k)-1(f)(2)]

See Q. 21:56 and Q. 21:57 for discussions of the multiple use limitation and the family aggregation rules.

Q. 21:17   How are excess contributions corrected?

A 401(k) plan will not be considered as failing the ADP test for any plan year (and, therefore, will maintain its qualification) if:

1. The amount of the excess contributions for such plan year (plus any income allocable to such contributions) is distributed to the appropriate highly compensated employees within 12 months after the close of the applicable plan year; or

2. The highly compensated employee elects to treat the amount of the excess contributions as an amount distributed to the employee and then contributed by the employee to the plan as an after-tax employee voluntary contribution. This is known as recharacterization. [IRC § 401(k)(8)(A); Reg. § 1.401(k)-1(f)(3); Prop. Reg. § 1.401(k)-1(f)(4)]

A plan may use qualified nonelective contributions, qualified matching contributions, the recharacterization method, the corrective distribution method, or a combination of these methods, to avoid or correct excess contributions. [Prop. Reg. § 1.401(k)-1(f)(5)(ii)]

Q. 21:18 What happens if a 401(k) plan fails to correct excess contributions?

If a 401(k) plan does not correct excess contributions (see Q. 21:17) within 2½ months after the end of the plan year for which they were made, the employer is subject to a 10 percent penalty tax on the amount of the excess contributions. Qualified nonelective contributions and qualified matching contributions properly taken into account for a plan year may permit a plan to avoid having excess contributions *even if* such contributions are made after the close of the 2½ month period. [IRC § 4979(f); Prop. Reg. § 1.401(k)-1(f)(6)(i)]

If excess contributions are not corrected before the end of the plan year following the plan year for which the excess contributions were made, the 401(k) plan will fail to qualify for the plan year for which the excess contributions were made and for all subsequent plan years during which the excess contributions remain in the plan. [Prop. Reg. § 1.401(k)-1(f)(6)(ii)]

Q. 21:19 How are excess contributions recharacterized?

The recharacterization (see Q. 21:17) of all or a portion of a highly compensated employee's share of excess contributions is done in the following manner:

1. The payor or plan administrator must report the recharacterized excess contribution as an employee voluntary contribution

to IRS and the employee. This is done by timely providing the employer and the employee whose contribution is recharacterized with such forms as IRS may designate for the purpose and taking such other action as IRS may prescribe.

2. The plan administrator must account for the recharacterized amounts as an employee voluntary contribution for purposes of Section 72 (relating to rules under which distributions from qualified retirement plans are taxed) and Section 6047 (relating to information returns with respect to owner-employees). [Notice 89-32, 1989-1 CB 671; Reg. § 1.401(k)-1(f)(3)(ii)]

However, excess contributions may not be recharacterized unless they are recharacterized under the plan with respect to which the excess contributions were made or under a plan with the same plan year as that plan. [Prop. Reg. § 1.401(k)-1(f)(3)(iii)(C)]

Q. 21:20 What are the tax consequences of the recharacterization of excess contributions?

A recharacterized excess contribution (see Q. 21:17) is included in the employee's gross income on the earliest date it would have been received by the employee if the employee had originally elected to receive the elective contribution in cash (see Q. 21:1). [Reg. § 1.401(k)-1(f)(3)(ii)]

A recharacterized amount is treated as an employee voluntary contribution for purposes of Sections 72 and 6047 (see Q. 21:19), the ACP test (see Q. 21:51), and the nondiscrimination requirements of Section 401(a)(4). For all other purposes under the Code, a recharacterized excess contribution is treated as an employer contribution that is an elective contribution. Thus, for example, they are so treated for purposes of the distribution (see Q. 21:33) and vesting (see Q. 21:31) requirements applicable to elective contributions. [Reg. § 1.401(k)-1(f)(3)(ii)]

Q. 21:21 When must the recharacterization of excess contributions occur?

Recharacterization must be accomplished no later than 2½ months after the close of the plan year to which the excess contribution relates. For purposes of this rule, recharacterization occurs on the date on which the last of the highly compensated employees with excess contributions to be recharacterized is notified (see Q. 21:19). [Reg. § 1.401(k)-1(f)(iii)(A)]

Q. 21:22 Does the recharacterization of excess contributions result in a penalty tax to the employee?

No. If a timely recharacterization of excess contributions is made, no penalty tax is imposed on the employee. [IRC §§ 72(t), 401(k)(8)(A), 401(k)(8)(D), and 4980A(c)(2)(F); Prop. Reg. § 1.401(k)-1(f)(4)(iv)]

Q. 21:23 Is there an excise tax on recharacterized excess contributions?

A 10 percent excise tax is imposed on the employer for excess contributions made to a plan. If excess contributions are recharacterized within 2½ months after the end of the plan year for which they were made, they are not treated as excess contributions for purposes of the excise tax. [IRC §§ 4979(a) and 4979(f); Prop. Reg. § 1.401(k)-1(f)(6)(i)]

Q. 21:24 How is an excess contribution corrected by distribution?

In addition to recharacterization, another method of correcting a highly compensated employee's share of excess contributions for a plan year is for the plan to distribute such amount plus any allocable income to the highly compensated employee.

For a distribution to effectively correct an excess contribution, it must be designated as a distribution of an excess contribution, and allocable income and the distribution must be made to the appropriate highly compensated employee within 12 months after the close of the plan year in which the excess contribution arose. [Prop. Reg. § 1.401(k)-1(f)(4)(i)]

Q. 21:25 How is a distribution of an excess contribution taxed?

If the distribution is made within 2½ months following the close of the plan year to which the excess contribution relates, it is included in the highly compensated employee's gross income on the earliest date any elective contribution made by the employee during that plan year would have been received had the employee originally elected to receive it in cash. If the distribution is made after the 2½-month period, it is included in the employee's gross income for the taxable year of the employee in which it is distributed. A corrective distribution of less than $100, however, is includible in gross income in the year of distribution rather than in the year deferred if it occurs within the 2½-month period. [IRC § 4979(f)(2)(B); Prop. Reg. § 1.401(k)-1(f)(4)(iv)]

A corrective distribution of excess contribution is not subject to the 10 percent excise tax on early distributions imposed by Section 72(t) (see Q. 9:68), the 15 percent excise tax on excess distributions imposed by Section 4980A, or the spousal consent requirements (see Q. 9:21). [IRC §§ 401(k)(8)(A) and 401(k)(8)(D); Prop. Reg. §§ 1.401(k)-1(f)(4)(iii) and 1.401(k)-1(f)(4)(iv)]

In addition, if the distribution is made to the employee within 2½ months following the close of the plan year to which the excess contribution relates, the 10 percent excise tax on excess contributions imposed on the employer does not apply. [IRC § 4979(f); Prop. Reg. § 1.401(k)-1(f)(6)(i)]

A corrective distribution is not considered a distribution for purposes of the minimum distribution requirements of Section 401(a)(9) (see Q. 9:57). Therefore, any distribution that must be made to the employee to satisfy the minimum distribution requirements is not satisfied by the corrective distribution. [Prop. Reg. § 1.401(k)-1(f)(4)(v)]

Q. 21:26 Is there a dollar limitation on the amount of elective contributions?

An employee's elective contributions under all plans in which the employee participates (even if not maintained by the same employer) during any taxable year (including SEPs that offer salary reduction arrangements; see Q. 25:9) are limited to $7,000, and the amount of the elective contributions in excess of $7,000 (excess deferrals) is included in such individual's gross income. [IRC § 402(g)(1); Prop. Reg. §§ 1.402(g)-1(a) and 1.402(g)-1(c)(1)]

The $7,000 limit on elective contributions is adjusted annually at the same time and in the same manner as the dollar limit on benefits payable under a defined benefit plan (see Q. 5:5). [IRC § 402(g)(5); Prop. Reg. § 1.402(g)-1(c)(1)]

The $7,000 limitation on the amount of a participant's elective contributions has been increased to $7,979 for 1990. [IR 90-15 (Jan. 30, 1990)]

Since a CODA is part of a defined contribution plan, the amount of a participant's elective contributions is also subject to the limitation on annual additions (see Q. 5:1). For example, a participant with compensation of $30,000 could not make an elective contribution of $7,979 in 1990, because the 25%-of-compensation limitation would be violated.

Q. 21:27 To what time period does the dollar limitation on elective contributions apply?

The limitation on elective contributions applies on the basis of the participant's tax year. In most cases, this is the calendar year. The limitation applies without regard to

- The plan year of the plan under which the elective contributions are made;
- When the participant elects to make the contributions; and
- When the elective contributions are made to the plan.

[IRC § 402(g)(1); Prop. Reg. § 1.402(g)-1(a); Notice 87-13, 1987-1 CB 432 (Q&A 5)]

Q. 21:28 How are excess deferrals corrected?

If an excess deferral is included in a participant's gross income for any taxable year, then, not later than March 1 following the close of the taxable year, the participant may allocate the amount of the excess deferral among the plans under which it arose (assuming more than one plan) and may notify each such plan of the portion allocated to it. Proposed regulations issued by IRS extend the March 1 date to April 15. [IRC § 402(g)(2)(A)(i); Prop Reg. § 1.402(g)-1(d)(2)(i)] Not later than April 15 following the close of the taxable year in which the excess deferral arose, the plan may distribute to the participant the amount allocated to it by the participant plus any income allocable to that amount. This distribution may be made notwithstanding any other provision of law. [IRC § 402(g)(2)(A)(ii); Prop. Reg. § 1.402(g)-1(d)(2)(ii)]

A corrective distribution of an excess deferral may also be made during the same year in which the excess deferral arose. Such a distribution may be made only if the following conditions are satisfied:

1. The participant designates the distribution as an excess deferral;
2. The corrective distribution is made after the date on which the plan received the excess deferral; and
3. The plan designates the distribution as a distribution of an excess deferral.

[Prop. Reg. § 1.402(g)-1(d)(3)]

Corrective distributions must be provided for under the terms of the plan. A plan may require that the notification and designations referred to above must be in writing and may also require that the participant certify or otherwise establish that the specified amount is an excess deferral. [Prop. Reg. § 1.402(g)-1(d)(4)]

Q. 21:29 What are the tax consequences of making excess deferrals?

Excess deferrals for a taxable year are included in the employee's gross income for the taxable year in which they were made. However, the income allocable to excess deferrals is included in the employee's gross income for the taxable year in which it is distributed. [IRC §§ 402(g)(1) and 402(g)(2)(C)(ii); Prop. Reg. § 1.402(g)-1(a)]

Example. In 1990, Susan defers $8,500 under a 401(k) plan. Earnings attributable to the excess deferral ($521) are $20. If Susan withdraws $541 ($521 + $20) by April 15, 1991, $521 is taxable in 1990 and $20 in 1991.

The 10 percent penalty tax on early distributions (see Q. 9:68) does not apply to a corrective distribution of an excess deferral. Similarly, it is not treated as a distribution for purposes of the 15 percent excise tax on excess distributions, nor is it subject to the spousal consent requirements (see Q. 11:25 and Q. 9:21). [Prop. Reg. §§ 1.402-1(d)(7) and 1.402(g)-1(d)(8)(i)]

If excess deferrals are not timely distributed, the amount of the excess deferrals is included in the employee's gross income for the taxable year in which the excess deferrals arose and will again be included in the employee's gross income in the year when they are actually distributed. Accordingly, failure to make a corrective distribution of excess deferrals within the specified period causes double taxation on such deferrals. [Prop. Reg. § 1.402(g)-1(d)(8)(ii)]

Q. 21:30 Are excess deferrals distributed after year-end to an employee nevertheless counted for purposes of the ADP test?

Whether or not excess deferrals are timely distributed to an employee after the end of the employee's taxable year, any excess deferrals of highly compensated employees (see Q. 4:28) are still counted for purposes of the ADP test (see Q. 21:8); excess deferrals of non-highly compensated employees are not taken into account. [IRC § 402(g)(2)(B); Prop. Reg. § 1.402(g)-1(d)(1)]

Q. 21:31 Must all contributions under a 401(k) plan be nonforfeitable?

A 401(k) plan is not qualified unless the employee's rights to benefits derived from elective contributions, as well as from qualified matching and qualified nonelective contributions (see Q. 21:12) used to satisfy the ADP test (see Q. 21:8), are nonforfeitable, i.e., 100 percent vested immediately. [IRC §§ 401(k)(2)(C) and 401(k)(3)(D); Reg. § 1.401(k)-1(c)]

Nonelective contributions and/or matching contributions not used to satisfy the ADP test may be forfeitable, i.e., subject to a vesting schedule. See Chapter 8.

Q. 21:32   What is a combined 401(k) plan?

A combined 401(k) plan is a plan that permits both elective contributions (those contributions that are made pursuant to a cash-or-deferred arrangement) and other types of employer contributions. By establishing a combined plan, the employer can fail safe the 401(k) plan so that it will always satisfy the ADP test (see Q. 21:8). [Reg. § 1.401(k)-1(b)(7)]

> **Example.** CLA Corporation has a profit sharing plan with a CODA. Each employee may elect to receive up to 2 percent of compensation in cash or to have that amount contributed to the plan as an elective contribution. In 1990, all highly compensated employees elect to have 2 percent of their compensation contributed to the plan, and all other employees elect to receive cash. CLA also makes a nonelective contribution to the plan equal to 2 percent of each employee's compensation. The nonelective contribution is qualified because it is subject to the same nonforfeitability and distribution provisions as the elective contributions.
>
> The elective contributions, taken alone, do not satisfy the ADP test (see Q. 21:8). Nevertheless, the 2 percent nonelective contributions may be taken into account in applying the ADP test because such contributions satisfy the nonforfeitability and distribution requirements. When these contributions are considered, the ADP for the highly compensated employees is 4 percent (2% + 2%) and the ADP for the nonhighly compensated employees is 2 percent (0% + 2%). Because 4 percent is not more than two percentage points greater than 2 percent and not more than 2 percent multiplied by 2.0, the ADP test is now satisfied. Because the ADP for the nonhighly compensated employees will never be less than 2 percent, this enables the plan to pass the ADP test in a year when it would otherwise fail—when the difference between the ADP for the highly compensated employees and the ADP for the nonhighly compensated employees exceeds the permissible spread.

Q. 21:3 When may distributions be made under a 401(k) plan?

Contrary to the usual rule for a profit sharing or stock bonus plan, a qualified 401(k) plan may not permit a distribution from the plan of amounts attributable to elective contributions merely because of the completion of a stated period of participation or the lapse of a fixed number of years. [IRC § 401(k)(2)(B)(ii); Reg. § 1.401(k)-1(d)(3)]

A qualified 401(k) plan must provide that amounts attributable to elective contributions (including qualified nonelective contributions and qualified matching contributions that are treated as elective contributions) may not be distributed to a participant or beneficiary before the occurrence of one of the following events:

1. The participant's retirement, death, disability, or other termination of service;

2. The termination of the plan without the establishment of a successor defined contribution plan (other than an employee stock ownership plan (ESOP); see Q. 22:1);

3. The date of the sale by a corporation to an unrelated entity of substantially all of the assets used by such corporation in a trade or business of such corporation with respect to an employee who continues employment with the entity acquiring such assets;

4. The date of the sale or other disposition by a corporation of such corporation's interest in a subsidiary to an unrelated entity with respect to an employee who continues employment with such subsidiary;

5. The participant's attainment of age 59½ if the CODA is part of a profit sharing or stock bonus plan; or

6. The participant's hardship if the CODA is part of a profit sharing or stock bonus plan.

[IRC § 401(k)(2)(B); Prop. Reg. § 1.401(k)-1(d)(1)(iii)]

If the amounts attributable to elective contributions (including qualified nonelective and qualified matching contributions) are transferred to another qualified retirement plan of any employer, the distribution limitations continue to apply to the transferred amounts. Thus, such other plan will not be qualified if the transferred amounts are distributed before the occurrence of one of the events specified above. [Prop. Reg. § 1.401(k)-1(d)(6)]

Q. 21:34 What amounts may be distributed in the case of a participant's hardship?

Prior to attaining age 59½, participants in a 401(k) plan are permitted to make in-service withdrawals of elective contributions only in the case of a hardship (see Q. 21:35 through Q. 21:39). Qualified matching contributions and qualified nonelective contributions and earnings thereon used to satisfy the ADP test (see Q. 21:14) may not be withdrawn under any circumstances. In addition, earnings on elective contributions after January 1, 1989 may not be withdrawn. Thus, the amount available to a participant for a hardship withdrawal consists of the amount of elective contributions and earnings thereon as of December 31, 1988, plus elective contributions made thereafter. [IRC § 401(k)(2)(B)(i)(IV); Prop. Reg. § 1.401(k)-1(d)(1)(iii)(A)(6)]

Q. 21:35 What constitutes hardship?

For a withdrawal to qualify as having been made on account of hardship, it must satisfy the following two-part test:

- Part 1—The withdrawal must be made on account of the participant's immediate and heavy financial need, and
- Part 2—The withdrawal must be necessary to satisfy such need.

Under the regulations, two methods are available for granting hardship withdrawals from qualified 401(k) plans. Under the first method, a determination of whether a participant qualifies for a hardship withdrawal under the two-part test is based on a review of all the relevant facts and circumstances in each individual situation. This is known as the facts-and-circumstances test.

Under the second method, if the plan uses certain types of expenditures and specific requirements as set forth in the regulations as a basis for granting hardship withdrawals, the withdrawal will be conclusively considered to have satisfied the two-part test specified above. This is known as the safe-harbor test.

A 401(k) plan may use the safe-harbor test for Part 1 and the facts-and-circumstances test for Part 2 and vice versa, or it may use the same test for both parts. [Reg. § 1.401(k)-1(d)(2)]

Q. 21:36 How is a heavy and immediate financial need (Part 1) determined under the facts-and-circumstances test?

The determination of whether a participant has an immediate and heavy financial need is made on the basis of all relevant facts and circumstances. Thus, a plan that uses the facts-and-circumstances test for Part 1 will have to establish rules regarding the purposes for which hardship withdrawals will be permitted. The plan can allow hardship withdrawals for any reason, provided the surrounding facts and circumstances create an immediate and heavy financial need. In this regard, the regulations note that, generally, the need to pay funeral expenses for a family member would constitute an immediate and heavy financial need but the need to purchase a boat or television would not. Additionally, the regulations provide that a financial need will not fail to qualify as immediate and heavy merely because such need was reasonably foreseeable or voluntarily incurred by the participant, for example, the need to purchase a home or send a child to college. [Reg. § 1.401(k)-1(d)(2)(ii)(A)]

Q. 21:37 How is a heavy and immediate financial need (Part 1) determined under the safe-harbor test?

Under the safe-harbor test, a hardship withdrawal will be deemed to be made on account of an immediate and heavy financial need of the participant if the withdrawal is made on account of any of the following reasons:

1. Medical expenses incurred by the participant, the participant's spouse, or any dependents of the participant;

2. Purchase of the participant's principal residence (excluding mortgage payments);

3. Payment of tuition for the next semester or quarter of post-secondary education for the participant or the participant's spouse, children, or dependents;

4. Payment of amounts necessary to prevent the eviction of the participant from the participant's principal residence or foreclosure on the mortgage of the participant's principal residence; or

5. Any additional events that may be prescribed by IRS in the future.

[Reg. § 1.401(k)-1(d)(2)(ii)(B)]

Q. 21:38 How is a hardship withdrawal determined to be necessary (Part 2) under the facts-and-circumstances test?

A withdrawal will be treated as necessary to satisfy an immediate and heavy need of the participant if the amount of the withdrawal does not exceed the amount necessary to relieve the financial need and such need cannot be satisfied from other sources that are reasonably available to the participant. This determination is made on the basis of all relevant facts and circumstances. For these purposes, a participant's resources are deemed to include assets of the participant's spouse and minor children that are reasonably available to the participant. For example, a vacation home owned by the participant and the participant's spouse as community property, joint tenants, tenants by the entirety, or tenants in common is deemed a resource of the participant, whereas property held for a participant's child under the Uniform Gifts to Minors Act is not treated as a resource of the participant.

A withdrawal generally may be treated as necessary to satisfy an immediate and heavy financial need if the employer reasonably relies on the participant's representation that the need cannot be relieved:

1. Through reimbursement or compensation by insurance or otherwise;

2. By reasonable liquidation of the participant's assets to the extent such liquidation does not create a financial hardship;

3. By the participant's cessation of elective and voluntary contributions under the plan;

4. By the participant making other withdrawals or nontaxable loans from all plans in which the participant participates; or

5. By borrowing from commercial sources on reasonable commercial terms.

[Reg. § 1.401(k)-1(d)(2)(iii)(A)]

Q. 21:39 How is a hardship withdrawal determined to be necessary (Part 2) under the safe-harbor test?

Under the safe-harbor test, a withdrawal will be deemed to be necessary to satisfy an immediate and heavy financial need if the employer relies on the participant's representation that the amount of the withdrawal does not exceed the amount necessary to satisfy the participant's financial need *and* all of the following requirements are satisfied:

1. The participant has made all withdrawals (other than hardship withdrawals) and all nontaxable loans currently available under all plans maintained by the employer.

2. The plan and all other plans maintained by the employer provide that the participant will not be permitted to make any contributions (elective and voluntary) to the plan for at least 12 months after receipt of the hardship withdrawal. However, the participant is still counted as an eligible employee for purposes of the ADP test.

3. The plan, and all other plans maintained by the employer, provides that the maximum elective contribution that a participant may make in the year in which the participant resumes making elective contributions is reduced by the amount of the elective contribution the participant made in the year in which the participant received a hardship withdrawal.

[Reg. § 401(k)-1(d)(2)(iii)(B)]

Q. 21:40 Are matching contributions and nonelective contributions subject to the nonforfeitability and distribution requirements applicable to elective contributions?

Employer matching contributions and nonelective contributions under a 401(k) plan need not be subject to the special nonforfeitability and distribution requirements (see Q. 21:31 and Q. 21:33) applicable to elective contributions unless they are needed to satisfy the ADP test (see Q. 21:12). However, if elective contributions are not accounted for separately (see Q. 21:41), the nonforfeitability and distribution requirements will also apply to all matching contributions and nonelective contributions, whether or not they are used to satisfy the ADP test. [Reg. § 1.401(k)-1(e)(3)]

A matching contribution is not forfeitable for minimum vesting purposes (see Q. 8:3) merely because it is forfeitable if the related contribution is treated as an excess contribution (see Q. 21:16), excess deferral (see Q. 21:26), or excess aggregate contribution (see Q. 21:53). [IRC § 411(a)(3)(G)]

Q. 21:41 What is a separate accounting under a 401(k) plan?

The portion of an employee's benefit that is attributable to elective contributions (including qualified matching and qualified nonelective contributions used to satisfy the ADP test) must be determined by an acceptable separate accounting between such portion and any other benefits of the employee under the plan by allocating investment gains and losses on a reasonable and consistent basis and by adjusting account balances for withdrawals and contributions. [Reg. § 1.401(k)-1(e)(3); Prop. Reg. § 1.401(k)-1(e)(8)]

Q. 21:42 Can an employer maintain two or more 401(k) plans?

Yes. But an employer that maintains two or more plans with CODAs and aggregates the plans for purposes of meeting the general qualification requirements (see Q. 3:1), must also aggregate the plans for purposes of the ADP test (see Q. 21:8). However, for plan years that begin after December 31, 1989, plans may be aggregated only if they have the same plan year. [Reg. § 1.401(k)-1(b)(5)(i); Prop. Reg. § 1.401(k)-(1)(b)(5)(iii)] For purposes of the ADP test, a highly compensated employee's elective contributions are aggregated. (See Q. 21:10.)

For plan years that begin after 1988, contributions and allocations under an ESOP (see Q. 22:1) may not be combined with contributions or allocations under any plan that is not an ESOP for purposes of determining whether either the ESOP or the non-ESOP satisfies the general qualification requirements and the ADP test. [Reg. § 1.401(k)-1(b)(5)(ii); see also Reg. §§ 54.4975-11(a)(5) and 54.4975-11(e)]

Q. 21:43 Can a CODA be part of a thrift or savings plan?

Yes. A thrift or savings plan (see Q. 2:7) is a plan in which employee or elective contributions and employer contributions are made on a matching basis. The matching contributions by the employer encourage greater participation by the nonhighly compensated employees and may be important in satisfying the ADP test (see Q. 21:8 and Q. 21:48).

For example, if the employer makes a $.50 matching contribution for every $1.00 of elective contributions made by the employee, the employee receives an immediate 50 percent return on the investment and has a greater incentive to participate in the plan.

Q. 21:44 How does a CODA affect the employer's tax-deductible contributions?

Since a CODA must be part of a profit sharing or stock bonus plan, the limitation on an employer's tax-deductible contributions to such type of plan applies—15 percent of total compensation paid to all participants (see Q. 10:7 and Q. 10:13). [IRC § 404(a)(3)(A)]

If any employee of the employer is covered by both a defined contribution plan and a defined benefit plan, a special tax-deduction limitation applies (see Q. 10:19). [IRC § 404(a)(7)]

Q. 21:45 How does a CODA affect the annual addition limitation?

Since a CODA must be part of a profit sharing or stock bonus plan, the limitation on annual additions to defined contribution plans applies (see Q. 5:1 and Q. 21:26). In computing the annual addition, elective contributions made under a qualified CODA are considered employer contributions. [IRC § 415(c); Reg. § 1.401(k)-1(g)(4)]

If the employee also participates in a defined benefit plan of the employer, a combined plan contribution limit applies (see Q. 5:12). [IRC § 415(e)]

Q. 21:46 Are elective contributions subject to payroll taxes?

Yes. Elective contributions (see Q. 21:13) made under a CODA are included in the Social Security taxable wage base for both employer and employee withholding purposes. Elective contributions are also subject to the Federal Unemployment Taxes Act (FUTA). [Social Security Act Amendments of 1983 § 324(d)]

Elective contributions are also included for purposes of measuring the annual increases in Social Security average wages, which will affect the calculation of both the taxable earnings base and benefit computations. [Social Security Act § 209, as amended by RRA '89 Act § 10208]

Q. 21:47 Does a 401(k) plan require registration with the Securities and Exchange Commission?

The Securities and Exchange Commission (SEC) has expressed its opinion that CODAs do not require registration of plan interests or employer stock purchased by the plan, but that a salary reduction plan under which an employee accepts a reduction in salary to obtain a contribution of a like amount by the employer to a qualified profit sharing plan may create plan interests that are securities. [Securities and Exchange Commission Release No. 33-6281; Diasonics, Inc., Securities and Exchange Commission, Division of Corporation Finance, December 23, 1982]

Q. 21:48   What is the special nondiscrimination test for qualified plans with employer matching contributions and/or employee contributions?

A special nondiscrimination test, the actual contribution percentage (ACP) test, applies to employer matching contributions and employee contributions under all qualified defined contribution plans (see Q. 2:2). The ACP test also applies to employee contributions under a defined benefit plan to the extent they are allocated to a separate account for each individual participant. The ACP test is essentially the same as the ADP test that is applied to elective contributions (see Q. 21:8).

A plan will be treated as meeting the nondiscrimination requirements of Section 401(a)(4) as to the amount of matching contributions and/or employee contributions only if the plan satisfies the ACP test. Satisfaction of the ACP test is the exclusive method of satisfying Section 401(a)(4) with respect to matching and employee contributions. [IRC § 401(m); Prop. Reg. §§ 1.401(m)-1(a)(1) and 1.401(m)-1(a)(2)]

The ACP test for the plan year will be satisfied if:

1. The ACP (see Q. 21:49) for the plan year for highly compensated employees (see Q. 4:28) does not exceed the ACP for such plan year for nonhighly compensated employees multiplied by 1.25; or

2. The ACP for the plan year for highly compensated employees does not exceed the ACP for such plan year for nonhighly compensated employees multiplied by 2.0, provided that the ACP for highly compensated employees does not exceed the ACP for nonhighly compensated employees by more than two percentage points. [IRC § 401(m)(2)(A); Prop. Reg. § 1.401(m)-1(b)(3)]

See Q. 21:56 and Q. 21:57 for discussions of the multiple use limitation and the family aggregation rules.

Q. 21:49   How is the ACP calculated for purposes of applying the ACP test?

The ACP is calculated by first determining the actual contribution ratio (ACR) (expressed as a percentage) for each employee. This is the ratio of the sum of the employee's employee contributions and matching contributions to the employee's compensation for the year. [IRC § 401(m)(3); Prop. Reg. § 1.401(m)-1(f)(13)]

For example, an employee whose compensation is $60,000 and who makes employee contributions of $5,000, which are matched by $1,000 of employer contributions, has an ACR of 10 percent ($5,000 plus $1,000 divided by $60,000). The ACP of the highly compensated employees is determined by taking the average of the ACRs for all highly compensated employees. If there are three highly compensated employees with ACRs of 5 percent, 7 percent, and 3 percent, the ACP is 5 percent (5% + 7% + 3% ÷ 3). The same procedure is followed for the group of nonhighly compensated employees. The ACP test is applied by comparing the ACP of the highly compensated employees to the ACP of the nonhighly compensated employees. ACRs and ACPs are calculated to the nearest one-hundredth of 1 percent. [Prop. Reg. § 1.401(m)-1(f)(13)(i)]

Q. 21:50   What contributions may be included for purposes of the ACP test?

A plan is generally required to apply the ACP test with respect to matching contributions and employee contributions. However, if qualified matching contributions are treated as elective contributions for purposes of satisfying the ADP test (see Q. 21:12), then they do not have to satisfy the ACP test (see Q. 21:48) and may not be used to help employee contributions and other matching contributions satisfy the ACP test. The matching contributions that are eliminated from the ACP test under this rule are only those contributions used to satisfy the ADP test. [Prop. Reg. §§ 1.401(m)-1(b)(1) and 1.401(m)-1(f)(13)(i)]

If the ACP test cannot be met with respect to matching and employee contributions, the plan has the option of treating as matching contributions all or any part of any qualified nonelective contributions (see Q. 21:14) and elective contributions (see Q. 21:13) made to any plan of the employer with respect to those employees who are eligible employees under the plan being tested. For plan years beginning after 1988, the plan year of the plan that uses qualified nonelective contributions and/or elective contributions to meet the ACP test must be the same as the plan year of the plans to which the qualified elective and nonelective contributions are made. [IRC § 401(m)(3); Prop. Reg. § 1.401(m)-1(b)(2)(viii)]

> **Example.** JLM Corporation maintains a profit sharing plan that permits elective and employee contributions. The plan permits elective contributions made by nonhighly compensated employees to be treated as employee contributions if required to meet the ACP test. The following contributions, as a percentage of compensation, are made to the plan.

	Elective contributions	Employee contributions
Highly compensated employees	10%	10%
Nonhighly compensated employees	10%	6%

The plan does not satisfy the ACP test with respect to employee contributions because the 10 percent ACP for the highly compensated employees is both more than two percentage points greater than the ACP for the nonhighly compensated employees and more than such ACP multiplied by 1.25. If one-fifth of the nonhighly compensated employees' elective contributions are treated as employee contributions, the elective contributions and employee contributions for the nonhighly compensated employees each becomes 8 percent. The plan can then meet the ACP test because the 10 percent ACP for the highly compensated employees is not more than the 8 percent ACP for the nonhighly compensated employees multiplied by 1.25.

Q. 21:51 When are contributions counted for purposes of applying the ACP test?

For purposes of the ACP test, an employee contribution is taken into account for the plan year in which it is made. Payment to an agent of the plan is treated as a contribution if the funds are transmitted to the plan within a reasonable time. If an excess contribution under a 401(k) plan is recharacterized as an employee contribution, then such recharacterized contribution is taken into account for the plan year in which it is included in the employee's gross income (see Q. 21:17).

A matching contribution is taken into account for the plan year in which it is allocated to the participant's account under the terms of the plan, provided that:

1. It is actually paid to the plan no later than the end of the 12-month period beginning on the day after the close of that plan year; and

2. It is made on account of the employee's voluntary or elective contributions for that plan year.

If a matching contribution does not satisfy these conditions, it may not be taken into account for purposes of the ACP test for the plan year in which it is made or any other plan year. Instead, it must satisfy the nondiscrimination requirements of Section 401(a)(4) (without application of the ACP test) for the plan year for which it is allocated as if it were the only employer contribution for that year. [Prop. Reg. § 1.401(m)-1(b)(5)]

Q. 21:52 What other requirements must a plan subject to the ACP test meet?

To satisfy the nondiscrimination requirements of Section 401(m), a plan must maintain the records necessary to demonstrate compliance with those requirements. Among other things, the records must be adequate to show that the ACP test has been met and must include information regarding the extent to which elective and non-elective contributions were taken into account to satisfy the ACP test. [Prop. Reg. § 1.401(m)-1(c)(2)]

To be a qualified retirement plan, it is not sufficient that a plan to which employee and/or matching contributions are made satisfy the ACP test. In addition, the plan must not discriminate in favor of highly compensated employees with respect to other benefits or rights of the plan, including the availability (as opposed to the amount) of voluntary and matching contributions. The determination of whether a rate of matching contributions discriminates in favor of highly compensated employees is made after correction of excess deferrals, excess contributions, and excess aggregate contributions. [Prop. Reg. § 1.401(m)-1(c)(1)]

Q. 21:53 What are excess aggregate contributions under the ACP test?

Excess aggregate contributions are the excess of the aggregate amount of employee contributions and matching contributions made on behalf of highly compensated employees for a plan year over the maximum amount of such contributions that are permitted under the ACP test (see Q. 21:48). Any qualified nonelective contributions and elective contributions treated as matching contributions for purposes of the ACP test are treated as matching contributions under this definition. However, qualified matching contributions that are treated as elective contributions for purposes of meeting the ADP test (see Q. 21:8) are not treated as matching contributions under this definition. [IRC § 401(m)(6)(B); Prop. Reg. § 1.401(m)-1(f)(12)]

If the ACP test is failed, there are excess aggregate contributions in the plan. However, correction of the excess aggregate contributions must be done on an individual employee basis. Allocation of the excess aggregate contributions among the highly compensated employees is done under the same leveling method that is used in allocating excess contributions under a 401(k) plan to individual highly compensated employees (see Q. 21:16). [IRC § 401(m)(6)(C); Prop. Reg. § 1.401(m)-1(e)(2)]

Q. 21:54 How are excess aggregate contributions corrected?

The principal method of correcting a highly compensated employee's share of excess aggregate contributions for a plan year is for the plan to distribute the share plus any allocable income to the employee. However, to the extent that excess aggregate contributions are forfeitable (i.e., not vested) under the terms of the plan, they may be forfeited rather than distributed. [IRC § 401(m)(6)(A); Prop. Reg. § 1.401(m)-1(e)(1)]

The following are not permissible methods of correcting an excess aggregate contribution:

1. Recharacterization (see Q. 21:17);
2. Failing to make matching contributions for highly compensated employees that are required under the terms of the plan; and

3. Forfeiting vested matching contributions made on behalf of highly compensated employees.

For a distribution to effectively correct an employee's share of excess aggregate contributions and allocable income, it must be designated as a distribution of an excess aggregate contribution and must be made after the close of the plan year in which the excess contribution arose and within 12 months thereafter. However, if the excess aggregate contributions are not distributed within 2½ months following the close of the plan year in which they arose, a 10 percent penalty tax will be imposed on the employer. [IRC §§ 401(m)(6)(A) and 4979(f); Prop. Reg. § 1.401(m)-1(e)(3)(i)]

Q. 21:55 What is the tax treatment of excess aggregate contributions?

Amounts attributable to excess aggregate contributions are generally included in the gross income of a highly compensated employee. However, amounts attributable to employee contributions are includible only to the extent of the income on such contributions. [IRC § 401(m)(7)(B)]

If the distribution is made within the first 2½ months after the close of the plan year for which the excess aggregate contributions were made, the year of inclusion is the taxable year of the employee ending with or within that plan year. If the distribution is made at a later date, the year of inclusion is the taxable year of the employee in which the distribution occurs. A corrective distribution of less than $100, however, is includible in gross income in the year of distribution if it occurs within the 2½ month period. [IRC § 4979(f)(2)(B); Prop. Reg. § 1.401(m)-1(e)(3)(v)]

A corrective distribution of excess aggregate contributions is not subject to the 10 percent excise tax on early distributions imposed by Section 72(t), nor is it treated as a distribution for purposes of the 15 percent excise tax on excess distributions imposed by Section 4980A. [IRC § 401(m)(7)(A); Prop. Reg. § 1.401(m)-1(e)(3)(v)]

A corrective distribution may be made without regard to the spousal consent requirements of Sections 401(a)(11) and 417 and is not regarded as a distribution for purposes of the minimum distribution requirements of Section 401(a)(9). Therefore, any distribution required under Section 401(a)(9) is not satisfied by a corrective distribution. [Prop. Reg. §§ 1.401(m)-1(e)(3)(iv) and 1.401(m)-1(e)(3)(vi)]

Q. 21:56 What is the multiple use limitation?

IRS is authorized to issue regulations to prevent the multiple use of the alternative limitation with respect to any highly compensated employee. The alternative limitation is the 2.0/two percentage point limitation (see Q. 21:8 and Q. 21:48). [IRC § 401(m)(9)(B); Prop. Reg. § 1.401(m)-2(b)(2)]

Multiple use of the alternative limitation does not occur unless (1) one or more highly compensated employees are eligible to participate in both a CODA and a plan to which employee contributions or matching contributions are made, and (2) the percentage obtained by adding the ADP and the ACP of the highly compensated employees exceeds an aggregate limit. Under the initial proposed regulations, this limit is the sum of:

1. 1.25 times the *greater* of the ADP or the ACP of the nonhighly compensated employees, and

2. Two percentage points plus the *lesser* of the ADP or the ACP of the nonhighly compensated employees, but this amount cannot exceed 2.0 times the lesser of the ADP or the ACP of the nonhighly compensated employees.

If the sum of the ADP and ACP of the highly compensated employees exceeds this aggregate limit, there is prohibited multiple use.

> **Example.** Under SBK Corporation's 401(k) plan, which provides for matching contributions, the ADPs for highly compensated employees and nonhighly compensated employees are 3.9 percent and 2.0 percent, respectively, while the ACPs for the two groups are 1.3 percent and 1.0 percent, respectively. The sum of the ADP and ACP for the highly compensated employees is 5.2 percent, and the prohibited multiple use would occur because the limitation would be 4.5 percent, as follows:
>
> 1. Greater of ADP or ACP of nonhighly
>   compensated employees   2.0

2. 1.25 × 2.0	2.5
3. Lesser of ADP or ACP of nonhighly compensated employees	1.0
4. 2.0 × 1.0	2.0
5. Aggregate limit (2.5 + 2.0)	4.5
6. Excess [5.2% (3.9% + 1.3%) − 4.5%]	.7

Under revised proposed regulations, the aggregate limit is the *greater* of the sum discussed above or the sum of:

1. 1.25 times the *lesser* of the ADP or the ACP of the nonhighly compensated employees, and

2. Two percentage points plus the *greater* of the ADP or the ACP of the nonhighly compensated employees, but this amount cannot exceed 2.0 times the lesser of the ADP or the ACP of the nonhighly compensated employees.

In the example, prohibited multiple use does not occur:

1. Lesser of ADP or ACP of nonhighly compensated employees	1.0
2. 1.25 × 1.0	1.25
3. Greater of ADP or ACP of nonhighly compensated employees	2.0
4. 2.0 × 2.0	4.0
5. Aggregate limit (1.25 + 4.0)	5.25
6. Excess [5.2% (3.9% + 1.3%) − 5.25%]	-0-

[Prop. Reg. § 1.401(m)-2(b)(3)]

The revised proposed regulations also clarify that multiple use of the alternative limitation will not occur unless the ADP and ACP of the highly compensated employees *each* exceeds 1.25 times the corresponding percentage of the nonhighly compensated employees. For plan years beginning before January 1, 1991, the employer can choose to use either method. [Prop. Reg. § 1.401(m)-2(b)(1); preamble to revised proposed regulations (May 14, 1990)]

When prohibited multiple use of the alternative limitation occurs, the ADP and/or ACP of the highly compensated employees is reduced by use of the leveling method (see Q. 21:16 and Q. 21:53) so that the combined ADP and ACP does not exceed the aggregate limit. The amount of the reduction must be distributed to the highly compensated employees according to the allocation produced by the leveling method; or, at the employer's election, the reduction may be allocated among all highly compensated employees under the plan or CODA that is being reduced or among only those highly compensated employees who are eligible under both the CODA and the plan for which employee contributions or employee and matching contributions are made. [Prop. Reg. § 1.401(m)-2(c)]

Q. 21:57 What are the family aggregation rules?

If an individual is a member of the family of a 5% owner or one of the ten most highly compensated employees, that individual is not treated as a separate employee and the individual's compensation (and any applicable contribution or benefit on that individual's behalf) is treated as if paid to (or on behalf of) a single 5% owner or highly compensated employee. Family members include the employee's spouse, lineal descendants or ascendants, and spouses of such lineal descendants, or ascendants. [IRC §§ 401(k)(5), 414(q)(6), and 416(i)(1)(B)(i); Prop. Reg. § 1.401(k)-1(g)(8)(iii)]

Under the initial proposed regulations, for such a family group, which is treated as one highly compensated employee, the combined ADR (see Q. 21:9) is the greater of:

1. The ADR determined by combining the elective contributions, compensation, and amounts treated as elective contributions of all the eligible family members who are highly compensated employees *without regard* to family aggregation, or

2. The ADR determined by combining the elective contributions, compensation, and amounts treated as elective contributions of all the eligible family members.

Generally, the elective contributions, compensation, and amounts treated as elective contributions of all family members are disregarded in determing the ADP (see Q. 21:9) of the nonhighly compensated employees.

> **Example.** Shirley has a child, Ellen. Both participate in a 401(k) plan maintained by EMK Corporation. Shirley is one of the ten most highly compensated employees and Ellen is a

nonhighly compensated employee. Shirley has compensation of $100,000 and defers $7,000 under the 401(k) arrangement; Ellen has compensation of $40,000 and defers $4,000 under the arrangement. The ADR of the family unit is 7.86 percent, calculated by aggregating the contributions and compensation of Shirley and Ellen ($7,000 + $4,000)/($100,000 + $40,000). If Ellen makes only $2,000 in elective contributions and has an ADR of 5 percent, the ADR of Shirley without regard to family aggregation is 7 percent; combining the contributions and compensation of Shirley and Ellen produces an ADR of 6.43 percent ($7,000 + $2,000)/($100,000 + $40,000). Thus, the ADR of the family unit is 7 percent (the greater of 7% and 6.43%).

Under revised proposed regulations, the family aggregation rule is always used so that the ADR of the family unit in the first part of the example remains at 7.86 percent; but, in the second part of the example, it is 6.43 percent and not 7 percent. [Prop. Reg. §§ 1.401(k)-1(f)(7), example 3, and 1.401(k)-1(g)(8)(iii)]

Under the initial proposed regulations, in the first part of the above example, if the ADR of the family unit created an excess contribution (see Q. 21:16), the reduction would be applied in proportion to both Shirley's and Ellen's contributions. In the second part of the example, Shirley's contributions would first be reduced and then, if necessary, both of their contributions would be reduced proportionately. Under revised proposed regulations, since the family aggregation rule is always used, the reduction will be applied in proportion to their contributions. [Prop. Reg. § 1.401(k)-1(f)(7), example 3]

For plan years beginning before January 1, 1991, employers can elect to use either method. [Preamble to revised proposed regulations (May 14, 1990)]

The family aggregation rules also apply for purposes of the ACP test (see Q. 21:48) and correcting excess aggregate contributions (see Q. 21:54), and employers may choose either method for plan years beginning before January 1, 1991. [Prop. Reg. §§ 1.401(m)-1(e)(4)(iii) and 1.401(m)-1(f)(13)(iii); preamble to revised proposed regulations (May 14, 1990)]

Chapter 22

Employee Stock Ownership Plans

An employee stock ownership plan (ESOP) is a special breed of qualified retirement plan. In addition to providing retirement benefits for employees, an ESOP can be used as a market for company stock, as a method of increasing the company's cash flow, and as a means of financing the company's growth. This chapter examines recent developments affecting ESOPs and highlights changes made by the Revenue Reconciliation Act of 1989.

Q. 22:1 What is an employee stock ownership plan?

An ESOP is essentially a defined contribution plan whose funds must be invested primarily in employer securities (see Q. 22:10). Generally, the funds may come from any or all of the following sources: (1) company contributions of cash or employer securities, (2) an exempt loan to the ESOP (see Q. 22:4), or (3) a defined contribution plan converted to an ESOP (see Q. 22:20). The amount of tax deductible contributions to an ESOP is generally determined in the same manner as for other defined contribution plans (see Q. 10:1 through Q. 10:15), although there is a special rule increasing the deductible amount of employer contributions used to repay exempt loans to the ESOP (see Q. 22:11). [IRC §§ 404(a)(3), 404(a)(9), 409, and 4975(e)(7)]

The funds are held in trust for the benefit of employees and their beneficiaries and are used to buy employer securities from stockholders or from the company itself. When a participant retires or leaves, the participant receives the vested interest in the ESOP in the form of cash or employer securities. However, an ESOP may preclude a participant from obtaining a distribution of employer securities if the company's corporate charter or bylaws restrict the ownership of substantially all employer securities to employees or the ESOP. [IRC § 409(h)(2)]

Participants can put the employer securities back to the company for their fair market value if the securities are not readily tradable on an established market (see Q. 22:2). To keep the employer securities from falling into the hands of competitors, either the ESOP or the company may be given the right of first refusal if the participant attempts to sell the securities. However, a participant generally can demand a distribution of benefits in the form of employer securities and cannot be required to sell the securities back to the company. [IRC § 409(h)(1); Reg. § 54.4975-7(b)(9)]

Q. 22:2   When can participants exercise their put option?

The put option must last for a period of at least 60 days following the date of distribution of employer securities. If the option is not exercised, the participant must be given the opportunity to sell the stock to the employer during a 60-day period in the following plan year. [IRC § 409(h)(4)]

If a put option is exercised with respect to stock distributed in a total distribution, the employer must pay for the repurchased stock in substantially equal periodic payments (not less frequently than annually) over a period beginning no later than 30 days after the exercise of the put option and ending no later than five years thereafter. Reasonable interest and adequate security must be provided for unpaid amounts. For this purpose, a total distribution is a distribution of the balance of the recipient's account within one calendar year. [IRC § 409(h)(5)]

If the stock is distributed in installments, the employer must pay for the stock no later than 30 days after the put option is exercised. [IRC § 409(h)(6)]

Q. 22:3   How is an ESOP different from a stock bonus plan?

A stock bonus plan (see Q. 2:9) permits, but does not require, current investments in employer securities. An ESOP must invest primarily in employer securities (see Q. 22:10). Further, an ESOP, but not a stock bonus plan, may borrow from the employer or use the employer's credit to acquire employer securities. [IRC § 4975(d)(3)]

Q. 22:4 What is an exempt loan?

Generally, the lending of money by the employer to a qualified retirement plan is a prohibited transaction. However, an employer's loan or guarantee of a loan to an ESOP will not be a prohibited transaction if the loan satisfies the requirements for being an exempt loan. The exempt loan requirements include the following:

- The loan must be primarily for the benefit of participants and beneficiaries of the ESOP;
- The proceeds of the loan must be used to acquire qualifying employer securities (see Q. 22:10) or to repay an exempt loan;
- The interest rate of the loan must be reasonable;
- The loan must be without recourse against the ESOP, and without collateral other than qualifying employer securities acquired (or refinanced) with the proceeds of the exempt loan; and
- The loan must provide for the release from encumbrance of employer securities used as collateral as the loan is repaid.

[IRC § 4975(d)(3); Reg. § 54.4975-7(b)]

Q. 22:5 Do commercial lenders have a tax incentive to make loans to ESOPs?

Yes. If a commercial lender (see Q. 22:7) makes a securities acquisition loan (see Q. 22:6) that enables the ESOP to acquire employer securities (see Q. 22:10), then 50 percent of the interest received by the commercial lender during the excludable period (see Q. 22:9) is not subject to income tax. The commercial lender may make the loan directly to the ESOP or to the employer (which in turn lends the money to the ESOP). Loans between related persons do not qualify for the exclusion. [IRC §§ 133(a) and 133(b)]

Q. 22:6   What is a securities acquisition loan?

A securities acquisition loan is

1. Any loan to an ESOP that qualifies as an exempt loan to the extent the proceeds are used to acquire employer securities (see Q. 22:10) for the ESOP or are used to refinance an exempt loan that was used to acquire employer securities, or

2. An "immediate allocation" loan to an employer that, within 30 days, transfers employer securities to the ESOP in an amount equal to the proceeds of the loan and such securities are allocable to accounts of participants within one year of the date of the loan.

A loan made to an employer sponsoring an ESOP may also qualify as a securities acquisition loan if the employer then, in turn, uses the proceeds to make an exempt loan to the ESOP with substantially similar repayment terms as the loan from the lender to the employer.

If the repayment terms of the two loans are not substantially similar, the loan to the sponsoring employer will still qualify as a securities acquisition loan if (1) the loan to the ESOP provides for more rapid payment of principal or interest than the loan to the sponsoring employer and (2) the allocations of employer securities within the ESOP attributable to the difference in payment schedules do not result in discrimination in favor of highly compensated employees (see Q. 4:28).

Under RRA '89, a loan made after July 10, 1989 will be treated as a securities acquisition loan only if the ESOP owns more than 50 percent of the issuing corporation's stock immediately after the ESOP receives the employer securities acquired with the loan proceeds. For purposes of the 50 percent test, certain nonvoting, nonconvertible preferred stock is disregarded, and IRS may provide that warrants, options, and convertible debt interests may be treated as stock. Also, the commercial lender's 50 percent exclusion does not apply to interest income received during a period in which the ESOP's stock ownership percentage falls to 50 percent or less. The 50 percent ESOP stock ownership requirement is reduced to 30 percent for loans made after July 10, 1989, but before November 18, 1989.

The term of a securities acquisition loan made after July 10, 1989, cannot exceed 15 years. Also, the ESOP must permit participants to vote stock allocated to their accounts that was acquired with a post-July 10, 1989 securities acquisition loan on a "one share/one vote" basis on all issues put to a shareholder vote.

RRA '89 rules do not apply to loans made pursuant to a binding written commitment in effect on July 10, 1989, and the 30 percent (not 50%) ownership test applies if there was a binding written commitment made between July 10, 1989 and November 18, 1989. IRS has provided guidelines as to what constitutes a binding written commitment. [*Notice 90-6*, 1990-3 IRB]

RRA '89 also added a 10 percent nondeductible excise tax on the employer with respect to the amount realized on dispositions of employer securities acquired with a securities acquisition loan made after July 10, 1989, in a transaction to which Section 133 applied if:

1. Within three years, the total amount of employer securities held by the ESOP decreases;
2. Within three years, the value of the ESOP's employer securities drops below 50 percent of the value of all employer securities; or
3. The ESOP disposes of employer securities not allocated to participants and does not allocate the proceeds to participants.

Certain distributions to participants, including distributions pursuant to a diversification election (see Q. 22:48), exchanges in corporate reorganizations, and dispositions required by state law are not treated as dispositions for purposes of the excise tax. [IRC §§ 133 and 4978B; Reg. §§ 54.4975-7 and 54.4975-11]

Q. 22:7 Which commercial lenders are eligible for the 50 percent interest exclusion?

A bank, an insurance company, a regulated investment company, or a corporation actively engaged in the business of lending money is eligible to exclude from gross income 50 percent of the interest received with respect to a securities acquisition loan (see Q. 22:6).

Entities eligible for the 50 percent interest exclusion are often referred to as qualified lenders. [IRC § 133(a)]

A corporation is actively engaged in the business of lending money if

1. It is not an S corporation;
2. It lends money to the public on a regular and continuing basis (other than in connection with the purchase by the public of goods and services from the lender or a related party); and
3. A predominant share of such loans are not securities acquisition loans. [Reg. § 1.133-1T, Q&A 2]

Q. 22:8 May loans that qualify for the 50 percent interest exclusion be transferred to other lending institutions?

Yes. A holder of a securities acquisition loan (see Q. 22:6) may sell or transfer such loan to another lending institution. A subsequent holder of the debt instrument may qualify for the interest exclusion if the holder is a qualified lender (see Q. 22:7). Further, a qualified lender will be eligible for the 50 percent interest exclusion even if a previous holder of the debt instrument was not a qualified lender. [IRC § 133; *Rev. Rul.* 89-76, 1989-1 CB 24]

Q. 22:9 Is there a limit on the time period for which the 50 percent interest exclusion applies?

Yes. The interest exclusion is allowable for the excludable period measured with respect to the date of the original securities acquisition loan. The excludable period generally is seven years or the term of the original securities acquisition loan, if longer. However, the excludable period is only seven years for immediate allocation loans and back-to-back loans with more rapid repayment provisions for the ESOP than the employer (see Q. 22:6). Also, the refinancing of an original securities acquisition loan does not extend the excludable period with respect to the original securities acquisition loan. [IRC § 133(e)]

Q. 22:10   What are employer securities?

Employer securities include common stock issued by the employer that is readily tradable on an established securities market. If the employer has no readily tradable common stock, employer securities include employer-issued common stock that has a combination of voting power and dividend rights at least the equal of the class of common stock with the greatest voting power and the class of common stock with the greatest dividend rights. Noncallable preferred stock that is convertible into common stock that meets the requirements of employer securities also qualifies if the conversion price is reasonable.

Employer securities also include stock issued by a member of a controlled group (see Q. 4:34) that includes the employer if the stock meets the same requirements as qualifying employer-issued stock. [IRC § 409(l); *Letter Ruling 8610082*]

Q. 22:11   What is the limitation on tax-deductible contributions to an ESOP?

Generally, the limitation on deductions for employer contributions to an ESOP is 15 percent of covered compensation. However, money purchase pension ESOPs have a 25 percent limitation. In addition, the overall limitation on deductible contributions to all defined contribution plans in combination is 25 percent of covered compensation. [IRC § 404(a)(7)]

The employer may deduct up to 25 percent of covered compensation for contributions to a leveraged ESOP (an ESOP that borrows to acquire employer securities) used to repay loan principal, and an unlimited amount for contributions used to pay interest on the loan. [IRC § 404(a)(9)]

Q. 22:12   Are dividends paid on employer securities held by an ESOP ever deductible by the employer?

Yes. The employer may be allowed to deduct dividends it pays on employer securities (see Q. 22:10) held by an ESOP that it maintains, or by an ESOP maintained by another member of a controlled group (see Q. 4:34) that includes the employer.

To be deductible, the dividend must be

1. Paid in cash to the ESOP participants or their beneficiaries;

2. Paid to the ESOP and distributed to the participants or beneficiaries not later than 90 days after the close of the plan year in which paid; or

3. Used to make payments on an exempt loan. (For employer securities acquired by the ESOP after August 4, 1989, the deduction for dividends used for loan repayment is applicable only if the dividends are on employer securities acquired with the proceeds of the loan being repaid.)

The deduction is allowed for the taxable year of the employer during which the dividend is paid, distributed, or used to repay an exempt loan. [IRC §§ 404(k) and 409(l)(4)]

If dividends on employer securities allocated to a participant are used to repay an exempt loan, the ESOP must provide that employer securities with a fair market value equal to the dividends be allocated to such participant in lieu of the dividends. [IRC § 404(k)(2)(B)]

It is important to note that IRS has authority to disallow the deduction if the dividends constitute an evasion of taxation. [IRC § 404(k)(5)(A)]

Q. 22:13   Are dividends paid to participants deductible even if participants can elect whether or not to receive them in a current cash payment?

Yes. Dividends actually paid in cash to plan participants are deductible despite a plan provision that permits participants to elect to receive or not receive payment of dividends. [IRC § 404(k); Reg. § 1.404(k)-1T, Q&A 2]

Q. 22:14 How are dividends paid to ESOP participants taxed?

Dividends paid in cash directly to ESOP participants by the employer and dividends paid to the ESOP and then distributed in cash to participants are treated as paid separately from any other payments from the ESOP. Thus, a deductible dividend is treated as a plan distribution and as paid under a separate contract providing only for payment of deductible dividends. A deductible dividend is a taxable distribution even though an employee has basis (see Q. 11:2), but the distribution is not subject to the 10 percent tax on early distributions (see Q. 9:68). [IRC §§ 72(t)(2)(A)(vi) and 402; Reg. § 1.404(k)-1T, Q&A 3]

A distribution of a participant's entire account balance from an ESOP is eligible for treatment as a lump-sum distribution (see Q. 11:4) even if the participant received dividend distributions with respect to employer securities held by the ESOP in earlier years. [*Letter Ruling 9024083*]

Employers must report deductible dividends on Form 1099-DIV. Participants must report the distribution on their tax returns as a plan distribution and not as investment income. IRS is directed to establish procedures for information returns and reports with respect to deductible dividend payments. [IRC § 6047(e); *Announcement 85-168*, 1985-48 IRB 40]

Q. 22:15 What is the limit on the amount that may be added to an ESOP participant's account each year?

The amount that can be added to a participant's account (the annual addition) is limited to the lesser of $30,000 (or, if greater, 25% of the maximum dollar limit payable under a defined benefit plan) or 25 percent of the participant's compensation. (See Q. 5:1.) [IRC §§ 415(c)(1) and 415(c)(2)]

If no more than one-third of the employer's contributions for the year are allocated to highly compensated employees (see Q. 4:28), contributions applied to pay interest on a loan, as well as forfeitures of ESOP stock acquired through a loan, are disregarded for purposes of computing the annual addition. [IRC § 415(c)(6)]

It appears that dividends on employer securities (see Q. 22:10) held by an ESOP are not considered to be part of the annual addition, so contributions to an ESOP may be effectively increased. [IRC § 404(k)]

For limitation years (see Q. 5:11) that began before July 13, 1989, if no more than one-third of the employer's contributions for the year was allocated to highly compensated employees, the dollar limit was doubled to $60,000. However, as a result of the $200,000 limit on compensation, effective in 1989, the limit was effectively reduced to $50,000 (i.e., 25% of $200,000). [IRC § 401(a)(17)]

Q. 22:16 Can a company obtain a tax deduction for stock contributions to its ESOP?

Yes. One of the basic advantages of using an ESOP is the ability to use either cash or employer securities (see Q. 22:10) for the company's contributions. A company strapped for cash can make its contributions in authorized but unissued securities and still get a tax deduction for the full amount of the contribution. Thus, for example, a company with an annual payroll of $500,000 that contributes $75,000 (15% of $500,000) to its ESOP in the form of employer securities is allowed a tax deduction of $75,000. The contribution in the form of employer securities not only keeps cash in the corporation but also provides a cash flow from the tax savings realized by the deduction.

The amount of the contribution is the fair market value of the employer securities even though there is no cost to the company.

Note, however, that DOL may consider a contribution of employer securities to a money purchase pension ESOP to be a prohibited transaction (see Q. 18:8).

Q. 22:17 Can an ESOP be integrated with Social Security?

A qualified retirement plan designated as an ESOP after November 1, 1977, may not be integrated with Social Security (see Chapter

6). An ESOP established and integrated before that date can remain integrated, but the plan cannot be amended to increase the integration level or the integration percentage. [Reg. § 54.4975-11(a)(7)(ii)]

Q. 22:18   How can a company use an ESOP to help finance the acquisition of another company?

A purchasing company that needs cash to acquire another company (the target) may obtain the necessary cash by arranging a bank loan to its ESOP. The ESOP gets the borrowed cash to the purchasing company by buying employer securities of the purchasing company. The purchasing company then buys the target's assets or stock with cash. The bank loan is paid off through tax-deductible cash contributions by the purchasing company to the ESOP.

Another approach is to have the ESOP itself buy the stock of the target with the borrowed funds, and then exchange the target stock for newly issued stock of its own company. This approach is riskier, however, because the exchange of stock may be considered a prohibited transaction under ERISA. Before proceeding in this way, a DOL exemption request should be considered (see Q. 18:9).

A third approach is for the company itself to borrow the cash and buy the target directly, using the cash flow created by a tax deduction for the stock contributions to the ESOP to help finance the purchase. This approach has the advantages of avoiding prohibited transaction problems and producing less dilution of the purchasing company's stock.

Q. 22:19   Are ESOPs used by publicly traded companies to defend against unwanted takeovers?

Yes. By establishing an ESOP that purchases stock on the open market, management hopes to place a block of stock in the presumably friendly hands of its employees. However, to the extent that publicly traded stock (i.e., a registration-type class of securities) is allocated to participants, each participant must be given the opportunity to direct the ESOP as to the voting of the allocated shares. With respect to unallocated stock, the trustees and other fiduciaries must take special care to be sure they are acting solely in the interest of ESOP participants and beneficiaries (see Q. 22:47). [IRC § 409(e)]

In one case, an ESOP that acquired 14 percent of the stock of a publicly traded company in response to a takeover threat was upheld as fundamentally fair to the shareholders of the public company. The ESOP required that unallocated stock be voted in the same proportion as allocated stock. [*Shamrock Holdings v. Polaroid*, 559 A2d 278 (Del. Ch. 1989)]

Q. 22:20 Can a profit sharing plan be converted to an ESOP?

Yes. If the company currently has a profit sharing plan and wants to replace it with an ESOP, the company has three alternatives. It can

1. Continue the profit sharing plan and make future contributions to both the profit sharing plan and the ESOP.

2. Terminate the profit sharing plan. This results in the immediate 100 percent vesting of all the accounts of plan participants. The assets under the profit sharing plan can be either distributed currently or maintained in the plan for distribution as employees retire or separate from service.

3. Adopt the ESOP as a continuation of the profit sharing plan. Replacement of the profit sharing plan will not be considered a termination of the plan for vesting purposes. Employer securities must be purchased with plan assets because an ESOP must invest primarily in employer securities (see Q. 22:1 and Q. 22:10).

Plan fiduciaries must beware that the conversion of a profit sharing plan into an ESOP may, depending on the purpose and financial consequences of the conversion, be a violation of the prudent man rule. In other words, if the business goes sour after the conversion, it is likely that participants will bring a claim against the fiduciaries for making an imprudent investment. The courts have been sympathetic to such claims. [*Eaves v. Penn*, 587 F2d 453 (10th Cir. 1978)]

Q. 22:21 How can an ESOP be used as an estate planning tool for the owner of a closely held corporation?

The bulk of an owner's taxable estate frequently consists of the value of the stock in his or her corporation. If the value of that stock is not established before the owner's death, an arbitrary figure—one based on a compromise between an IRS valuation expert and the executor's expert—may be used to determine the amount of estate taxes due. The establishment of an ESOP before the owner's death may ease this burden on the estate because the fair market value of the stock acquired by the ESOP would be determined by an independent appraiser beforehand, reducing the chances of a dispute with IRS. [IRC § 401(a)(28)]

The ESOP can also provide cash to pay the estate taxes and administration expenses of a deceased majority shareholder. The tax law provides various solutions to the liquidity problems of an estate that consists mostly of the stock of a closely held corporation. If the estate fails to qualify for this special treatment, it may be able to raise the cash through the sale of stock to the ESOP.

For example, assume that the estate of a deceased shareholder fails to meet the requirements that permit it to pay the estate tax in installments over a period of up to 15 years. The estate tax is then due within nine months of the shareholder's death. By selling the deceased shareholder's stock to the ESOP, the estate can raise the cash it needs.

The ESOP can also rescue an estate of a deceased shareholder that cannot avail itself of the benefits of a Section 303 redemption. This provision of the Code permits the redemption of a portion of a deceased shareholder's stock for the express purpose of paying estate taxes and administration expenses. If an estate fails to qualify, the proceeds of a redemption of the deceased shareholder's stock are likely to be subject to income tax as a dividend. This result can be avoided by having the ESOP buy the stock from the estate. The sale to the ESOP does not have the danger of being treated as a dividend.

Generally, a sale to the corporation or to the ESOP will result in no gain at all because the estate's basis for the stock it sells will equal the fair market value of the stock on the deceased shareholder's date of death, and the purchase price paid by the corporation or the ESOP will likely be this amount. [IRC §§ 303, 1014, and 6166]

Q. 22:22 Is there an estate tax deduction for sales of employer securities to an ESOP?

Under prior law, the value of the taxable estate of the deceased owner of employer securities was determined by deducting from the value of the gross estate an amount equal to 50 percent of the qualified proceeds of a qualified sale of employer securities to the ESOP. [IRC § 2057(a)]

However, that estate tax deduction was modified by OBRA '87 and then eliminated by RRA '89 for estates of decedents who died after December 19, 1989. The OBRA '87 amendments restricted the application of the deduction to sales of qualified employer securities (see Q. 22:23) and limited the maximum allowable reduction in tax liability to $750,000. In addition, the allowable deduction was limited to 50 percent of the taxable estate. The OBRA '87 changes also included limitations on sale proceeds that may be taken into account in determining the allowable deduction. Finally, the amendments established additional requirements regarding the filing of the executor's statement (see Q. 22:25). For estates of decedents who died before December 20, 1989, the deduction, as modified by OBRA '87, applies to sales after February 26, 1987, and before January 1, 1992. [IRC § 2057]

Q. 22:23 What are qualified employer securities?

For purposes of the estate tax deduction, qualified employer securities are securities issued by a domestic corporation that has no outstanding stock tradable on an established securities market that are also includible in the decedent's gross estate. Also, for decedents dying after October 22, 1986, the securities are not qualified unless they would have been includible if the decedent had died at any time during the period between October 22, 1986, and the date of death. Securities that would have been includible in a spouse's gross estate under these rules will be treated as having satisfied these requirements. The securities will be treated as not having been includible for any period during which the risk of loss was diminished as described in Section 246(c)(4). The executor must specifically elect the deduction for the qualified securities. [IRC §§ 2057(d) and 246(c)(4)]

IRS has retroactively applied the rule enacted in OBRA '87 that employer securities purchased by an estate after a decedent's death are not qualified securities. OBRA '87 merely clarified Section 2057 as originally enacted by TRA '86, and reflected legislative intent as shown by the legislative history of TRA '86. [*Letter Ruling 8952003*]

To qualify, the decedent must have owned the employer securities directly at the time of death.

> **Example.** Herb owned 49 percent of X Corporation, a personal holding company that owned 1000 shares of Y Corporation at the time of Herb's death. Shortly thereafter, X liquidated and Herb's estate received 490 shares of Y, which it then sold to Y's ESOP. The 490 Y shares are not qualified employer securities because X, not Herb, owned the shares at the time of Herb's death. [*Letter Ruling 9006004*]

Q. 22:24 What proceeds may be taken into account in determining the estate tax deduction?

The sale proceeds that are taken into account in determining the allowable deduction must be reduced by the net sale amount. The net sale amount is defined as the proceeds from the disposition of employer securities by the ESOP during the year immediately preceding the participant's death less the cost of employer securities acquired by the ESOP during that period. For purposes of determining the net sale amount, all ESOPs maintained by an employer are treated as one plan. [IRC § 2057(c)(1)]

The proceeds attributable to the sale of transferred assets cannot be considered in determining the allowable deduction. Transferred assets are assets held by the qualified retirement plan when it was not an ESOP, or assets of the ESOP attributable to assets held by a qualified retirement plan other than an ESOP. Transferred assets do not, however, include any assets held by the ESOP on February 26, 1987. Proceeds from a sale of employer securities that occurs after the filing deadline for the estate tax return are excluded from consideration. Proceeds from the sale of securities distributed to the decedent from a qualified retirement plan or transferred to the decedent in connection with the performance of services, or pursuant to a qualified stock option, incentive stock option, employee stock purchase plan, or restricted stock option, are also not considered in determining the amount of the deduction. [IRC §§ 2057(c)(2) and 2057(c)(3); see also IRC §§ 83, 422, 422A, 423, and 424]

Q. 22:25 Is any statement required to be filed by the executor?

Yes. The executor must file with IRS a verified written statement of the employer, whose employees are covered by the ESOP, acknowledging the estate's sale of employer securities to the ESOP and certifying the net sale amount and the amount of assets that are not transferred assets (see Q. 22:24). [IRC § 2057(e)]

Q. 22:26 Are there any penalties for the improper allocation or disposition of employer securities purchased by the ESOP in a qualified sale?

Yes. An excise tax is imposed on the employer in the event of certain dispositions of qualified employer securities (see Q. 22:23) acquired by an ESOP in a sale to which the estate tax deduction applied (see Q. 22:22). [IRC § 4978A]

The excise tax will be imposed if (1) there is any disposition of the acquired qualified employer securities within three years of acquisition, or (2) there is any disposition prior to the allocation of the acquired securities and the proceeds of the disposition are not allocated to participants and beneficiaries. The excise tax imposed on the employer is 30 percent of the amount realized on the disposition. [IRC §§ 4978A(b), 4978A(c)(1), 4978A(c)(2), and 4978A(f)(4)(A)]

In addition, if an ESOP uses assets to which an estate tax deduction applied to repay a loan used to acquire securities from transferred assets (see Q. 22:24), an excise tax of 30 percent of the amount repaid on the loan will be imposed on the employer. [IRC §§ 4978A(b)(1)(B) and 4978A(c)(3)]

This tax will not be imposed on (1) a disposition as a result of certain reorganizations; (2) a disposition made to meet the diversification requirements (see Q. 22:48); or (3) a distribution to an employee as a result of death, retirement, disability, or separation from service. [IRC § 4978A(e); see also IRC § 4978(d)]

For a discussion of restrictions applying to a disposition for which a nonrecognition election has been made, see Q. 22:41 through Q. 22:43.

There are also two penalties if any portion of the assets attributable to employer securities acquired in a sale generating an estate tax deduction are allocated to a 25 percent shareholder of the employer or, during the nonallocation period (see Q. 22:27), for the benefit of the decedent whose estate makes such a sale or any related person. The first penalty is that participants who received the prohibited allocations must currently include the securities' fair market value in income at the time of the allocation. The second penalty is an excise tax imposed on the employer, equal to 50 percent of the amount involved (see Q. 22:43). [IRC §§ 267(b), 409(n), and 4979A]

Q. 22:27   What is the nonallocation period?

The nonallocation period, for purposes of the estate tax deduction (see Q. 22:22 through Q. 22:26) and nonrecognition sales of stock to an ESOP (see Q. 22:30 through Q. 22:43), is the period beginning on the date of sale and ending on the later of (1) the date that is ten years after the date of sale, or (2) the date of the plan allocation attributable to the final payment of acquisition indebtedness incurred in connection with the sale. [IRC § 409(n)(3)(C)]

Q. 22:28   Can an ESOP assume the estate tax liability of a deceased stockholder?

Not for estates of decedents dying after July 12, 1989. For estates of decedents dying before July 13, 1989, an ESOP that acquires employer securities (see Q. 22:10) from the deceased stockholder's estate may assume liability for the decedent's estate tax in an amount equal to the lesser of (1) the fair market value of the securities transferred that are included in the decedent's gross estate, or (2) the total estate tax owed. The executor must affirmatively elect this procedure and file, by the due date (including extensions) of the estate tax return, a written agreement signed by the plan administrator agreeing to the plan's assumption of the liability. The company sponsoring the ESOP must also guarantee payment of the estate tax. The assumption by the ESOP of the estate tax liability is not treated as a prohibited transaction.

For estates of decedents dying after September 27, 1985, and before July 13, 1989, the estate tax liability may not be transferred to the ESOP unless the executor is eligible to elect to make deferred payment of the estate tax. If the executor elected installment payments of the estate tax, the plan administrator could also elect by the estate tax return due date (including extensions) to pay the ESOP's tax liability in installments. [IRC §§ 2210(c) and 6166(k)(6)]

Q. 22:29   How can an ESOP be used to provide a market for the stock of controlling shareholders in a closely held corporation?

An ESOP is a mechanism that enables controlling shareholders to sell all or a portion of their shares to the employees, who would be the logical buyers if they could obtain the financing.

The transaction clearly benefits the shareholders by allowing them to cash out their interests in the company. It also benefits the corporation because the shares may be purchased with pretax dollars (i.e., annual cash contributions to the ESOP), resulting in a substantial reduction in the cash required to finance the transaction. Further, a commercial lender may be eligible to exclude from its taxable income 50 percent of the interest received on the loan to purchase the shares of a selling shareholder, so the lender may charge a reduced rate of interest (see Q. 22:5 through Q. 22:9).

Another advantage of this type of transaction is that it provides for the continuity of management by enabling new employees to acquire stock as older employees and shareholders retire without diluting the equity of the remaining shareholders. That is, the ESOP, by purchasing outstanding shares from existing shareholders, avoids the diluting effect that would be involved if the ESOP purchased newly issued shares from the company.

There may, however, be some dilution of earnings to the extent that the ESOP creates expenses that the company would not otherwise have. Even this may not be the case if the company previously had a profit sharing plan and the ESOP is installed simply as a replacement for the profit sharing plan (see Q. 22:20).

Q. 22:30 May gain on the sale of securities to an ESOP be deferred?

Yes. A stockholder who sells qualified securities (see Q. 22:32) to an ESOP may elect to defer recognition of all or part of the gain, which would otherwise be recognized as long-term capital gain, by purchasing qualified replacement property (see Q. 22:33) within the replacement period (see Q. 22:34). If the stockholder makes an election (see Q. 22:31), gain is immediately taxable only to the extent that the amount realized on the sale exceeds the cost of the replacement property. [IRC § 1042; Reg. § 1.1042-1T, Q&A 1]

Note: If the selling stockholders' interests in the ESOP are in excess of 20 percent of the total account balances for all employees, IRS may consider the sale to the ESOP to be a distribution under Section 301 and not a sale. [Rev. Proc. 87-22, 1987-1 CB 718]

Q. 22:31 Are all taxpayers eligible to elect deferral of gain upon the sale of securities to an ESOP?

All taxpayers except C corporations (see the Glossary) can make the election. [IRC § 1042(c)(7)]

Q. 22:32 What are qualified securities?

Qualified securities are employer securities (see Q. 22:10) that (1) are issued by a domestic corporation that has no readily tradable stock outstanding, and (2) have not been received by the seller as a distribution from a qualified retirement plan or pursuant to an option or other right to acquire stock granted by the employer. [IRC § 1042(c)(1)]

Q. 22:33 What is qualified replacement property?

Qualified replacement property is any security issued by a domestic operating corporation that did not have passive investment income (e.g., rents, royalties, dividends, or interest) that exceeded 25 percent of its gross receipts in its taxable year preceding the purchase. Securities of the corporation that issued the employer securities (see Q. 22:10), and of any corporation that is a member of a controlled group of corporations with such corporation (see Q. 4:34), cannot be qualified replacement property. An operating corporation is a corporation that uses more than 50 percent of its assets in the active conduct of a trade or business. Banks and insurance companies are considered operating corporations. [IRC §§ 409(l) and 1042(c)(4)]

Q. 22:34 What is the replacement period?

The replacement period is the period beginning three months before the date of sale to the ESOP and ending 12 months after the sale. The qualified replacement property (see Q. 22:33) must be purchased during this period. [IRC § 1042(c)(3); Reg. § 1.1042-1T, Q&A 3(c)]

Q. 22:35 What other conditions apply before the deferral of gain is permitted?

After the sale, the ESOP must own at least 30 percent of either (1) each class of outstanding stock of the corporation, or (2) the total value of all outstanding stock of the corporation. Also, for sales after July 10, 1989, the selling shareholder must have held the stock for at least three years. As part of the election (see Q. 22:36), the selling shareholder must file with IRS a verified written statement of the corporation sponsoring the ESOP, consenting to the application of the excise taxes on early dispositions and prohibited allocations of the qualified securities (see Q. 22:41 through Q. 22:43). [IRC § 1042(b); Reg. § 1.1042-1T, Q&A 2(a)]

Q. 22:36 How does the selling shareholder elect not to recognize gain?

The election not to recognize the gain realized upon the sale of qualified securities (see Q. 22:32) is made in a statement of election attached to the selling shareholder's income tax return filed on or before the due date (including extensions) for the taxable year in which the sale occurs. The election is irrevocable. If the selling shareholder does not make a timely election, the shareholder may not subsequently make an election on an amended return or otherwise. [*Letter Ruling 8932048*]

The statement of election must provide that the selling shareholder elects to treat the sale of securities as a sale of qualified securities and must contain the following information:

- Description of the qualified securities sold, including the type and number of shares;
- Date of the sale of the qualified securities;
- Adjusted basis of the qualified securities;
- Amount realized upon the sale of the qualified securities;
- Identity of the ESOP to which the qualified securities were sold; and
- Names and taxpayer identification numbers of the others involved if the sale was part of a single interrelated transaction including other sales of qualified securities, and the number of shares sold by the other sellers.

If the selling shareholder has purchased qualified replacement property (see Q. 22:33) at the time of the election, a statement of purchase must be attached to the statement of election. The statement of purchase must describe the qualified replacement property, give the date of the purchase and the cost of the property, declare such property to be the qualified replacement property, and be notarized within 30 days after the purchase of the qualified replacement property.

If the selling shareholder has not purchased qualified replacement property at the time of the filing of the statement of election, the notarized statement of purchase described above must be attached to the shareholder's income tax return filed for the following taxable year. The statement of purchase must be filed with the IRS District where the election was originally filed if the return is not filed with such District. [IRC § 1042(a)(1); Reg. § 1.1042-1T, Q&A 3]

IRS ruled that an election that substantially complied with the rules was valid even though the notarized statement did not declare that the property purchased with the sales proceeds was intended to be qualified replacement property. [*Letter Ruling 9028082*]

Q. 22:37 What is the basis of qualified replacement property?

If the selling shareholder makes an election not to recognize the gain, the basis of the qualified replacement property (see Q. 22:33) purchased during the replacement period (see Q. 22:34) is reduced by an amount equal to the amount of gain that was not recognized. If more than one item of qualified replacement property is purchased, the basis of each item is reduced by an amount determined by multiplying the total gain not recognized by a fraction whose numerator is the cost of such item of property and whose denominator is the total cost of all such items of property. [IRC § 1042(d); Reg. § 1.1042-1T, Q&A 4]

Q. 22:38 What happens if the taxpayer who elects nonrecognition treatment later disposes of the qualified replacement property?

If the taxpayer disposes of any qualified replacement property (see Q. 22:33), gain must be recognized unless exempted (see Q. 22:39), to the extent not previously recognized in connection with the acquisition of the qualified replacement property, notwithstanding any other provision of the law that might defer recognition. A special recapture rule applies if the taxpayer controls the corporation that issued the qualified replacement property and the corporation disposes of a substantial portion of its assets other than in the ordinary course of its trade or business. [IRC § 1042(e)]

Q. 22:39 Do all dispositions of qualified replacement property result in the recapture of gain?

No. The following dispositions are exempted from the recapture provisions:

- Dispositions upon death;
- Dispositions by gift;

- Subsequent sales of the qualified replacement property to an ESOP pursuant to Section 1042; and

- Transfers in a corporate reorganization, provided no corporation involved in the reorganization is controlled by the taxpayer holding the qualified replacement property.

[IRC § 1042(e)(3)]

Q. 22:40 What is the statute of limitations when a selling shareholder elects nonrecognition of the gain on the sale of qualified securities?

If any gain is realized, but not recognized, by the selling shareholder on the sale of any qualified securities (see Q. 22:32), the statute of limitations with respect to such nonrecognized gain will not expire until three years from the date of IRS receipt of:

- A notarized statement of purchase that includes the cost of the qualified replacement property (see Q. 22:36);

- A written statement of the selling shareholder's intent not to purchase qualified replacement property (see Q. 22:33) within the replacement period (see Q. 22:34); or

- A written statement of the selling shareholder's failure to purchase qualified replacement property within the replacement period.

If the selling shareholder files a statement of intent not to purchase or failure to purchase qualified replacement property, the statement must be accompanied, if appropriate, by an amended return for the taxable year in which the gain from the sale of the qualified securities was realized. The amended return must report any gain from the sale of qualified securities that is required to be recognized in the taxable year in which the gain was realized due to a failure to meet the nonrecognition requirements. [IRC § 1042(f); Reg. § 1.1042-1T, Q&A 5]

Q. 22:41 What happens if the ESOP disposes of qualified securities within three years of their acquisition?

An excise tax is imposed on the amount realized on the disposition (see Q. 22:42) of qualified securities (see Q. 22:32) if:

- The ESOP acquires any qualified securities in a sale for which nonrecognition treatment was elected (see Q. 22:36);
- The ESOP disposes of any of such qualified securities during the three-year period after the date on which any qualified securities were acquired; and
- Either (1) the total number of shares of employer securities (see Q. 22:10) held by the ESOP after such disposition is less than the total number of shares of employer securities held immediately after the sale for which nonrecognition treatment was elected, or (2) the value of the employer securities held by the ESOP immediately after such disposition is less than 30 percent of the total value of all employer securities outstanding at that time.

[IRC § 4978(a); Reg. § 54.4978-1T, Q&A 1]

Q. 22:42 What is the amount of the excise tax on the disposition of qualified securities?

The tax is 10 percent of the amount realized on the disposition that is allocable to qualified securities acquired within the three-year period following their acquisition. [IRC § 4978(b); Reg. § 54.4978-1T, Q&A 2]

A disposition is any sale, exchange, or distribution. However, the excise tax will not apply to any disposition of qualified securities that is made by reason of:

- Death of the employee;
- Retirement of the employee after the employee has attained age 59½;
- Disability of the employee; or
- Separation from service by the employee for any period that results in a one-year break in service (see Q. 4:10).

In addition, dispositions necessary to comply with the diversification requirements (see Q. 22:48) and exchanges pursuant to corporate reorganizations will not trigger the excise tax. [IRC § 4978(d); Reg. § 54.4978-1T, Q&A 3]

The excise tax is imposed on the corporation or corporations that made the verified written statement of consent to the application of such excise tax on the disposition of employer securities (see Q. 22:36). [IRC § 4978(c); Reg. § 54.4978-1T, Q&A 4]

Q. 22:43 Are there any restrictions on the allocation of employer securities acquired by the ESOP in a transaction in which the seller elected nonrecognition of gain?

Yes. None of the stock acquired by the ESOP in a nonrecognition transaction may be directly or indirectly allocated to or accrue to the benefit of the selling shareholder or a member of the shareholder's family during the nonallocation period (see Q. 22:27), or to an owner of more than 25 percent of any class of employer stock at any time.

For purposes of determining whether the prohibition against an accrual of qualified securities (see Q. 22:32) is satisfied, the allocation of any contributions or other assets that are not attributable to qualified securities sold to the ESOP must be made without regard to the allocation of the qualified securities. In effect, this allocation restriction operates to prohibit any direct or indirect accrual of benefits under all qualified retirement plans of an employer. [IRC § 409(n); Reg. § 1.1042-1T, Q&A 2(c)]

> **Example.** Alex, Bob, and Carol own 50, 25, and 25 shares, respectively, of the 100 outstanding shares of common stock of Carol Corporation. The corporation establishes an ESOP that obtains a loan, and the loan proceeds are used to purchase the 100 shares of qualified securities from Alex, Bob, and Carol, all of whom elect nonrecognition treatment with respect to the gain realized on their sale of such securities. No part of the assets of the ESOP attributable to the 100 shares of qualified securities may accrue under the ESOP for the benefit of Bob or Carol during the nonallocation period or to Alex at any time. Those restrictions also apply to any person who is a member of their families. Furthermore, no other assets of the ESOP may accrue to the benefit of such individuals in lieu of the receipt of assets attributable to such qualified securities.

The prohibited allocation is treated as a distribution to the person receiving such allocation. Also, there is an excise tax imposed on the employer equal to 50 percent of the amount involved in a prohibited allocation of qualified securities acquired by an ESOP after October 22, 1986. [IRC §§ 409(n)(2) and 4979A]

Q. 22:44 How can an ESOP be used to facilitate a buyout of shareholders in a closely held corporation?

An ESOP can be used to repurchase all or a portion of the stock of minority shareholders, inactive shareholders, and outside shareholders. In these instances, the primary advantage is that the corporation repurchases the shares with pretax dollars. From the minority shareholder's point of view, it is generally irrelevant whether the shares are purchased by the company or by the ESOP, since the shareholder would generally be entitled to the same tax treatment in either case. However, the sale of the stock to the ESOP is more likely to be treated as a sale (and not a distribution of property) than a sale of stock to the company. [Letter Ruling 8931040]

The repurchase of stock from existing shareholders can be financed in a number of ways, depending on the size of the payroll, the assets of the ESOP, and the needs and objectives of the selling shareholder. If the selling shareholder needs immediate liquidity, the ESOP may use any cash on hand and borrow funds either from the company or from an outside lender to purchase the shareholder's stock for cash.

If the selling shareholder does not need immediate liquidity, the shareholder may prefer to receive interest by selling the stock to the ESOP on an installment-sale basis in return for an interest-bearing note. An installment sale has the advantages of spreading out the tax over a number of years and fixing the price of the shares at the time of the sale.

Finally, the shareholder may simply sell a portion of the shares each year on a serial-sale basis. This is the approach usually taken when the shareholder is not yet ready to sell a block of stock at one time.

Note: In order to meet qualification requirements and avoid a prohibited transaction, an independent appraiser must determine the purchase price in each transaction on the basis of the stock's fair market value at the time of sale. [IRC § 401(a)(28)(C) and 4975(d)(13); ERISA § 408(e)]

Q. 22:45 How can an ESOP be used to finance a business?

Under conventional financing, a corporation that needs to raise $1 million for working capital or expansion purposes borrows the funds from a bank or other lender and repays the loan with after-tax dollars. Although the interest component of each debt payment is a deductible expense to the corporation, the principal repayment is not deductible and is, therefore, considered an after-tax payment.

By use of an ESOP, it is possible to arrange the financing so that both the interest and principal repayments are tax deductible. This is accomplished either by having the ESOP rather than the corporation borrow the $1 million or by having the corporation reloan the proceeds to the ESOP. The ESOP uses the loan proceeds to purchase $1 million worth of newly issued stock from the company. The company has the $1 million needed for working capital or expansion purposes, and the ESOP owns $1 million worth of company stock. Thereafter, the company may make an annual tax-deductible contribution to the plan consisting of (1) an amount of up to 25 percent of covered payroll for the purpose of repaying the loan principal, plus (2) an unlimited amount used to pay interest on the loan. [IRC § 404(a)(9)]

In the case of a typical private company, the lender may demand both a pledge agreement, pledging the shares of stock as collateral for the loan, and a guarantee agreement from the corporation. Under the guarantee agreement, the corporation agrees to make annual contributions to the ESOP sufficient to amortize the loan and, in the event that the corporation fails to make such contributions, to pay the loan directly.

See Q. 22:5 through Q. 22:9 for a discussion of the 50 percent interest exclusion available to certain lenders.

Q. 22:46 May an ESOP enter into an agreement obligating itself to purchase stock when a shareholder dies?

No. An ESOP may, however, be given an option to buy stock when the shareholder dies. [Reg. § 54.4975-11(a)(7)(i)]

Q. 22:47 Must plan participants be given voting rights with respect to their stock?

If the employer securities (see Q. 22:10) are registered with the Securities and Exchange Commission (SEC), participants must be given full voting rights with respect to stock allocated to their accounts.

An ESOP maintained by an employer that does not have registration-type securities (e.g., a closely held corporation) is required to pass through voting rights to participants with stock allocated to their accounts only with respect to any corporate merger or consolidation, recapitalization, reclassification, liquidation, dissolution, sale of substantially all assets of a trade or business, or other similar transaction prescribed by regulations. The plan may authorize the trustees of an ESOP maintained by such an employer to vote such allocated stock on a one vote per participant basis. [IRC § 409(e)]

These voting requirements do not apply to stock held by the ESOP in a suspense account, i.e., stock not yet allocated to participants. The trustees have discretion in voting unallocated stock and allocated stock not subject to the pass-through rule, but they must vote such stock in accordance with their fiduciary duty to plan participants and beneficiaries (see Q. 17:10).

Q. 22:48 What is diversification of investments in an ESOP?

A qualified participant (see Q. 22:49) in an ESOP must be permitted to direct the ESOP as to the investment of up to 25 percent of his or her account during the 90-day period following each plan year in the qualified election period (see Q. 22:50). With the final diversification election during the qualified election period, a participant may elect to diversify up to 50 percent of his or her account. [IRC § 401(a)(28)(B)]

Q. 22:49 Who is a qualified participant?

A qualified participant is any employee who has completed at least ten years of participation in the ESOP and has attained age 55. [IRC § 401(a)(28)(B)(iii)]

Q. 22:50 What is the qualified election period?

The qualified election period is the six-plan-year period beginning with the plan year after the first plan year beginning after 1986 in which the employee is a qualified participant (see Q. 22:49). [IRC § 401(a)(28)(B)(iv)]

Q. 22:51 What must an ESOP do to satisfy the diversification requirements?

A qualified participant (see Q. 22:49) must be given the opportunity to make a diversification election within 90 days after the close of each plan year within the qualified election period (see Q. 22:50) with respect to a cumulative amount of at least 25 percent of his or her account (50% for the last election period). The ESOP can satisfy this requirement by offering any of the following:

1. To distribute all or part of the amount subject to the diversification election;

2. At least three other distinct investment options; or

3. To transfer the portion of the account balance subject to the diversification election to another qualified defined contribution plan (see Q. 2:2) of the employer that offers at least three investment options.

The ESOP must complete diversification in accordance with a diversification election within 90 days after the end of the period during which the election could be made for the plan year. [IRC § 401(a)(28)(B)(ii); Notice 88-56, 1988-1 CB 540, Q 13]

Q. 22:52 What is the effect of the diversification or distribution of a participant's employer securities?

Amounts diversified pursuant to a diversification election are generally treated as amounts not held by an ESOP, and are no longer subject to the statutory provisions governing amounts held by an ESOP. Thus, for example, a qualified participant cannot demand that the distribution of diversified amounts be made in the form of employer securities. [Notice 88-56, 1988-1 CB 540, Q 16]

Amounts distributed in satisfaction of the diversification requirements that consist of employer securities are subject to a participant's put option (see Q. 22:1). Distributions in satisfaction of the
diversification requirements do not violate the restrictions regarding
distributions before a participant's termination of employment or
certain other events. [Notice 88-56, 1988-1 CB 540, Q 14; see IRC §
409(h)]

Q. 22:53 Are all employer securities held by an ESOP subject to diversification?

No. Only employer securities acquired by or contributed to an
ESOP after December 31, 1986 are subject to the diversification
requirements. Therefore, employer securities allocated to participant
accounts after December 31, 1986 will not be subject to diversification if they were acquired or contributed before that date. [Notice 88-
56, 1988-1 CB 540, Q 1]

Also, if an ESOP received cash contributions prior to January 1,
1987, and thereafter—but within certain time limits—used the contributions to acquire employer securities, those securities would be
deemed to have been acquired before January 1, 1987, and would
not be subject to the diversification rules. [Notice 88-56, 1988-1 CB
540, Q 3]

Q. 22:54 Are dividends paid to an ESOP subject to the diversification rules?

Yes. Dividends paid after December 31, 1986, in the form of
employer securities, or in cash or other property used to acquire
employer securities, are subject to the diversification rules. This will
be true even though the dividends are paid with respect to employer
securities acquired by the ESOP before January 1, 1987. [Notice 88-
56, 1988-1 CB 540, Q 1]

However, the diversification rules will not apply to securities
acquired with cash dividends paid before January 1, 1987, if the
acquisition occurred within 60 days of the date of payment of the
dividend. [Notice 88-56, 1988-1 CB 540, Q 1 and Q 3]

Q. 22:55   How is the determination made as to which employer securities are subject to diversification?

An ESOP may separately account for employer securities contributed or acquired after December 31, 1986, and those contributed before January 1, 1987. If the ESOP does not maintain separate accounts for securities based on the date of acquisition, any securities allocated after 1986 will be presumed to consist, first, of securities acquired or contributed after 1986, and second, of securities acquired or contributed before 1987. [*Notice 88-56*, 1988-1 CB 540, Q 4]

An ESOP may, under certain circumstances, use an alternative formula to determine the portion of a qualified participant's (see Q. 22:49) account attributable to employer securities acquired or contributed after December 31, 1986. Under this formula, the number of securities in a qualified participant's account deemed acquired or contributed after December 31, 1986, is determined by multiplying the number of shares allocated to a qualified participant's account by a fraction representing, as of the plan valuation date closest to the date on which the individual becomes a qualified participant, the portion of the total shares that were acquired by or contributed to the ESOP after December 31, 1986. This formula is available only if the IRS model plan amendments to conform to the TRA '86 changes were adopted by the ESOP sponsor on or before January 1, 1989. [*Notice 88-56*, 1988-1 CB 540, Q 5; *Notice 87-2*, 1987-1 CB 396]

> **Example.** ABC Corporation adopted the model plan amendments with respect to its ESOP. On January 1, 1989—the plan's valuation date—the ESOP holds 100,000 shares of ABC Corporation's stock. Of those 100,000 shares, 75,000 were acquired by the ESOP after December 31, 1986. Carol, a participant in the ESOP with 40 shares allocated to her account, becomes a qualified participant on January 15, 1989. The number of shares allocated to Carol's account that are subject to the diversification requirements is 30. If Carol does not elect to diversify within 90 days after the close of the 1989 plan year, and eight more shares are allocated to her account on January 1, 1990, the number of shares in her account subject to diversification increases to 36. [*Notice 88-56*, 1988-1 CB 540, Q 9]

Q. 22:56 May any qualified participants in ESOPs that hold employer securities acquired after December 31, 1986 be excluded from making the diversification election?

Yes. If an ESOP holds and allocates to a qualified participant's account a *de minimis* amount of employer securities acquired after December 31, 1986, it will not be required to offer diversification to that participant. A fair market value of $500 or less will be considered to be a *de minimis* amount for this purpose, although an ESOP may elect to use a lower threshold. If the *de minimis* level is exceeded later in the qualified election period, then all employer securities allocated to the qualified participant that were acquired or contributed after December 31, 1986, are subject to diversification. [Notice 88-56, 1988-1 CB 540, Q 7 and Q 8]

Q. 22:57 May employer securities acquired before 1987 be diversified?

Yes. The shares diversified need not be those actually acquired after 1986. The number of shares that must be available for diversification is nevertheless determined by the number of shares acquired or contributed after December 31, 1986. The diversified shares, however, must be employer securities that, immediately prior to diversification, were subject to the put option and right to demand requirements of Section 409(h). [Notice 88-56, 1988-1 CB 540, Q 10]

Q. 22:58 May an ESOP permit a qualified participant to elect diversification of amounts in excess of that required by statute?

Yes, an ESOP may permit diversification of amounts in excess of the minimum requirements. However, such amounts are not treated as available for diversification or as diversified in accordance with Section 401(a)(28)(B). Amounts in excess of the minimum diversification requirements remain subject to the participant's right under Section 409(h) to demand distribution in the form of employer securities. [Notice 88-56, 1988-1 CB 540, Q 11]

Q. 22:59   Is a loan from a shareholder to an ESOP a prohibited transaction?

Not necessarily. Although ERISA generally prohibits loans (or loan guarantees) between a qualified retirement plan and a disqualified person (a 10% or more shareholder, for example), a loan (or a loan guarantee) by a disqualified person to an ESOP is not a prohibited transaction (see Q. 18:1) if the loan qualifies as an exempt loan (see Q. 22:4). [ERISA § 408(b)(3); IRC § 4975(d)(3)]

Q. 22:60   Must distributions under an ESOP commence by specified dates?

Yes. As a qualification requirement, with regard to distributions attributable to stock acquired after December 31, 1986, an ESOP must provide that, if a participant elects (and, if applicable, the participant's spouse consents), the distribution of the participant's account balance will begin not later than one year after the end of the plan year

- In which the individual terminates employment by reason of reaching retirement age, disability, or death; or
- That is the fifth plan year following the plan year in which the individual otherwise terminates employment (unless the individual is reemployed by the employer before such time).

For purposes of this rule, the individual's account balance is deemed not to include any employer securities acquired with the proceeds of an exempt loan (see Q. 22:4) until the end of the plan year in which such loan is repaid in full. In addition to these requirements, the ESOP must comply with the minimum distribution requirements (see Q. 9:57). [IRC §§ 401(a)(9), 409(o)(1)(A), and 409(o)(1)(B)]

Q. 22:61   Must distributions under an ESOP be made at certain intervals?

With regard to distributions attributable to stock acquired after December 31, 1986, an ESOP must provide that (unless the participant elects otherwise) the distribution of the participant's account balance will be in substantially equal periodic payments (not less frequently than annually) over a period not longer than five years. If the participant's account balance exceeds $500,000, the distribution period may be extended one year for each $100,000 (or part thereof) by which the account balance exceeds $500,000. However, the distribution period cannot exceed ten years. [IRC § 409(o)(1)(C)]

Q. 22:62   Are distributions from an ESOP subject to the 10 percent additional tax on early distributions?

Yes. However, distributions before January 1, 1990, were exempt from the additional tax if the distributions were attributable to assets that had been invested in employer securities (see Q. 22:10) for the five-plan-year period preceding the plan year in which the distributions were made. [IRC § 72(t)(2)(C)].

ESOP assets will be considered invested in employer securities in a variety of circumstances. If an ESOP receives cash or other assets for employer securities as part of a reorganization, the assets will satisfy the requirement if they are invested in employer securities within 90 days (or an extended period if granted by IRS) of the acquisition of cash or other assets. Cash received by an ESOP as the result of an exempt loan, earnings, dividends, or other cash contributions will satisfy the requirement if invested in employer securities within 60 days of the contribution. Cash or cash equivalents allocated to a participant's account will be deemed to be invested in employer securities if the value of those benefits does not exceed 2 percent of the value of the allocated securities. Also, amounts transferred to an ESOP following a reversion from a terminated defined benefit plan will meet the investment requirement if the amounts are invested in employer securities within 90 days of the transfer. [Notice 88-56, 1988-1 CB 540, Q 18; IRC § 4980(c)(3)]

Q. 22:63   Which factors are used to value employer securities that are not readily tradable?

Employer securities (see Q. 22:10) that are not readily tradable must be valued by an independent appraiser. [IRC § 401(a)(28)(C)]

The valuation of employer securities must be reasonable, written, made in good faith, and based on all relevant factors used to determine fair market value. Relevant factors include:

- Nature of the business and history of the enterprise;
- Economic outlook in general and condition of specific industry;
- Book value of the securities;
- Earning capacity of the company;
- Dividend-paying capacity of the company;
- Existence of goodwill;
- Market price of similar stocks;
- Marketability of securities, including an assessment of the company's ability to meet its put obligations; and
- Existence of a control premium, which means a block of security that provides actual control of the company (control must be actual control that is not dissipated within a short period of time).

[DOL Prop. Reg. § 2510.3-18]

Q. 22:64 Is a participant's interest in an ESOP exempt from bankruptcy?

This matter is unsettled. One court has held that an ESOP that was funded solely through employer contributions and allowed withdrawals only in strictly defined circumstances was exempt. [*In re Pettit*, 61 Bankr. 341 (Bankr. WD Wash. 1986)]

Another court held that an ESOP is exempt only if the ESOP would qualify as a spendthrift trust under state law. In this case, the debtor's interest in the ESOP had arisen solely from the debtor's voluntary contributions and from interest and dividends on such contributions. [*In re Cassada*, 86 Bankr. 541 (Bankr. ED Tenn. 1988)]

Chapter 23

Multiemployer Plans

Many companies maintain qualified retirement plans established under collective bargaining agreements. Frequently, more than one employer is required to contribute to the plan. How these multiemployer plans work, their basic advantages, and the system for guaranteeing benefits are examined in this chapter.

Q. 23:1 What kind of retirement plan is used to provide retirement benefits for union workers?

Retirement plans are subject to collective bargaining. Often a retirement plan negotiated by a union is set up on an industrywide (sometimes regional) basis. An employer, out of necessity or voluntarily, will negotiate to join this industrywide retirement plan. In other cases, the employer may find it possible or desirable to have a separate (individual) retirement plan for its own employees as a result of negotiations with the union.

If the employer decides to go with an individual retirement plan, the plan is virtually identical to those plans adopted in nonunion situations. The only difference is that the retirement plan covers union workers and the benefits result from the collective bargaining process. All of the requirements for qualification as a tax-favored retirement plan that apply to retirement plans that do not cover union employees apply to the individual collectively bargained retirement plan.

If, on the other hand, the employer decides to provide benefits under an industrywide or areawide retirement plan, commonly referred to as a multiemployer plan, an entirely different set of rules applies (in addition to some of the basic requirements). [IRC §§ 413(a) and 413(b); see also ERISA §§ 4201 through 4225] For example, hours of service that are credited to a participant for purposes of eligibility, vesting, and accrual of benefits are determined under different rules. [IRC § 413(b)] The minimum funding requirements applicable to qualified retirement plans are modified. [IRC § 412(b)(7)] Also, the provisions governing plan termination differ greatly from the rules for single-employer plans. [Compare ERISA §§ 4041 and 4041A]

Q. 23:2 What is a multiemployer plan?

Generally speaking, a multiemployer plan is a plan established under a collective bargaining agreement that is maintained by two or more unrelated employers. From a technical or legal standpoint, however, the multiemployer plan is defined as a plan

- To which more than one employer is required to contribute;
- That is maintained under a collective bargaining agreement between an employee organization and more than one employer; and
- That meets any additional requirements that may be issued by DOL.

[ERISA § 3(37); IRC § 414(f)]

The multiemployer plan should be distinguished from the single-employer plan. Although the multiemployer plan is established through negotiations between employers or an association of employers or a trade association and the union representing the plan participants, the single-employer plan is established or maintained by only one employer, either unilaterally or through a collective bargaining agreement. Generally, the sponsoring single employer has the ultimate responsibility for the administration of the plan. In contrast, responsibility for a multiemployer plan lies with a board of trustees comprised of both union and employer representatives. [ERISA § 3(37)(A); Labor-Management Relations Act § 302(c)(5)]

Q. 23:3 What are the basic advantages of a multiemployer plan?

The multiemployer plan has been developed to meet the needs of industries (e.g., construction, transportation, or mining) that usually use craftsmen and draw their employees from a limited pool of workers within a specific geographical area. A multiemployer plan can benefit a particular industry because it:

- Permits mobile employees to take their pension benefits with them when they move from one participating employer to another within the same industry;

- Stabilizes pension costs among participating employers, reducing competitive wrangling for select employees;

- Makes possible economies of scale because of the pooling of pension resources, either increasing benefits or reducing employer costs; and

- Reduces administrative costs through use of experienced and knowledgeable administrators and trustees.

Q. 23:4 How are hours of service credited to an employee under a multiemployer plan?

For purposes of participation and vesting, a multiemployer plan is treated as if all participating employers constitute a single employer. Thus, with certain exceptions, all covered service with an employer participating in the plan as well as all contiguous noncovered service with an employer participating in the plan is taken into account. For purposes of the accrual of benefits, only covered service is counted. [DOL Reg. § 2530.210; IRC §§ 413(a) and 413(b); *Rev. Rul. 85-130*, 1985-2 CB 137]

Q. 23:5 Is a retirement plan maintained by two or more affiliated companies considered a multiemployer plan?

No. In considering whether more than one employer is required to contribute to the plan, employers that are under common control (see Q. 4:34) are considered as only one employer. Thus, a plan that requires contributions from two or more companies that are controlled by the same interests is not a multiemployer plan because only one employer is required to contribute to the plan; multiemployer plans require more than one unrelated employer. (See Q. 23:2.) [ERISA § 3(37)(B)]

Q. 23:6 Are benefits under a multiemployer plan guaranteed?

Yes. PBGC has the authority to insure the benefits of a defined benefit multiemployer plan. Although the multiemployer plan usually combines the features of a defined benefit plan (see Q. 2:3) and a defined contribution plan (see Q. 2:2), i.e., both benefits and contributions are fixed, the courts have said that the multiemployer plan is a defined benefit plan. Therefore, the benefits under a multiemployer plan are guaranteed by PBGC. [*Connolly v. PBGC*, 581 F2d 729 (9th Cir. 1978); *PBGC v. Defoe Shipbuilding Co.*, 639 F2d 311 (6th Cir. 1981)]

Note, however, that the benefits under a multiemployer plan are guaranteed only if the plan becomes insolvent. (See Q. 23:7.) [ERISA § 4022A(a)(2)]

Q. 23:7 When is a multiemployer plan insolvent?

A multiemployer plan is considered insolvent when its available resources are insufficient to pay benefits when due for the plan year or when the plan is determined by the plan sponsor to be insolvent while the plan is in reorganization. The plan's available resources include cash, marketable securities, earnings, payments due from withdrawn employers, and employer contributions, minus reasonable administration expenses and amounts owed to PBGC for financial assistance. [ERISA § 4245]

Q. 23:8 What level of benefits is guaranteed?

The level of guaranteed benefits is generally lower than the guarantees provided under single-employer defined benefit plans. However, benefits accrued through July 29, 1980, that are payable to retirees or beneficiaries as of that date or to vested participants who were within three years of normal retirement age as of that date are guaranteed in accordance with the higher ERISA single-employer rules. [ERISA §§ 4022A(a), 4022A(c), and 4022A(h)]

PBGC now guarantees 100 percent of the first $5 of monthly benefits per year of service. The next $15 of monthly benefits or, if less, the accrual rate over $5 per month per year of service is guaranteed at 75 percent for strong plans and 65 percent for weaker plans. [ERISA § 4022A(c)]

Q. 23:9   What benefits are not guaranteed by PBGC?

PBGC will not guarantee benefits that have been in effect under the multiemployer plan for less than 60 months. Also, benefit improvements that have not been in effect for at least 60 months are not guaranteed.

This differs from coverage provided for single-employer plans, which phases in benefit guarantees of 20 percent a year, with a minimum phase-in of $20 each month, during the five-year period following the implementation of a benefit improvement. [ERISA §§ 4022(b) and 4022A(b)]

Q. 23:10   What is the financial liability of an employer that withdraws from a multiemployer plan?

An employer that withdraws from a multiemployer plan is liable for its proportionate share of unfunded vested benefits (UVBs), determined as of the date of withdrawal. The liability is imposed upon withdrawal without reference to the plan's termination.

The employer's withdrawal liability is based on the plan's total unfunded liability for vested benefits, not the lesser guaranteed benefits that apply to single-employer terminations. The method used to determine the employer's share can vary from plan to plan. (See Q. 23:22.)

The result is that an employer that withdraws from an underfunded multiemployer plan may have to continue to contribute to the plan at approximately the same dollar level after withdrawal as before withdrawal until the liability is fully paid. In some cases, the withdrawing employer can make payments over a 20-year period. (See Q. 23:33.)

Q. 23:11   Can withdrawal liability be assessed against any employer that withdraws from a multiemployer plan?

Withdrawal liability applies only to withdrawals that occur on or after September 26, 1980. The U.S. Supreme Court has ruled that the withdrawal liability provisions of ERISA are constitutional. [*Connolly v. PBGC*, 475 US 211 (1986)]

Q. 23:12   What steps are involved in determining multiemployer plan withdrawal liability?

The withdrawal liability process consists of five phases:

1. Determining whether the employer has withdrawn;
2. Computing the withdrawn employer's share of the plan's UVBs;
3. Determining whether any reductions apply to the withdrawal liability;
4. Notifying the employer of the amount of the withdrawal liability; and
6. Collecting the liability.

[ERISA §§ 4201 and 4202]

Q. 23:13   When is a participating employer considered to have withdrawn from a multiemployer plan?

An employer is considered to have withdrawn, and therefore is subject to withdrawal liability, when it (1) permanently ceases to have an obligation to contribute to the multiemployer plan or (2) permanently ceases all covered operations under the plan.

Special rules apply for determining whether there is a complete or partial withdrawal (see Q. 23:15) of employers in the following industries:

- Building and construction
- Trucking
- Household goods moving
- Public warehousing
- Retail food
- Certain segments of the entertainment industry

[ERISA § 4203]

The key issue is whether the employer's obligation to contribute has ceased. If the employer is no longer obligated to make contributions to the multiemployer plan, it cannot escape withdrawal by either continuing to make payments or getting another company to agree to make contributions on its behalf. [*Connors v. B & W Coal Co.*, 646 F. Supp. 164 (D. DC 1986)] However, the result may be different if another company signs an agreement undertaking the obligation on behalf of the original employer. [*ILGWU Nat'l Retirement Fund v. Distinctive Coat Co.*, 6 EBC 2631 (SD NY 1985)]

In an arbitration, it was held that although the passage of some time may be necessary for a determination of whether a cessation of covered operations is permanent, once it is determined to be permanent, the date of withdrawal will relate back to the date when contributions ceased. [*E.H. Hatfield Enters., Inc. v. UMW 1950 and 1974 Pension Plans*, 9 EBC 1980 (1988) (Jaffe, Arb.)]

Q. 23:14 Can an employer be held liable for withdrawal liability as a result of circumstances such as decertification of the union or a plant closing?

Yes. The issue is whether the employer's obligation to contribute to the multiemployer plan has ceased or whether all covered operations under the plan have ceased. If the answer is yes to either, then the circumstances that led to the cessation of the obligation to contribute or to the cessation of all covered operations are irrelevant. For example, an employer may be subject to withdrawal liability if the employer's employees vote to decertify the union representing them. Similarly, withdrawal liability may be triggered by a plant closing or merger of a facility. [ERISA §§ 4203, 4205, and 4212]

Q. 23:15   Does a participating employer have any liability if there is a partial withdrawal from the multiemployer plan?

Yes. Withdrawal liability applies when a participating employer partially withdraws from the multiemployer plan. Generally, a partial withdrawal occurs when

1. There is at least a 70 percent decline in the employer's contribution base units (for example, hours worked);
2. The employer ceases to have an obligation to contribute to the plan under at least one, but not all, of its collective bargaining agreements and continues the same type of work in the geographical area covered by the agreement; or
3. The employer ceases to have an obligation to contribute to the plan for work performed at one or more, but fewer than all, of its facilities covered under the agreement.

[ERISA § 4205]

Q. 23:16   What is a facility for purposes of a partial withdrawal?

The term facility has been determined by PBGC to be a discrete economic unit of an employer. For example, the term will ordinarily apply to a single retail store rather than to a group of stores in a metropolitan area. [PBGC Opinion Letter Nos. 86-2, 82-33, and 82-22; *May Stern & Co. v. Western Pennsylvania Teamsters and Employers Pension Fund*, 8 EBC 2202 (1987) (Nagle, Arb.)]

Q. 23:17   Is withdrawal liability affected if employers are under common control?

Employers under common control (see Q. 4:34) are considered as only one employer. Withdrawal liability can be assessed against all members of the commonly controlled group, even if only one member of the commonly controlled group is required to contribute to the multiemployer plan. [ERISA § 4001(b); *IUE AFL-CIO Pension Fund v. Barker & Williamson, Inc.,* 788 F2d 118 (3d Cir. 1986); *Board of Trustees of the W. Conference of Teamsters Pension Trust Fund v. Salt Creek Terminals, Inc.,* No. C85-2270R (WD Wash. 1986); *Connors v. Calvert Dev. Co.,* 622 F. Supp. 877 (D. DC 1985)]

Q. 23:18 Does a withdrawal occur if there is a change in business structure?

No, provided the change in corporate structure does not cause an interruption in the employer's contributions or obligations under the multiemployer plan. [ERISA § 4218]

Changes in corporate structure include the following:

- Reorganization involving a mere change in identity, form, or place of organization;
- Liquidation into a parent corporation;
- Merger, consolidation, or division; and
- Change to an unincorporated form of business enterprise.

[ERISA § 4069(b)]

The incorporation of a sole proprietorship or partnership does not constitute a withdrawal if the successor corporation continues to have an obligation to contribute and does so. [PBGC Opinion Letter No. 83-18]

Similarly, changes in the composition of an employer-partnership (e.g., sale of partnership interests to new partners) do not result in a withdrawal if the partnership continues to have an obligation to contribute and continues to honor that obligation. [*Park S. Hotel Corp. v. New York Hotel Trades Council,* 851 F2d 578 (2d Cir. 1988); *Connors v. B & W Coal Co., Inc.,* 646 F. Supp. 164 (D. DC 1986); but see *E.H. Hatfield Enters., Inc. v. UMW 1950 and 1974 Pension Plans,* 9 EBC 1980 (1988) (Jaffe, Arb.)

Q. 23:19   Does a withdrawal occur if there is a suspension of contributions during a labor dispute?

No withdrawal occurs as a result of the temporary suspension of contributions during a labor dispute. However, a withdrawal may occur if the cessation of contributions is permanent even though the cessation occurred during a labor dispute. [ERISA § 4218; PBGC Opinion Letter Nos. 82-21 and 82-2; *Combs v. Adkins Coal Co., Inc.*, 597 F. Supp. 122 (D. DC 1984)]

Q. 23:20   Who determines when a withdrawal from a multiemployer plan occurs?

The plan sponsor determines whether and when an employer has withdrawn from the multiemployer plan. [ERISA §§ 3(16)(B) and 4202]

Q. 23:21   Is a sale of employer assets considered a withdrawal from a multiemployer plan?

If the assets sold by the employer represent all of its covered operations, there may be a complete withdrawal. However, if only part of the employer's operation is sold, a partial withdrawal (see Q. 23:15) may result.

The selling employer is relieved of primary withdrawal liability if the following conditions are satisfied:

- The purchasing company assumes substantially the same contribution obligation;
- The purchasing company posts a bond; and
- The contract of sale provides that the selling employer is secondarily liable if the purchasing company completely or partially withdraws during the following five plan years and fails to pay its withdrawal liability.

Also, the withdrawal liability of the selling employer is subject to a maximum amount. For this special sale of assets exception to apply, the purchaser must be an unrelated party. [ERISA §§ 4204 and 4225]

In one case, the purchasing company continued to contribute on behalf of the selling company's employees pursuant to its own collective bargaining agreement, which was essentially identical to that of the selling employer. The court held that no withdrawal had occurred. [*Dorns Transp., Inc. v. Teamsters Pension Trust Fund of Philadelphia and Vicinity*, 787 F2d 897 (3d Cir. 1986)] In another case the court ruled that when the purchasing company assumed substantially the same contribution obligation as the seller and subsequent events caused a reduction in workforce and contributions, withdrawal liability could not be assessed against the selling employer because the sale of assets did not cause the reduction in contributions and the reduction was neither abusive nor significantly harmful to the plan. [*I.A.M. Nat'l Pension Fund Benefit Plan A v. Dravo Corp.*, 7 EBC 1892 (D. DC 1986)]

Q. 23:22   How is a withdrawing employer's share of the multiemployer plan's UVBs computed?

The withdrawing employer's share of the multiemployer plan's UVBs (see Q. 23:10) may be computed under a statutory method or a PBGC-approved alternative method. The four statutory methods are:

1. The presumptive method
2. The modified presumptive method
3. The rolling-five method
4. The direct attribution method

The presumptive method is generally used to determine withdrawal liability unless the plan is amended to permit the use of an alternative method. [ERISA § 4211; PBGC Reg. § 2642.1]

The plan may adopt a statutory alternative method, but such an alternative may not be applied to an employer without its consent if it withdrew before the adoption of the alternative method. [ERISA § 4214(a)]

PBGC has issued a final regulation modifying the presumptive and modified presumptive methods of allocating UVBs, and plans may adopt these modifications without prior PBGC approval. [PBGC Reg. § 2642.5(a)]

Q. 23:23　Can withdrawal liability be imposed if the multiemployer plan has no UVBs?

The courts are split on this issue. One view holds that, under the direct attribution method (see Q. 23:22), UVBs (see Q. 23:10) are calculated based on pension benefits attributable to the withdrawing employer only, and not with respect to the plan as a whole. Since the withdrawing employer is deemed responsible for the vested benefits of its employees, it could accordingly be liable for withdrawal liability even if plan assets would be sufficient to fund this liability. [*Ben Hur Constr. Co. v. Goodwin*, 784 F2d 876 (8th Cir. 1986)]

PBGC criticized this result, and another court agreed. To assess withdrawal liability on employers withdrawing from financially healthy plans is inconsistent with the language and purpose of ERISA. [PBGC Notice of Interpretation, 50 Fed. Reg. 47, 342 (1986); *Berkshire Hathaway, Inc. v. Textile Workers Pension Fund*, 874 F2d 53 (1st Cir. 1989)]

Q. 23:24　May multiemployer plan withdrawal liability be waived or reduced?

There are numerous circumstances under which multiemployer plan withdrawal liability can be either waived or reduced. These waivers are designed to protect small employers and employers in certain industries.

For example, an employer's liability is waived in full if its share is less than the lesser of $50,000 or .75 percent of the total unfunded liability of the plan. If the employer's share is between $50,000 and $150,000, it is reduced but not eliminated. The plan may increase the $50,000 and $150,000 limits to $100,000 and $250,000, respectively. [ERISA § 4209]

Also, waivers of withdrawal liabilities are provided in the construction industry on a mandatory basis when the employer leaves the area. A similar waiver is provided in certain cases for plans covering the entertainment industry. In both cases, there is no withdrawal liability unless the employer either continues to perform the same work in the same jurisdiction or resumes the same work in the same jurisdiction within five years and does not renew its obligation to contribute to the plan. PBGC may exclude certain employers in the entertainment industry from the waiver provision if PBGC determines that it is necessary to protect the plan's participants. [ERISA §§ 4203(b) and 4203(c)]

Employers that withdraw from a plan in the trucking, public warehousing, or household goods moving industries may post a five-year bond instead of making withdrawal liability payments. If PBGC later determines that the employer's withdrawal has substantially damaged the plan, it may require that the bond be paid to the plan. [ERISA § 4203(d)]

Q. 23:25 What happens if an employer reenters a plan after a prior withdrawal?

PBGC has issued regulations providing for the reduction or abatement of withdrawal liability under certain circumstances. A reentering employer that seeks an abatement of its complete withdrawal liability must formally apply for the waiver by the date of the first scheduled withdrawal liability payment that falls due after the employer resumes covered operations under the multiemployer plan. The application must

1. Identify the withdrawn employer and the date it withdrew;
2. Identify the reentered employer and all trades and businesses under common control with the employer as of both the date of withdrawal and the date of resumption of covered operations;
3. Set forth the list of operations for which the employer is obligated to contribute to the plan; and
4. Include the date the employer resumes covered operations.

[ERISA § 4207; PBGC Reg. § 2647.2]

Q. 23:26 What withdrawal liability payments must the employer make while the abatement determination is made?

The reentering employer may post a bond or establish an escrow account equal to 70 percent of the required withdrawal liability payments, in which case, pending the abatement determination, no withdrawal liability payments need be made. [PBGC Reg. § 2647.3]

Q. 23:27 What is required for abatement of an employer's withdrawal liability upon reentry to the multiemployer plan?

An employer that completely withdraws from a multiemployer plan and subsequently reenters the plan will have its liability abated if it resumes covered operations under the plan and assumes a post-entry level of contribution base units (see Q. 23:15) that exceeds 30 percent of the employer's prewithdrawal amount. [PBGC Reg. § 2647.4]

Q. 23:28 What are the effects of an abatement?

If the plan sponsor determines that the reentering employer is eligible for abatement:

- The employer has no obligation to make future withdrawal liability payments to the multiemployer plan with respect to its complete withdrawal;
- The employer's liability for a subsequent withdrawal will be calculated under modified rules;
- The bond will be canceled or amounts held in the escrow account (see Q. 23:26) will be returned to the employer; and
- Any withdrawal liability payments made by the employer will be refunded by the plan.

[PBGC Reg. § 2647.2]

Q. 23:29 What are the effects of a nonabatement?

If the plan sponsor determines that the employer is not eligible for abatement:

- The sponsor notifies the employer of its determination;

- Within 30 days of the sponsor's notice, the bond posted or the escrow account established by the employer (see Q. 23:26) must be paid to the multiemployer plan;

- Within 30 days of the sponsor's notice, the employer must make the balance of the withdrawal liability payment not covered by the bond or escrow account;

- The employer must resume its withdrawal liability payments under the plan schedule; and

- The employer will be treated as a new employer for purposes of any future application rules.

[PBGC Reg. § 2647.2]

Q. 23:30 How can a reentering employer elect nonabatement?

A reentering employer can elect nonabatement by not filing the application for a waiver of its withdrawal liability (see Q. 23:25) upon its reentry to the multiemployer plan. [PBGC Reg. § 2647.2]

Q. 23:31 Does the value of the employer affect the amount of its withdrawal liability?

Yes. If all, or substantially all, of the employer's assets are sold in an arm's-length transaction to an unrelated party and the purchasing company does not assume the withdrawal liability (see Q. 23:21), the employer's withdrawal liability is limited to the greater of (1) the unfunded vested benefits attributable to its employees or (2) a percentage of the employer's liquidation or dissolution value, as determined under the following table:

Liquidation or dissolution value of employer after sale	Percentage
Not more than $2,000,000	30% of the amount
More than $2,000,000, but not more than $4,000,000	$600,000, plus 35% of the amount in excess of $2,000,000

More than $4,000,000, but not more than $6,000,000	$1,300,000, plus 40% of the amount in excess of $4,000,000
More than $6,000,000, but not more than $7,000,000	$2,100,000, plus 45% of the amount in excess of $6,000,000
More than $7,000,000, but not more than $8,000,000	$2,550,000, plus 50% of the amount in excess of $7,000,000
More than $8,000,000, but not more than $9,000,000	$3,050,000, plus 60% of the amount in excess of $8,000,000
More than $9,000,000, but not more than $10,000,000	$3,650,000, plus 70% of the amount in excess of $9,000,000
More than $10,000,000	$4,350,000, plus 80% of the amount in excess of $10,000,000

However, the withdrawal liability is *not* included in determining the liquidation or dissolution value of the employer. [ERISA § 4225]

Q. 23:32 Does an insolvent employer have withdrawal liability?

Yes, but that liability may be limited. An insolvent employer in liquidation or dissolution is liable for the first 50 percent of its normal withdrawal liability, and the remainder of its liability is limited to the employer's value, as of the commencement of liquidation or dissolution, reduced by the first 50 percent. [ERISA § 4225(b)]

An employer is insolvent if its liabilities, including withdrawal liability, exceed its assets as of the commencement of liquidation or dissolution. However, the employer's liquidation or dissolution value is determined without regard to withdrawal liability. [ERISA § 4225(d); *Trustees of Amalgamated Ins. Fund v. Geltman Indus., Inc.,*

784 F2d 926 (9th Cir. 1986)] An employer in chapter 11 reorganization, however, is not said to be in liquidation or dissolution and so may not have its withdrawal liability cut in half. [*Granada Wines, Inc. v. New England Teamsters & Trucking Indus. Pension Fund*, 748 F2d 42 (1st Cir. 1984)]

Q. 23:33　What is the 20-year cap on a withdrawing employer's liability?

The withdrawing employer's liability is paid over the number of years required to amortize the liability in level annual installments. The annual liability payments are basically equal to the annual payments of the employer's plan contributions before withdrawal. If the annual payments will not amortize the withdrawal liability in 20 years, the withdrawal liability is reduced to the amount that can be paid off in the 20-year period. [ERISA § 4219(c)]

Q. 23:34　When is the employer notified of its liability for withdrawal from a multiemployer plan?

The plan sponsor must notify the employer of the amount of its liability "as soon as practicable" after the employer's withdrawal. At the same time, the plan sponsor will demand payment in accordance with a schedule of payments. [ERISA § 4219(b)]

Notice of, and demand for, withdrawal liability made to one member of a commonly controlled group is sufficient to constitute notice and demand to all members of the group. Thus, courts have held an entity within a commonly controlled group liable for the withdrawal liability of another group member even though only the withdrawing employer received actual notice of the withdrawal liability. The rationale for this is that all trades or businesses under common control are treated as a single employer and, thus, notice to one is notice to all. (See Q. 23:17.) [*I.A.M. Nat'l Fund v. Slyman Indus., Inc.*, 901 F2d 127 (DC Cir. 1990); *Teamsters Pension Trust Fund—Board of the W. Conference v. Allyn Transp. Co.*, 832 F2d 502 (9th Cir. 1987); *IUE AFL-CIO Pension Fund v. Barker & Williamson, Inc.*, 788 F2d 118 (3d Cir. 1986); *Central States, Southeast & Southwest Areas Pension Fund v. Bay*, 684 F. Supp. 483 (ED Mich.

1988); *Board of Trustees of the W. Conference of Teamsters Pension Trust Fund v. Salt Creek Terminals, Inc.*, No. C85-2270R (WD Wash. 1986); *Connors v. Calvert Dev. Co.*, 622 F. Supp. 877 (D. DC 1985)]

Q. 23:35 Is the initial determination of a withdrawing employer's liability presumptively correct?

When an employer withdraws from a multiemployer plan, the plan sponsor determines the amount of the withdrawing employer's liability (see Q. 23:10 and Q. 23:12). The initial determination is presumed to be correct. To overcome this presumption, the employer must demonstrate, by a preponderance of evidence, that the actuarial assumptions and methods used by the plan's actuary are unreasonable or that a significant error has been made in applying the assumptions or methods. [ERISA § 4221(a)]

A number of employers have raised unsuccessful constitutional challenges to the presumption of correctness accorded plan sponsors' determinations of withdrawal liability. [*Keith Fulton & Sons, Inc. v. New England Teamsters and Trucking Indus. Pension Fund*, 762 F2d 1137 (1st Cir. 1985); *Board of Trustees of the W. Conference of Teamsters Pension Trust Fund v. Thompson Bldg. Materials, Inc.*, 749 F2d 1396 (9th Cir. 1984); *Washington Star Co. v. International Typographical Union Negotiated Pension Plan*, 729 F2d 1502 (DC Cir. 1984); *Textile Workers Pension Fund v. Standard Dye & Finishing Co.*, 725 F2d 843 (2d Cir. 1984); *Republic Indus., Inc. v. Teamsters Joint Council No. 83 of Virginia Pension Fund*, 718 F2d 628 (4th Cir. 1983); *Centennial State Carpenters Pension Trust Fund v. Woodworkers of Denver, Inc.*, 615 F. Supp. 1063 (D. Colo. 1985).

However, two courts have held that the presumption of correctness of the determination of the amount of the withdrawing employer's liability by plan sponsors who owe a fiduciary duty to the plan and who are therefore biased in favor of the plan is unconstitutional. [*United Retail & Wholesale Employees Teamsters Union Local No. 115 Pension Plan v. Yahn & McDonnell, Inc.*, 787 F2d 128 (3d Cir. 1986), *aff'd per curiam sub nom, PBGC v. Yahn & McDonnell, Inc.*, 481 US 735 (1987); *Robbins v. Pepsi-Cola Metropolitan Bottling Co.*, 636 F. Supp. 641 (ND Ill. 1986)] In affirming the Third Circuit's decision that the presumption in favor of the correctness of a plan sponsor's initial determination regarding withdrawal liability is unconstitutional, the Supreme Court split 4–4. Thus, the decision is binding only with respect to the parties in the case. As a result, the conflict among the circuits continues.

Q. 23:36   May an employer contest the determination of its liability for withdrawing from a multiemployer plan?

Yes. When the employer receives notice of its withdrawal liability from the plan sponsor, it may, within 90 days of its receipt of such notice, ask the plan sponsor to review any specific matter relating to its determination, point out any inaccuracy in their determination, or provide additional information to the trustees bearing on their determination. [ERISA § 4219(b)(2)] The plan sponsor has 120 days to reconsider its earlier determination of withdrawal liability. If it takes no action, then the employer must request arbitration within 60 days after the expiration of the 120-day period or it may be estopped from disputing the amounts owed in a later court action to collect the withdrawal liability (see Q. 23:37). [ERISA § 4221(a)(1)(B)]

The plan sponsor, however, is supposed to undertake a "reasonable review" of the employer's contentions and notify the employer of its decision, setting forth the basis for its decision and the reasons behind any change in its liability determination. The employer must request arbitration within 60 days of its receipt of this second notice even though 120 days may not have lapsed since the employer requested a review of its withdrawal liability. [ERISA § 4221(a)(1)(A)]

The plan sponsor, too, may request arbitration within 60 days of either (1) notification to the employer of its decision after review of the employer's dispute of the liability determination, or (2) the expiration of 120 days after the employer requests review of the plan sponsor's initial determination. Alternatively, both the plan sponsor and the employer may jointly request arbitration within 180 days of the initial demand for payment of withdrawal liability. [ERISA §§ 4219(b) and 4221(a); PBGC Reg. § 2641.2]

Q. 23:37 Does the employer run any risk if it does not demand arbitration of the plan sponsor's claim for withdrawal liability?

Yes. An employer that fails to initiate arbitration within the statutory periods risks being barred from disputing the plan's determination of withdrawal liability in a subsequent court action by the plan sponsor to recover that liability. [*New York State Teamsters Conference Pension & Retirement Fund v. McNicholas Transp. Co.*, 848 F2d 20 (2d Cir. 1988); *ILGWU Nat'l Retirement Fund v. Levy Bros. Frocks, Inc.*, 846 F2d 879 (2d Cir. 1988); *Robbins v. Admiral Merchants Motor Freight, Inc.*, 846 F2d 1054 (7th Cir. 1988); *Teamsters Pension Trust Fund—Board of Trustees v. Allyn Transp. Co.*, 832 F2d 502 (9th Cir 1987); *IAM Nat'l Pension Fund v. Clinton Engines Corp.*, 825 F2d 415 (DC Cir. 1987)]

Additionally, courts will dismiss an employer's action to challenge a determination of withdrawal liability when arbitration has been bypassed. [*Mason and Dixon Tank Lines, Inc. v. Central States, Southeast and Southwest Areas Pension Fund*, 852 F2d 156 (6th Cir. 1988); *Flying Tiger Line v. Teamsters Pension Trust Fund*, 830 F2d 1241 (3d Cir. 1987)]

Even if the employer attempts to initiate arbitration but does not do so properly, i.e., in accordance with the rules of the plan, it may be held to have waived its right to contest the claim. For example, merely expressing a desire for arbitration and requesting information on how to proceed is not the equivalent of initiation of arbitration within the meaning of the plan's rules. [*Robbins v. Braver Lumber and Supply Co.*, No. 85 C 08332 (ND Ill. 1987)]

However, an employer has been permitted to proceed in the absence of arbitration when no factual issues were raised [*I.A.M. Nat'l Pension Fund Benefit Plan C v. Stockton Tri Indus.*, 727 F2d 1204 (DC Cir. 1984)]

Q. 23:38 When are withdrawal liability payments due?

The plan sponsor sets the schedule of payments. The first payment is due 60 days after demand (see Q. 23:34), and subsequent payments are usually made quarterly.

Even if the employer contests the determination of liability either with the plan sponsor or through arbitration, the employer is not relieved of its obligation to begin payment of the withdrawal liability. [ERISA §§ 4219(c)(2), 4219(c)(3), and 4221(d); *DeBreceni v. Merchants Terminal Corp.*, 889 F2d 1 (1st Cir. 1989)]

A default will not occur, however, until 60 days after a demand for payment is made (see Q. 23:39).

If, after review, the plan sponsor or arbitrator determines that the employer has overpaid, the employer is entitled to a lump-sum refund with interest. [PBGC Reg. § 2644.2(d)]

Q. 23:39   What happens if a withdrawal liability payment is missed?

If a payment is not made by the due date, interest is charged until the payment is actually made. A default generally occurs 60 days after the employer gets written notice from the plan sponsor of failure to make a payment when due. If the payment is not made within the 60 days, the entire amount of the withdrawal liability plus interest becomes due immediately. [ERISA § 4219(c)(5); PBGC Reg. §§ 2644.2 and 2644.3; *Local 807 Labor-Management Pension Fund v. ABC Fast Freight Forwarding Corp.*, No. 82 C 3356 (ED NY, March 7, 1984)]

Q. 23:40   Are owners of the employer personally liable for withdrawal liability?

Generally, shareholders of corporations are not personally liable for amounts the employer cannot pay. [*Operating Eng'r Pension Trust v. Reed*, 726 F2d 513 (9th Cir. 1984) but see, *Laborers Clean-Up Contract Admin. Trust Fund v. Uriarte Clean-Up Serv., Inc.*, 736 F2d 516 (9th Cir. 1984)] Controlling or dominant shareholders are not considered employers for withdrawal liability purposes. [*DeBreceni v. Graf Bros. Leasing, Inc.*, 828 F2d 877 (1st Cir. 1987); *Connors v. P & M Coal Co.*, 801 F2d 1373 (DC Cir. 1986)]

However, a state law under which the ten largest shareholders of a closely held corporation can be held liable for unpaid plan contributions was held not to be preempted by ERISA. [*Sasso v. Vachris,* 66 NY2d 28 (1985)]

A corporate officer is not personally liable for withdrawal liability payments solely by virtue of his or her capacity as an officer of the withdrawing employer. [*Connors v. B.M.C. Coal Co.,* 634 F. Supp. 74 (D. DC 1986); *Connors v. Darryll Waggle Constr., Inc.,* 631 F. Supp. 1188 (D. DC 1986)]

Partners or sole proprietors are personally liable, but assets that would be exempt under bankruptcy law are also exempt from satisfaction of the withdrawal liability obligation. [ERISA § 4225(c); *Board of Trustees of the W. Conference of Teamsters Pension Trust Fund v. H.F. Johnson, Inc.,* 830 F2d 1009 (9th Cir. 1987)]

Q. 23:41   Are withdrawal liability claims entitled to priority in bankruptcy proceedings?

It has been held that withdrawal liability is considered a general unsecured claim and is not entitled to priority in bankruptcy proceedings because it is not an administrative expense claim. [*Trustees of the Amalgamated Ins. Fund v. McFarlin's, Inc.,* 789 F2d 98 (2d Cir. 1986)]

Q. 23:42   What is a mass withdrawal from a multiemployer plan?

There are two types of mass withdrawals:

1. The withdrawal of every employer from the plan; and
2. The withdrawal of substantially all employers pursuant to an agreement or arrangement to withdraw.

[PBGC Reg. § 2640.7]

If a mass withdrawal occurs, all withdrawing employers lose the benefit of the deductible amount (see Q. 23:24) and the 20-year cap (see Q. 23:33), and the plan's unfunded vested benefits are fully allocated among all of the withdrawing employers. [ERISA §§ 4209 and 4219(c); PBGC Reg. §§ 2648.1 through 2648.5]

PBGC has issued regulations regarding the administration of multiemployer plans that have terminated by mass withdrawal—that is, the withdrawal of every employer or the cessation of all employers' obligations to contribute to the plan. The rules generally require the sponsor of such a plan to monitor the financial condition of the plan and, depending on the condition of the plan, reduce or suspend benefits or apply to the PBGC for financial assistance. [PBGC Reg. §§ 2675.1 through 2675.44]

Q. 23:43 What is the liability of an employer upon termination of a multiemployer defined benefit plan?

In the case of a multiemployer plan, plan termination no longer means dissolution of the plan, nor does it result in PBGC involvement as the provider of benefits. Instead, termination now means the freezing of the plan's vested benefits and the elimination of further accruals and nonvested benefits or the conversion of the plan into a defined contribution plan. Employers must continue to contribute to the frozen plan in order to fund the plan's unfunded liabilities. The plan administrator must notify PBGC after the effective date of termination. [ERISA § 4041A; PBGC Reg. §§ 2673.2, 2675.1, and 2675.2]

PBGC funds are available only if a plan becomes insolvent (see Q. 23:7). These PBGC funds are only loans and must be repaid. [ERISA §§ 4022A(a) and 4261]

Q. 23:44 May a multiemployer plan exclude some newly adopting employers from withdrawal liability?

Yes. A multiemployer plan may adopt a rule under which an employer may withdraw from the plan without liability within six years after joining the plan or, if less, the number of years required for vesting under the plan. This free-look rule is applicable to the employer only if it (1) contributes less than 2 percent of all employer contributions to the plan each year, and (2) has not previously used this rule with respect to the plan.

In addition, for the free-look rule to be enforceable, the plan must (1) be amended to permit the rule, (2) have an eight-to-one assets-to-benefits payable ratio in the year before the employer joins the plan, and (3) provide that an employee's service before the employer joined the plan will not be counted in determining benefits. Plans primarily covering employees in the building and construction industry are not permitted to adopt the free-look rule. [ERISA § 4210]

Chapter 24

Individual Retirement Plans

Anyone who receives compensation may set aside a modest amount of money each year for retirement in a tax-deferred account known as an individual retirement plan (IRA). However, not all IRA contributions are deductible. This chapter examines how IRAs work.

Q. 24:1 What is an individual retirement plan?

An individual retirement plan is a personal retirement plan. This type of plan allows employees, self-employed individuals, and certain other individuals, whether or not they participate in qualified retirement plans (including Keogh plans, simplified employee pensions (SEPs), tax-sheltered annuities, and government plans) to establish IRAs and make annual contributions to them. For active plan participants, however, these contributions might not be deductible (see Q. 24:7). [IRC §§ 219 and 408]

There are two types of individual retirement plans: (1) individual retirement accounts (see Q. 24:2), and (2) individual retirement annuities (see Q. 24:3). Both types are commonly referred to as IRAs.

A working spouse may set up an IRA for his or her nonworking spouse (see Q. 24:17). In addition, certain divorced or separated persons may make deductible contributions to IRAs even though they receive no wages or salary (see Q. 24:5).

Deductible contributions to an IRA are tax deductible whether or not the individual itemizes deductions. [IRC § 62(a)(7)]

Earnings on all amounts contributed to any IRA accumulate on a tax-deferred basis. [IRC § 408(e)]

Q. 24:2 What are the basic characteristics of an individual retirement account?

An IRA is a trust or custodial account established for the exclusive benefit of an individual and his or her beneficiaries. The trustee (or custodian) must be a bank, thrift institution, insurance company, brokerage firm, or other person who demonstrates to IRS that he or she will administer the account in a manner consistent with the requirements of the law. No part of the account funds can be invested in life insurance contracts. Assets of the account cannot be commingled with other property except if there is a common trust fund or common investment fund. [IRC § 408(a)]

IRA assets should not be invested in collectibles (works of art, rugs, antiques, metals, gems, stamps, coins, or other items of tangible personal property specified by IRS). Amounts invested in collectibles are treated as distributions for tax purposes (that is, taxed as current income; if the individual is under age 59½, a 10 percent penalty tax for a premature withdrawal also applies). However, gold or silver coins issued by the U.S. government or any type of coin issued under the laws of any state will not be considered collectibles. An interest in a portion of a gold coin portfolio is not considered a collectible. [IRC § 408(m); *Letter Ruling 8940067*]

The individual's interest in the IRA must be nonforfeitable. Distributions must satisfy the minimum distribution requirements in order to avoid penalties for insufficient distributions (see Q. 24:30 and Q. 24:31). [IRC §§ 408(a)(4) and 408(a)(6)]

An account that is identified as an IRA and meets the statutory requirements is treated as an IRA, even if the owner later claims it is not an IRA because the owner made an untimely rollover contribution that is an excess contribution (see Q. 24:6). [*Michel,* 58 TCM 1019 (1989)]

Q. 24:3 What are the basic characteristics of an individual retirement annuity?

An individual retirement annuity is an annuity contract or endowment contract issued by an insurance company. However, an endowment contract issued after November 6, 1978 cannot qualify. The contract must be nontransferable and nonforfeitable. Premiums may not be fixed nor may they exceed $2,000 a year. Distributions must satisfy the minimum distribution requirements and must be made by specified dates in order to avoid penalties for insufficient distributions (see Q. 24:30 and Q. 24:31). [IRC § 408(b); Reg. § 1.408-3(e)(ix)]

Participation in a group annuity may be used instead of an individual annuity contract.

Bear in mind, however, that only part of the premium for an endowment contract builds an annuity; the rest buys current life insurance protection. The part of the premium that pays for current life insurance protection is *not* tax deductible. [IRC §§ 219(d)(3), 408(a)(3), and 408(b); *Letter Ruling 8439026*]

> **Example.** Assume the annual premium for an endowment contract issued on October 1, 1978 is $1,700, and $300 of that buys current life insurance. Only $1,400 is considered an IRA contribution. An additional contribution could be made to another IRA to take full advantage of the difference between the $1,400 contribution and the maximum $2,000 annual contribution.

If an individual borrows any money from or against an individual retirement annuity, the annuity contract ceases to be a qualified individual retirement annuity as of the first day of the year. Because of the borrowing, the individual must include in his or her gross income for the year the fair market value of the annuity as of the first day of such year. [IRC § 408(e)(3); *Griswold*, 85 TC 869 (1985)]

Q. 24:4 Who is eligible to set up an IRA?

Any individual under age 70½ receiving compensation may establish an IRA (also see Q. 24:5). [IRC § 219(d)(1)]

An IRA may also be established as a vehicle for deferring taxes on eligible distributions from qualified retirement plans, including distributions received after attainment of age 70½. For details, see Chapter 26.

Q. 24:5 How much can be contributed to an IRA?

Each year an individual may contribute 100 percent of compensation up to a maximum of $2,000 to an IRA. [IRC §§ 219(b), 408(a), and 408(b)]

The contribution limit is $2,250 if a spousal IRA is also established (see Q. 24:17). [IRC § 219(c)(2)] However, there is no dollar limit with respect to a rollover contribution (see Q. 26:2).

Compensation includes taxable alimony and separate maintenance payments. A divorced or separated spouse who receives taxable alimony, but no other compensation, is able to make contributions to an IRA. Deferred compensation and amounts received as a pension or annuity are not treated as compensation and cannot be used as a basis for contributions to an IRA. A separation pay allowance received by an employee is considered deferred compensation for this purpose. Also, a fee paid by a husband to his wife for services rendered in connection with their jointly held investments is not compensation to her. [IRC § 219(f)(1); Reg. § 1.219-1(c); *Letter Rulings 8535001 and 8519051*]

A contribution made to an IRA for the year in which an individual attains age 70½, or any year thereafter, is a nondeductible excess contribution (see Q. 24:6) that cannot be treated as a designated nondeductible IRA contribution (see Q. 24:13). [IRC §§ 219(d)(1) and 408(o)]

An estate cannot make an IRA contribution on behalf of the decedent or to the spousal IRA of the decedent's spouse for the year in which the decedent died. [*Letter Ruling 8439066*]

Q. 24:6 What penalty is imposed on an excess contribution to an IRA?

If an individual contributes more to his or her IRA than the amount allowable (see Q. 24:5), the excess contribution is subject to a 6 percent excise tax. Further, the penalty will be charged each year the excess contribution remains in the IRA. [IRC § 4973]

The individual can avoid the penalty by withdrawing the excess contribution, along with the net income allocable to the excess, before the due date (including extensions) of his or her federal income tax return for the year of the excess contribution. The net income on the excess contribution is treated as gross income for the taxable year in which the excess contribution was made. [IRC §§ 408(d)(4) and 4973(b)]

If the individual does not withdraw the excess contribution before such filing deadline, he or she must pay the 6 percent excise tax for the year of the excess contribution. To avoid the 6 percent excise tax for the following year, the remaining excess contribution can be eliminated by either withdrawing such amount from the IRA or making a contribution for such year equal to the maximum allowable amount (see Q. 24:5) reduced by the remaining excess contribution. [IRC § 4973(b)]

Q. 24:7 Can active participants in qualified retirement plans also make deductible IRA contributions?

Not necessarily. If an individual is an active participant (see Q. 24:9) in a qualified retirement plan for any part of a plan year ending with or within the individual's taxable year, IRA contributions cannot be deducted if the individual's adjusted gross income exceeds certain specified amounts (see Q. 24:10 and Q. 24:11). For married couples (see Q. 24:10), if either spouse is an active participant, both are treated as active participants. [IRC § 219(g)]

Q. 24:8 What is active participation?

Generally, active participation refers to participation in a qualified retirement plan, SEP (see Chapter 25), tax-sheltered annuity, or governmental plan. An individual's status as an active participant must be reported on Form W-2.

Q. 24:9 Who is an active participant?

An active participant in a defined benefit plan (see Q. 2:3) is an individual who participates or meets the eligibility requirements for participation at any time during the plan year ending with or within the individual's taxable year. Thus, an individual is an active participant if the individual is eligible but declines to participate or fails to complete the minimum period of service or to make an employee contribution necessary to accrue a benefit. An individual is not an active participant if the employer has frozen benefit accruals (unless pre-freeze benefit accruals increase as compensation increases). [*Letter Ruling 8948008*]

An individual is an active participant in a money purchase or target benefit pension plan (see Q. 2:4 and Q. 2:5) if an employer contribution or forfeiture is required to be allocated to the individual's account for the plan year ending with or within the individual's taxable year. Thus, an individual who separates from service before the beginning of a calendar year may still be an active participant for such calendar year if, under the terms of the plan, the individual is eligible to receive an allocation for the plan year ending in such calendar year.

An individual is treated as an active participant under a profit sharing or stock bonus plan (see Q. 2:6 and Q. 2:9) if any employer contribution is added or any forfeiture is allocated to the individual's account during the individual's taxable year. A contribution is added to the individual's account on the later of the date the contribution is made or allocated.

An individual is *not* an active participant in a defined contribution plan (see Q. 2:2) if only earnings (rather than contributions or forfeitures) are allocated to the individual's account.

An individual is treated as an active participant for any taxable year in which the individual makes a voluntary or mandatory employee contribution or an elective contribution under a 401(k) plan (see Q. 21:1). But an individual is *not* an active participant merely because he or she is eligible but chooses not to make such elective contribution.

The determination of whether an individual is an active participant is made without regard to whether the individual's rights are nonforfeitable. [IRC § 219(g); *Notice 87-16*, 1987-1 CB 446]

For married couples filing jointly, if either spouse is an active participant under the rules described above, both spouses are treated as active participants for purposes of determining the amount that each may contribute to an IRA. However, in the case of a married couple filing separate tax returns and who do not live together at any time during the taxable year, the active participant status of one spouse will not affect the status of the other spouse. [IRC § 219(g)(4)]

Q. 24:10   What level of income affects an active participant's deduction limitation?

Adjusted gross income over the applicable dollar amount results in a limit on the IRA deduction for active participants. The applicable dollar amounts are:

1. $40,000 for taxpayers filing a joint return;
2. $25,000 for any unmarried taxpayer; and
3. Zero for married individuals filing separate returns.

However, married individuals filing separately who live apart during the entire year are treated as not married for this purpose. [IRC § 219(g); *Notice 87-16*, 1987-1 CB 446]

For purposes of the IRA deduction limit, adjusted gross income is calculated without taking into account any deductible IRA contributions made for the taxable year or certain exclusions for foreign earned income and U.S. savings bond redemptions, but taking into account any taxable Social Security benefits and passive loss limitations applicable to the taxpayer. [IRC § 219(g)(3)]

Q. 24:11   If an individual is an active participant in a qualified retirement plan, what are the applicable IRA deduction limits?

The amount that may be deducted will be the contribution limitation (see Q. 24:5) reduced by an amount that bears the same ratio to the contribution limitation as the amount by which the taxpayer's adjusted gross income exceeds the applicable dollar amount (see Q. 24:10) bears to $10,000. Thus, a married couple with at least one active participant spouse and adjusted gross income of at least 50,000 cannot make a deductible IRA contribution.

> **Example.** Marjorie, an active participant in her employer's qualified retirement plan, is married to Stanley and they file a

joint return. Their adjusted gross income for 1990 is $47,500 and each earns over $2,000. Both Marjorie and Stanley may make a deductible IRA contribution of up to $500, computed as follows:

Adjusted gross income	$47,500
Less: Applicable dollar amount	40,000
Difference	$ 7,500
Reduction in $2,000 limitation 　($2,000 multiplied by $7,500/$10,000)	$ 1,500
Maximum deductible IRA contribution 　($2,000 less $1,500)	$　500

[IRC § 219(g)(2); *Notice 87-16*, 1987-1 CB 446]

The reduction in the $2,000 limitation is rounded to the next lowest $10 in the case of a reduction that is not a multiple of $10. [IRC § 219(g)(2)(C)]

For individuals whose adjusted gross income is not above the level that would totally eliminate a deductible IRA contribution, there is a $200 minimum IRA deduction allowable.

> **Example.** Michael, an unmarried individual who is an active participant in his employer's qualified retirement plan, has adjusted gross income of $34,900. He may make a deductible IRA contribution of $200.

[IRC § 219(g)(2)(B)]

Q. 24:12　May an individual who is ineligible to make a fully deductible IRA contribution make a nondeductible IRA contribution?

Yes. An individual who is ineligible to make a deductible IRA contribution to the full extent of the contribution limitation (see Q. 24:5) may make designated nondeductible IRA contributions (see Q. 24:13). [IRC § 408(o)]

Q. 24:13 What are designated nondeductible IRA contributions?

Designated nondeductible IRA contributions are nondeductible IRA contributions to the extent of the excess of (1) the lesser of $2,000 (or $2,250 when a spousal IRA is also involved) or 100 percent of compensation over (2) the IRA deduction limit with respect to the taxpayer (but see Q. 24:14). [IRC § 408(o)]

Q. 24:14 May an individual who is eligible to make a deductible IRA contribution elect to treat such a contribution as nondeductible?

Yes. An individual is permitted to make such an election and might do so if, for example, the individual had no taxable income for the year after taking into account other deductions. [IRC § 408(o)(2)(B)(ii)]

Q. 24:15 Is an individual required to report designated nondeductible contributions on his or her tax return?

Yes. An individual who makes a designated nondeductible contribution (see Q. 24:13) to an IRA (or who receives any amount from an IRA) must include the following information on his or her income tax return for the applicable taxable year:

1. The amount of designated nondeductible contributions for the year;
2. The amount of distributions from IRAs for the year;
3. The excess (if any) of (a) the aggregate amount of designated nondeductible contributions for all preceding taxable years, over (b) the aggregate amount of distributions from IRAs that were excludable from gross income for such taxable years;
4. The aggregate balance of all IRAs of the individual as of the end of the taxable year; and

5. Such other information as IRS may prescribe.

[IRC § 408(o)(4)]

If the required information is not provided on the individual's tax return for a taxable year, all IRA contributions are considered to have been deductible and, therefore, are taxable upon withdrawal from the IRA. However, an individual may change a designation of a contribution from deductible to nondeductible (or vice versa) by filing an amended return before the expiration of the statute of limitations on assessment of tax for such year. [Notice 87-16, 1987-1 CB 446]

There is a $50 penalty for failure to report the required information, and a $100 penalty for overstating the amount of designated nondeductible contributions—unless the taxpayer can demonstrate that the error was due to reasonable cause. [IRC §§ 408(o)(4) and 6693(b)]

Q. 24:16   What is the tax treatment of IRA withdrawals by an individual who has previously made both deductible and nondeductible contributions?

The amount includible in an individual's income is determined by subtracting from the amount of the IRA withdrawal an amount that bears the same ratio to the amount withdrawn as the individual's aggregate nondeductible IRA contributions bear to the aggregate balance of all IRAs of the individual (including rollover IRAs and SEPs).

The formula for determining the nontaxable portion of an IRA distribution is:

$$\frac{\text{Total nondeductible contributions}}{\substack{\text{Aggregate IRA} \\ \text{year-end account} \\ \text{balances plus} \\ \text{amount of IRA} \\ \text{distributions}}} \times \text{IRA distribution} = \substack{\text{Nontaxable portion} \\ \text{of distribution}}$$

[Notice 87-16, 1987-1 CB 446]

Example. Assume Irene has made aggregate deductible IRA contributions into two IRAs for 1988 and 1989 of $1,800 and aggregate nondeductible IRA contributions of $2,200 during those two years. In January 1990, Irene withdraws $1,000 from one IRA. At the end of 1990, the account balance of both IRAs is $4,500. Of the $1,000 withdrawn during 1990, $400 is treated as a partial return of nondeductible contributions, calculated as follows:

$$\frac{\text{Total nondeductible contributions (\$2,200)}}{\text{Aggregate IRA year-end account balances (\$4,500) plus amount of IRA distributions during year (\$1,000)}} = \frac{\$2,200}{\$5,500} \times \$1,000 = \$400$$

The balance of the withdrawn amount ($1,000 − $400 = $600) is includible in income on Irene's 1990 tax return.

For further discussion of the taxability of withdrawals from IRAs, see Q. 24:32.

Q. 24:17 What is a spousal IRA?

If only one spouse is working, the working spouse may make an additional contribution to an IRA (a spousal IRA) on behalf of the nonworking spouse (provided a joint income tax return is filed). A spousal IRA is available even if both spouses work, if the spouse for whom the spousal IRA is set up consents to being treated as having no compensation, for IRA purposes, for the taxable year. The total amount of allowable annual contributions to the working spouse's IRA and to the spousal IRA is $2,250 (or 100% of the working spouse's earnings if less). The contributions to both IRAs need not be split equally between the spouses. However, the maximum IRA contribution on behalf of either spouse is $2,000. [IRC § 219(c); *Harris*, 51 TCM 1154 (1986)]

If either spouse is an active participant in a qualified retirement plan, the allowable contributions are not fully deductible if the couple's adjusted gross income is more than $40,000 (see Q. 24:10). If the couple's adjusted gross income is between $40,000 and $50,000, the deductible portion of the allowable contributions

($2,250) is proportionately reduced (see Q. 24:11). None of the contribution is deductible if the couple's adjusted gross income is $50,000 or more. [IRC § 219(g)]

What happens if the working spouse has reached age 70½? As long as the working spouse continues to receive compensation, he or she can make deductible contributions to the nonworking spouse's IRA. The nonworking spouse must, however, be less than age 70½, and the maximum contribution on behalf of the nonworking spouse is $2,000. [IRC § 219(d)(1)]

What happens if the working spouse dies? A contribution may be made to a spousal IRA by the surviving spouse if a joint income tax return is filed for the year for which the contribution was made. [*Letter Ruling 8527083*]

Q. 24:18 When must IRA contributions be made?

A deductible or nondeductible contribution to an IRA must be made by the due date, not including extensions, for filing the return. [IRC § 219(f)(3)]

> **Example.** Jay wants to make a contribution to his IRA for 1990. He can do so any time in 1990 or he can wait until his 1990 tax return is due, April 15, 1991. Even if he obtains an extension to file his return to August 15, 1991, his IRA contribution is due by April 15, 1991.

An IRA contribution is timely if it is received by the IRA sponsor in an envelope bearing a post office cancellation date no later than the due date of the individual's federal income tax return, not including extensions. [*Letter Rulings 8536085, 8551065, 8611090,* and *8628047*]

Q. 24:19 Can an IRA deduction be claimed before the contribution is actually made?

Yes, as long as the contribution is made by the due date, not including extensions, for filing the return. [*Rev. Rul. 84-18, 1984-1 CB 88*]

Example. Carol files her 1990 return on February 4, 1991, and claims a deduction of $2,000 for an IRA contribution that she has not made. If she makes the contribution by the due date of the return, April 15, 1991, the deduction is allowed.

Q. 24:20 Does the payment of a fee to the trustee of an IRA reduce the amount otherwise allowable as a contribution to the IRA?

No. The payment of a fee to the trustee for the establishment and maintenance of an IRA, or for various other administrative services performed, is not considered a contribution to an IRA for purposes of the annual contribution limit (see Q. 24:5) or the excess contribution penalty (see Q. 24:6). Moreover, the trustee fees may be deductible as expenses incurred for the production of income. [*Rev. Rul. 84-146*, 1984-2 CB 61; *Letter Rulings 8329049* and *8432109*; IRC § 212]

However, the payment of brokerage commissions incurred for the purchase or sale of IRA assets are considered contributions to the IRA subject to the annual contribution limit. [*Letter Ruling 8711095*; *Rev. Rul. 86-142*, 1986-2 CB 60] This rule also applies to commissions paid to insurance agents attributable to the purchase of individual retirement annuities. [*Letter Ruling 8747072*]

Q. 24:21 Will the receipt of free checking by a customer who directs the IRA to invest in a bank's financial products constitute a prohibited transaction?

Maybe. IRS has announced that it will not raise issues concerning possible prohibited transactions arising from services offered by banks to IRA holders until DOL rules on a pending administrative exemption request on the issue. Previously, DOL had rendered an opinion that a prohibited transaction occurred when an IRA holder, who is a fiduciary with respect to the IRA, used IRA assets to obtain valuable services such as free checking. [IRC § 4975(c)(1); *Announcement 90-1*, 1990-2 IRB; DOL Advisory Opinion No. 89-12A]

Q. 24:22   May an individual borrow money to fund an IRA?

Yes. The deductibility of the interest paid on the loan is determined under the general rules applicable to interest payments. The interest payments are not subject to the rule prohibiting interest deductions on loans incurred to purchase or carry tax-exempt assets because the income earned on the IRA is tax-deferred, not tax-exempt. [IRC § 163; Letter Ruling 8527082]

Q. 24:23   May an individual make a contribution to an IRA with a credit card?

Yes, according to IRS. An individual established an IRA at a bank and funded the IRA with a cash advance drawn on his bank credit card. The bank executed the transaction pursuant to written instructions of the individual. IRS ruled that if, by April 15, a cash advance was drawn on the individual's credit card, credited to his IRA, and designated as a contribution for the previous year, the individual could deduct the contribution for the previous year, provided the bank honored its obligation to make payment on the credit card cash advance. [Letter Ruling 8622051]

Q. 24:24   What is an employer-sponsored IRA?

An employer may establish IRAs for its employees (and for the nonworking spouses of these employees). The contributions are deductible by the employer and includible as compensation income by the employee, subject to Social Security and unemployment taxes. Whether the employee can deduct the contribution is determined under the rules generally applicable to IRA contributions (see Q. 24:7 through Q. 24:11). The assets of the employer-sponsored IRAs may be held in a common trust fund. [IRC §§ 219(f)(5) and 408(c)]

If the employer contributes less than the maximum allowed (100% of compensation up to $2,000; increased to $2,250 in the case of a spousal IRA), the employee can contribute the difference.

> **Example.** Michael's employer contributes $1,500 to an IRA on his behalf. Because Michael earns more than $2,000 a year, the

maximum allowable contribution is $2,000. Michael can contribute an additional $500 to the IRA.

There is no requirement that an employer-sponsored IRA cover a certain number or group of employees. In fact, the employer may discriminate in favor of highly compensated employees. [IRC § 408(c)]

Q. 24:25 Can employer-sponsored IRAs help an employer that has a qualified retirement plan satisfy coverage requirements?

No. An employer maintaining a qualified retirement plan cannot satisfy the coverage requirements that must be met by taking into consideration the fact that employees not covered under the plan are covered by an employer-sponsored IRA.

For details on coverage requirements, see Chapter 4.

Q. 24:26 What is a payroll-deduction IRA?

An employer may choose to play a limited role in promoting retirement savings (IRAs) for its employees by establishing a payroll-deduction program in conjunction with a financial institution (a bank, insurance company, mutual fund, or brokerage firm, for example). Each employee is allowed to set up an IRA with the sponsoring institution, and the amount the employee wishes to contribute to the IRA each pay period is deducted from his or her paycheck by the employer.

Q. 24:27 Does a payroll-deduction IRA expose the employer to ERISA liabilities and compliance requirements?

A payroll-deduction IRA is not considered a pension plan subject to ERISA as long as the employer does not endorse the program. The employer will not be considered to have endorsed the program and will be free of ERISA responsibilities if *all* of the following conditions are met:

1. Materials distributed to the employees, either by the employer or by the IRA sponsor, clearly say that:

   - the program is completely voluntary;
   - the employer is not endorsing the sponsor or its investment program;
   - there are other IRA investments available to employees outside the payroll-deduction program;
   - an IRA may not be appropriate for everyone; and
   - the tax consequences are the same whether or not payroll deductions are used to make the IRA contributions;

2. The employer is not the IRA sponsor or an affiliate of the sponsor;

3. No significant investments will be made in securities of the employer; and

4. If the payroll-deduction IRA is the result of a collective bargaining agreement, no investments designed to provide more jobs, loans, or similar direct benefits to union members are permitted.

In addition, the employer must promptly transfer the funds it deducts from its employees' paychecks to the IRA sponsor or it risks the imposition of some ERISA responsibilities. [DOL Advisory Opinion No. 81-80A]

Q. 24:28 How does a simplified employee pension differ from an employer-sponsored IRA?

A SEP allows a company to contribute the lesser of $30,000 or 15 percent of an eligible employee's compensation to an IRA established by the employee. The employer-sponsored IRA limit is the lesser of $2,000 ($2,250 for a spousal IRA) or 100 percent of compensation (see Q. 24:5). SEPs must comply with coverage and nondiscrimination requirements, while an employer-sponsored IRA may discriminate in favor of highly compensated employees.

For details on how a SEP works, see Chapter 25.

Q. 24:29 Are there restrictions on IRA distributions?

No. Unlike qualified retirement plans, an individual may with-draw all or any part of an IRA at any time. Also, spousal consent to a withdrawal is not necessary, and there are no limitations as to the form of distribution.

However, minimum annual distributions must start by April 1 of the year after the year in which the individual reaches age 70½ (see Q. 24:30) and a penalty tax is imposed for insufficient distributions (see Q. 24:31). [IRC §§ 408(a)(6) and 408(b)(3); see IRC § 401(a)(9)]

Also, additional taxes may apply to distributions before an individual reaches age 59½ (see Q. 24:37) and to distributions in excess of certain limits (see Q. 11:25).

Q. 24:30 What is the minimum distribution requirement?

Once distributions from an IRA are required to begin (see Q. 24:29), the owner must withdraw a certain amount during each year or be subject to a penalty for insufficient distributions (see Q. 24:31).

IRS has issued proposed regulations detailing the methods for satisfying the minimum distribution requirement. The proposed regulations indicate that distributions from an IRA are subject to requirements similar to those governing minimum distributions from qualified retirement plans, including the minimum distribution incidental benefit requirement (see Q. 9:65). [Prop. Reg. § 1.408-8, Q&A A-1 and B-13]

Generally, the minimum required distribution for a year is calculated by dividing the account balance of the IRA as of December 31 of the previous year by the owner's life expectancy (or by the joint life expectancies of the owner and his or her designated beneficiary). [Prop. Reg. § 1.401(a)(9)-1, Q&A F-1]

An individual who is the owner or beneficiary of more than one IRA must calculate the required minimum distribution with respect to each IRA. However, the amounts required to be distributed may then be aggregated and the distribution taken from any one or more of the IRAs. [*Notice 88-38*, 1988-1 CB 524]

The minimum distribution for a year is not reduced even if a portion of the IRA assets are transferred to a former spouse pursuant to a divorce decree during the year. The minimum distribution is still based on the IRA balance on December 31 of the year before the transfer. [*Letter Ruling 9011031*]

See Question 24:36 for the minimum distribution requirements after the death of the IRA owner.

Q. 24:31 What is the penalty imposed for insufficient distributions from an IRA?

An annual nondeductible 50 percent excise tax is imposed on the difference between the minimum required distribution from an IRA (see Q. 24:30) and the amount distributed. [IRC § 4974]

IRS can waive the penalty tax if the shortfall resulted from a reasonable error and the individual is taking steps to correct the situation. [IRC § 4974(d)]

Q. 24:32 How are distributions from an IRA taxed?

Generally, a recipient of a payment or distribution from an IRA must include the amount received in gross income for the year of receipt.

IRA distributions are taxed as ordinary income. IRA distributions are not eligible for capital gains treatment or the forward averaging method that may apply to lump-sum distributions from qualified retirement plans. [IRC § 408(d)(1); *Costanza*, 50 TCM 280 (1985)]

If the IRA is paid out all in one year, the individual pays income tax on the entire amount in one year. By receiving distributions as an annuity or over a period of years, tax payments are spread over several years.

If the individual has made only deductible IRA contributions, the entire amount of each IRA distribution is fully taxable. If, however, the individual has made nondeductible contributions to any IRA, a portion of all IRA distributions, even distributions made from an IRA to which only deductible contributions have been made, will be considered a tax-free return of the individual's nondeductible contributions (see Q. 24:16). For purposes of determining what portion of an IRA distribution is taxable, the following special rules apply:

1. All IRAs and SEPs maintained by the individual are aggregated;

2. All distributions during the year are treated as one distribution;

3. The aggregate account balance is determined as of the end of the year, and includes distributions made during the year; and

4. The individual's overall nondeductible contributions are determined as of the end of the year.

[IRC § 408(d)(2)]

If a distribution from an IRA is premature, the amount distributed is taxed as ordinary income and a penalty tax may be imposed (see Q. 24:37). [IRC § 72(t)]

IRA distributions are also subject to the penalty tax on excess distributions (see Q. 11:25).

The payment of a fee directly from the IRA to a company for services in connection with transferring IRA assets between mutual funds is not a taxable distribution to the IRA owner. [*Letter Ruling 8747072*]

A distribution from an IRA is not taxable if there is a valid rollover of the distribution to another IRA, or to the same IRA (see Q. 26:3 and Q. 26:4).

Q. 24:33   Are amounts remaining in an IRA at death subject to federal estate taxes?

The entire amount in the IRA is included in the decedent's gross estate. [IRC § 2039] Amounts accumulated in a decedent's IRA as of the date of death may be subject to the 15 percent excise tax on excess retirement accumulations (see Q. 12:19).

An IRA may constitute qualified terminable interest property (QTIP) for which an estate tax marital deduction may be elected (see

Q. 12:18). In one ruling, IRS allowed a QTIP election when all IRA income was paid to a QTIP trust that, in turn, paid out all such income received from the IRA, plus all trust income, to the surviving spouse annually during her lifetime. [IRC § 2056(b)(7); Rev. Rul. 89-89, 1989-2 CB 231]

Q. 24:34   What is an inherited IRA?

An IRA becomes an inherited IRA after the death of the IRA owner unless the beneficiary is the IRA owner's surviving spouse. The nonspouse beneficiary cannot make a tax-deductible contribution to an inherited IRA, and distributions from an inherited IRA do not qualify for rollover treatment. (See Q. 24:36 for the applicable minimum distribution requirements.) [IRC §§ 219(d)(4) and 408(d)(3)(C)]

Q. 24:35   Do special rules apply if the beneficiary is the IRA owner's surviving spouse?

Yes. A surviving spouse who inherits an IRA from a deceased spouse can elect to treat the IRA as his or her own. In that event, the surviving spouse can make contributions to the IRA, and the minimum distribution requirements during the surviving spouse's lifetime (see Q. 24:30) and after the surviving spouse's death (see Q. 24:36) apply exactly as if the surviving spouse were the original owner of the IRA. The surviving spouse may make such election even if the deceased spouse had started taking distributions from the IRA. [IRC § 408(d)(3); Prop. Reg. § 1.408-8, Q&A A-4]

Alternatively, a surviving spouse who is the beneficiary of a deceased spouse's IRA may roll the IRA distribution into the surviving spouse's own IRA. Such rollover was allowed when the deceased spouse named his estate as beneficiary of his IRA, and his surviving spouse was the sole beneficiary of the estate. [*Letter Rulings 9010084, 9006050, and 8842058*]

Q. 24:36 What minimum distribution requirements apply after the IRA owner's death?

Generally, the minimum distribution rules applicable to qualified retirement plans apply to distributions from IRAs (see Q. 9:61 and Q. 9:62). [IRC §§ 408(a)(6) and 408(b)(3)]

Thus, if a decedent had been receiving lifetime distributions under an irrevocable election, post-death distributions must be made at least as rapidly as under such method. If no such irrevocable election had been made, the IRA must be distributed in one of two methods:

1. The entire IRA must be distributed by December 31 of the year that includes the fifth anniversary of the decedent's death; or

2. Distributions may be made over a period not extending beyond the life expectancy of the designated beneficiary if distributions begin by December 31 of the year that includes the first anniversary of the decedent's death.

If the designated beneficiary is the surviving spouse, distribution may be deferred until the decedent would have reached age 70½. (Alternatively, the surviving spouse may choose to treat the IRA as his or her own. See Q. 24:35). [IRC § 401(a)(9)(B)]

Q. 24:37 What is the penalty imposed on a premature distribution from an IRA?

A distribution from an IRA before the individual for whose benefit the IRA was established reaches age 59½ is subject to a 10 percent penalty tax (i.e., the tax is increased by an amount equal to 10% of the amount includible in gross income). The penalty tax does not apply, however, if an early distribution is made because of the IRA owner's death or disability. In addition, the penalty tax does not apply if the payment is part of a series of substantially equal periodic payments (not less frequently than annually) made over the life (or life expectancy) of the IRA owner or the joint lives (or life expectancies) of the IRA owner and his or her beneficiary. However, if the amount of the periodic payments is modified (other than by reason of death or disability) before the later of (1) the end of the five-year period beginning with the date of the first payment, or (2) the employee's attainment of age 59½, the penalty tax that would have been imposed on all payments, plus interest, is imposed. [IRC § 72(t)]

IRS has provided acceptable methods of calculating substantially equal periodic payments. [*Notice 89-25*, 1989-1 CB 662, Q&A 12; *Letter Rulings 9021058, 9013008, 9004042,* and *8921098*]

An individual with more than one IRA can take periodic payments from one IRA without taking periodic payments from the others. Also, the account balances of the other IRAs are not considered in calculating the amount of the periodic payment from the distributing IRA. [*Letter Ruling 8946045*]

Q. 24:38 May an IRA be transferred incident to divorce?

Yes. A transfer of an individual's interest in an IRA to his or her spouse or former spouse under a divorce decree or a written instrument incident to the divorce is not a taxable distribution or transfer (see Q. 28:5). After the transfer, the transferred interest is treated as the IRA of the transferee spouse or former spouse. [IRC § 408(d)(6); *Letter Ruling 9006066*]

Q. 24:39 Can an IRA be reached by judgment creditors?

It depends on state law because ERISA does not apply to IRAs. Some courts have ruled that an IRA can be reached by all judgment creditors because the money deposited in the IRA is (1) contributed voluntarily, (2) set aside for the depositor's own benefit, (3) subject to the depositor's control, and (4) the IRA is revocable at will. Additionally, some courts will consider the special needs of the depositor. [*In re Ree*, No. 89-00723-W (ND Okla. (1990)); *In re Lownsberry*, No. 89-B-07144-J (DC Col. (1989)); *Schoneman v. Schoneman*, No. 62-852 (Kans. Ct of App (1989)); *In re Gillett*, 46 BR 642 (SD Fla., (1985)); *In re Montavon*, 52 BR 99 (D. Minn. (1985))]

Conversely, other courts have ruled that an IRA is exempt property under state law. [*In re Ewell*, No. 89-1736-8P7 (BR MD Fla.

(1989)); *In re Maitin,* No. 3-88-02890 (BR ED Tenn. (1989)); *In re Laxson,* No. 388-36662 RCM-7, 102 BR 85, ND Tex. (1989)]

Note that at least one court has ruled that even though an IRA is not exempt from bankruptcy, the portion of the IRA attributable to a rollover from a qualified retirement plan retained its exempt status. [*In the Matter of Woods,* 59 Bankr. 221 (WD Wis. (1986))]

Another court has held that an IRA, upon the depositor's death, passed directly to the named beneficiary and did not become part of the deceased depositor's estate subject to the claims of creditors. [*Estate of Davis,* 6 EBC 2491, No. A024159 (Cal. Apps. Ct. 1985)]

Chapter 25

Simplified Employee Pensions

Complex and burdensome rules may cause the owner of a small business to think twice before adopting a qualified retirement plan. But then both the company and the owner forgo significant tax benefits. The simplified employee pension (SEP) offers a practical alternative with respect to the institution of a retirement program. Requirements for establishing and maintaining a SEP are explained in this chapter.

Q. 25:1 What is a simplified employee pension?

A SEP is an individual retirement account or individual retirement annuity (IRA) established for an employee to which the employer makes direct tax-deductible contributions. [IRC § 408(k)]

Q. 25:2 Who is eligible to participate in a SEP?

Each employee age 21 or over who, for 1990, earns at least $342 during the year (adjusted for cost-of-living increases) and has performed services for the employer in at least three of the immediately preceding five calendar years must participate in the SEP. Employees covered by a collective bargaining agreement in which retirement benefits were the subject of good faith bargaining and employees who are nonresident aliens may be excluded from participation. All employees, including part-time employees, not excluded under one of the above statutory exclusions must participate in the SEP. [IRC § 408(k)(2); Prop. Reg. § 1.408-7(d); IR 90-15, Jan. 30, 1990]

Example. JTS Corporation, a calendar year corporation, maintains a SEP. Mindy commenced employment October 1, 1987. Mindy worked 250 hours in 1987 and 900 hours each year in 1988, 1989, and 1990. If Mindy is at least age 21 and earns $342 or more, she must participate in the SEP in 1990.

Contributions must be made on behalf of all employees who meet the participation requirements during the calendar year, whether or not they are employed as of a particular date. [Prop. Reg. § 1.408-7(d)(3)]

Contributions must also be made on behalf of eligible employees over age 70½, even though the employees may already have started to receive required distributions from the SEP and may not make contributions to their own IRAs. [IRC § 219(b)(2)]

For purposes of participation in a SEP, the rules regarding controlled businesses, affiliated service groups, and leased employees are applicable. [IRC §§ 414(b), 414(c), 414(m)(4), and 414(n)(3)]

Q. 25:3 Does the prohibition against discrimination in favor of highly compensated employees apply to a SEP?

Yes. A SEP may not discriminate in favor of highly compensated employees (see Q. 4:28). Contributions must bear a uniform relationship to the compensation of each employee. However, the amount of employee compensation that may be taken into account in computing the employer's annual contribution in 1990 may not exceed $209,200 (adjusted for cost-of-living increases). [IRC § 408(k)(3); IR 90-15, Jan. 30, 1990]

Example In 1990, Jill Corporation has three employees: the business owner earning $300,000 and two other employees earning $20,000 each. Since all three employees meet the eligibility requirements and the SEP may take into account only the first $209,200 of compensation paid to an employee, only $249,200 ($209,200 plus $40,000) would be counted for purposes of determining the amount of the contribution to the SEP. Assuming Jill Corporation wants to contribute the maximum amount allowed on behalf of the owner (see Q. 25:6), it must use a 14.34 percent formula for its contribution. The contribution on behalf of the owner would be $30,000 (14.34% × $209,200), and the contribution for the other two employees would be $2,868 each (14.34% × $20,000).

If the SEP is top-heavy, the employer contributions on behalf of each eligible non-key employee must generally be at least 3 percent of compensation. [IRC §§ 408(k)(1)(B), 416(c)(2), and 416(e)] For details on top-heavy plans, see Chapter 20.

Q. 25:4 May a SEP be integrated with Social Security?

Yes. Contributions to a SEP may be integrated with Social Security. The new integration (or permitted disparity) rules applicable to defined contribution plans also apply to employer contributions to non-salary reduction SEPs (see Q. 25:9 through Q. 25:11). These rules permit a limited disparity between the contribution percentages applicable to compensation below and above the Social Security taxable wage base. [IRC §§ 401(l)(2) and 408(k)(3)]

A SEP will not be considered discriminatory if the contribution percentage for compensation in excess of the Social Security taxable wage base does not exceed the contribution percentage for compensation below the taxable wage base by more than the lesser of (1) the contribution percentage for compensation below the wage base or (2) the greater of (a) 5.7 percent or (b) the percentage equal to the rate of tax attributable to old age insurance as of the beginning of the plan year.

> **Example.** Sharon Corporation establishes a SEP for the 1990 calendar year. The SEP provides that each participant will receive an allocation of 5 percent of compensation up to the taxable wage base ($51,300 in 1990) and 10.7 percent of compensation in excess of the taxable wage base. The SEP does not integrate properly because the contribution percentage for compensation in excess of the taxable wage base (10.7%) exceeds the contribution percentage for compensation below the taxable wage base by more than 5 percent. However, if the excess contribution percentage was reduced to 10 percent, the plan would integrate properly.

Q. 25:5   Are contributions made to a SEP on an employee's behalf forfeitable?

No. Employer contributions under a SEP must fully vest when made and are nonforfeitable. Employers may not condition any contribution to a SEP on the employee's retaining any portion of the contribution in the account and may not prohibit withdrawals from a SEP. The employee may take a distribution from the SEP at any time and at the employee's discretion, but the distribution must then be included in income (see Q. 25:18). [IRC § 408(k)(4)]

Q. 25:6   How much may be contributed to an employee's IRA through a SEP?

The employer's annual contribution to a SEP on behalf of each employee is limited to the lesser of (1) 15 percent of the employee's compensation (not including the SEP contribution) or (2) $30,000 (or, if greater, one-quarter of the dollar limitation in effect for defined benefit plans). If the employer's contribution exceeds the above limitation, the excess contribution is includible in the employee's income and regarded as having been contributed by the employee to the IRA under the SEP. [IRC § 402(h)(2)]

A 6 percent excise tax is imposed on an excess contribution to an IRA, and this tax is applicable to SEPs. [IRC § 4973]

The employee may contribute an additional $2,000 to a personal IRA even though a participant in a SEP. However, for the purpose of determining the deductibility of the IRA contribution, the employee will be considered an active participant because of the employee's participation in the SEP (see Q. 24:9). [IRC §§ 219(g)(5)(A)(v) and 408(j); Notice 87-16, 1987-1 CB 446]

Q. 25:7   How much can an employer deduct for contributions to a SEP?

Subject to the $30,000 annual addition limitation for each employee (see Q. 25:6), the employer may deduct no more than 15 percent of the total compensation paid to all participating employees during the calendar year ending with or within the employer's taxable year (or during the taxable year in the case of a SEP maintained on the basis of the employer's taxable year). [IRC § 404(h)(1)(C)]

An excess contribution is deductible in succeeding taxable years in order of time, subject to the 15 percent limitation. If the employer maintains both a SEP and a profit sharing plan, the deduction limitation for the profit sharing plan contribution is reduced by the amount of the allowable deduction for the SEP contribution with respect to the participants in such plan. [IRC § 404(h)(2)]

Q. 25:8   When are contributions to a SEP deductible?

Contributions to a SEP are deductible:

1. In the case of a SEP maintained on a calendar-year basis, for the taxable year within which the calendar year falls; or
2. In the case of a SEP maintained on the basis of the taxable year of the employer (that is not a calendar year), for such taxable year.

   [IRC § 404(h)(1)(A)]

The contribution must be made no later than the due date of the employer's return for the taxable year (including extensions). [IRC § 404(h)(1)(B)]

Q. 25:9   Which employers may adopt salary reduction SEPs?

An employer that has fewer than 26 employees who were eligible to participate at any time during the preceding calendar year may establish a SEP whereby each employee is permitted to elect to have contributions made to the SEP or to receive the contributions in cash under procedures similar to a 401(k) plan. At least 50 percent of the eligible employees of the employer must elect to defer part of their compensation to the SEP. [IRC § 408(k)(6)]

Q. 25:10   What are the limits on elective deferrals to a SEP?

Elective deferrals under a SEP are treated like elective deferrals under a 401(k) plan and are subject to an annual $7,000 limitation for an employee. The $7,000 amount is adjusted for cost-of-living increases; and, for 1990, the maximum deferral amount has been increased to $7,979. [IRC §§ 401(a)(30), 402(g), and 408(k)(6)(A)(iv); IR 90-15, Jan. 30, 1990]

Q. 25:11 Is there a special nondiscrimination test for salary reduction SEPs?

Yes. Under a salary reduction SEP, the deferral percentage for *each* highly compensated employee (see Q. 4:28) cannot exceed 125 percent of the average deferral percentage for all eligible nonhighly compensated employees. The deferral percentage for an employee for a year is the ratio of: (1) the amount of elective employer contributions actually paid over to the SEP on behalf of the employee for the year to (2) the employee's compensation for the year. [IRC §§ 408(k)(6)(A)(iii) and 408(k)(6)(D)]

The above calculation is different from the calculation applicable to a 401(k) plan (see Q. 21:9). Under a 401(k) plan, after the actual deferral percentage (ADP) is calculated separately for each employee, the *average* of the ADP for all highly compensated employees cannot exceed 125 percent of the average of the ADP for all nonhighly compensated employees. Also, an alternative test is available under a 401(k) plan. If the average ADP for highly compensated employees does not exceed the average ADP for nonhighly compensated employees multiplied by 2 and the average ADP for highly compensated employees does not exceed the average ADP for the nonhighly compensated employees by more than two percentage points, the ADP test will be satisfied even if the first test is not satisfied.

> **Example.** Ildiko Corporation establishes a salary reduction SEP. The deferral percentage for each highly compensated employee equals 5.5 percent. The average deferral percentage for the non-highly compensated employees equals 4 percent. The special nondiscrimination test is not satisfied because 5.5 percent is greater than 5 percent (125% × 4%). If the salary reduction SEP was a 401(k) plan, the requirement would be met because 5.5 percent does not exceed 4 percent by more than two percentage points and 5.5 percent is less than 4 percent multiplied by 2.

Q. 25:12 How is a SEP established?

Generally, any employer may establish a SEP. SEPs are available to both C and S corporations, partnerships, and sole proprietorships. In order to establish a SEP, the employer must execute a written instrument within the time prescribed for making deductible contributions. This instrument must include the name of the employer, the participation requirements, the allocation formula, and the signature of a responsible official. [IRC § 408(k)(5); Prop. Reg. § 1.408-7(b)]

The SEP may be set up in one of three ways:

- By executing Form 5305-SEP or Form 5305A-SEP in the case of a salary reduction SEP (see Q. 25:9);
- By a master or prototype plan for which a favorable opinion letter has been issued; or
- By an individually designed plan.

Q. 25:13 When may an employer use a model SEP?

IRS has designed a model SEP agreement to be used by employers wishing to implement SEPs with relatively little paperwork. This is done by completing Form 5305-SEP or 5305A-SEP for salary reduction SEPs. The form is not filed with IRS but is retained by the employer and distributed to all participating employees. This fulfills the employer's reporting and disclosure obligations relating to the adoption of the agreement and also satisfies the notification requirements. However, a model SEP may not be used

- By an employer currently maintaining another qualified retirement plan.
- By an employer that has ever maintained a defined benefit plan (even if it has been subsequently terminated).
- By members of an affiliated service group, a controlled group of corporations, or trades or businesses under common control, unless all eligible employees of all members participate in the SEP.
- By an employer that uses the services of leased employees.
- If any eligible employee has not established an IRA.

- If the contribution formula is integrated with Social Security.

- By an employer with no nonhighly compensated employees (this applies only to a salary reduction SEP).

Use of a nonmodel SEP requires the employer to distribute certain other summaries regarding the SEP. Once an employee becomes eligible to participate in the SEP, the employer must furnish certain specific information to the employee including an explanation of participation requirements, the formula allocating employer contributions, the name of the person designated to supply any additional SEP information, and an explanation of the terms of the IRA accepting the SEP contribution.

Q. 25:14 Can a dissolved partnership's SEP be continued by its successor sole proprietors?

No. A SEP adopted by a partnership is not considered a plan covering its employees after the partnership is dissolved, even though the former partners continue to operate the same business as sole proprietors. A sole proprietor must adopt a new SEP in order to continue making deductible contributions for his or her employees. [Letter Ruling 8450051]

Q. 25:15 What are the annual reporting requirements of a SEP?

Once a SEP is established, there is limited annual reporting to both IRS and participants. There is no requirement that the employer file the Form 5500 series for the SEP (see Q. 15:1). The trustee or issuer of the IRA is required to furnish annual information regarding contributions to the SEP and the fair market value of assets in the SEP. For this purpose, Form 5498 must be filed with IRS by May 31. [Prop. Reg. § 1.408-5]

The information on Form 5498 must also be supplied to the participants. The employer maintaining the SEP must notify each participant of the SEP contribution made on the employee's behalf on Form W-2 by the later of January 31 following the contribution year or 30 days after the contribution. [IRC § 408(l); Prop. Reg. § 1.408-9]

Q. 25:16   Are SEP contributions taxable to the employee?

No. Both employer contributions and employee elective deferrals under the SEP are excludible from the employee's gross income. [IRC § 402(h)]

Notwithstanding the exclusion from gross income, SEP contributions made under a salary reduction agreement are subject to the Federal Insurance Contributions Act (FICA) and the Federal Unemployment Taxes Act (FUTA) taxes, but SEP contributions under a nonsalary reduction arrangement are not subject to such taxes. [IRC §§ 3121(a)(5)(C) and 3306(b)(5)(C)]

Q. 25:17   How are SEP assets managed?

The assets of a SEP are managed by a financial institution and not by individual trustees, although the employee may be permitted to direct the investment of the employee's account. The SEP must be established with a bank, thrift institution, insurance company, brokerage firm, or other entity that is eligible to be an IRA custodian. Each individual who participates in the SEP may set up or use a personal IRA for investment purposes. If the participant does not have an IRA, the employer *must* establish one for the participant.

Similar to an individual's personal IRA, the participant may make trustee-to-trustee transfers and change the investment manager of the SEP. Since IRA rules govern the types of investments in a SEP, SEP assets cannot be loaned to participants or invested in life insurance contracts, collectibles, or any other assets in which IRAs may not invest. [IRC §§ 408(a)(3), 408(e)(4), and 408(m)]

Q. 25:18   How are distributions from a SEP taxed?

Generally, the same rules that apply to IRA distributions apply to distributions from a SEP. Distributions from a SEP are includible in ordinary income in the year received; and, as with an IRA, favorable tax elections (e.g., special averaging) are not available for distributions from a SEP.

If a withdrawal from a SEP is premature (that is, a distribution is made before the individual reaches age 59½, becomes disabled, or dies) the amount withdrawn, in addition to ordinary income tax, is subject to a 10 percent penalty tax. Similar to distributions from an IRA, an exception to the 10 percent penalty tax exists if the individual receives a distribution from the SEP in substantially equal periodic payments. [IRC §§ 72(t)(1) and 72(t)(2)(A)(iv)]

Distributions from a SEP must begin no later than the April 1st of the calendar year following the year in which the participant reaches age 70½. If the required minimum distribution is not made, a penalty tax is imposed equal to 50 percent of the amount by which such minimum required distribution exceeds the actual amount distributed during the taxable year. [IRC §§ 401(a)(9) and 4974(a)]

If the employee has at any time made nondeductible IRA contributions, the amount includible in income upon a distribution from a SEP is determined in accordance with an allocation formula (see Q. 24:16). [IRC §§ 402(h)(3) and 408(d)]

The assets of a decedent's SEP are included in the decedent's gross estate. [IRC § 2039]

The 15 percent excise tax on excess distributions from qualified retirement plans and excess accumulations upon the employee's death is also applicable to SEPs. [IRC § 4980A]

Q. 25:19 How may assets be moved from a SEP without penalty?

An employee may wish to move funds from an IRA under the SEP to another IRA for higher interest rates, different investment alternatives, or more favorable withdrawal and transfer terms. Similar to IRAs, there are two ways to move assets from the SEP without penalty. One method is through a rollover, whereby the employee withdraws all or part of the amount from the SEP account and rolls over that amount to another IRA, or even the same IRA, within 60 days. Assets withdrawn, but not timely rolled over, will be included in the employee's income and may be subject to penalty taxes. Also, such rollovers may not be made more frequently than once every 12 months; otherwise, the subsequent rollover will be included in the employee's income and may be subject to penalty taxes. [IRC § 408(d)(3)]

The second, and more advisable, way to move funds from an IRA under a SEP to another IRA is through a trustee-to-trustee transfer of funds. Under this method, the employee directs the trustee of the IRA to transfer the IRA funds directly to the trustee of a second IRA. There are no restrictions on the number of trustee-to-trustee transfers that may be made to or from a SEP.

For more details, see Chapter 26.

Q. 25:20 May a distribution from a qualified retirement plan be rolled over into a SEP?

Yes. If, within 60 days after receipt, a participant rolls over a distribution from a qualified retirement plan to an IRA funded as a SEP, the rollover amount will not be includible in income. [IRC § 402(a)(5); *Letter Ruling 8630068*]

However, if a participant wishes to retain the ability to roll the distribution back into another qualified retirement plan, a conduit IRA must be used (see Q. 26:19).

Q. 25:21 What advantages does a SEP offer to the business owner?

The greatest advantage a SEP offers over qualified retirement plans is the minimal amount of paperwork and bookkeeping necessary to start and maintain the plan. Costs for consultants (lawyers, accountants, or actuaries) are sharply reduced, possibly even eliminated. Another advantage of a SEP is the flexibility it affords with respect to contributions. The employer can contribute any amount it wishes, up to a maximum set by law (see Q. 25:6), or it can choose not to make any contribution at all. Although this is generally true for profit sharing plans also, it is not true for pension plans. Furthermore, a SEP may be established after the end of the employer's taxable year.

Q. 25:22 What are the drawbacks to the adoption of a SEP?

Eligibility rules for a SEP tend to be less restrictive than the rules for qualified retirement plans, and this can increase the employer's costs. Many of the employees who need not be covered under a qualified retirement plan must be covered under a SEP. For example, a SEP must include part-time and seasonal workers, regardless of how few hours they worked during the year (assuming they satisfy the compensation requirement and have worked for the employer in at least three of the previous five years; see Q. 25:2).

Another drawback to a SEP is that employees must be fully vested at all times (see Q. 25:5). A qualified retirement plan does not operate this way; vesting can be gradually phased in to favor longer-term employees (see Chapter 8).

Furthermore, the extent to which assets in a SEP are protected from creditors may not be as great as under a qualified retirement plan. (See Q. 24:39, Q. 27:40, and Q. 27:41.)

Chapter 26

Rollovers

It is possible to postpone payment of taxes on certain distributions from a qualified retirement plan by transferring (rolling over) all or part of the distribution to an individual retirement account (IRA) or to another qualified retirement plan. In addition, money contributed to one IRA can be withdrawn and transferred to another IRA without tax or penalty. This chapter examines how rollovers work and describes the tax advantages and drawbacks involved.

Q. 26:1 What is a rollover?

A rollover is a tax-free transfer of cash or other property from a qualified retirement plan to an individual and then from the individual to another qualified retirement plan. There are two types of rollovers to an IRA. First, amounts may be transferred from one IRA to another. Second, amounts may be transferred from a qualified retirement plan to an IRA. A rollover from one qualified retirement plan to another is also possible, as is a rollover to a qualified retirement plan from an IRA, if all amounts in the IRA are attributable to an earlier rollover contribution from a qualified retirement plan (see Q. 26:19). [IRC §§ 402(a)(5) and 408(d)(3)(A)(ii)]

Q. 26:2 What are IRA rollover accounts?

An IRA rollover account is an individual retirement plan to which certain distributions from a qualified retirement plan or from another individual retirement plan have been transferred. The transfer is on a *tax-free* basis. There is no dollar limit on the amount that may be transferred into an IRA rollover account. [IRC §§ 402(a)(5) and 408(d)(3)]

A distribution from a qualified retirement plan may be rolled over to any type of individual retirement plan except an endowment contract (see Q. 24:3). [IRC § 402(a)(5)(E)(iv)]

Nondeductible employee contributions to a qualified retirement plan that are included in the distribution may *not* be rolled over to an IRA. Instead, they are returned to the employee tax-free. See Q. 26:19 for details of a conduit IRA.

Q. 26:3 How does a rollover from one IRA to another work?

All or part of the money contributed to a particular IRA may be withdrawn and transferred (rolled over) to another IRA without tax or penalty. This gives the IRA participant flexibility by enabling the participant to shift investments. For example, the participant may shift from one annuity IRA to another or, seeking higher interest or dividends, from one trusteed IRA to another.

To make the switch, certain requirements must be met. To qualify for a tax-free rollover:

1. The amount distributed to the individual from the old account must be transferred to the new account not later than 60 days after receipt.

2. If property, other than cash, is received from the old account, that same property must be transferred to the new account (although provision is made for a sale of the property and a rollover of the proceeds).

3. If a tax-free rollover of a particular IRA has been made during the preceding 12-month period, a second (tax-free) rollover from that IRA is *not* permitted. [IRC § 408(d)(3)(B); *Letter Ruling 8502044*]

Q. 26:4 May an individual borrow from an IRA?

No, but IRS has ruled that the requirements for a valid rollover are met when an individual receives a distribution from an IRA and the distribution is redeposited in the same IRA within 60 days. Such a transaction will constitute a tax-free rollover and not be subject to the excess contribution limits (see Q. 24:6). [IRC §§ 408(e) and 4975(d); *Letter Rulings 9010007* and *8826009*]

> **Example.** Susan has a $10,000 Certificate of Deposit (CD) maturing in 45 days. Susan has a $4,000 tuition payment due now and does not want to cash in the CD early. Susan withdraws $4,000 from her IRA and makes the tuition payment. When the CD matures, Susan immediately repays the $4,000 to her IRA. The withdrawal and redeposit are tax-free.

Q. 26:5 May more than one tax-free transfer between IRAs be made during a 12-month period?

Yes, but only if the individual has the funds in an IRA transferred from the IRA *directly* to another IRA. Because this type of transfer is not considered a rollover, the 12-month waiting period (see Q. 26:3) does not apply. [IRS Publication 590 (Revised December 1989)]

Further, if the individual has more than one IRA, a separate 12-month waiting period applies for each IRA. [Prop. Reg. § 1.408-4(b)(4)(ii)]

Q. 26:6 May a beneficiary of an IRA roll over the proceeds at the death of the owner of the IRA?

Yes, but only if the beneficiary is the surviving spouse of the IRA's owner. [IRC § 408(d)(3); *Letter Ruling 9011035*]

IRS has ruled that a surviving spouse may roll over funds received from the deceased spouse's IRA if the funds were paid to the surviving spouse as a beneficiary of the decedent's estate rather than as the designated beneficiary of the IRA. [*Letter Rulings 9010084* and *8842058*]

IRS has also ruled that, if the deceased spouse's IRA is paid to a trust and the trust distributes the IRA funds to the surviving spouse, the surviving spouse may roll over the distribution. [*Letter Rulings 9016067* and *8920045*]

An IRA acquired by a beneficiary upon the death of a nonspouse is an inherited IRA and does not qualify for rollover treatment. (See Q. 24:34.) [IRC § 408(d)(3)(C); *Letter Rulings 9014071 and 8623054*]

Q. 26:7 What types of distributions from a qualified retirement plan may be rolled over?

Only a qualified total distribution (see Q. 26:8) or a partial distribution (see Q. 26:10) may be rolled over. [IRC § 402(a)(5)(E)]

Q. 26:8 What is a qualified total distribution?

A qualified total distribution is:

1. A lump-sum distribution (see Q. 11:4) except that a distribution from a money purchase pension plan does not have to be combined with other pension plans and the 5-year participation requirement is not applicable;

2. One or more distributions made within the taxable year of the employee because of a plan's termination or the complete discontinuance of contributions to a stock bonus or profit sharing plan; and

3. A distribution of accumulated employee deductible contributions (see Q. 5:17).

[IRC §§ 402(a)(5)(E) and 402(a)(6)(E); *Letter Rulings 9025092, 9019059, and 9019050*]

Any portion of a qualified total distribution may be rolled over into either another qualified retirement plan or an IRA. A qualified total distribution from a tax-sheltered annuity (TSA) may be rolled over to another TSA or an IRA. [IRC §§ 403(b)(8) and 408(d)(3)(A)]

Q. 26:9 Is a rollover available for a distribution from a terminated retirement plan?

Yes, participants who have not separated from service but who receive a distribution from a qualified retirement plan because of the plan's termination can roll over all or part of the distribution to postpone tax on the distribution. This is a qualified total distribution (see Q. 26:8). [IRC § 402(a)(5)(E)(i)(I)]

Q. 26:10 What is a partial distribution?

A partial distribution from a qualified retirement plan is eligible for tax-free treatment if:

1. The distribution is at least 50 percent of the balance to the credit of the employee and is not part of a series of periodic payments (see Q. 26:13);

2. The distribution is on account of the employee's death, separation from service, or disability;

3. The employee elects partial distribution treatment (see Q. 26:11); and

4. The rollover is made within 60 days of the distribution. [IRC § 402(a)(5)(D); *Letter Rulings 8945053* and *8945009*]

Under a special rule, a distribution from an employee stock ownership plan (ESOP) that satisfies the diversification requirement may be rolled over even if it does not otherwise qualify for rollover treatment. [IRC §§ 401(a)(28)(B)(ii) and 402(a)(5)(D)(i)]

Q. 26:11 How does the employee elect partial distribution treatment?

To treat a contribution of a partial distribution to an IRA as a rollover contribution, the employee must make an election. The election is made by designating in writing to the IRA sponsor (at the time of contribution) that the contribution is a rollover contribution. [IRC § 402(a)(5)(D)(i)(III); Reg. § 1.402(a)(5)-1T, Q&A-3]

Q. 26:12 What are the tax consequences of electing partial distribution treatment?

Electing partial distribution treatment has the following tax consequences:

1. The distribution may be rolled over tax-free to an IRA and may

not be rolled over to another qualified retirement plan (this same rule applies to a partial distribution from a TSA);

2. Subsequent distributions from the qualified retirement plan do not qualify for the special tax treatment accorded lump-sum distributions (see Q. 11:12);

3. Net unrealized appreciation in employer securities attributable to nondeductible employee contributions is subject to immediate tax; and

4. An IRA that contains a partial distribution rollover may not be rolled over to a qualified retirement plan or a TSA.

[IRC § 402(a)(5)(D) and 408(d)(3)(A)]

Q. 26:13 May a retired employee who has received distributions from a qualified retirement plan roll over the remaining benefits to an IRA?

An employee retired and elected to receive his qualified retirement plan benefits in 15 annual installments. After receiving three installments, the employee elected to receive a final single-sum payment of the balance of his account. Even though the final payout was more than 50 percent of the employee's benefits, the employee could not roll over the payment to an IRA as a partial distribution because the final payment was one of a series of periodic payments. (See Q. 26:10.) [IRC § 402(a)(5)(D)(i); *Letter Rulings 9014055, 9013009,* and *9001056*]

However, IRS has ruled that, even though a retired participant had been receiving monthly benefits, he could roll over the final single-sum payment when the retirement plan was liquidated. [*Letter Ruling 8909050*]

Q. 26:14 May a person who is over age 70½ roll over a qualified retirement plan distribution?

An individual over age 70½ may roll over a distribution from a qualified retirement plan *except* to the extent such distribution is a required minimum distribution. (See Q. 9:54 and Q. 9:57.) [IRC §§ 401(a)(9) and 402(a)(5)(G); *Rev. Rul. 82-153,* 1982-2 CB 86]

Q. 26:15 Is a rollover of qualified retirement plan benefits available to the spouse of a deceased employee?

Yes. The spouse of an employee who receives a qualified total distribution (see Q. 26:8) or a partial distribution (see Q. 26:10) from a qualified retirement plan on account of the employee's death is permitted to roll over all or part of the distribution to an IRA. This applies only to a surviving spouse and *not* to a nonspouse beneficiary. [IRC §§ 402(a)(5) and 402(a)(7); *Letter Ruling 9005071*]

The spouse may establish an IRA rollover account even if the spouse would not be eligible to establish a regular IRA. However, the surviving spouse may not roll over the distribution to another qualified retirement plan or from the rollover IRA to another qualified retirement plan in which the spouse is a participant. [IRC § 402(a)(7)]

Q. 26:16 How does a rollover from a qualified retirement plan to an IRA work?

The payout must be transferred into one or more IRAs within 60 days after receipt of the final payment from the qualified retirement plan (see Q. 26:17). It is not necessary, however, to transfer the entire amount into the IRA; but the portion not rolled over is taxed as ordinary income in the year received. No special tax treatment (e.g., forward averaging) is available with respect to the portion of the distribution that is currently taxed. [IRC § 402(a)(6)(C)]

A distribution from a qualified retirement plan may be rolled over into an IRA that has previously been established by a participant for purposes of the participant's annual contributions. But when the rollover is made into this type of IRA, the participant cannot later roll over the amount of the original distribution into a second qualified retirement plan maintained by the same or a new employer. The only way around this pitfall is to set up a separate IRA (a conduit IRA) to receive the rollover (see Q. 26:19). [IRC § 408(d)(3)(A)]

Q. 26:17 When does the 60-day rollover period begin?

If a distribution qualifying for rollover treatment is received by an individual in more than one payment, for purposes of the 60-day rollover period, that individual is deemed to have received *all* distributions on the day the last payment is received. [*Letter Ruling 8434052*]

Q. 26:18 Can the 60-day rollover period be extended?

According to IRS, the 60-day rollover period may not be extended under any circumstances. IRS has held that transfers not completed within 60 days of the date of distribution are not valid rollovers, even though they were caused by clerical error and not the fault of the individual. IRS says that neither the statute nor the regulations grant IRS the authority to waive or extend the 60-day period. [*Letter Rulings 9013078, 8824047,* and *8819074*]

But, when an individual received a distribution of cash and stock, delivered the distribution to a brokerage company with instructions to deposit the distribution into his IRA and the brokerage company mistakenly credited the stock to the individual's personal account, the bookkeeping error was disregarded and the IRA rollover was ruled timely. [*Wood v. Commissioner,* 93 TC No. 12 (1989)]

Q. 26:19 Can amounts in a rollover IRA be transferred to a qualified retirement plan?

Only a qualified total distribution (see Q. 26:8) may be rolled over to a qualified retirement plan through an IRA. But the conduit IRA can receive no assets other than those that were distributed to the individual from the first plan. Also, the second qualified retirement plan must provide for the acceptance of rollovers. [IRC § 408(d)(3)(A)(ii)]

Transferring money from one qualified retirement plan to another through an IRA may provide a big tax advantage. The amount rolled over might remain eligible for special tax treatment (e.g., electing forward averaging tax treatment for a lump-sum distribution received from the second qualified retirement plan), although generally a trust-to-trust transfer provides more assurance of retaining eligibility for favorable tax treatment.

An IRA that contains a partial distribution rollover (see Q. 26:10) may not be rolled over to a qualified retirement plan. [IRC § 402(a)(5)(D)(ii)]

Q. 26:20 Can a distribution from a disqualified retirement plan be rolled over?

A distribution from a retirement plan that is retroactively disqualified is includible in income and is *not* eligible for a rollover to an IRA or a qualified retirement plan. Rollover treatment is permitted for a distribution from a retirement plan that is *qualified at the time of distribution*, not at the time when contributions by the employer were made. [Reg. §§ 1.402(a)-1(a)(1)(ii), 1.402(a)-1(a)(1)(v), and 1.402(b)-1(b); *Cass v. Commissioner,* 774 F2d 740 (7th Cir. 1985); *Baetens v. Commissioner,* 777 F2d 1160 (6th Cir. 1985); *Woodson v. Commissioner,* 651 F2d 1094 (5th Cir. 1981); but see *Greenwald v. Commissioner,* 366 F2d 538 (2d Cir. 1966)]

Q. 26:21 What are the tax advantages and disadvantages of rolling over a qualified retirement plan distribution to an IRA?

A rollover of a qualified retirement plan distribution to an IRA provides three distinct tax advantages:

1. Postponement of tax payments;

2. Possible reduction of tax liability on the eventual payout; and

3. Continued tax-free buildup of retirement savings.

The rollover defers tax on the qualified plan payout and on the income earned in the IRA. Subsequently, tax liability on amounts in the IRA can be spread out by making withdrawals over a period of years.

Nevertheless, an IRA rollover has drawbacks. First, amounts in the IRA generally cannot be withdrawn without penalty before age 59½ (see Q. 24:37). Second, IRA withdrawals are taxed as ordinary income with no special tax-reducing rules available (e.g., forward averaging). [IRC §§ 72(t) and 408(d); *Costanza v. Commissioner,* 50 TCM 280 (1985)]

Whether the advantages of a rollover will outweigh the disadvantages depends on each individual situation.

Q. 26:22   Can an IRA rollover be revoked?

Upon recept of a lump-sum distribution from a qualified retirement plan, an individual has the option of electing to roll over the distribution to another eligible retirement plan or to have the tax on such distribution computed by using the forward averaging method (see Q. 11:12 and Q. 11:13). Once the individual elects to roll over the distribution into an IRA, those funds become part of the IRA and are then subject to the rules governing IRAs. The amount timely rolled over to an IRA cannot be considered an excess contribution and, therefore, cannot be withdrawn as such. [IRC §§ 402(a)(5) and 4973(b)] An individual cannot recharacterize a rollover contribution made to an IRA once the rollover has been made. Once an individual has chosen the form of a transaction for tax purposes, the individual cannot later disavow the form of the transaction merely because the tax consequences of the form chosen have become disadvantageous. [*Letter Rulings 8536098* and *8536097*]

For the IRA rollover to be tax-free, the individual must *irrevocably elect* to treat the IRA contribution as a rollover contribution. Once any portion of the lump-sum distribution is irrevocably designated as a rollover contribution, the amount rolled over is not taxable and no part of the distribution is eligible for special income tax treatment. An irrevocable election is made by a written designation to the IRA sponsor (at the time of contribution) that it is a rollover contribution. [Reg. § 1.402(a)(5)-1T, Q&A-3 and Q&A-4; *Letter Ruling 8815035*]

Chapter 27

Business Owners

One of the best tax shelters available—especially for the business owner—is a qualified retirement plan. This chapter examines how a qualified retirement plan benefits the business owner and reduces income tax liability. A self-employed business owner may also adopt a qualified retirement plan to accumulate funds on a tax-favored basis. How much the business owner can contribute to a plan, what type of plan is best suited for the business owner, as well as several strategies for reducing the cost of the retirement plan to the business owner are also examined.

Q. 27:1 How do the working owners of a closely held corporation benefit from a qualified retirement plan?

There are two basic ways for a working owner to get money out of a closely held corporation: (1) compensation and (2) dividends.

If a working owner earns a salary or bonus from a closely held corporation, the corporation will get a deduction for the amounts paid to the owner. In turn, the owner is taxed on compensation at ordinary income tax rates. A dividend paid to the working owner is treated differently: it is not deductible by the corporation. The dividend is also taxable to the working owner at ordinary income tax rates. Payments of dividends, therefore, are subject to double taxation.

Adoption of a qualified retirement plan provides the corporation with a deduction for the amount it contributes to the plan. The working owner, as a participant in the plan, is not currently taxed on the amounts contributed for the owner's benefit. Further, earnings from investments made by the plan build up tax-free. When the owner eventually receives the plan benefits, the distribution may be eligible for special tax treatment if it is made in a lump sum (see Q. 11:12). [IRC § 402(e)]

Therefore, adoption of a qualified retirement plan provides the corporation with the same tax benefits as does the payment of current compensation. But the working owner of a closely held corporation is able to *defer* payment of taxes until benefits are received, and these benefits may be eligible for special tax treatment.

Q. 27:2 How can the adoption of a qualified retirement plan increase the wealth of the owner of a closely held corporation?

Dramatic results can be achieved by a qualified retirement plan.

Example. Tom, the owner of a closely held corporation, earns a $50,000 annual salary, and the company is able to pay a 15 percent bonus ($7,500) each year. From the additional $7,500 each year, Tom will keep about $5,400 after taxes. If that $5,400 is invested at a very conservative 5 percent per year (assuming a 28% bracket), Tom will earn about 4 percent net after taxes. Over a 25-year period, he will be able to build up about $225,000 after taxes.

If, instead of giving Tom a $7,500 bonus, the corporation has a qualified profit sharing plan and contributes that $7,500 to the plan each year on his behalf, the corporation gets the same $7,500 deduction that it would have received had it paid the bonus.

If the profit sharing trust earns the same 5 percent that Tom would have earned individually, then, because the profit sharing trust pays no income taxes, the total buildup of these annual investments in the trust on Tom's behalf, over the 25-year period, will come to $376,000. (Remember, the full $7,500 per year—not $5,400 after taxes—is accumulating in the trust.

Furthermore, it is accumulating at the full 5% interest rate.)

If this $376,000 buildup in funds is paid out to Tom in one year upon his retirement, he may be eligible to elect special tax treatment. (See Q. 11:12.)

The above example is oversimplified, especially in the case of a small or medium-sized corporation. To give this type of dramatic buildup to the business owner, other employees must also be covered. This, of course, boosts costs. But there are methods that can be used to reduce costs. These methods (e.g., integration with Social Security benefits) may be incorporated into the plan.

Q. 27:3 How does the adoption of a qualified retirement plan reduce a corporation's tax liability?

To illustrate how a qualified retirement plan reduces a corporation's tax liability, assume the corporation had taxable income of $45,000 in 1990 and *no* qualified plan. Its income tax liability would be $6,750. If, however, the owners decided to adopt a qualified retirement plan and make a tax-deductible contribution of $21,000 to the plan, the corporation's taxable income would now be $24,000 ($45,000 *minus* $21,000). Its income tax liability would be reduced to $3,600. By adopting the plan and making the contribution, this corporation would cut its tax liability by almost 50 percent. [IRC § 11(b)]

Q. 27:4 Can a self-employed individual set up a qualified retirement plan?

Yes. A plan covering a self-employed individual must, however, satisfy certain requirements in addition to the normal corporate retirement plan qualification requirements. [IRC §§ 401(c) and 401(d)]

A self-employed individual is an individual who has income (see Q. 27:10) from self-employment for the taxable year (see Q. 27:8).

Q. 27:5 What tax advantage does a self-employed individual gain by adopting a qualified retirement plan?

The basic tax advantages of adopting a qualified retirement plan, which are similar to those received by the owner of a closely held corporation, are:

- The self-employed individual receives a federal income tax deduction, subject to the applicable limitations of the Code, for contributions made to the qualified retirement plan.
- To the extent the contribution the self-employed individual makes to a qualified retirement plan is tax-deductible, the tax on this income is deferred (it will be taxable when it is ultimately received from the plan).
- Income earned on contributions to the plan (whether or not tax-deductible when made) will escape tax while in the plan, thereby permitting a greater total compounding of earnings than would otherwise be possible.
- Reduced tax rates may apply to lump-sum distributions (see Q. 11:12) to the self-employed individual or the individual's beneficiary.

Q. 27:6 Is it worthwhile for a self-employed individual to incorporate?

· Although there generally is parity between qualified corporate retirement plans and qualified retirement plans for the self-employed, the incorporated business owner will still have advantages that will be unavailable to the unincorporated business owner. Among the advantages are the following:

- The incorporated business owner may be permitted to borrow from the plan. (See Q. 27:25.) [IRC §§ 401(a)(13) and 4975(d)]
- Plan contributions for the incorporated business owner allocable to life, accident, health, or other insurance are deductible. (See Q. 1:20 and Q. 1:21.) [IRC § 404(e)]
- The incorporated business owner can terminate employment

for lump-sum distribution purposes. (See Q. 11:8.) [IRC § 402(e)(4)(A)]

- Plan contributions on behalf of an incorporated business owner can create or increase a net operating loss. [IRC § 172(d)(4)(D)]
- The incorporated business owner may receive tax-free group term life insurance benefits. [IRC § 79)
- The incorporated business owner may receive tax-free benefits under a medical expense reimbursement plan. [IRC §§ 105(b) and 105(g)]

Note: An individual who incorporates principally to obtain tax deductions not otherwise available to a self-employed individual should review those circumstances in which IRS may allocate income and deductions of a personal service corporation to an employee-owner. (See Q. 27:34.)

Q. 27:7 How should an existing qualified retirement plan be handled if a self-employed individual incorporates the business?

The simplest and most practical arrangement may be to have the corporation adopt the qualified retirement plan. If the corporation establishes a new plan, the assets of the prior qualified retirement plan can be transferred to the trustees of the new plan or rolled over by the self-employed individual. (IRS approval should probably first be secured by filing an application for a favorable determination letter.)

If the qualified retirement plan that covered the self-employed individual is being terminated, IRS should be notified (see Q. 19:55).

Another alternative is to freeze the plan. Since the individual is no longer self-employed, the individual can make no further contributions to the plan. However, amounts in the plan will continue to accumulate on a tax-free basis. Distributions can later be made from the plan in accordance with its provisions. However, if a qualified retirement plan covering a self-employed individual is frozen, the plan must still comply with the requirements of the Code. [*Rev. Rul.* 89-87, 1989-2 CB 81; IRC § 401(a); Prop. Reg. § 1.401(a)(26)-2(b)]

Q. 27:8 Who is a self-employed individual?

Anyone who carries on a trade or business as a sole proprietor or who is a member of a partnership is self-employed. Although the individual need not carry on regular full-time business activities to be considered self-employed, an individual must have earned income. (See Q. 27:10 and Q. 27:11.) [IRC § 401(c); Reg. § 1.1402(c)-1]

Q. 27:9 Who is an owner-employee?

An owner-employee is a self-employed individual who is either a sole proprietor or, in the case of a partnership, a partner who owns more than 10 percent of either the capital interest or the profits interest in such partnership. [IRC § 401(c)(3); Reg. § 1.401-10(d)]

Q. 27:10 What is earned income?

The criterion for contributions to a qualified retirement plan on behalf of a self-employed individual is earned income. This means that contributions by or for a sole proprietor or partner may be made to a qualified retirement plan only if personal services are performed. Thus, for example, inactive owners who derive income solely from investments may not participate in a qualified retirement plan. [Reg. § 1.401-10(c)(3); Frick, 56 TCM 1368 (1989); Pugh, 49 TCM 748 (1985); Frick, 50 TCM 1334 (1985)] Earned income is defined as the net earnings from self-employment in a trade or business in which personal services of the taxpayer are a material income-producing factor. In effect, earned income is the net profit of the business. The fact that capital is an important aspect of the self-employed individual's business is not significant in determining earned income. [IRC § 401(c)(2); see also IRS Pub. 560]

Distributions of income to a limited partner are not considered net earnings from self-employment. However, guaranteed payments made to a limited partner are considered net earnings from self-employment if paid for services rendered to or for the partnership. [IRC § 1402(a)(13); Reg. § 1.401-11(d)(2)(ii)]

Payments to a former employee under a deferred-compensation plan represent compensation for past services and are not considered earned income. [*Letter Ruling 8522057*]

For purposes of computing the limitations on deductions for contributions to a qualified retirement plan, earned income is computed after taking into account amounts contributed to the plan on behalf of the self-employed individual (i.e., the self-employed individual's earned income is reduced by the deductible contributions to the plan). [IRC § 401(c)(2)(A)(v)]

> **Example.** In 1990, a self-employed individual's net earnings from the business are $100,000. The business contributes $20,000 to a defined contribution plan on the individual's behalf. The self-employed individual's earned income for purposes of applying the plan contribution limits (see Q. 27:16) is $80,000 ($100,000 − $20,000). [IRC § 404(a)(8)(D)]

For taxable years beginning after 1989, earned income is computed after the deduction allowed to the self-employed individual for one-half of the individual's self-employment taxes. [IRC §§ 164(f), 401(c)(2)(A)(vi), and 1401]

Q. 27:11 May an individual be both self-employed and an employee of another employer?

With respect to the same employer, regardless of the form of entity (e.g., sole proprietorship, partnership, or corporation), the classifications as self-employed and employee are normally mutually exclusive. However, an individual may be an employee of one entity and still be self-employed with regard to another entity.

> **Example.** Alison is employed by Sherry Corporation as an accountant and also has her own part-time accounting practice. Even though she may participate in Sherry Corporation's qualified retirement plan, she is also able to establish a qualified retirement plan for her self-employment income. [Reg. § 1.401-10(b)(3)(ii)]

Q. 27:12 Can the bulk of qualified retirement plan contributions and benefits be set aside for the business owner and other essential employees under the terms of the plan?

Generally, no. A qualified retirement plan may not discriminate in favor of employees who are considered highly compensated. Discrimination in favor of highly compensated employees (see Q. 4:28) must be avoided in coverage, contributions, and benefits. [IRC §§ 401(a)(4) and 410(b)]

An obvious example of discrimination would be a money purchase pension plan (see Q. 2:4) that provides for a contribution equal to 25 percent of compensation for highly compensated employees, but only 10 percent of compensation on behalf of all other employees. Such a plan would not qualify for tax-favored status. An important exception applies if the plan is integrated with Social Security (see Q. 6:1).

For details on minimum contribution and benefit requirements that may apply to the plan, see Chapter 20.

Q. 27:13 May a qualified retirement plan lose its tax-favored status if only the business owner and other essential employees will receive benefits?

Even if the plan is not discriminatory as it is written (see Q. 3:1), the *operation* of the plan can result in discrimination, and the plan may lose its tax-favored status.

> **Example.** A plan covers all employees and provides a schedule for the vesting of benefits that meets the requirements of the Code (see Q. 8:3). If the only employees attaining vested benefits are the business' highly compensated employees (because rank-and-file workers leave before they have enough years of service to earn vested benefits, for example), the plan—in actual operation—may discriminate in favor of the highly compensated employees and may lose its tax-favored status (see Q. 27:12). [Rev. Rul. 66-251, 1966-2 CB 121]

In one case, IRS denied tax-favored status to a profit sharing plan because the rapid rate of turnover among lower-paid employees caused the bulk of the benefits to go to the business owner and the essential employees. However, IRS was rebuffed by the court. The court found that, if there was any discrimination in the operation of the plan, it was in favor of *permanent* employees and against *transient* employees, not in favor of the highly compensated employees and against rank-and-file employees. This type of discrimination is not prohibited. [*Lansons, Inc.*, 69 TC 773 (1978), *aff'd*, 622 F2d 774 (5th Cir. 1980)]

On the other hand, if discrimination in benefits results from a pattern of abuse by the business owner, for example, if rank-and-file employees are fired before their benefits become nonforfeitable, the plan is likely to lose its tax-favored status. [IRC § 411(d)(1)(A)]

Q. 27:14 How much can a business owner contribute to the qualified retirement plan?

It depends on the type of retirement plan the business owner adopts. If either a single defined contribution plan or a combination of defined contribution plans is adopted, the annual addition (see Q. 5:1) to the business owner's account during any year may not exceed the lesser of (1) $30,000 (or, if greater, 25% of the maximum dollar limitation permitted under a defined benefit plan) or (2) 25 percent of compensation. [IRC § 415(c)]

The maximum annual benefit that may be provided to a participating business owner under a defined benefit plan is the lesser of (1) $90,000 (with adjustments for inflation) or (2) 100 percent of the business owner's average compensation for the highest three consecutive years. [IRC § 415(b)]

Bear in mind that, under a defined benefit plan, the limitation is placed on the annual benefit payable, not the annual contribution necessary to fund the benefit. The annual contribution is determined actuarially, based on the business owner's age and anticipated annual benefit, the plan's normal retirement age, the form of benefit payable, and the actuarial assumptions used.

For a discussion of the limitations on contributions and benefits, see Chapter 5.

Q. 27:15 Is there any limit on tax-deductible contributions to a qualified retirement plan by a corporation?

Yes. Compensation paid to any employee is tax-deductible by the corporation only if the amount paid is reasonable. In determining reasonableness, all forms of compensation are considered, including contributions to the corporation's qualified retirement plan. Whether a particular business owner's compensation is reasonable is a question of fact in each case. [IRC § 162; Reg. § 1.404(a)-1(b); *Barton-Gillet Co.*, 442 F2d 1343 (4th Cir. 1971); *Bianchi*, 66 TC 324, aff'd, 553 F2d 93 (2d Cir. 1977)]

For a discussion on the limits of tax-deductible contributions, see Chapter 10 and Q. 27:17.

Q. 27:16 How much may be contributed to a qualified retirement plan on behalf of a self-employed individual?

The contribution limits that apply to corporate plans apply to plans covering self-employed individuals. Thus, the annual addition limit for defined contribution plans is the lesser of $30,000 or 25 percent of compensation. (See Q. 5:1.) But because earned income is computed after taking into account amounts contributed to the plan on behalf of the self-employed individual (see Q. 27:10), the effective percentage limit on contributions is 20 percent of earned income computed before the contributions (1 ÷ 1.25 = .80; 1.0 − .80 = .20).

If the self-employed individual adopts a profit sharing plan only, the effective percentage limit on the contribution is 13.043 percent of earned income computed before the contribution (1 ÷ 1.15 = .86957; 1.0 − .86957 = .13043).

> **Example.** Stephanie's earned income for 1990 is $100,000, and she adopted a profit sharing plan that year. Stephanie's maximum deductible contribution to the plan is $13,043. Her earned income is $86,957 ($100,000 − $13,043), and 15 percent of $86,957 is $13,043.

The contribution limit to a defined benefit plan is based upon a maximum annual retirement benefit equal to the lesser of $90,000 or 100 percent of compensation (see Q. 5:5).

Q. 27:17 Do any special limitations apply to the deduction for contributions made to a defined benefit plan on behalf of a self-employed individual?

Yes. Unlike a corporate defined benefit plan to which an employer can make deductible contributions in excess of an employee's compensation if such contributions are necessary to fund the employee's benefit, an employer's deductible contribution on behalf of a self-employed individual is limited to the self-employed individual's earned income for the year (computed without regard to the deduction for employer contributions made on the individual's behalf). [IRC §§ 162, 212, 401(c)(2), 404(a)(8)(C), and 404(a)(8)(D); Reg. § 1.404(a)(8)-1T]

> **Example.** Caroline, a sole proprietor, has net earnings of $50,000 from her business. The maximum deductible contribution she can make on her own behalf to her defined benefit plan is $50,000. (Caroline's earned income is $50,000 for deduction purposes.)

Q. 27:18 What type of qualified retirement plan should the business owner install?

From a business viewpoint, it depends initially on the business owner's objectives. The plan may be used to achieve one or more of the following:

- Building a tax-sheltered retirement fund for the business owner and essential employees;
- Recruiting essential employees from competitors;
- Reducing employee turnover; and
- Establishing a market for the corporate business owner's stock in a closely held corporation.

Another consideration is the ability of the business to support the retirement plan. In choosing a plan, the business owner must decide what contributions the business can afford to make.

From a personal viewpoint, the business owner's objectives must be ascertained. These may include one or more of the following:

- Maximizing retirement benefits;

- Maximizing contributions made on the owner's behalf; and
- Having flexibility with regard to annual contributions.

If the business owner wants to maximize retirement benefits (the amount available at retirement), the owner's age may be the key factor in determining what type of plan to adopt. A younger business owner may accumulate the most dollars for retirement using a defined contribution plan; older business owners may do better using a defined benefit plan.

Similarly, if maximizing contributions is the goal, the older business owner can accomplish that by using a defined benefit plan; the younger business owner might do better using a defined contribution plan, although a defined benefit plan could also accomplish the objective.

If flexibility is the goal, a profit sharing plan should be considered. This type of defined contribution plan gives the business owner control over the amount of annual contributions. Although a profit sharing plan generally reduces the maximum amount that may be contributed on behalf of the business owner, it can be combined with a money purchase pension plan to afford the business owner the opportunity to make larger contributions.

Other factors, however, may influence the business owner's decision. For example, how much will it cost to cover the employees? This will depend on how many of them must be covered, their compensation, and their ages. If the business owner's goals would be achieved using a defined benefit plan, but the cost of funding benefits for employees who are older than the business owner is substantial, it may be necessary to modify the objectives and use a defined contribution plan. But, if the employees are younger than the business owner, a defined benefit plan may be better than a defined contribution plan. In either situation, integrating the plan with Social Security (see Q. 6:1) may cut the cost of covering the business owner's employees and enable the objectives to be accomplished.

Q. 27:19 What type of qualified retirement plan (or plans) should a business owner use to maximize retirement benefits?

There is no one answer. The age of the business owner and the expected rate of return on the plan's investments, however, are the key factors in determining what type of qualified retirement plan will provide the most at retirement.

In a defined benefit plan, the actuary first determines the amount needed at retirement to pay the business owner's annual benefit as set by a formula in the plan. The actuary then determines the amount that must be contributed to the plan each year to reach the amount needed at retirement. The actuary uses various factors to compute the annual contribution, including an interest factor (the rate of return on plan investments). This interest factor is usually conservative, 7–8 percent, even when market rates are greater.

Investment gains and losses affect the amount of each year's contribution. Thus, if the investment return was 11 percent, the investment gain reduces the business owner's future contributions. If the investment return was only 4 percent, the investment loss increases the subsequent contributions. Whether or not the interest assumption holds true, the annual adjustment in required contributions does not affect the final result—the amount in the plan at retirement. If the business owner's compensation remained constant over the period of participation, the amount available at the end would be known at the beginning.

In a defined contribution plan (other than a target benefit plan), no actuarial calculations are made and no interest factor is assumed. The annual contribution is generally determined by multiplying the business owner's compensation for the year by the contribution percentage established in the plan. Gains from the investment of plan assets inure to the business owner's benefit and losses are absorbed to the owner's detriment. Thus, if compensation stays constant, under a money purchase pension plan, the business owner will know the annual contribution, but not how much will be available at retirement. That will depend on the investment performance.

Example. Dan, a business owner, aged 45, will retire at age 65 and has $30,000 a year to contribute to the qualified retirement plan. Under a defined contribution plan that provides for a $30,000 annual contribution, Dan will have at retirement $600,000 plus the actual earnings or minus the actual losses on the plan's investments. Thus, if Dan thinks the plan can realize a greater than 7 or 8 percent return on its investments, the defined contribution plan may be preferable to the defined benefit plan.

In this example, the business owner's age had no bearing on the final result. If, under the defined contribution plan, the maximum contribution is $30,000, and, under the defined benefit plan, the amount that could be contributed is $50,000, the business owner would have more available at retirement under the defined benefit plan (unless the plan's investment return was very high). If the business owner is aged 35 at the time the plan is adopted, the extra ten years of compounded earnings—assuming a better-than-average return—may make the defined contribution plan a better choice.

Q. 27:20 How can the use of a normal retirement age earlier than 65 benefit the business owner?

In a defined benefit plan, using a retirement age earlier than 65 may substantially increase the amount of contributions that must be made each year to fund the retirement benefits, which, in turn, increases the business owner's tax deduction. This is because there are fewer years in which to fund the retirement benefits.

There are several obstacles that must be overcome to take advantage of this planning opportunity. First, IRS says that a retirement age earlier than 65 can be used as a basis for computing required contributions only if the lower age approximates the age at which company employees customarily retire. [Rev. Rul. 78-331, 1978-2 CB 158; Rev. Rul. 78-120, 1978-1 CB 117; Letter Rulings 8552001 and 8610002]

Second, because the defined benefit plan will require larger contributions, the company will have to produce a higher cash flow to fund the plan. If it cannot meet the increased funding required, it may be subject to a penalty tax (see Q. 7:16).

Finally, the business owner must be able to show that the total compensation package—salary plus retirement plan contributions made on the business owner's behalf—is reasonable (see Q. 10:1 and Q. 27:15).

The IRS position regarding the use of a normal retirement age earlier than 65 is that an actuarial assumption that employees retire at a normal retirement age that ignores the actual incidence of retirement in the workforce could cause the assumptions to be unreasonable and the amounts to be not currently deductible. Assumptions are to be monitored and adjusted accordingly to reflect current experience. The analysis for funding purposes is at what age is retirement most likely to take place, a determination of probability, that is derived from the average retirement age of the group. [*Letter Ruling 8808005*; *Rev. Rul. 78-331*, 1978-2 CB 158; also see *Jerome Mirza & Assocs, Ltd. v. U.S.*, 882 F2d 229 (7th Cir. 1989)]

Q. 27:21 How does integration with Social Security benefit the business owner?

Integration can help business owners reach what is undoubtedly their primary goal in setting up a retirement plan: rewarding themselves and their essential employees. By integrating the retirement plan with Social Security, the business owners can give proportionately greater benefits or make proportionately greater contributions to the plan on their behalf than they do for rank-and-file workers. A qualified retirement plan that covers self-employed individuals may be integrated with Social Security in the same way that a corporate qualified retirement plan may be.

For details on how integration works, see Chapter 6.

Q. 27:22 Is a voluntary contribution feature attractive to the business owner?

A business owner can make voluntary nondeductible contributions to a qualified retirement plan, but such contributions are now subject to limitations and nondiscrimination tests. These nondiscrimination requirements reduce the attractiveness of allowing voluntary employee contributions. (For details regarding the limitations on voluntary contributions, see Q. 5:15.)

Q. 27:23   Is it advantageous for the business owner to include life insurance protection in the qualified retirement plan?

By including life insurance in the plan, the corporate business owner is able to shift a personal expense (not tax-deductible) to the corporation. Just as the corporation's plan contributions are deductible, contributions (within limits) to pay for the life insurance are deductible. The corporate business owner will, however, have to include in gross income the cost of the current life insurance protection received under the plan.

There is a different rule for a self-employed individual. Plan contributions made on behalf of a self-employed individual that are allocable to the purchase of pure life insurance (the term element—not the entire premium) are not deductible. (See Q. 12:3.) [IRC §§ 404(a)(8)(C) and 404(e); Reg. § 1.404(e)-1A(g)]

For further details, see Chapter 12.

Q. 27:24   May the company borrow from its qualified retirement plan to acquire assets needed in its business?

Generally, no. A penalty tax (see below) is imposed on any prohibited transaction, which includes the lending of money between a plan and the company. Thus, a company may not borrow from its plan for any purpose. [IRC § 4975(c)(1)(B)]

DOL, however, may grant an exemption from the loan restrictions. Generally, an exemption is granted only if it is (1) administratively feasible; (2) in the interests of the plan, its participants, and beneficiaries; and (3) protective of the rights of participants and beneficiaries of the plan. [IRC § 4975(c)(2)]

Exemptions for loans from a qualified retirement plan to the company to buy business assets have been approved by DOL. The company must have a good credit rating, the interest rate must be comparable to what a bank would charge, and adequate security must be provided. For examples of when an exemption will be allowed, see Q. 18:11.

The penalty tax on a prohibited transaction is imposed at the rate of 5 percent of the amount involved in the transaction for every year (or part of a year). If the 5 percent tax is imposed and the prohibited transaction is not corrected within the taxable period, an additional tax equal to 100 percent of the amount involved in the transaction is imposed.

Both the initial and additional taxes are payable by the individual who participated in the prohibited transaction. The taxable period begins when the prohibited transaction occurs; it ends, if it is not corrected, on the earlier of the date the notice of deficiency with respect to the 5 percent tax is mailed or the date the 5 percent tax is assessed. [IRC §§ 4975(a), 4975(b), and 4975(f)]

Q. 27:25 May a business owner borrow from the qualified retirement plan?

Yes, if the owner is a participant in the *corporation*'s qualified retirement plan and the plan contains a provision authorizing loans to participants. However, a shareholder-employee (that is, a more-than-5% shareholder) of an S corporation may not borrow from the corporation's qualified retirement plan. [IRC §§ 401(a)(13) and 4975(d)]

The general rules for loans apply to a self-employed individual other than an owner-employee (see Q. 27:9). However, the law prohibits a qualified retirement plan from lending to an owner-employee or to the owner-employee's spouse and certain other relatives. [IRC §§ 401(a)(13) and 4975(d)]

See Chapter 11 for further discussion.

Q. 27:26 May a director of a corporation establish a qualified retirement plan based on the director's fees?

An outside director may establish a qualified retirement plan on the basis of such fee income. Since many outside directors are in high income tax brackets, the creation of a qualified retirement plan may be an especially attractive tax-saving device for these individuals. [Rev. Rul. 68-595, 1968-2 CB 378]

Special rules apply to an inside director. An inside director is an individual who is both an employee (or leased employee, owner, or manager) and a director of the same corporation. If the inside director maintains a qualified retirement plan apart from any plan maintained by the corporation, then, to the extent that contributions, forfeitures, and benefits under the inside director's individual plan are attributable to services performed for the corporation as a director, the inside director is treated as an employee of the corporation and his or her interest in his individual plan is treated as though it was provided under both (1) a separate qualified retirement plan maintained by the corporation and covering only the inside director, and (2) any actual plan maintained by the corporation in which the director participates.

If either of these plans fails to meet the qualification requirements (see Chapter 3), any plan actually maintained by the corporation that covers the inside director and the plan maintained by the inside director may be disqualified. [Prop. Reg. § 1.414(o)-1(g)]

Q. 27:27   What happens if a business owner controls two corporations?

For purposes of determining whether a retirement plan is qualified, all employees of corporations that are members of a controlled group of corporations are treated as if they were employed by a single employer. If the business owner controls both Kenneth Corp. and Robert Corp. but establishes a retirement plan only for the employees of Kenneth Corp., the plan may not be approved by IRS. (See Q. 4:32 through Q. 4:34.) [IRC § 414(b)]

Q. 27:28   Does any special coverage requirement apply if an owner-employee controls another business?

Yes. If an individual is an owner-employee (see Q. 27:9) of more than one business and participates in a qualified retirement plan maintained by one of the individual's businesses (Plan X), all employees of any other business controlled by the owner-employee must be covered by a plan that gives them benefits at least as favorable as those provided for the owner-employee under Plan X. [IRC §§ 401(d)(1) and 401(d)(2); Reg. § 1.401-12(l); see also IRC § 414(c)]

Control means (1) ownership of the entire interest in an unincorporated trade or business or (2) ownership of more than 50 percent of either the capital interest or the profits interest in a partnership.

> **Example.** Debi is the sole owner of a record store and is also a 51 percent partner in a hardware store. The hardware store maintains a qualified retirement plan. No contributions to the hardware store's qualified retirement plan can be made on Debi's behalf unless her record store gives its employees equal benefits under a qualified retirement plan.

This special coverage requirement is one of the few restrictions that apply to qualified retirement plans that cover owner-employees but not to corporate retirement plans.

Q. 27:29 What happens if the business owner sets up a management corporation?

If the business owner establishes a second corporation to perform management functions for the owner's closely held manufacturing corporation and owns at least 80 percent of the stock of each corporation, both corporations will be considered to be members of a controlled group of corporations. (See Q. 27:27 and Q. 4:32 through Q. 4:34.) [IRC §§ 414(b) and 1563(a)]

If the management corporation establishes a qualified retirement plan for the business owner (its only employee) and the manufacturing corporation has no plan for its employees, the plan probably will not be qualified because of inadequate coverage and participation. (See Q. 4:1.)

In addition, both (1) the organization that principally performs management functions for one other organization and (2) such other organization are considered to be an affiliated service group. (See Q. 27:31 and Q. 27:32.)

Q. 27:30 Are there advantages gained by using a professional corporation together with a professional service partnership?

The answer may be yes, but all employees of members of an affiliated service group (see Q. 27:31) will be treated as employed by a single employer for purposes of plan qualification. [IRC § 414(m)]

Q. 27:31 What is an affiliated service group?

An affiliated service group consists of a service organization (FSO) and one or both of the following:

1. A service organization (A-ORG) that is a shareholder or partner in the FSO and that either regularly performs services for the FSO or is regularly associated with the FSO in performing services for third persons; and

2. Any other organization (B-ORG) if a significant portion of the business of the B-ORG is the performance of services for the FSO or the A-ORG (or for both) of a type historically performed in the service field of the FSO or the A-ORG by employees, and 10 percent or more of the interests in the B-ORG is held by individuals who are highly compensated employees of the FSO or A-ORG.

[IRC § 414(m); *Rev. Rul.* 81-105, 1981-1 CB 256]

> **Example.** Medical partnership P consists of corporate partners A, B, and C. Each partner owns one-third of the partnership. The partnership employs nurses and clerical employees. Corporations A, B, and C have only one employee each, the respective shareholders. The partnership does not maintain a retirement plan. Corporations A, B, and C maintain separate retirement plans.
>
> Partnership P may be designated as the FSO. Since Corporations A, B, and C are partners in the FSO and regularly perform services for the FSO, Corporations A, B, and C are A-ORGs. Because Corporations A, B, and C are A-ORGs for the same FSO, Corporations A, B, and C and the FSO constitute an affiliated service group. Consequently, all the employees of

Corporations A, B, and C and the employees of P are considered as employed by a single employer for purposes of testing the qualification of the three separate retirement plans maintained by Corporations A, B, and C.

IRS has issued proposed regulations directed at determining what types of organizational structures will be disregarded in order to prevent the avoidance of employee benefit requirements. These regulations cover affiliated service groups, leased employees (see Q. 4:36), and other organizational arrangements. [Prop. Reg. §§ 1.414(m)-6, 1.414(n)-4, and 1.414(o)-1]

Q. 27:32 Will IRS rule on the qualified status of the retirement plan of a member of an affiliated service group?

Yes. IRS has set out procedures for obtaining determination letters on the qualification of a retirement plan established by a member of an affiliated service group.

An employer (1) that has adopted a new retirement plan, (2) that has amended an existing retirement plan to satisfy the affiliated service group rules, or (3) whose affiliated service group status has changed may request a determination on whether the retirement plan is qualified, taking into consideration employees of any other organization who must be treated as employees of that employer. Generally, a determination letter issued with respect to the retirement plan will cover the affiliated service group rules only if the employer submits, with the determination letter application, certain information. If IRS considers whether the retirement plan of the employer (or group of employers) satisfies the requirements of the affiliated service group rules, the determination letter issued to the employer(s) will indicate that these questions have been considered and that the retirement plan satisfies qualification requirements relating to the affiliated service group rules. Without this statement, a determination letter does not apply to any qualification issue arising by reason of the affiliated service group rules.

The application for a determination letter must include:

1. A description of the business of the employer, specifically dis-

cussing whether it is a service organization or an organization whose principal business is the performance of management functions.

2. Identification of other members (or possible members) of the affiliated service group.

3. A description of the nature of the business of each member (or possible member) of the affiliated service group, specifically discussing whether the member is a service organization or management organization.

4. The ownership interests between the employer and the members (or possible members) of the affiliated service group.

5. A description of services performed for the employer by the members (or possible members) of the affiliated service group, or vice versa, including financial data as to whether the services are a significant portion of the member's business and are of a type historically performed in the employer's service field by employees.

6. A description of how the employer and the members (or possible members) of the affiliated service group associate in performing services for other parties.

7. A description of management functions, if any, performed by the employer for the members (or possible members) of the affiliated service group, or received by the employer from any other members (or possible members) of the group (including data as to whether such management functions are performed on a regular and continuing basis) and whether it is not unusual for such management functions to be performed by employees of organizations in the employer's business field.

8. If management functions are performed by the employer for the members (or possible members) of the affiliated service group, a description of what part of the employer's business constitutes the performance of management functions for the members (or possible members) of the group (including the percentage of gross receipts derived from management activities as compared to the gross receipts from other activities).

9. A brief description of any other retirement plan(s) maintained by the members (or possible members) of the affiliated service group, if such other retirement plan(s) is designated as a unit for qualification purposes.

10. A description of how the retirement plan(s) satisfies the coverage requirements if the members (or possible members) of the affiliated service group are considered part of an affiliated service group with the employer.

11. A copy of any ruling issued by the National Office to the employer as to whether the employer is a member of an affiliated service group; a copy of any prior ruling that considered the effect of affiliated service group status on the employer's retirement plan; and, if known, a copy of any such ruling issued to any other member or possible member of the same affiliated service group, accompanied by a statement as to whether the facts upon which the ruling was based have changed.

[Rev. Proc. 85-43, 1985-2 CB 501; Rev. Proc. 83-36, 1983-1 CB 763; and Rev. Proc. 80-30, 1980-1 CB 685]

Q. 27:33 What is a personal service corporation?

A personal service corporation is a corporation that provides, as its principal activity, personal services substantially performed by the employee-owners (see Q. 27:35). This definition is not limited to incorporated professionals but will also apply to incorporated salesmen, consultants, and other service-rendering individuals. [IRC § 269A(b)(1); Prop. Reg. § 1.269A-1(b)(1)]

Q. 27:34 Can the income of a personal service corporation be allocated to the employee-owner?

If substantially all of the services of a personal service corporation (see Q. 27:33) are performed for one other organization (see Q. 27:36) and the principal purpose for forming the corporation is the avoidance of income tax by reducing the income of, or obtaining the benefit of any deduction for, any employee-owner (see Q. 27:35) that would not otherwise be available, IRS may allocate income and deductions between the personal service corporation and its employee-owners. [IRC §§ 269A and 482; Prop. Reg. §§ 1.269A-1(a) and 1.269A-1(f); Haag, 88 TC 604 (1987); Foglesong v. Commissioner, 691 F2d 848 (7th Cir. 1982), rev'g 77 TC 1102 (1981); Achiro,

77 TC 881 (1981); *Keller*, 723 F2d 58 (10th Cir. 1983), *aff'g* 77 TC 1014 (1981)]

Since the personal service corporation must perform services for only one other organization and need not have any ownership interest in such organization, this provision will both broaden the affiliated service group rules (see Q. 27:31) and apply to other situations.

Now that parity between the amount of retirement benefits and contributions available to the employee-owner under qualified corporate retirement plans and qualified retirement plans covering self-employed individuals has been achieved, IRS should not be able to allocate qualified retirement plan deductions to the incorporated employee-owner, since the employee-owner could then receive the same benefits without incorporating. However, if the incorporated employee-owner uses the corporation to obtain other tax benefits not available to an unincorporated employee-owner, those tax deductions may be lost. (See Q. 27:6 and Q. 27:38.)

Q. 27:35   Who is an employee-owner?

An employee-owner is an employee who, directly or indirectly, owns more than 10 percent of the stock of the personal service corporation. [IRC § 269A(b)(2); Prop. Reg. § 1.269A-1(b)(2)]

Q. 27:36   What is one other organization for purposes of the personal service corporation rules?

For the potential reallocation of income and deductions between the personal service corporation and the employee-owner to occur, substantially all of the services of the corporation must be performed for one other corporation, partnership, or other entity. [IRC § 269A(a)(1); Prop. Reg. § 1.269A-1(a)(1)]

All related persons are treated as one other entity. [IRC §§ 144(a)(3) and 269A(b)(3); Prop. Reg. § 1.269A-1(b)(3)]

Q. 27:37 Is there a safe harbor for a personal service corporation?

Yes. In general, a personal service corporation (see Q. 27:33) will be deemed not to have been formed for the principal purpose of avoiding income tax if the federal income tax liability of no employee-owner (see Q. 27:35) is reduced in a 12-month period by more than the lesser of (1) $2,500 or (2) 10 percent of the federal income tax liability of the employee-owner that would have resulted in that 12-month period had the employee-owner performed the personal services in an individual capacity. [Prop. Reg. § 1.269A-1(c)]

Q. 27:38 Is a retirement plan considered in determining whether the principal purpose of a personal service corporation is the avoidance of income taxes?

Generally, the existence of a qualified retirement plan will not be taken into account in determining the presence or absence of a principal purpose of the personal service corporation to avoid income tax for purposes of the safe-harbor rule (see Q. 27:34 and Q. 27:37). [Prop. Reg. § 1.269A-1(d)]

Q. 27:39 Is there any type of tax-favored qualified retirement plan for the business owner that is simple to adopt and inexpensive to operate?

Yes, a simplified employee pension (SEP) requires only a minimal amount of paperwork and expense to adopt and administer. For details on SEPs, see Chapter 25.

Q. 27:40 Are corporate qualified retirement plan benefits exempt from the participants' creditors?

Not necessarily. Though ERISA and the Code require every qualified retirement plan to prohibit the assignment or alienation of benefits under the plan, most courts hold that this, in and of itself, does not keep a participant's interest in a qualified retirement plan from becoming part of the bankruptcy estate and therefore subject to disposition in the bankruptcy proceedings. The key issue is whether the qualified retirement plan is a spendthrift trust under federal Bankruptcy Code Section 541(c)(2) or under a particular state's law.

Once a participant's interest in the qualified retirement plan is deemed to be part of the estate in bankruptcy, whether the participant can then "exempt" such interest from property subject to distribution to creditors depends on (1) whether the participant's interest in the plan qualifies for exemption under state law, if the debtor has chosen the exemption scheme of the state, or (2) whether payments from the plan are reasonably necessary for the support of the debtor-participant and dependents, if the debtor has chosen the federal exemption scheme (assuming the debtor's state has not "opted out" of it). [*The Travelers Ins. Cos. v. Fountain City Federal Credit Union*, No. 89-7052 (11th Cir. 1989); *In re Hutton*, No. 89-1193 (8th Cir. 1990); *In re Graham*, 726 F2d 1268 (8th Cir. 1984); *Matter of Goff*, (*Goff v. Taylor*), 706 F2d 574 (5th Cir. 1983); *In re Martinez*, No. 89-01424 (Bankr. SD Fla. 1989); *In re Seilkop*, No. 89-00067 (Bankr. SD Fla. 1989); *In re Sellers*, No. 3-89-00532 (Bankr. ED Tenn. 1989); *In re Gribben*, No. C-2-86-1269 (Bankr. ED Ohio 1989); *In re Kendrick*, 106 B.R. 605 (Bankr. WD Mo. 1988); *In re Crenshaw*, (*Rogers v. Norman*), 51 B.R. 554 (ND Ala. 1985); *In re Loe*, (*Halverson v. Mico, Inc.*), 83 B.R. 641 (Bankr. D. Minn. 1988); *Matter of Craddock*, 62 B.R. 583 (Bankr. ND Ga. 1986)]

Q. 27:41 Can property in a qualified retirement plan covering self-employed individuals be reached by judgment creditors?

One court has ruled that property in a qualified retirement plan covering self-employed individuals can be reached by judgment creditors because the money in the plan is deposited voluntarily and is set aside for the self-employed individual's own benefit, and the plan is revocable. Also, the self-employed individual has both a legal and equitable interest in the property [*Parkinson, Jr. v. Bradford Trust Co. of Boston*, 50 B.R. 67 (Bankr. ED Va. 1985)] However, in a later case, the same court concluded that property in a qualified retirement plan covering a self-employed individual could be exempt from the bankruptcy estate. [*In re Diaz*, 13 Collier Bankr. Cas. 2d (MB) 410 (ED Va. 1985)]

Another court has ruled that property in a qualified retirement plan covering a self-employed individual can be attached because the plan is created by the depositor for his or her sole benefit, all funds remain those of the depositor, the account is not held in trust for the benefit of another, and no other individual has an interest in such funds. [*Wear v. O'Brien*, 94 B.R. 583 (Bankr. WD Mo. 1988)] Still another court concluded that funds in a qualified plan could be exempt "to the extent reasonably necessary for the support of the debtor and any dependent." [*In re Lawrence*, 57 B.R. 727 (ND Iowa 1986)]

Although most courts have applied state law, some courts have found that the anti-alienation restrictions of ERISA that are enforceable against general creditors should be equally enforceable against a trustee in bankruptcy, so that a self-employed individual's interest in the individual's qualified retirement plan is excluded from the bankruptcy estate. [*FDIC v. Farha*, No. 87-1530 (10th Cir. 1989); *In re Ralstin*, 61 B.R. 502 (D. Kan. 1986)]

Q. 27:42 Is a professional's interest in the qualified retirement plan of a professional corporation exempt from creditors?

One court has ruled no because the plan was not used for retirement purposes. The professional corporation had a profit sharing plan that the doctor controlled. Previously, the doctor had borrowed most of his interest in the plan. Just prior to filing his petition in bankruptcy, the doctor caused the corporation to contribute all of its available cash to the plan. These two transactions, viewed together, demonstrated that the plan operated to meet the doctor's short-term personal needs and was not used principally for retirement purposes. [*In re Daniel*, 7 EBC 1096 (9th Cir. 1985)] See also Q. 27:40 and Q. 27:41.

Chapter 28

Qualified Domestic Relations Orders

The rate of divorce in the United States continues to increase; and, in many cases, qualified retirement plan benefits represent the major marital asset. The Retirement Equity Act of 1984 established a new category of plan benefit recipients—alternate payees under qualified domestic relations orders (QDROs). This chapter analyzes the requirements for QDROs and their tax consequences.

Q. 28:1 What is a qualified domestic relations order?

A QDRO is a domestic relations order (DRO; see Q. 28:2) that creates or recognizes the existence of an alternate payee's (see Q. 28:3) right to, or assigns to an alternate payee the right to, receive all or a portion of the benefits payable with respect to a participant under a qualified retirement plan, and that complies with certain special requirements (see Q. 28:2). [IRC § 414(p)(1)(A); Reg. § 1.401(a)-13(g)(1); *Brotman v. Molitch*, No. 88-9876 (ED Pa. 1989)]

The rules relating to QDROs generally became effective on January 1, 1985. However, a plan administrator (see Q. 14:1) *may* treat a DRO entered before 1985 as a QDRO, whether or not it meets the above definition, but *must* treat it as a QDRO if, on January 1, 1985, the plan administrator was paying benefits in compliance therewith. If a plan administrator chooses not to treat a pre-1985 order as a QDRO, the alternate payee should try to have the DRO amended to satisfy the requirements for a QDRO.

Q. 28:2   What is a domestic relations order?

A DRO is a judgment, decree, or order (including approval of a property settlement agreement) made pursuant to a state domestic relations law (including a community property law) that relates to the provision of child support, alimony payments, or marital property rights to an alternate payee (see Q. 28:3). [IRC § 414(p)(1)(B)]

A DRO must also satisfy certain special requirements. The DRO must clearly specify:

1. The name and last known mailing address (if any) of the participant and the name and mailing address of each alternate payee covered by the order;
2. The amount or percentage of the participant's benefits to be paid by the qualified retirement plan to each such alternate payee or the manner in which such amount or percentage is to be determined;
3. The number of payments or period to which the order applies; and
4. The qualified retirement plan to which the order applies.

[IRC § 414(p)(2)]

In addition, a DRO may not require:

1. The qualified retirement plan to provide any type or form of benefit, or any option, not otherwise provided under the plan (see Q. 28:8);
2. The qualified retirement plan to provide increased benefits (determined on the basis of actuarial value); or
3. The payment of benefits to an alternate payee that are required to be paid to another alternate payee under another order previously determined to be a QDRO (see Q. 28:1).

[IRC § 414(p)(3)]

An order will not be disqualified merely because it does not specify the current mailing address of the participant and each alternate payee as long as the plan administrator (see Q. 14:1) has reason to know the addresses independently of the order (for example, the alternate payee is also a plan participant and the plan records include a current address for each participant). [REA Comm. Reports]

An order will not be treated as providing increased benefits unless it provides for the payment of benefits in excess of those to which the participant would be entitled in the absence of the order. A DRO will remain qualified with respect to a successor qualified retirement plan of the same employer or a qualified retirement plan of a successor employer. [REA Comm. Reports]

An order will not fail to be a QDRO even if the form of the benefit does not continue to be a form permitted under the qualified retirement plan because of a plan amendment or a change of law. In the case of a plan amendment, an alternative payee remains entitled to receive benefits in the form specified in the order. In the case of a law change that makes the benefit form specified in the order impermissible, the plan must permit the alternative payee to select a form of benefit specified in the plan. In either case, the elected form cannot affect, in any way, the amount or form of benefits payable to the participant. [TRA '86 Comm. Reports]

If a DRO satisfies all of the above requirements, then the order will satisfy the special requirements of a QDRO (see Q. 28:1).

Q. 28:3   Who is an alternate payee?

An alternate payee is a spouse, former spouse, child, or other dependent of a participant who is recognized by a DRO (see Q. 28:2) as having a right to receive all or a portion of the benefits payable under the qualified retirement plan with respect to the participant. [IRC § 414(p)(8)]

Whether the alternate payee is the spouse or a former spouse of the participant, as opposed to a child or other dependent of the participant, affects the tax consequences of a distribution from the qualified retirement plan pursuant to a QDRO (see Q. 28:1). See Q. 28:16 through Q. 28:18 for details.

Q. 28:4   Does a QDRO violate the anti-assignment rule?

Generally, a retirement plan will not be a qualified retirement plan unless the plan provides that plan benefits may not be assigned or alienated. However, this prohibition against the assignment of plan benefits does not apply to the creation, assignment, or recognition of a right to any benefit payable with respect to a participant pursuant to a QDRO (see Q. 3:9 and Q 28:1). [IRC § 401(a)(13); Reg. § 1.401(a)-13(g); but see *Fox Valley & Vicinity Construction Workers Pension Fund v. Brown*, No. 88-2322 (7th Cir. 1990)]

Q. 28:5 Do the QDRO rules apply to all qualified retirement plans?

Yes. The QDRO (see Q. 28:1) requirements apply to all qualified retirement plans and also apply to tax-sheltered annuities. [IRC §§ 401(a)(13) and 414(p)(9)]

The QDRO rules have also been extended to governmental plans and church plans; however, distributions from such plans are treated as made pursuant to a QDRO *without* the necessity of satisfying the special QDRO requirements (see Q. 28:1 and Q. 28:2). [IRC §§ 414(d), 414(e), and 414(p)(11)]

Although the QDRO rules do *not* apply to IRAs (see Q. 24:1), the transfer of an individual's interest in an IRA to the individual's spouse or former spouse under a divorce or separation agreement is not considered a taxable transfer made by such individual; and, thereafter, the IRA is treated as maintained for the benefit of the spouse or former spouse. It is also possible for a QDRO to require a distribution of benefits to the participant and then a transfer of a portion or all of the distribution to an IRA for the benefit of the former spouse. [IRC § 408(d)(6); *Letter Ruling 9016077*]

An IRA may also be used to implement a QDRO if a direct transfer of the participant's interest in a retirement plan to the participant's spouse is otherwise prohibited. When a QDRO required a participant-contractholder to transfer his interest in a tax-sheltered annuity to his spouse, but the terms of the annuity prevented a transfer to anyone other than the contractholder, the participant-contractholder could surrender the tax-sheltered annuity for its cash surrender value, roll over the distribution to an IRA, and then transfer the IRA to his spouse. [IRC § 408(d)(6); *Letter Ruling 8916083*]

Q. 28:6 Does a QDRO affect the qualification of a retirement plan?

A qualified retirement plan will not be treated as failing to satisfy the general qualification requirements (see Q. 3:1) and the restriction on distributions under a 401(k) plan (see Q. 21:33) solely because of a payment to an alternate payee (see Q. 28:3) pursuant to a QDRO (see Q. 28:1). This is the case even if the plan provides for payments pursuant to a QDRO to an alternate payee prior to the time the plan may make payments to a participant. For example, a qualified retirement plan may pay an alternate payee even though the participant may not receive a distribution because the participant continues to be employed by the employer (see Q. 28:8). [IRC § 414(p)(10); Reg. § 1.401(a)-13(g)(3)]

Q. 28:7 Must a qualified retirement plan include provisions regarding QDROs?

No. A qualified retirement plan need not include provisions with regard to QDROs, and this exclusion will not cause the retirement plan to fail to satisfy the general qualification requirements. [Reg. § 1.401(a)-13(g)(2)]

Q. 28:8 What is the earliest retirement age exception?

A DRO may not require a qualified retirement plan to provide any type or form of benefit, or any option, not otherwise provided under the plan (see Q. 28:2). [IRC § 414(p)(3)(A)]

A DRO will not fail to satisfy the above requirement solely because the DRO requires that payment of benefits be made to an alternate payee (see Q. 28:3):

1. In the case of any payment before the participant has separated from service, on or after the date on which the participant attains (or would have attained) the earliest retirement age (see Q. 28:9),

2. As if the participant had retired on the date on which such payment is to begin under the DRO, and

3. In any form in which such benefits may be paid under the qualified retirement plan to the participant.

[IRC § 414(p)(4)(A)]

A DRO will be a QDRO (see Q. 28:1) even though the order provides that payments to the alternate payee may begin on or after the date on which the participant attains the earliest retirement age under the qualified retirement plan, whether or not the participant actually retires on that date. Therefore, a participant cannot delay an alternate payee's receipt of benefits by failing to take advantage of an early retirement option provided by the plan. [IRC § 414(p)(4)(A)(i)]

Payments of benefits prior to a participant's separation from service, but after earliest retirement age, must be made as if the participant had actually retired on the date payments are to begin under the QDRO. Only benefits actually accrued on that date are taken into account, and any employer subsidy for early retirement is not taken into account. An employer subsidizes an early retirement benefit to the extent that the benefit provided is greater than the actuarial equivalent of a retirement benefit commencing at normal retirement age. For example, if a participant would be entitled to a monthly retirement benefit under a qualified retirement plan of $1,000 at age 65 and the plan permits the participant to retire at age 62 with the full $1,000 monthly retirement benefit, the employer is subsidizing the early retirement benefit. Actuarial equivalency is computed using the interest rate specified in the qualified retirement plan. If the plan does not specify an interest rate for determining actuarial equivalency (as would be the case if the employer were subsidizing the benefit), a 5 percent interest rate is used. [IRC § 414(p)(4)(A)(ii)]

Benefit payments to an alternate payee after the earliest retirement age generally may be in any form allowed under the qualified retirement plan; however, benefits may not be paid in the form of a joint and survivor annuity with respect to the alternate payee and the alternate payee's subsequent spouse. [IRC § 414(p)(4)(A)(iii); Reg. § 1.401(a)-13(g)(4)(iii)(B)]

Q. 28:9 What does earliest retirement age mean?

Earliest retirement age means the earlier of:

1. The earliest date benefits are payable under the qualified retirement plan to the participant, and

2. The later of (a) the date on which the participant attains age 50, or (b) the date on which the participant could begin receiving a distribution from the plan if the participant separated from service.

[IRC § 414(p)(4)(B)]

Q. 28:10 Must a qualified retirement plan establish a procedure to determine the qualified status of a DRO?

A qualified retirement plan must establish reasonable procedures to determine the qualified status of DROs (see Q. 28:2) and to administer distributions made pursuant to QDROs (see Q. 28:1). [IRC § 414(p)(6)(B)]

Although a qualified retirement plan need not include provisions regarding QDROs (see Q. 28:7), the plan procedures *must* be in writing and the procedures must permit an alternate payee (see Q. 28:3) to designate a representative to receive copies of the notices sent to the alternate payee with respect to a DRO. [REA Comm. Reports]

Q. 28:11 What happens when a qualified retirement plan receives a DRO?

If a DRO (see Q. 28:2) is received by a qualified retirement plan, the plan administrator (see Q. 14:1) must promptly notify the participant and each alternate payee (see Q. 28:3) of the receipt of the DRO and the plan's procedures (see Q. 28:10) for determining its qualified status. In addition, the plan administrator must determine whether the DRO is a QDRO (see Q. 28:1) and notify the participant and each alternate payee of the determination. [IRC § 414(p)(6)(A)]

During the period in which the determination of whether a DRO is a QDRO is being made (by the plan administrator, by a court of competent jurisdiction, or otherwise), the plan administrator must separately account for the amounts (segregated amounts) that would have been payable to the alternate payee during such period if the DRO had been determined to be a QDRO. [IRC § 414(p)(7)(A)]

If, within the 18-month period beginning with the date on which the first payment under the DRO would be required, the DRO (or any modification thereof) is determined to be a QDRO, the plan administrator must pay the segregated amounts (including any interest thereon) to the alternate payee or payees. [IRC §§ 414(p)(7)(B) and 414(p)(7)(E)]

If, within the 18-month period, it is determined that the DRO is not a QDRO or the determination is not made, then the plan administrator must pay the segregated amounts (including any interest thereon) to the person or persons who would have been entitled to such amounts if there had been no DRO. If a determination that a DRO is a QDRO is made after the 18-month period, it may be applied prospectively only. Therefore, the qualified retirement plan should not be liable to the alternate payee for payments for the period prior to the determination if the qualification is determined after the 18-month period. However, if a DRO is determined to be a QDRO after the 18-month period, the alternate payee may have a cause of action against the participant under state law for the amounts that were paid to the participant but that otherwise should have been paid to the alternate payee. [IRC §§ 414(p)(7)(C) and 414(p)(7)(D); REA Comm. Reports]

Q. 28:12 Can the amounts segregated for an alternate payee under a QDRO be forfeited?

If an alternate payee (see Q. 28:3) cannot be located, the qualified retirement plan is not permitted to provide for the forfeiture of the alternate payee's segregated amounts (see Q. 28:11) *unless* the plan provides for the segregated amounts to be fully reinstated when the alternate payee is located. [REA Comm. Reports]

Q. 28:13   How does a QDRO affect the Qualified Preretirement Survivor Annuity and Qualified Joint and Survivor Annuity requirements?

A QDRO (see Q. 28:1) may provide that a former spouse will be treated as the participant's current spouse for some or all of the QPSA (see Q. 9:9) and QJSA (see Q. 9:8) requirements. [IRC § 414(p)(5); Reg. §§ 1.401(a)-13(g)(4)(i)(A) and 1.401(a)-13(g)(4)(ii)]

To the extent a former spouse is treated as the participant's current spouse by reason of a QDRO, the actual current spouse will *not* be treated as the participant's current spouse. [IRC § 414(p)(5); Reg. § 1.401(a)-13(g)(4)(i)(B)]

> **Example 1.** Assume Barrie is divorced from Larry, but a QDRO provides that Barrie shall be treated as Larry's current spouse with respect to all of Larry's benefits under a qualified retirement plan. Barrie will be treated as the surviving spouse under the QPSA and QJSA unless Larry obtains Barrie's consent to waive the QPSA or QJSA or both. The fact that Larry married Carrie after Larry's divorce from Barrie is disregarded. If, however, the QDRO had provided that Barrie would be treated as Larry's current spouse only with respect to benefits that accrued prior to the divorce, then Barrie's consent would be needed by Larry to waive the QPSA or QJSA with respect to benefits accrued before the divorce and Carrie's consent would be required with respect to the remainder of the benefits.

> **Example 2.** Assume the same facts as in Example 1, except that the QDRO ordered that a portion of Larry's benefit must be distributed to Barrie rather than ordering that Barrie be treated as Larry's spouse. The QPSA and QJSA requirements would not apply to the part of Larry's benefit awarded Barrie. Instead, the QDRO would determine how Barrie's portion of Larry's benefit would be paid. Larry would be required to obtain Carrie's consent if Larry wanted to elect to waive either the QPSA or QJSA with respect to the remaining portion of his benefit.

If, because of a QDRO, more than one individual is treated as the surviving spouse, the qualified retirement plan may provide that the total amount to be paid in the form of a QPSA or survivor portion of a QJSA may not exceed the amount that would be paid if there were only one surviving spouse. The QPSA or survivor portion of the QJSA payable to each surviving spouse must be paid as an annuity based on the life of each respective spouse. If the QDRO splits the participant's benefit between the participant and a former spouse (either through separate accounts or percentage of the benefit), the surviving actual current spouse of the participant would be entitled to a QPSA or QJSA based on the participant's benefit reduced by the separate account or percentage payable to the former spouse. The calculation is made as if the separate account or percentage had been distributed to the participant. [Reg. § 1.401(a)-13(g)(4)(i)(C)]

If an alternate payee is treated pursuant to a QDRO as having an interest in the plan benefit, including a separate account or percentage of the participant's benefit, then the QDRO cannot provide the alternate payee with a greater right to designate a beneficiary for the alternate payee's benefit amount than the participant's right. The QPSA or QJSA provisions do not apply to the spouse of an alternate payee. If the former spouse who is treated as a current spouse should die prior to the participant's annuity starting date (see Q. 9:3), then any actual current spouse of the participant would be treated as the current spouse, except as otherwise provided in the QDRO. [Reg. § 1.401(a)-13(g)(4)(iii)]

Q. 28:14 Must an alternate payee consent to a distribution from a qualified retirement plan?

The general rules that apply to the distribution of benefits to a participant from a qualified retirement plan also apply to the distribution of benefits to an alternate payee (see Q. 28:3) pursuant to a QDRO (see Q. 28:1). (For exceptions, see Q. 28:6, Q. 28:8, and Q. 28:13.)

If the distribution to the alternate payee does not exceed $3,500, the alternate payee's consent is not required. However, if the distribution exceeds $3,500, the alternate payee's consent is required (see Q. 9:72).

In determining whether the present value of the benefit payable to the alternate payee exceeds $3,500, the present value of the participant's remaining benefit is disregarded. Similarly, for purposes of determining whether the present value of the benefit payable to the participant exceeds $3,500, the present value of the benefit payable to the alternate payee under a QDRO is disregarded. [TRA '86 Comm. Reports]

Q. 28:15 Does a QDRO affect the maximum amount of the participant's benefits under a qualified retirement plan?

Even though a participant's benefits are awarded to an alternate payee (see Q. 28:3) pursuant to a QDRO (see Q. 28:1), the benefits awarded to the alternate payee are still considered benefits of the participant for purposes of applying the limitations of Section 415 to the participant's benefits. See Chapter 5 for details. [Reg. § 1.401(a)-13(g)(4)(iv)]

Q. 28:16 What are the income tax consequences of a QDRO to the participant?

If the alternate payee (see Q. 28:3) pursuant to a QDRO (see Q. 28:1) is other than the participant's spouse or former spouse (e.g., a child), any distribution from a qualified retirement plan to such alternate payee will be included in the *participant's* gross income for the year of distribution. If, however, any portion of the distribution represents a recovery of the participant's investment in the contract (see Q. 11:2), that portion will be excluded from the participant's gross income. [IRC §§ 402(a)(1) and 402(a)(9)]

The balance to the credit of an employee (see Q. 11:5) does not include an amount payable to an alternate payee under a QDRO. So, an alternate payee's decision to receive payments in a form other than a lump sum will not affect the participant's eligibility for the special tax treatment afforded a lump-sum distribution (see Q. 11:4) or the participant's eligibility to roll over a distribution from the qualified retirement plan. [IRC § 402(e)(4)(M); *Letter Rulings 8935041* and *8743102*]

See Chapters 11 and 26 for details on taxation of distributions and rollovers.

Q. 28:17 What are the income tax consequences of a QDRO to an alternate payee spouse or former spouse?

If the alternate payee (see Q. 28:3) is the spouse or former spouse of the participant, any distribution from a qualified retirement plan to such alternate payee pursuant to a QDRO (see Q. 28:1) will be included in the *alternate payee's* gross income for the year of distribution. The participant's investment in the contract (see Q. 11:2) must be apportioned between the participant and such alternate payee. The investment in the contract will be allocated on a pro rata basis between the present value of the distribution to the alternate payee and the present value of all other benefits payable with respect to the participant. [IRC §§ 72(m)(10) and 402(a)(9); *Letter Ruling 9013007*]

If a distribution of the balance to the credit of an employee (see Q. 11:5) would be treated as a lump-sum distribution (see Q. 11:4), then the payment under a QDRO of the balance to the credit of an alternate payee spouse or former spouse of the participant will be treated as a lump-sum distribution. The balance to the credit of the alternate payee does not include any amount payable to the participant. [IRC § 402(e)(4)(O)]

For details on taxation of distributions, see Chapter 11.

Q. 28:18 Can an alternate payee roll over a distribution pursuant to a QDRO from a qualified retirement plan?

A distribution from a qualified retirement plan pursuant to a QDRO (see Q. 28:1) to an alternate payee (see Q. 28:3) who is not the spouse or former spouse of the participant (e.g., a child) may not be rolled over to another qualified retirement plan or to an IRA. Since such alternate payee pays no income tax on the distribution, the ineligibility of the alternate payee to roll over the distribution is of no importance to the alternate payee. However, because the participant remains taxable on a distribution to a nonspouse or nonformer spouse alternate payee, this ineligibility to roll over will cause the participant to include the distribution in income. This remains true even if the participant receives, at the same time, a distribution from the plan eligible to be rolled over and does roll over such distribution (see Q. 28:16).

If, however, the alternate payee is the spouse or former spouse of the participant and receives within one taxable year the balance to the credit of the alternate payee (see Q. 28:17) pursuant to a QDRO, the alternate payee is eligible to roll over any portion or all of the distribution to an IRA. The distribution may not be rolled over to another qualified retirement plan. [IRC § 402(a)(6)(F); *Letter Ruling 9013007*]

It appears that the partial distribution (see Q. 26:10) rules do not apply in the event of a distribution from a qualified retirement plan to an alternate payee spouse or former spouse pursuant to a QDRO. Therefore, the alternate payee must receive the entire amount to be eligible to make a rollover.

For details on rollovers, see Chapter 26.

Q. 28:19 Does the 10 percent early distribution tax apply to a distribution made to an alternate payee pursuant to a QDRO?

The 10 percent tax on early distributions (see Q. 9:68) from qualified retirement plans does *not* apply to any distribution to any alternate payee (see Q. 28:3) pursuant to a QDRO (see Q. 28:1). [IRC § 72(t)(2)(D); *Letter Rulings 9013007* and *8935041*]

Because of this exception, the 10 percent early distribution tax will not be imposed on the participant if the alternate payee is a nonspouse or nonformer spouse (e.g., a child) (see Q. 28:16) and will not be imposed on a spouse or former spouse alternate payee (see Q. 28:17).

Q. 28:20 How does a QDRO affect the excess distribution tax and the excess accumulation tax?

To calculate an individual's distributions for excess distribution tax purposes, amounts paid to an alternate payee (see Q. 28:3) who is not the spouse or former spouse of the individual (e.g., a child) from a qualified retirement plan pursuant to a QDRO (see Q. 28:1) are included but amounts paid to an alternate payee spouse or former spouse are disregarded. Any amounts paid to an alternate payee spouse or former spouse from a qualified retirement plan pursuant to a QDRO are includible distributions of the alternate payee for excess distribution tax purposes. (See Q. 11:25 through Q. 11:28.)

To calculate a decedent's aggregate interests for excess accumulation tax purposes, amounts paid to an alternate payee who is not the spouse or former spouse of the decedent (e.g., a child) from a qualified retirement plan pursuant to a QDRO are included but amounts paid to an alternate payee spouse or former spouse are disregarded. Any amounts paid to an alternate payee spouse or former spouse from a qualified retirement plan pursuant to a QDRO will be includible distributions of the alternate payee for excess distribution tax purposes and, if rolled over to an IRA (see Q. 28:18), will be includible, to the extent not withdrawn during the alternate payee's lifetime, in the alternate payee's calculation of aggregate interests for excess accumulation tax purposes. However, if the alternate payee is the spouse, as opposed to the former spouse, of the decedent, a special spousal election will be available. (See Q. 12:19 through Q. 12:26.)

An individual whose total benefits in all retirement plans (see Q. 11:29) on August 1, 1986, had a value in excess of $562,500 was eligible to elect a special grandfather rule. The grandfather election permits the individual to offset distributions received during the individual's lifetime by the portion of the initial grandfather amount recovered during the year of distribution. Furthermore, if the grandfather election was made, the decedent's aggregate interests may be reduced by the unrecovered grandfather amount on the date of the decedent's death. The effect of the special grandfather rule is the potential reduction of the excess distributions tax and/or the excess accumulations tax. (See Q. 11:29 through Q. 11:34 and Q. 12:22 through Q. 12:24.)

If, pursuant to a QDRO, a portion or all of a participant's qualified retirement plan benefits are awarded to the participant's spouse or former spouse, there is no statutory authority for allocating to the alternate payee any portion, pro rata or otherwise, of the participant's unrecovered grandfather amount. Since there is no statutory authority, the question as to whether a court may order an allocation of the unrecovered grandfather amount in a QDRO remains unanswered.

Example. Larry had qualified retirement plan benefits of $2,000,000 on August 1, 1986 and made the grandfather election. In 1991, Larry and Carrie are divorced and, under a QDRO, $1,000,000 of Larry's benefits is allocated to Carrie. If Larry has not recovered any portion of his initial grandfather amount, he retains the entire $2,000,000 initial grandfather amount.

Q. 28:21   Are qualified retirement plan benefits subject to equitable distribution?

Some portion or all of a participant's benefits under a qualified retirement plan may be awarded to the participant's spouse pursuant to a QDRO (see Q. 28:1). However, at least one court has ruled that qualified retirement plan benefits accrued prior to the marriage are not subject to an equitable distribution of marital assets absent evidence of a gift or conveyance. [*Zaborowski v. Zaborowski*, No. 88-1802 (DCA Fla., 5th District, 1989)]

Q. 28:22   Can a QDRO be enforced by an attachment of the participant's monthly retirement benefits?

One court has held that an order made pursuant to the state domestic relations law that relates to alimony payments is a QDRO (see Q. 28:1), which may be enforced by attachment of the participant's (husband's) qualified retirement plan benefits. The court determined that, since the state domestic law allowed attachment of the husband's income in any form, the attachment order against his qualified retirement plan benefits was a QDRO, which allowed the wife to recover amounts for alimony. [*Taylor v. Taylor*, 44 Ohio St 3d 61 (1989)]

Q. 28:23   Can a QDRO be discharged in bankruptcy?

One court has held that a participant's obligation to pay one-half of his qualified retirement plan benefits to his former spouse as part of a divorce decree's property settlement was a "debt" under the U.S.

Bankruptcy Code that was dischargeable in bankruptcy. The property settlement awarded the former spouse one-half of the participant's qualified retirement plan benefits as he received them. The participant filed a Chapter 7 bankruptcy petition and listed that obligation as a dischargeable debt. The Bankruptcy Code defines a debt as a liability on a claim and a claim as a right to payment, whether or not such right is contingent or unmatured. The court held that the former spouse had a claim for a share of future qualified retirement plan payments, however contingent or unmatured that claim may be. Although a debt for alimony, maintenance, or support is not dischargeable under the Bankruptcy Code, the obligation in this case was a property settlement and, therefore, a debt that was dischargeable in bankruptcy. [*Bush v. Taylor*, No. 88-2145 (8th Cir. 1990)]

Glossary

The following is a list of terms (arranged in alphabetical order) that is intended to provide the reader with additional guidance in understanding the complex concepts that apply to qualified pension and profit sharing plans.

Accrued Benefit: A benefit that an employee has earned (or accrued) through participation in the plan.

In a defined contribution plan (e.g., a profit sharing plan), the accrued benefit of a participant is the balance in his or her individual account at a given time.

In a defined benefit plan, the accrued benefit is determined by reference to the benefit that will be provided to a participant when he or she reaches normal retirement age as specified by the plan.

The accrued benefit should not be confused, however, with the benefit (or portion thereof) that a participant has a right (nonforfeitable) to receive if he or she leaves prior to retirement. This benefit is determined by reference to the plan's vesting schedule and the years of service credited to a participant.

Actuarial Assumptions: Contributions to a defined benefit plan depend upon certain assumptions made by the plan's actuary, which may include mortality, investment return, employee turnover, retirement age, and salary scale.

Actuarial Equivalence: Two different sets of values are in an actuarial equivalence when they have an equal present value under a given set of actuarial assumptions.

Affiliated Service Group: Generally, an affiliated service group consists of two or more related service or management organizations, whether or not incorporated. Employees of the members of an affiliated service group are treated as employed by a single employer for plan qualification purposes.

Annual Addition: Term used in connection with the limitation on the contributions that may be made for a participant under a defined contribution plan.

Annuity: A series of periodic payments, usually level in amount or adjusted according to some index (e.g., cost-of-living), that typically continue for the lifetime of the recipient. In contrast, an installment payment is one of a specific number of payments that will be paid whether or not the recipient lives to receive them.

See also "Joint and Survivor Annuity."

Beneficiary: A person designated by a participant or one who, by the terms of the plan, is or may be eligible for benefits under the plan if the participant dies.

C Corporation: See "S Corporation."

Cash-or-Deferred Plan: A qualified profit sharing or stock bonus plan that gives a participant an option to take cash or to have the employer contribute the money to a qualified profit sharing plan as an "employer" contribution to the plan (i.e., an "elective deferral").

These arrangements are often called "401(k) plans." See Chapter 21.

CB: Cumulative Bulletin. This is a government publication in which revenue rulings and other pertinent IRS pronouncements are published. The Cumulative Bulletin is published semiannually and incorporates the materials that were published weekly by IRS in its Internal Revenue Bulletins (IRBs).

Closely Held Corporation: A nonpublic corporation that is owned by a small number of shareholders.

Code: The Internal Revenue Code of 1986 (26 U.S.C. §1 et seq.), as adopted by TRA '86 (Pub. L. No. 99-514). ("Former Code" refers to repealed provisions, including those in the previous Internal Revenue Code of 1954.)

Collectively Bargained Plans: Plans that provide retirement benefits under a collective bargaining agreement. Generally speaking, if more than one employer is required to contribute to the collectively bargained plan, the plan is treated as a multiemployer plan, subject to special rules. If only one employer (including affiliates) is required to contribute to the plan, however, the plan is treated in the same way that other plans that do not cover union employees are treated.

Combination Plans: The use of two or more plans in combination to provide retirement benefits for employees and their beneficiaries. A defined contribution plan (e.g., a money purchase plan) may be combined with a defined benefit pension plan or with another defined contribution plan (e.g., a profit sharing plan).

Limitations on contributions or benefits depend on the type of combination used.

Common-Law Employee: A person who performs service(s) for an employer, if the employer has the right to direct both the objective of the services and the manner in which they are performed.

Commonly Controlled Businesses: All employees of corporations that are members of a "controlled group of corporations" are treated as employed by a single employer for purposes of plan qualification. A comparable requirement applies to partnerships, sole proprietorships, and other businesses under common control.

See also "Controlled Group of Corporations."

Conduit IRA: See "Rollover IRA Account."

Contributory Plan: A pension plan under which employee contributions are required as a condition of participation.

Controlled Group of Corporations: There are three types of controlled groups: (1) the parent-subsidiary controlled group, (2) the brother-sister controlled group, and (3) the combined group.

Two tests must be met to have a "parent-subsidiary" controlled group: (1) stock equal to 80 percent of the combined voting power of each corporation, or at least 80 percent of the value of all outstanding stock of each corporation, is owned by one or more of the corporations of the group; and (2) the common parent corporation owns at least 80 percent of the voting power or value of at least one of the corporations in the group.

Two tests must be met to have a "brother-sister" controlled group: (1) five or fewer persons (individuals, estates, or trusts) own at least 80 percent of the combined voting power or value of two or more corporations; and (2) taking into account the ownership of each stockholder only to the extent that it is identical in each of the corporations involved, the five or fewer persons own more than 50 percent of the combined voting power or value of the corporations involved.

A "combined group" is a group of two or more corporations if: (1) each corporation is a member of either a parent-subsidiary group or a brother-sister group; and (2) at least one of the corporations is the common parent of a parent-subsidiary group and also is a member of a brother-sister controlled group.

All employees of corporations that are members of a controlled group of corporations are treated as employed by a single employer for plan qualification purposes.

Curtailments: The reduction of benefits or the augmenting of eligibility requirements so as to amount to a partial or a complete termination of the plan.

Death Benefits: Payments to a beneficiary of a deceased participant that may be provided under a qualified plan, but they must be incidental to the retirement benefits, which are the major purpose of the plan.

DEFRA: Deficit Reduction Act of 1984. Measure passed by Congress to reduce the budget deficit. One portion of the Act was the Tax Reform Act of 1984.

See also "Tax Reform Act of 1984."

Defined Benefit Plan: A plan that is designed to provide participants with a definite benefit at retirement (e.g., a monthly benefit of 20 percent of compensation upon reaching age 65). Contributions under the plan are determined by reference to the benefits provided, not on the basis of a percentage of compensation.

Defined Contribution Plan: A plan that provides an individual account for each participant and in which benefits are based solely upon the amount contributed to the account (plus or minus any income, expenses, gain, and losses allocated to the account).

Determination Letter: Letter issued by the IRS District Director's office determining that a plan submitted to it meets the requirements for qualification (or does not meet those requirements).

Discretionary Formula Plan: A profit sharing plan that provides that the amount of each year's contribution will be determined by the board of directors (or responsible official(s)) of the sponsoring employer, in its discretion. (Contributions must be "recurring and substantial" to keep the plan in a qualified status.)

Discrimination: A situation in which a plan, through its provisions or through its operations, favors officers, shareholders, or highly compensated employees to the detriment of other employees.

Disqualification: Loss of qualified (tax-favored) status by a plan, generally resulting from operation of the plan in a manner that is contrary to the provisions of the plan or that discriminates against rank-and-file employees.

See also "Discrimination."

Disqualified Persons: See "Party in Interest."

DOL: Department of Labor. The nontax (regulatory and administrative) provisions of ERISA are administered by the Department of Labor. The Department issues opinion letters and other pronouncements, and requires certain information forms to be filed.

Earmarking: Allowing a participant in a defined contribution plan to direct the investment of the amount in his or her account.

Effective Deferral: A contribution to a cash or deferred arrangement made pursuant to an employee's election to have such contribution made in lieu of receiving cash.

Employee: An individual who provides services for compensation to an employer and whose duties are under the control of the employer.

Employee Contributions: See "Mandatory Employee Contributions" and "Voluntary Contributions."

Employee Stock Ownership Plan; ESOP: A profit sharing, stock bonus, or money purchase pension plan, the funds of which must be invested primarily in employer company stock. Unlike other plans, an ESOP may borrow from the employer or use the employer's credit to acquire company stock.

See also "Stock Bonus Plan."

Employer-Sponsored IRA: An IRA that is sponsored by the employer for purposes of helping its employees make a tax-deductible contribution to an IRA and to invest the funds in a particular type of investment.

The employer-sponsored IRA should be distinguished from a simplified employee pension plan (SEP), which requires employer contributions and must meet certain requirements with respect to participation, discrimination, withdrawals, and contributions.

Enrolled Actuary: A person who performs actuarial services for a defined benefit plan. His or her services include making a determination of how much has to be contributed to the plan each year to provide the stated benefits at retirement, and the preparation of a statement that has to be filed with the plan's annual return to IRS. Actuaries who perform these services are enrolled with the Joint Board for the Enrollment of Actuaries.

ERISA: Employee Retirement Income Security Act of 1974. This is the basic law covering qualified plans and incorporates both the pertinent Internal Revenue Code provisions and labor law provisions. ERISA is the basic law designed to protect the rights of beneficiaries of employee benefit plans offered by employers, unions, and the like. ERISA imposes various qualification standards and fiduciary responsibilities on both welfare benefit and retirement plans, and provides enforcement procedures as well. In the retirement area, it also provides standards for tax qualification.

ERTA: Economic Recovery Tax Act of 1981.

Excess Plan: A plan under which contributions or benefits are based on compensation in excess of the Social Security integration level.

Exclusive Benefit Rule: Plan fiduciaries must discharge their duties solely in the interest of participants and beneficiaries for the exclusive purpose of providing benefits to participants and beneficiaries and paying administration expenses.

See also "Fiduciary."

FASB: Financial Accounting Standards Board; the body that sets uniform standards for treatment of accounting items. In the employee benefits context, FASB has prepared an exposure draft concerning disclosure of unfunded benefit liabilities.

FASB 87: The statement issued by FASB regarding employers' accounting for pensions.

Fiduciary: Any person who exercises discretionary authority or control over the management or disposition of plan assets or who gives investment advice to the plan for a fee or other compensation.

Fiscal year: A 12-month period used for accounting purposes.

5% Owner: Any person who owns, directly or indirectly, more than 5 percent of the stock of the employer. If the employer is not a corporation, the ownership test is applied to the person's capital or profits interest in the employer.

See also "Key Employee" and "Top-Heavy Plan."

Forfeitures: The benefits that a participant loses if he or she terminates employment before becoming eligible for full retirement benefits under the plan. For example, a participant who leaves the service of an employer at a time when he or she will receive only 60 percent of benefits forfeits the remaining 40 percent.

401(k) Plan: An arrangement (defined by Section 401(k)) under which a covered employee can elect to defer income by making pretax contributions to a profit sharing or stock bonus plan. A cafeteria plan may provide a 401(k) plan as a qualified benefit option. *See* Chapter 21.

Frozen Plan: A qualified pension or profit sharing plan that continues to exist even though employer contributions have been discontinued and benefits are no longer accrued by participants. The plan is "frozen" for purposes of distribution of benefits under the terms of the plan.

Funding Deficiency: The excess of total liabilities under a defined benefit, money purchase, or target benefit pension plan over total credits for all plan years. This amount is subject to an excise tax, unless IRS waives the tax. The technical term is "accumulated funding deficiency."

Highly Compensated Employee: An employee who, during the year or the preceding year, is (or was): (1) a 5% owner, (2) receiving compensation in excess of $75,000 (adjusted for cost-of-living increases), (3) in the top-paid group of employees and receiving compensation in excess of $50,000 (adjusted for cost-of-living increases), or (4) an officer and receiving compensation greater than $45,000 (adjusted for cost-of-living increases).

H.R. 10 Plan: *See* "Keogh Plan."

Individual Account Plan: A plan that provides for an individual account for each participant and in which benefits are based solely on the amount contributed to an account and any income, expenses, gains, losses, and forfeitures allocated to the account.

IRA: An individual retirement account or an individual retirement annuity. Any working person and certain divorced spouses receiving alimony may establish IRAs and gain deductions for contributions to the IRAs and tax deferrals on the earnings.

Insured Plan: A plan funded exclusively by insurance contracts.

Integrated Plan: A plan that takes into account either benefits or contributions under Social Security. Social Security benefits are used to integrate a defined benefit plan; Social Security contributions are used to integrate defined contribution plans.

Interested Parties: Generally means all employees at the time the employer applies for a determination letter. IRS requires that interested parties be notified when the application is made.

IRC: Internal Revenue Code of 1986. This is the basic federal tax law.

IRB: Internal Revenue Bulletin. A weekly collection of materials published by IRS. *See also* "CB."

IRS: Internal Revenue Service: This is an agency of the Treasury Department, headed by the Commissioner of Internal Revenue, charged with primary responsibility for administering, interpreting, and enforcing the Code. (Note, however, that the Secretary of the Treasury—and not IRS—issues regulations under the Code.)

Joint and Survivor Annuity: An annuity paid for the life of the participant with a survivor annuity for his or her spouse. The survivor annuity must be at least 50 percent, but not more than 100 percent, of the annuity received by the participant during his or her lifetime. Also, the joint and survivor annuity must be the actuarial equivalent of a single life annuity that would have been paid to the participant.

Keogh Plan: A qualified retirement plan, either a defined contribution plan or a defined benefit plan, that covers a self-employed person. (Other employees might also be covered.)

Key Employee: A participant who, at any time during the plan year or any of the four preceding years, is (or was): (1) an officer who earns at least $45,000 a year, (2) one of the 10 employees owning the largest interest in the employer and receiving annual compensation of more than $30,000, (3) a more-than-5% owner of the employer, or (4) a more-than-1% owner earning more than $150,000.

See also "5% Owner," "Officer," "1% Owner," and "Top-Heavy Plan."

Letter Ruling: A private ruling issued by IRS in response to a request from a taxpayer as to the tax consequences of a proposed or completed transaction. Private letter rulings are published informally by several publishers. They are not considered as precedents for use by taxpayers other than the one that requested the ruling, but they do give an indication of IRS's current attitude as to a particular type of transaction.

Leveraged ESOP: An employee stock ownership plan that borrows to acquire employer company stock.

See also "Employee Stock Ownership Plan."

Lump-Sum Distribution: A type of distribution that is required for purposes of using the forward averaging method in computing the income tax that is due.

The basic requirements to qualify as a lump-sum distribution are (1) the distribution must be made within one taxable year of the recipient; (2) it must include the entire balance credited to an employee's account; and (3) it must be made on account of an employee's death, separation from service (except in the case of a self-employed person), or attainment of age 59½ (or, in the case of a self-employed person only, on account of disability).

Mandatory Employee Contributions: Contributions made by an employee in order to become eligible to participate under a plan.

Master Plan: A retirement plan that is sponsored by a financial institution such as an insurance company, bank, mutual fund, or stock brokerage firm, and that may be adopted by an employer merely by executing a participation agreement.

Minimum Funding: The minimum amount that must be contributed by an employer that has a defined benefit, money purchase, or target benefit pension plan. The minimum is made up of amounts that go to cover "normal costs" (for the benefits earned by employees for the current year) plus other plan liabilities such as "past service costs"—liabilities for benefits that have been earned for services performed prior to the adoption of the plan. If the employer fails to meet these minimum standards, in the absence of a waiver from IRS, an excise tax will be imposed on the amount of the deficiency.

Minimum Funding Standard Account: An account that is maintained for a defined benefit, money purchase, or target benefit pension plan for purposes of keeping track of the plan's liabilities and credits. If the account shows a deficiency (excess of liabilities over credits), an excise tax is imposed on that amount.

Money Purchase Pension Plan: A defined contribution plan under which the employer's contributions are mandatory and are usually based on each participant's compensation. Retirement benefits under the plan are based on the amount in the participant's individual account at retirement.

Multiemployer Plan: A pension plan, maintained under a collective bargaining agreement, that covers the employees of more than one employer. Generally, the various employers are not financially related but rather are engaged in the same industry.

Named Fiduciary: A fiduciary who is named in the plan instrument or identified through a procedure set forth in the plan.

One of the distinguishing features of the named fiduciary is that he or she has the authority to designate others to carry out fiduciary responsibilities (e.g., invest the plan funds).

Noncontributory Plan: A pension plan under which employees are eligible to participate and receive accrued benefits without contributing to the plan.

Nonelective Contribution: A contribution to a cash-or-deferred arrangement other than an elective deferral. (An elective deferral is a participant-elected contribution that the participant could have chosen to receive instead as cash.) If the amount of the nonelective contribution depends on the amount of a participant's elective deferral, it is an "employer matching contribution."

Nonforfeitable Benefits: Benefits that cannot be lost by a participant even if he or she terminates service with the employer before qualifying for full retirement benefits. The nonforfeitable benefits are determined by applying the years of credited service to the vesting schedule used by the plan.

See also "Vested Benefits."

OBRA '87: The Omnibus Budget Reconciliation Act of 1987 contained provisions affecting the minimum funding standards, including the Pension Protection Act of 1987. See "Pension Protection Act of 1987."

Officer: An administrative executive of a corporate employer who is in regular and continued service. One employed for a special and single transaction or one who has only nominal administrative duties is excluded.

Offset Plan: A plan that reduces the participant's benefit by an amount specified (i.e., by formula) in the plan.

Old Age, Survivors, and Disability Insurance; OASDI: Payroll tax imposed on employers that is equal to a set percentage of the wages paid to employees. The OASDI tax rate is used for purposes of integrating a defined contribution plan and a simplified employee pension (SEP). Social Security payroll taxes also include Medicare taxes.

See also "Integrated Plan."

1% Owner: Any person who owns, directly or indirectly, more than 1 percent of the stock of the employer. If the employer is not a corporation, the ownership test is applied to the person's capital or profits interest in the employer.

A 1 percent owner is a key employee only if his or her annual compensation from the employer is more than $150,000.

See also "Key Employee" and "Top-Heavy Plan."

Owner-Employee: A sole proprietor or a partner who owns more than 10 percent of either the capital interest or the profits interest in a partnership.

Partial Termination: Reducing benefits or making participation requirements less liberal, although not amounting to a complete termination of the plan, may be considered a partial termination, resulting in the vesting of accrued benefits for at least part of the plan.

The typical types of partial terminations include: the employer closing a plant and thereby substantially reducing the percentage of employees participating under the plan, the reduction of benefits for participating employees, the substantial reduction of contributions to the plan, and the exclusion of a group of employees from participation after they were included in the plan.

Party in Interest: A person who, because of his or her or its relationship with the plan (e.g., as a fiduciary, provider of services, or the plan sponsor), is prohibited from entering into certain transactions with the plan.

See also "Prohibited Transactions."

Pension Benefit Guaranty Corporation; PBGC: A nonprofit corporation, functioning under the jurisdiction of the Department of Labor, that is responsible for insuring pension benefits.

Pension Protection Act of 1987 (PPA): Enacted as part of OBRA '87, designed to protect the integrity of the federal pension system by, for example, raising PBGC premiums and tightening the plan termination requirements.

Plan year: Any 12-consecutive-month period that has been chosen by the plan for keeping its records. The 12-month period may be the calendar year, a fiscal year, or a policy year (if insurance is used to fund all plan benefits). The plan year does not have to coincide with the employer's taxable year or begin on the first day of the month. Change of a plan year usually requires the consent of IRS.

Profit Sharing Plan: A defined contribution plan under which the employer agrees to make discretionary contributions (usually out of profits). A participant's retirement benefits are based on the amount in his or her individual account at retirement.

Prohibited Group: Officers, shareholders, or highly compensated employees. Discrimination in favor of the prohibited group may cause disqualification of a plan.

Prohibited Transactions: Specified transactions that may not be entered into (directly or indirectly) by a party in interest with the plan. Those include, for example, sales or exchanges, leases, and loans between the parties. The Department of Labor may exempt a specific transaction from the prohibited transactions restriction.

See also "Party in Interest."

Prototype Plans: *See* "Master Plan."

Prudent-Man Rule: The standard under which a fiduciary must act. The fiduciary is required to act "with the care, skill, prudence, and diligence under the circumstances then prevailing that a prudent man acting in a like capacity and familiar with such matters would use in the conduct of an enterprise of a like character and with like aims."

P.S. 58 Costs: Costs applied to current life insurance protection provided under the plan for purposes of determining the amount of the participant's tax liability for the coverage.

Qualified Cash-or-Deferred Arrangement: See "401(k) Plan."

Qualified Domestic Relations Order; QDRO: A court order issued under state domestic relations law that relates to the payment of child support or alimony or to marital property rights. A QDRO creates or recognizes an alternate payee's right, or assigns to an alternate payee the right, to receive plan benefits payable to a participant. The alternate payee may be the participant's spouse, former spouse, or dependent.

Qualified Pension Plan (Qualified Plan): A plan that meets the requirements of the Internal Revenue Code (generally Section 401(a)).

The advantage of qualification is that the plan is eligible for special tax considerations. For example, employers are permitted to deduct contributions to the plan even though the benefits provided under the plan are deferred to a later date.

Qualified Total Distribution: One or more distributions from a plan (1) within one taxable year of the employee made on account of the termination of the plan or a complete discontinuance of contributions to the plan or (2) that constitute a lump-sum distribution. A distribution of accumulated deductible employee contributions is also a qualified total distribution. A qualified total distribution may be rolled over to an IRA.

See also "Lump-Sum Distribution."

Reportable Event: An event that may indicate that the plan is in danger of being terminated. ERISA requires plan administrators of certain defined benefit plans to notify the PBGC of the occurrence of such event so as to give the PBGC enough time to protect the benefits of participants and beneficiaries. The notice must usually be given within 30 days of the occurrence of the reportable event unless the PBGC waives notice.

A reportable event includes an occurrence such as: (1) disqualification of the plan for tax purposes; (2) benefit decrease by plan amendment; (3) substantial decrease (more than 20 percent) of the number of employees that are participating under the plan, if the present value of unfunded benefits equals or exceeds $250,000; or (4) an IRS determination that the plan has been partially or completely terminated.

REA: Retirement Equity Act of 1984. Among major changes made by the Retirement Equity Act: reduced age requirement for participation in a plan; increased the period of service considered for vesting purposes; broadened survivor-benefit requirements; allowed the assignment or alienation of benefits in divorce proceedings.

Reversion of Employer Contributions: A qualified plan (or trust) is prohibited from diverting corpus or income for purposes other than the exclusive benefit of employees. However, this prohibition does not preclude the return of a contribution made by an employer if the contribution was made, for example, by reason of a mistake of fact or conditioned on the qualification of the plan or the deductibility of the contribution.

Rev. Proc.: A revenue procedure issued by IRS. It is somewhat similar to a revenue ruling, but deals with procedural matters or details the requirements to be followed in connection with various dealings with IRS. Rev. Procs. also set forth (at times) guidelines that IRS follows in handling certain tax matters.

Rev. Rul.: A public revenue ruling issued by IRS. These rulings express IRS's views as to the tax results that apply to a specific problem.

Rollover: A tax-free transfer of cash or other assets from one retirement plan to another. An IRA account owner may shift assets from his or her present IRA to another. Certain payouts from a pension plan may also be rolled over to an IRA or to another employer's plan.

Rollover IRA Account: An individual retirement account that is established for the sole purpose of receiving a distribution from a qualified plan so that the assets can subsequently be rolled over into another qualified plan.

S Corporation: A corporation whose shareholders have elected not to be taxed as a regular (or "C") corporation, but like a partnership, with profits and losses passing through directly to the shareholders, rather than at the corporate level.

Salary-Reduction Arrangement: Under this type of cash-or-deferred arrangement, each eligible employee may elect to reduce his or her current compensation or to forgo a salary increase and have these amounts instead contributed to the plan on his or her behalf on a pretax basis.

See also "Cash-or-Deferred Plan."

Savings Plan: *See* "Thrift Plan."

Self-Employed Person: A sole proprietor or a partner in a partnership.

Settlement: An action taken to relieve a plan of primary responsibility for a pension benefit obligation.

Shareholder-Employee: A more-than-five-% shareholder of an S corporation.

Simplified Employee Pension Plan; SEP: A retirement program that takes the form of individual retirement accounts for all eligible employees (subject to special rules on contributions and eligibility).

Split-Funded Plan: A plan that is funded in part by insurance contracts and in part by funds accumulated in a separate trusteed fund.

Spousal IRA: An IRA that is established for the nonworking spouse of an employee who qualifies for an IRA. A contribution of $2,250, instead of $2,000, is permitted, but the maximum contribution for either spouse is $2,000.

Step-Rate Plan: A plan that provides different levels of benefits that are based on levels of compensation. For example, a contribution under a money purchase plan of 8 percent of compensation for amounts up to $15,300 and 13 percent of compensation for amounts in excess of $15,300. The step-rate plan is one of the ways of integrating benefits with Social Security benefits.

Stock Bonus Plan: A defined contribution plan that is similar to a profit sharing plan except that the employer's contributions do not have to be made out of profits and benefit payments generally must be made in employer company stock.

See also "Profit Sharing Plan" and "Employee Stock Ownership Plan."

Subchapter S Corporation: See "S Corporation."

Summary Plan Description; SPD: A detailed, but easily understood, summary describing a pension plan's provisions that must be provided to participants and beneficiaries.

Table 1: A table, found in the Treasury regulations under Section 79, that gives the monthly cost of providing $1,000 of insurance coverage, based on the employee's age. Table 1 is used to value coverage in excess of $50,000 that is provided to (and generates tax liability for) employees under a group term life insurance policy that qualifies under Section 79.

TAMRA: Technical and Miscellaneous Revenue Act of 1988. Contained many corrections and clarification to OBRA '87 and TRA '86.

Target Benefit Plan: A cross between a defined benefit plan and a money purchase plan. Similar to a defined benefit plan, the annual contribution is determined by the amount needed each year to accumulate a fund sufficient to pay a targeted retirement benefit to each participant on reaching retirement. Similar to a money purchase plan, contributions are allocated to separate accounts maintained for each participant.

Taxable Year: The 12-month period used by an employer to report income for income tax purposes. The employer's taxable year does not have to coincide with the year used by the plan to keep its records.

Tax Reform Act of 1984 (TRA '84): Tax measure signed into law on July 18, 1984. Among major changes made by the Tax Reform Act: delayed until 1988 cost-of-living increases in contributions and benefits; repealed the estate tax exclusion for death benefits from a pension plan or an IRA; allowed partial distributions from a pension plan to be rolled over to an IRA; applied restrictive distribution rules to 5% owners only.

Tax Reform Act of 1986 (TRA '86): The Act that made such major changes to the Code that it renamed the Code as the "Internal Revenue Code of 1986." It was signed on October 22, 1986.

TEFRA: Tax Equity and Fiscal Responsibility Act of 1982. Lowered limits on contributions and benefits for corporate plans; certain loans from plan to be treated as distributions; reduced estate tax exclusion for retirement plan death benefits to maximum of $100,000; repealed special Keogh plan and S corporation restrictions; added "top-heavy" plan requirements.

Thrift Plan: A defined contribution plan that is contributory in the sense that employer contributions are geared to mandatory contributions by the employee. Employer contributions are made on a matching basis—for example, 50 percent of the total contribution made by the employee.

Top-Heavy Plan: Beginning in 1984, a plan that primarily benefits key employees is considered top-heavy and qualifies for favorable tax treatment only if, in addition to the regular qualification requirements, it meets several special requirements.

See also "Key Employee."

Treasury Regulations: Regulations promulgated by the U.S. Department of the Treasury. IRS is a part of the Treasury Department, and regulations interpreting the Internal Revenue Code are technically Treasury regulations.

Trust: A fund established under local trust law to hold and administer the assets of a plan.

Trustees: The parties named in the trust instrument or plan that are authorized to hold the assets of the plan for the benefit of the participants.

The trustees may function merely in the capacity of a custodian of the assets or may also be given authority over the investment of the assets. Their function is determined by the trust instrument or, if no separate trust agreement is executed, under the trust provisions of the plan.

Unit Benefit Plan: A type of defined benefit pension plan that calculates benefits on the basis of units earned by the employee during his or her employment, taking into consideration length of service as well as compensation.

Vested Benefits: Accrued benefits of a participant that have become nonforfeitable under the vesting schedule adopted by the plan. Thus, for example, if the schedule provides for vesting at the rate of 10 percent per year, a participant who has been credited with six years of service has a right to 60 percent of the accrued benefit. If he or she terminates service without being credited with any additional years of service, he or she is entitled to receive 60 percent of the accrued benefit.

Voluntary Contributions: Amounts that a participant voluntarily contributes to a plan in addition to the contributions made by the employer. IRS permits "reasonable" amounts of employee contributions. Up to 10 percent of the employee's compensation is generally considered reasonable. Voluntary contributions, unlike employer contributions, are not deductible on the employee's tax return.

Year of Service: A 12-month period during which an employee is credited with at least 1,000 hours of service.

Index

(References in the index are to question numbers.)

-A-

Abatement determination
multiemployer plan withdrawal
liability, 23:25–23:30
Accountant
fee, 1:12
Form 5500 series annual return
filing, 15:13
as plan administrator, 14:16
as plan fiduciary, 17:4
Accrued benefits
aggregated plans, top-heavy rules,
20:22
calculation, top-heavy plan, 20:2
defined, 8:2
defined benefit plan limitation, 5:10
defined benefit plan, top-heavy rules,
20:1
effect of plan disqualification on
PBGC guarantee, 19:25
effect of plan termination, 19:4
elimination or reduction, 8:25
future benefit reduction, 8:26
integration level, 6:6
loan effect on QJSA or QPSA, 9:11,
9:12
minimum vesting standards, 8:3
plan amendment
reducing, 11:36, 19:53
terminating, 19:53
plan termination language, 19:40
prior benefit structure, 4:24
QDRO and early retirement, 28:8
qualified retirement plan loan, 11:42

years of service, 8:23
Accumulated funding deficiency, 7:16
**Actual contribution percentage (ACP)
test**
calculation, 21:49
contributions included, 21:50
excess aggregate contributions,
21:53–21:55
other requirements, 21:52
qualified plans with employer
matching contribution and/or
employee contributions, 21:48
qualified retirement plan
contributions, 5:14, 5:15
timing of contribution, 21:51
Actual deferral percentage (ADP) test
calculation, 21:9
compensation defined, 21:11
correcting excess contributions, 21:17
employee contributions, 21:12
excess contributions, 21:16
excess 401(k) plan deferral
distribution after year-end, 21:30
generally, 21:8
simplified determination, 21:15
Actual deferral ratio (ADR)
calculation for multiple 401(k) plans,
21:10
401(k) plans, 21:9
Actuary
calculating defined benefit plan
costs, 2:14
error, and excess plan contributions,
1:23

I-1

(*References in the index are to question numbers.*)

Actuary (*cont.*)
fee, 1:12
as fiduciary, 17:4
as plan administrator, 14:14
plan cost assumption, 2:15, 7:7
Administrative expenses
See also Fee
excess retirement accumulation, 12:25
payment from plan assets, 10:24, 17:23
Administrator of plan
accountant as, 14:16
actuary as, 14:14
basic responsibilities, 14:3
choice of distribution form, 14:12
defined, 14:1
explanation of qualified plan distribution tax rules, 14:11
final distribution of assets, 19:37, 19:38
Form 5500 filing, 15:3
"handling of fund" defined, 14:19
information gathering, 14:5
late third-party filing of Form 5500 series annual return, 15:10
notice
of plan benefits, 19:34
of plan termination, 19:1, 19:17
of significant event for insurance purposes, 19:16
notice to IRS of plan termination, 19:55
officers or owners as, 14:2
oral inquiries from participants, 14:10
plan termination, effect of collective bargaining agreement, 19:27
recordkeeping failure penalty, 14:6
records maintenance, 14:4
trustee as, 14:15
withholding benefits, 14:7
ADP. *See* Actual deferral percentage (ADP) test
ADR. *See* Actual deferral ratio
Affiliated companies, retirement plan as multiemployer plan, 23:5
Affiliated service group
defined, 27:31
IRS determination letters, 27:32
qualified retirement plan, 27:30

Age at retirement. *See* Retirement age
Age requirement
defined benefit plan, 5:6
qualified retirement plan, 4:2
Aggregated plans, top-heavy determination, 20:22
Aggregate interests, deceased participant, 12:20, 12:21
Aggregation group. *See* Highly compensated employees; Top-heavy plans
Alienation, qualified retirement plan benefit rule, 3:10
Alternate payee, QDRO
distribution consent, 28:14
distribution rollover, 28:18
early distribution tax, 28:19
forfeiture by, 28:12
generally, 28:3
income tax consequences, 28:17
Amendment to plan
accrued benefit reduction or termination, 19:53
accrued benefits, elimination or reduction of, 8:25
avoiding excess distributions tax, 11:36
determination letter filing requirements, 13:7
distribution of excess assets to employer, 19:46
effect of PBGC guarantee prior to plan termination, 19:24
employer discretion as to benefits, 9:47
future accrued benefits, reduction of, 8:26
non-Section 411(d)(6)-protected benefits, 8:27
qualified retirement plan, for IRS compliance, 3:7
resulting in termination, 19:52
terminating plan, for qualification, 19:54
top-heavy plan requirements, 20:59
transitional rule, 9:49
waiver of funding standards, 7:19, 7:22
Amortization
extension, for minimum funding standard, 7:24

Index

investment earnings of pension plans, 7:11

plan loan repayment schedule, 11:39

unfunded old liability, 7:10

Annual addition

CODA and, 21:45

compensation defined, 5:3

defined contribution plan account, 5:1

ESOP limit, 22:15

to qualified retirement plans, generally, 1:13

replaced voluntary contribution, 5:4

$30K ceiling, 5:2

Annual benefit

average compensation defined, 5:7

defined, 5:6

defined benefit plan maximum, 5:5

defined benefit plan years of participation or service requirement, 5:8

top-heavy defined benefit plan years of service, 20:41

top-heavy plan, 20:38

Annual distribution requirement, 9:57

Annual return

accompanying schedules, 15:4

Form 5500 series

accountant's opinion, 15:13

automatic extension, 15:7

due date, 15:5

filing location, 15:14

late filing penalty, 15:8

statute of limitations on, 15:11

Annuity

See also Surviving spouse

benefits, lump-sum distribution to beneficiary, 11:11

distributions, 9:57

individual retirement annuity, 24:3

payments, taxation of qualified plan distributions, 11:3

plan termination restriction on, 19:28

starting date

benefit distributions, 9:3

surviving spouse, 9:4

Anti-alienation rule, qualified retirement plan benefits, 3:10

Appeal, adverse determination letter, 13:12

Arbitration, multiemployer plan

withdrawal liability, 23:37

Assets of plan

administrative expense payment, 17:23

defined benefit plan

allocation upon termination, 19:39

transfer of excess, 19:48

valuation, 7:12

employee contributions as, 17:22

ESOP investment in employer securities early distribution tax, 22:62

excess after plan termination, 19:45

final distribution, 19:37, 19:38, 19:55

final distribution notice, 19:42

improper use penalty, 17:24

investment in another entity, 17:15

investment manager liability, 17:34

loans to make investments, 17:36

multiemployer plan sale as withdrawal, 23:21

prohibited transaction sale exemption, 18:11

qualified professional asset managers, 18:12

reallocation of distributed assets, 19:41

segregation of, 17:14

SEP

management of, 25:17

moving without penalty, 25:19

Assignment

anti-assignment rule, QDRO, 28:4

vested interest, 3:9

Attachment

QDRO, monthly retirement benefits, 28:22

qualified plan benefits, 3:10

Attorney ♦

fee, 1:12

as plan fiduciary, 17:4

Audit, by PBGC after plan termination, 19:43

Average annual compensation

defined, 6:21

retirement benefit limit, 5:7

Average benefit percentage test

defined, 4:19

minimum coverage requirement, 4:17

(*References in the index are to question numbers.*)

-B-

Balance to credit of employee
defined, 11:5
QDRO and, 28:16, 28:17
Bankruptcy
corporate qualified retirement plan
benefits, 27:40
ESOP participant, interest exemption,
22:64
IRA access by judgment creditors,
24:39
multiemployer plan withdrawal
liability, claim priority, 23:41
QDRO and, 28:23
self-employed individual, qualified
retirement plan protection, 27:41
Base benefit percentage, 6:11
Base contribution percentage, 6:5
Basis
qualified replacement property, 22:37
qualified retirement plan
distributions, taxation and, 11:2,
11:3
Beneficiary
change in, spousal consent
requirement, 9:22
death benefit tax, 12:16
distribution requirements, 9:61, 9:62
as fiduciary, 17:7
IRA, 24:24, 24:35
IRA rollover, 26:6
life insurance proceeds, qualified
retirement plan, 12:10
lump-sum distribution, taxation of,
11:10
P.S. 58 cost recovery, 12:14
top-heavy plan rules, 20:31
Benefit distributions. See Distribution
requirements
Benefits
See also Accrued benefits;
Distribution requirements
accrued benefit defined, 8:2
amount limitation, 9:51
annual retirement benefit, top-heavy
plan, 20:38
availability
amendment of qualified plan, 9:39
current, 9:34
effective, 9:35

choice
QJSA waiver, 9:23
QPSA waiver, 9:24
claim denial, 9:75
commencement, 9:54
defined benefit offset plan, 6:19
early, 9:67
integrated plan, 6:14
payment, 9:52
disability, annuity starting date, 9:3
distributions, years of service
requirement, 8:20
early retirement, qualified plan, 9:71
to employer, as fiduciary breach,
17:13
employer discretion, 9:44
forfeiture, 8:17
nonforfeitable benefits, 8:19
form of
denial by qualified plan, 9:36
employer denial of, 9:43
pattern of plan amendments, 9:42
formal application, 9:74
formula integrated rules and, 6:13
defined benefit offset plan, 6:18
401(k) plan separate accounting,
21:41
incidental death benefits rule, 9:64
income tax withholding, 14:7
level, multiemployer plan guarantee,
23:8
liabilities, 19:18
life insurance
effect on retirement benefits, 12:5
tax consequences of qualified plan
providing, 12:6
minimum-to-heavy vesting
requirement, 20:34
multiemployer plan guarantee, 23:6
non-Section 411(d)(6) protected, 8:27
one-year break in service and, 8:16
payment
commencement, 9:52
deferral, 9:53
form, 9:32, 9:33
method, 9:50
still-employed participant, 9:70
PBGC guarantee
amendment guarantee prior to
termination, 19:24
disqualification of plan, 19:25

(References in the index are to question numbers.)

limits on, 19:22
maximum guaranteed monthly, 19:23
single-employer defined benefit plan, 19:20, 19:21
plan investor
  defined, 17:20
  significant level of participation, 17:19
plan termination restriction on, 19:28
postponement election, 9:69
records, qualified retirement plan, 14:4
Section 411(d)(6)
  availability, 9:46
  protection, 9:41
  protection, effective dates, 9:48
single-employer defined benefit plan, 19:20
valuation, interest rate used, 9:73
waiver, 7:23
Bonding
fiduciary exception, 14:20
funds or other property, 14:18
party in interest, 14:21
retirement plan official, 14:17
single participant plan, 14:22
Breach of duty
co-fiduciary, 17:27–17:29
  contribution or indemnity, 17:29
  fiduciary liability, 17:27
fiduciary, ERISA punitive damages, 17:30
fiduciary liability, 17:25
nonfiduciary liability, 17:26
Brokers commissions, deductibility of plan expenses, 10:24
Business financing, use of ESOP, 22:45
Buy-back provision, restoral of forfeited benefits, 8:21

-C-

Capital gains
lump-sum distribution, 11:19
nonrecognition election
  ESOP allocation restrictions, 22:43
  selling shareholder, 22:36
recapture, disposition of qualified replacement property, 22:39
recognition election, ESOP sale,

statute of limitations, 22:40
securities sale to ESOP, deferral on, 22:30, 22:31, 22:35
Capitalization rule, deduction limits on employer contributions, 10:20
Cash-or-deferred arrangement (CODA)
and tax-deductible employer contributions, 21:44
annual addition limitation, 21:45
defined, 2:18
401(k) plan definition, 21:1
as profit sharing plan, 21:6
thrift or savings plan and, 21:43
Cash-or-deferred election, 401(k) plan, 21:2, 21:3
Class exemption, prohibited transaction, 18:12
Classification test, 4:18
Closely held corporation
ESOP
  as estate planning tool, 22:21
  as market for controlling shareholder stock, 22:29
  in shareholder buyout, 22:44
  prohibited transaction exemptions, 18:11
  qualified retirement plan advantages, 27:1, 27:2
CODA. *See* Cash-or-deferred arrangement
Collective bargaining agreement. *See* Labor union
Commissions
brokers, deduction of plan expenses, 10:22
IRA deductions, 24:20
Commonly controlled businesses, minimum coverage and participation requirements, 4:32
Common ownership, controlled group of corporations, 4:34
Compensation
defined, 6:24
for annual addition limitation, 5:3
for profit sharing plan deduction limits, 10:13
401(k) definition, 21:11
highly compensated employee defined, 4:29
1.0 rule, retirement plan contribution, 5:13

(References in the index are to question numbers.)

Compensation (*cont.*)
top-heavy plan limits, 20:50
Consultant, as fiduciary, 17:4
Contributions
See *also* Elective contributions;
Employee contributions;
Employer contribution; Qualified
retirement plan
IRA, 24:5
liability for failure, 7:17
SEP, tax treatment of, 25:16
timeliness, 10:3
Control, 27:28
Controlled group of corporations
common ownership and, 4:34
funding standard accounts, 7:15
liability for failure to make
contributions, 7:17
qualified retirement plan, 27:27
years of service vesting requirement,
8:10
Cost-of-living adjustments, defined
benefit plan, 5:5
Costs of plan
actuarial assumptions, 7:7
administration, payment from plan
assets, 17:23
deduction of employer payment,
10:24
past service, and funding
requirement, 7:10
P.S. 58, 12:7
qualified plan providing life
insurance, 12:7
Coverage requirements
employee benefit rule, 4:20
favorable tax treatment for retirement
plans, 4:15
labor union employees, and qualified
retirement plan, 1:16
qualified retirement plan, 4:1
termination of employment and, 4:21
Covered compensation, 6:22
Current liability, 7:2

-D-

Damages. See Penalty
Death benefits
estate tax exclusion, qualified
retirement plan, 12:17

estate tax marital deduction, 12:18
excess retirement accumulation
defined, 12:20
incidental death benefits rule, 9:64
as plan distributions, 20:18
qualified retirement plan, 12:1
insurance proceeds, 12:10
payments, taxation of, 12:16
top-heavy plans, 20:18
vesting forfeiture, 8:22
Deductions. See Tax deduction rules
Deferrals
Capital gains tax, securities sale to
ESOP, 22:30, 22:31, 22:35
excess 401(k) plan deferrals
correction of, 21:28
tax consequences, 21:29
to SEP, elective, 25:10
Defined benefit plan
See *also* Integrated plan; Qualified
retirement plan
accrued benefit limitation, 5:10
accrued benefits, 8:2
active participant, 24:9
actuarial assumptions, 2:15, 7:7
actuary as administrator, 14:14
alternative integration level, offset
plan, 6:20
alternative integration levels, 6:15
annual benefit defined, 5:6
annuity distributions, 9:57
asset allocation upon termination,
19:39
asset valuation, 7:12
automatic survivor benefits, 9:18
average compensation defined, 5:7
cash balance plan defined, 2:18
commencement of benefits, 6:14
company with older essential
employees, 2:25
conversion to another plan, 19:6
cost-of-living adjustment, 5:5
costs, 2:14
covered compensation, 6:22
defined, 1:2, 2:3
defined benefit excess plan, 6:2, 6:9
defined benefit offset formula,
integration rules, 6:18
defined benefit offset plan, 6:2
determining nondeductible
contributions, 10:10

Index

(References in the index are to question numbers.)

distress termination, 19:19, 19:20
dual participation in defined
   contribution plan, 5:12
early retirement, 9:71, 27:20
ERISA Title IV on termination, 19:9
excess assets after termination, 19:45,
   19:46
excess contributions deduction, 10:18
flat benefit plan defined, 2:12
floor offset plan defined, 2:17
forfeiture amounts, 8:18
forfeitures, restoral of, 8:21
full funding limitation, 7:14
funding method, effect on
   deductibility, 10:17
funding past service costs, 7:10
funding requirements, 7:2
integration level, 6:6
integration rules, 6:13
investment earnings and funding
   requirement, 7:11
life insurance benefit, 1:20
life insurance coverage, 12:4, 12:5
limit on tax-deductible contribution,
   10:16
maximizing benefits, 27:19
maximum annual retirement benefit,
   5:5
maximum offset allowance, defined
   benefit offset plan, 6:17
minimum coverage requirement, 4:20
minimum funding standards, 7:1
multiple top-heavy plan employer,
   minimum benefit/contribution for
   non-key employees, 20:49
objectives, 27:18
offset plan benefit commencement,
   6:19
overfunding relief, 19:48
prior benefit structure minimum
   participation requirement, 4:24
QPSA, 9:9
quarterly contributions, 7:26
reallocation of distributed assets,
   19:41
recordkeeping failure penalty, 14:6
self-employed individual contribution
   limits, 27:17
single-employer plan termination,
   19:16, 19:17, 19:18, 19:19, 19:20
Social Security integration, 6:2

Social Security retirement age
   defined, 5:9
standard termination, 19:17
target benefit plan, contrasted to, 2:5
termination of plan, 19:1, 19:11
   additional notice requirements,
      19:33
   benefit restrictions, 19:28
   factors, 19:3
   factors determining date, 19:31
   insurance coverage exemptions,
      19:13
   integration rules, 6:25
   notice of intent, 19:29
   to recover excess assets, 19:47
top-heavy plan, 20:1
   minimum benefit requirement,
      20:37, 20:42
   years of service, 20:41
transfer of excess assets as taxable
   income, 10:21
unit benefit plan defined, 2:13
years or participation or service
   requirement, 5:8, 20:41
Defined contribution plans
See also Integrated plan; Qualified
   retirement plan
accrued benefits, 8:2
ACP nondiscrimination test, 21:48
annual addition ceiling, 5:2
annual addition limitations, 5:1,
   21:26, 21:45
automatic survivor benefits, 9:18
company with older essential
   employees, 2:25
defined, 1:2, 2:2
defined contribution excess plan, 6:2,
   6:3
dual participation in defined plan,
   5:12
earmarking investments, 17:43
employer contribution, 5:1
floor offset plan defined, 2:17
health insurance benefit, 1:21
integration level, 6:6
integration rules and contribution
   formulas, 6:7
integration with Social Security, 6:2,
   6:3
life insurance benefits, 1:20
life insurance coverage, 12:4, 12:5

(*References in the index are to question numbers.*)

Defined contribution plans (*cont.*)
maximizing benefits, 27:19
minimum coverage requirement, 4:20
multiple top-heavy plan employer,
minimum benefit/contribution for
non-key employees, 20:49
objectives, 27:18
QPSA, 9:9
tax deductible contribution limits,
10:15
termination, 19:1, 19:3
termination insurance coverage
exemption, 19:13
thrift or savings plan, 2:7
top-heavy plan
employees receiving minimum
contributions, 20:46
minimum contribution requirement,
20:43
transfer of excess assets as taxable
income, 10:21
waiver of minimum funding
standards, 7:19
Delegation, fiduciary responsibilities,
17:33
Department of Labor
employer property contribution
prohibition, 18:8
exception to loan prohibition from
qualified retirement plan, 27:24
prohibited transaction class
exemption, 18:12
prohibited transactions, retroactive
exemptions, 18:10
reporting requirements, 15:17, 15:18
Determination letter
adverse determination, 13:12
affiliated service group retirement
plan, 27:32
defined, 13:1
employer application, 13:3
filing requirements, 13:7
Form 5310 filing, 15:15
length of application process, 13:11
limitations of, 13:5
notice to employees, 13:7
partial termination of plan, 19:5
place of filing, 13:9
plan termination notice, 19:55
"qualifies in operation" defined, 13:4
review procedure, 13:10

subsequent revocation, 13:13
termination of plan, 13:7, 19:7
timing of approval request, 13:6
user fee, 13:2
Determination year, 4:30
Director, qualified retirement plan,
27:26
Disability
benefits, annuity starting date, 9:3
distribution as lump-sum
distribution, 11:9
Disclaimer, summary plan description,
16:7
Discontinuance of contributions, profit
sharing plan, 19:50
Discrimination
benefit availability, 9:34, 9:35
benefit form, amendment of qualified
plan, 9:39
benefit payment form, 9:33, 9:34
401(k) plan special nondiscrimination
tests, 21:8
ADP calculation, 21:9
by qualified retirement plan in favor
of highly compensated
employees, 27:12
effect on tax-favored status, 27:13
reallocation of distributed plan
assets, 19:41
salary reduction SEP, 25:11
Dispositions
ESOP-qualified securities, excise tax,
22:41, 22:42
qualified replacement property
after nonrecognition election, 22:38
capital gain recapture, 22:39
Distress termination, defined benefit
plan, 19:19, 19:20
Distribution requirements
administrative discretion exception,
9:45
alternate beneficiary, 9:22
annual distribution, 9:57
annuity contracts and automatic
survivor benefit, 9:15
annuity starting date, 9:3, 9:4
attainment of age 70½, 9:55
automatic survivor rules, 9:18
exception to, 9:7
beneficiary change, 9:22
benefit amount limitation, 9:51

Index

(References in the index are to question numbers.)

benefit commencement date, 9:54
benefit form
    amendment of, 9:39
    effective availability, 9:35
benefit option
    amendment notice regarding, 9:40
    pattern of amendments and, 9:42
benefit payment commencement, 9:52
benefit payment form, 9:32, 9:33,
    9:34
    denial by qualified plan, 9:36
    effective dates, 9:38
benefit payment method, 9:50
benefit postponement election, 9:69
benefits to still-employed
    participants, 9:70
deferral election, 9:56
distribution to beneficiary, 9:61, 9:62
early commencement of benefits,
    9:67
early distribution penalty, 9:68
early retirement benefits, 9:71
employer denial of benefit form, 9:43
employer discretion, 9:44
estate tax on survivor annuity, 9:10
floor offset plans and automatic
    survivorship, 9:14
formal application for benefits, 9:74
401(k) plan matching and
    nonelective contributions, 21:40
frozen or terminated plan and
    automatic survivor benefits, 9:16
general spousal QPSA/QJSA waiver
    consent, 9:25
immediate involuntary distributions,
    9:72
incidental death benefits rule, 9:64
interest rate valuation, 9:73
involuntary distribution by qualified
    plan, 9:37
late distribution penalty, 9:00
life expectancy, 9:58
life expectancy recalculation, 9:59
loan effect on QJSA or QPSA, 9:11
married participants, 9:19
minimum distribution incidental
    benefit requirement, 9:65
minimum distribution requirement,
    9:57
multiple plan participant, 9:60
normal retirement age defined, 9:66

participant rights upon claim denial,
    9:75
payment deferral, 9:53
PBGC administration, 9:17
penalty for failure, 9:63
plan amendment, employer
    discretion, 9:47
plan amendment, transitional rule,
    9:49
QJSA notice to participant, 9:28
QJSA/QPSA subsidized by plan, 9:30
QJSA waiver, benefit choice, 9:23,
    9:24
QPSA notice to participant, 9:29
QPSA or QJSA waiver, 9:22
qualified joint and survivor annuity
    defined, 9:8
qualified preretirement survivor
    annuity defined, 9:9
remarried surviving spouse, 9:2
Section 411(d)(6) benefit availability,
    9:46
Section 411(d)(6) benefits, 9:41
spousal consent
    to loan, 9:12
    to QJSA or QPSA waiver, 9:21
    specified on document, 9:27
    to waiver, gift tax and, 9:26
survivor annuity benefit, 9.31
transferee plan, 9:13
transferee plan, 9:13
unmarried participant, and survivor
    benefits, 9:6
waiver of automatic survivor benefit,
    9:20
Distributions
See also Taxation of distributions
before retirement age, minimum
    benefit for top-heavy plan, 20:39
calculation of excess, 11:27
choice of form, 14:12
correcting excess 401(k) plan
    contribution, 21:24
    tax treatment of, 21:25
deductible employee contributions,
    5:17
disqualified retirement plan, rollovers
    of, 26:20
ESOP
    at certain intervals, 22:61
    commencement of, 22:60

(References in the index are to question numbers.)

Distributions

ESOP *(cont.)*
early distribution tax, 22:62
excess aggregate contributions, tax treatment, 21:55
excess defined, 11:26
401(k) plan
excess deferrals, 21:28
excess deferrals, after year-end, 21:30
timing of, 21:33
grandfather recovery amount, 11:30
IRA
limitations, 24:29
minimum distribution requirement, 24:30, 24:31
minimum distribution requirements at death, 24:36
premature distribution penalty, 24:37
taxation of, 24:32
liability for excess, 11:25
partial, from qualified retirement plan, 26:10
post-death, excise tax, 12:27
qualified retirement plan, 1:1
rollover into SEP, 25:20
rollovers, 26:7
SEP, taxation of, 25:18
10 percent excise tax, 1:19
top-heavy plan determination, 20:17
vesting years of service, 8:20
Diversification of investments
defined, 22:48
ESOP
dividends, 22:54
effect of, 22:52
excess amounts, 22:58
exclusions, 22:56
requirements, 22:51
subject securities, 22:53, 22:55, 22:57
fiduciary responsibility, 17:37
Dividends
cash election, deductibility, 22:13
employer securities, deductibility, 22:12
ESOP, taxation of, 22:14
Domestic relations order. *See* Qualified domestic relations order (QDRO)

-E-

Early retirement benefits, 9:71, 27:20
Earmarking investments, 17:43
Earned income, 27:10
Economic Recovery Tax Act of 1981 (ERTA), 1:10
Elective contributions
compensation defined for purposes of, 21:11
defined, 21:13
401(k) plan, 21:5
dollar limits, 21:26
time period, 21:27
timing of distributions, 21:33
nonforfeitability and distribution requirements, matching and nonelective contributions, 21:40
payroll tax, 21:46
Employee
See also Participant
benefit requirement, qualified retirement plan, 4:20
compensation, 1.0 rule, retirement plan contribution, 5:13
effect of plan choice on, 1:8
leased employee defined, 4:36
participation in defined benefit and defined contribution plans, 5:12
participation in qualified plan, commencement of, 4:7
termination, and minimum coverage requirement, 4:21
waiver of participation, effect on plan tax status, 4:26
Employee contributions
ACP test, 21:48, 21:50
cash-or-deferred election, 21:3
deductibility, qualified retirement plan and, 5:17
401(k) plan ADP test, 21:12
as plan assets, 17:22
qualified retirement plan limitation, 5:14
qualified retirement plan requirement, 4:6
tax treatment of deductible distributions, 11:24
top-heavy plans, 20:20
vesting standards, 8:8

Index

Employee-owner
allocation of personal service
corporation income, 27:34
defined, 27:35
Employee Retirement Income Security Act (ERISA)
See also Pension Benefit Guaranty
Corporation; Prohibited
transactions
contribution or indemnity from
breaching co-fiduciary, 17:29
fiduciary, 17:1
damages for fiduciary, 17:30
liability for breach of duty, 17:25
relief from past liability, 17:32
responsibilities, and Keogh plan,
17:5
generally, 1:9
payroll-deduction IRA, 24:27
prohibited transactions, 18:1–18:4,
18:6–18:10, 18:12
reporting requirements, criminal
penalties, 15:9
Title IV, 19:9
Employee stock ownership plan (ESOP)
allocation restrictions, nonrecognition
transaction, 22:43
annual addition limit, 22:15
cash dividends, deductibility of,
22:13
closely held corporation shareholder
buyout, 22:44
corporate and stockholder benefit,
2:26
deferred gain on securities sale,
22:30, 22:31, 22:35
defined, 2:10, 22:1
disposition of qualified securities,
excise tax, 22:41, 22:42
distribution commencement, 22:60
distribution intervals, 22:61
dividends on employer securities
deductibility of, 22:12
taxation of, 22:14
early distribution tax, 22:62
employer securities defined, 22:10
employer securities sale, filing
statement, 22:25
estate planning tool for closely held

corporation owner, 22:21
estate tax deduction for employer
security sale, 22:22
estate tax liability of deceased
stockholder, 22:28
exempt loan, 22:4
financing business, 22:45
financing company acquisition,
22:18
gain nonrecognition, selling
shareholder, 22:36
integration with Social Security,
22:17
investment diversification
defined, 22:48
dividends, 22:54
effect of, 22:52
excess amounts, 22:58
exclusions, 22:56
requirements, 22:51
securities acquired before 1985,
22:57
subject securities, 22:53, 22:55
loan
incentive, 22:5
prohibited transaction rules, 18:7
from shareholder, 22:59
as market for controlling shareholder
stock, 22:29
nonallocation period, estate tax
deduction, 22:27
penalty for improper allocation of
employer securities distribution,
22:26
profit sharing plan conversion, 22:20
put option, exercising, 22:2
qualified election period, 22:50
qualified employer securities defined,
22:23
qualified participant, 22:49
qualified replacement property, 22:33
basis, 22:37
nonrecognition election and later
disposition, 22:38
qualified securities defined, 22:32
qualified securities sale, statute of
limitations on gain
nonrecognition election, 22:40
replacement period, 22:34
securities acquisition loan, 22:6

(References in the index are to question numbers.)

Employee stock ownership plan (ESOP) *(cont.)*
securities acquisition loan,
  50-percent interest exclusion, 22:7
  eligibility, 22:7
  limit on eligibility period, 22:9
  transfer to other lending institutions, 22:8
versus stock bonus plan, 22:3
stock contributions deduction, 22:16
as takeover defense, 22:19
tax-deductible contribution limit, 22:11
tradability valuation of employer securities, 22:63

Employer
annual return schedules, 15:4
insolvency, multiemployer plan withdrawal liability, 23:32
of leased employee, defined, 4:37
missed profit sharing plan contribution, 10:12
related, top-heavy rules for separate plans, 20:13
ten largest owners, top-heavy plans, 20:27
termination of qualified retirement plan, 19:1

Employer contribution
See also Employer securities; Property; Self-employed individual
base contribution percentage defined, 6:5
current deductibility, 10:2
deductibility of amount in excess of Section 415 limits, 10:23
defined benefit plan
  deduction limits, 10:16
  quarterly payments, 7:26
defined contribution plan, 5:1
ESOP
  stock deductibility, 22:16
  tax-deductibility limit, 22:11
excess amounts
  deductibility rules, 10:8
  defined benefit plan, 10:18
excess contribution percentage defined, 6:4
family aggregation rule, 10:25

401(k) plan
elective contributions defined, 21:13
qualified matching contributions, 21:14
qualified nonelective contributions, 21:14
full funding limitations, 7:14
minimum funding standards, 7:6
  IRS waiver, 7:18
multiple plan deduction limits, 10:19
multiple plans, deduction of excess contributions, 10:22
noncompliance penalty, 7:16
nondeductible contributions
  amount, 10:9
  timing of determination, 10:10
profit sharing plan of affiliated company, 10:14
promissory note as payment, 10:6
qualified retirement plan, maximum allowed, 27:14
tax deduction limits, 10:20
tax deduction rules, 10:1
tax effect of CODA, 21:44
timeliness, funding standards versus tax deductibility, 7:25
top-heavy defined contribution plan minimum, 20:43
prohibited transaction rules, 18:7, 18:8

Employer securities
See also Employee stock ownership plan (ESOP)
defined, 22:10
dividend deductibility, 22:12
estate tax deduction on sale, 22:24
  ESOP, 22:22
filing statement, 22:25
lump-sum distribution, tax treatment, 11:16
penalty for improper allocation or distribution, 22:26
prohibited transaction rules, 18:7
qualified employer securities defined, 22:23
qualified replacement property, 22:33
qualified retirement plan investment, 17:40
qualified securities defined, 22:32
qualifying employer securities

(References in the index are to question numbers.)

defined, 17:42
tradability valuation, 22:63
Equity interest, 17:17
Equity participation, significant level
of, 17:19
ERISA. *See* Employee Retirement
Income Security Act (ERISA)
ESOP. *See* Employee stock ownership
plan (ESOP)
Estate tax
additional
death of plan participant, 11:37
excess retirement accumulation,
12:19
death benefits exclusion, qualified
retirement plans, 12:17
ESOP
closely held corporation, 22:21
employer security sale, 22:22
liability for deceased stockholder,
22:28
sale of employer securities,
relevant proceeds, 22:24
excess retirement accumulation,
12:25
IRA assets, 24:33
life insurance proceeds under
qualified retirement plan, 12:12
qualified employer securities defined,
22:23
surviving spouse as beneficiary of
aggregate interests, 12:24
survivor annuity, 9:10
Excess aggregate contributions
correction of, 21:54
defined, 21:53
tax treatment of, 21:55
Excess benefit percentage, 6:10
Excess contribution percentage, 6:4
Excess retirement accumulation,
generally, 12:25, 12:26
grandfather rule, 12:23
single life annuity, 12:22
Excise tax
disallowance of plan contribution
deduction, 10:11
distribution failure, 9:63
ESOP disposition of qualified
securities, 22:41, 22:42
excess contributions to profit sharing
plan, 10:8

excess IRA contribution, 24:6
excess recipient distributions, 11:25
excess retirement accumulation
liability, 12:26
funding requirement penalty, 7:16
improper distribution of employer
securities, 22:26
nondeductible contributions, 10:10
qualified plan distributions, 1:19
qualified retirement plan loans, 11:42
recharacterized 401(k) plan excess
contributions, 21:23
Experience gain or loss, 7:11

-F-

Family aggregation rule
defined, 5:18, 21:57
highly compensated employee, 4:31
minimum coverage requirement, 4:22
tax deduction rules, 10:25
Fee
determination letter, 13:2
excess retirement accumulation,
12:25
IRA trustee, 24:20
payment from plan assets, 17:23
plan administration, deduction of
employer payments, 10:24
qualified retirement plan adoption,
1:12
Fiduciary
asset segregation, 17:14
basic duty, 17:10
bonding of, 14:17
bonding exception, 14:20
co-fiduciary breach, 17:28, 17:29
contribution or indemnity from
breaching co-fiduciary, 17:29
degree of risk, 17:38
delegation of responsibilities, 17:33
diversification responsibility, 17:37
employer benefit as breach of duty,
17:13
ERISA
damages for breach, 17:30
fiduciary defined, 17:1
Keogh plan, 17:5
improper use of plan assets, 17:24
investment advice determining status,
17:2

(References in the index are to question numbers.)

Fiduciary (*cont.*)
  investment in another entity, 17:15
  liability for breach of duty, 17:25
  liability insurance, 17:31
  look-through rule, 17:16
  named fiduciary defined, 17:3
  prohibited individual, 17:8
  prohibited transactions, 18:1–18:12
  prohibited transaction exemptions,
    18:11
  prudent man rule, 17:39
  relief from past liability under
    ERISA, 17:32
  relief from personal liability, 17:31
  self-directed account plan defined,
    17:6
  self-directed participant or
    beneficiary, 17:7
  service to plan, prohibited
    transaction rules, 18:7
  standard of care, 17:11
Final average compensation, 6:23
Flat benefit plan, 2:12
Floor offset plan
  automatic survivor annuity
    requirements, 9:14
  defined, 2:17
  top-heavy safe harbor rules, 20:49
Forfeiture
  benefits, 8:17
  401(k) plan contribution, 21:31
  401(k) plan matching and
    nonelective contributions, 21:40
  money purchase pension plan
    contributions, 2:4
  nonforfeitable benefit, 8:19
  QDRO alternate payee, 28:12
  SEP contribution, 25:5
  top-heavy plan minimum
    contributions, 20:44
  vesting benefits, 8:17, 8:18
Form 5500 series. *See* Annual return
Forward averaging
  effect of plan choice on employee,
    1:8
  lump-sum distribution, 11:22, 11:23
  to individuals at age 50 before
    1/1/86, 11:13
  taxation of, 11:15
Frozen retirement plan
  automatic survivor benefits, 9:16

top-heavy rules, 20:15
401(k) plans
  ACP test, 21:48
    calculation, 21:49
    contributions included, 21:50
    determination, 21:15
    elective contributions, 21:12
    excess aggregate contributions,
      21:53–21:55
    other requirements, 21:52
    timing of contribution, 21:51
  ADR calculation, 21:9
    for multiple plans, 21:10
  cash-or-deferred election, 21:2
  CODA
    annual addition limitation, 21:45
    tax-deductible employer
      contributions, 21:44
    thrift or savings plan, 21:43
  combined plan defined, 21:32
  compensation defined, 21:11
  correcting excess contributions, 21:17
  defined, 2:8, 21:1
  distributions, timing of, 21:33
  elective contributions, 21:13
    dollar limit, 21:26
    payroll tax, 21:46
    tax treatment, 21:5
    time period, 21:27
  excess contributions, 21:16
    distribution correcting, 21:24
    failure to correct, 21:18
    tax treatment, 21:25
  excess deferrals
    ADP test on distribution after
      year-end, 21:30
    correction of, 21:28
    tax consequences, 21:29
  family aggregation rules defined,
    21:57
  favorable tax treatment, 3:2
  forfeitability of contributions, 21:31
  hardship distribution, 21:34
    hardship defined, 21:35
    heavy and immediate financial
      need, 21:36, 21:37
  multiple plans, 21:42
  multiple use limitation, 21:56
  qualified nonelective contributions
    and qualified matching
    contributions, 21:14

Index

(References in the index are to question numbers.)

qualified nonelective contributions,
top-heavy rules, 20:6
recharacterization of excess
contributions, 21:19
excise tax, 21:23
penalty tax, 21:22
tax consequences, 21:20
timing, 21:21
SEC registration, 21:47
self-employed individual, 21:7
separate accounting of benefits, 21:41
special nondiscrimination tests, 21:8,
21:48
tax advantages, 21:4
top-heavy minimum contribution
rules, 20:48
Full funding limitation, 7:14
Funding method, defined benefit plan
deductible contributions, 10:17
Funding requirements
actuarial assumptions, 7:7
in addition to minimums, 7:2
alternative to waiver, 7:23
amendment of plan with existing
waiver, 7:22
amortization extension, 7:24
asset valuation, 7:12
controlled group of corporations,
7:15
defined benefit plan quarterly
payments, 7:26
exceptions to minimum funding
standards, 7:3
filing funding waiver request, 7:20,
7:21
full funding limitation defined, 7:14
funding standard account defined,
7:13
future accrued benefits, reduction of,
8:26
insurance contract plan, 7:4
liability, 7:17
liability overstatement penalty, 7:8
minimum funding standard failure,
7:16
minimum funding standards, 7:1
noncompliance penalty, 7:16
normal retirement age, 7:9
notice of waiver request, 7:20
past service costs, 7:10
pension plan investment earnings

7:11
termination of pension plan, 7:27
timeliness of contributions, 7:25, 10:3
waiver of minimum standards, 7:18
waiver procedure, 7:19

-G-

Garnishment, qualified plan benefits,
3:10
Gift, spousal consent to waiver, 9:26
Grandfather rule
defined, 11:29
discretionary method, 11:31
excess distribution tax, 11:33
excess retirement accumulation of
deceased participant, 12:23
lump-sum distribution, 11:34
recovery of initial amount, 11:30

-H-

Hardship
401(k) plan distributions, 21:34
defined, 21:35
heavy and immediate financial
need, 21:36–21:39
IRS waiver of minimum funding
standards, 7:19
waiving minimum funding standards,
7:18
Health insurance, qualified retirement
plan benefit, 1:21
Heavy and immediate financial need
fact and circumstances test, 21:36,
21:38
safe-harbor test, 21:37, 21:39
Highly compensated employees
benefit payment form, 9:33
compensation defined, 4:29
defined, 4:28
determination year and look-back
year defined, 4:30
family aggregation rule, 4:22, 4:31,
5:18, 21:57
401(k) ADP test, 21:8
ADP calculation, 21:9
401(k) plan excess contribution,
21:16
multiple use limitation, 21:56

I-15

(References in the index are to question numbers.)

Highly compensated employees (*cont.*)
plan failure to meet minimum
coverage or participation
requirements, 4:27
qualified retirement plan
discrimination, 27:12
effect on tax-favored status, 27:13
SEP discrimination prohibition, 25:3
Hour of service
defined, 4:9
maternity or paternity leave, 4:14
multiemployer plan, 23:4

-I-

Immediate participation requirement,
leased employee, 4:40
Incidental death benefits rule, 9:64
Income tax deductions. *See* Tax
deduction rules
Incorporation
for retirement plan qualification, 1:4
self-employed individual, advantages
to, 27:6
self-employed individual, handling
existing qualified plan, 27:7
Individual retirement account (IRA)
See also Rollovers
access by judgment creditors, 24:39
active participant deduction
limitation, income level, 24:10
active participant defined, 24:9
active participation defined, 24:8
applicable deduction limits for
qualified retirement plan
participant, 24:11
asset transfer at divorce, 24:38
basic characteristics, 24:2
beneficiary rollover, 26:6
borrowing during rollover period, 26:4
contribution amount, 24:5
contributions, timing of, 24:18
credit card payment, 24:23
deduction claim, timing of, 24:19
designated nondeductible
contributions, 24:13
distributions
restrictions on, 24:29
taxation of, 24:32
eligible individual, 24:4
eligibility of active participants in

qualified retirement plans, 24:7
employee-sponsored, 24:24
qualified retirement plan coverage,
24:25
versus SEP, 24:28
estate taxes on, 24:33
excess contribution penalty, 24:6
financing, 24:22
free checking benefit, 24:21
individual retirement annuity, basic
characteristics, 24:3
individual retirement plan defined,
24:1
inherited, 24:34
insufficient distribution penalty,
24:31
minimum distribution requirement,
24:30, 24:36
multiple tax-free transfers, 26:5
nondeductible contribution, 24:12,
24:15
nondeduction election, 24:14
payroll deduction, 24:26
ERISA liabilities and compliance
requirements, 24:27
premature distribution penalty, 24:37
QDRO rules and, 28:5
qualified retirement plan rollovers to,
tax considerations, 26:21
rollover, 1:3
accounts, 26:2
amounts, transfer to qualified
retirement plan, 26:19
between IRAs, 26:3
partial distribution treatment, 26:11
from qualified retirement plan,
procedure, 26:16
revocation, 26:22
SEP contribution to, 25:6
spousal IRA, 24:17
surviving spouse, special rules, 24:35
trustee fee, 24:20
withdrawals, tax treatment of, 24:16
Insolvency of employer, multiemployer
plan withdrawal liability, 23:32
Installment payments, and lump-sum
distribution, 11:6
Insurance
contract plan
conversion of pension plan, 7:5
defined, 7:4

Index

fiduciary liability, 17:31
multiemployer plan benefits, 23:6
plan termination, 19:9–19:16
for prohibited transaction losses, 18:6
Insured qualified retirement plan, 2:19
Integrated plan
alternative integration levels
defined benefit excess plan, 6:15
defined benefit offset plan, 6:20
average annual compensation
defined, 6:21
base benefit percentage (BBP), 6:11
base contribution percentage (BCP),
6:5
benefit to business owner, 27:21
commencement of benefits, 6:14
compensation defined, 6:24
contribution formulas under defined
contribution excess plan, 6:7
covered compensation, 6:22
defined, 6:1
defined benefit excess plan
formulas, 6:13
general rules, 6:9
defined benefit offset plan
benefit commencement, 6:19
benefit formulas, 6:18
rules, 6:16
defined contribution excess plan, 6:3,
6:8
eligibility, 6:2
excess benefit percentage, 6:10
excess contribution percentage, 6:4
final average compensation defined,
6:23
integration level, 6:6
maximum excess allowance, 6:12
maximum offset allowance, 6:17
qualified retirement plan and Social
Security, 6:1
termination, effect of, 6:25
top-heavy plan restrictions, 6:26
Integration level, 6:6
Interest from retirement plan loan,
deductibility of, 11:40
Internal Revenue Code (IRC)
prohibited transactions,
18:3–18:5, 18:7–18:12
Internal Revenue Service (IRS)
notice of plan termination, 19:55
retirement plan approval, 3:6

Internal Revenue Service (IRS)
reporting
annual return schedules, 15:4
Form 5500 series annual return, 15:2
automatic extension, 15:7
due date, 15:5
filing extension, 15:6
late filing penalty, 15:8
late third-party filing, 15:10
statute of limitations, 15:11
generally, 15:1
prohibited transaction, Form 5500
statute of limitations, 15:12
qualified retirement plan distribution
reporting forms, 15:16
special return filing, 15:15
Investment earnings, funding
requirement and, 7:11
Investment manager, liability, 17:34
IRA. See Individual retirement account
IRS penalty. See Penalty
IRS waiver. See Waiver

-K-

Keogh plan
defined, 2:16
and ERISA fiduciary responsibility
rules, 17:5
Key employee
defined, 20:24
non-key employee for top-heavy
plan, 20:29
participation in multiple top-heavy
plans, 20:51
top-heavy plan 1.0 rule, 20:53
combined fractions over 1.0, 20:55
concentration test, 20:57
extra minimum benefit or
contribution, 20:58
multiple plan maximum limits,
20:56
top-heavy rules, 20:16
exclusion from second plan
participation, 20:52
former key employee, 20:30

-L-

Labor union See also Multiemployer
plans

(*References in the index are to question numbers.*)

Labor union (*cont.*)
aggregation of collectively bargained
retirement plans, 20:11
collective bargaining agreement,
termination of plan, 19:27
multiemployer plan vesting
standards, 8:4
notice of funding waiver request,
7:21
qualified retirement plan
eligibility, 4:5
exclusions, 1:16

Leased employee
defined, 4:36
employer defined, 4:37
participation in qualified retirement
plan, 4:39
participation requirement, 4:40
qualified plan approval, 4:41
years of service, 4:38

Liability
benefit liabilities defined, 19:18
employer
multiemployer plan withdrawal,
23:10–23:44
for taxes on reversion, 19:48
for underfunded terminated plan,
19:44
excess retirement accumulation tax,
12:26
excess retirement plan distributions,
11:25
failure to make plan contributions,
7:17
overstatement penalty, 7:8
plan asset investment, 17:34
relief from breach of fiduciary duty,
17:31
withholding failure, 14:8

Life expectancy
annual recalculation, 9:59
determination, 9:58

Life insurance
beneficiary under qualified
retirement plan, 12:10
cost recovery upon qualified plan
distribution, 12:13
insured qualified retirement plan
defined, 2:19
P.S. 58 rates, 12:8
qualified retirement plan

advantages to participant, 12:15
benefit, 1:20
benefit protection, 27:23
contribution deduction, 12:3
coverage, 12:2
estate tax on, 12:12
limits on, 12:4
loan taxability, 12:9
taxation of proceeds, 12:11
tax consequences, 12:6
retirement plan benefits and, 12:5

Limitation year
qualified retirement plan, 5:11

Line-of-business exception
minimum coverage and participation
requirements, 4:35

Loan
for acquisition of securities, 22:6
by shareholders, 22:59
as tax incentive for commerical
lender, 22:5
life insurance from qualified plan,
12:9
prohibited transaction
exemptions, 18:11, 22:4
rules, 18:7
QPSA or QJSA, effect on, 9:11
for qualified retirement plan
investment, 17:36
from qualified plan, 11:42
deductibility of interest, 11:40
limits on, 11:38
maximum repayment period, 11:39
spousal consent, 11:41
by sponsor from qualified retirement
plan, 27:24, 27:25
spousal consent to loan on accrued
benefit, 9:12

Local law
and qualified retirement plan trust,
3:4

Look-back year, 4:30

Look-through rule
exceptions, 17:16
nonexception investments, 17:21

Lump-sum distribution
additional distribution, tax benefits
and, 11:7
balance to the credit of an employee,
11:5
to beneficiary of deceased

(References in the index are to question numbers.)

participant, taxation issues,
11:10, 11:11
benefit availability, 9:46
capital gains treatment, 11:19
defined, 11:4
of employer securities, tax treatment,
11:16
excess distributions, special rule,
11:28
explanation of tax rules, 14:11
five-year averaging, 11:17
forward averaging election, 11:22,
11:23
grandfather rule, 11:34
individual at age 50 before 1/1/86,
special taxation rules, 11:13
and installment payments, 11:6
and qualified retirement plan
distribution to disabled
employee, 11:9
taxable portion, 11:15
tax advantages, 1:3
taxation of, 11:12
tax effect on employee, 1:8
ten-year averaging, 11:18

-M-

Management corporation, 27:29
Married participants
death benefit, 12:1
Master retirement plan, 2:21
Matching contributions
ACP test, 21:48, 21:50
401(k) plan, 21:14
elective contribution
nonforfeitability and
distribution rules, 21:40
Maternity leave
retirement plan service requirement,
4:14
Maximum excess allowance,
integrated plan, 6:12
Maximum offset allowance,
integrated plan, 6:17
Merger of qualified plan, 4:25, 8:28
Minimum age requirement,
qualified retirement plan, 4:2
Minimum coverage requirement
commonly controlled businesses, 4:32
effect of failure on tax status, 4:27

line-of-business exception, 4:35
Minimum funding standards
additional employer contribution, 7:6
generally, 7:1
IRS waiver, 7:18, 7:19
Minimum participation requirement
commonly controlled businesses,
4:32
effect of failure on tax status, 4:27
line-of-business exception, 4:35
merger with another plan, 4:25
prior benefit structure, 4:24
qualified retirement plan, 4:23
sponsor with multiple businesses,
4:33
Money purchase pension plan
active participant, 24:9
contrasted to target benefit plans, 2:5
defined, 2:4
minimum funding standards, 7:1
thrift or savings plan as, 2:7
**Multiemployer Pension Plan
Amendments Act of 1980
(MPPAA),** 1:10
Multiemployer plan
See also Sponsor
abatement determination, 23:25
effect of abatement, 23:28
interim payments, 23:26
nonabatement effects, 23:29
nonabatement election by
reentering employer, 23:30
requirements, 23:27
affiliated company retirement plan,
23:5
appropriate retirement benefit plan
for union workers, 23:1
basic advantages, 23:3
benefit guarantee, 23:6
benefit level guarantee, 23:8
benefits without PBGC guarantee,
23:9
defined, 23:2
employer liability upon termination,
23:43
employer withdrawal, 23:10
arbitration, 23:37
bankruptcy claim priority, 23:41
change in business structure, 23:18
computation of UVB (unfunded
vested benefit) share, 23:22

(References in the index are to question numbers.)

Multiemployer plan
employer withdrawal (*cont.*)
contesting liability determination, 23:36
contribution suspension during labor dispute, 23:19
determination, 23:20
effect of value, 23:31
employer liability for withdrawal, 23:10, 23:11
employers under common control, 23:17
exclusions, 23:44
facility for partial withdrawal, 23:16
initial determination, 23:35
insolvent employer, 23:32
mass withdrawal, 23:42
missed payment, 23:39
notice, 23:34
owners of employer, 23:40
partial withdrawal, 23:15
payment commencement, 23:38
period, 23:13
plan without UBVs, 23:23
process, 23:12
reentering a plan, 23:25
sale of employer assets, 23:21
special circumstances, 23:14
20-year cap, 23:33
waiver or reduction, 23:24
hours of service, 23:4
insolvency, 23:7
minimum vesting standards, 8:4
top-heavy rules, 20:5
unfunded vested benefits, 23:10, 23:22, 23:23
years of service requirement, 8:10
Multiple plans
deductible contribution limits, 10:19
excess contribution deduction rule, 10:22
401(k) plans, 21:10, 21:42
top-heavy plans
adopted before 1984, 20:54
determination, 20:22
key employee exclusion from second top-heavy plan, 20:52
key employee 1.0 rule, maximum limits, 20:56

non-key employee minimum benefit/contribution, 20:49
Multiple use limitation, 21:56
Mutual fund
prohibited transaction class exemption, 18:12
qualified retirement plan investment, 17:45

-N-

Nonhighly compensated workforce, 4:40
Nonqualified retirement plan
contributions
deductibility, 1:5
limitations, 1:7
taxation of, 1:6
effect of plan choice on employee, 1:8
employee coverage, 1:7
Notice
amendment of benefit options, 9:40
claim denial, 9:75
determination letter, application for, 13:7
failure to make plan contributions, 7:17
failure to meet funding standards, 7:16
final distribution of assets, 19:42
funding waiver request filing, 7:20
to IRS, plan termination, 19:55
multiemployer plan withdrawal liability, 23:34
PBGC notice of noncompliance
extension of notice period, 19:36
timing of notice, 19:35
PBGC reporting, 15:25
plan benefits, required termination information, 19:34
plan merger, 8:28
plan termination, 19:17
QJSA, to plan participant, 9:28
QPSA, to participant, 9:29
of significant event to PBGC, 19:16
termination of defined benefit plan, 19:29
termination of plan, 19:1

Index

(References in the index are to question numbers.)

-O-

Officers
as highly compensated employees,
4:28
as qualified plan administrators, 14:2
top-heavy plan, 20:25, 20:26
Offset. *See* Floor offset plan
**Omnibus Budget Reconciliation Act of
1987 (OBRA '87),** 1:10
**Omnibus Budget Reconciliation Act of
1989 (OBRA '89),** 1:10
One-year break in service
defined, retirement plan eligibility
requirement, 4:10
maternity or paternity leave, 4:14
vesting requirement, 8:14–8:16
Operating company, 17:18
Oral trust, tax treatment of, 3:3
Ordinary income
deductible employee contributions as,
11:24
lump-sum distribution as, 11:19
Owner, 5% or 1% owner, top-heavy
plan rules, 20:28
Owner-employee
defined, 27:9
multiple businesses, qualified
retirement plan rules, 27:28
Ownership, common, and controlled
group of businesses, 4:34

-P-

Participant
active, in IRA, 24:9
advantages of qualified plan life
insurance protection, 12:15
age limit, 4:3
attainment of age 70½, 9:55
average annual compensation, 6:21
average compensation, top-heavy
plan minimum benefit, 20:40
bankruptcy, ESOP interest exemption,
22:64
benefit payments during
employment, 9:70
benefit postponement election, 9:69
benefits upon plan merger, 8:28
compensation, top-heavy plan

contribution requirements, 20:45
in defined benefit and defined
contribution plans, 5:12
early distribution penalty, 9:68
eligibility requirements, 1:15
ERISA protection, 1:9
ESOP qualified participant, 22:49
exemption from automatic survivor
rules, 9:7
as fiduciary, 17:7
married, commencement of benefits,
9:19
multiple plans, distribution rules,
9:60
in multiple top-heavy plans, key
employee as, 20:51
notice of QJSA, 9:28
notice of QPSA, 9:29
number of, for termination insurance
premium, 19:15
payment deferral, 9:53
rights upon claim denial, 9:75
tax advantages of qualified retirement
plan, 1:3
taxation of plan benefits, 1:6
tax consequences of qualified plan
providing life insurance, 12:6
unlocated, asset distribution
procedure, 19:38
unmarried, and survivor benefit
requirements, 9:5
vesting buy-back provisions, 8:21
Participation requirement
five-year, tax options, 11:14
immediate, leased employee, 4:40
minimum
commonly controlled business,
4:32
effect of failure on tax status, 4:27
line-of-business exception, 4:35
plan merger, 4:25
prior benefit structure, 4:24
qualified retirement plan, 4:23
sponsor with multiple businesses,
4:33
months of plan participation, 11:20
qualified retirement plan, 4:1
Partnership
Keogh plan defined, 2:16
owner-employee defined, 27:9

(References in the index are to question numbers.)

Partnership (cont.)
SEP plan, contribution by successor, 25:14

Party in interest
class exemption, prohibited transactions, 18:12
defined, 18:2
penalty for prohibited transaction, 18:4
prohibited transaction exemption, 18:9
sale by, prohibited transaction exemption, 18:11
service to plan, 18:7

Paternity leave, retirement plan service requirement, 4:14

PBGC. See Pension Benefit Guaranty Corporation (PBGC)

Penalty
borrowing from qualified retirement plan, 27:24
criminal, ERISA reporting violations, 15:9
distribution failure, 9:63
early distribution, 9:68
excess IRA contribution excise tax, 24:6
fiduciary
breach of duty, 17:25
prohibited transaction, 18:4
punitive damages, 17:30
improper allocation or disposition of ESOP-purchased employer securities, 22:26
improper use of plan assets, 17:24
IRA distribution shortfall, 24:31
IRA premature distributions, 24:37
IRA reporting failure, 24:15
late filing of Form 5500 series annual return, 15:8
late PBGC premium payment, 15:23
liability overstatement, 7:8
prohibited transactions, 18:4
punitive damages for, fiduciary breach, 17:30
recharacterizing 401(k) plan excess contributions, 21:22
recordkeeping failure, 14:6
taxation of distributions, 11:1
underpayment of quarterly payment, 7:26

waiver of late charges by PBGC, 15:24

Pension Benefit Guaranty Corporation (PBGC)
See also Employee Retirement Income Security Act (ERISA); Termination of plan
defined, 19:10
form filing after plan termination, 15:22
guaranteed benefits, 19:20
initiation of plan termination, 19:26
insurance coverage, 19:12
late payment charges, 15:23
limitations on benefit guarantee, 19:22
multiemployer plan benefits not guaranteed, 23:9
multiemployer plan guarantee, 23:6
notification, 15:25
premium form filing, change in plan year, 15:21
premium forms due date, 15:20
required reporting forms, 15:19
survivor benefit plan, 9:17
termination of plan, 19:2

Pension plan
annual contributions, 1:13
defined contribution plan deduction, 10:15
employer property contribution prohibition, 18:8
funding standard account, 7:13
health insurance benefit, 1:21
as insurance contract plan, 7:4, 7:5
normal retirement age, and minimum funding, 7:9
payment limitation, 19:8
payroll-deduction IRA, 24:27
termination insurance coverage, 19:12

Pension Protection Act (PPA), 1:10, 19:11

Personal service corporation
allocation of income to employee-owner, 27:34
defined, 27:33
rules, other organization, 27:36
safe harbor rules, 27:37
qualified retirement plan consideration, 27:38

Plan administrator. See Administrator

(References in the index are to question numbers.)

of plan

Plan expenses. *See* Costs of plan

Pooled investment funds, 17:44

Premiums
PBGC forms, 15:20
change in plan year and, 15:21
PBGC late payment penalty, 15:23
plan termination insurance, 19:14,
19:15

Prior benefit structure
defined, minimum participation
requirement, 4:24

Professional corporation
plan interest, protection from
creditors, 27:42

Profit sharing plan
active participant, 24:9
advantages to small companies, 2:24
annual contributions, 1:13
benefit types, 1:19
cash or deferred arrangement as,
21:6
compensation defined for deduction
limits, 10:13
complete discontinuance of
contributions, 19:50
contribution flexibility, 2:23
defined, 2:6
employer contribution to affiliated
company, 10:14
ESOP conversion, 22:20
excess contributions, deductibility
rules, 10:8
full vesting upon complete
discontinuance, 19:51
health insurance benefit, 1:21
missed contribution, 10:12
objectives, 27:18
recently formed company, 2:24
tax deductible contributions, 10:7
thrift or savings plan as, 2:7

Prohibited transaction
borrowing from qualified retirement
plan, 27:24
class exemption, 18:12
closely held corporation, exemptions
for, 18:11
correction of, 18:5
defined, 18:1
disqualified person defined, 18:3
employer property contribution, 18:8

insurance against transaction loss,
18:6
IRA free checking benefit, 24:21
IRC versus ERISA provisions, 18:3
loan exception, 18:7
party in interest defined, 18:2
party in interest exemptions, 18:9
penalty against party in interest or
disqualified person, 18:4
retroactive exemptions, 18:10
statutory exemptions, 18:7

Promissory note
as payment, tax deduction rules, 10:6

Property
contribution to qualified plan, 10:4
defined for bonding requirement,
14:18
employer, qualified retirement plan
investment, 17:40
qualifying employer real property,
17:41

Prototype retirement plan, 2:21

Prudent man rule, 17:11, 17:12, 17:39

Publicly offered security, 17:17

Put option, ESOP, 22:2

-Q-

QDRO. *See* Qualified domestic
relations order (QDRO)

Qualification
amendment to terminating plan,
19:54
domestic relations order, 28:2
ESOP distribution commencement,
22:60
minimum vesting schedules, 8:5
QDRO, qualified retirement plan
procedure, 28:10
retirement plan, and QDRO, 28:6
revocation, effect on distribution
taxation, 11:21
top-heavy plans, 20:23

**Qualified Domestic Relations Order
(QDRO)**
alternate payee, 28:3
forfeiture, 28:12
income tax consequences, 28:17
anti-assignment rule, 28:4
and bankruptcy proceeding, 28:23
defined, 28:1

(*References in the index are to question numbers.*)

Qualified Domestic Relations Order (QDRO) (*cont.*)
  domestic relations order
    defined, 28:2
    receipt by qualified retirement plan, 28:11
  earliest retirement age
    defined, 28:9
    exemption, 28:8
  early distribution tax, 28:19
  excess distribution tax and excess accumulation tax, 28:20
  IRA and, 28:5
  QPSA and QJSA requirements, 28:13
  qualified retirement plans, 28:7
    applicability of rules, 28:5
    equitable distribution, 28:21
    maximum benefits, 28:15
    procedure for DRO qualification, 28:10
  reduction of future accrued benefits, 8:26
  retirement benefits
    assignment of, 3:9
    attachment of, 2:22
  retirement plan qualification, 28:6
  rollover of qualified retirement plan distribution to alternate payee, 28:18
  tax consequences to participant, 28:16

Qualified Joint and survivor annuity (QJSA)
  benefit distributions, 9:1, 9:2
  defined, 9:8
  effect of loan on, 9:11
  formal benefit application default, 9:74
  frozen or terminated plan, 9:16
  involuntary distribution, 9:72
  notice to participant, 9:28
  plan-subsidized, 9:30
  QDRO, 28:13
  waiver
    annuity starting date, 9:4
    benefit choice, 9:23
    general spousal consent, 9:25
    spousal consent, 9:21

Qualified preretirement survivor annuity (QPSA)
  benefit distributions, 9:1, 9:2

  defined, 9:9
  effect of loan on, 9:11
  frozen or terminated plan, 9:16
  involuntary distribution, 9:73
  notice to participant, 9:29
  plan-subsidized, 9:30
  and QDRO, 28:13
  waiver
    benefit choice, 9:24
    general spousal consent, 9:25
    spousal consent, 9:21

Qualified professional asset managers, 18:12

Qualified retirement plan
  See also Administrator of plan; Defined benefit plan; Defined contribution plan; Determination letter; Employee stock ownership plan; (ESOP) 401(k) plans; Multiemployer plans; Prohibited transactions; Taxation of distributions; Tax deduction rules; Termination of plan; Top-heavy plans
  accrued benefits
    elimination or reduction of, 8:25
    reduction of future accrued benefits, 8:26
  additional estate taxes, 12:19
  administrative discretion exception, 9:45
  administrator, 14:1–14:22
  adoption cost, 1:12
  affiliated service group determination letter, 27:32
  aggregate interests of deceased participant, 12:21
  alternate payee distribution consent, 28:14
  amendment
    to avoid excess distributions tax, 11:36
    for IRS compliance, 3:7
  annuity payments
    and lump-sum distribution to beneficiary, 11:11
    taxation of, 11:3
  automatic survivor benefits, 9:6
  average benefit percentage test, 4:19
    minimum coverage requirement, 4:17

(References in the index are to question numbers.)

bankruptcy protection, 27:40

benefit accrual and years of service, 8:23

benefit form, 9:36

benefit form amendment, 9:39

benefit postponement election, 9:69

benefits upon merger, 8:28

benefit types, 1:19

bond provided by party in interest, 14:21

borrowing by sponsor, 27:24, 27:25

business owner objectives, 27:18

buy-back provision, 8:21

change in vesting schedule, 8:6

choice for company with older essential employees, 2:25

classification test, 4:18

closely held corporation, advantages to, 27:1, 27:2

commencement of participation, 4:7

comparable plan defined, 19:6

consecutive service requirement, 4:4

contribution deductibility, 1:5, 1:22, 5:17

contribution limitations, 1:7, 5:12

controlled group of corporations, 27:27

coverage requirements, 4:1

current deductibility, 10:2

custom-designed plans, 2:20

death benefit, 8:22, 12:1
  estate tax exclusion, 12:17
  estate tax marital deduction, 12:18
  payments, taxation of, 12:16
defined, 1:2

Department of Labor reporting exemptions, 15:18

director of corporation, 27:26

discrimination in favor of highly compensated employees, 27:12
  effect on tax-favored status, 27:13

disqualification for operational error, 14:13

distribution recipient, taxation of, 11:25

distribution
  to disabled employee as lump-sum, 11:9
  reporting requirement, 15:16
  rollover by person over age 70½, 26:14

domestic relations order
  qualification procedure, 28:10
  receipt by plan sponsor, 28:11

early retirement benefits, 9:71

earned income defined, 27:10

effect of cash position on choice, 2:22

effect of plan choice on employee, 1:8

eligible employees, 1:14

eligibility requirements, 1:15

employee
  contribution limit, 5:14, 5:15
  contribution requirement, 4:6
  coverage, 1:7

employee benefit requirement, 4:20

employer property contribution prohibition, 18:8

excess contributions, 1:23
  deductibility rules, 10:8

excess retirement accumulation defined, 12:20

exclusions from participation, 1:16, 1:17

existing, upon incorporation by self-employed individual, 27:7

Form 5500 series return requirement, 15:2

"handling of funds" defined, 14:19

health insurance benefits, 1:21

incidental death benefits rule, 9:64

incorporation by sponsor, 1:4

installment rollover, 26:13

insured plan defined, 2:19

interest, assignment of, 3:9

investment in employer securities or real property, 17:40

investment limitations, 17:35

involuntary distributions, 9:37
  immediate, 9:72

IRA deduction, 24:7
  limits on, 24:11

IRS approval, 3:6

IRS reporting requirement, 15:1

Keogh plan defined, 2:16

leased employee
  IRS approval for use of, 4:41
  participation by, 4:39

life insurance
  beneficiary, 12:10
  benefits, 1:20

(References in the index are to question numbers.)

Qualified preretirement survivor annuity (QPSA)
  life insurance (*cont.*)
    contribution deduction, 12:3
    coverage, 12:2
    as funding source, 2:19
    limits, 12:4
    loans, taxability of, 12:9
    proceeds, estate tax on, 12:12
    proceeds, taxation of, 12:11
    protection, 12:15, 27:23
    tax consequences, 12:6
  limitation year, 5:11
  loans
    deductibility of interest, 11:40
    limitations on, 11:38
    to make investments, 17:36
    requirements, 11:42
    spousal consent to, 11:41
  local law and, 3:4
  lump-sum distributions
    defined, 11:4
    to disabled employee, 11:9
    installment payments and, 11:6
    taxation of, 11:12
  maintenance obligation, 1:11
  married participants, commencement of benefits, 9:19
  maternity or paternity leave, service requirement, 4:14
  maximizing retirement benefits, 27:19
  maximum age limit, 4:3
  maximum benefits pursuant to QDRO, 28:15
  maximum employer contributions, 27:14
  maximum loan repayment period, 11:39
  merger, for minimum participation requirement, 4:25
  minimum age and service requirements, 4:2
  minimum funding standard exclusions, 7:3
  minimum funding standards, 7:1
  minimum participation requirement, 4:23
  mutual fund investment, 17:45
  non-Section 411(d)(6) protected benefits, 8:27
  notice of benefit option amendment, 9:40
  number of allowable plans, 1:18
  optional benefit payment forms, 9:32
  oral trust, 3:3
  owner-employee controlling other businesses, 27:28
  participation requirements, 4:1, 4:5
  participation, effect of waiver on tax status, 4:26
  past service and eligibility requirement, 4:13
  payment deferral, 9:53
  payment method, 9:50
  personal service corporation safe harbor rules, 27:38
  plan choices, 2:1
  pooled investment funds defined, 17:44
  professional corporation, protection from creditors, 27:42
  property contribution, deductibility of, 10:4
  provision choices, 2:28
  QDRO
    alternate payee forfeiture, 28:12
    application of rules, 28:5
    distribution, excess distribution and accumulation tax, 28:20
    equitable distribution rule, 28:21
    provisions, 28:7
    rollover by alternate payee, 28:18
  "qualifies in operation" defined, 13:4
  ratio percentage test, minimum coverage requirement, 4:16
  reason for adoption, 1:1
  recently formed companies, 2:24
  records maintenance, 14:4
  recovery of P.S. 58 costs, 12:13
  remarried surviving spouse, benefits to, 9:2
  requirements for favorable tax treatment, 3:1
  rollover of distributions, 26:7
    partial distribution, 26:10
    by person over 70½, 26:14
    procedure for rollover to IRA, 26:16
    to SEP, 25:20
    by surviving spouse, 26:15
    tax considerations of rollover to IRA, 26:21
    transfer of IRA rollover amounts,

(*References in the index are to question numbers.*)

26:19
self-employed individual, 27:4
  advantages to, 27:5
  bankruptcy protection, 27:41
  maximum contribution, 27:16
SEP and, 27:39
service requirements, 1:15
single life annuity, present value of,
  12:22
single participant, bonding
  requirement, 14:22
Social Security benefits, 3:8
Social Security integration, 2:27, 6:1,
  6:2, 27:21
sponsor contributions, 1:13
sponsor with multiple businesses,
  4:33
surviving spouse, benefits to, 9:1
tax advantages of, 1:1, 1:3
taxation of contributions, 1:6, 11:1
tax-deductible contribution limits,
  27:15
tax-free distributions, 11:2
tax liability reduction, 27:3
tax lien on interest, 3:9
tax rule explanation, 14:11
timeliness of payment by check, 10:5
top-heavy plan tax requirements, 3:1
trustee, 3:5
types of plans and objectives, 27:18
vesting
  change in vesting schedule, 8:6
  defined, 8:1
  forfeitures and employee death,
    8:22
voluntary contributions, tax
  advantages of, 5:16, 27:22
year of service, 4:8, 4:11, 4:12, 4:13
**Qualified terminable interest property
  (QTIP),** IRA as, 24:33
Quarterly payments, defined benefit
  plan, 7:26

-R-

Ratio percentage test, minimum
  coverage requirement, 4:16
Real estate operating company, 17:18
Replacement period, ESOP sale, 22:34
Replacement property
  ESOP as, 22:33, 22:37

nonrecognition election and later
  disposition, 22:38
Reporting requirements
  See also Department of Labor;
    Employee
  Retirement Income Security Act
    (ERISA); Internal Revenue
    Service (IRS) reporting
  final asset distribution, 19:55
  IRS, 15:1
  nondeductible IRA contributions,
    24:15
  qualified retirement plan
    distributions, 15:16
  SEP
    annual reporting, 25:15
    model SEP, 25:13
Retirement age
  defined, 9:66
  earliest retirement age defined, 28:9
  early retirement, qualified retirement
    plan benefit, 27:20
  and minimum funding standards,
    7:9
  QDRO early option, 28:8
Retirement benefits. *See* Benefits;
  Qualified retirement plan
Retirement Equity Act of 1984 (REA),
  1:10
Retirement plan
  See also Nonqualified retirement
    plan; Qualified retirement
    plan
  critical legislation, 1:10
  distribution withholding rules, 14:9
  failure to meet minimum coverage or
    participation requirements, 4:27
  favorable tax treatment coverage
    requirements, 4:15
  notice of application for
    determination letter, 13:7
  timing of approval request, 13:6
Retirement plan participant. *See*
  Participant
Retirement plan sponsor. *See* Sponsor
Revenue Reconciliation Act (RRA),
  1:10, 22:6
Revocation of qualification,
  distribution taxation, 11:21
Rollovers
  defined, 26:1

(References in the index are to question numbers.)

Rollovers (*cont.*)
disqualified retirement plan
distribution, 26:20
IRA
beneficiary, 26:6
borrowing during rollover period,
26:4
IRA to IRA, 26:3
rollover accounts, 26:2
transfer to qualified retirement
plan, 26:19
multiple tax-free transfers, 26:5
partial distribution, 26:10–26:12
QDRO alternate payee, qualified
retirement plan distribution,
28:18
qualified retirement plan assets into
SEP, 25:20
qualified retirement plan benefits, by
surviving spouse, 26:15
qualified retirement plan distribution,
26:7
to IRA, tax treatment, 26:21
by person over age 70½, 26:14
qualified retirement plan
installments, 26:13
qualified retirement plan to IRA,
procedure, 26:16
qualified total distribution, 26:8
revocation, 26:22
SEP assets, 25:19
60-day period commencement, 26:17
60-day period extension, 26:18
terminated retirement plan
distribution, 26:9
top-heavy plans, 20:19

-S-

Safe harbor plan, money purchase
pension plan as, 4:40
Safe harbor rule
coverage requirement, qualified
retirement plan, 4:18
personal service corporation, 27:37
top-heavy plan minimums, 20:49
Safe harbor test, heavy and immediate
financial need, 21:37, 21:39
Salary reduction
401(k) arrangement, 2:8
SEP

eligible employers, 25:9
nondiscrimination test, 25:11
Savings plan. *See* Thrift or savings
plan
SEC. *See* Securities and Exchange
Commission
Section 411(d)(6) benefits, 9:41
Securities
lump-sum distribution, tax treatment
of, 11:16
publicly offered, 17:17
Securities acquisition loan
50 percent interest exclusion, 22:7
limit on eligibility period, 22:9
transfer to other lending
institutions, 22:8
generally, 22:6
**Securities and Exchange Commission
(SEC),** 401(k) plan registration,
21:47
Self-employed individual
also an employee of another
employer, 27:11
defined, 27:8
defined benefit plan contribution
limits, 27:17
distribution to disabled employee,
11:9
earned income defined, 27:10
employer contributions, deductibility
of, 10:1
401(k) plan, 21:7
handling qualified retirement plan
upon incorporation, 27:7
incorporation advantages, 27:6
Keogh plan defined, 2:16
maximum qualified retirement plan
contribution, 27:16
owner-employee defined, 27:9
qualified retirement plan
bankruptcy protection, 27:41
establishing, 27:4
providing life insurance, tax effect,
12:6
tax advantages, 27:5
Separation from service, 11:8
Service requirement.
See also Year of service
and benefit distributions, 8:20
break in service, and vesting,
8:14–8:16

(References in the index are to question numbers.)

funding, 7:10

hour of service defined, 4:9

one-year break in service defined, 4:10

payment from plan assets, 17:23

prohibited transaction exceptions, 18:7

qualified retirement plan, 1:15, 4:2, 4:4, 14:4

termination of employment, 4:21

year of service defined, 4:8

Shareholder, multiemployer plan withdrawal liability, 23:40

Simplified employee pension (SEP)

advantages to business owner, 25:21

annual reporting requirements, 25:15

asset management, 25:17

moving assets without penalty, 25:19

contribution deduction timing, 25:8

contribution forfeitures, 25:5

deductible amount, 25:7

defined, 2:11, 25:1

discrimination prohibition, 25:3

distribution taxation, 25:18

drawbacks, 25:22

elective deferral limits, 25:10

eligible participants, 25:2

versus employer-sponsored IRA, 24:28

establishment of, 25:12

integration with Social Security, 25:4

IRA contribution, 25:6

model SEP, use of, 25:13

rollover from qualified retirement plan, 25:20

salary reduction

eligible employers, 25:9

nondiscrimination test, 25:11

successors to dissolved partnership, 25:14

as tax-favored qualified retirement plan, 27:39

tax treatment of contributions, 25:16

top-heavy plan, 20:7

Single-employer defined benefit plan. *See* Defined benefit plan

Single Employer Pension Plan Amendments Act (SEPPAA), 1:10, 19:11

Single-employer plan, distinguished

from multiemployer plan, 23:2

Single life annuity, excess retirement accumulation valuation, 12:22

Social Security

See also Integrated plan benefits and top-heavy plan minimum benefit/contribution requirements, 20:47

defined benefit plan, 6:2

defined contribution plan, 6:2, 6:3

effect of benefits on qualified plan, 3:8

ESOP plan, 22:17

qualified retirement plan, 2:27, 6:1, 27:21

retirement age, and defined benefit plan annual payment, 5:6

retirement age defined, 5:9

SEP, 25:4

Sole proprietorship, Keogh plan defined, 2:16

Sponsor

See also Multiemployer plan

borrowing from qualified retirement plan, 27:24, 27:25

contribution flexibility, 2:23

deductibility of contributions, 1:5

effect of plan choice on employee, 1:8

employer-sponsored IRA, 24:24

qualified retirement plan coverage, 24:25

excess plan contributions, 1:23

incorporation, for qualified retirement plan, 1:4

liability for underfunded terminated plan, 19:44

multiemployer plan withdrawal liability claim, 23:36, 23:37

number of allowable plans, 1:18

plan amendment to avoid excess distributions tax, 11:36

plan contributions, 1:13

tax advantages of qualified retirement plan, 1:3

terminating insurance premium, 19:14

Spousal consent

general QPSA/QJSA waiver, 9:25

loan on accrued benefit, 9:12

plan specification, 9:27

QJSA waiver, benefit choice, 9:23

(References in the index are to question numbers.)

Spousal consent (*cont.*)
  qualified plan loan, 11:41
  waiver of QJSA or QPSA, 9:21
Spouse
  See also Qualified Domestic
    Relations Order (QDRO);
    Surviving spouse
  QDRO income tax consequences,
    28:17
  spousal IRA, 24:17
Statute of limitations
  Form 5500 series, 15:11, 15:12
  gain nonrecognition election, sale of
    qualified securities, 22:40
Stock bonus plan
  active participant, 24:9
  benefit to corporation and
    stockholders, 2:26
  defined, 2:9
  versus ESOP, 22:3
Stock plan. *See* Employee stock
  ownership plan (ESOP)
Straight life annuity, defined benefit
  plan annual benefit payment, 5:6
Subsidiary, qualified retirement plan,
  1:18
Summary plan descriptions (SPD)
  change in plan, 16:8
  defined, 16:1
  disclaimer clause, 16:6
  filing location, 16:3
  five-year update period, 16:11
  language requirement, 16:14
  as legally binding document, 16:5
  modification, 16:9
  other required documents for
    participants, 16:13
  to participant and beneficiary, 16:2
  plan termination, 16:12
  reportable material modification, 16:9
  required information, 16:4
  update timing, 16:10
Surviving spouse
  See also Distribution requirements;
    Qualified joint and survivor
    annuity; Qualified retirement
    survivor annuity
  annuity starting date, 9:4
  as beneficiary of aggregate interests,
    12:24
  benefit distributions, 9:1

  estate tax on annuity, 9:10
  IRA benefits, 24:35
  lump-sum distribution, 11:10
  qualified plan death benefits, 12:1
  remarriage, and benefit distributions,
    9:2
  rollovers
    IRA rollover, 26:6
    of qualified retirement plan, 26:15
Survivor annuity
  annuity contracts, 9:15
  floor offset plans, 9:14
Survivor benefit
  annuity requirements, 9:31
  automatic, 9:6, 9:18
    exception from, 9:7
    waiver of, 9:20
  frozen or terminated plan, 9:16
  transferee plan, 9:13

-T-

Target benefit plan
  active participant, 24:9
  contrasted to defined benefit plans,
    2:5
  contrasted to money purchase
    pension plan, 2:5
  defined, 2:5
  minimum funding standards, 7:1
Taxable income, qualified plan
  providing life insurance, 12:7
Taxable wage base (TWB)
  defined, 6:6
  defined contribution excess plan
    integration level, 6:8
Taxable year, nondeductible
  contributions, 10:10
Taxation
  See also Estate tax; Excise tax, Tax
    deduction rules
  and choice of retirement plan, 2:24
  distribution of excess 401(k) plan
    contribution, 21:25
  effect of plan choice on employee,
    1:8
  ESOPs
    dividends, 22:14
    loan incentives, 22:5
  estate tax on survivor annuity, 9:10
  excess aggregate contributions, 21:55

(References in the index are to question numbers.)

excess 401(k) deferrals, 21:29
excise tax for distribution failure, 9:63
401(k) plan benefits, 3:2
gift tax, spousal waiver consent, 9:26
integrated plan, 6:1
IRA
  distributions, 24:32
  withdrawal by individual with previous nondeductible contributions, 24:16
lien assessment on qualified plan benefits, 3:9
life insurance under qualified retirement plan, 12:6, 12:7, 12:9, 12:11
partial distribution election, 26:12
penalty
  employee contribution noncompliance, 7:6
  pension liability overstatement, 7:8
  for prohibited transaction, 18:4
  recharacterizing 401(k) excess contributions, 21:22
QDRO consequences to plan participant, 28:16
qualified retirement plan advantages, 1:1, 1:3, 3:1, 4:15, 5:16
retirement plans, 1:6
rollover of qualified retirement plan to IRA, 26:21
SEP
  contributions, 25:16
  distributions, 25:18
10 percent excise tax on nondeductible contributions, 1:23
waivers
  minimum funding standard, 7:18
  plan participation, 4:26
Taxation of distributions
additional estate tax upon death of participant, 11:37
annuity payments, 11:3
attained age method, 11:32
balance to the credit of an employee, 11:5
calculation of excess, 11:27
deductible employee contributions, 11:24
early distribution tax, 9:68
excess distributions

defined, 11:26
grandfather rule and, 11:33
plan amendment to avoid, 11:36
tax on, 11:35
five-year participation requirement, 11:14
forward averaging, 11:13
grandfather amounts
  discretionary method, 11:31
  recovery of, 11:30
grandfather rule defined, 11:29
lump-sum distributions
  annuity payments, 11:11
  to beneficiary of deceased, 11:10, 11:11
  capital gains treatment, 11:19
  defined, 11:4
  disability distribution, 11:9
  employer securities, 11:16
  five-year averaging, 11:17
  forward averaging, 11:22, 11:23
  individual at age 50 before 1/1/86, 11:13
  installment payments and, 11:6
  qualified retirement plan, 11:13
  special rule, 11:28
  taxable portion, 11:12, 11:15, 14:11
  tax benefits and additional distribution, 1:3, 11:7
  tax effect on employee, 1:8
  ten-year averaging, 11:18
months of plan participation, 11:20
plan loans
  deductibility of interest, 11:40
  generally, 11:42
  limitations on, 11:38
  maximum repayment period, 11:39
  spousal consent for, 11:41
  qualified retirement plan generally, 11:1
  qualified retirement plan recipient, 11:25
revocation of qualification, 11:21
separation from service defined, 11:8
tax free, for qualified retirement plans, 11:2
Tax deduction rules
See also Individual retirement account
certain dispositions of employer securities, 22:26

(References in the index are to question numbers.)

Tax deduction rules (*cont.*)
  compensation defined, 10:13
  contributions in excess of Section
    415 limits, 10:23
  current deductibility, 10:2
  defined benefit plan
    deductible contribution limits,
      10:16
    excess contributions, 10:18
    funding method, 10:17
  defined contribution plan
    contribution limits, 10:15
  disallowance of plan contributions
    deduction, 10:11
  employer contributions, 1:5, 1:22,
    10:1
    to affiliated company profit
      sharing plan, 10:14
    limits on, 10:20
  ESOP
    cash dividends, 22:13
    contribution limit, 22:11
    employer security dividends, 22:12
    qualified employer securities
      defined, 22:23
    sale of employer securities, 22:22,
      22:24
    stock contributions, 22:16
  estate tax deduction
    employer security sale to ESOP,
      22:22
    nonallocation period, 22:27
  excess plan assets
    as taxable income, 10:21
    multiple plan contributions, 10:22
    profit sharing plan contributions,
      10:8
    retirement accumulation, 12:25
  family aggregation rules, 10:25
  401(k) plan CODA, 21:44
  life insurance contribution, 12:3
  missed contribution, 10:12
  multiple plans
    contribution limits, 10:19
    excess contributions, 10:22
  nondeductible contributions
    amount, 10:9
    timing of determination, 10:10
  payment
    by check, timeliness of, 10:5
    by promissory note, 10:6

  plan expense payment by employer,
    10:24
  profit sharing plan, 10:7
    excess contributions, 10:8
  property contribution, 10:4
  qualified plan loan interest, 11:40
  qualified retirement plan limits,
    27:15
  SEP, 25:7, 25:8, 25:16
  termination of plan, 19:7
  timeliness of contributions, 7:25, 10:3
**Tax Equity and Fiscal Responsibility
  Act of 1982 (TEFRA),** 1:10
Tax penalty. *See* Penalty
Tax Reform Act of 1984, 1:10
Tax Reform Act of 1986, 1:10
**Technical and Miscellaneous Revenue
  Act of 1988 (TAMRA),** 1:10
Termination of employment, 11:8
  benefit forfeiture, 8:17
  minimum coverage requirement, 4:21
Termination of plan
  accrued benefit, effect on, 19:4,
    19:53
  affected party, 19:32
  "all other benefits under the plan,"
    19:40
  amendment as, 19:52
    distribution of excess assets to
      employer, 19:46
    qualification, 19:54
    to reduce or stop benefit accrual,
      19:53
  benefit liabilities defined, 19:18
  benefit restrictions, 19:28
  collective bargaining agreement,
    19:27
  contributing factors, 19:3
  defined benefit plan
    allocation of assets, 19:39
    overfunding relief, 19:48
  determination letter, 13:7
  disqualification of plan, benefit
    guarantee, 19:25
  employer withdrawal, 19:49
  ERISA Title IV, 19:9
  excess plan assets, 19:45
    recovery of, 19:47
  factors determining date, 19:31
  final distribution of assets, 19:37,
    19:38, 19:42

(References in the index are to question numbers.)

formal Board declaration, 19:2
liability
  employer liability for
    under-funding, 19:44
  employer reversion liability, 19:48
  multiemployer plan employer
    liability, 23:23
maximum guaranteed monthly
  benefit, 19:23
notice requirements, 19:33
  benefits information, 19:34
  intent, 19:29
  to IRS, 19:55
  to PBGC of final asset distribution,
    19:42
number of participants, for insurance
  purposes, 19:15
payment limitation, 19:8
PBGC, 19:10
  benefit limits, 19:22
  benefits, 19:20
  coverage, 19:12
  coverage exemptions, 19:13
  guarantee of prior amendment,
    19:24
  initiation, 19:26
  notice of noncompliance, 19:35,
    19:36
  premium, 19:14
  reporting requirements, 15:22
of pension plan, minimum funding
  requirement, 7:27
post-termination audit, 19:43
profit sharing plan, complete
  discontinuance of contributions,
  19:50
provision for, 19:1
reallocation of distributed assets,
  19:41
relevance of date, 19:30
replacement or conversion of existing
  plan, 19:6
rollover of distributions, 26:9
summary plan descriptions, 16:12
survivor benefit requirements, 9:16
tax-favored status, effect on, 19:7
top-heavy rules, 20:14
Types
  distress, 19:19, 19:20
  partial, 19:5
  standard, 19:17

vesting, 19:21
Third party filing
Form 5500 series annual return late
  filing, 15:10
Thrift or savings plan
CODA and, 21:43
defined, 2:7
employee contributions and, 4:6
Top-heavy plans
accrued benefits, calculation of, 20:2
aggregated plans, 20:22
aggregation group, 20:12
  permissive aggregation group, 20:10
  required aggregation group, 20:9
aggregation of collectively bargained
  retirement plans, 20:11
amendment to incorporate
  requirements, 20:59
annual retirement benefit, 20:38
beneficiary, 20:31
compensation limits, 20:50
death benefits, 20:18
defined benefit plans, 20:1
  minimum benefit requirement,
    20:37, 20:42
  years of service for minimum
    annual benefit, 20:41
defined contribution plan, 20:3
determination, 20:8
determination date, 20:21
employee contributions, 20:20
former key employees, 20:30
401(k) plans
  elective distributions, minimum
    contributions, 20:48
  qualified nonelective contributions,
    20:6
frozen retirement plan, 20:15
integration restrictions, 6:26
key employee, 20:16
  defined, 20:24
  exclusion from second plan
    participants, 20:52
  1.0 rule, 20:53, 20:55, 20:56, 20:57,
    20:58
  participant in multiple plans, 20:51
minimum benefit for early
  distribution, 20:39
minimum contribution requirement,
  20:43, 20:46
  forfeitures and, 20:43

(*References in the index are to question numbers.*)

minimum contribution requirement (*cont.*)

    participant's compensation, 20:45

    multiple employer plan rules, 20:5

    multiple plans adopted prior to 1984, 20:54

    non-key employees, 20:29, 20:49

        multiplan employer minimum benefit contribution for, 20:49

    officer of employer, 20:25

    organizations with officers, 20:26

    ownership

        5% or 1% owner, 20:28

        ten largest owners of employer, 20:27

    participant's average compensation, 20:40

    plan distributions to employees, 20:17

    qualification requirements, 20:23

    requirements for favorable tax treatment, 3:1

    rollovers and transfers, 20:19

    separate retirement plans of related employers, 20:13

    simplified employee pensions, 20:7, 25:3

    Social Security benefits and minimum benefit/contribution requirements, 20:47

    subject qualified retirement plans, 20:4

    termination of plan, 20:14

    top-heavy group defined, 20:12

    vesting

        change in schedule, 20:35

        favorable schedule, 20:36

        minimum vesting requirements, 20:32, 20:33

        subject benefits, 20:34

Transfer

    IRA

        assets at divorce, 24:38

        rollover to qualified retirement plan, 26:19

        tax-free, between IRAs, 26:5

    top heavy plans, 20:19

    trustee-to-trustee, SEP assets, 25:19

Transferee plan, 9:13

Trustee

    IRA, fee for, 24:20

    life appointment, 17:9

    prudent man standard, 17:12

    qualified retirement plan, 3:5, 14:15

    death of employee, 8:22

    defined, 8:1, 8:5

    employee contribution standards, 8:8

    forfeiture amounts, 8:18

    forfeiture of nonforfeitable benefits, 8:19

    minimum service requirements, 4:2

    minimum vesting standards, 8:3

    multiemployer plan standards, 8:4

    non-Section 411(d)(6) protected benefits, 8:27

    one-year break in service, 8:14, 8:15, 8:16

    profit sharing plan, complete discontinuance of, 19:51

    qualified retirement plan, 1:15, 2:28

        schedule changes, 8:6

        vesting records, 14:4

    schedule, 8:6, 8:7, 8:13

    SEP contribution, 25:5

    termination of plan, 19:4, 19:21

    top-heavy plan

        change in schedule, 20:35

        minimum vesting requirement, 20:32

        schedule favorable to employer, 20:36

        subject benefits, 20:34

        years of service, 20:33

    unfunded vesting benefits, 23:10, 23:22, 23:23

    years of service

        exceptions, 8:11, 8:12

        requirement, 8:9, 8:10, 20:33

-U-

Union. See Labor union

Unit benefit plan, 2:13

-V-

Valuation, ESOP tradability, 22:63

Venture capital operating company, 17:18

(References in the index are to question numbers.)

Vesting

accrued benefit

defined, 8:2

elimination or reduction of, 8:25

reduction of future benefits, 8:26

years of service, 8:23

assignment of interest, 3:9

balance to the credit of an employee, defined, 11:5

benefit distribution and years of service, 8:20

benefit forfeiture, 8:17

benefits upon plan merger, 8:28

buy-back provision, 8:21

-W-

Waiver

automatic survivor benefits, 9:20

funding standards

additional information needed, 7:21

alternative to waiver, 7:23

amendment of pension with existing waiver, 7:22

general spousal consent, 9:25

minimum funding standards, 7:18, 7:19

multiemployer plan withdrawal liability, 23:24

participation, effect on plan tax status, 4:26

QJSA

annuity starting date, 9:4

spousal consent, 9:21

QPSA

benefit choice, 9:24

spousal consent, 9:21

request, notice requirements, 7:20

Withdrawal

hardship, 401(k) plan, 21:34-21:40

from IRA, 24:29

individual with previous nondeductible contributions, 24:16

multiemployer plan, employer liability, 23:10–23:44

as plan termination, 19:49

Withholding

liability for failure, 14:8

retirement plan benefits distribution, 14:7, 14:9

-Y-

Years of service

accrued benefits, 8:23

benefit distributions and, 8:20

defined benefit plans

minimum, 5:8

top-heavy plan, minimum annual benefit, 20:41

leased employee, 4:38

retirement plan eligibility requirement, 4:8, 4:11–4:13

top-heavy plan

minimum annual benefit, 20:41

vesting requirement, 20:33

vesting requirement, 8:9–8:12, 20:33